Baedeker

China

www.baedeker.com

Verlag Karl Baedeker

SIGHTSEEING HIGHLIGHTS ✶ ✶

Beijing and its imperial palace, the booming metropolis of Shanghai, the imperial summer palace in Chengde, the famous terra-cotta army near Xi'an – the list of outstanding sights in China is endless. To help get some idea, here are a few of the top highlights, which justify travelling for longer in China, too.

1 ✶ ✶ Pamir Mountains near Kashgar
On the road to Karakorum through the dramatic high mountains of Pamir towards Pakistan. ▶ page 385

2 ✶ ✶ Chengde
Chengde is the city with the most important imperial buildings in China after Beijing, including the fascinating temple of Puning Si. ▶ page 212

3 ✶ ✶ Dunhuang · the Mogao Caves
An oasis in the desert, and not far away are the monks' grottoes of Mogao, a UNESCO World Heritage Site.
▶ page 280

4 ✶ ✶ Beijing
The abundance of high-quality attractions here can be matched by few places in the world: the imperial palace, lama monasteries… and not far away is the Great Wall of China. ▶ page 149

5 ✶ ✶ Datong · the Yungang Caves
The Yungang caves near Datong are a UNESCO World Heritage Site.
▶ page 260

6 ✶ ✶ Pingyao
A journey through time back to ancient China: old-fashioned streets and alleys, yet this is no museum but a vividly lively place.
▶ page 521

7 ✶ ✶ Tai Shan
The most famous of the holy mountains of China. ▶ page 508

8 ✶ ✶ Qufu
Confucius was born and buried here.
▶ page 459

9 ✶ ✶ Xi'an · the terra-cotta army
Who has not heard of the warriors guarding the tomb of China's first emperor?
▶ page 581

10 ✶ ✶ Huanglong · Jiuzhaigou
Scenic wonders in northern Sichuan where natured has weaved magic.
▶ page 370

11 ✶ ✶ The Purple and Gold Mountain of Nanjing
Last resting place of the first Ming emperor and of Sun Yatsen.
▶ page 441

12 ✶ ✶ Shanghai
A booming metropolis, modern, hectic and vibrant. ▶ page 471

13 ✶ ✶ Suzhou
The gardens of Suzhou are unmatched in splendour. ▶ page 497

14 ✶ ✶ Hangzhou
A city to be compared with Europe's Florence: a hint of tradition, wealth and beauty
▶ page 320

15 ✶ ✶ Huang Shan
»Whoever has seen Huang Shan will have no eyes for any other mountain« said Xu Xiake, the famous geographer of ancient China, and he was right. ▶ page 359

©Baedeker

1 Pamir Mountains
2 Chengde
3 Dunhuang
4 Beijing
5 Datong
6 Pingyao
7 Tai Shan
8 Qufu
9 Xi'an
10 Huanglong/Jiuzhaigou
11 Nanjing Purple Mountain
12 Shanghai
13 Suzhou
14 Hangzhou
15 Huang Shan
16 Jangtse Gorges
17 Lhasa
18 Dazu
19 Wulingyuan
20 Wuyi Shan
21 Lijiang
22 Guilin
23 Shilin
24 Foshan
25 Hong Kong

BAEDEKER'S BEST TIPS

Of all the Baedeker tips in this book, here a list of some of the most interesting. Experience and enjoy China, the »Middle Kingdom« in all its glory.

🔋 Early-morning exercise on the Coal Hill
Among the best things that China has to offer – for early-risers ▶ **page 174**

🔋 Dong'anmen night market
The market in Beijing for lovers of fried scorpion and silkworms. Bon appetit! ▶ **page 176**

🔋 »House of Sages' Rest«
The right place to go in Beijing for a cup of tea ▶ **page 183**

A cup of tea ...
... in China's attractive tea houses

🔋 Water and wine
Enjoy a sweet glass in Jilin amid the idyllic atmosphere by the shores of a mountain river. ▶ **page 208**

🔋 Breathing country air
Staying the night with a peasant family in Shaoshan gives an insight into Chinese rural life. ▶ **page 212**

🔋 Navel-gazing
See the giant Guanyin at the Puning Si monastery from navel height.
▶ **page 225**

🔋 Too spicy?
Anyone finding the spicy Sichuan cuisine too hot – i.e. virtually everybody – ought to be prepared with a few handy Chinese words. ▶ **page 234**

🔋 »By cable-car over the river«
By cable-car over the Yangtze – the best way of obtaining good photos in Chongqing. ▶ **page 248**

🔋 Web artists
The spectacular webs of the spiders native to Dali, three dimensional and often more than 20 m long. ▶ **page 256**

🔋 Iron horses from within
A visit to the former locomotive works in Datong. ▶ **page 264**

🔋 Tea with ambience
Where in Hangzhou can you stop for a nice cup of tea? ▶ **page 323**

Body control
Another Shaolin-trick: standing on two fingertips

🖺 Picnic on a Sunday
Right in the middle of Hong Kong what is probably the biggest regularly occurring picnic in the world takes place on Sundays. ► **page 347**

🖺 Evening in Causeway Bay
This part of Hong Kong in the evening roars into life – in stores, cinemas, restaurants and pedestrian zones.
► **page 351**

🖺 Throw the keys away ...
Padlocks bring good fortune on Huang Shan they say. ► **page 366**

🖺 Go by road not air
Taking the plane to Huanglong means missing out on a lot. The journey there through river gorges and ancient villages
► **page 370**

🖺 The Arhat Oracle
It can tell the future. Curious?
► **page 404**

Locks in the sea of clouds
On Huang Shan long-lasting padlocks are there to secure affection

🖺 Kung fu in action
Interesting demonstrations of the martial art in the Shaolin monastery
► **page 422**

🖺 Paper Palaces
... for the dead. Nowhere are such magnificent examples created as in Kayuan Si monastery in Quanzhou
► **page 459**

🖺 Raindrop music
Nature itself provides the music in the Yu Yuan garden in Shanghai ► **page 487**

🖺 Tourist Center
A strange name for a tea-house where all the beauties of the Wuyi Shan can be enjoyed ► **page 573**

🖺 The Bonsai Garden
In Yangzhou the art of raising dwarf trees is presented in a particularly attractive ambience. ► **page 613**

An experience for the senses
There is nothing that can't be bought at the night markets.

Tea is not just drunk, it is celebrated.
▶ **page 100**

BACKGROUND

PRACTICALITIES

Price categories

▶ **Where to stay (double room)**
Budget: less than 200 yuan
Mid-range: 200 – 600 yuan
Luxury: more than 600 yuan

▶ **Where to eat**
Inexpensive: less than 40 yuan
Moderate: 40 – 120 yuan
Expensive: more than 120 yuan
(per meal per person)

*A young woman in traditional costume
near Dali in southwest China*
► page 254

Entrance to the garden of the Imperial Palace in Beijing
▸ **page 164**

Gods of the years in a temple in Macau →

Background

QUICK, EASY TO READ AND EASY
TO CHECK INFORMATION ABOUT
CHINA; ITS COUNTRY AND
PEOPLE, ITS ECONOMICS, ITS
POLITICS, ITS SOCIETY AND
ITS EVERYDAY LIFE

EVER CHANGING CHINA

»Middle Kingdom« – that was no European idea; it is what the Chinese called their own country, centre of the civilized world. Nowadays the words still express self-confidence and pride in a complex but unique culture which has been developing over a period dating back to three or four thousand years before the birth of Christ.

China's imperial influence extended far beyond its own borders. Europe would never have become what it is today without China, without paper or printing or inventions like the compass, nor without the Chinese influence on Baroque fashions and the ideas that led to the European Enlightenment. After a century of decline and a crisis of confidence resulting from its own internal politics, China is now regaining its importance, its traditions and the productivity of its people

An aging land
China's family planning policy will result in an aged society

is on the increase. China is no longer to be disregarded as a world power. To discover the real China as a traveller is a true challenge, thanks to its foreignness, its sheer size and the contradictory nature of the land. China is no monolith and never was. China nowadays is more exciting, fascinating, confusing and rewarding than ever. It is as big as all of Europe put together and has all the variety of a whole continent. Unlike present-day Europe, though, it is undergoing change at a frantic rate, and in many different directions at once: China is modern, even ultra-modern in cities like Shanghai and Hong Kong, but also in Beijing, Guangzhou and many other places. Indeed coming back to Europe after experiencing 21st-century China almost feels like walking into a stuffy old museum. China is also very ancient, though, and awareness of that past is growing, with archaeological digs, an increasing number of fine museums and with the listing of more and more buildings and sites for historical protection. There are therefore more and more things for visitors to see.

Changing socialism

China is international: foreign goods have great prestige and, at least in the major cities, they have become easy to find. Interest in the outside world has also continued and the number of Chinese explor-

A monument to failure
The Great Wall of the Ming dynasty was built in the 16th and 17th centuries to keep the Mongols out of the empire. Later the Manchus succeeded in overcoming it several times before finally taking over from the Ming dynasty.

The power of religion …
… is evident in the splendour of temples and monasteries. The abundance of gold, fine decorative work, pure magnificence and symbolism is overwhelming.

Everyday ceremony
Some tea houses in China maintain the old traditions of ceremonial enjoyment.

The art of the garden
Lakes, canals and bridges, mountains and water, wild and tamed nature, vivid and restrained colours. Chinese garden art is characterized by the harmonious union of different elements such as here in Liu Yuan park in Souzhou.

Steaming hot from the wok
Cooked food stalls in city alleys and on markets provide delicious meals, some of them exotic, at low prices. Try it!

A shower of petals
A ceremony in front of the Fuhu Temple on Emei Shan. Expressions of belief can be encountered here on all sides.

ing beyond their own shores is rapidly increasing. At the same time, national pride is on the up as well and, although there are some blemishes and blind spots involved in this, it is hard to argue that such pride is not well merited. Something else that is on the rise is religion. How many more temples, churches and mosques there are now than even twenty years ago! The only thing indeed that seems not to be booming is socialism, not in name of course, but the old order is clearly in retreat and the clock can never be turned back. Mao Zedong remains a national icon and the Communist Party clings to his mystique, seeking not to lose their monopoly on power, but the trend is to read his poems rather than his political legacy.

Variety at every turn

A traveller in China may seek to see and experience all the land has to offer, but such a cornucopia of experiences, impressions and knowledge is virtually impossible to take in. What characterizes the land anyway? Is it the cold of Siberia or wintry Manchuria? Is it the tropical beaches of Hainan province? Is it the rain-swept east coast? Is it the sandy wastes and oases of the interior, farther from the sea than any other lands on earth? Is it the Tibetans or the disco-dancing youth of Shanghai? Is it the murals of a cave temple or golf courses and ski pistes? It is hard to keep all of China's aspects in mind. Yet to discover just a fraction of what there is to learn is enough to make any visit worthwhile. There you can experience not only the sights; there is also every chance of getting to know the people. In spite of language barriers and the difficulty of deciphering the writing, the Chinese are usually very open to foreigners, always keen to learn and are not timid about trying out their English skills on the »long noses« they meet, even those who may not have much English to try out. One last thing to note is that China is a wonderful place for gourmets. In spite of certain prejudices, Chinese cuisine is commonly highly exotic, particularly as regards vegetables. Pork, beef, lamb, poultry, fish and sea food are all staples of the Chinese diet, and appeal to non-Chinese as well. The very variety of the culinary spectrum in the cuisine of the various regions makes it worth exploring the country in detail. Anyone who makes a start on the food will barely be able to bring their first visit to an end and that is only one of the things they will find hard to leave.

Devotions
A Tibetan woman at prayer

Facts

How many people live in China? What are their religious beliefs? To what extent is the Chinese economy organized on market lines? When did the Boxer rebellion take place? What is a scholar's garden? All these questions will be answered on the pages that follow.

Nature

China's lands can be pictured as **six major territories**: Manchuria in the north east, northern China, southern China, the Tibetan plateau, the Mongolian plateau and the central Asian west, its glacial valleys and basins ringed by towering mountains.

Northeastern China (Manchuria)

The northeast of China, known as , undergoes extremes of temperature from the dry, sub-polar cold of the winter to the humid heat of the summer months. The region consists of three independent subdivisions, the core being formed by the **Manchurian lowlands**, the northern part of which, the Songhua plain, includes the east of the Gobi Desert, a sparsely peopled, sandy and barren steppe, while the southern lowlands are given over to intensive farming. At the western rim of the region, the upper reaches of the Great Hinggan River herald the climb up to the **Mongolian Basin**. This range of mountains has peaks ranging from 1500 m/4900 ft up to 2034 m/6700 ft. The steep slopes facing east receive enough rainfall from the Pacific air currents to allow for the growth of dense, deciduous broad-leaved the icy comugh the mountains themselves extend northward into **East Manchurian Highla** of Siberia. The mountainous eyries of the wealth. re characterized by their rich mineral

Northern China

The core region of northern China and on of the most intensively cultivated and most populous areas of the country, and of the world, is called the Great or **»Yellow Plain«**. This plain is no more than the cone-shaped flood plain of the Huang He river, the Yellow River, deposited out of the huge quantities of sediment borne by the river as its course repeatedly changed over the millennia. One feature that characterizes the landscape and the culture is the way the people of northern China have built dams and dykes to contain the **Huang He**, the course of which is now at greater elevation than the surrounding plain. The people's ever-present risk that their intensively cultivated land will be flooded has called for huge defensive efforts (dykes, channelling via canals). The borderline between the territory and the neighbouring Mongolian basin is formed by the **loess highlands of Shanxi** and the **Ordos Plateau** (around which the Yellow River follows a grand loop), which grows ever more barren and desert-like further to the north. Among the conspicuous characteristics are the sands blown down from the sandy steppes of the north deposited by the wind as sedimentary alluvial deposits up to 200 m/600 ft deep and then eroded into impressive shapes. The huge quantities of eroded material are then transported by the Yellow River and its tributaries and deposited as loess over the Great Plain.

← Advertising allowed: a courtyard in Beijing with a poster

Facts and Figures China

Religion
► C 60 % of the population is not religious. About 30% are followers of the syncretistic traditional religion, Buddhist 8 %, Moslem 1.5 %. The number of Christians lies well above 1 %, estimates go above 5 %.

Language
► Official language: Chinese
► Languages of the national minorities

State
► Form of government: People's republic
► Capitol: Beijing
► Administration: 22 provinces, 5 autonomous regions, 4 directly controlled cities, special administrative region Hong Kong and Macau
► Highest legislative body: National People's Congress (parliament)mmunist
► General secretary State: Hu Jintao Party an' ' ' '

Area
► 9.6 million sq km/3.7 million sq mi
► Bordering countries: Tajikistan, Kyrgyzstan, Kazakhstan, Mongolia, Russia, North Korea, Vietnam, Laos, Myanmar (Burma), India, Bhutan, Nepal, Pakistan and Afghanistan

Population
► 1.3 billion
► Population density: 135 pro sq km/355 per sq mi
► Ethnic groups: 92 % Han Chinese, 1.3 % Zhuang, 0.8 % Hui, 0.8 % Manchu, 0.7 % Miao, 4.5 % Others: Mongols, Koreans, Turkic peoples, Tibetans; in all 55 national minorities

Economy
► Gross domestic product: 3.86 trillion US-$ (2008)
► Per capita income: 3,100 US-$ (2008), considerably less in rural areas
► Unemployment rate: officially 4 %; the actual rate is considerably higher
► Economic structure (in parts of the gross domestic product): agriculture 14%, industry 53%, service industry 33%

Southern China The sub-tropical verdant hills of the rainy south differ enormously from the northern territories, as exhibited by the architecture, the climate, the hydrography and the flora. The sheltered, flat scenery of the northern plains and sedimentary plateaux contrasts with the south's precipitous and restless contours. Outside of the large lowland valleys, intensive cultivation of this territory requires extensive construction of terraces and embankments.

The Tibetan Plateau is the highest central massif in Asia. An immense wall of mountains, comprising the **Himalayas, Trans-Himalayan peaks, Karakoram and Pamir ranges** with peaks rising to between 7000 and 8846 metres (23,000 to 29.000 ft) protect a towering plateau with an average height of 4000 to 4500 m (13,000 to 15,000 ft) from the south. The highlands of Tibet have nothing like the character of a plain. They are characterized by chains of mountains running east-west in parallel, interspersed with glacial valleys and the jagged contours that surround them. To the south, rivers tributary to systems like the Sindh/Indus or Tsangpo/Brahmaputra waterways plunge through steep, narrow valleys down towards the Indian Ocean, whereas beyond the Trans-Himalayan region, few rivers drain the slopes. Large areas at higher elevations are covered in snow and virtually all year round they experience the glacier formation of the frozen mountainous steppes.

Tibetan Highlands

Between the mighty ranges of the central Asian mountains there are several important fold basins, which have several features in common, in spite of the wide variety of elevations at which they appear. Owing to the rain shadow of the surrounding mountains and their location deep inland, these high, unwatered valleys form **infertile dry terrains**, which also are also subject to extreme fluctuations in temperature. Sandy deserts merge into salty clay plains, saline un-

Intramontane basins

Rice terraces in Yunnan province

Nomads on the steppes of Inner Mongolia

drained lakes alternate with mounds of debris at the foot of the mountains. The most important of the central Asian valleys which are at least partly under Chinese control are– from west to east – the Tarim Basin and the Turfan Depression, the Dzungarian Basin and – further to the southeast – the Qaidam Basin.

Mongolian Basin　The Mongolian Basin covers a breadth of some 2000 km/1250 mi and extends far beyond the borders of China and the autonomous region of Inner Mongolia into the neighbouring country to the north. The broad and relatively flat basin with an average elevation of 1200 to 1500 m (4000 to 5000 ft) is bounded in the west by the Altai and Beishan mountains, in the south by the Nanshan range and the Gobi Desert, by the Greater Hinggan Range in the east and by the southern Baikal Mountains in the north. The region overall is characterized by the semi-arid conditions and the pronounced manner in which the contours separate the region into sub-basins. The wintry cold of the northern steppes and uplands allows for a traditional way of life based on nomadic transhumance, continuous migration to new grazing lands, while the barren, arid lands of the Gobi Desert, adjoining to the south, are hostile to life.

The Monsoon Dictates

Monsoon climate　The various climatic conditions that prevail in China are all dominated by the monsoon, which has a widely differing influence on the various regions owing to the broad expanse of the country from east to west and north to south, and because of the enormous differences in altitude. The seasonal **change in the prevailing wind direction** which occurs at monsoon time is determined by the contrast in temperatures between the broad continent of Asia and the Pacific Ocean.

In winter the winds blow from a cold high pressure area over central Asia and Siberia towards the Pacific. The prevailing northerly winds blow dry, cold air over the country, leading to **sunny, but cold weather**. In the extreme south the effect of these air flows are weaker so that the area, while not reaching tropical temperatures, does remain free of wintry frosts.

Dry and cold

In summer the winds come primarily from the south, bringing wet and warm air from the Pacific deep inland and causing rainfall whose volume gradually peters out towards the north. High temperatures and humidity lead to **conditions so sultry it is difficult for the body to cope**, especially as the nights are little cooler than the days.

Wet and warm

The transition from winter to summer weather, i.e. the onset of the cyclonic monsoon rains, is expressed as a frontal zone, which starts in southern China during the months of May and June and drifts northward until well into July. As the drift progresses, rainfall in the south gradually wanes. Towards the end of summer, the frontal zone once again starts to drift southward. From about September/October the cool, dry winter weather then reasserts itself.

Cyclonic monsoon rains

Autumn is the time for typhoons (from tai feng = big wind). These tropical cyclones only form in the low latitudes where the sea has a temperature of at least 26 – 27°C. They can extend to a height of 12 km/7 mi and be as much as 700 km/450 mi in diameter. In southern China more than **three typhoons a year** are to be expected. They hit the Chinese south coast from the southeast and their storm winds and flood tides in conjunction with heavy rainfall regularly cause serious damage. However, they rapidly lose their force as they move inland.

Typhoons

The monsoon rains of summer grow less the further inland a region is and the more it is sheltered from the sea by mountains, as the rainfall then falls on the high ground. This results in a division between the climate of eastern China, with its wet summer weather, and the west, which remains dry all year round. In the west, too, the highland climate of the Tibetan Plateau differs from that of the steppes and the desert of Xinjiang to the north. In the eastern half of the country, the verdant south contrasts with the yellow-coloured alluvial loess terrain of northern China. In summer the temperatures in both parts of eastern China are similar but in winter the north is very much colder than the south. A rough boundary between the

The climatic division

China *Climate*

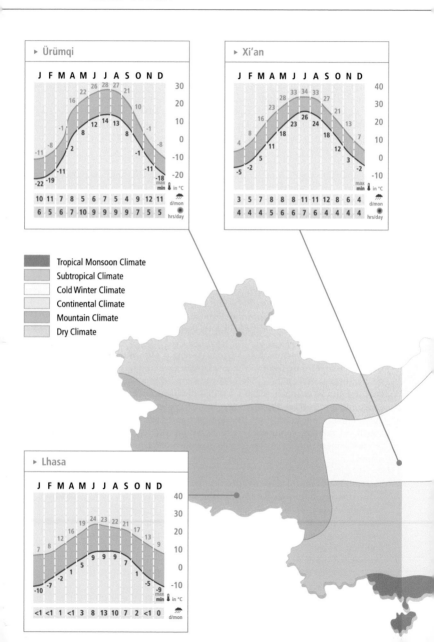

▶ Ürümqi

	J	F	M	A	M	J	J	A	S	O	N	D		
			-1		16	22	26	28	27	21				30
					12	14	13			10				20
		-8	2	8					8		-1	-8		10
	-11													0
			-11							-1		-11		-10
	-22	-19										-18		-20

max min in °C

| 10 | 11 | 7 | 8 | 5 | 6 | 7 | 5 | 4 | 9 | 12 | 11 | d/mon |
| 6 | 5 | 6 | 7 | 10 | 9 | 9 | 9 | 9 | 7 | 5 | 5 | hrs/day |

▶ Xi'an

	J	F	M	A	M	J	J	A	S	O	N	D		
					28	33	34	33	27					40
			16	23		26			21					30
	4	8	11	18			24		18	13				20
		5									12	7		10
	-5	-2									3	-2		0
														-10

max min in °C

| 3 | 5 | 7 | 8 | 8 | 8 | 11 | 11 | 12 | 8 | 6 | 4 | d/mon |
| 4 | 4 | 4 | 5 | 6 | 6 | 7 | 6 | 4 | 4 | 4 | 4 | hrs/day |

Tropical Monsoon Climate
Subtropical Climate
Cold Winter Climate
Continental Climate
Mountain Climate
Dry Climate

▶ Lhasa

	J	F	M	A	M	J	J	A	S	O	N	D		
					19	24	23	22	21					40
			12	16						17				30
	7	8				9	9	9		13	9			20
			1	5					7		1			10
		-2												0
	-10	-7										-9		-10

max min in °C

| <1 | <1 | 1 | <1 | 3 | 8 | 13 | 10 | 7 | 2 | <1 | 0 | d/mon |

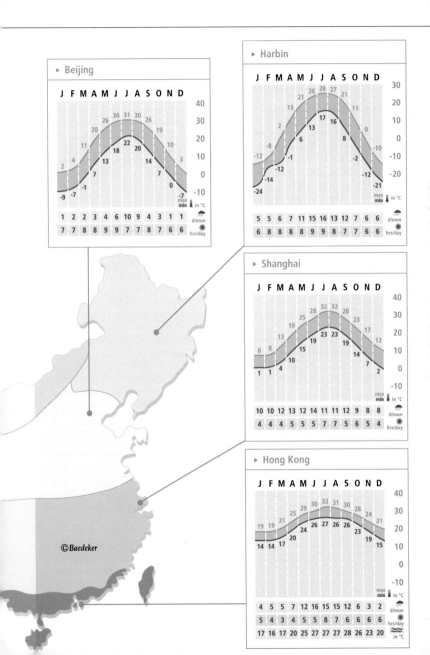

► Beijing

J	F	M	A	M	J	J	A	S	O	N	D	
2	4	11	20	26	30	31	30	26	19	10	3	max
-9	-7	-1	7	13	18	22	20	14	7	0	-7	min
1	2	2	3	4	6	10	9	4	3	1	1	d/mon
7	7	8	8	9	9	7	7	8	7	6	6	hrs/day

► Harbin

J	F	M	A	M	J	J	A	S	O	N	D	
-12	-8	2	13	21	26	28	27	21	11	0	-10	max
-24	-14	-12	-1	6	13	17	16	8	-2	-12	-21	min
5	5	6	7	11	15	16	13	12	7	6	6	d/mon
6	8	8	8	8	9	9	8	7	7	6	6	hrs/day

► Shanghai

J	F	M	A	M	J	J	A	S	O	N	D	
8	8	13	19	25	28	32	32	28	23	17	12	max
1	1	4	10	15	19	23	23	19	14	7	2	min
10	10	12	13	12	14	11	11	12	9	8	8	d/mon
4	4	4	5	5	5	7	7	5	6	5	4	hrs/day

► Hong Kong

J	F	M	A	M	J	J	A	S	O	N	D	
19	19	21	25	29	30	32	31	30	28	24	21	max
14	14	17	20	24	26	27	26	26	23	19	15	min
4	5	5	7	12	16	15	15	12	6	3	2	d/mon
5	4	3	4	5	5	8	7	6	6	6	6	hrs/day
17	16	17	20	25	27	27	28	28	26	23	20	in °C

©Baedeker

two runs from the Qinling mountains (south of Xi'an) towards the east (north of the Yangtse delta). Southward of this line the climate is sub-tropical and rice is the main crop to be cultivated, while to the north the plants that grow are those of temperate zones.

Flora and Fauna

Forests China still possesses all the key types of forest as appropriate to its various climatic zones, coniferous forests in the north, deciduous woodland in the temperate zones and tropical rainforest in the south. Forests occupy some 13% of the land space. Coniferous (larch, spruce and pine) and deciduous broadleaf (maple, birch, lime, ash) forests extend across the northern territories. Native fauna includes elk, reindeer, Siberian tigers and Amur leopards. One other plant that grows in the region is a small shrub with red berries, which goes by the name of **ginseng** (renshen), famous and sought after for the rejuvenating effect of its roots. Also dubbed the »elixir of youth« the plant is to be recommended as a tonic, but is also used as a medicine. The tropical rainforests, meanwhile, such as those which extend through Yunnan and Guangdong provinces, are home to a great many more species: numerous birds, monkeys, rhinoceros, tigers, elephants, muntyak deer and leopards.

Steppes and deserts Steppes cover much of the northern plain and the eastern part of Inner Mongolia. This provides a habitat for many game species and predators – camels, pheasants, rabbits, eagles, least weasels, foxes, bears, lynx, deer, mountain goats and wolves.

Mountains Tibet, the highest territory in the world, also has the roughest climate of any part of China, with severe temperature fluctuations dependent on the time of year. The Tibetan plateau is dominated by mountain vegetation, which extends down into the provinces of Yunnan and Sichuan. This is the land of the **yak**, a type of cattle with a thick woolly coat. Yaks are used as beasts of burden as well as for food and they also provide wool and milk. Other mountain creatures live in the Himalayan region, including kiang asses, wild yaks, orongo antelope and dwarf hare. In the mountains of central China there are still such typically Chinese animals as pandas, Asian black bears and red pandas, serow chamois, takin goats, snub-nosed monkeys and clouded leopards.

Birds With more than 1000 species of bird, China has more ornithological variety than any other country. These include Phasianidae and other Galliformes, the most familiar being the **game pheasant**. The most important species in this family include various kinds of partridge, grouse, Tibetan snowcock, rock partridge and francolins; there are also great bustards, little bustards and hazel grouse. Mountain bamboo partridges and Asian blue quails are popular as caged birds. The

Young pandas are particularly comical – the breeding station in Chengdu is a good place to see them.

enormous variety of waterfowl should also be mentioned, among which the colourful Mandarin duck is one well-known variety. Nearly all the types of crane which live here are protected species.

Doubtless the best-known of all endangered species is the **giant panda**. Stocks are being ensured by an elaborate breeding and protection programme. A similar programme was also successful in the case of the red ibis, a few hundred of which still live in Shaanxi. Young of the endangered Yangtze alligator, bred in captivity, are being released into the wild. Among other endangered species is Yangtze giant soft-shelled turtle, of which only four individuals are known. Tigers are also endangered, while the Yangtze river dolphin or baiji is believed to be extinct.

Rare animals

Of the 520 species of bamboo that exist in the world, 300 can be found in the tropical and sub-tropical south of China. The old bamboo forests cover some two percent of the forested area, although they are rapidly retreating. Owing to the extent of its range – it grows almost up to the snow line – bamboo is of great importance, in particular because it is such an **outstandingly useful plant**. As the trademark flora of this part of China and a popular subject for the nation's painters, it is used as building material for boats, houses, furniture and musical instruments. Bamboo roots, seeds and marrow are also used in cooking. Bamboo is also the main item in the diet of the giant panda.

Bamboo

Population · Politics · Economy

The core population
What is now regarded as the Chinese population, also named the **Han** after one of the imperial dynasties, is actually a mixture of ethnicities and cultures. As far as can be deduced from the archaeological record, the features of the original people, who settled on the banks of the Huang, are nowadays best represented in the central and eastern regions of the country. The repeated waves of invaders from the steppes to the north and periods of rule by the Mongolians and Manchurians have nevertheless led to an **intermingling of the various peoples** with the indigenous Chinese population. Other less extensive miscegenation has occurred between the northerly Han groups and Turkmen-Uighur and Persian peoples, who came from the west along the »Silk Road«.

Ethnic groups
The Han Chinese nowadays make up around 92% of the total population of China, while the remaining 8% belong to the country's 55 recognized national minorities, primarily settled around the western and southern peripheries. In the southwest, the remote geography has enabled such indigenous peoples as the **Zhuang, Miao, Yi and Yao** to survive. They still live, albeit in small numbers, in their mountainous regions. Unlike the Tibetans, the Mongolians, the Kazakhs and the Uighurs, who all developed independent scripts, the cultures of the ethnic groups in the southwest – on the borders with Laos, Cambodia, Myanmar and Vietnam – have never developed their own form of writing.

Population policies
With 1.3 billion people, China is the most populous country in the world. Some **birth control** initiatives have been in place since the first communist census of 1953 but political resistance meant that they barely scratched the surface of the population problem. Mao, for example, regarded birth control as »murder of the Chinese people«. This meant that, interrupted only by the catastrophe of the »Great Leap Forward« which claimed 20 to 30 million dead from famine from 1959 to 1962, the population exploded under his rule, from 563 million in 1950 to 983 million in 1980, a rise of 75% in the space of a single generation.

In 1979 a rigid **one-child policy** was introduced, though it was met with furious resistance and has been relaxed in subsequent years to include a number of exceptions. Among these is a rule that peasant families may have a second child if the first was a girl. This is because there is no state pension for rural peasants and, since daughters are fully adopted into the families of their husbands when they marry, a son still remains essential for security in old age. Regulations are also less strict for the 55 minority groups than they are for the Han Chi-

Even today, old people still enjoy more respect than they do in the West. →

nese. Rapidly increasing prosperity, movement to the cities and a generally higher standard of education since the 1990s have all led to married couples increasingly sticking voluntarily to the one-child rule, or even giving up the idea of children altogether for the sake of their careers. On the other hand, more children continue to be born in rural districts than is desired by family planners. Nevertheless the rate of growth has levelled out to a great degree and it is expected that the population will reach a projected peak of 1.5 billion in 2050 before declining again. Before then, however, China will be faced with another massive problem, that of an **increasingly aging population**.

State and Government

State constitution

The Peoples Republic of China, or to transliterate the Chinese name in Pinyin romanization: Zhonghua Renmin Gongheguo, was declared on 1 October 1949. The constitution defines the state as a »people's republic« with a socialist basis, a democratic dictatorship of the proletariat with aspects of Marxism, Leninism and Maoism under unlimited leadership by the Communist Party.

National People's Congress

The National People's Congress (a single-chamber parliament), the highest policymaking organ of the state, has close to 3000 members, elected by the provinces, the autonomous regions, self-governing cities and military units for terms of five years. This body makes the laws, determines economic planning and reserves the right to declare war. It meets once a year and determines the **standing committee** of the National People's Congress, the chairman of which has the role of head of state. During the parliamentary recess the standing committee is responsible for legislation and elects the **state council** as the executive organ of the National People's Congress. The council consists of a president, which it nominates, several vice-presidents, a general secretary and a variable number of other ministers with various portfolios. The government is answerable to the People's Congress.

CPC

The ruling party is the Communist Party of China (CPC) with its **Central Committee** (175 members), **Politburo** (16 members) and **Military Commission**. The highest decision-making body of the party is the Standing Committee of the Politburo led by a General Secretary.

Government

The area covered by the state is divided into 31 administrative regions: 22 provinces (sheng; roughly corresponding to the 18 historic provinces of the imperial era), five autonomous regions with special statutes for national minorities (Neimenggu/Inner Mongolia, Ningxia, Xinjiang/Sinkiang, Guangxi and Xizang/Tibet) plus four self-governing cities (the capital Beijing along with Shanghai, Tianjin and

Provinces Map

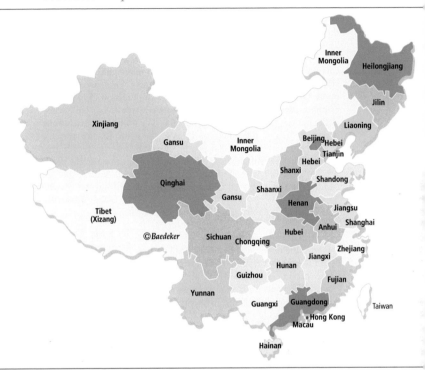

Chongqing). In addition, there are two special administrative regions in Hong Kong and Macao. China also claims sovereignty over the de facto autonomous Taiwan, which it regards as its 23rd province.

China remains a single-party dictatorship, although the continually growing market economy and the steep rise in prosperity have meant that the population has gained considerable freedom. This is particularly to be seen in terms of **entrepreneurial freedom**, the freedom to choose between jobs and freedom to travel. Religious activities have also come strongly to the fore, although the state continues to regard all kinds of religious practice with great suspicion and can be violent in its repression of them if they stray from the established structures (Falun gong, Catholics faithful to the Vatican etc.). With regard to **freedom of information and opinion**, the situation is markedly better than it was in the 1980s. The state's constant attempts to maintain control, its strict monitoring of the internet for example, increasingly look like Canute trying to turn back the tide. Political demonstrations in one or other part of the country are virtually a daily event

Democracy and human rights

and are an indication that the public at large are increasingly aware of their rights. By making it possible to call the government to task, the government itself has given citizens a means to defend itself against bad decision-making and despotism. The legal system is still not independent of the government, however, and is riddled with corruption. There is **no national opposition movement** able to provide a counterweight to the Communist Party. Free elections currently take place only at the lowest levels of administration (with a genuine choice of candidates, and, it goes without saying, only within the bounds f the officially permissible). The number of **executions** is greater than all the other countries of the world put together. In 2006, there were some 1,000 proven cases. In order to reduce this figure, China has stiffened the criteria for the imposition of the death penalty. Thus the Supreme Court has to confirm all death sentences, and the number of capital crimes has been reduced.

Economic Development

Since the days when the empire was first unified in around 100 BC and with the opening of the »Silk Road«, China had for long periods been **the greatest trading nation in the world** (with links in particular to central Asia and the Arab world). The situation gradually changed from the 15th century. Reasons for this included the isolationist policies of the Ming emperors after the end of the great maritime expeditions (1433) and the unstoppable rise of Europe from the 18th century.

Missed chances The opening of Chinese ports to trade, which was forced by Britain and other European states in 1842, brought to light on the one hand how seriously China had fallen behind in technology and politics, but also opened up new opportunities. With its **silk, porcelain and tea** the country still had goods for which it was world-renowned. Nevertheless its ossified methods of production hindered the exploitation of these massive opportunities for trade. While the world market in tea, for example, expanded by a factor of three and more between 1873 and 1910, China's share of that market plunged from 92 to 28 per cent.

Impoverished China Even in the 18th century China was still a decidedly rich country. Its impoverishment began in the 19th and increased to dramatic levels during the 20th. The main reason for the decline is usually seen in the opium smuggled into the country from India by unscrupulous Britons, which gradually drained China's finances and the morale of its ruling elite. In fact, though, there were at least two other factors, which were both as important: **the inability to reform the government, and civil war**. The Taiping Rebellion and its suppression devastated huge areas of the country between 1850 and 1864. After the fall of the empire, central power declined further and no sooner had some stability had been restored under Chiang Kaishek than Japanese troops occupied large areas of the country and plunged it back into chaos.

The founding of the new state in 1949 brought with it a long hoped-for consolidation and initially led to an economic boom. The policies of the Mao era, however, put a brake on development after 1958. In particular, time revealed that the **collectivization of agriculture** and the abandonment of the market economy had been extremely damaging to the country, to the extent that agricultural earnings per head of the dramatically multiplying population during the 20 years until the end of the Mao era were practically stagnant and the great mass of the population were as poor in 1977 as they had been in 1957.

The Mao era

The extent to which productivity had been crippled under Mao began to emerge when Deng Xiaoping, the leading figure behind the post-Mao reforms, allowed peasants to once more decide for themselves what to cultivate and to sell their surpluses at proper market rates. In the space of just eight years between the introduction of the reforms in 1979 until 1987, the wheat and rice harvests shot up by 50% and domestic earnings for peasants quadrupled. It proved much more difficult to restructure the massive, often highly subsidized state industries and bring them into a **market economy**. During the 1980s and 90s, the Party allowed more and more freedom to run private businesses and to engage in entrepreneurial activity in trade and industry. At the same time the state withdrew from an active role in the economy. The socialist planned economy was transformed into a market economy across the country. By 1996, state-owned companies were only contributing 29% of industrial production.

The Deng Xiaoping era

The volume of trade with other countries grew by a factor of 7.6 between 1980 and 1996, while the country's share of world trade approximately tripled during the same period. Nowadays China is on its way to becoming the largest trading nation in the world. The economic dynamism and long-term growth rates, consistently broaching 10% per annum, have benefited the entire country, albeit to differing extents. Even the formerly backward western parts of China have been gaining, since the government has been targeting development there. At the same time, though, this is causing a number of problems to come to a head. The growing chasm between rich and poor and the continued lack of a social safety net, along with endemic corruption, has repeatedly led to local unrest and occasionally riots. In spite of some local successes, in air pollution limitation for example, environmental problems are on the increase. The main problem, though, is the over-exploitation of resources.

Successes and difficulties

History

The history of China encompasses what can be a confusing chain of ruling dynasties, rise, unification and fall, threats from abroad by foreign peoples and armies along with internal power struggles among the elite. Take a trip now through China's history from the beginnings to the present day.

Prehistory and Early Historical Period

7th–2nd millennia BC	Neolithic age, featuring a variety of local cultures
5th–4th centuries BC	Yangshao culture
1600–1025 BC (approx.)	Shang dynasty
1025 (approx.)–249 BC	Zhou dynasty
221 BC	First unification of the empire

All over China you will hear and read about »5000 years of Chinese culture« or even »5000 years of Chinese history«. However, would such an individual as Confucius, for example, have understood himself as being Chinese? It is unlikely that he would. Zhong Guo, the »Middle Kingdom«, had a different meaning in those days. Nevertheless, even before Confucius there was likely to have been some kind of **cultural identity** amid the duchies and kingdoms of northern and central China, which would later form the core of the country familiar today. In those regions, at least the political elite would already have had common convictions and conventions and would have regarded themselves as civilized people, as they could write and follow elaborate rules of behaviour, which set them apart from »barbarians« with other ways of life.

Prehistory

Between 9000 and 3000 years ago, what was to become China was a patchwork of various local cultures, but all practising farming. On the fertile alluvial soil around the Yellow River and its tributaries, as well as in the basins of the Huai He and the Yangtse **cultivation of millet and rice** had begun 8500 years ago at least. At the same time pottery had been introduced. The Yangshao culture (5000–3000 BC) is famous for its bulbous but beautifully ornamental pots, which spread from the great curve of the Yellow River to all points of the compass. At around the same time, there is evidence that jade, silk and paint were all being produced in southern China.

The development of writing

The oldest evidence of writing in China can be found on so-called oracle bones dating from about 3500 years ago. At that time, under the **Shang dynasty**, there was a spectacular heyday of Chinese crafts with the manufacture of artistically designed bronze vessels, which were used for ritual purposes and are sometimes inscribed, thus allowing the reasons for their casting to be deduced. Less important

← *Hong Kong harbour – already full of shipping back in 1900*

Guardians of the mausoleum of the First Emperor: soldiers of the terracotta army

inscriptions were mainly written on strips of bamboo until the invention of paper in the 1st century BC.

From Confucius to the first emperor

The decisive phase, in which the emerging China developed its concept of itself and the world and formulated its ideals, took place within a span of just 300 years, from Confucius (c. 500 BC) to the unification of the empire in 221 BC. China at this time consisted of warring kingdoms, which had developed out of the **vassal states of the Zhou king**, whose suzerainty they no longer seriously acknowledged. It was an age of upheaval, of changing values and wars of hegemony. Court advisers were in demand, among them Confucius. The question was how to create a strong state and an ideal society. Confucius looked back to antiquity. The early Taoists had the radically opposing idea that civilization itself was a state of sin. However history followed its own logic and the fringe state of Qin, with little weight of tradition and a desire for reform, managed under the guiding hand of its king Zheng to defeat all its rival dominions. The ruler, to reflect the glory of this achievement, granted himself a new title, as »first emperor of Qin«, making him in effect the first emperor of China.

The 5000-year myth

So how old is China really? Since modern history is effectively defined to begin with the emergence of writing, the relevant figure in that sense is 3500 years. Features of the civilization now regarded as Chinese, however, were already present in much earlier times. On the other hand, the emergence of a definitively Chinese identity took place over a period spanning more than a thousand years. The **unification of the empire** is the key milestone in the process. It is from that point that an ideal encompassing the unity of the Chinese state exists. Quite early on though, the Chinese identity had already developed– after Confucius at the latest – an idea of a perfect past. Where other civilizations had their creation myths, Chinese myths feature cultural heroes who rescued people from vegetating in swamps, irrigated the land and taught them how to drain land, till soil and catch fish. These »**founding emperors**«, unmentioned in the earliest texts, were invented during the Zhou period. The first in the sequence is Fuxi, who is said to have ruled for 115 years from 2852 BC – with some generous rounding that would have been 5000 years ago.

The First Empire and its Fall

221–207 BC	Qin dynasty
206 BC– AD 220	Han dynasty
221–263	Three Kingdoms period
304–589	Northern and southern dynasties

National unity under the Qin and Han dynasties remained intact for about 440 years. The first half of this period, in particular, was characterized by **violent conquest**. China expanded southward as far as the South China Sea, eastward into Korea and north into the Mongolian steppes – ruining the livelihoods of the steppe peoples who lived there – as well as westward into central Asia along the »Silk Road«, which enjoyed its first boom period in the wake of these conquests. The dynasty secured its northern boundary by bribery, and by building a longer frontier wall than any other dynasty. The silk, which was regularly given to the nomadic peoples to pacify them, was greatly surplus to their own requirements, and thus they became traders, Chinese silk being bought and sold as far away as Rome.

The mighty empire of the Han suffered from its own internal strife. Power struggles between the court eunuchs and the families of the empresses weakened the imperial rule, allowing Taoist rebel movements (the »Yellow Turbans«) to emerge after 184 AD and eventually bring down the state. After Han rule ceased, China entered a transitional period lasting about 300 years (until 589). There was a division of power and of the empire itself so that the era is called the period of the »Three Kingdoms« and of the **»northern and southern dynasties«**. From 304 various steppe peoples took advantage of the power vacuum to conquer northern China, where they established various short-lived dynasties of their own. One of the effects was that

Decline of the Han regime

members of the intellectual elite fled south to a part of the country which seen only little Sinification until that time. New states were formed there as well and the Confucian **culture of intellectuals and scholars** gained a new self-confidence. Thanks to the foreign dynasties and their devout rulers, Buddhism took firm root in China and inspired an abundance of new art forms. The magnificence of the cave temples at Datong and Luoyang is a conspicuous example.

Second Empire

581–618	Sui dynasty
589	Second empire
618–907	Tang dynasty

The Sui dynasty managed to reunify China by 589. The building of the Grand Canal from the Yangtze to Beijing and the construction of a massive new capital city cemented their place in history, but their works did not continue for long. It was the subsequent Tang dynasty that created a major new empire extending as far as modern-day Kazakhstan. The Silk Road and Chinese Buddhism were both now at their height. The new capital of Chang'an (►Xi'an) was a world-class metropolis, a meeting point of peoples and religions, and at the time of **Emperor Xuanzong** (ruled 713–756) and his favourite consort Yang Guifei, the »poet princes« Li Bai and Du Fu became the stellar guiding lights of Chinese poetry. It was at some point during this period that the printing of books was invented – for the dissemination of religious propaganda.

A wave of change
Securing the full extent of all its conquests required intense efforts, which became too much for the empire over the course of time. For a few decades the regime lived beyond its means but in 755 the rebellion of An Lushan, a Sogdian-Turkic general in the service of the Chinese, put an end to this **»golden age«** as if it had been nothing but a fabulous dream. The consequence was that China lost all its central Asian possessions and Tibetan armies swept across the land as far as its capital. China's position as a world power was lost and the Silk Road lost its importance. The years of war against the rebels depopulated large areas of northern China, depleting the power base of the Tang themselves and creating the conditions for their subsequent decline and China's transformation into a state ruled by Confucian officials.

The centre of gravity shifts
At the same time, in the 8th century, the cultivation of rice paddies in the Yangtze region went through an epoch-making boom, shifting the centre of gravity of the Chinese state firmly southward. It was

from the south that most of the bureaucracy was later recruited. When in 760, in the midst of the unrest, the Chinese massacred thousands of Persian and Arab merchants trading in the country, it was an outward signal of a new change in thinking, which swept the elite with it. China was turning inward. Increasingly during the 9th century, **Confucianism gained in importance** and Buddhism was heavily criticized as an immoral foreign religion.

Such ideas soon asserted themselves at court, too. From 842 to 845, 4600 monasteries were dissolved and some destroyed, 260,000 monks and nuns were stripped of their religious status, 150,000 peasants who had been dependents of the monasteries were registered as taxpayers and all non-Chinese religions were totally forbidden. Although it was quickly rehabilitated, Buddhism was never able to fully recover from this period of repression.

Anti-Buddhist repression

The Rise of the Steppe Peoples

960–1279	Song dynasty
1126–1234	Northern China: Yin dynasty
1271–1367	Mongolian Yuan dynasty

The subsequent period of decline, which had actually begun decades before the »official« ending of the Tang dynasty, was comparatively brief for the core regions of China. It ended with the founding of the **Song dynasty**, which selected Kaifeng as its new capital. Along the northern borders, however, competitors who had organized themselves along Chinese lines were making themselves felt and forcing the payment of tribute by the Song-ruled empire. The second of these empires, ruled by the Jurchen Yin dynasty, conquered all of northern China as far as the river Huai in 1126, forcing the imperial court of the Song to flee south and move its capital to Hangzhou.

Building on a basis that had been forged during the Tang period, intellectuals of the Song era developed a philosophical system which went far beyond the original Confucian ideal with its concept of political and social order. The great **philosopher Zhu Xi** (1130–1200) codified it and thereby established an orthodoxy which would keep a hold until the 20th century. There was no longer an aristocracy as such. The apparatus of the state was based on officials who would obtain their posts on the basis of anonymous examinations. These examinations tested candidates on the key texts of Confucianism. The upper class, those able to afford education for their sons, received no privileges as such and were not immune from the decline

Neo-Confucianism and the rule of bureaucracy

of their families. Clans would also allow talented boys from poor families the opportunity to rise to the political and social elite. This mobility is one of the strengths of a state run by such Confucian officialdom and it was therefore able to survive any changes in the ruling dynasties virtually unscathed.

Economic life   Another innovation affected economic life, where there was more liberalism than in the past. An **urban citizenry** emerged. Where there had previously been nightly curfews, even in cosmopolitan Chang'an during the Tang era, now storytellers and clowns, taverns and bordellos would turn the Song capital into a vigorous metropolis even in the hours of darkness. Large private companies were formed for handcrafts and mining. Overseas trade blossomed and Quanzhou became the biggest port in the world.

The Mongol era   The Mongols under Kublai Khan were the first of the steppe peoples to achieve the conquest of all of China in the 13th century, although the undertaking had taken decades of struggle. In their giant new empire, the new capital would be a former border outpost which would later be called Beijing. Chinese citizens were now third class, behind the Mongolian ruling class and members of other defeated peoples. Thanks to the **Pax Mongolica** the Silk Road was opened up once again. Now Europeans, too, were coming as far east as China, and even revisionists who dispute that Marco Polo was one of them will certainly have to concede the fact of John of Montecorvino's inauguration in Beijing in 1293 or 1294 as the first Catholic archbishop of the city, or the presence of a Latin-inscribed gravestone of an Italian girl who was buried in Yangzhou in 1342.

The Beijing Era

| 1364–1644 | Ming dynasty |
| 1644–1912 | Qing dynasty |

Violent rebellion forced the Mongols back to the steppes after 1350. The rebel leader, son of a peasant, took the imperial throne for himself in 1368 and chose the name Ming, »**the Brilliant**«, for his empire and subsequent dynasty. He made his residence in Nanjing but, after his death, one of his younger sons gained control of the empire in 1402 and moved the seat of empire back to Beijing, thus moving once again from the heart of China to its fringe. His reason for the move was an ambition to inherit the entire Mongol empire, but the plan failed. Nevertheless, the layout of the city as established at that time and the new imperial palace he built are still in existence to this day.

Khubilai Khan receives visitors from Europe; among them, on horseback, Marco Polo

The same ruler who reigned as the **Yongle emperor** until 1424 also sought to establish China even overseas as the reconstituted centre of the civilized world. This led to the mounting of overseas expeditions under the leadership of the eunuch Zheng He (c. 1371–1434), a mega-project of the state for which an entire fleet of sea-going junks was built. Between 1405 and 1433 the fleet undertook seven voyages reaching as far as the Red Sea and East Africa.

Overseas expeditions

After the Yongle emperor, though, everything changed. The heirs to the throne were brought up in palaces and had never led armies. An **isolationist philosophy** began to win the upper hand at court. Trapped in Confucian arrogance, the rulers wanted nothing more to do with the »barbarians« of the outside world. The Mongols, however, were dependent upon trade with China. With such trade now denied them, they invaded the border regions. China responded with the building of a wall. A general plan for the project never existed, however. Starting in 1474, building work continued for 170 years, albeit with lengthy pauses. Isolationism also affected maritime trade. China's trading ships were forbidden to sail to foreign countries. It instituted a golden age for smugglers.

Isolationist policies

When the first Portuguese sailors appeared at the estuary of the Pearl River in the 16th century, China was not willing to tolerate their presence in Guangzhou. They were thus confined to a base on a nearby peninsula, which was to become Macao. This would also be the first base for European missionaries to China. Jesuits now made the journey to Beijing. The trailblazer was one **Matteo Ricci** (1552–1610). As educated men, and ones who took a great interest

The Jesuits

in the Confucian teachings, he and various others gained great respect at court. Jesuits would later be entrusted with the management of the Chinese calendar. It was their reports that gave Europe its first detailed knowledge of the Middle Kingdom.

Manchus on the dragon throne When a people's rebellion brought the bankrupt Ming dynasty crashing in 1644, a loyal general called on the Manchus for help. Freely invited into the country, they made use of the opportunity and took the whole of China for themselves. Qing, **»Great clarity«**, is the name given to their dynasty and empire. They quickly made alliances with some of the Mongols and built a new extensive empire, taking in Mongolia and central Asia and for the first time including Taiwan. In 1720 they also gained dominance over the hitherto independent Tibet.

A new heyday Under the Qianlong Emperor in the 18th century China experienced another heyday. The Manchu empire reached its greatest extent – not least thanks to clever religious diplomacy, for which impressive testament still stands in Chengde to this day. The general economic prosperity also brought an unparalleled increase in population, so that the population of China now exceeded the whole of Europe.

From the Opium Wars to Chairman Mao

1839–1842	First Opium War
1856–1860	Second Opium War
1900	Boxer rebellion
1911/1912	Revolution and founding of the republic
1931	Occupation of Manchuria by Japan
1937–1945	Japanese expansion and the Second World War

Even by the 18th century, the British had already become assiduous drinkers of tea. The expensive weed nevertheless needed to be paid for in China with silver as China imported nothing from Europe. At this point the British East India Company started to smuggle opium into China via Guangzhou, and rapidly the balance of trade was turned on its head. The emperor sent one of his officials to the city and in 1839 he had all of the opium he found stored there burned. Britain took this as a declaration of war and the first **Opium War** was begun. China, with nothing to match British cannon, was forced to open up Shanghai and other ports to overseas trade and to lease Hong Kong to the British crown in the Peace of Nanjing.

This was only the first of several demeaning defeats. A second Opium War saw British and French troops penetrate as far as Beijing, where they set the summer palace in flames. China found it particularly humiliating to be forced into allowing foreign embassies to open in Beijing. Soon France, Japan, Russia and Germany had also negotiated so-called Unequal Treaties, leased zones, concessions and special rights, and China was divided into foreign spheres of influence.

Subsequent wars

Much worse than this, though, was to follow the Taiping Rebellion, which from 1850 till 1864 plagued southern China and the Yangtze region. The rebel movement under its leader Hong Xiuquan combined traditional religious beliefs with nationalist politics against any entities with an interest in Manchu rule. It is still considered the **biggest rebellion in the history of the world** and ravaged whole areas of land, almost leading to the fall of the dynasty.

Taiping Rebellion

When the emperor ordered long-overdue reforms to the system in 1898, the widow of the former emperor Cixi placed him under house arrest. It was soon her hope that an anti-foreign movement, the **»Righteousness and Harmonious Fists«** would be able to drive out the hated foreigners, and she had its rioters armed. Massacres in Beijing of Chinese Christians and a siege of the embassy quarter lasted

Boxer Rebellion

In the first half of the 19th century, British merchants smuggled opium into China, causing millions of Chinese to become addicts

till an allied army from eight of the affected countries occupied Beijing and dictated the »Boxer protocol«. It obliged the Manchu empire to make high reparation payments and would be the trigger of its downfall.

Revolution and foundation of a republic

In southern China and among a Chinese diaspora, a republican movement was formed with the aim of bringing down Manchu rule. The leading figure was one **Sun Yatsen**. Three steps would lead to the fall of the empire: on 10 October 1911 a republican rebellion took root in the town of Wuchang (Wuhan), on 1 January 1912 in Nanjing the Republic of China was declared, and on 12 February 1912 the child emperor Puyi abdicated under pressure from the military eminence grise, **Yuan Shikai**. Yuan Shikai, although in fact a royalist, became president of the fledgling republic and turned it into a farce. The country collapsed again. Although central government nominally existed in Beijing, power was in truth exercised by warlords.

The rebellion of 14 May 1919

When the treaty of Versailles included the agreement that the former German lease zone of Jiaozhou, which had been occupied by Japan in 1914, was not to be returned to China, a powerful **patriotic movement** took root in Beijing and other cities. Its aims went beyond political protest to demand a complete renewal of the culture, »Down with Confucianism! Down with the classic script! And up with science and democracy!« was the cry, mainly among students of the new universities, which had been set up along western lines. New literature came into being using the language of the present day. Its most important protagonist was Lu Xun. Recipes for Western-style utopias were mooted and thus in 1921 the **Chinese Communist Party was established**. Mao Zedong was one of its founding members.

The era of Chiang Kaishek

Sun Yatsen made another attempt to bring China to together with Soviet support starting in 1923, using military means or negotiation. When Sun died, power shifted to a new man, Chiang Kaishek. In 1927 he had the **workers' movement** in Shanghai violently repressed. Communists, formerly his allies; fled to the mountains and established bases there. In 1928 Chiang indeed succeeded to a large degree in re-establishing national unity and he made Nanjing the new capital. A phase of relative peace then followed, during which China's economy also began to find its feet again.

Japanese occupation

In 1931 Japan's Kwantung army engineered the so-called **Mukden incident** and made it their excuse to occupy Manchuria and later, from 1937, a large part of China's core territories. The government initially fled to Wuhan, then on to Chongqing, which was declared the wartime capital. Memories of the **Nanjing massacre** of December 1937, when the Japanese army was exposed as a rabble of murderers and rapists, still darken Sino-Japanese relations to this day.

From 1930 Chiang Kaishek undertook a number of campaigns against Communist-controlled areas of southern China. By 1934 the Communists were no longer able to withstand the pressure. The Long March of the Red Armies began. They marched for thousands of kilometres through fierce terrain, suffering horrifying losses in the process. The march only ended a year later when it reached Yan'an in Northern Shaanxi.

The Long March

Chiang Kaishek was forced to put up a common front with the Communists against the Japanese during the Second World War but the alliance was not to hold for long. Mao developed his partisan tactics during this period. They saw only limited success against the occupiers but their patriotic élan gave the Communists a huge degree of renown, which was later to help legitimize their domination of the country.

The Second World War

Chiang Kaishek looked to have emerged as the great victor in August 1945 when the war ended. Nevertheless, he scorned the concept of a united government with the Communists, which even the USA had supported. His own **corrupt administration** rapidly threw away any credit it might have had in the eyes of the populace. The result was a new civil war, in which the disciplined Communist troops increasingly gained the upper hand. Chiang and his clique, along with more than a million followers, fled to Taiwan.

Renewed civil war

The massacre of Nanjing claimed the lives of up to 70,000 people

The People's Republic of China

1949	Establishment of the state
1958	Policy of the »Great Leap Forward«
1966–1969	Cultural revolution
1976	Death of Mao
1978	Start of the reform era
1989	Repression of the democratic movement
1997	Return of Hong Kong to China
2008	Summer Olympic Games in Beijing

From the founding of the state until September 1976 only one man mattered in China, one who could do what he wished and whose word was his followers' command: Mao Zedong. He was a visionary, a figure with which the entire nation could identify and he was completely untouchable. Anyone criticizing him, however good the reason, would be stripped of office and could be thankful if he merely became an »unperson«. Mao believed in the power of the mind and in the revolutionary élan of the simple people, the »masses«. In both these beliefs he was quite wrong. Although the Soviet-planned development strategy of the years up to 1957 had been directed towards industrialization and had brought economic growth, he believed that China could mobilize a huge effort to create a communist utopia. The**»Great Leap Forward«**, however, would be a disaster leading to a famine that would kill 20 to 30 million people.

Cultural Revolution Subsequently, as reason crept back into economic policy, Mao conceived a new masterplan. He saw the party bureaucracy and the intellectual classes as being rife with revisionist elements, capitalists in disguise, and hence he fomented a revolution among the country's youth: the **Great Cultural Revolution of the Proletariat**. It would be the most insane revolution of all time. Within two years, priceless cultural treasures were destroyed; an entire generation of children went uneducated; intellectuals, suspected capitalists and politicians ranging up to the state president himself were humiliated and many committed suicide. The party apparatus fell into chaos. A startling development occurred in 1972, though, when China put an end to its self-imposed isolation and opened up diplomatic and trading relations with capitalist nations.

The early reform era After Mao's death in 1976, the party carefully started to distance itself from Mao's policies. All of the excesses were blamed upon a group called the **»Gang of Four«**, which included Mao's widow. Behind the scenes there were furious arguments about the direction to

Resistance to state oppression: the crushing of the democracy movement in 1989

be taken, how far to break from Mao and how much to align to a market economy. By means of some clever manœuvring **Deng Xiaoping**, managed to force through a package: economic reforms would be undertaken (reduction of government interference, more market economics, openness to the outside world), but the Communist Party's monopoly of power would remain. The decollectivization of agriculture was the first great success. His special economic zones were also beneficial, bringing foreign capital and expertise into the country. However, in 1986 a series of demonstrations calling for greater freedoms for the populace and a reduction of arbitrary state interference brought forth an uncompromising response from the conservative forces in the government. On 4 June 1989 the international community was shocked by the bloody suppression of a **student-led democracy movement** in the centre of Beijing.

This »victory« did not benefit the conservatives at all. The mostly aging old guard was forced to make way for a technocratically oriented younger generation who continued the Deng reforms. China started a **staggering ascent to become a power in world trade**. It became the »workshop of the world«, not only because of its low wages but thanks to a huge entrepreneurial effort and a decisive desire for education. Never before in history had a country changed so radically as China has done since 1990, and it has not only been a mere few who have benefited. In addition, the country has also been rediscovering its own past. Pride in its »5000 years of culture«, even if the description is based on ancient myths, has taken root in virtually every Chinese – and surely not without reason. China is well on the way to living up again to its old name, the »Middle Kingdom«.

China since 1990

Art and culture

This section covers some of the background which will help you to understand the things you will see and experience in China. Buddhist temples and the Peking opera, artistic gardening and symbolism, the architectural forms from traditional palaces to modern buildings, art, ancient and contemporary and the varied world of Taoism.

Architecture

Traditional and Modern

The dramatic leaps and upheavals which have taken place in the development of the new China and its identity are nowhere more apparent than in the world of architecture. Whereas traditionally all the various regions had maintained their own styles, specifically suited to the area in question, nowadays the dull, **modern architecture of refurbished buildings everywhere** predominates in the inner cities: white tiled facades with blue-tinted glass. Attempts to combine modern high-rise architecture with classical building forms have mostly been disappointing.

It is in Hong Kong where the most successful attempts have been made to create internationally recognized modern buildings which set themselves apart from the uniform template. Admittedly that part of the country was untouched by the political and cultural upheavals of the post-war period. Meanwhile there have been efforts to give large hotels or skyscraper offices a »Chinese« touch by adding the familiar curving roof. They were doomed to failure and have been abandoned. The exciting projects of the early 21st century, the national theatre, the national museum, the buildings for the Olympic Games in Beijing, the latest office towers in Shanghai, that city's satellite town of Luchao and others, have primarily been entrusted to architectural agencies from Europe or America. To see original Chinese aesthetics in architecture, it is necessary to go back into the past and into the country.

Basic Elements of the Classic Building Style

Traditional building styles, varied as they may be, follow systems based on a few basic concepts. This can be seen in its purest form in northern China. Two features in particular stand out: first of all the symmetry involving a pronounced axis with a cult symbolism, aligned towards the throne in a palace, the image of the god in a temple or the altar to the family's ancestors (at least where it once stood) in a peasant home. The second feature is the arrangement of the building or group of buildings in keeping with the higher **symmetry of the heavens**, i.e. the main façade faces south, or alternatively east. This second aspect also characterizes the layout of cities. A typical central core for a Chinese city (especially in northern China) is laid out in chessboard fashion, surrounded by rectangular walls, aligned towards the points of the compass and divided into four quarters by two main streets that cross in the middle.

Axis and compass points

← *An elaborate head-dress: a performer of Beijing opera preparing to go on stage*

TIMBER FRAME CONSTRUCTION

The traditional method of construction in Beijing uses a timber frame. The roof with its characteristic curved form is supported by a framework of wooden columns and beams.

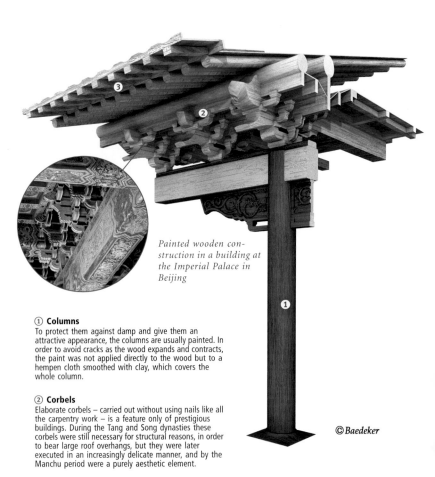

Painted wooden construction in a building at the Imperial Palace in Beijing

© Baedeker

① Columns
To protect them against damp and give them an attractive appearance, the columns are usually painted. In order to avoid cracks as the wood expands and contracts, the paint was not applied directly to the wood but to a hempen cloth smoothed with clay, which covers the whole column.

② Corbels
Elaborate corbels – carried out without using nails like all the carpentry work – is a feature only of prestigious buildings. During the Tang and Song dynasties these corbels were still necessary for structural reasons, in order to bear large roof overhangs, but they were later executed in an increasingly delicate manner, and by the Manchu period were a purely aesthetic element.

③ Rafters
In order to achieve an attractive curve of the roof, the ends of the rafters were lengthened by adding »flying rafters« to them. Where the visible timbers were painted, swastikas were used to decorate the rectangular rafter ends and so-called Buddha's eyes for the round ones.

With the exception of solitary peasant dwellings, building in China does not typically involve individual buildings as it does in Europe. Instead a group of buildings is clustered around a central courtyard. The ensemble will usually consist of a main building aligned towards the south and two side buildings aligned at right-angles to that. The southern perimeter of the courtyard is either formed by the rear of another building or by a high wall taller than a man. It is always the longest side which is the front. Other characteristics include the single-storey building style and the fact that all such groups are walled. These basic features apply equally to city dwellings – a typical example being the courtiers' dwellings of old Beijing – or to palaces and temples. Especially in the latter, these characteristics are found all over the country. The most important exceptions were places of business, which tend to be huddled together with no courtyards, being built right next to the street without regard for the compass points.

Ensemble building

These are best known from Beijing but can be encountered in other places, too. They are walls which block the view through the gates of an estate from outside. In the case of temples they are built in front of the main portal on the opposite side of the street, thus visually isolating the building when looking out, but also dividing the sacred areas from the profane. The phrase »spirit walls« refers to a **folk belief** that the walls will prevent evil spirits from entering, since such spirits, it is thought, can only move in straight lines. Zigzagging bridges and tall steps up to temples also exist for similar reasons. The Chinese term, though, means little more though than a false wall, and makes no reference to any spirits.

Spirit walls

Timber-frame Construction

Traditional buildings individually are usually built on the basis of a timber frame with a rectangular floor plan. The key building worker was thus not a bricklayer but a carpenter. A stone terrace was elevated above the ground and wooden columns around it were joined by means of longitudinal and transverse beams. Above this the roof truss was constructed, consisting of chambers that tapered towards the top. All the wooden parts of the building were put together **without nails**. Once the roof was covered, all the other work would continue beneath it.

Construction

A pedestal consisting of natural stone carved into a rectangle is usually the height of one step for dwellings. It is precisely matched to the floor plan of the building since the eaves, lacking any guttering, need to protrude over its edge. The base for the pillars is formed by packed and shaped boards upon which the pillar itself simply stands.

Pedestal

The number of bays – the space between the pillars – is considered the classical measurement of a building's size, even though the dis-

Pillars and bays

The angle of the roof, here on a monastic building near Yangzhou – is the result of a complex construction.

tance between columns varies with the height of the building. The figure given applies to the number of bays as seen from the front (identical with the number from the rear) and the side. The number of columns inside the building depends on its size and how the rooms are laid out. There are always an odd number of bays along the longest sides so that a central entrance is created. The Chinese word for a bay is jian and is often inaccurately translated as »room«. Thus the legend that the imperial palace has 9999 rooms, as is often said, really means that it has that number of bays – one fewer than the palace of the sky emperor.

Elegantly curving roofs
The sweeping curved roofs are indubitably the most characteristic features of Chinese buildings. Why the ancient Chinese should have put in all the extra building effort necessary to build such a curving roof has been the matter of some debate. Was it simply for aesthetic reasons? The most convincing answer, though, rests on a conflict of aims for the building. To keep water dripping from the eaves as far away from the building as possible, in particular so that the wooden parts of the body could stay dry in the wind and rain, the roof needed to overhang as far as possible. If the angle of the roof were to be constant, however, this would mean having extended eaves that would cast a shadow over much of the building preventing sunlight from getting indoors. The curvature of the roof eliminates this disadvantage.

»Multi-inclined« roof
Aesthetics and prestige are definitely behind one other feature of the more important buildings, the multi-inclined roof, taking the form of a **hipped roof**. The actual roof is raised above a lower section with a shallower incline supported by its own thin columns, which often covers only the gallery of the building. Without being immediately

obvious, this double-inclination construction has the effect of raising the roof ridge by several metres, relative to a single-inclination roof, causing the building to appear more imposing.

The aesthetic of roofs is completed by ornamentation. Some roofs are decorated with relief-work, decorative discs which line the bottom of the convex rows of tiles and the crescent-shaped slats in between, which form the actual edges of the eaves. The ends of the rafters underneath the eaves have swastikas painted on them, so-called **Eyes of Buddha**. The ridges of a roof are formed by special tiles which are higher than the others, providing extra visual emphasis. In northern China the raised ends of the ridges are particularly conspicuous (creatures named chiwen seem to be swallowing the ridge in their mouths) as are the dragon heads where the raised upper section of the transverse ridges come to an end and the ceramic animal figures which adorn the continuation of them, forming a sequence which is completed at the bottom by the figure of an immortal riding on a phoenix. In southern China other types of (often quite opulent) decoration are popular. For temples and guild houses the roof top and ornamental panels under the eaves are sometimes decorated with painted sculptures of picture-book luxuriance.

Roof decoration

Diversity of Form and Function

The building methods described here were used almost universally in the China of old. The complicated joinery of the beams is lacking however in most simple residences. The layout around a courtyard, the preferred alignment of the main building lengthways in a southerly direction and the **principle of axial symmetry**, however, were applied without variation to buildings serving a variety of functions and covering all degrees of prestige. This might be taken as a certain poverty of structural imagination but it could also be seen another way. This traditional building form attained such perfection of design and allowed for such flexibility for individual buildings in terms of breadth, depth and height and the layout of rooms inside that it could be used for virtually any purpose. Apart from single-storey hall-type buildings (which with regard to building techniques also includes residential houses), distinction is made between various other types of building, as follows:

Multi-storey buildings form a class in their own right (the Chinese term is lou). They include residences with an upper floor, bell towers and drum towers, turrets marking the corners of city walls and the barbicans over city gates. They may be fully or only partly walled – at least on the ground floor – but they all have a wooden roof.

Multi-storey buildings

This is the category in which the most variety of form is apparent. Floor plans can be square, hexagonal, cruciform, fan-shaped or cir-

Pavilions

cular and a variety of other shapes are to be found, too. The common characteristic is that they are open on at least two sides and often all sides. Another distinction is made between **garden pavilions** – based on timber frames without (solid) walls but possibly including balustrades – and **tower pavilions**, usually walled. Europeans sometimes apply the word pavilion to any other types of Chinese buildings, including some with multiple storeys, which do not fit into the categories of residences or pagodas.

Pagodas One structure which developed from Indian »stupas« is a distinctive form of **»Buddhist church tower«** marking a holy district. They do not contain bells but house relics and some smaller designs identify tombs. Three specific types of pagoda can be seen. The slender Chinese pagodas, sometimes on a square base but mostly featuring a regular polygonal floor plan, have pointed roofs and a structure divided by an odd number of protruding roof-like ledges. Pagodas are typically built of masonry. So-called »porcelain pagodas« are entirely covered with glazed tiles. Wooden pagodas have a masonry core. **Bottle pagodas or dagobas** originated in Tibet and consist of a tall multi-level pedestal with a structure on top of a form not unlike an upside-down brandy glass, above which is a spire topped with a bronze canopy. Indian-Nepalese **diamond throne pagodas** consist of a very tall, square pedestal, richly decorated with relief work, which can be climbed by means of a internal stairway. Sitting on top of the base are five small pagodas, the central one being taller than the others. These five small pagodas are similar in form to the dagobas and their pedestals are also adorned with reliefs or statuary.

Regional Buildings

It can roughly be said that the attention to compass alignment is more heavily stressed the further south one goes. The architects also seem to favour more decoration, indeed ostentation, further southward. In **central China** one common type of structure is the stepped gable. In the **Yangtze region** high, pointed roofs are popular. In the far south, however, in Guangdong province for example, there is no curvature to the roofs at all, but tall roof ridges decorated with statues. In **Fujian** the ridges themselves are curved and have high pointed ends (»swallow-tail roofs«). In the same region the biggest traditional residential buildings in China are to be found, with up to six storeys, circular or square and possessing rugged outer walls made of clay, thick and windowless at the bottom and with at most three entrances. These too have axes obeying the compass-alignment principle. In the courtyard is a temple dedicated to the residents' ancestors. The simplest dwellings are cave dwellings in the alluvial loess, which are common in the provinces of **Shanxi and Shaanxi**, where there are whole villages of them, although such homes are now increasingly being abandoned.

Buildings in the Tibetan Style

The architecture of the Tibetans is not so uniform. In north Sichuan, for example, Tibetan buildings are different from those in Lhasa. Here we are primarily concerned with the building methods used in the towns and villages of the autonomous region of Tibet. The religious architecture of Mongolia was also influenced by Tibetan sources, as was the style used in the building in several imperial-era monasteries in Chengde or the Yihe Yuan summer palace in Beijing.

Basic structures

A typical Tibetan building has a flat roof and consists mainly of daubed clay or clay tiles. The walls are then covered in white or red plaster and the flat roof is edged with black thatch. Symmetry of design is uncommon and is standard only for prestigious monastery buildings. For larger, multi-storey buildings the walls are angled inward, the window openings (with trapezium shaped frames) are small so that the interiors are immersed in mysterious semi-darkness. One peculiarity is the **fabric adornment of the buildings** in the form of decorative curtains for galleries and porches as well as five-coloured prayer pennants: blue for the sky, white for the clouds, red for the sun, green for water and yellow for the earth. On residential front doors a recumbent crescent will be painted with a comet-like circle and tail floating above it, symbols for the sun and moon and for the unity of opposites.

The white dagoba in the Beihai Park in Beijing is an example of a chorten

Religious buildings
Large monasteries consist of multiple buildings, which are usually grouped in irregular clusters so that the monasteries are like towns in their own right. Occasionally **the arrangement will take the form of a mandala** (▶Chengde, Puning Si). The holy of holies is sometimes covered with a bronze roof that glitters gold in the sunlight and which is curved in the Chinese style. The decoration of the roof usually includes a Wheel of Life in the centre, looking much like the wheel of an old sailing ship. This is flanked by two gazelles recalling the gazelle arbour where Buddha gained enlightenment.

Castles
Since the state machinery in Tibet was unable to effectively guarantee internal and external security, various castles or fortresses (dzongs) were built throughout Tibet and monasteries are frequently also situated and designed to allow for defence against attackers. Although the dzongs have now vanished apart from a few ruins, Tibet's largest fortress, indeed its most famous building of all, still remains: the **Potala Palace**.

Central Asian and Islamic Architecture

Central Asia
In the autonomous region of Xinjiang, yet another building style is predominant, a style which came hand-in-hand with Islam from the Turkic and Arab regions and can be seen unmistakably in the religious buildings of the region. One especially typical characteristic is the **geometric and floral ornamentation**, carved out of wood or added as stucco, which is particularly conspicuous in its use of polychrome, blue-and-white or green glazed tiles. The typically oriental curved roofs catch the observer's eye as well as the use of stalactites made of stucco, which also appear in the Moorish architecture of Andalusia. The pillars, often made of wood, are octagonal with plenty of ornamentation, while the walls are made of sun-dried bricks.

Islamic architecture
The Islamic architecture in the rest of China displays little Arab influence except in a few exceptional cases. The mosques tend to follow the customary style of hall structures around a courtyard. Minarets often resemble the Buddhist pagodas. The main building of any mosque is its large prayer hall. The alignment of the buildings is not southerly but along an east-west axis, so the people can face in the westerly direction of Mecca as they pray.

Western Stylistic Influences and Colonial Architecture

After the first of the Opium Wars (and earlier in Guangzhou and Macao) a typical colonial-style architecture developed, though it was limited to a few places. In southern China this can be seen in the arcades around the buildings' perimeters, allowing them to be ventilated without letting in the sun. In particular as a result of mission-

Inspired by Egyptian architecture: the Great Hall of the People on Tian'anmen Square in Beijing

ary work and railway building, Western architecture from several countries spread in the form of churches and railway stations, even in the interior of the country. One of the best surviving examples of such a national style from the West is the unusual case of Qingdao: although German colonial rule was ended as long ago as 1914, building styles such as mansard roofs or (imitation) half timbering are still used to the present day.

As the Chinese Republic was consolidating in the so-called Nanjing Decade (1928–1937), there was a linked architectural movement opposed to Western influence, which sought to combine **Western building techniques with Chinese stylistic elements** in order to create a new type of national architecture. The Bauhaus style prevalent in Europe at the time was thus shunned here and appears only in a few isolated examples in Shanghai.

The Nanjing Decade

»National Form, Socialist Content«

With the founding of communist China in 1949 the country sought out a new style of socialist architecture, inspired by what was then a perceived fraternity with the Soviet Union. In pursuing the »national form, socialist content« ideal propagated by Stalin, the Chinese nevertheless avoided wholesale imitation of the Stalinist »wedding-cake style« and built much plainer buildings. In addition the **national style of the Republican era** was resuscitated. There was nevertheless a movement in opposition to this as well, which clearly rejected the traditionalist forms as well as the adoption of an international style, scorned as being Western-capitalist. The aim was to create something new from the best of the whole world. This is why, for example, the assembly hall of the People's Congress in Beijing plainly exhibits signs of inspiration by ancient Egyptian temple architecture.

Architecture of the Reform Era

From 1978 a new discussion about architectural design principles was opened. A much more basic problem came to the fore, though, **town planning**. Poor concepts developed over the course of decades needed to be corrected, including the neglect of the old city centres and their excessively dense residential populations, which was turning them into slums, excess pressure on the transport networks, and industrialization, which had proceeded in the absence of town-planning principles and had led to overuse of resources and a degree of pollution which in some places had reached alarming levels.

Reforms are clearly leaving their mark In terms of architecture, the new town planning brought with it much more versatile demands for buildings as well as a variety of concepts and interests in profitability among architects themselves – and foreign investors – plus a recognition of individual creativity, all of which led to an extraordinarily increased **variety of styles and buildings** in comparison with earlier times. The spectrum ranges from hair-raisingly expensive villa estates to 50-storey skyscrapers which would not be out of place in Chicago. The influence of investors from Hong Kong is clearly exhibited. The estates on the outskirts of cities are designed very much along American lines.

Garden Palaces and the Art of Gardening

Chinas gardens are works of art where bears little resemblance to what is familiar in Europe. Instead of gazing across broad lawns, the view is met with walls and buildings, which set a framework for the garden itself. It is not glittering rows of flowers which set the primary patterns here; rather it is jagged, rocky artificial hills. Instead of statues of classical goddesses or putti, **bizarrely shaped natural rock formations provide the ornamentation**. Instead of walking along straight gravel paths, visitors have to teeter up and down amid the rocks or even descend into caves. There are no benches in the open to provide places to rest, but pavilions and verandas. Instead of a pocket of nature surrounding a building, here buildings and walls enclose the garden, like a miser guarding his hoard. Even the water is different. Here no fountain spouts from the centre of a pond, instead the gentle trickling of a stream can be heard or the sound of raindrops on a pool.

Scholars' Gardens

The unique features of these gardens arise from the fact that most of the garden designers were usually people of literary training who, after a life of toil as an official, finally sought peace in retirement. Most went to the Yangtze region, where more often than not they had been born, and even now this area has more gardens than the rest of the country, including some of the finest in the land. In addition of course, there are also the large imperial gardens, although these too were inspired by the scholars' gardens of retired officials in the south.

The gardens reflect a Taoist ideal, seeking harmony between nature and the works of man. By presenting the **basic themes of scenic variety** in all their opposing aspects – hills and waterways, summits and caves, barren and verdant, wet and dry, colourful and bleak, wild and tame – they create within the enclosing rectangle of masonry an

Philosophical aspects

Pavilions and colonnades like here in Liu Yuan in Souzhou make the garden experience pleasant even when the spring weather is less than inviting.

edifying observation of the totality of nature, revealing its true nature as seen from a viewpoint corresponding to the male-female, earth-and-sky harmonious polarity of Yin and Yang.

Sensory sophistication

In addition to the philosophical aspects there is also the dramatic, theatrical arrangement. It would be stupid to show everything at once, thus walls and winding paths split the space up, creating a **vivid kaleidoscope**, sometimes big, sometimes small. Some scenes are no bigger than a room, through which the winding paths lead visitors from one surprise to the next. While a section of garden may still be hidden by a wall, window-like openings provide an exciting taster of what is to come. On another occasion, the sight of a distant pagoda and a waterway beyond the garden may be incorporated as »hidden« scenery.

Not only beautiful but practical

Amid all the aesthetic beauty of the gardens, there is also an impressive practicality about them. There is no reason to rush indoors to shelter from wind and rain; there are always pavilions, fairy-tale castles, galleries and verandas to keep out the weather. Indeed some aspects only come into their own when it rains, especially the banana trees. It is not because of their fruit that they stand before the windows of the observation huts, but for the striking sound of the rain beating on their great leaves.

Symbolism

The **symbolism of the plants** is also important. Weeping willows, for example, both embody the spring and symbolize feminine tenderness. The lotus plants in the ponds are certainly delightful for their flowers and their fragrance, but the associations they invoke go much further. The Chinese word for lotus is lian, a homophone of the word for love and of another word meaning a »joining together« of people, i.e. marriage. The buildings too have their own symbolism. An entrance in the form of a bottle or vase – ping in Chinese – evokes the homophone meaning »peace« and »rest«: i.e. »enter in peace«.

Educational worth

Unfortunately, Western observers find it difficult to appreciate one last, but highly important aspect. The garden builders revelled in a superb education. The scenery and the names of the halls make reference to stories and legends, which are primarily variations on a single theme: a simple life as far as possible from the world of politics. In the »Garden of the Master of Nets« in Suzhou, for example, the owners stylized themselves as simple merchants, in this case recalling a wise elder who was happier catching fish than risking his life in dignified office. Among the scholarly gardeners, it is positively stylish to play with hermit traditions. Retirement offered time for Taoist contemplation and for a **luxurious renunciation of the world**. In a garden it was possible to create something that the contemptible world otherwise withheld: a paradise.

The lotus flower, symbol of love, and (for Buddhists) of purity

Imperial Garden Palaces

»Every emperor or ruler needs to possess a garden, in which to wan- **Ideology...**
der and to seek rest in mind and body once the audiences of the day
have been conducted and public duties have been completed. In such
a place, a ruler could relax his mind and calm his spirits. Without
such a place, sensual lusts would consume him and sap his will.«
These were the words the youthful Qianlong emperor used to argue
a **moral basis for imperial leisure gardens**. The common label used
for such places is »summer palace«, although this is only roughly ap-
plicable and the English term has no equivalent in Chinese. The gardens, therefore, were not simply for pleasure but instead provided
the ruler with a calming and morally irreproachable form of relaxa-
tion and a boon to his spirits

This may have been the ideology propounded but it hardly explains **... and reality**
the number of such amenities. Under the last of the dynasties there
were five gardens northwest of Beijing, one in Chengde, as well as
other parks around the lakes outside the Forbidden City. The fact
that they all covered acres of land also goes unexplained by Qianlong's justification. In fact, though, their functions were various.
Under the last dynasty these garden palaces with their extensive
waterways would, depending on the location, their nature and the
preferences of the emperors themselves, would be used as a **second
palace for the emperor** (along with all his wives, children, eunuchs
etc.) whenever he tired of the palace in Beijing, a home for the em-

press dowager, the mother of the reigning monarch, for receiving and accommodating ambassadors bringing tribute and various other purposes. In addition, the gardens around the summer palaces would be used for sporting events, festivals with firework displays, acrobatic, theatrical and ice-skating performances or boat trips. They even allowed the emperors to go shopping in imitation shopping streets. Other uses included acting as a base for hunting or riding expeditions, recuperation spots, for gatherings of intellectuals, as art galleries and libraries, as tea houses and pavilions, for the pursuit of religion (ancestor worship, Buddhism) in the temples which were included at the sites, and for military exercises.

The world in one garden The variety of function provided by the gardens is reflected in the extraordinary diversity of design and layout of buildings and parkland. They display little of the strict hierarchy of the Confucian conception of the world. They pursue quite different ideals: **solidarity with the countryside and people**, expressed in the grey of the roof tiles, sometimes early on by the integration of cultivated fields, which allowed the emperor to see the struggles of the working people. With scenes and building styles from all the various regions of the country and of the world, the gardens illustrated that Manchu China was an international empire. That is the reason for Tibetan-style buildings in the Summer Palace in Beijing, a village of Mongolian yurts in Chengde or the dykes that replicate those of the West Lake at Hangzhou. As in the scholars' gardens, individual tableaux and pleasure palaces embody in both name and design the classic Chinese wisdom or make reference to it. Curiously, **the paradise theme** is also part of this, even though the literary ideal of renunciation of politics was quite contrary to the claim to absolute rule propounded by the emperors.

Ink Painting

Like calligraphy (► Baedeker Special p. 62) the related art of ink painting was not primarily practised in ancient China by professional artists but by scholars earning their income as officials or politicians, in other words, amateurs in the best sense. They did not sell their works, they donated them. Anyone seeking to make a living from art was seen as an artisan and as such was not usually highly regarded in society.

Painting in landscape form Chinese painting is vastly different from that practised in Europe. Even the formats are different. The Chinese use **horizontal scrolls**, which are not to be observed at once but in sections, vertical scrolls, album pages or fans. Paintings are made on paper or silk, often using only black ink. The ink does not usually cover the whole surface and areas of white such as clouds or water are created by leaving the ground uncovered. Calligraphy, dedications, verses, reminiscences, often referring to familiar wisdoms are an integral part of the pictures. All paintings include the red seal of the artist and often the collector's seal as well.

Landscapes

The most popular genre was landscape painting. The images embody a Taoist-inspired view of nature. Amid a breathtaking backdrop of mountains, lakes, streams, waterfalls and clouds, the beholder's eye is led along a winding path and over narrow bridges to a pavilion, where a wise man, tended by servants, looks out at the staggering scenery about him. The human is tiny, the nature immense. By rolling and unrolling the metres and metres of scroll, the viewer can undertake **virtual journeys through the extended landscape**. Examples such as this explain why such paintings do not display a realistic perspective. The same applies equally to paintings made in vertical formats: as the perspective changes for someone walking through a landscape, so too does the perspective for someone viewing such a painting.

Plants

Other motifs for ink painting are also primarily concerned with nature. They mainly show plants and flowers – in particular those with

Mongolian emperor hunting tigers, shown on a roll about 3m/10ft long dating from around 1300

Water calligraphy is a transient art form, as the writing disappears when it dries. It is best to watch the artists as they work.

WRITING AS AN ART FORM

Skill with the brush was essential for every Chinese who wanted to make a name for himself in imperial times: it was impossible to pass the Mandarin examinations without good handwriting. As Chinese typewriters were expensive, unwieldy and slow to operate without a great deal of practice, everything was written by hand right up to modern times. Only the computer brought this to an end.

To this day, shops for stationery and artists' equipment sell the utensils that were needed on the desk of a Chinese scholar: **brushes** varying in size from pencil-thin for personal correspondence to thick as an arm for display calligraphy; special paper, which is absorbent but does not allow the ink to run; and an **inkstick** and **inkstone**. Liquid ink is not used: the black inksticks, sometimes decorated with ornamental gilding, are rubbed on very fine black basalt with water. The other implements are a **brush rest** on which to place wet brushes, a brush box to hold the brushes when they are not in use, a water can and a little porcelain bowl for washing the brushes. **Seals** are extremely important even today. Their purpose, like that of a signature, is authentication. Except in the case of collector's items made by a famous seal carver, the value of a seal is dependent mainly on its beauty and the rarity of the stone. The work of cutting the seal, by contrast, is cheap. The seal comes with a box of red seal ink.

Calligraphy is more than just beautiful handwriting: it is an art form in its

own right. To know the names of the most famous masters of the art is still a matter of general knowledge, and their personal styles have been much imitated. Professional calligraphers are masters of several styles, from the ancient clerical script (or even the archaic seal script) to regular script and the highly personal cursive script, in which one character flows into the next and no longer fills an imaginary square space of its own. Chinese calligraphy demands not just a steady hand, but years of practice.

The National Gallery in Beijing often holds exhibitions of modern calligraphy, and the works of the great masters are among the treasures of the Palace Museum. To appreciate the popularity of this art form, go to a park in the early morning. In places that are paved with slabs of stone or concrete, it is usual to see at

Masters of calligraphy can be found in museums and parks.

least one or even several water calligraphers at work. **Writing in water** is a new trend. To do it, in place of a brush the artists use rags wrapped around the end of a sawn-off broomstick. As the writing evaporates quickly, water calligraphers leave no permanent traces and can use the same stone slabs, which correspond to the squares on Chinese writing paper, again and again.

symbolic powers, such as bamboo, pine or peonies – but also birds, fish, insects and rocks.

Palace paintings The paintings by professional palace artists have a different character entirely. They are colourful, extremely accurate and rich in detail. They tend to show palace life, ceremonies, imperial hunts and inspection tours, interspersed with idealized scenes from the life of the people.

Modern Art

With the incipient opening up of the country around 1980, a fascinating art scene developed in China's major cities. Initially all kinds of Western movements and styles, which had been denigrated for decades, were greedily emulated and copied. At the same time, though, there was renaissance in traditional ink painting and 20th century ink-painting masters like **Qi Baishi and Xu Beihong** gained respect once again, with their works being exhibited and other new artists imitating their own styles. The modern art scene was then – and still remains – very market-oriented. Paintings use motifs that are likely to sell. Nevertheless then, as now, modern Chinese art has been far from descending into mere imitation. On the contrary, much has been created in the last 20 to 25 years that was fascinating, novel and even exciting.

Oil paintings with Chinese motifs For example, one unusual aspect includes oil paintings featuring Chinese motifs, which are executed with conspicuously excellent skill. They include interiors, street scenes, people at work, women in traditional costume and particularly feature **people and scenes from minority regions**. They are always aesthetically perfect and often romanticized but at the same time they are highly expressive and the almost photographic accuracy makes them hugely fascinating. They are particularly popular among Chinese people at home and abroad. In recent times, though, the tide of such paintings has slightly ebbed.

Traditional and modern European and American art enthusiasts are mostly attracted by modern-looking, often abstract works, regardless of the techniques used (oil, screenprint, mixed media), which also have some aspect that is recognizably Chinese, e.g. Chinese characters or **traditional, albeit alienated, motifs**. These varied trends have awakened a great deal of creativity. Paintings or sculptures dealing with the dichotomy of traditional and modern have interested many artists and this is clearly popular with foreign visitors.

Young and wild Others have rejected themes such as this entirely, concentrating on their own creativity, their own personal views of the world, their own subjective questions, observations and aesthetics. Among Western connoisseurs, gallery owners, exhibitors and museums, it is these »wild young artists« who have garnered the most attention and their works have been exhibited several times in Europe. Their art, of its nature, is very difficult to sum up. Much of it is provocative and some is also humorous or ironic. Galleries, which have to sell to survive, do not display such works very often unless the artist has already gained a measure of fame.

Theatre and Opera

The acme of China's theatrical art is a kind of musical play – featuring either live actors as in Peking opera, or marionettes or shadow puppets. Theatre involving the spoken word was unknown in old China and only reached the country's shores in the 20th century, but quickly became one of the mainsprings for cultural reawakening.

Theatre Then and Now

Abroad Chinese opera is mostly equated with Peking opera, but in fact this is only the most recent form of the art. It did not come into being until around 1800. The form with the greater historical importance is **Kun opera**, although this is very seldom seen. In Hong Kong and the province of Guangdong, **Canton opera** is still performed. Puppet theatre is mostly seen in rural districts where the peasants cannot afford to engage professional opera troupes.

All traditional forms of theatre are suffering badly at the present time. Young people are no longer going to watch the shows, theatres are expected to survive without government subsidies and the influx of new actors has reduced to a trickle on account of lack of job security, low wages and the long training. Theatres promoting Peking opera survive nowadays primarily thanks to foreign tourists. The programme is therefore planned with them in mind, so that for fear of boredom **individual scenes from various operas** are shuffled together and, in view of the fact that most of the public cannot speak Chinese, scenes relying on language are mainly avoided. Instead a lot of acrobatics are included, which gives a decidedly one-sided view of the theatrical art to the visitors.

! *Baedeker* TIP

Authentic
It is still possible to see Peking opera in its authentic form, albeit not every day. The best performances are by the Chinese Theatre Academy (Zhongguo Xiqu Xueyuan), Wanquansi 400, Beijing, Tel. 010/63351122.

Peking Opera

Hideously anti-quated or fasci-nating spectacle?

The best known of the Chinese opera styles is also the most recent of them. Peking opera only emerged around 200 years ago. More than the traditional central Chinese Kun opera or southern China's Canton opera, it is the capital's own **musical theatre** which is identified with **traditional Chinese stagecraft**. Nevertheless, while people all over the world thrill to the skills of Chinese acrobats, opinions are mixed regarding Peking opera itself. This not only applies to foreigners, many of whom would rather close their ears to the sound of the high-pitched falsetto voices of the women, but also to the younger Chinese, for whom the entire genre with its Ming-era costumes, almost incomprehensible arias and tales of imperial generals, young scholars and virginal young women seems hopelessly antiquated. In the face of such adversities, though, Peking opera still has its enthusiasts among older people who grew up with it and among an international community that finds this unique and highly exotic spectacle totally fascinating.

Spectacle with music, song and acrobatics: Beijing opera

Peking opera relies totally on stagecraft. There are virtually no famous dramatists or composers. Almost everything hinges on the stage presence of the actors taking part. One person may encompass the roles of **singer, narrator, dancer, mime-artist or acrobat**. One of the fascinations for the audience is the lack of scenery and the sparing use of props. This inspires the imagination. Other factors too require thinking: if someone on the brightly lit stage should stretch both arms out forwards, it signals that in fact the scene is taking place in the dark of the night. Arias alternate with spoken dialogue and monologues as in European operettas. Such spoken sections are varied with gusto by the actor-singers and even on occasion, if the mood is good and the public is sympathetic, they may even be sprinkled with music-hall jokes.

Singers and the stage

Apart from this, the movements on the stage are subject to very strict conventions. One thing that aids understanding of the pieces is a knowledge of the four types of roles into which all the main characters fall. **Sheng** is the name for the likable male hero, identified by his white-painted face with rosy cheeks. Typically the role might be a young, assiduous intellectual who has already passed two of his examinations to become an official. **Dan** is the name given to all the female roles. Women are always made up in white. Young ladies from respectable families wear magnificent hairstyles. Until the republican period, all Dan roles were played exclusively by men, which explains the typical falsetto singing style. Nowadays it is rare for Dan roles to be played by a man. **Jing** roles are male parts, in which the actors wear stunning face make-up, the colour and shape of which reflects the temperament and nature of the character. Thus red stands for loyalty, bravery and honesty; black is for boldness and steadfastness; yellow is cruelty and white is treachery. Jing types are physically active and energetic. **Chou** are clowns and fools, always men, who already look amusing on account of their white make-up around the eyes and nose. Like Jing players, they can be virtuous or crafty. Each of the four role-types involves a specific body language, which connoisseurs understand immediately. Certain arias and kinds of music may also be distinguished depending on the characters and the nature of the plot.

Typical roles in Peking opera

A ying role: the Monkey King

Acrobatics and music Certain scenes, which appear in many a Peking opera show, are fascinating to everybody in the audience: **the acrobatic fight scenes** where heroes or heroines defend themselves against hordes of attackers. This requires perfect control over the body, which can only be achieved with years of tough training that needs to be started at an early age. While the visuals – costumes, acting, mime and acrobatics – immediately delight every theatregoer, the same does not apply to the music. On the contrary, for many a European, the music spoils the whole experience. It is a question of familiarity. The orchestra will normally resemble a **chamber orchestra** with just a handful of musicians. They are usually seated to one side. What they play has a purely incidental function, like film music. Arias are accompanied or scenes highlighted by percussion instruments (claves, drums, cymbals), erhu violin, yueqin mandolin or some other pizzicato instrument, a bamboo flute or a suona, a kind of oboe with a penetrating tone. The small drum used to keep the beat serves the function of an orchestra's conductor. What delights the true connoisseurs of Peking opera, though, is a well sung aria with plenty of coloratura, although this is an acquired taste.

Plot The plots of most operas follow the standard stories to be found anywhere: **folk tales** and poetically tinged historical topics predominate. They often involve the love affairs of talented but impecunious young aspirants to officialdom and frequently include warfare and the heat of battle. Unlike the spoken passages, arias are written in classical Chinese, which practically no one can understand simply by listening to it, so that the text is often displayed in surtitles projected over the stage, or alongside it. For performances primarily aimed at foreigners these surtitles may often feature an English translation of the words.

Buddhism

The teachings of Gautama Buddha, Prince Siddhartha, who lived in India in around 500 BC, spread here from the time of Christ, but increasingly after the 3rd century, following penetration by foreign peoples along the Silk Road to China. Initially it was often opposed, by Taoists in particular, but from the 4th century it increasingly took hold and in the early Tang period (7th/8th centuries) it reached a spectacular peak. Chinese Buddhism is of the **Mahayana school**, the »Great Vehicle«, which allows for enlightenment – here frequently equated with salvation – to be achieved not only by monks but also by lay people. Life on earth is thereby seen as a world of suffering, which traps people within the cycle of reincarnation owing to their own passions (desire, hate and obsession) and through illness and death. Recognition of the truth, the vanity of being and the possibil-

The 500 figures of monks carved in wood in the Biyun Si monastery in Beijing are among the most impressive works of Buddhist art.

ity of liberation from the cycle of birth and rebirth leads to entry into Nirvana. A Buddha, »an enlightened one«, is someone who achieves this recognition by their own powers and who overcomes their own passions to enter Nirvana.

People can gain support and assistance in their search from, among other sources, bodhisattvas. In China four such figures in particular are venerated. The most popular of these is **Guanyin Pusa**, the bodhisattva of mercy, originally a masculine figure, who changed into a feminine one during Tang-period China. She is often portrayed with multiple heads and arms. One depiction features her with a veritable garland of arms and an eye on the palm of each hand. The symbolism is that she sees everyone's troubles and will help anyone who comes to her.

Bodhisattvas

Temple Monasteries

Although many Buddhist ideas have penetrated the general folk beliefs of the people, the Buddhist religion is only really obvious in its temple monasteries. They serve not only as convents for monks and nuns but as a place of worship for lay people. Nowadays, few of them are used for their original purpose but are maintained by the state as **listed buildings**. Whenever monks or nuns are present there, they have the status of government officials and their monasteries too are

GAUTAMA AND THE TEN THOUSAND BUDDHAS

Is there more than one Buddha? The answer is yes, for »Buddha«, a Sanskrit word meaning »awakened (to enlightenment)« is a title rather than a name. The founder of the religion, Buddha Gautama, was, according to Buddhist teaching, only one of countless Buddhas.

As **Prince Siddharta Gautama** he is said to have been a comtemporary of Confucius, living from 563–483 BC. Scholars tend to date him however, to around 400 BC. He was born in Lumbini – today, Nepal – into the Skakya clan, which is why is is also referred to as »Shakyamuni« or the »Shakya sage«. His earlobes, stretched down with heavy ornaments, point to his aristocratic lineage, and were transferred to the portraits of other Buddhas too.

The life of the historical Gautama is overlain with **legends**. On an excursion from the parental palace, he is said to have been so horrified by human suffering that he became a wandering ascete. Years later, he is said to have achieved enlightenment (»awakening«) while sitting beneath a bodhi tree. Human beings are prisoners of their illusions, which are caused by desire, hate and obsession. Only those who overcome this illusion can escape the eternal cycle of rebirth and thus the earthly vale of tears. In Nirvana (»blowing away«) one's individual existence and identity is extinguished.

In particular in **Chinese Mahayana Buddhism**, which was also adopted in Japan and Korea, as in Tibetan Buddhism too, Gautama was joined by **many other Buddhas**. For example there are the Buddhas of the ten thousand aeons, or the transcendental Buddhas, who never walked the Earth. The most popular of them is the redeemer Buddha Maitabha, with his paradise, the »pure land«, an intermediate station on the road to Nirvana, into which he rescues the faithful.

In Tibetan Buddhism, it is even possible to shake the hand of a Buddha, for some monks are venerated as **living Buddhas**. One such is the Panchen Lama (as an incarnation of Amitabha), not however the Dalai Lama, as the latter is regarded as the incarnation of a bodhisattva, and is thus a step lower on the spiritual hierarchy.

under control of the government. The monasteries are obliged, though, nowadays to be self-financing where possible, by means of admission charges, sale of souvenirs or payment for religious services.

Outer courtyard

The statuary of the first two halls of a Buddhist temple complex is largely standardized. On the northern side of the outer courtyard (with the bell and drum towers) is the hall of the heavenly kings (Tianwang Dian). This serves as a foyer to the inner temple domain. Six figures here have a specific role appropriate to this function: In the middle is a smiling **pot-bellied Buddha** to greet all those entering. This figure seems slightly alien to the concept of monastic renunciation and is indeed an »invention« imported from Chinese Taoism. Its plain costume indicates that it represents a monk. He laughs at the unimportance of human travails and worries and thus reassures the temple's visitors that what awaits inside is a reason for rejoicing. Next, though, comes a shock The Four Heavenly Kings glare from the right and left with fearsome visages, in martial pose, ready to do battle, their eyes wide open in threat and their mien dark. Under their feet they trample demons representing human desires and passions, which have no place inside the temple.

Inner courtyard

Once visitors have got beyond the guarding figures, they find themselves in an initial inner courtyard. They will see a large bronze censer, the central item of temple furniture, indeed the very item that makes the temple into a place of worship. The incense smoke rising from here is to honour the figures in the next hall. There it is possible to see the highest to which any human bring can aspire, to become a Buddha. In the »Great Hero's Treasure Hall«– as this hall is conventionally named – it is common to see three Buddhas seated on a throne of lotus blossom or a stylized pedestal indicating Sumeru the World Mountain, also adorned with lotus leaves. These are usually representative of the **Buddhas of the Three Ages**: past present and future. One other possible triad may be formed by the three celestial Buddhas: Amitabha, Shakyamuni and the Medicine Buddha, who represents the key Buddhist concepts of benevolence and the relief of suffering.

Main hall

Apart from the Buddhas in the middle, the most important statues in the main hall are the 18 luohan (saints), who line up in two rows, nine on each side. Unlike the iconographically strictly depersonalized depiction of the Buddhas, these luohan are depicted in many different ways. In some temples they display a dignified and restrained appearance, in others they are like living people while a third kind of depiction is almost caricature. The main hall and sometimes other halls will also have a magnificent altar upon which the five devotional objects are placed: a censer in the middle with a vase and a candle on each side.

Beyond the main hall What comes after the main hall is less strictly defined. Usually there will be a meeting hall for monks where sermons are given and lectures are held, in which there will be a statue that rounds off the overall concept and guides believers back to the world to await their salvation. There is no repetition of the figures already seen, but other Buddhas will be depicted, in particular the Vairocana, the »sun-like«. Practically no temple monastery lacks an **image of Guanyin**, often with a thousand arms and eyes. Where the walls are covered in Buddhas, they represent the »10,000 Buddhas« of all the ages. One other figure that sometimes appears in the last hall is the reclining (or sleeping) Buddha: showing him as he enters Nirvana. Alongside the halls along the axis there may be other buildings or edifices of importance. These may include pagodas of various styles or side halls with Buddha images.

Tibetan Buddhism (Lamaism)

In contrast to the Chinese temple monasteries, those of Tibetan Buddhism are distinguished by their much greater variety of images.

Meditation in the Nanputuo Si monastery

They often belong to the **Tantric School** and communicate different messages from those common in Chinese Buddhism. Tantrism emphasises the effectiveness of secret, occasionally orgiastic, rituals starkly highlighting the difference between the sexes and employing mystic formulae called mantras. One conspicuous feature, which does not appear in Chinese Buddhism, involves the fierce gods. Frightful in appearance and hung with chains of human skulls dramatically symbolizing earthly mortality, they represent former enemies of Buddhism, now constrained by magic and ready to fight evil and perform good works in the spirit of the teaching. Some of these gods are shown in ritual, ecstatic copulation with their female counterparts, the Yogini (so called Yum-Yab images). The concept of the mantras is also expressed by **mandalas**, geometrical images with point and often axial symmetry, which are used as meditation aids and, in the form of palaces representing the Paradise of the West, also point the way to salvation. Temple monasteries are found not only on the Tibetan plateau and its surrounding areas, but also in Mongolia, in Beijing and in Chengde.

Taoism

Taoism is mainly identified in the West with the Taoist philosophy of the legendary (although historically unverifiable) **Lao Tse** (literally: »old master«). It emerged around 2300 years ago as a political philosophy, and as a critical adversary of Confucian culture, with the message: »Back to nature! Away with wars and weapons, away with rules and rites!«. It saw contemporary civilization as pernicious. People need only look for themselves at how nature and the cosmos functioned. That was how rulers should manage their empire. **Wu wei**, »No intervention!«, was the motto. No one should interfere in the natural way of things, in the Tao (or Dao), the »way« by which all natural change occurred.

Philosophy of non-intervention

Unworldly and politically impracticable, the concept failed as a theory of government. Nevertheless, early Taoism on several occasions provided the ideology for autonomous organizations critical of the state, for Messianic movements which would occasionally break into violent revolt. Later on this tradition gave rise to a kind of secret society. In addition, the idea continued to flourish that people could retreat from the world, let their hair grow, live a life like the birds and become one with eternal nature. This is the Taoism of the hermits, which also attracted in an idealized form many a pensioned Confucian official, although they limited their hermit role to a retreat into their own gardens, which they enjoyed as a refuge from politics.

Oneness with nature

Monasteries and gods When Buddhism came to China almost 2000 years ago, it represented a major challenge for Taoism. The idea had to adapt and adopted many aspects of the competing religion, Including the institution of **temple monasteries and celibate communities of monks**. The world of gods in Taoism is also inspired by Buddhism. The response to the popular Buddhist god of mercy was to create an equivalent feminine deity. This meant that Taoism gained another aspect beyond its original political philosophy and became infused – as did many Buddhist concepts – with much of the folk religion of the people.

Health and immortality As Taoism nourished itself from all kinds of sources, it also gave much back to Chinese culture. It is so closely tied to much of how China appears today that it is impossible to delineate between them. This is particularly true in the country's medical traditions (►Baedeker Special p. 104). Shadow boxing, Qigong, Kung Fu, even dietary rules practised throughout China: all of these are linked to the Taoist tradition, with its age-old ideal of immortality and the ideal of utilizing secret cosmic forces for the benefit of oneself.

Confucianism and the Cult of the State

The ideology of the state and society in imperial China can no more be reduced to the teachings of Confucius than those of Christendom can to the life and words of Jesus Christ. What was more important were the ideas of later Confucian philosophers, old books of rites (some attributed to Confucius himself), pre-Confucian texts like the Book of Songs (Shijing) and the Book of History (Shujing), which were interpreted in the sense of an idealized past and which often functioned as a political model even after the end of the Confucian state, less in terms of the political practices of the Confucian state but in private and state sacrifice.

Dominant hierarchy The core concept of Confucian teachings on society is the organization of people into hierarchies. The woman is below the man, the younger below the elder, the subject beneath the king. It also demanded, though, that those who ruled should have a suitable degree of education. Thus the **Confucian system of officials** took shape: social elevation, certainly from the Song period, came about almost entirely thanks to the passing of anonymous examinations for scholars and officials. The subjects of these tests were the classic texts of Confucianism. In Europe at the time of the Enlightenment, where the aristocracy ruled by right of birth, this »rule of the philosophers« made a major impression. The ideal was, however, contradicted by the hereditary nature of the imperial throne. The emperors' belief in themselves as »sons of heaven« was predicated on an archaic world dominated by religion, although it had become integrated into Confucianism, matching as it did the latter's hierarchical ideology.

The utmost expression of this idea came in the form of the **cult of the state**, for which a separate Ministry of Rites was responsible. The ruler would by means of annual ceremonies restore the harmony between man and the cosmos. The essential aspects of this which people needed – at least those who tilled the soil – was the right amount of sun and rain, heat and cold. Peace on earth was also patterned on the harmony of the heavens. The holy places of this cult of the state now make up some of the country's most important tourist attractions: the imperial altars in Beijing, the temples of the five holy mountains and Confucian temples all over the country, especially though in Qufu, where the initiator of the cult of the state was worshipped for his teachings.

Harmony between people and the cosmos

The ceremonies were extraordinarily complex and expensive affairs, in which countless **animals** were sacrificed and vast quantities of silk were burned. The main protagonists were the emperors themselves or their top officials. Ritual music dating back 2000 years, still played to this day in Taiwan, is possibly the oldest traditional music known anywhere in the world.

The people were excluded

Music plays a key role in Confucianism in general. It embodies the ideal relationship between hierarchy and harmony such as should prevail throughout state and society. No harmony can be conceived without the dominant fundamental. The rule of the state thus fulfilled a similar role in Confucian eyes, responsible for maintaining or restoring harmonious relationships. This was the only way the state could thrive. With the system of **tributes**, by which China handled its relationships with other states – with tribute payments backed by graciously evident return gifts – the ideal of harmony and hierarchy was to be spread to the far corners of the world, where China, by very reason of its Confucian teachings, was held to be the epitome of civilization. That the foreign powers of Europe who penetrated into China during the 18th century should be unwilling to submit to this ideal was beyond the imagination of the »Middle Kingdom«. This lies at the root of China's reluctance to reform in the late imperial era, a reluctance which would claim Confucianism itself as a victim.

Hierarchy and harmony

Famous people

People who have left their mark on China – or our modern idea of it: Marco Polo with his travelogue, Kublai Khan, the first emperor of the Yuan dynasty, Mao Zedong and his wife ruling communist China – and many other figures from politics, art and literature.

Chiang Kaishek (1887–1975)

Politician

The man who was China's most powerful individual for a quarter of a century is, like his mentor Sun Yatsen, best known in the West by the Cantonese version of his name. Chiang (in fact Jiang Jieshi) was born in 1887 near Ningbo (Zhejiang province) to a merchant family. He himself chose a military career, studied in Japan and joined the republican revolution in 1911. In 1923 he rose to the leadership of the general staff of the National Party, the **Kuomintang**, quickly thereafter becoming head of the Whampoa military academy, which was to prepare for the military reunification of China. After the death of Sun Yatsen, he became the great man's successor. Chiang was indeed successful in reunifying most of China in 1927/28, but his bloody attempts to eradicate the communist movement led to his ultimate failure. Against the military aggression of Japan his response was aimless. He survived the Second World War in China's wartime capital of Chongqing thanks only to American support and his marriage to Mei-ling Song, who was from one of China's richest families; her sister Qingling had, in 1915, married Sun Yatsen, who was 30 years her senior. After 1945, the extreme corruption prevalent in his government led to Chiang squandering the power he had gained. After fleeing to Taiwan in 1949 he established a stable dictatorship there. Chiang died in Taipei in 1975.

Cixi (1835–1908)

Empress dowager

She was the dominant political figure of the late Manchu era and her power was a serious affront to the patriarchal Confucian. It was rare enough for women to flout all the rules of etiquette and morals in the masculine domain of Chinese politics, but what she achieved could only be accomplished with great intelligence and extreme ruthlessness. It was no less than the usurpation of imperial power and the exercise of it for 45 years.

While she would later be called **mother of the emperor** or »Empress Dowager«, when she came to court in 1851 she was a mere concubine. Her ascent began when she bore the emperor his only heir. When the emperor died in 1861 she managed to stage a coup d'état and seize power from the designated regent. When her son died in 1875 she broke all the rules of succession and named a three-year-old nephew of hers as emperor. It was only when he came of age in 1889 that she withdrew to the summer palace of Yihe Yuan. In 1898 she put an end to the so-called Hundred-Day Reform with another political manœuvre and placed the emperor under arrest. In allowing the Boxer Rebellion of 1900, she initiated a fiasco. When she died in 1908, the demise of the dynasty was merely a matter of time.

← *From a concubine to the most powerful woman in the empire: Cixi*

Deng Xiaoping (1902–1997)

Politician   Deng is considered the father of modern China – and in terms of his effectiveness he was indeed the most successful Chinese politician of the 20th century. Born in Sichuan province in 1902, he studied in France where he joined the communist movement. Back in China, he took part in the Long March. With the founding of the People's Republic he rose to an elevated position in the Party and the government. When the Great Leap Forward policy collapsed, he became prominent as a follower of the pragmatic policies of President Liu Shaoqi but with the Cultural Revolution both of them were stripped of power. He returned to politics in 1974 but fell from grace again in 1976, and it was not until two years after the death of Chairman Mao that he managed to press through a series of **market economic reforms** in the face of continuing opposition from members of the Party establishment. When the students demonstrated in 1989, he acted to maintain state power and allowed the military suppression of the movement. In the aftermath, though, he managed to disempower the advocates of state planning, who were totally opposed to his policies and saw him as responsible for the whole calamity, and send them into retirement. He himself simultaneously surrendered most of his positions in state and administration but his influence on the political line was undiminished. In the 1990s he was to see the dramatic success of his policies: Chinas breathtaking modernization and the enhancement of both its economy and its political influence. Deng died in Beijing in 1997.

Kublai Khan (1215–1295)

First emperor of the Yuan dynasty   A nephew of Genghis Khan, was the first to make Beijing the centre of a massive empire encompassing all of China. He himself was the first emperor of the Mongolian Yuan dynasty, which he founded. In 1280 he completed the **conquest of China** after wiping out southern China's Song dynasty. He also made two failed attempts to conquer Japan. Under Kublai Khan peace would reign throughout much of Asia and trade along the »Silk Road« blossomed, especially trade with Persia. On several occasions Italian merchants also arrived in China, including a young man called Marco Polo. Kublai Khan exhibited tolerance to Buddhism and Christianity. John of Montecorvino, the first Catholic archbishop of Beijing, also took office during the emperor's reign. Kublai Khan died in Beijing in 1295.

Confucius (551–479 BC)

Philosopher   The most revered historical figure in China came from Qufu in Shandong province and spent most of his adult life in the role of a wandering adviser to the local princes. His real name was Kong Qiu, but he was more commonly known as Kong Zi or Kong Fuzi, »Mas-

Chiang Kaishek with his wife, photographed in 1927

ter Kong«. It was from this appellation that the Jesuits derived the Latinized version of the name. Little reliable is known about his life. His presumed lifespan, from 551 to 479 BC is not certain (especially the year of his birth) and his life and works are shrouded in legend. Nor did Confucius leave behind any writings of his own. The nearest we know of his person and teaching comes from the »Analects«, which were posthumously recorded by his followers. According to these, at a time of war and social upheaval, he sought to create a new social design based on an **idealized understanding of antiquity**. The school of philosophy he founded was originally one of many and was only elevated to being the state ideology during the Han period

Lao She (1899–1966)

Born under the name Shu Qingchun in Beijing in 1899, Lao She **Writer** grew up in poverty. From 1924 to 1929 he taught and studied in London and it was there that he began writing. In 1936 his most famous novel »Rickshaw Boy« was published. In it he described the life (and failure) of a young man who comes to Beijing from his home in the country and seeks his fortune there with hard work and thrift. »Beneath the Red Banner« is another one of his **novels with a Beijing reference**. There was political controversy at the time concerning his 1957 play »The Tea House«, which is set in Beijing during the years 1898, 1918 and 1948. Some of his works have been widely translated. In 1966, under attack from the Red Guards, Lao She committed suicide.

Li Bai (701–762)

Poet The greatest »poet prince« of the Tang era created works that would set standards for centuries to come. His **beautiful poetry** is still learned by heart to this day. Li Bai was born in 701 at a time when China had reached its greatest western extension. Then named Li Tai-po, he was the son of a Chinese merchant in a region believed to be in modern Kyrgyzstan. He grew up, though, in Sichuan province. In 742 his unparalleled talents brought him to the Chinese court, although he was not to remain there long. Most of the time he lead the nomadic life of an inspired Bohemian. He died in 762, allegedly when he attempted, in a drunken stupor, to embrace the reflection of the moon in a pond – a good story, at least.

Lu Xun (1881–1936)

Writer Lu Xun, China's greatest modern novelist, was born in 1881 as Zhou Shuren in Shaoxing; southern China. He achieved fame under his pseudonym, Lu Xun. At the age of 16 Lu went to Japan, where he studied medicine and science, but while there he succumbed to his literary interests and began to write. Lu returned to his homeland in 1909 and worked as a teacher there until 1920. Amid the cultural undercurrents which were flowing through China all through this period, he initially stayed aloof but in 1918 he came to prominence with his book, **»Diary of a Madman«**, now considered the cornerstone of modern Chinese literature. Between 1920 and 1926 he lived in Beijing, where he taught in a college of higher education, before moving to Guangzhou to teach in the Sun Yatsen University. Lu was soon forced to leave the city, though, to escape the anti-communist witch-hunt of the Kuomintang. He returned to Shanghai, where he worked exclusively as a writer, essayist and translator until his death in 1936, contributing greatly to the cultural and political debate during those years. No author Chinese author has been translated so often into Western languages.

Mao Zedong (1893–1976)

Chairman of the Communist Party and founder of Communist China For many this son of a Hunan peasant born in mid-China in 1893 remains the **most identifying figure of the nation**. The »Great Helmsman«, Communist Party chairman since 1935, was for them the man that the communists had to thank for their victory in 1949. Others, especially intellectuals, detest Mao because in the years after 1945 he was responsible for millions of deaths, for a catastrophic policy of collectivization, for the desolation of cultural life and, in the maelstrom of the Cultural Revolution he whipped up, for the **destruction of irreplaceable cultural treasures**. Mao's political life's work has, apart from the unification of the country, left little worthwhile legacy. He remains revered for his lyricism and his distinctive calligraphy. Truckers and taxi drivers made him their **patron saint** and many still have a dog-eared picture of the Chairman as a talisman attached to the rear-view mirror.

Marco Polo (1254–1324)

World traveller

Did the young Venetian who accompanied his father and uncle to China really see the Beijing of the Mongol era with his own eyes, or truly experience the ceremonials of the imperial court? Doubts about his account are regularly expressed and those who do not believe him have regularly written him off as a swaggerer. Scholars who have made frequent deep analyses of his book have found the truth of it to be unconfirmed in all but a few places and some of it has been written nowhere else. However, the book was not a travel diary but a kind of **handbook for travelling merchants**. European trips to the Far East were nothing new in the 13th/14th centuries. In a chronological list of Europeans travelling to Mongolia or China, Marco Polo only ranks at number 34. The Polos returned home by sea in 1292, after a stay of 17 years, with the entourage of a Mongolian princess who was due to marry in Persia. They arrived back in Venice in 1295 and it was three years later that a man called Rustichello persuaded Marco Polo to dictate his report, while both of them were prisoners of war. It was to become one of the most famous books in the history of the world.

Venerated and hated: Mao Zedong

Qianlong Emperor (1711–1799)

Manchu Emperor

Qianlong, »Heavenly Prosperity«, was the regnal name chosen by the emperor and the one by which he is now known. His long reign, 1736 to 1795, saw the **last great heyday of imperial China**. The Manchu empire reached its greatest extent (as far as modern-day Kyrgyzstan and Kazakhstan), Tibet came under Chinese dominion and a long period of internal peace in China saw its population virtually double, highly unusual in a pre-industrial society. The emperor himself was unusual too.

As the fourth son of the Yongzheng Emperor, he was born in a princely palace which was later to be re-consecrated as a lama temple and was given the name of Hongli. When he ascended the throne on 18 October 1735, he was just 24. He turned out to be a highly responsible young man with plenty of discipline for work, although he was modest in his personal desires. A certain moralist rigour in the emperor, as portrayed in the Buddha-like poses in which he allowed himself to be painted, led to a literary inquisition, in which countless important works were destroyed. Hongli himself, though, considered himself a patron of the arts and was a respected calligrapher.

Qin Shihuangdi (259–210 BC)

First emperor of China

The emperor whose tomb near Xi'an would house the famous terracotta army is seen as one of the most important figures and most brilliant politicians in the history of the world, although it is of no little importance that he was also one of its cruellest tyrants. He was born in 259 BC, the son of the king of Qin, and ascended the throne at the age of twelve.

His ambitions rapidly became obvious: to obliterate the rival Chinese kingdoms and to unify all of China under his rule. After he had first strengthened Qin itself by introducing an efficient bureaucracy along with other reforms and military armament, he set about his aim and achieved it in 221 BC. Fully conscious of his own historical importance, he adopted a new title: Shihuangdi, **»first noble emperor«**.

His desire for conquest was not yet sated, though. Qin expanded its borders in all directions – southward as far as the South China Sea, eastward to Korea, northward onto the steppes, where he built a wall stretching several hundred kilometres to secure the conquered lands. 700,000 prisoners would be set to work on the building of a new palace and his gigantic mausoleum. When he died as emperor in 210 BC, revolts broke out at once and three years later his dynasty came to an end. His grave was ravaged and plundered. The idea of a united China, however, as realized by that first emperor, would extend down through the ages, and survived all the vagaries of history until the present day.

Sun Yatsen (1866–1925)

The »Father of the Nation« was the honorific given to the founder of the Chinese republic, Sun Yatsen. He was born in 1866 in the Pearl River delta village of Zhongshan. Since he had studied medicine, he is often called »Dr. Sun« in English. His actual name was Sun Wen. The name that prevails in the West derives from the Cantonese pronunciation of a pseudonym of his, although in Chinese he is exclusively called Sun Zhongshan nowadays. With his great personal integrity he considered his task in life to be the ending of Manchurian rule and to allow a Chinese republic to bring prosperity and social justice. However, he personally had no involvement in the revolution of 1911. Nevertheless after the **declaration of the republic** on 1 January 1912, he was nominated its first president, although in February 1912 he gave up the post in return for the abdication of the child emperor Puyi. He was unable to prevent the subsequent splintering of China, though. It remained his aim to re-establish the national unity of the country but he did not live to see this happen. He died aged 59 during negotiations in Beijing in 1925. When his body lay in state in the city's Sun Yatsen Park, some 700 000 people filed past to pay their respects. The mighty mausoleum, which was built for him in Nanjing and completed in 1929, bears witness to the astonishing degree of honour in which he was held by all levels of society. Sun's legacy is still maintained to this day, especially in Taiwan, but even the communists saw (and still see) him as a legitimate forerunner, particularly as his widow Song Qingling later came down on the side of Mao.

Founder of the Chinese Republic

Tsongkhapa (1357–1419)

There can be barely any Tibetan monastery, which does not possess a picture of this great religious thinker and reformer. »Tsongkhapa« – »Man from onion valley« – is actually only a nickname, referring to the area around Xining, where the Kumbum monastery would later be built. This was where Tsongkhapa was born in 1357. The facts of his childhood are swamped by legend but it is certain that he displayed an extraordinary thirst for knowledge from an early age. He learned from exponents of various teachings in Tibetan Buddhism and with his reaction to a decline of morals in Tibet's monasteries at the time, he eventually founded a reform movement called the **»School of Virtue«** (Gelugpa), which is mostly called the Yellow Hat school after the headwear worn by its devotees. After his death the school increasingly gained in presence until it held the dominant position in both the religion and politics of Tibet. This remains so till the present day. Even the institutions of the Dalai Lama and Panchen Lama derive from the Yellow Hat school.

Philosopher and intellectual

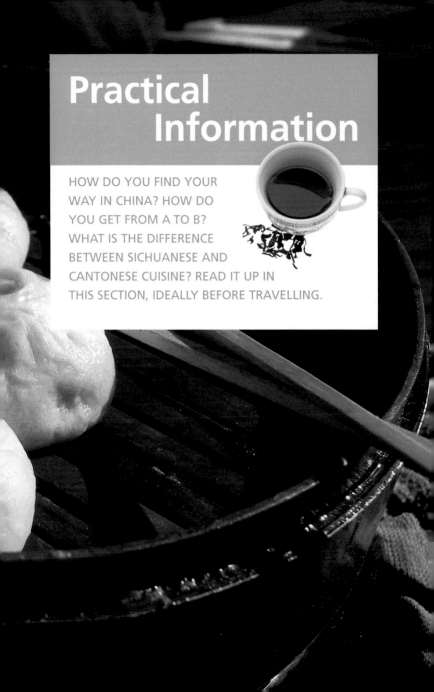

Practical
Information

HOW DO YOU FIND YOUR
WAY IN CHINA? HOW DO
YOU GET FROM A TO B?
WHAT IS THE DIFFERENCE
BETWEEN SICHUANESE AND
CANTONESE CUISINE? READ IT UP IN
THIS SECTION, IDEALLY BEFORE TRAVELLING.

Accommodation

Foreigners on package tours mostly stay in quite comfortable and sometimes impressively prestigious four-star hotels, few of them more than 25 years old. In poorer areas, they may have to settle for three-star accommodation of similar vintage. Such hotels generally provide double rooms with bathrooms and toilets en suite. Most of these places, though, are rather **big and faceless**, heated in winter, air-conditioned in summer. Places with flair or any kind of personal atmosphere are rare. Management often leaves a lot to be desired even now. The number of stars does not indicate whether saunas, swimming pools, etc., which were in existence when the hotel opened, are still available for use by the public.

i **Price categories**

■ The accommodation described in the travel-guide section is rated according to the following categories:
■ Luxury: More than 600 yuan per double room
■ Mid-range: 200–600 yuan
■ Budget: Up to 200 yuan

Booking via internet   People preferring to book their own hotels can do that easily nowadays, and often at considerable discounts, via the internet, e.g. at **www.sinohotel.com** and **www.sinohotelguide.com**. Make sure that your hotel is centrally located and not miles out in some industrial suburb, which occurs more often than one might think. Even when booking through a travel agent in China itself, it is necessary to keep an eye on this.

Backpacker hostels   In some places there is some splendid accommodation for backpackers while in others there is virtually nothing. The best places to go for this are Beijing, Yangshuo, Dali, Lijiang and Hong Kong. The internet will help here, too. Good sites to check include www.travel-uk.org/Hostels-China.html, www.hihostels.com and www.yhachina.com.

Arrival · Before the Journey

Getting there by plane   The aeroplane is not only the quickest but also the cheapest way to get to China. All the large European airports offer non-stop flights to Beijing with **flying times of ten to eleven hours**, depending on where you depart from. Depending on bookings (which change every day), prices of at least 500 euros are to be expected for a return flight – and generally it will be much more. Some flights from eastern Europe are markedly cheaper. Non-stop flights are also available from Europe to Chengdu, Shanghai, Hong Kong and Canton (Guangzhou); although the flying time is up to two hours longer.

Expensive, protracted, unforgettable: the journey to Beijing on the Trans-Siberian Railway

Travelling via Moscow it is possible to take the **Trans-Siberian Railway** to Beijing. The journey takes a week and involves higher prices and more bureaucratic difficulties than by plane but it is, of course, a more exciting adventure. It is possible as well to cut off some of the journey by flying part of it, e.g. Moscow – Irkutsk. From Beijing there is at least one train a day to virtually every part of the country. One alternative, although it is rarely used and is even more complicated, is to make the journey via Kazakhstan and Ürümqi, following the route of the old »Silk Road« between Turfan and Xi'an.

Package or individual deals?

Even for experienced lone travellers, in the case of China a package deal is to be recommended for a first trip to the country. There are three reasons for this. Firstly the **language hurdle**. Outside the main centres, do not expect to be able to get by with English. Looking up in books what signs written in Chinese might say is also something that is only possible if you already know some Chinese. As a rule travellers in China have to deal with the fact that they are effectively illiterate.

The second reason is that package tourists get to see more and understand more. For anyone travelling there for the first time China invites **endless questions**. Precisely when the matter concerns culture or history where the interplays are somewhat complex, then the kind of explanations that a good tour guide can provide are essential. Furthermore, many a detail will simply be missed if there is no one to point it out.

Time – a limited resource

The third reason is that of **limitations on time and money**. If the trip is only to take in Beijing or Shanghai, it may be possible to find the attractions of the inner city alone, but more remote destinations, which better convey the character of China in former times, are sometimes difficult to reach if one is organizing the trip oneself, even for those who speak fluent Chinese. Unless the time available for such a trip is unlimited, it is better to spend the money on an organized package tour.

Long distances

If you do wish, on a subsequent visit perhaps, to experience the country under your own steam, as it were, it is essential to bear in mind the distances involved and the fact that the transport infrastructure is still less developed than that of Europe. It is better to concentrate on a single region and allow plenty of time for it. At the end of the day, the experience will be more enjoyable than having to be continuously packing and unpacking, buying tickets, waiting in airports and the like.

Advanced booking

Even for those travelling individually it is advisable to book hotels and train or air tickets for inside China in advance, ideally using bank transfers to pay. This applies less to the larger cities, where there is a large selection of hotels, but is crucial in places with **limited accommodation**, on and around holy mountains, remote national parks or when stopping over in historic old towns.

Conditions for entry and exit

Entering China

Entry into China is only permitted for those possessing a **passport and a valid visa**. When travelling with a group, it is usual to hand passports in advance to the tour organizer, who will then organize a group visa for the party. A single visa can be requested up to fifty days before the planned trip and will be valid for a maximum of three months. Such requests can be made personally and require a new passport-sized photograph. Alternatively visas can be handled via an agency dealing directly with one of the diplomatic representations listed below (► p. 106, NB: visas cannot be obtained by post). A visa for a single entry into the country costs £30 in Britain and will take four to five working days to process. Visas for multiple entries or express visas obtained at short notice cost extra. Higher prices can also be expected if the visa is requested from a country other than your own. In this case, it may be necessary to provide **additional documentation** such as copies of residence permits etc. This applies even to

EU citizens in other EU countries, even where such documentation may not have previously been required under EU law. All the visa information included here applies to type L visas (tourist visas). For transit visas, working visas etc. additional conditions will apply.

When entering China proper from **Hong Kong** a visa can be obtained in Hong Kong itself but one or two days processing time will be required. Try, for example, the China Travel Service, Overseas Tourist Department, 1/F., Alpha House, 27-33 Nathan Rd., Kowloon, Tel. +852-23 15 71 88, Fax +852-23 15 72 92, www.ctshk.com. To enter Hong Kong itself, only a passport is necessary, although it needs to be valid for at least another month after leaving. Typically citizens of most English-speaking countries will receive a permit to remain for 90 days (British citizens 180 days), which is stamped into their passport. Citizens of most English-speaking countries can also enter **Macau** for up to 30 days without a visa (Irish citizens 90 days, UK citizens 180 days). A passport is required in all cases.

Entry via Hong Kong/Macau

Chinese customs regulations allow for any amount of foreign currency to be taken in and out of the country. Up to 400 cigarettes and two bottles of spirits can be brought in duty free. No more than 6000 Chinese yuan may be taken out of the country and export of antiques is not permitted unless they are authorized by means of a red seal. On returning to the EU or to Hong Kong and Macau the following amounts of items can be brought across the border duty free: 200 cigarettes, 100 cigarillos, 50 cigars or 50 g of tobacco, 1 litre of alcoholic drinks with more than 22% alcohol by volume and 2 litres of wine, 50 g of perfume or 0.25 litres of eau de toilette. Be aware that upon returning (to the EU) only purchased items up to a total worth of 175 euros are duty-free. Citizens of non-EU countries should enquire about their own customs regulations.

Customs regulations

Travel insurance

It is recommended that travel health insurance be obtained before entering China. For treatment in Chinese hospitals payment in cash is expected. Accident insurance is also useful since it can be expected that repayments obtained under Chinese insurance will be considerably less than those common (and obligatory) in Europe.

Children in China

Chinese people are very kind to children and having children with you will usually ensure a sympathetic response. Nevertheless visits to temples and palaces are often rather dull for small children. Therefore most parks offer diversions such as paddle boats, roundabouts and dodgems. One other good idea is a visit to the zoo. At various places along the Great Wall and the Silk Road, camel rides are on offer.

Electricity

220 volts, 50 hertz: European appliances can be used as is, although adapters are needed for the plugs. Hotel bathrooms usually have a socket for electric razors. These can also be used for charging rechargeable batteries.

Emergency calls

► **Police**
Tel. 110

► **Fire brigade**
Tel. 119

► **Tourist telephone service**
In Beijing there is also a 24/7 tourist telephone service, which you can call if you have language difficulties: Tel. 010/65 13 08 28.

Etiquette and Customs

»Face« and politeness

For a holidaymaker in China it is generally sufficient to observe the usual polite etiquette. However, it is different if you meet Chinese people privately or if indeed you are seeking to do business. One example involves **invitations**. Chinese friends or business partners who you do not know well should not be invited to a normal eatery. This will damage your honour; you will »lose face«. It is much better to choose a place as expensive as your guest could afford or even a bit more. The choice should make an impression without being embarrassingly beyond the means of your guest, since the expectation would be that any return invitation would involve somewhere of similar standard. If you, yourself, are invited to an expensive place, it often signifies that some **equivalent response** is expected of you. If you wish to invite someone yourself, be sure not to give your guests the opportunity to pay the bill behind your back. This happens quicker and more often than you might think. The safest way is to agree the courses in advance with the waiter and to pay there and then. Hosts should do guests the honour of personally placing the best dishes before them. If you yourself are a guest, be sure to leave a decent amount on your plate, more than you would in Europe. If you do not want any more to drink, simply leave the last glass of beer or cup of tea full. If you are the host, you should, without question, provide for more drinks until no one wants any more.

Consideration for one's own »face« also extends to the impression you give. Superiors are expected to drive better cars. If they were to come in a small car or even by bike, the **loss of face** would be virtually impossible to regain. In business, it is even more crucial than elsewhere to avoid humiliating others, especially embarrassing a boss in front of his employees. People who do this also make themselves look bad and may discredit themselves permanently.

Business

Respect the elderly, make friendly gestures and observe the »normal« rules of politeness – then you will feel welcome in China

Dress codes Fortunately clothing is not a major factor. Chinese people choose practical clothes. They also keep their shoes on when visiting a temple or someone else's home. Sloppy clothes should, however, be avoided. **Smart casual** is seldom wrong. Even in the imperial palace wearing shorts or mini-skirts will not cause offence. When representing a company, though, it is expected, as in Europe, that »collar and tie« or an obviously expensive outfit should be worn.

Taking photographs It is often forbidden to take photographs inside many of the attractions, and usually in temples too. Outdoors, though, you can usually take all the photographs you like. However, when photographing strangers, it is important to take the context into account. In parks or in front of tourist attractions, where Chinese people themselves take plenty of photographs, you can press the shutter all you like, but on ordinary streets you should always **ask for permission first**. Photographing people when they are doing hard, physical work is exceedingly impolite and can lead to ugly scenes.

Festivals · Holidays · Events

PUBLIC HOLIDAYS

In China there are only seven official holidays

▶ **1 January**
New Year

▶ **Spring Festival**
On first new moon after 21 January, plus the day before and after (▶right)

▶ **Qingming Festival**
▶right

▶ **1 May**
Labour Day

▶ **Dragon Boat Festival**
On the fifth day of the fifth month
▶right

▶ **Mid-autumn Festival**
▶p. 101

▶ **1 October**
National holiday (founding of the nation 1949; with the two following days). The streets are decorated with flags and pots of flowers and there are fireworks in the evening.

TRADITIONAL FESTIVALS

Festivals almost exclusively follow the traditional lunisolar calendar, which for simplicity is usually referred to as the Chinese lunar or farming calendar. On account of this the dates fluctuate from year to year by as much as a month. Apart from the spring festival, these festivals tend to be regarded differently in different parts of the country. They are mostly observed in the south, especially in Hong Kong, where the traditions lived on unbroken.

▶ Spring Festival

The most important festival is the Chinese New Year celebration, which is nowadays called the Spring Festival (chun jie) in order to distinguish it from 1 January. This is a family festival for which everyone who can goes home. People give gifts of money in red envelopes, visit relatives and old friends, and eat positive feasts in their homes. Public life comes to a standstill for several days – restaurants and even hotels have a skeleton service. Before and afterwards, though, some lovely markets are held at the temples, selling toys and folk art and all kinds of good foods, while acrobats, lion dancers and puppet shows provide extra entertainment.

▶ Lantern festival

The winter festival season ends with the first full moon of the new (lunar) year. That is when the lantern festival or festival of lights (yuanxiao jie) is celebrated with exhibitions of magnificent lanterns. Round sticky rice balls (yuanxiao) are eaten; these symbolize the full moon and are both sweet and filling.

▶ Qingming Festival (Tomb Sweeping Day)

On 5 April (in leap years and the year following, 4 April) the graves of ancestors are spruced up and offerings are made to them. In Hong Kong the visit to the cemetery is more like a graveside picnic.

▶ Dragon Boat Festival

This festival (Duanwu Jie) is not of great importance in the dry northerly regions but in the south (e.g. in Hong Kong) they hold dragon boat races. Dragon boats are narrow rowing boats with a dragon's head. This is all in memory of the poet and official Qu yuan (332–296 BC), who is said to have drowned himself in his despair at the ruination of the state. During the festival zongzi are eaten, a high-calorie dish made of sticky rice wrapped in leaves with meat or sweet red beans.

▶ Mid-autumn Festival (Moon Festival)

At the Zhongkiu festival on the 15th day of the eighth month, the full moon is supposedly bigger and rounder than normal. People eat round moon cakes, a cake with marzipan-like filling and an egg yolk inside, symbolising the moon.

▶ Double Ninth

The Chongyang Jie festival on the ninth day of the ninth month is another festival for the dead similar to the one in April

▶ Children's Day (Ertong Jie)

1 June: This is the day when only children (which is all most families are allowed) get spoiled more than otherwise. Many parents go out with their dressed-up children, e.g. to pleasure parks.

REGIONAL FESTIVALS AND EVENTS

▶ Ice sculpture show

The ice festival of Harbin in January/February is world famous. Other smaller festivals of a similar kind are held elsewhere, like the one on the reservoir in the Longqing gorge near Beijing.

► **Kite Festival in Weifang**
Early April: Weifang (in Shandong) is famous for its manufacture of kites and its festival features an international kite-flying competition.

► **Water Splashing Festival (Poshui Jie)**
Mid-April: a festival held by the Dai people in Xishuangbanna. An exuberant festival with dancing, dragon boat races and the washing of Buddha statues. Once they are clean the festival reaches its climax with a huge water fight.

► **Chinese Grand Prix**
Mid-April: Formula 1 in Shanghai

► **The birthday of Tin Hau**
On the 23rd day of the 3rd month a celebration is held for the birthday of the patron of sailors in all the Tin-Hau or Mazu temples along the coast, especially in Hong Kong.

► **Beer Festival in Qingdao**
China's Octoberfest begins on the second weekend in August and like the Munich original lasts for 16 days.

► **Beijing/Shanghai Marathon**
Mid-Oct. or mid-Nov.

Food and Drink

Food is hugely important in China. It is a **central aspect of Chinese culture** in that it is not only for nourishment or gourmet pleasure but diet itself traditionally plays a major cultural role – primarily focusing on the question of what to eat in warm weather and what to eat when it's cold, what to eat when pregnant, what to eat for what illness etc. The social aspect, too, is more prominent than in Europe. Food creates and cements social bonds. Everybody will share all parts of a meal, although the finest dish is always placed before the guest of honour and serving expensive specialities is common to impress guests of the house or business partners in a restaurant, much more food being laid on the table than can ever possibly be eaten.

Hot meals are eaten three times a day and since socialist frugality has been set aside, a large portion of people's income is spent on culinary delights, a situation from which the **extensive selection of restaurants** in the bigger cities is clearly benefiting. The transformation of Beijing, Shanghai or Guangzhou into international metropolises can therefore not only be seen but tasted. Nowadays the food is not even exclusively Chinese. It is now possible to enjoy foods from all over the globe.

Three hot meals

← *The fifth day of the fifth month: dragon boats compete for the prize*

Nothing wrong with slurping: eating habits in China

Table manners In China table manners differ from those prevalent in the West. Many things that would be taboo in the West – eating with your mouth full, slurping, laying chewed bones on the tablecloth or spitting inedible foods onto the table – are commonplace and should not raise a frown. If you are invited to someone's home, it is not considered impolite to leave the television switched on during the meal. Sneezing or blowing your nose at the table are not desirable, though. If you need to sneeze, leave the table quickly.

Eating in company The main rule in a restaurant is never to order separately, never to eat separately and never to pay separately. Chinese meals involve **eating together**. People do not eat »their« order but share everything with everybody else. Enjoyment is therefore all the greater, the bigger the size of the group. Two people are usually too few, four would be better and eight to ten is ideal. Elect one person to make the order for everyone and pay for the meal when it is finished. Even in restaurants with European food, payment should be made in this way.

Eating with chopsticks is child's play

It is usually assumed that one more portion will be ordered than there are people at the table and dishes are selected from various categories. Thus, for a table with four people, the order might be one soup, one vegetable dish, a pork dish, a poultry dish and a fish dish. Much like a buffet, the meals are not brought one after the other but are all laid on the table more or less at once. Everyone then takes some food from each dish before passing everything on to the next person. To keep the tastes separate, it is OK to go back to any of the dishes that tasted good. Rice is ordered separately. When inviting Chinese people, it will impress them if you order the rice much later or do without altogether.

One more meal

> ### *i* Price categories
>
> - The restaurants described in the travel section are categorized according to the following criteria (per person for a single meal):
> - Expensive: More than 140 yuan
> - Moderate: 50–140 yuan
> - Budget: Up to 50 yuan

Specific mealtimes in China are usually earlier in the day than in Europe. Restaurants are therefore frequently open before noon and get busy after about 6pm.

When are mealtimes?

Chinese cooking

The differences in cuisine between the various regions of China are as immense as the country itself. Here are some of the most important styles of cuisine and their characteristics:

The cuisine in Beijing and northern China is heavily influenced from Mongolia. This is most obvious in such dishes as **lamb hotpot**, a communal meal which is particularly popular in winter. Traditionally little or no rice is used with wheat flour being used instead in the form of noodles (hand-drawn or sliced), steamed bread or dumplings with various fillings and names. Jiaozi, baozi and guotie for example, typical meals on the folk menu, offer succulent delights for very small amounts of money. The best known recipe around the world, **Peking duck**, is eaten in restaurants and during celebratory meals.

Beijing and northern China

Palace cuisine is only found in Beijing. Several hundred recipes have survived the demise of the monarchy. A typical feature is that **a lot of small portions** are placed on the table. The preparation often involves a great deal of skilled work, especially in the aesthetic presentation of the food.

Palace or imperial cuisine

The culinary art of the south China province of Guangdong and Hong Kong makes it a queen among the regional cooking of the country. It is particularly famed (or notorious) for the extraordinary **variety of ingredients**, including many types of seafood. Some of the

Guangdong and Chaozhou

most expensive specialities are included in that category, shark fin soup, swallows' nests and abalone (large sea snails). The flavouring is mild, since the natural taste is supposed to come through. Cantonese tea culture is famous too, at least the edible accompaniment to it, so-called dim sum. In Cantonese the word means »**touch the heart**« and is used to describe the delicacies served with tea, some of it savoury, some of it sweet. A huge variety is on offer: dumplings with shrimp filling, spare ribs in black-bean sauce, chicken's feet, dumplings with roast pork and sesame seed balls filled with lotus seed paste – to name but a few. Dim sum is eaten from early morning till afternoon – in Hong Kong and Guangzhou it typically forms the midday meal when supplemented by a plate of fried noodles or rice – but not in the evenings. The local people also eat **snake and dog**, both preferably (and dog exclusively) in the colder months.

! *Baedeker* TIP

Don't be scared of snakes and dogs ...

... or scorpions and silkworms! Some travellers in China fear being served such things in their meals without their knowing, but there is nothing to worry about. Specialities of that kind are conspicuously expensive and in menus prepared for package tourists they are usually quietly omitted.

Sichuan

In the mid-west of China they like it hot. With lashings of chili and Sichuan pepper authentic meals can often be virtually inedible for strangers. Not to worry, though, first of all, Sichuan restaurants outside Sichuan have all toned down their recipes to accommodate the more sensitive palates of their customers and secondly there are also some original dishes which are mild and less furiously spiced. The mild **Sichuan duck**, smoked over camphor wood, is one of the more famous.

Shanghai and Hangzhou

Boiled and braised foods are common in Shanghai and Hangzhou. A sweetish note is added by the popular sweet and sour sauce, to accompany either fish or pork. One of the specialities of Shanghai cuisine, eaten in autumn, is Chinese mitten crab.

Yunnan

Yunnan cuisine is something of a generalization as the province extends from the edge of the Tibetan plateau on one side into the subtropical climes of southeast Asia on the other, encompassing many differing peoples, and proffers a huge variety of culinary delights. One type of cooking that is known far beyond the borders of the province is the **cuisine of the Tai peoples of South Yunnan** with its flavours more reminiscent of Thailand. Typical recipes include wild mushrooms and rice eaten in a tube of bamboo.

Central Asia

The further west one goes in China, the more desert-like the terrain becomes and the food too becomes more influenced by Islamic and nomadic features, i.e. not many vegetables and no pork, but plenty

Preparing Peking duck

of **lamb and mutton**. Shish kebabs in a salt and spice mixture, though, are certainly available in other parts of the country, primarily served in roadside snack bars.

The types of regional cuisine mentioned here by no means include all the types of cooking to be found in China but do exemplify the basic kinds of mixtures. **Fujian cooking** resembles Chaozhou and Gwangdong cuisine, especially in the south. **Hunan cooking** shares with Sichuan a preference for spiciness. **Shandong cooking** primarily displays northern influence, although it also benefits from a generous amount of fish and other seafood. In parts of Manchuria, though, the proximity of Korea makes itself felt: dog meat and heavily spiced Chinese cabbage, eaten as a warming winter repast, is one typical example.

Regional variations

As artistically crafted as the finest palace cuisine, vegetarian recipes offer astonishing imitations of meat dishes. China's vegetarian cuisine is heavily influenced by Buddhism so alcohol is never included.

Vegetarian cooking

Drinks

The best thing to drink with Chinese food is the light Chinese beer. With Cantonese food the preference is for tea. Nowadays many restaurants also serve a very decent Chinese wine – red, white or rosé.

Tea
In areas where tea is cultivated, of course tea is the most commonly consumed drink, but elsewhere tea is not necessarily as common as one might think, in particular in accompaniment with food. Cantonese meals are the exception here. In the home of tea, however, such as the provinces of **Fujian and Zhejiang**, it is popularly drunk as a refreshing between-meals drink, perhaps with some small snack.

Coffee
Coffee is coming more and more into fashion. Only Shanghai has a long tradition of coffee drinking but nowadays there are even chains of Chinese coffee houses with branches in all the provincial cities, where **highly aromatic Arabica varieties** are served.

Otherwise, coffee is also on offer in good hotels. In smaller and more remote places – even in those tourist centres where foreigners are less common – coffee is better avoided. If it is served at all, it can be quite horrible.

Refreshing drinks
When travelling in summer, it is popular to take a plastic bottle of drinking water. Most kinds of water on offer are not natural mineral waters, but distilled water enhanced with minerals. There is also a broad range of soft drinks, colas and similar. One splendidly refreshing draught in the heat of summer is **drinking yoghurt**, which the Chinese call suannai.

Spirits
Spirits, of course, aid the digestion. Restaurants do not usually serve spirits by the glass so that they mostly have to be ordered by the bottle. Some spirits are very expensive but one that can be had for a song is **erguotou**. It originates from Beijing but is available virtually all over the country served in practical hip flasks. It is easiest to buy in tobacco and drinks kiosks.

Rice wine
Rice wine is drunk warm. The yellow **Shaoxing wine** is available in bottles. Elsewhere, as in Xi'an and Yunnan (or across the country in Yunnan restaurants), freshly made rice wine will be served. It has a milky colouring and does not keep well.

Chinese recipes

Baozi
Circular dumplings with a wheaten yeast dough jacket (usually just called a bun in English) available with various meat and vegetable fillings.

The very finest kinds of tea are served in China →

Beijing kaoya (Peking duck) The skin's the thing! Marinated in honey and then grilled, the duck is then served at the table where the cook will slice off slivers of skin. These are then dipped in a special sauce and wound round with fresh leek in cold pancakes (baobing). Other courses may be served as you wish (vegetables, soup) to complete the meal.

Doufu A bean curd often better known by its Japanese name of tofu. It is made of fermented soya beans. As a purely vegetable protein, doufu is very healthy and forms the basis for many recipes, e.g. mapo doufu – »pock-marked old lady tofu« another spicy recipe from Sichuan.

Jiaozi Jiaozi are crescent shaped dumplings) in a bun with various fillings (typically minced pork and Chinese cabbage). They are either boiled or steamed and are ordered by weight. Filled dumplings similar to jiaozi but fried in a pan and called guotie are particularly filling.

Huoguo Huoguo is **hotpot**. The original Mongolian hotpot (Chinese: shuan yangrou) has given rise to various forms differing in the nature of the broth and the ingredients used. One thing that they have in common is that those eating the meal all gather around the pot with the steaming broth and fish out of it the briefly simmered, thinly sliced slivers of meat, leaves of cabbage, mushrooms or tofu. These are dipped into a cold sauce in one's own bowl to cool, then eaten. One of the popular varieties is yuanyang huoguo, where the pot has a dividing wall so that it is possible to choose between two different types of broth, one spicy and one mild.

> ! **Baedeker TIP**
>
> **It won't fill you up**
>
> Peking duck sounds as if it ought to be a filling meal in itself, but as it is only the roasted skin that is eaten, it needs vegetables and other accompaniments to make a meal of it.

Jiaohuazi ji and lamian **Beggar's chicken** is a whole chicken wrapped in a lotus leaf and than stewed in its own juice inside a clay shell. **Hand-drawn noodles** (lamian), usually served in noodle soup, are a typical cookshop dish.

Lengpan Lengpan refers to various kinds of hors d'oeuvre, practically the only Chinese dishes which are served cold. They are always served in small portions so that it is no problem to order several at once. They can include roasted peanuts, marinated lotus root, or marinated cucumber sticks, thinly sliced cold roast meat, tofu skin or – especially popular in summer – tomatoes in sugar.

Pidan »Hundred-year-old« (preserved) eggs are duck or chicken eggs enclosed in a special airtight clay shell and pickled for three weeks, which are eaten in thin slices as an hors d'oeuvre, ideally with a little fresh ginger. They have a very intensive egg taste.

Sichuan duck (smoked duck) is smoked with tea leaves and camphor wood – one of the few specialities from Sichuan which is not at all spicy.

Zhangcha Ya

Health

In most parts of China **no particular health precautions** are necessary. No immunizations are required, although immunization against hepatitis is recommended.

In the south, however, there are some areas where there is a risk of malaria. Dengue fever also occurs there, for which reason it is advisable use insect repellent. Expert advice can be obtained at www.net-doctor.co.uk/travel, www.cdc.gov/travel or www.publichealth.gc.ca. **Tap water** should only be drunk after boiling, although it can be used for cleaning teeth. Fruit should only be eaten if it has been freshly peeled.

It is important to bring all important medication from home along with medicines for illnesses such as diarrhoea or colds. The reason is that brands well known in Europe are unheard-of in China so that it is necessary to check the ingredients to get the right drugs, which can be difficult. Leave any medicines unopened in their original packaging until you have entered the country. People needing large quantities of medicine, e.g. diabetics, are advised to travel with a letter from their doctor attesting to their needs. This will avoid any trouble with customs.

Medicines

If you get ill, it is normally best to go first to the Chinese travel guides. In all the larger cities there are doctors able to speak English. If you are staying in a hotel when the illness comes on, ask reception to call for a taxi to the hospital. In cities with an international presence there will also be medical centres or clinics especially for foreigners, which also provide dental services. It is always necessary to pay for any such treatment in cash so that it is advisable to take out travel health insurance.

What to do in case of illness

▶ MEDICAL CENTRES

▶ **Beijing**
Beijing Lufthansa Center
Room S 106
No. 50, Lianmaqiao Road
Tel. 010/64 65 15 61/62/63

▶ **Shanghai**
Hongqiao Clinic
Hongqiao Lu 788
Tel. 021/64 45 59 99

Physical agility is not a matter of age. Gymnastics with a sword or a tango in the park are good ways of staying fit.

HERBS, QI AND A LONG LIFE

Up at the crack of dawn and out into the park, in summer and winter: the Chinese show steely discipline when it comes to their daily exercises. This custom is part of a tradition that aims to strengthen the life force. It is connected with the old Daoist dream of immortality. The importance to the Chinese of a long and healthy life can be seen even more clearly in the herbal departments of pharmacies, where a single ginseng root can fetch as much as the price of a luxury car – a fitting present for an eightieth birthday, for example.

Chinese civilization is the world's oldest living culture. However, turbulent times since the Opium Wars have left little of this tradition untouched – except in the field of medicine. Although modern international medicine is practised in China, too, classical medical lore and an astonishingly widespread basic knowledge about the art of healthy eating are today perhaps even more alive than ever. Traditional Chinese medicine continues to develop, is taught at univer-

sities, researched and practised in dedicated hospitals. Acupuncture is just one part of it. Herbal medicine, a body of knowledge thousands of years old which is also supported by documentation that goes back far into the past, has greater importance. Today pharmaceutical research is extremely interested in these traditions. The distinctive feature of the awareness of health issues in China is, however, the long tradition of constant attention to health. An important

part of this is physical well-being, which explains the wide availability of massage and early-morning exercises in parks, including waltzing, disco dancing and yangge, a folk step dance, as well as all manner of stretching exercises which enable many old people to remain remarkably agile. Others take a more serious approach to tradition and look after their qi – an ancient concept that originally meant »breath«. However, qi means more than breath. Just as we speak of breathing life into something, so qi refers to the life force. Exercises to strengthen it are summarized in the term qigong. There are many forms of qigong. Visitors to China who go to a park early in the morning will see or hear some of them, for example primal-scream qigong, whose practitioners shout out their tensions and repressed emotions in order to free themselves from the burden. Most other forms of

Qigong, gymnastics, nutrition: a tradition of permanent attentiveness to the body

qigong are quiet, sometimes very slow – as in taijiquan or »shadow boxing« – and sometimes positively meditative. Many Chinese practise qigong on their own, while others go to masters of the art, most of whom develop their own style. It is not clearly distinct from gymnastics. This applies to almost all forms of qigong that involve movement – sword gymnastics, for example, which is always a wonderful sight.

Information

ADDRESSES FOR INFORMATION

► **In UK and Ireland**
China National Tourist Office
www.cnto.org.uk

► **In North America**
China National Tourist Office
www.cnto.org
Anyone travelling in China can obtain information most easily at travel bureau counters in the larger and better hotels. That is also the best way to obtain travel tickets or book flights. City tourist offices for foreigners are still rare.

► **In Hong Kong and Macau**
Hong Kong ► p. 337
Macau ► p. 423

EMBASSIES AND CONSULATES

A complete list of Chinese embassies and consulates abroad can be found at www.fmprc.gov.cn/eng (click rubric Missions Overseas)

► **Chinese Embassy in London**
31 Portland Place
Tel. 020/7299 4049
www.chinese-embassy.org.uk
There are Chinese consulates in Manchester and Edinburgh

► **Chinese Embassy in Washington**
2201 Wisconsin Ave. NW
Tel.202 338 6688
www.china-embassy.org
There are Chinese consulates in Chicago, Houston, Los Angeles, New York and San Francisco.

► **Chinese Embassy in Ottawa**
515 St Patrick St
Ottawa Ontario K1N 5H3
Tel. 613 789 34 34
www.chinaembassycanada.org/eng
There are Chinese consulates in Toronto, Vancouver and Calgary.

► **Chinese Embassy in Canberra**
15 Coronation Dr
Yarralumla ACT
Tel. 02 6273 4783
http://au.china-embassy.org/eng/
There are Chinese consulates in Sydney, Melbourne and Perth.

► **British Embassy in Beijing**
11 Guanghua Lu
Tel. 010/5192 4000

► **Canadian Embassy in Beijing**
19 Dongzhimenwai Dajie
Tel. 010/65 32 35 36

► **US Embassy in Beijing**
3 Xiushui Beijie
Tel. 010/65 32 38 31

► **Irish Embassy in Beijing**
3 Ritan Donglu
Tel. 010/65 32 26 91

► **New Zealand Embassy in Beijing**
3 Ritan Don Erjie
Tel. 010/65 32 27 31
There are UK, US, Canadian, Australian and New Zealand consulates in Hong Kong, Shanghai and Guangzhou; in addition, there are UK and Canadian consulates in Chongqing, and a US consulate in Shengyang.

Language and Writing

Two aspects in particular make Chinese appear difficult to European ears: the tonal inflections and the writing. In addition, the fact that Chinese is not related to any European language means that there is a total absence of any familiar-sounding words to give you something to go on. However, it is not so bad as all that. The Chinese language does have the advantage of having incomparably simple morphology. Long lists of verb conjugations as in Spanish or French are unnecessary. One verbal form applies to all expressions, whether it be »I am«, »we are«, »you were« or »they will be« – the basic form suffices for everything.

Difficult language with simple morphology

Past or future, singular or plural, active or passive, all these forms are deduced from context. Sometimes additional words are added to specify them. It is also practical that sentence structure and word-formation are not unlike some European languages. »Hŭo« meaning fire and »chē« meaning vehicle are thus combined to make: »hŭochē«, meaning fire vehicle, i.e. locomotive or indeed the word railway itself. Zhàn means to stand, stand still, stop or, as a noun, a stop. Thus hŭo, chē and zhàn combine to make hŭochēzhàn, fire-vehicle stop, or railway station.

Grammar

The tones of the Chinese language, though, strike Europeans as highly exotic. Mā means mother, má is hemp or also pock-marked, mǎ means a horse and mà means to curse. These makes it possible to form the lovely sentence: »Má mā mà mǎ«, »The pock-marked mother curses the horse«. Mandarin Chinese recognizes **four tones**: the first one, a constant tone: mā, the second, a rising tone: má, the third a longer tone, which descends then rises again: mǎ and a fourth short descending tone: mà. Any foreigner able to master these tones well will gain high praise among the Chinese, although it is not always important to utter the four tones properly since much of the sense is derived from the context. In addition Chinese people who have grown up using a specific accent will not always use the tones »correctly«. Tonal inflections are not necessarily strange to Europeans; the difference is that accents are not placed on words but on individual syllables. In English the word »converse« means »opposite« if the first syllable is accented, whereas it means » to have a conversation« if the second is accented. If this kind of accent is pared down to single-syllable words, then perhaps Chinese inflection does need seem so strange after all.

Phonetics

The rest of the pronunciation is not so difficult. Only a few of the sounds are unknown in Europe and are usually easy to imitate. The official romanization is usually a good guide to pronunciation: thus the name of the capital is now spelt Beijing, which is how it is pro-

Easy to imitate

nounced, rather than Peking. Among the peculiarities of the script is that x is pronounced like the ch in the Scottish »loch«, ch itself is pronounced as in »church« and q is pronounced like the ti in »Christian«. Thus the Fragrant Hills in the west of Beijing are called Xiāng Shān, which sounds like Chiang-shan, whereby the diphthong in »ia« Xiāng is sounded as a single syllable (not chi-ang!). Another place to go in the western hills is called the »Eight Great Sites« Bādàchù, and the great city gate alongside Mao's mausoleum is the gate of Qiánmén – Tian-men. Mao rhymes with »how« by the way. The existence of the four tones in standard Chinese compensates for an astonishing deficit elsewhere. The language has only 410 different syllables if the inflections are disregarded. The language is therefore **very short of possible sound combinations**. The use of the tones only increases the variety by a factor of four, i.e. 4 x 410 = 1640 syllables. However, all four tones are not always applied to any given syllable. Nevertheless the tones do serve to compensate for the deficit and in modern Chinese most words are longer than one syllable anyway, usually being made up of two or three.

Mandarin Chinese

The language taught in schools and spoken on television and radio is called **Mandarin**. Other than a few older people in remote areas, everyone today understands this version of the language, even though many speak it with an accent. In Hong Kong and Macau **Cantonese**, which differs considerably from Mandarin, is the official language. Young people have mostly learned English in school nowadays and some speak it very well, although you cannot count on meeting people with a sufficient degree of knowledge in foreign language. This also goes for taxi drivers.

A thank you will suffice

Chinese people are always ready with praise for people who can say as little as »Hello« (nǐ hǎo), »Goodbye« (zài jiàn) or »Thank you« (xièxie) in Chinese. Make sure that you have your destinations written down in Chinese, including your return destination or to less well known places (like restaurants). It is best to include the address too.

Writing

What gives Chinese its true fascination, though, is its writing. The fact that the biggest Chinese dictionaries include as many 50,000 characters may be intimidating, but many are no longer used. In fact a Chinese who can understand, pronounce or write no more than 5000 to 6000 characters can still be regarded as very well educated. Normally knowledge of 3000 characters is a good vocabulary, enough to read a newspaper, for example.

Chinese – are the characters pictograms?

One idea that is widespread in the West is that Chinese is a pictogrammatic language where the characters actually depict what they represent as Egyptian hieroglyphs often do. For the last 3000 years, though, this has hardly been the case and very few of the commonly used characters nowadays have a detectably pictorial character. In fact Chinese characters are much like Western numerals in nature. Their sense does not arise from their shape and needs to be learned, as does their pronunciation. Most Chinese characters, though, do exhibit some **easy links** regarding both meaning and pronunciation. Thus types of trees and other wooden objects (chairs, tables, beams, boards etc.) are written with a character that signifies wood (mù, derived from a picture of a tree). Actions usually contain an aspect signifying the word hand (shǒu). In addition the phonetic sense is also indicated vaguely, usually by means of some sort of rhyme, which is used with its own meaning elsewhere, of course, but in such cases is used only for its similarity of sound. Another principle for the construction of characters is simply the combination of meanings. One example is the character lín. This include the wood symbol (originally a tree) twice and thus signifies multiple trees, or a forest. The assignment of characters by such indicators of meaning has traditionally been the most common way of ordering them so that they can be found in a dictionary. Nowadays, however, an alphabetic ordering (based on the transcription of words into the Latin alphabet) is becoming increasingly common, as it is more practical and all Chinese children need to learn the Latin transcription to master proper Mandarin anyway.

Examples of radicals (semantic elements)

mù	木	wood, semantic element in e.g. sōng 松 pine, yǐ 椅 chair, liáng 梁 beam
shǒu	手	hand, in simplified form semantic element in e.g. dǎ 打 hit, zhǐ 指 show
rén	人	person, in simplified form semantic element in e.g. nǐ 你 you, fú 俘 prisoner

Examples of combinations of semantic and phonetic elements

fáng	房	house, room	=	hù	戶	door, household	+	fāng 方
fǎng	訪	visit	=	yán	言	speak	+	fāng 方
jīng	精	fine, select (adj.)	=	mǐ	米	grain of rice	+	qīng 青
qíng	晴	cloudless	=	rì	日	sun	+	qīng 青

Examples of semantic combinations

lín	林	grove, forest from repetition of wood (tree) mù 木
hǎo	好	good, from nǚ 女 woman and zǐ 子 child
rén	仁	goodness, humanity, from rén 人 person and èr 二 two

The Chinese figures

0	零	líng	4	四	sì	8	八	bā	1.000	千 qiān
1	一	yī	5	五	wǔ	9	九	jiǔ	10.000	万 wàn
2	二	èr	6	六	liù	10	十	shí		
3	三	sān	7	七	qī	100	百	bǎi		

Note The destinations described in this travel guide are printed in Chinese in the chapter ► »Chinese names for asking directions« on page 616ff. and a brief ►selection of phrases is on page 627ff.

Literature

History **John Keay:** *China: A History* (HarperPress 2008) This book is precisely what it claims to be, by someone who knows the region like the back of his hand.

Travel **Colin Thubron:** *Behind the Wall* (Vintage 2007). The author has spent much of his life travelling in Asia, and his writing is highly acclaimed. This book was written in 1987, during the Deng era, but before the Beijing massacre, at a time when memories of the Cultural Revolution were still vivid.

Peter Fleming: *One's Company* (Pimlico 2004) and »News from Tartary« (Birlinn 2001). China in the chaos of the 1930s as observed by the »brother of the more famous Ian«.

Buddhism **Damien Keown:** *Buddhism: A Very Short Introduction* (Oxford University Press 2000). Precisely what it says, and probably quite long enough (150 pages) for the non-specialist.

Memoirs **Pu Yi:** »From Emperor to Citizen« (Oxford 1987) A classic: the memoirs of the last emperor, who ascended the throne in 1908 as a four-year-old. He later lived the life of a playboy, was then installed by the Japanese as a puppet monarch and ended his days under communism as a gardener.

Jung Chang: *Wild Swans: Three Daughters of China* (HarperCollins 2003). A modern classic. This impressively written family saga tangibly expresses China's tribulations on the way from Confucianism to Communism.

Chinese fiction **Cao Xueqin:** *Dream of the Red Chamber* (Penguin 1995) The feelings of the individual fall foul of family duties. Since this book first appeared in 1791 generations of readers have suffered along with its hero.

Lao She: *Camel Xiangzi* (trans. by Shi Xiaojing, Chinese University Press 2004); another translation is »Rickshaw, the Novel« by JM James (University of Hawaii Press 1986). Yet another »translation« by Evan King (»Rickshaw Boy«, Reynals Hitchcock 1945) bears only a passing resemblance to the original. This most famous of all Beijing novels is set in the 1920s.

Dai Sijie: *Balzac and the Little Chinese Seamstress* (Vintage 2002): A tragi-comic love story set in the provinces soon after the Cultural Revolution.

Qiu Xiaolong: *Death of a Red Heroine* (Sceptre 2006) Socially critical crime thriller set in Shanghai during the period of political repression in the early 1990s.

Wei Hui: *Shanghai Baby* (Robinson 2003) A tale of life and passion for a modern well-to-do girl from Shanghai that breaks all the taboos.

Xiaolu Guo: *A Concise Chinese-English Dictionary for Lovers* (Vintage 2008). Don't be fooled by the title: this is a novel, written by a Chinese in English. A first-person tale of a Chinese girl sent to London by her parents to learn English. She learns a lot more besides. Culture-shock is an understatement.

The crime novels of **Robert van Gulik**! Historical whodunnits in the Brother Cadfael mould, sometimes based on real events, set in the 7th century. They are not only extremely thrilling but also provide an excellent picture of life in ancient China and how the Confucian state operated. »Murder in Canton« (Chicago 1993) is recommended.

Foreign fiction about China

Colin Thubron: *Shadow of the Silk Road* (Vintage 2007). The author (see above) revisits western China on the first stage of a journey that takes him across central Asia to the Mediterranean.

Silk Road

Sven Hedin: *The Silk Road: Ten Thousand Miles Through Central Asia* (Tauris Park 2009) The story of Hedin's famous journey of discovery from Kashgar to Beijing at the end of the 19th century, which first brought the Silk Road to the attention of the modern West.

Sun Shuyun: *A Year in Tibet* (HarperPerennial 2009). A book on Tibet written by a Han Chinese, whose only way out of a no-win situation is to tell the truth as she sees it.

Tibet

Heinrich Harrer: *Seven Years in Tibet* (Flamingo Moderrn Classics 1997). Austrian mountaineer trapped in India when war breaks out; imprisoned by British; escapes to Tibet; becomes Dalai Lama's friend; gets portrayed by Brad Pitt in a film (but that bit's not in the book).

Michael Yamashita: *Marco Polo* (White Star 2005) A great photographer travelling in the footsteps of the famous Venetian creates a fabulous photographic record of China.

Coffee-table books

DK Reference: *China: A Portrait of the People, Place and Culture* (Dorling Kindersley 2008) Fantastic hitherto unseen images of a fascinating country.

Media

China Daily is a daily newspaper available from all the better hotels and is often distributed free to guests, although in the provinces, it may only arrive several days after publication. It also has news from the rest of the world. Another similar paper is Shanghai's English-language **Shanghai Daily**. The leading daily paper in Hong Kong is the **South China Morning Post**.

In international hotels in Beijing, Shanghai and Canton it is common for the American news channel CNN to be provided via internal cable networks. Chinese television's own English-speaking channel, **CCTV 9**, can be received anywhere. One English radio broadcaster is China Radio International, which can be heard in Beijing on 91.5 MHz FM.

When staying in Beijing or Shanghai, the city listings magazines, published mainly by foreigners, are really useful. They include restaurant criticisms and concert tips among other things. Keep an eye out for these primarily in hotels or the bars and restaurants frequented by foreigners: »that's« and »City Weekend« or in Hong Kong »HK Magazine«.

Money

The Chinese currency is called the Renminbi (RMB), meaning people's currency. The unit of currency is called the yuan (cf. British money is called sterling and its unit is the pound). The exchange rate is about 8 to 10 yuan per euro (9 to 11 yuan to the pound). A yuan is divided into 10 jiao, which are generally called by their slang name, »mao«. One jiao (or mao) is then worth ten fen, although this smaller unit is rarely seen in day-to-day transactions any more. The various denominations up to the yuan are available in coins or notes. Larger denominations are in notes only. Most notes depict Mao on one side, but older notes are also in circulation, many of the counterfeit. Cash is best obtained from ATMs bearing the Maestro symbol, but ATMs without the Maestro symbol will often accept debit cards. Usually, up to 2500 yuan per day can be withdrawn, but there is a charge of about 5 pounds per

! **Baedeker TIP**

Exchange of currency

Keep hold of some of those exchange receipts. They are needed in order to exchange any superfluous yuan you may have left before leaving the country. The excess money is not paid back in European currencies, though, but in US or Hong Kong dollars.

withdrawal. Hotels that cash travellers' cheques are becoming increasingly rare. To cash travellers' cheques it is usually necessary to visit special bank branches.

Hong Kong and Macau

Both of the special administration zones have their own currency: the **Hong Kong dollar** (HK$) or the **Macau pataca** (Ptc). The two of them are roughly equivalent in value although the Hong Kong dollar may be worth a trifle more. This is pegged at a ratio of 7.8:1 to the US dollar. People travelling to Macau normally pay with Hong Kong dollars, which are acceptable everywhere. Be careful with the change, though, as patacas are not accepted in Hong Kong. One of the confusing things about Hong Kong banknotes is that all of its issuing banks have their own designs, with only the dimensions being standardized.

Personal Safety

China is a safe place to visit. Women, too, can usually travel in safety. Nevertheless it is as well not to be silly. Mobile telephones, in particular, are often stolen. In markets or shopping centres, it is not a bad idea to keep a close eye on your purse or wallet. The biggest danger is probably that of being swindled when buying goods, especially in the case of alleged antiques.

Post · Telecommunications

Letters and postcards to Europe take at least five days from Beijing, Shanghai and Hong Kong by air mail. Stamps (4.5 yuan for a postcard, 6 yuan for letters weighing up to 20 g) can usually be obtained from anywhere that also sells postcards, e.g. in hotel shops. If you need to send a larger package and the hotel's business centre is unable to help, try at the main post office.

There are all sorts of ways to use the telephone in China. The easiest   **Telephones**
but most expensive is to bring your own mobile phone with you from home. The phone will automatically dial into the local Chinese network. Depending on the hotel where you are staying, there may be a telephone in the room, which will cost a similar amount (in some hotels the phone may need to be switched through, sometimes only after payment of a deposit.) Telephone kiosks allow calls to Eu-

TELEPHONE INFORMATION

DIAL CODES

▶ **From abroad**
To China: Tel. 00 86
To Hong Kong: Tel. 00 852
To Macau: 00 853

▶ **From China/Hong Kong/Macau**
To Britain: 00 44
To Ireland: 00 353
To North America: 00 1

The first 0 of the local dial code is omitted after dialling an international code.

rope for only eight yuan per minute and buying a **telephone card** from dispensers allows calls at a similar rate. It is even easier with an **IP card**, allowing the use of practically any telephone once the card's ID has been entered. This is also convenient for local calls. IP cards can be purchased for 100 yuan at airports as soon as you arrive. For more frequent visitors to China it is worth buying a Chinese **SIM card** (chuzhi ka) in combination with top-up credit. It is also possible to select English as the operating language.

Prices

Prices in China cover a wide range. In international hotels and luxury restaurants prices are as high as in the cities of Europe; but the further one explores life in China itself, the more apparent are the benefits to the visitor of China's lower average wages. Admission charges in particular can represent a major cost factor. They range from 20 yuan for smaller groups of buildings up to 100 yuan for the important attractions and as much as 200 yuan to enter national parks and nature reserves.

 WHAT DOES IT COST?

Taxi
from 1.2 yuan
per km/0.6mi

**1 bottle of beer
in a pub**
from 20 yuan

3 course dinner
from 60 yuan

Double room
from 200 yuan

Shopping · Souvenirs

Shopping is a virtually infinite topic for which the most apt advice is, »bring as little luggage as possible«. Even those who shun shopping as a social disease could get their sacred principles shaken in China. Anyone who actually enjoys shopping should take care that they do not end up with a huge bill for excess baggage at the check-in counter. That could easily run to a couple of hundred pounds. The second most important piece of advice then is to have anything heavy sent separately and make sure in advance that the shop or dealer offers such a service.

At the beginning of a trip through China lasting two or three weeks and covering several thousand kilometres, one might think of leaving all the souvenir shopping till the end of the trip. Clever thinking, but dead wrong. Apart from a few items that are standardized through-

Antiques, bric-à-brac, nostalgic and exotic items: a flea market in Hong Kong

out the country, like stamps, it is always better to buy anything you like straight away. Anything typical of a certain place in China will be virtually impossible to get anywhere else. Even if you can find something like it, there will be less choice, the quality will be worse and the price will be higher.

Haggling Practically anywhere it is possible to obtain considerable discounts by haggling, especially at **roadside stalls and flea markets**. In such places the price demanded initially may be several times bigger than the true value. Even the state shops allow discounts, although not to such an extent. No such rebates are available for everyday items bought in supermarkets or department stores.

Antiques and art Pay twice as much attention when buying antiques or art. In the first place, a lot of counterfeiting goes on and the supposedly antique items are then sold at inflated prices. Secondly, it is only permitted to take antiques out of the country with a special permit. For any pieces dating back more than 200 years such an **export licence** is usually unobtainable. Any attempt to smuggle goods out of the country is likely to cause serious trouble. The same applies to items of newer vintage if they are considered to be part of the national heritage. This includes 20th-century art. Anyone delighting in the beauty of antique works of art but not actually able to tell the difference between an original and a copy should probably simply ask for a copy to begin with. They are often brilliantly executed but, while technically perfect, they may not be cheap either, although they will certainly be much cheaper and more »authentic« than a fake sold for an inflated price as an original. Some objects are only available for sale as **counterfeits**, e.g. travel altars (about 20 cm high, the three parts of which can be folded together). For items that really are genuine, those available for export are marked with a red seal and the sales invoice serves as an additional written confirmation of authenticity.

Stamps The Chinese Post Office is continually bringing out wonderful and thematically interesting stamps. It is a major area for collectors. Counters selling **special stamps** can be found in most of the larger post offices and on some days there are collectors' fairs in post offices.

Books Wherever photography is forbidden, in cave temples, temple monasteries and palaces (or if you have no way to take photographs anyway), it is worth taking a look at photograph volumes on sale there. There are usually some of quite decent quality, not too large but with English captions and sold at a fair price. In cities keep an eye out for **foreign language book stores**, where Chinese phrase books and translations of Chinese literature can be found as well as some equally fine photographic volumes.

Artistically folded and stacked kites maybe found in places like the large friendship shops. Colourful butterflies, dragonflies or birds hanging over a counter signal a place for kite fans to delight in.

Kites

A little of China's medicinal knowledge can easily be brought home. Among the more popular offerings are metal or stone balls to be rolled around on the palm of the hand so that circulation and acupuncture nodes are stimulated. **Foot-massage rollers** are also popular and make a fine exercise apparatus for desk workers. Back beaters (wooden balls or a rod for massaging one's own back), backscratchers and – for those who want something really big – massage chairs with in-built electric motors.

Health products

Shopping in department stores can bring more than a few interesting things to light: woks in various shapes and sizes, kitchen choppers, vegetable peelers, serving carousels, vacuum flasks, steam baskets, chop sticks – to name but a few.

Domestic goods

In China and Hong Kong it is possible to get high-quality clothing at quite cheap prices. Some of the clothes are imitations of famous brand names and designers or sometimes genuine branded goods, which exhibit some small defect making them unexportable, so that they are then finished and offered for sale, either legally or illegally, on the domestic market. The best value, though, is in labour-intensive products: cashmere and silk. Other good value items include accessories such as belts and ties (haggle). Shoes are cheap too, but beware of brand counterfeits!

Clothes

The fine wool of the cashmere sheep comes not only from Kashmir itself, but from breeding animals kept in other places, primarily in the southern parts of Inner Mongolia. In spring **cashmere pullovers** are often sold at an extra discount. It is also worth looking out for products made of yak wool, as available for example in the province of Qinghai.

Cashmere and yak wool

Silk from the home of silk. A silk blouse or jacket won't add much to the weight of your luggage. Good-quality garments – make sure they're crease-proof – are not cheap even in China. Nevertheless the available selection, especially in the silk-producing regions along the southern Yangtze, is large and varied. Men can opt for silk ties while for women an embroidered qipao, the traditional, side-buttoned dress with high collar and slit sides is a fascinating buy.

Silk

Furniture in the classic Ming style is particularly attractive. The style is once more being made new. Some other very nice things include carved pieces from old windows or beds and, thanks to the wave of demolitions of old town housing, there are many such **original items** to be found at the moment.

Furniture and wood carvings

Calligraphy brushes: tools or things of beauty?

Music   Expand your musical tastes. The range of music pressed onto silver discs ranges from classic Chinese art music played on guqin zithers via stirring folk music to Cantopop, rock and jazz. It is best to avoid pirate pressings of Western discs as the quality is bad and customs may cause trouble.

Musical instruments   It doesn't have to be a Chinese bamboo flute; there are plenty of Western instruments on sale too and at very low prices. Even if you can't play an instrument, you can buy a **gong**, not only decorative but when celebrations are held, they can really add to the occasion.

Pearls   The most attractive souvenir jewellery can be found in the shape of freshwater pearls. They can be distinguished from saltwater pearls by their greater range of colours and shapes. What counts as unattractive in a saltwater pearl, namely a less rounded or potato-like shape, is precisely what makes fresh water pearls so appealing, that and the fact that they are so much cheaper.

Calligraphy brushes   Writing brushes range from pencil-thin varieties for personal correspondence to versions as thick as your arm for large-format calligraphy. The ink is not liquid but comes in a block which is then rubbed with water onto an inkstone. The latter are made of fine black basalt and the larger and more richly decorated ones can cost as much as a car, although there are of course much cheaper ones. Finally, you cannot do without the special paper that should absorb the ink well but not let it run. **Xuan paper** (Xuan zhi, named after a place in An-hui) is the most famous kind. Other accessories include such things as a water can, a brush holder, a porcelain basin for rinsing out the brushes and a brush case in which, once cleaned, the brush can be stored till its next use.

Stones and minerals

It sounds like nature but is, in fact, a **traditional element of classical Chinese art**. The style encompasses stones ground flat and painted with pretty drawings reminiscent of trees or landscapes on the one hand and bizarre examples on the other, especially stones with holes in them. Those intended for gardens can be several metres tall so that they are not easy to transport but smaller examples can be found too, for decorating flower beds or desks. Where such stones are sold there may well also be attractive mineral crystals on sale as well.

Stamps and stamping ink

The seal of a personal stamp carries as much documentary weight in the Far East as a signature. In many places it is possible to choose a Chinese name and have a **stone stamp** carved on the spot. The value of the piece depends less on the labour involved than on the value of the stone itself. The seals are accompanied with a porcelain container for the stamping ink.

Tea leaves and china

The finest quality is to be found in areas where tea is cultivated. It is worth paying that bit more than one normally would. Ideally, being in China, it is nice to get the right kind of china to drink out of, too. One typical china is made of brown-coloured **Yixing clay**. In particular, teapots are available in an astounding variety of shapes and are popular with collectors. One technical sign of quality to note is that the lid should fit properly without wobbling around. Some Chinese tea-lovers reject Yixing clay for the best kinds of tea, preferring porcelain cups and teapots. Such tea services can be obtained in many places, although the best-quality ones are imported from Taiwan and also found in Hong Kong..

Carpets

Chinese carpets have their own style: with their motifs offering the promise of good fortune and their pretty ornamentation which emerges solidly at the edges thanks to the incised edges. Since the 19th century, China's centres of carpet making have been **China's centres of carpet making have been** Beijing and Tianjin, but examples can also be found further south. The fine silk carpets with their shimmering surfaces are especially gorgeous. These are mostly not intended for laying on the floor but for hanging on walls or using as a tablecloth.

Folk art · arts and crafts

Whereas the high-quality craftsmanship of the country once fulfilled only the decorative needs of emperors and officials, ordinary people always enjoyed simple, home-made items. Some such items can still be purchased today, although it takes a lot of luck and patience to locate a shop selling genuine folk art. On short trips it is more likely that commercialized forms of it are all that you will see.

Knotwork The **art of knotting** looked for a long time as if it would die out but it has recently seen a major renaissance. Typical decorative knots are bright red, flat and intended for hanging, from a bedpost for example.

Silhouettes Silhouette cut-outs are the traditional decoration for windows. Most examples are mass produced nowadays (although this has not harmed the beauty of individual pieces), but there are still some real artists among the people, although it is very hard to find examples of their work.

Toys China traditionally has a huge variety of toys: clay animal figures, clever games of patience made of wood or wire, grasshoppers made of straw. Games for grown-ups – including Chinese chess, go and mahjongg – deserve a mention too although they are produced industrially nowadays.

Embroidery Cloth handbags, the twelve animals of the Chinese calendrical cycle on a tapestry, decorative covers, embroidered pieces of traditional costume among the ethnic minorities, often featuring extremely artistic work, all these things make for usually highly colourful souvenirs that do not weigh too much in your luggage.

Cloisonné This **colourful enamel work** is not a Chinese invention but stems from the Near East. It was only introduced into the Middle Kingdom in the 15th century. Cloisonné work is unfortunately rather heavy as a rule, although a few years ago, so-called bodiless cloisonné was developed, which omits the metal core.

Fans Mostly people think of the common folding fans which are practical to carry and which are still used widely in summer. Nevertheless there are also non-folding fans, mostly made of silk and painted. **Paper fans**, too, are painted or decorated with calligraphy making them into decorative works of art.

Glass, glass painting The art of painting glass from the inside with a fine brush was traditionally used for snuff boxes in particular. New examples are now being made too but it is worth looking at them with a magnifying glass to see if they count among the huge number of **fakes**. The problem does not arise with the wonderful glass globes which can be obtained complete with small stands at very low cost in China.

The most »Chinese« of all minerals has been highly prized for more than 3000 years. In the earliest days of the empire, the royal insignia were made from it. However, jade is a general term that refers to all kinds of soft nephrite as well as the hard and expensive jadeite, which has only been worked since the Ming period. Jade workers also make use of other minerals like agate. Estimating the value of a jade piece is a matter for experts. Novices are often offered soapstone (steatite) or other soft materials masquerading as jade. One important **authentication criterion** is that jade should allow light to shine through it. The standard colours are white and green, but it is often other colourings that make a piece so attractive, especially when a skilled artist has been inspired by the colours to create the design. Be aware that the handcraft should be very fine. Typical items of jade jewellery include bracelets, rings and pendants.

A beautifully made doll is a good present for young and old

The little ones crawl and the big ones laugh:
pot-bellied Buddhas are a merry crew and an inexhaustible source of mirth

Lacquer   The most familiar form of lacquerware is Fuzhou lacquer. This exists in four different forms: plain lacquerware, lacquer with mother-of-pearl inlay, painted lacquer (especially for furniture) and, the most expensive and intricate variant, **carved lacquer**. One nice and easy-to-carry souvenir is bodiless lacquerware, where once several layers of lacquer have hardened, the lacquered body (normally wood but in this case clay) is then removed.

Porcelain   Porcelain is even called china in English, but its homeland is not a very good place to buy it. Top quality china is exported and in the country itself it is difficult to get. There do exist some **fine older pieces**, though. Since they do not come into the antique category, they can still be exported. Replicas of old porcelain pieces can also be worth the investment (although it is likely to be an expensive out-lay). What can be obtained quite cheaply is vernacular, hand-painted porcelain, such as can be bought in the Chinese department stores of Hong Kong.

Sport and Outdoors

In China you can play golf, go swimming, skiing or cycling, ride a camel or climb a mountain – although hardly anyone travels to China to take advantage of all these sporting possibilities. Nevertheless there are certainly some travel agents who bear such a clientele in mind. For instance Edelweiss (www.edelweissbike.com) offer **motorbike tours** in China. Bike China Adventures (www.bikechina.com) specialize in **cycling tours**, and further information on cycling in China can be obtained from http://www.bicycle-adventures.com/cycling-in-China.htm, while information on **trekking trips** can be found at (www.wildchina.com). Seaside holidays on the beaches of Hainan are provided as a supplemental offer by several travel agents.

Some non-sporting activities can be attractive, too. A trip to China is obviously perfect for anyone learning Chinese. www.languagesabroad.co.uk offers a number of courses, but many more sites will be found on the internet. This is also true of courses in tai qi and qi gong, for example under www.worldlinkedu.com/martial_arts.php.

Time

China is eight hours ahead of GMT and seven hours ahead of British Summer Time: 10am in London or Liverpool is 5pm (summer) or 6pm (winter) in Beijing, Shanghai or Hong Kong. Despite its huge breadth from east to west, China has only **one time zone**. In the west where the sun rises and sets more than two hours later than in Beijing, people compensate simply by getting up, working, eating and sleeping later.

Tipping

It is unusual to give tips for most services in China. In particular Chinese waiters and catering staff do not receive a tip unless they serve the food individually to each guest, as is done at elegant banquets. On such occasions it is customary for the invited guests to proffer the staff a small bonus.

Calculating taxi fares to the nearest mao (a tenth of a yuan) is considered laughable. Taxi drivers sometimes even let people off without paying some of the money if it is too complicated to sort out the change.

Travel guides   Chinese travel guides, however, rely on very generous tips. Speak to your group or the agent back in Europe and elect someone to pass on an envelope on behalf of all the group members at the end of the trip. Bus drivers will also expect a tip at the end of a package tour

Transport

By car

On mainland China cars drive on the right, while in Hong Kong and Macau they drive on the left. Vehicles follow the highway code of »**strongest wins**« – anyone driving a rental car should be aware of this if they have any respect for their own skin. Cars turning into or out of corners also have right of way over cyclists and pedestrians – even if not de jure, then de facto, and that is what matters. Any foreigner who hits a Chinese cyclist in their own car, though, so the cyclist falls over, should certainly not expect to rely on any such »strongest wins« principle.

The traffic in Beijing …

A few other rules for cyclists: always keep your eyes on the road ahead and keep ringing your bell. Make use of any promising gap, especially when in the company of other cyclists. If a city has guarded **cycle parks**, you are obliged to use them. They do require a fee but it is minimal.

Ring that bell hard

By rail

The rail system is an important means of transport and to be recommended, especially because there is so much of rural life to see just by looking carefully out the window, and the landscape is sometimes quite unique and magnificent. Thanks to an ambitious modernization programme, many journey times have been considerably reduced, but often it is necessary to use **night trains**. Make sure to take direct services wherever possible since the timetables make no allowance for people making connections. A modern booking system is still supposedly under construction, i.e. in some places it is only possible to book tickets on trains leaving from the station where you are. Anyone wishing to book in advance thus needs to do so through a travel agent.

… and flyovers in Shanghai are equally confusing

Hard-sleepers and soft-sleepers

Most trains provide three comfort classes: second-class seating carriages (yingzuo, »hard-seaters«), couchettes (yingwo, »hard-sleepers«) and sleeping-cars (ruanwo, »soft-sleepers«). On day-time trains without sleeping carriages there may also be first-class seating (ruanzuo, »soft-seaters«). In the Japanese-built expresses between Shanghai and Nangjing, there are first and second-class seats, and only as many tickets as there are seats. Second-class seating carriages are the cheapest; on some routes they are rationed by seating availability, but on others, passengers are taken whether there are seats or not, so you may have to stand. Couchette carriages have six beds per compartment but the compartments are open on the corridor side. Sleeping cars have four beds per compartment and the compartment can be locked. There are also two other major advantages: each bed has a reading lamp and each compartment has a volume control so that train announcement speakers can be turned down or off entirely. The constant announcements, reminders and entertainment programmes are among the most irritating things about travelling by train in China.

Make a reservation!

Sleepers, couchettes or first-class seats may only be used if booked in advance. Stations along the route have small allocations, and if these are exhausted, it is possible to board the train with a second-class seating ticket and take pot luck. It is sometimes possible to change class on the train (mostly in car 8).

Restaurant and buffet cars

Eating possibilities on trains vary from line to line. A restaurant car is provided as standard but the food may only come in polystyrene boxes or you have to serve yourself from a self-service buffet. In most cases, though, food is nicely cooked and served hot. In addition, restaurant cars usually have a **sufficiency of beer**. In both seating and sleeping carriages there is hot water, so that it is possible to brew up a tea or coffee or prepare pot noodles.

Railway stations

Railway stations can only be entered with a valid ticket. The **ticket office is therefore usually in a side building** on the station forecourt. The platforms are normally closed so people bide their time in a waiting room till passengers are called to board the train in question. Stations always have small shops where you can obtain provisions for the journey.

By air

Air travel has modernized much more quickly than the railways. The number of airports and plane connections in the country has veritably exploded since the 1990s. The rapid expansion has meant that in nearly all cases **only the latest aircraft** are used. One important aspect is that passports must always be shown, even for inland flights – passports should therefore be carried in hand luggage or on one's person at all times. The prices are low in comparison with Europe, so the flight costs little more than the fare for a sleeper carriage on the corresponding railway line, in spite of the dramatic shortening of the journey time.

Long-distance coach

With the **expansion of the motorway network** the importance of long-distance coaches has increased markedly. On many routes (e.g. Beijing–Tianjin, Chengdu––Chongqing) they have virtually supplanted train travel as the buses are not only quicker and cheaper but also more frequent.

In general there is a distinction to be made between coaches travelling by day and overnight buses. The first are normal coaches but the latter have **narrow bunks**. The advantage of these night services is that they allow access to some quite remote places. However, the buses have frequently been involved in dramatic accidents resulting from **driver fatigue**. It takes a certain adventurousness to put one's trust in such a bus.

Daytime and overnight buses

Buses run between city bus stations according to a fixed timetable. Tickets can be bought at the counters there. Larger cities may have several bus stations. Large cities in close proximity also have normal bus services running between them. Also, in addition to regular buses, there may be **minibuses** too. They are more expensive but not necessarily any quicker or more comfortable since they run as needed and may divert all around the houses.

Tickets

Boats and ferries

The most interesting stretches for tourists along the three Yangtze gorges is described in the travel guide section (► p. 599). The Yangtze is also a key inland waterway downstream of the gorges. Several **ferry connections also remain important**: across the Pohai Gulf (e.g. Weihai–Dalian), across the estuary of the Pearl River (Hong Kong––Macau and Hong Kong–Zhuhai) and Hainan.

City transport

By 2007 there were underground or overhead railways in ten cities. Other systems are under construction or in planning. In most towns buses provide much of the public transport. Normally a **conductor** will travel with the bus; although in some buses (e.g. all buses in Hong Kong) it is necessary to pay the exact fare into a machine. If you do not speak Chinese and do not know the route, there is always a risk that you might not end up where you want.

Taxis
Taxis are highly recommended as they are very cheap. Usually the price is calculated by meter, although in some smaller towns, fixed price fares are now in place. For longer day trips it is possible to negotiate a **daily rental price**. Apart from the price, the destination and the journey time should be agreed in advance too.

Bicycles
Bicycles can be recommended for anyone with the ability to read a street map as long as they have no fear of heavy traffic. The cost of renting a bike is low but it is necessary to pay a deposit.

Travellers with Disabilities

In China disabled people are practically never seen in public. This includes blind people or wheelchair users. This is hardly surprising as the country still has few or no facilities for the disabled. Attempts to change this are in their very early stages and the only places with any semblance of service for disabled people are the international hotels. Considerable improvements were made in Beijing in preparation for the 2008 **Paralympic Games**. There, some of the main attractions (imperial palace, Altar of Heaven, the Changling Ming mausoleum) also have a few toilets suitable for disabled use. The classic attractions in particular, though, have lots of high steps and thresholds so that, in spite of one or two ramps, a helping hand is always required. Public transport is not suitable for disabled users at all. Any disabled people intending to travel in China should therefore always be accompanied by able-bodied assistance and should accurately inform themselves in advance from a travel agent in their own country of the details with regard to accommodation and travel. There is information to be had online from www.disabilitytravel.com or from the following organizations:

▶ HELP FOR TRAVELLERS WITH DISABILITIES

► **Royal Association for Disability and Rehabilitation RADAR**
Issues fact packs for disabled travellers
12 City Forum, 250 City Rd
London
Tel. 020 7250 3222
www.radar.org.uk

► **In the USA: Society for Accessible Travel & Hospitality SATH**
Suite 601, 347 Fifth Ave.
New York
Tel. 212 447 7284
www.sath.org

Weights and Measures

China uses the metric system. Older measures have been adapted to a metric scale: A Chinese mile (barely used nowadays) is only 500 m long, a pound (jin) is 500 g, an ounce (liang) 50 g. Temperatures are stated in Celsius.

When to Go

A key aspect as it is easy to make bad mistakes with the. To start with, one really bad time to go is around the Chinese New Year festival, when all the shops are closed and the whole transport infrastructure is clogged with people making their way home for the feast. Similarly bad times include the first week in April and the time around 1 October, since these are holiday times in China and all the attractions are hopelessly crowded. The summer months are also a poor choice. In most parts of the country it is then very hot and humid with lots of heavy rain. The fresh air of the mountains and the seaside means that resorts there are particularly full in July and August. In terms of weather, the best time is October, but for that very reason, that month is the peak holiday season and hotel prices are correspondingly high. One very good compromise is to go in November. In the north it is already cold but in the south it is still pleasant and almost entirely dry. April is not bad either, especially in the north. In the south at that time it can still be unpleasantly cold, dull and rainy. Those who wish to travel the Silk Road should avoid the spring, which is the sandstorm season.

Better in winter

In general winter is better than summer for a visit. Places of accommodation and some attractions provide a discount, which can be as much as 60% in four or five-star hotels. Many attractions can also be viewed without troublesome crowds.

Tours

PACKAGE OR INDIVIDUAL, BEIJING, SHANGHAI,
HONG KONG OR THE DEPTHS OF INLAND
CHINA, CHINA PROVIDES ANY NUMBER OF
TRAVEL OPTIONS. THE FOLLOWING SECTIONS
DESCRIBE FIVE DIFFERENT TOURS FOR
EXPERIENCED TRAVELLERS AND BEGINNERS.

TOURS THROUGH CHINA

You don't know how to start? In the following pages, we'll present five particularly attractive tours through China.

■■■ TOUR 1 Traditional Highlights
The ideal route for anyone visiting China for the first time is to start from Beijing, then on to Xi'an, Shanghai, Guilin and Hong Kong. The highlights come thick and fast. ► **page 136**

■■■ TOUR 2 Alternative Highlights
Travel along a chain of UNESCO World Heritage Sites. Travelling by bus and train makes the encounter with the real China so much more intense. ► **page 138**

■■■ TOUR 3 The Silk Road
On the trail of explorers and merchant caravans, a trip to innermost China ► **page 140**

Kashgar   Kuqa
TOUR 3

©*Baedeker*

■■■ TOUR 4 Back to China's Roots
China's roots lie in the »yellow soil«: in the loess deposits of the Yellow River. Here a unique cultural landscape has been created amid the canyons and cave villages. ► **page 142**

■■■ TOUR 5 Tibet
An encounter with non-Chinese people and traditions is the focus of this tour with its climax in the mountains of Tibet. ► **page 144**

Prayer flags ...
... can be seen everywhere in Tibet

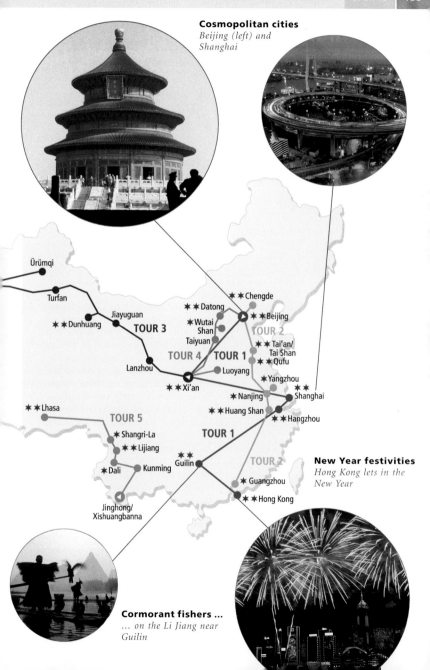

Cosmopolitan cities
Beijing (left) and Shanghai

New Year festivities
Hong Kong lets in the New Year

Cormorant fishers ...
... on the Li Jiang near Guilin

Travelling in China

How do you cross half a continent?

China will strain any kind of pre-planning. Between Manchurian Harbin with its ice palaces and the palm-lined beaches of Sanya there is not only a distance of 3400 km/2100 mi as the crow flies but also a vast spectrum of lands and peoples, just as there are along the line from Shanghai to Kashgar in central Asia, 4180 km/2600 mi away. It is not only the sheer size of China that is so breathtaking, but its **variety of cultures**. Even to the average Chinese, the life of the Mongolians with the staple diet of cheese, mutton and hard liquor is no less exotic than it is to the average European visitor. Tibet and Uyghurian Xinjiang are also unique entities. There is an endless list of UNESCO World Heritage Sites in China. That too illuminates how fascinating it can be to travel here. The five suggested tour routes listed below reveal a mere cross section of what the country has to offer.

Where to begin?

With all of China to choose from, where should anyone start? That at least is an easy question to answer. **Beijing**, the capital, not only boasts the greatest number of treasures – there are six World Heritage Sites here alone – but it is also the place that offers easiest access to the core elements of Chinese culture, whether it be Confucianism and empire or the socialist and nationalist aspects of the modern day. Each of them can be seen here in its purest form. A first trip should, of course, also include **Shanghai**. The dynamism of the city and its consistent forward-looking attitude are exciting for anyone. To encounter both its ancient culture and its latest ambitions for the future, a third part of the tour should concentrate on **China's countryside**. There, though, the choice becomes utterly overwhelming. Most travellers to China opt for the conical karst scenery of Guilin, a wonderful mixture of natural splendour and sub-tropical culture. Xi'an – with the first emperor's terracotta army – and Hong Kong then round off a perfect route for first-time visitors.

The courage to explore will pay dividends

It is possible to make a more intensive trip, though, getting nearer to the land and its people, travelling more across country and less through airport departure lounges. There can be few countries where such adventurousness is so satisfying as in China. Just one of its provinces can be larger than some European countries. As long as that remains clear and the visitor is wise enough to focus on a single region, there will still be little time to waste and plenty to enjoy. There are twenty-four carat jewels by the score to be found, even off the beaten track, including glorious scenery like UNESCO's natural World Heritage Sites at **Jiuzhaigou, Wulingyuan or Mount Huang Shan**, small towns of huge historical importance like Pingyao und Lijiang or medium-sized cities like Xiamen or Kunming. For people with specialised interests, there is a massive scope, too, encompassing exploration of Buddhism, birdwatching or water sports.

The size of the country means aircraft are a very frequently used form of transport. It is nicer to travel by train to follow the changes in the scenery. Cross-country buses, however, cover some routes more quickly and cheaply. For places a little outside any town you may have chosen as a base, it is best to negotiate an all-day price for a taxi, which is by no means expensive. Within cities or for short trips, hiring a bicycle is often a more effective alternative to travelling by bus or taxi.

How to travel

One more word about planning. Anyone travelling in China under their own steam without being able to speak and read Chinese will be making their life unnecessarily difficult. It is a frustrating experience and would very likely waste quite a lot of time. Such trips are no cheaper either and such people are more likely to fall victim to a swindler. Certainly for a first trip to China, it is best to travel with a **qualified tour guide**. There are two alternatives, though: one or two weeks in Beijing and/or Shanghai are not only well worth the trip for a first-time visitor, they are also easy to organize, even with excursions.

Making your own way

Like being in a luxury hotel: the reception area on a Yangtze cruise ship

Tour 1 Traditional Highlights

Duration: 12 Days   **Distance:** 4150 km/2580 mi

This is the most commonly chosen package-tour route, tried and trusted for first-time visitors. Obviously two disadvantages need to be taken into account. Most of the time is spent in the company of other tourists (albeit mostly Chinese), and there are few trips across country since most of the connections are by plane.

Starting from Beijing

The journey starts in ❶✶✶ **Beijing**. The standard program in the capital includes the imperial palace, the Altar of Heaven, the summer palace of Yihe Yuan, the lama temple of Yonghe Gong, Tian'anmen Square, the graves of the Ming emperors and the Great Wall of China. This requires at a minimum of two and a half days. If you choose centrally located accommodation, there may be plenty of time for shopping in the old town. People travelling under their own steam might be able to treat themselves to an extra day for a visit to the imperial art collection or trip to the »Fragrant Mountain« Xiang Shan. The city has so much to offer that even a fortnight would not be enough.

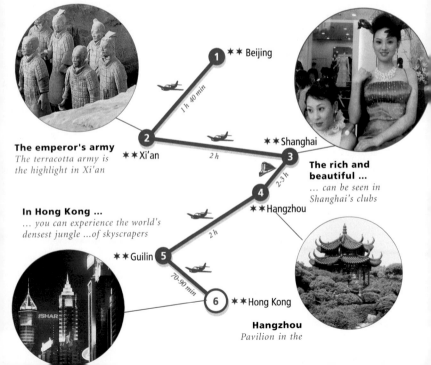

The emperor's army
The terracotta army is the highlight in Xi'an

❷ ✶✶ Xi'an

❶ ✶✶ Beijing

1 h 40 min

2 h ✶✶ Shanghai

❸

The rich and beautiful ...
... can be seen in Shanghai's clubs

2-3 h

❹ ✶✶ Hangzhou

In Hong Kong ...
... you can experience the world's densest jungle ...of skyscrapers

2 h

❺ ✶✶ Guilin

70-90 min

❻ ✶✶ Hong Kong

Hangzhou
Pavilion in the

A flight taking an hour and forty minutes covers the 960 km/600 mi to ❷✳✳ **Xi'an**. Of all the cities in China, this one has the most archaeological treasures. This is no wonder for the city was the political hub of the country until 1100 years ago. Just as the palace and the Altar of Heaven in Beijing echo the former dominance of the emperors, so does the terracotta army that guards the grave of the first emperor outside Xi'an.

Flight to Xi'an

The next place to go is ❸✳✳ **Shanghai**, close to two hours flight away (1200 km/750 mi) and an entirely different world from Xi'an. The interesting factors here are those of the 20th and 21st centuries: Huangpu Promenade lined with colonial-period buildings on one side and the skyscrapers of Pudong on the other, the view from the television tower or the upper floors of the Jin Mao Tower, wandering along Nanjing Road to Peoples' Square or a visit to the posh suburb of Xintiandi. Shanghai takes up a day and a half. One more day allows for a trip to the scholars' gardens of Suzhou.

To Shanghai

A train (200 km/125 mi, 2 to 3 hours) takes you to ❹✳✳ **Hangzhou** and the delightful Western Lake. It is particularly attractive if a light haze shrouds the obligatory gondola trip. A stop at a tea-house and a good meal will quickly make it clear that Hangzhou, even today, is a place where a laid-back lifestyle prevails – often in a highly attractive mixture of classical and modern. On a visit to the »Peak Flown from Afar« and the temple monastery of Lingyin Si both new and old Buddhist art can be seen. One whole day (with an overnight stay) is just enough to allow for a flying visit to a tea plantation, e.g. in Dragon Fountain Village.

By train to Hangzhou

Two hours flight (1300 km/800 mi) to the southwest ends with a landing in the conical karst landscape of ❺✳✳ **Guilin**. The main attraction, a trip on the Li River to Shaoxing, will take up three quarters of the day, but the city itself is also a delight. To take that in and allow for some leisure time, spend a day and a half here. For those travelling under their own steam and with time to spare, it is worth taking a couple of extra days for cycling, hiking, rafting or lazing in Yangshuo.

The karst country

A 490-km/300-mile flight taking 70 to 90 minutes ends at the most modern airport in the world – in ❻✳✳ **Hong Kong**. Commonly all too little time is allowed for the former British colony. It is unjustifiably regarded as lacking history and being mercilessly modern. There is plenty of exotic life to be experienced, though, in its older districts. A wander through the markets of Mong Kok, a trip by peak tram to the Peak, a tour of the financial quarter around Statue Square, a bit of shopping, a trip around the harbour and some midday dim sum in a tea-house quickly adds up to a stop of two days. But stay even longer if you can – it will be worth it!

Hong Kong

Tour 2 Alternative Highlights

Duration: 15 Days   **Distance:** 3220 km/2000 mi

This tour unrolls like a chain of pearls made up of UNESCO World Heritage Sites, ranging from the time of Confucius to the present day. It is the ideal tour for travellers on a second visit to China, or for first-timers looking for something a bit less conventional. Most of the journey is made by train. That means the trip, where few foreigners will be seen, is harder work but much more interesting too.

Starting from: Beijing

Anyone who has been in ❶✴✴ **Beijing** before can spend the two days on an alternative program, planning one whole day for a visit to the Qing dynasty tombs to the east and the temple monastery of Dule Si (230 km/143 mi altogether). The second day can be spent in Beihai Park and the narrow streets of the neighbouring district with its bell towers and drum towers, along with a taste of modern Beijing at Wanfujing Road. There are any number of alternatives, however.

Excursion to Chengde

The trip starts with a four-hour rail journey (260 km/160 mi) to ❷✴✴ **Chengde** with its imperial palace, multi-faceted palace gardens and the magnificent »Outer Temples«. Stay there for two nights and come back on the afternoon of the third day.

Night train to Tai'an

In Beijing there will be just enough time for a generous evening meal, then it is time to take the night train. It takes about 7 hours (570 km/355 mi) to get to ❸**Tai'an**, where it arrives very early in the morning. This leaves the whole day for climbing the holy mountain of the east, **Tai Shan**. The following morning is set aside for visiting the Tai Shan temple of Dai Miao, then take a taxi or cross-country bus to ❹✴✴ **Qufu** (80 km/50 mi, about an hour). To avoid to much rush in the city of Confucius means spending a whole day there.

Evening meal in Nanjing

Taking a train at lunchtime on the following day from Yanzhou station (16 km/10 mi west of Qufu) leaves enough time for an evening meal in ❺✴ **Nanjing** (7 hours., 510 km/320 mi). The former capital of China (most recently 1945–1949) has now become one of the biggest of China's boom cities in the lower Yangtze region. In most people's minds the city is somewhat unjustifiably overshadowed by Shanghai, although it has many more facets. The lively old central quarter of Fuzimiao, the enormous Sun Yatsen mausoleum and the impressively designed memorial to the Nanjing massacre provide for a more vivid encounter with the more recent history than virtually anywhere else. Stay there for a whole day and two nights.

Bus to Yangzhou

It takes two hours (100 km/60 mi) by bus to ❻✴ **Yangzhou**. Although the town does not attract many visitors, its classic gardens plus the wonderful Slender West Lake combine in most practical fashion the advantages of both Suzhou and Hangzhou. The look of the spot is a charming combination of ancient and modern. One day is enough to take it all in but anyone wishing for a longer rest could pick no better spot for it.

There are two alternatives for the next phase: departing for Nanjing at around 11am and taking a train from there to arrive in Huang-shan town in the evening (staying the night at the foot of the mountain) or going to Nanjing in the evening to take a night train, which arrives at about 5am. In either case, in the morning a cable car can then be taken up ❼ ✷✷ **Huang Shan** mountain. The following night can be spent on the mountain itself. This leaves a good day and a half to explore the bizarre, fairy-tale mountain terrain before taking a very late plane to cover the 970 km/660 mi to ❽ ✷ **Guangzhou**. The ancient port, today almost a second Shanghai, is a pleasing mixture of tradition and modernity. Visitors can enjoy dim sum, stroll along the Pearl River to the colonial quarter of Shamian, and take an excursion to Foshan, before flying back home after a two-night stay.

Huang Shan and Macau

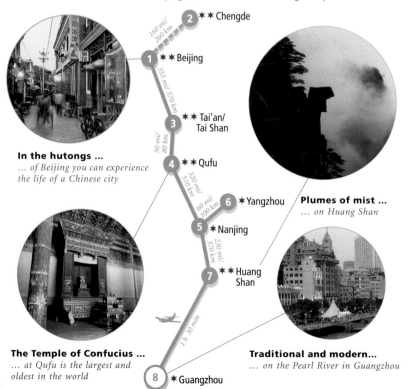

In the hutongs ...
... of Beijing you can experience the life of a Chinese city

The Temple of Confucius ...
... at Qufu is the largest and oldest in the world

2 ✷✷ Chengde
160 mi/ 260 km
1 ✷✷ Beijing
355 mi/ 570 km
3 ✷✷ Tai'an/ Tai Shan
50 mi/ 80 km
4 ✷✷ Qufu
320 mi/ 510 km
6 ✷ Yangzhou
60 mi/ 100 km
5 ✷ Nanjing
230 mi/ 370 km
7 ✷✷ Huang Shan
1 h 30 min
8 ✷ Guangzhou

Plumes of mist ...
... on Huang Shan

Traditional and modern...
... on the Pearl River in Guangzhou

Tour 3 The Silk Road

Duration: 13 – 15 Days   **Distance:** 6300 km/3900 mi

The right way to do this tour would be on the back of a donkey or a camel but at least the route needs to be covered by land in order to get the right impression of distance. What could be more classic than to follow in the well-trodden footsteps of pilgrims to India, of explorers, of countless merchant caravans and mounted armies? It can be travelled either via the Jade Route, travelling into China from the west, or the Silk Route out of China. The latter is better nowadays as central Asia is more exotic.

Start in Xi'an
The tour starts from ❶ ✳ ✳ **Xi'an**, which was known as Chang'an in the Tang period. Anyone who is already familiar with the main attractions there (▶ Tour 1), can take a day trip to the graves of the Tang emperors and the monastery of Famen Si, visiting the forest of steles, but do not miss a chance to revisit the fascinating history museum. This all adds up to two days.

Night train to Lanzhou
A night train covers the stretch to ❷**Lanzhou** (680 km/420 mi, nearly 9 hours); where spending a day allows for a trip to the ✳ **Buddha caves of Bingling Si** (depending on time of year; 75 km/47 mi by road, 54 km/34 mi by boat). The alternative is to go straight to ❸**Jiayuguan** (770 km/480 mi from Lanzhou, 13.5 hours). Here at the end of the Great Wall of the Ming dynasty, the most recent wall fortification in China's history, is where for centuries the world beyond the frontiers of empire began. At the fort the contrast between two cultures, the agrarian and the nomadic, is still palpable.

Dunhuang
Roughly a day with one overnight stop is long enough to spend there, then take a cross-country bus to ❹ ✳ ✳ **Dunhuang** (420 km/260 mi, 5 to 6 hours). There, in the late afternoon, you can scramble over the massive sand dunes. The following morning, set out before dawn towards the ✳ **Jade Gate Fortress of Yumen Guan** (96 km/60 mi each way). Here, on the salt marsh amid the gravelly desert, you can immerse yourself in the historic Silk Road experience. In the afternoon there should still be time to see the **Mogao Caves** – an outstanding art experience.

Across the desert
Spend a second night in Dunhuang, then finally set aside a day's travel for the 680-km/420-mile train ride across the desert to ❺ **Turfan**. This should take almost eight hours of travelling, plus the 120 km/75 mi by road from Dunhuang to the station at Liuyuan and 50 km/31 mi from Turfan station to Turfan itself. Here, in Xinjiang, we are in another world. This first strikes home simply walking through

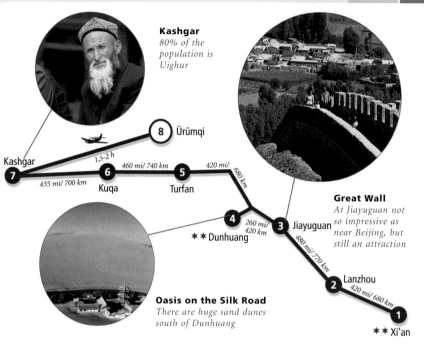

Kashgar
80% of the population is Uighur

8 Ürümqi

1,5–2 h

Kashgar
7   435 mi/ 700 km   6   460 mi/ 740 km   5   420 mi/
Kuqa   Turfan   680 km

Great Wall
At Jiayuguan not so impressive as near Beijing, but still an attraction

4   260 mi/ 420 km   3 Jiayuguan
** Dunhuang   480 mi/770 km

Oasis on the Silk Road
There are huge sand dunes south of Dunhuang

Lanzhou
2   420 mi/ 680 km
1
** Xi'an

the town and its markets in the evening. Since the train for the next stage only leaves in the evenings the first decision to make is whether to stay for one day or two. Choosing the first means being limited to seeing sights close to the town, the Emin Minaret, the ruins of Jiaohe, Kares Park and the valley of grapes; whereas an extra day provides the chance of seeing some more distant attractions, like the Bezeklik Caves, the ruins of Gaocheng and the Astana tombs.

The night train to ❻ **Kuqa** (740 km/460 mi, 11.5 hours) reaches its destination before 6am Beijing time, which translates to about 4am locally, but there is no time to be tired. The Kizil Caves northwest of the town may not be interesting in terms of art history, but the scenery is well worth staying awake for. The same applies to the town's other attractions. After one night it is time to take a morning train to the next destination, ❼ **Kashgar** (700 km/435 mi, roughly 11 hours). If the tour is so planned that arrival in Kashgar is on Sunday, then it is well timed to experience the bustle of market day. After two nights' stay there are two alternatives, either to leave China in the direction of Pakistan with a journey through the ✶✶ **Pamir Mountains** – or to climb to the summit of Musztag Ata at an elevation of 7546 m / 24,713 ft and spending one more night. Anyone not carrying on into Kyrgyzstan can fly to ❽ **Ürümqi** (1100 km/690 mi, 1.5 to 2 hours) to spend another day there.

Into deepest China

Tour 4 China's Roots

Duration: 10 – 11 Days   **Distance:** 2900 km/1800 mi

China's roots lie in the »yellow soil«« (huangtu): in the loess deposits of the Yellow River. This has formed a unique cultural landscape, for nowhere else in the world has such thick alluvial deposits as here. With its vertically dug terraces, gorges, cave passages and cave villages, the ochre scenery leaves its deepest impression when it is as barren as a desert between late autumn and spring. The next stage of the journey is partially by train with the rest by bus or taxi.

From Beijing to Datong

The nicest and quickest way to get from ❶✳✳ **Beijing** (West Station) to ❷✳✳ **Datong**, 370 km/230 mi away, is by an afternoon train arriving in the evening. That allows for a good night's sleep before devoting the next day to this treasure house of Buddhist art of the 5th and the 11th to 15th centuries in the city's own temple monasteries and in the ✳✳ **Yungang Caves** 15 km/9 mi west of the city.

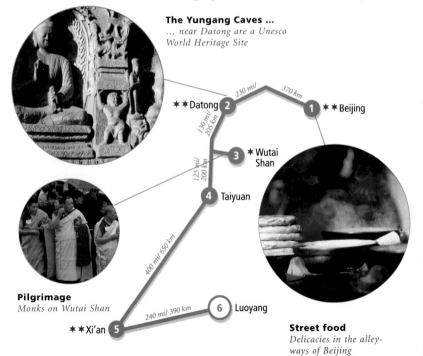

The Yungang Caves ...
... near Datong are a Unesco World Heritage Site

✳✳Datong ❷
230 mi/ 370 km
❶ ✳✳Beijing
130 mi/ 205 km
❸ ✳ Wutai Shan
125 mi/ 200 km
❹ Taiyuan
400 mi/ 650 km
240 mi/ 390 km ❻ Luoyang
✳✳Xi'an ❺

Pilgrimage
Monks on Wutai Shan

Street food
Delicacies in the alleyways of Beijing

For the following three-day stage to Taiyuan, it is best to organize a chauffeur-driven car through a travel agent unless you are travelling with a group on a package tour. This stage involves a drive of 205 km/ 127 mi –stopping off at the »Hanging Monastery« on the way – to the »Five Terrace Mountain«, ❸ * **Wutai Shan**, the oldest Buddhist centre in China, where two nights will be spent in the cluster of monasteries at Taihuai. Along the stage from Taihuai to Taiyuan (200 km/125 mi), do not miss making brief detours to the two oldest surviving temple buildings in China: * **Foguang Si** and * **Nanchan Si**.

Wutai Shan

Arriving early enough in ❹ **Taiyuan**, the provincial capital of Shanxi, allows for a quick look around the town. The following day means striking out early, ideally having negotiated a day-fare for a taxi, to drive the 25 km/16 mi to the * **Jinci temple** and another 90 km/56 mi to the historic town of ** **Pingyao**, where a night, or if possible two, should be spent. The atmosphere is great. There is after all a great deal to see here, one of the sights being the if anything overdecorated temple outside the town.

Base at Taiyuan

For the subsequent train journey, in the morning take the only direct train to Xi'an (586 km/360 mi, 10 hours). The time should be spent gazing out of the carriage window. To the right the **Valley of the River Fen** can be seen, while to the left the view takes in canyons and cave villages. A typical loess landscape such as this cannot be experienced anywhere else in such comfort. At around 5pm the train comes to the Yellow River with its characteristic suspension of alluvial loess and spends a good half hour travelling along its banks before crossing.

A day by train

Late in the evening the train arrives in ❺ ** **Xi'an**. This was the most important political hub in China between the 3rd century BC and the 10th century AD. It requires a visit of two days. On the topic of loess, it is particularly interesting to take a trip to the grave of the Tang emperor Qianling and visit the Banpo Museum with its relics of prehistoric settlement. The undisputed highlight of Xi'an, though, is the world-famous ** **terracotta army of the first emperor**, Qin Shihuangdi. The army guarding his tomb was only discovered by chance in 1974.

The army of the first emperor

❻ **Luoyang**, the second major capital of its era, can be reached via a good five-hour rail journey (390 km/240 mi), travelling by day. The natural excursion the following day is to see the * **Buddha caves of Longmen**. In addition take a taxi to the northern edge of town, where some cave villages can still be seen just as they were set up in the plain not far from the tomb museum. They involved the excavation of square courtyards 7 m/20 ft deep, around which cave dwellings (yaodong) were dug into the walls. Nowadays, however, hardly anybody lives in such places.

Destination Luoyang

Tour 5 Tibet

Duration: 23 Days   **Distance:** 3500 km/2175 mi

An encounter with non-Chinese people and traditions is the focus of this tour through the southwest of China. It is by far the most adventurous of the tours. This is to be taken seriously: in particular the second part of the journey after Lijiang, and even more so after Shangri-La, requires a great deal of adaptability and a healthy constitution.

No one should expect any sort of comfort on this part of the journey. In fact you can be sure of unexpected delays, e.g. due to rock falls or altitude sickness. The section in Tibet itself should definitely be organized via a travel agent and not attempted under your own steam, although the first section as far as Lijiang can be undertaken thus without difficulty. This tour cannot be undertaken in summer or winter – in the former case because there is too much rain and in the latter because many of the mountain roads will be impassable.

Start in Jinghong   The tour opens in the region of ✴ **Xishuangbanna** Xishuangbanna on the border with Myanmar. This is more Southeast Asia than China – culturally and linguistically. Three days and two overnight stops are a minimum. At the tour base in ❶**Jinghong** or on trips out from there, e.g. to Wild Elephant Valley, it is in any case relaxing enough that you might easily be tempted to forgo the rest of the journey.

Flight to Kunming   Nevertheless the bookings have already been made, e.g. the flight to ❷**Kunming**, provincial capital of Yunnan (390 km/240 mi, 50 minutes). Stop here for two days. Half of one day should be set aside for a trip out to the »Dragon Gate« in the **Western Mountains** (15 km/9 mi from the centre), while a whole day is needed for the long excursion to the **»petrified forest« of Shilin**, 120 km/75 mi southeast of town.

Breakfast in Dali   Late in the evening, a train with sleeping coaches runs to ❸ ✴ **Dali** (360 km/225 mi, 8 hours approx.). From the station at Dali City (Xiaguan) buses ply up to the old town of Dali (17 km/11 mi), the actual destination. Since it will already be breakfast time and a whole day lies ahead, there is no need to spend more than two nights. A boat trip can be taken out onto Lake Erhai, while a cable car leads up to the mountains for a little hiking.

The streets of Lijiang   A third day in Dali can be spent in leisure because the subsequent bus trip to ❹ ✴✴ **Lijiang** (180 km/112 mi) only takes three and a half hours. The bus arrives in Lijiang at the bus station at the southern edge of the old town centre. The rest of the day and all the days thereafter can be spent enjoying the magic of the town's maze of streets, although it would be worth setting aside one day for a trip to **Baisha** and the snow-topped mountain of **Yulong Xueshan** (35 km/ 22 mi north). 95 km/59 mi away from there lies the **Tiger Leaping Gorge**. Set aside three days and two nights for all of this as most of the travel is by shanks' pony.

For one night go back to Lijiang, where you should have left your heavy luggage. Then take the bus into the literary utopia of ❺ ✳ **Shangri-La** (200 km/125 mi, 5 hours). Stop for two nights.

Utopia »in the flesh«

This is, by now, deep in the area inhabited by Tibetans, more than 3000 m/10,000 ft above sea level, but it is still another 1670 km/1040 mi to ❻ ✳✳ **Lhasa**. It is a difficult route over many a rough road and some passes as much as 4500 m/14,800 ft high. The landscape, though, is as dramatic as anywhere in the world, but it is not a good place to fall ill, so it is as well to bring any medicines that might be needed. Nor can it be recommended for people with back problems. At least eight days must be allowed for travelling. Road building is progressing apace, so it might be a little quicker now, but as soon as a truck sheds its load, all plans go out of the window very quickly.

The long road to Lhasa

A broad smile for the visitor
Tibetan boy in Lhasa

Three-Pagoda Temple
One of the highlights of Dali

Sights from A to Z

FASCINATING SCENERY, MIGHTY RIVERS AND HOLY MOUNTAINS CONTRASTED BY PULSATING CITIES. CHINA IS A VAST COUNTRY WITH A WEALTH OF INTERNATIONALLY IMPORTANT CULTURAL TREASURES.

✶ ✶ Beijing

Hd 26

Province: Beijing   **Population:** 14 million
Altitude: 50 m

There are some place names the very sound of which evokes a magical sensation, excites expectations, dreams and emotions, even (or perhaps especially) in people who have never been there. They also awake the desire to go there. Peking was just such a name, and it has lost none of its magic in its more authentic and now generally used form, Beijing.

Take care, though: Beijing is a surprisingly modern metropolis, with vast, wide and dead straight boulevards lined by tall, modern buildings to match the size of the city itself. Some still remember it as a paradise for cyclists but now, with the building of a motorway ring, it is being transformed into a **city of car drivers**. Foreigners from all over the world, diplomats or company representatives who come with their whole families and spend large amounts of money here, can enjoy an appropriate infrastructure with local publications in English, culinary offerings from all over the world and bars open virtually round the clock.

The Chinese themselves primarily regard Beijing (»capital of the north«), as the centre of its immense empire, with primacy in politics but also in culture, science and – in spite of Shanghai – in business. After centuries of decline – impoverishment, war, revolution and isolation – everyone, native or foreign, is now seeing that the metropolis has for some years been developing back into a **magnet capable of exerting its attraction on an international scale**. The magical sound of its name, though, goes back much further and chimes with the city's rank as the premier city, not only of China but of all east Asia.

Beijing – the capital of the north

▶ VISITING BEIJING

INFORMATION

Beijing Tourist Information Centre
28 Jianguomenwai Dajie (south of the New Otani Hotels) Tel. 010/65 13 08 28 (24-hour-telephone hotline for queries and complaints)
www.bjta.gov.cn

← *The obligatory group photo on Tian'anmen Square*

Instead of talking to the headquarters, it is sometimes more convenient to use one of the 20 sub-offices in the city, for example:

Sanlitun office
Gongrentiyuchang Beilu (immediately to the east of the Xin Donglu instersection, next to KFC)

Main railway station office
16 Laoxianju Hutong
(diagonally opposite the station itself, to the east of the Henderson Shopping Centre)

Airport counter
Opposite the exit for international passengers

TRANSPORT

Public transport
The underground is cheap and fast but there are some major gaps in its coverage of the city, even after the Olympics. In the area of interest to tourists there are to date only three lines. September 2009 will see the opening of line 4 to the Summer Palace. Most of the public transport is handled by buses, including trolley-buses, but to use them without speaking Chinese is a hazardous undertaking. Also, there are express buses on some routes, which do not stop everywhere.

Taxi
Usually a taxi is the best choice for getting around as a taxi fare costs no more than a bus or tram journey does in Europe. The rates depend on the kind of vehicle, although the difference is only noticeable on longer journeys. Taxis operating outside the city usually have no licence to venture into the urban district, but there is no problem in the opposite direction.

Bicycles
Bicycles are very useful and practical, especially as Beijing is flat and it seldom rains except in the middle of summer. Cycles can be hired e.g. on Wangfujing to the north of Dong'anmen Dajie.

The Grand Hyatt luxury hotel in the middle of the huge Oriental Plaza complex

SHOPPING

The main shopping boulevard is Wangfujing. Interesting places there include the basement level under the massive Sun Dong An Plaza, because of all the many traditional foods (including tea) sold there or the imitations of the little shops of old Beijing at the northern end. Yashow Market (Yaxiu Fuzhuang Shichang) offers a huge selection of inexpensive clothes, plus sporting goods, sofa cushions and crafts (58 Gongrentiyuchang Beilu, next to the footbridge). The Friendship Shop (Youyi Shangdian, 17 Jianguomenwai Dajie), actually a large department store, is really expensive but concentrates on quality and has a large assortment of goods of interest to foreigners: crafts, kites, Chinese medicines and foreign publications. Beijing Curio City (Beijing Guwan Cheng, east of the third ring road, 1.3 km/1400 yd south of Jinsong Lu), which resembles a department store but houses more than a hundred professional art dealers, is a destination for true enthusiasts. The classic place to go for antiques, though, is the famous Liulichang.

WHERE TO EAT

► Expensive

① *Crystal Jade Palace*
Don Chang'an Jie
Oriental Plaza BB78–BB82
Tel. 010/64 60 66 88, App. 2460
Underground Dongdan, Wangfujin
Cantonese dimsum in a classy ambience, beneath huge crystal chandeliers.

② *Fangshan*
Beihai Park, northern shore of Qiongdao Island
Tel. 010/64 01 18 89 u. 64 01 18 79
Imperial cuisine in a pleasure palace, where food is ordered not by the dish but the whole menu.

③ *Green T. House*
6 Gongrentiyuchang Xilu
Tel. 010/65 52 83 10
Underground Tian'anmendong
The interior and the cuisine are creative and innovative, creating a feast for all the senses, an unforgettable experience.

► Moderate

④ *Bookworm*
Nan Sanlitun Lu
Building no.4
upper floor via external staircase
Tel. 010/65 86 95 07
A lending library with a restaurant serving Western cuisine. Free internet access and cheap menu du jour.

④ *Da Dong Roast Duck Restaurant*
Dongsi 10 Tiao A-22
Nangxincan Business World
Underground station: Dongsishitiao
Tel. 010/51 69 03 29
This is counted among the best restaurants for Peking duck, but the other dishes, too, are top class. Make sure to book well in advance.

⑥ *Nuage*
22 Qianhai Dongyan
Tel. 010/64 01 95 81
Vietnamese restaurant often very busy in the evenings. Very lucky people might get a seat next to the window with a view of the lake.

⑦ *South Silk Road*
Qianhai Xiyan (»Lotus Lane«) A-19
Tel. 010/66 15 55 15
Yunnan cuisine from southwest China: The name refers to the trading route for tea and horses, which runs from Yunnan to Tibet. It is possible to sit outside by the lakeshore.

⑧ *Xihe Yaju*
Ritan Donglu

Beijing Map

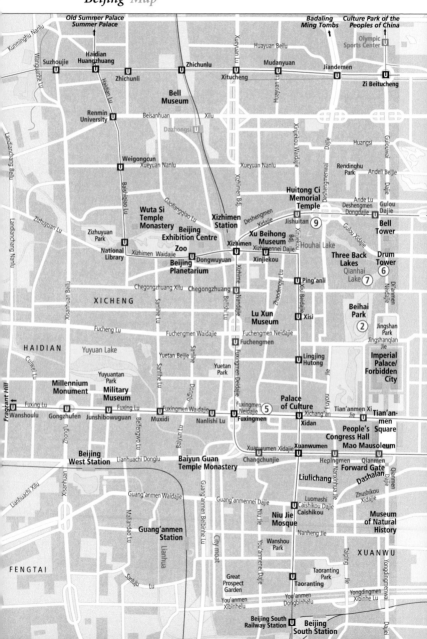

Old Summer Palace
Summer Palace
Badaling
Ming Tombs
Culture Park of the
Peoples of China
Olympic
Sports Center
Kunminghu Nanlu
Wanglange Lu
Suzhoujie
Haidian
Huangzhuang
Zhichunlu
Huayuan Beilu
Mudanyuan
Jiandemen
Zi Beitucheng
Xueyuan Lu
Zhichunli
Xitucheng
Haidian Lu
Bell
Museum
Beisanhuan
Xilu
Renmin
University
Dazhongsi
Huangsi
Gulouwai
Huayuan Lu
Rendinghu
Park
Andeli Beijie
Weigongcun
Xueyuan Nanlu
Xueyuan Nanlu
Xinjiekou Waidajie
Deshengmenwai Dajie
Huitong Ci
Memorial
Temple
Ande Lu
Deshengmen
Dongdajie
Gulou
Dajie
Gaoliangqiao Lu
Wuta Si
Temple
Monastery
Xizhimen
Station
Deshengmen
Xidajie
Jishuitan
9
Bell
Tower
Zizhuyuan Lu
Landanchang Beilu
Baishiqiao Lu
Zizhuyuan
Park
Beijing
Exhibition Centre
Zoo
Xizhimen
Xu Beihong
Museum
Houhai Lake
Three Back
Lakes
Drum
Tower
6
Landanchang Nanlu
National
Library
Xizhimen Waidajie
Xizhimennei Dajie
Qianhai
Lake
7
Di'anmen
Neidajie
Dongwuyuan
Xinjiekou
Beijing
Planetarium
Ping'anli
Gulou Xidajie
Xizhimenwai Dajie
Chegongzhuang Xilu
Chegongzhuang
Xinjiekou Nandajie
XICHENG
Sanlihe Lu
Beilishi Lu
Lu Xun
Museum
Xisi
Beihai
Park
2
Jingshan
Park
Jingshanqian
Jie
Fucheng Lu
Fuchengmen Waidajie
Fuchengmen Neidajie
HAIDIAN
Yuyuan Lake
Yuyuantan
Park
Yuetan Beijie
Sanlihe Lu
Yuetan
Park
Dongsi
Fuchengmen
Fuxingmen Deidajie
Fuchengmen
Lingjing
Hutong
Imperial
Palace/
Forbidden
City
Culwei Lu
Millennium
Monument
Military
Museum
Fuxingmen Waidajie
Fuxingmen
Neidajie
Xidan
Xichang'an
Palace
of Culture
Tian'anmen Xi
Jie
Tian'an-
men
Square
Fragrant Hill
Fuxing Lu
Wanshoulu
Gongzhufen
Junshibowuguan
Fuxing Lu
Muxidi
Nanlishi Lu
Fuxingmen
Xichang'an
Xuanwumen
People's
Congress Hall
Mao Mausoleum
Zhonglu
Beijing
West Station
Lianhuachi Donglu
Baiyun Guan
Temple Monastery
Xuanwumen Xidajie
Changchunjie
Xuanwumen
Hepingmen
Qianmen
Forward Gate
Dashalan
Lianhuachi Xilu
Xisanhuan Zhonglu
Guang'anmen Waidajie
Guang'anmen Beibinhe Lu
Guang'anmennei Dajie
Liulichang
Luomashi
Caishikou Dajie
Naxinhua Lu
Qianmen
Zhushikou
Xidajie
Malandao Lu
Guang'anmen
Station
Caishikou
Niu Jie
Mosque
Nanheng Jie
Museum
of Natural
History
City moat
Lianhua
Lu
Niu Jie
You'anmen Dajie
Wanshou
Park
Wanshou Jie
XUANWU
Taiping
Yongdingmenwai
FENGTAI
Smiju
Lu
Great
Prospect
Garden
You'anmen
Xibinhu
Taoranting
Park
Taoranting
You'anmen
Dongbinhelu
Yongdingmen
Xibinhe Lu
Yongdingmenwai
Dajie
Beijing South
Railway Station
Beijing
South Station
5

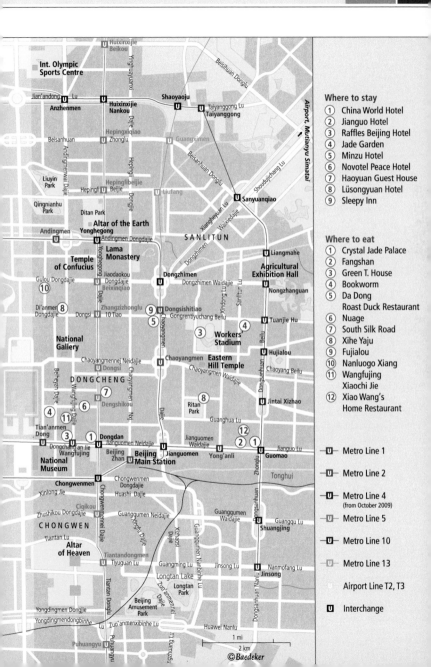

Where to stay

1. China World Hotel
2. Jianguo Hotel
3. Raffles Beijing Hotel
4. Jade Garden
5. Minzu Hotel
6. Novotel Peace Hotel
7. Haoyuan Guest House
8. Lüsongyuan Hotel
9. Sleepy Inn

Where to eat

1. Crystal Jade Palace
2. Fangshan
3. Green T. House
4. Bookworm
5. Da Dong
   Roast Duck Restaurant
6. Nuage
7. South Silk Road
8. Xihe Yaju
9. Fujialou
10. Nanluogo Xiang
11. Wangfujing
    Xiaochi Jie
12. Xiao Wang's
    Home Restaurant

U— Metro Line 1

U— Metro Line 2

U— Metro Line 4
(from October 2009)

U— Metro Line 5

U— Metro Line 10

U— Metro Line 13

Airport Line T2, T3

U Interchange

© Baedeker

(northeast corner of Ritan Park)
Tel. 010/85 61 76 43
Very popular spot in the park
serving Huaiyang cuisine from
mid-China.

► Inexpensive
⑨ *Fujialou*
Donsi Shitiao 23
Underground Dongsishitiao
Tel. 010/84 03 78 31
Beijing vernacular dishes. Noodles,
tofu etc. Very popular, always full.

⑩ *Nan Luogu Xiang*
This is not a restaurant but Beijing's
new trendy scene: a long, fairly
traditional old residential alley with
small restaurants and cafés that have
geared themselves to foreigners:
sometimes with a family atmosphere,
sometimes »cool«. Food and drink are
cheap everywhere. Good places include Zuihonglou (no. 15-1, Taiwa-
nese cuisine) and Zha Zha Café (no.
101).

⑪ *Wangfujing Xiaochi Jie*
Underground Wangfujing
Western side of Wangfujing, behind a
decorative gate
A street of eateries in old Beijing style
with lots of cookshops. Hardly any of
it is original but the atmosphere is
authentic.

⑫ *Xiao Wang's*
Home Restaurant
2 Guanghua Dongli
(go north from the eastern side of the
Jinglun Hotel, then turn right)
Tel. 010/65 94 36 02
Branch in the Houhai district:
15 Qianhai Beiyan
Tel. 010/66 17 55 58
Friendly private restaurant geared to
foreign custom with a large choice
including vegetarian meals.

WHERE TO STAY
► Luxury
② *China World Hotel*
1 Jianguomenwai Dajie
Tel. 010/65 05 22 66
Fax 010/65 05 08 28
www.shangri-la.com/en
Underground Guomao
738 rooms. Part of the World Trade
Centre, regarded by businesspeople as
the best hotel in town

③ *Jianguo Hotel*
5 Jianguomenwai Dajie
Tel. 010/65 00 22 33
Fax 010/65 00 28 71
www.hoteljianguo.com
Underground Yong'anli
426 rooms. With its pretty garden
courtyards, the hotel has an intimate
feel. French gourmet restaurant.

① *Raffles Beijing Hotel*
33 Dong Chang'an Jie
Tel. 010/65 26 33 88
Fax 010/85 00 43 80
http://beijing.raffles.com
Underground Wangfujing
910 rooms. The »legendary hotel« of
the capital: atmospheric building in a
central location

► Mid-range
④ *Jade Garden*
(Cuiming Zhuang)
1 Nanheyan Dajie
Tel. 010/58 58 09 09
Fax 010/58 58 09 99
www.jadegardenhotel.cn
Inexpensive four-star comfort. Central
location. 113 rooms.

④ *Minzu Hotel*
51 Fuxingmennei Dajie
Tel. 010/66 01 44 66
Fax 010/66 01 48 49
www.minzuhotel.cn
Underground Xidan

615 rooms. The former grand socialist hotel has undergone thorough rebuilding to become a pleasant modern hotel.

⑤ *Novotel Peace Hotel*
3 Jinyu Hutong
Tel. 010/65 12 88 33
Fax 010/65 12 68 63
www.novotel.com
495 rooms. Central location near Wangfujing, well equipped with sauna and swimming pool.

► Budget
⑦ *Haoyuan Guest House*
53 Shijia Hutong
Tel. 010/65 12 55 57
Fax 010/65 25 31 79
www.haoyuanhotel.com
19 rooms. Stay in a refurbished old courtly building. All the rooms are at ground level with those in the idyllic courtyard at the rear being more spacious, elegantly furnished, especially quiet and thus more expensive.

⑧ *Lüsongyuan Hotel*
22 Banchang Hutong
Tel. 010/64 04 04 36
Fax 010/64 03 04 18
www.the-silk-road.com/hotel/lusong yuanhotel/index.html
31 rooms with the atmosphere of old Beijing, which is very popular with foreigners and has its own internet teahouse.

⑨ *Sleepy Inn*
103 Deshenmennei Dajie
Tel. 010/64 06 99 54
This personally managed bright and cheerful youth hostel in an attractive old-town location has rooms with two, four and six beds. Cycle hire.

BARS AND PUBS
Three Lakes (Shichahai)
Better, bigger, more atmospheric and popular than Sanlitun ever was: the areas around the Front Lake (Qianhai) and at the southern and northern ends of the Rear Lake (Houhai) bubbles with life at the weekends, but it is pretty lively during the week, too, especially when there is good weather and people can sit outside. There are any number of simple and inexpensive bars and restaurants. On »Lotus Lane« (west bank of the Front Lake) there are some more expensive establishments. Here and around the marble bridge of Yinding Qiao it is bustling and noisy, but it is quieter in the middle of Houhai's south bank (Houhai Nan-yan). One good place to go for a nice time is the No Name Bar next to the Nuage Restaurant, 3 Qianhai Dongyan.

Sanlitun
It's the same old story: small bars grows up Topsy-like, frequented by bohemians, in a cheap neighbour-hood. The area's success attracts the glitterati, and that's the end of bohemia. Everything gets chic and expensive. In Sanlitun, the investor calls it »The Village«, an ensemble of garish glass boxes with brand-name shops, trendy bars and a hotel for a well-heeled clientele. It's surrounded by the remains of old Sanlitun, e.g. The Tree with Belgian beer and pizza from the wood-fired oven – cheap, and with a proper pub atmosphere. (second alleyway after the shopping mall at 3.3). There are more addresses at the Workers' Stadium, including the dance temple of Coco Banana (Gongrentiyuchang Xilu 8, rear)

Hutong Bar
Nan Luogu Xiang
This could become the favourite bar,

at least in this old-town lane. Beer, wine and herbal teas are served in a historic ambience. There's also seating outside.

Schiller's
Liangmahe Nanjie (west of the inter-section with Sanlitun Lu)
A nicely located spot with a view of the Liangma Canal and German food, where it is possible to sit outside.

GOING OUT

Beijing opera, variety, acrobats
All the three forms of art come together: tea-house variety shows often include operatic arias and acro-batics. Beijing opera, which often includes acrobatic scenes as well, is experienced at its best and most typical in a teahouse atmosphere, sitting four to a table. Some of the best places are listed below:

Chaoyang Theatre
36 Dongsanhuan Beilu
Tel. 010/65 07 24 21
Beijing's leading stage for acrobats

Hu Guang Guild House
3 Hufangqiao
Tel. 010/63 51 82 84
A theatre built in 1830 for a mer-chants' guild is the loveliest place imaginable to see Beijing opera and it is geared to foreigners.

Tianqiao Paradise Teahouse
113 Tianqiao Shichang
(in the building at the rear)
Tel. 010/63 04 06 17
Beijing's finest teahouse auditorium. Colourful programme with acrobatics, opera and magic as well as explan-ations in English.

>Brief history of Beijing/Peking

Traces of human settlement in Beijing go back to very early times: the hominid known as Peking Man (*Homo erectus pekinensis*) took refuge in caves here. Early modern men used it as a base for their hunting. About 3100 years ago the earliest **forerunner of the modern city** came into being. It was then the residence of what was initially an unimportant dynasty of princes called Yan. After the unification of China into an empire (221 BC), Beijing (or its predecessor in a slightly different location) was primarily a garrison town and trading post on the northern border, where the agricultural land of the Yel-low River flood plain approaches the steppes.

Beijing a thou-sand years ago A new era began when a group of steppe dwellers called the Khitan conquered parts of northern China and built a secondary capital on a new site corresponding to the western part of what is now south-ern Beijing in the year 947.

The best part of 200 years later, the Jurchens drove out the Khitans and occupied other parts of China, naming Beijing as the centre of their great empire. This **earliest heyday** of Beijing lasted till the next conquerors invaded from the steppes, the Mongols, who laid waste the Jurchens' city in 1215.

700,000 BC	First traces of Peking Man
11th century BC	First fortified town, residence of the prince of Yan
947 AD	Southern capital of the Kitan (Liao dynasty)
1215	Destruction by the Mongols
1267–1274	Rebuilt as the »Great Capital« of the Mongols
1406–1420	Beijing rebuilt as the capital of the Ming dynasty
1644	Beijing becomes the capital of the Manchu empire
1860	British and French troops destroy many of the palaces
1900	Boxer Rebellion, massacre of Christians
1928	Nanking is made the capital, Beijing becomes »Beiping«
1949	Mao declares the People's Republic of China
1965–1969	Demolition of the city walls, Cultural Revolution
1989	Democracy movement is suppressed
2008	Beijing hosts the 29th Olympic Games

Mongol era

Beijing was rebuilt for the first time on its present site under Kublai Khan as of 1267. It was bigger than ever before and completely new. Eight years later a young Venetian called **Marco Polo** walked in amazement through its streets and saw things that excelled anything in Europe in terms of size and splendour. Marco Polo was not the first European to travel to China, but his stunning account of what was then called by the Mongolian name of **»Khanbalik«** set the city on the road to fame, at least in Europe. Such fame spread by other means, too. As early as 1306 the Vatican established a permanent presence in Beijing when John of Montecorvino entered service as the first Catholic bishop of the city.

Ming and Qing eras

When the Mongols were driven out in 1368 by the victorious Ming rulers, the city, once again plunged into devastation, initially lost its importance and returned to being what it had been for most of its existence, a garrison on the northern borders. It was only with the putsch that brought the third of the Ming emperors to the throne that Beijing regained the honour of capital city status in the tradition of the former »Barbarian kings«. This was the first time, though, that Beijing had been the residence of a genuinely Chinese dynasty. After this restoration in 1420, Beijing regarded itself as the **centre of the civilized world**; a claim which manifested itself in the city's layout and in the buildings and size of the imperial palace and Altar of Heaven, as can be seen to this day. It was at the latter that the **emperor, the representative of the earthly world**, performed elaborate nightly rituals to ensure harmony between heaven and earth. To the city came ambassadors bearing tribute from Korea, Vietnam and other countries of east and southeast Asia. In 1652 even the then Dalai Lama was greeted here – at a temple which had been built especially for him. At around the same time, the reports of the Jesuits, who were employed by the Chinese emperor, attracted attention in Europe, forming a pillar of the philosophy of the Enlightenment period with their demand for a **rule of the wise** and also inspiring the Baroque fashion for all things Chinese. The Goethes' house in Frankfurt had a »Peking Room«.

Outer and Inner Cities
Another factor was that the city had once again become bigger. Trade was conducted outside the city gates, especially in the **southern suburbs** where there were countless shops, theatres, guest houses and bordellos. In 1553 the southern city received its own walls and came to be called the »Outer City«, as opposed to the »Inner City« centred on the palace.

Manchu era
Under the Manchu rulers Beijing's buildings underwent no great change, but initially the whole Chinese population was expelled from the Inner City. The metropolis went through another golden age under the great Qianlong Emperor in the 18th century. A new era was heralded in hideous fashion as British and French troops plundered the summer palace and the garden palace before burning them down. The Chinese empire reach a new low with the **Boxer Rebel-**

New Beijing: on the right, the CCTV building by Rem Koolhaas

lion of 1900 and the occupation of Beijing by allied troops, with the consequence that for the first time a suburb for foreigners from Europe came into being (to the east of the modern Tian'anmen Square).

After the abdication of the emperor in 1912, Beijing still remained the nominal capital but the government had virtually no de facto authority any more.**In 1928 Nanjing was made the capital once again** and the name Beijing (meaning »capital of the north«) was changed to Beiping (»northern peace«).

Beijing and Beiping

This remained the case until the victory of the Communist Party, who proclaimed their new Chinese state here in 1949. They made the former imperial capital their own centre of power and soon furnished it with industrial settlements, a major east-west road and monumental new buildings to reshape it as a socialist show place, a **centre for the international proletariat**. With the death of Mao, though, another new era began for the city. Since that time Beijing has unmistakably developed into a true world metropolis, although the process did see a setback with the bloody **suppression of the student-led democracy movement** on Tian'anmen Square in June 1989. After the Asian Games took place here in 1990, another sporting milestone was set with the 2008 Olympics, which were enthusiastically exploited for propaganda purposes. Beijing has already become a largely modern city with elegant shopping temples, a cosmopolitan restaurant and pub scene and American-style luxury hotels.

Beijing under Communism

Tips for exploring the city

Beijing makes it easy for visitors to find their way with its easily understood street grid aligned to the points of the compass. The historic **north-south axis** links the main attractions from the Altar of Heaven in the south across Tian'anmen Square (Square at the Gate of Heavenly Peace) past the imperial palace and Jingshan (Coal Hill) as far as the drum and bell tower in the north of the city. Anyone staying for as long as a week – and Beijing deserves no less – should ideally rent a bicycle for a day or two. In most hotels it is possible to book organized bus tours to the more distant attractions such as the Great Wall and the Ming tombs. A more flexible solution, which is also cheaper as long as there are more than two people travelling, is to hire a taxi, having negotiated a suitable price for the whole day first.

The area around the northern lakes near the drum tower is listed as a protected area and it is a lovely place to walk and shop. The area ranges from the north gate of Beihai Park in the south to Jishuitan underground station in the north with the residence of prince Gong bounding it to the west.

Walking and shopping in the old town

Highlights Beijing

✱ ✱ Tian'anmen Square

The **centre of communist China**: this is where the triumph of communism's victory over the chains of imperialism and feudalism was to be immortalized for the public. Tian'anmen Square (Tiananmen Guangchang, meaning »Square at the Gate of Heavenly Peace«, although it is often mistranslated as »Square of Heavenly Peace«) was extended to its present dimensions for the tenth anniversary of the People's Republic in 1959. The size of it and the buildings around its rim are in keeping with the policies of that era. The revolutionary masses were to supposed to gather here to cheer their leaders. Its has been of great importance in the recent history of China. A **demonstration of students** taking place on the open space in front of the Gate of Heavenly Peace brought into existence the May Fourth movement of 1919, which catapulted China belatedly into the 20th century. On 1 October 1949 the masses celebrated here as Mao declared the **establishment of the People's Republic of China**. On 18 August 1966, Mao was on hand to review the first of nine parades featuring more than a million youngsters of the Red Guard from all over China. On 4 June 1989 saw the square witnessed the **bloody ending of another student movement**, whose occupation of the square had kept the Party and state authorities on tenterhooks for several weeks. The square was seldom used for political purposes in the normal way of things, instead being the venue for the flying of kites. Underground line 1: Tian'anmen West, Tian'anmen East, Underground line 2: Qianmen.

In the centre of the square is a stele 38 m/125 ft high built to honour the heroes of the people and unveiled on 1 May 1958. Its construction saw the Communists strike an amusing blow against tradition. Metaphorically, the emperors had once had an uninterrupted view through the palace gates from their throne rooms, but now they would now be greeted by the inscription, **»Eternal Glory to the People's Heroes«**, written in the calligraphy of Mao Zedong on the northern side of the obelisk. The southern side saw more calligraphy, this time by the then prime minister Zhou En-lai, praising the revolutionary heroes of Chinese history. Bas-reliefs on the plinth depict episodes of revolutionary history from the Opium Wars and beyond.

Monument to the People's Heroes

! **Baedeker TIP**

Flag ritual

For Chinese tourists in the capital, to experience the raising of the flag at sunrise has been almost a patriotic duty for some years. The ritual is timed to the last second. Whether the sun's shining or not, the exact astronomical moment is decisive.

Clockwise around the square starting in the north, the buildings around it come in the following sequence: a fort-like building which was erected as the south gate of the so-called imperial city in 1417 became a symbol of the state on 1 October 1949 when Mao Zedong proclaimed the founding of the People's Republic of China from there. **Beijing's only public portrait of Mao** still hangs here. The gate with its five arches was usually closed during the imperial age. It was from here that the emperors had made their proclamations. In front of the gate there is a moat channelled in a marble-lined culvert and spanned by five white marble bridges. Two white pillars entwined with dragons and carved with reliefs adorn the space in front of the gate along with two white marble lions. Grandstands either side are used for major celebrations at Tian'anmen-Square, primarily nowadays for the **National Days**. The road through the gate runs along Beijing's north-south axis through another gate just as big, the Duan Men gate, towards the imperial palace.

Gate of Heavenly Peace (Tian'an Men)

This mighty palace of a museum has stood on the eastern side of the square since 1959 It was opened in 1961 when it housed the **Museum of History and the Museum of the Chinese Revolution**. Its new name dates from 2003. The renaming was the first step in a comprehensive extension and refurbishment programme, at the end of which the museum should be one of the largest in the world with a world-class exhibition of the **best of Chinese art and culture**. It is currrently closed for rebuilding works, probably until 2010.

National Museum (Zhongguo Guojia Bowuguan)

Mao Mausoleum (Mao Zhuxi Jiniantang) This monumental building 34 m/112 ft in height was built in less than a year after the death of the great chairman on 9 September 1976. It uses materials from all the provinces of China. The architecture is patterned after that of the Lincoln Memorial in Washington. Considerable theatrical efforts were made to glorify the dead leader. In the centre of the entrance hall there is a white marble statue of Mao 3.5 m/11.5 ft high which depicts him smiling gently in front of an idealized Chinese landscape on an embroidered tapestry covering 7 x 24 m/23 x 79 ft. The square building centres on the **mummified remains** of the Chairman in a crystal coffin. Outside opening hours the body disappears down to a refrigerated chamber in the cellar. As the preservation of the mummy is not without its problems, a wax effigy has also been made, so that it is not always easy to be certain which is on view. Mao lies precisely along the north-south axis of old Beijing – a **symbol of rank according to the Confucian legacy**, which would probably not greatly appeal to the deceased revolutionary. It is not permitted to take photographs or to stand still inside the building; bags and cameras must be deposited next to the National Museum before entry. Opening times: Tue–Sun 8am–12 noon (with frequent changes) 9 Sep and 26 Dec 7.30am–11.30am, 2pm–4pm.

Front Gate (Qianmen) South of Mao's mausoleum is a tall grey gate, once the central passage between the Inner and Outer Cities Nowadays it has two sections. The northern part is the **gate tower** and **turret** of the bastion protruding towards the south. The walls linking the two and enclosing the large courtyard were pulled down in 1915/16. The bottom two floors of the gate tower and the main northern gate house an attractive **exhibition of photographs of old Beijing**. Opening times: 8.30am–4pm daily.

The Great Hall of the People (Renmin Dahui Tang) The Renmin Dahui Tang (or »Great Hall of the People«) on the western side of the square is home to the **People's Congress**, the Chinese parliament, although it only meets sporadically. The hall is also used for state receptions other political events, being open to the public at other times. Among the things on view are some of the magnificent provincial assembly halls with their varied styles of furnishing and the **plenary hall which seats 9,700**. The exterior with its galleries of columns up to roof height is inspired by ancient Egypt. The entrance is on the side street to the south. Bags must be left at the aluminium kiosk there. Opening times vary but closing is always before 3pm (Sat and Sun 1pm).

Beiing Planning Exhibition Hall To the east of the Qianmen gate the attractions of the modern Museum of Town Planning seek to tempt visitors inside. They include a bronze model showing Beijing in 1949. Another model of the city, some of it with paths for people to walk through, shows the current state of planning all the buildings completed for the 2008 Olympics. 20 Qianmendong Dajie. Opening times: Tue–Sun 9am–5pm.

Westward from Tian'anmen Square

From the northern end of Tian'anmen Square, Beijing's major east-west axis, the Chang'an-Boulevard stretches away in both directions. The names **»East«** and **»West Road of Eternal Peace«** (Dong Chang'an Jie, Xi Chang'an Jie) only actually apply to the central sections either side of the Gate of Heavenly Peace (Tian'an Men), but are often used to describe the entire dead-straight 40-km/25 mi length of the road. Having been completed to its present extent in the 1950s, the road is a **product of communist city planning**. Part of the intent was to act as counterpoint to the north-south axis of imperial times.

Alongside the Great Hall of the People to the west and directly on the boulevard, one of the **most spectacular building projects in all of China** can be seen: the National Grand Theatre (National Centre for the Performing Arts), designed by French architect Paul Andreu. It is structurally extremely bold and is enormously controversial. It looks like a gigantic oval bubble rising out of a lake and contains a concert hall, an opera house and a theatre.

✳ **National Theatre**

Diagonally opposite the theatre towards the west, the boulevard runs alongside a long red wall. Behind it is the **»modern equivalent of the Forbidden City«**. Featuring the former **imperial pleasure gardens**, it was here in 1949 that the new political elite of China, including Mao Zedong, moved in. From the outside all that can be seen is a motto written by Mao in his own calligraphy on the spirit wall obscuring the view inside through the southern entrance: »Wei renmin fuwu« – »Serve the people!«. Underground line 1: Tian'anmen-West.

Zhongnanhai

The National Theatre seems to float on the surface of the water like a bubble

Eastward of Tian'anmen Square

Beijing Hotel A building with a history. On Wangfujing stands a 17-storey block from 1974, which was completely rebuilt in spectacular fashion from the foundations up during 2000/2001. To the west comes the oldest wing, dating back to 1917, which is followed by a section built in 1954/55 and including the **famous great banqueting hall** and a palatial foyer which makes the perfect entrance for state visitors accommodated here.

Oriental Plaza Hong Kong tycoon Li Kashing commissioned what was the hitherto **largest construction project in the city**. Built between1996 and 2000 it is a gigantic complex of shops, offices, apartments and hotels 520 m/570 yds in length, extending from the Dongdan intersection as far as Wangfujing. It is not just the two-storey shopping mall, which also has some inexpensive restaurants, that acts as a magnet to visitors; they are also drawn by the fountains in front of the **luxurious Grand Hyatt hotel** in the middle.

Old observatory (Gu Guanxiang Tai) At the point where the east-west road crosses the former line of the city walls in the east stands an important **testament to the early cultural interaction between China and Europe**. Eight astronomical instruments are situated on top of a 14 m/46 ft terrace which was built in 1442. The exquisite bronze casts include a celestial globe, a sextant and three armillary spheres. Six of the pieces were made in 1670 according to plans drawn up by the Flemish Jesuit missionary, **Ferdinand Verbiest**. Two more were added in 1744. Southwest corner of the Jianguomen intersection. Opening times: April–Oct. Tue–Sun 9am–4.30pm, otherwise 9am–11am, 1pm–4pm. Underground lines 1 and 2: Jianguomen.

✳ ✳ Imperial palace (Gu Gong)

Design and symbolism This is the greatest **assemblage of classical Chinese architecture** and is among the most imposing palace sites in the world. Numerals, colours, ornamentation, points of the compass and names are some of the symbols used to set the residence's place in the world and indicate how Confucian China saw the role of its supreme ruler. The names of the largest halls (usually written on roof plaques in both Chinese and Manchurian) speak of harmony, since harmony was to reign on earth thanks to the salvation brought by the **dominion of the son of heaven**. Even the floor plan expresses harmony in the form of its symmetry, which not only involves the arrange-

✔ DON'T MISS

- The great throne halls
- Hall of Mental Cultivation with the personal chambers of the last emperors.
- The inner throne halls
- The Ningshou Gong section of the palace with the Nine Dragon Wall and treasury
- Palace garden and north gate

Imperial Palace / Forbidden City Map

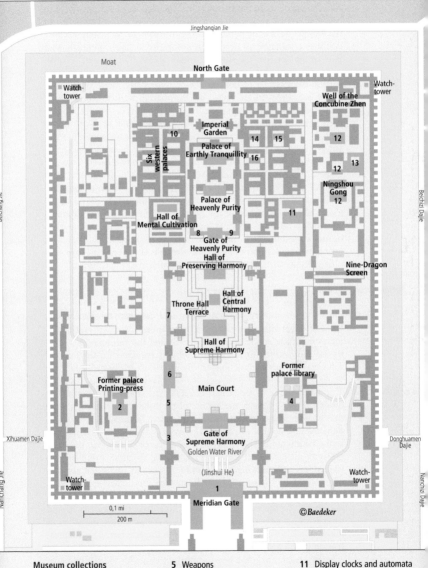

Jingshanqian Jie

Moat

North Gate

Watch-tower

Watch-tower

Well of the Concubine Zhen

Imperial Garden

10

14 15

12

Six western palaces

16

13

12

Palace of Earthly Tranquillity

Ningshou Gong

12

Palace of Heavenly Purity

11

Hall of Mental Cultivation

8   9

Gate of Heavenly Purity

Hall of Preserving Harmony

Nine-Dragon Screen

Hall of Central Harmony

Throne Hall Terrace

7

Hall of Supreme Harmony

Former palace library

Former palace Printing-press

6

2

Main Court

4

5

3

Gate of Supreme Harmony

Golden Water River

(Jinshui He)

Xihuamen Dajie

Donghuamen Dajie

Watch-tower

Watch-tower

1

Meridian Gate

0,1 mi

200 m

©Baedeker

Beichang Jie

Bechizi Dajie

Nanchang Jie

Nanchizi Dajie

Museum collections

1 In the Gate Tower:
   Textile painting, embroidery
2 Painting, calligraphy
3 Art of printing, palace documents
4 Ceramics

5 Weapons
6 Court and ceremonial music
7 Utensils
8 Imperial birthday celebrations
9 Imperial weddings
10 Puyi, the last emperor

11 Display clocks and automata
12 Treasuries
13 Theatre collection
14 Jade
15 Cloisonné
16 Bronze

ment of the main halls, the gates and the courtyards along an axis, but also aligns them towards the sky. The alignment is from north to south along the same axis as the city itself. The second principle of the design is that of hierarchy. The thrones all face south. Those coming to an audience were thus compelled to face the north, that part of the sky that the sun and moon abhor, but the part of earth upon which they shine and which is occupied by the emperor, the earthly **counterpart of heaven**. The numbers, too, have their voice. There are three throne halls and the marble terraces upon which they stand have three steps. The imperial dragons have five talons on their paws and on the magnificent **Nine Dragon Wall** there are indeed nine of them. Nine times nine golden nails adorn each one of the gate wings. These odd numbers represent yang, the masculine principle upon which the sun shines. The roofs only have two eaves. Thus the emperors subordinated themselves to heaven as their subjects were subordinated to them. Then there are the colours and ornamentation, the imperial yellow of the roofs exaggerating the yellow colour of the loess soil, the festive red of the painted columns, the **cloud dragons**, who bring rain and blessing and are seen everywhere, painted on beams, carved as reliefs on doors, rocks and wall canopies and decorating thousands of other objects. In the halls at the rear, they are supplemented by the Chinese phoenix, the emblem of the empress.

Arrangement

Hierarchical thinking is apparent in the arrangement of the grounds, which measure 960 m by 750 m/1050 x 820 yd. At the »front« – in the south – stand the **representative and administrative buildings**, while at the »rear« – the north – are the ladies' chambers and living-quarters. In the centre, along the axis, stand the throne halls, (three in the south, three in the north), while secondary buildings at the sides provide service functions (in the south) or living-quarters.

»Forbidden City«

The actual name of the palace is Zijincheng, meaning **»Purple Forbidden City«**. Purple is the colour of the mighty surrounding walls that give the palace its fortress-like character. The palace is »forbidden« because no one was allowed to enter at their own will, but only at the command of the emperor. The emperor was also in principle the only male resident capable of fathering children. Adult princes were domiciled elsewhere. The southern part in particular, though, was entered by top officials, candidates for the highest examination for officialdom, foreign ambassadors, palace guards and the imperial bodyguard. In the northern parts of the palace, the emperor would meet with his advisers and when there were weddings, the wives of major officials would pay their respects to the empress. The **administration of the palace itself** was the responsibility of several thousand eunuchs. Apart from the most important eunuchs and the emperor himself, no one was allowed to move through the palace freely. The women lived in luxury in individual walled palaces but were in fact like prisoners – although here too there were a few exceptions.

The magnificent throne in the Palace of Heavenly Purity

surface of any **classical Chinese hall** at about 2370 sq m/25,000 sq ft. The roof is supported by 72 pillars, 12 along each of the long sides. The present building dates from 1695. In the middle of it, between six central gilded pillars on a pedestal with seven levels, is the gold painted **imperial throne itself**. Behind it a wall canopy is also painted gold. The hall is adorned with a coffered ceiling. The ornamental dragons are quite ubiquitous.

The hall that follows is an elegant **centrally built hall resembling a pavilion** with a tented roof and perimeter gallery. This is where the emperor would receive the honours of top officials on the great ceremonial occasions and also where he prepared himself for the major state cult events.

Hall of Central Harmony

The third throne hall, a building 50m/55 yd wide with a double-eaved hipped roof, was used for state banquets. From 1798 the palace examinations would also be held here – the highest examination for officialdom. Near the bottom of the steps leading up at the rear is the largest **dragon relief stone** in the palace. It is 16.6 m/50 ft long, 3 m/10 ft wide and 1.7 m/6 ft thick. It was transported here from its quarry outside Beijing by hauling it along specially cast rails.

Hall of Preserving Harmony

Inner throne halls A gilded pair of bronze lions, a male on the right and a lioness on the left, guard the main gate to the inner palace. The first hall is the largest, the »**Palace of Heavenly (masculine) Purity**«. Until the beginning of the 18th century it served as the residential palace of the emperor and thus has heated side chambers. This is where the actual government of the state was carried on. The square hall after it is adorned with ornamentation featuring dragons and phoenixes. It was the throne hall and reception chamber of the empress. It contains two huge ornamental clocks, a water clock on the left and a chiming mechanical clock constructed in 1798 along European lines on the right. The **living and sleeping quarters of the empress** were located during the Ming era in the third of the three small throne halls. The Manchus rebuilt the inner one, though, and erected a sacrificial shrine here, where they would slaughter two pigs every day in front of images of more than a dozen gods, according to their own (non-Chinese) custom. The meat would then be cooked on a giant stove. At the eastern end of the building the imperial wedding chamber was maintained in joyful red.

! *Baedeker* TIP

Tea in the imperial garden
The palace has no shortage of ugly snack-bars, not to mention a Starbucks. For those in search of something more genuine, there's a tea and coffee house on the south side of the palace garden, which is also a nice place to warm up in winter.

Beyond the next gate come the 1.2 hectares/3 acres of the **palace gardens** featuring some bizarre trees, pavilions, mosaic-tiled paths and an imposing **artificial rocky hill**. In the middle there is a Daoist temple. A gate leads northwards out of the Inner Court of the palace into a guard zone between the inner and outer walls, which enclosed the living-quarters within the outer walls, and which is exited through the mighty **Shenwu Men (North Gate)**.

Imperial palace: secondary palaces

The six western palaces On both sides of the inner throne halls are the former quarters of the emperors' **auxiliary wives and concubines**. Most of these western palaces retain the majority of their original furnishings, giving an idea of what life was like here less than a hundred years ago. In some places covered channels can still be seen in the north walls where the heaters would be lit to keep the rooms warm.

Hall of Mental Cultivation The Hall of Mental Cultivation, which adjoins the palaces to the south, is of historic importance. Protected by additional walls and gates and built with little ostentation, this building with its courtyard and auxiliary halls was used by the emperors as of the early 18th century as **living room, official chamber and personal audience room**. It was thus for the last two centuries of empire the actual centre of power in China. The throne itself stands in the central space of the building and is appropriately aligned towards the south. Meetings with the imperial counsellors, and thus the formulation of key decisions, actually took place in the auxiliary room to the east, though. After **Empress Dowager Cixi** usurped the throne in 1861, she would officiate at such meetings having, for the sake of etiquette, hidden herself behind a curtain at the eastern end of the room. In front of it, merely for the sake of appearances, would sit the Son of Heaven. At the western end of the hall is where the former living quarters of the emperor were. They are decorated in quite reserved fashion and are of »normal« dimensions.

In the secondary courtyards on the eastern side of the small throne halls part of the imperial art collection is kept, including the jade collection, which allows fashions in taste to be followed across some 3000 years. To the south, in the large Fengxian Dian complex, the imperial collection of magnificent clocks and automata (mostly brought from Europe) has been given a new home.

Six eastern palaces and the Hall of Fengxian Dian

A gate to the east from the central courtyard north of the large throne halls leads to the Palace of Tranquil Longevity (Ningshou Gong). Its forecourt is adorned by a spirit wall, the **Nine Dragons Wall**, which is almost 30 m/100 ft long and 3.5 m/11.5 ft high. The relief, consisting of coloured ceramic tiles, is the palace's most splendid open-air artwork, and represents the emblem of blessed imperial rule. The Palace of Tranquil Longevity extending to the north combines **prestigious grandeur with cosiness**. The palace gained its present appearance from 1772 to 1776 when the Qianlong Emperor had it built for his retirement. Its halls now serve as **treasury chambers**. Among the features to the north of it are part of the furniture collection, the palace theatre (right) and the garden of the Qianlong Emperor (left).

Palace of Tranquil Longevity

In the outer courtyard in front of the main gate there is a spirit wall. It is **the palace's most magnificent piece of open-air art** the Nine Dragons Wall features a relief depicting the creatures which symbolise the blessings of imperial rule put together using ceramic tiles.

Nine Dragons Wall

✶ Jing Shan and Beihai Park

At a central location in Beijing a hill 43 m/141 ft high to the north of the imperial palaces is the city's premier view point. Its current size is due to its use as a spoil heap for the earth excavated to create the moat for the imperial palace. Since coal was stored here at the time of the Mongol emperors, the people dubbed it Mei Shan, or Coal Hill, which is how it is also sometimes known in the West. Its modern Chinese name really means **»View Hill«**. Topped with a pavilion, the summit is precisely on the north-south axis of the city and its

Jing Shan (Coal Hill)

! *Baedeker* TIP

Early-morning exercise on Coal Hill
The mound with the surrounding park is the nicest place to join the people of Beijing in their morning exercise or simply to watch them at it: shadow-boxing, sword exercises, Yangge dance, waltzes, and all kinds of health-promoting Qigong. Water-calligraphers are at work on the pavement, old men give their songbirds some fresh air. Important: come before breakfast! The park opens between 6 and 7am depending on the season.

palace. In terms of Chinese Feng Shui, it is located in correspondence with the Golden Water River at the south of the palace.

A good 500 m/550 yds west of Jing Shan is **Beihai Park** (Beihai Gongyuan), which is the most popular green spot in the city, mainly thanks to its large lake (where boats can be hired). The park is overlooked by its landmark which can be seen for a large distance around it, the white dagoba on **Qiongdao island**. The park grounds date back to the 11th century. Its current layout, with its innumerable pleasure palaces, pavilions, rockeries and temples, was essentially devised between the 13th and 18th centuries.

The circle of Fort Tuancheng
A wall rises to the west of the south entrance to the park. It encloses a near-circular earth terrace levelled to the same height as the top of the wall itself. A hall on top of it contains a **Burmese jade Buddha**, sponsored by monks in 1896. A pavilion in front of the hall houses a jade bowl 1.5 m/5 ft in diameter, which weighs 3.5 tons and dates from 1265. The circular »fort« never served any military purpose.

Qiongdao Island and the White Dagoba
The white marble **»Bridge of Eternal Peace«** (Yong'an Qiao) leads from the southern entrance to the park across to the »Jade Island« of Qiongdao. Towering over the three-arched gate at the foot of the hill is a 36 m/118 ft **bottle pagoda** (dagoba), erected in 1651 in honour of the Dalai Lama, who had travelled to Beijing on a state visit. Winding stairway paths lead up to the summit on both sides. The dagoba itself cannot be climbed. In front of it there is a red pedestal topped by a hall built from glazed tiles. All around it there are images of Buddha, and it contains a bronze statue representing a **Tibetan manifestation of the bodhisattva Manjushri**.

Northern shore
To the west of the northern entrance there is are several **Buddhist temples and pleasure palaces**. In the midst of them is the park's most magnificent feature, 27 m/30 yd long and 5 m/16 ft high, a double-sided Nine Dragon Wall. In addition to the little dragons that decorate it, it also has 635 of the cloud and water creatures who bestow blessing wherever they are. The nicest spots on the northern shore are the spacious **Five Dragon Pavilions** built out over the water and linked by bridges. Amateur musicians often meet here and give performances of Beijing opera. Opening times: 9.30am– 5.30pm. The park itself is open during daylight hours as appropriate to the season.

The area north of Beihai Park and around the Three Lakes in the north of the old town is where top officials and princes once lived. Although the area had begun to take on the appearance of a slum under communist rule, it is now undergoing a renaissance as a magnet for the rich, for idlers, connoisseurs and those who simply like to wander and take in the surroundings. There is no better place in the city for a nice long walk. Around the little marble bridge of **Yinding Qiao**, which separates the Front Lake (Qianhai) and the Rear Lake (Houhai), various bars and restaurants have taken root. Along the west bank of the Front Lake a whole row of restaurants (»Lotus Lane«) has recently come into being.

Three Lakes (Shichahai)

The end of Beijing's central north-south axis has been marked since the time of the Ming dynasty by the bell tower, the northernmost of the two towers at the end of the road. The towers provided a sort of **time signal** for the city until 1924. The bell sounded early in the morning at 5am to signal the start of the day and sounded again in the evening at 7pm. Every two hours between the drums would roll their own signal. It is possible to climb both the towers and from the top there is a fine all-round view of the surrounding, still traditional-looking part of town. Opening times: 9am–4.30pm daily. Underground line 2: Gulou.

Bell tower and drum tower (Zhonglou, Gulou)

A pavilion tops the summit of Coal Hill

Residence of Prince Gong (Gong Wangfu)	The biggest and most attractive sight in the area is just ten minutes' walk from the Middle Lake. Things to see there include the **classical garden** with its two ponds, pavilions, colonnades, garden stones, two artificial hills and a pretty theatre. Prince Gong (1833–1898) played a leading role in the exchange between foreign powers after the second **Opium War**. It was he who established the first Chinese foreign ministry. The actual residential buildings of his estate have not survived.
	Qianhai Xijie. Opening times: 8.30am–4.30pm daily.

East of the imperial palace

Wangfujing

The Beijing of the 20th and 21st centuries can be seen in and around the most famous shopping street in the city, the name of which means »Well of the Prince's Residence«. The main attraction for Beijing natives and Chinese visitors to the capital is the pedestrian zone with its multiple department stores and the seven-storey **shopping temple of Sun Dong An Plaza** on the corner with »Goldfish Street« (Jinyu Hutong). Another popular place is the street of snack bars that turns off from the southern end of the block towards the west, recognizable by the colourful decorative gate. It is a new development but in the old style. The church on the eastern side of the street (78 Wangfujing) was established in 1665 by **Ferdinand Verbiest**. The rebellious Boxers perpetrated a massacre here in 1900, killing hundreds of Chinese Christians. The present aisled building with its three domes above the façade dates from the year 1904. Underground line 1: Wangfujing.

Diagonally opposite the north end of Wangfujing is the **National Gallery** (Zhongguo Meishuguan) building, a prestigious edifice in the Sino-Stalinist style, which was completed in 1962 (1 Wusi Dajie). It mainly houses rolling exhibitions of commercial contemporary art (mostly Chinese), including calligraphy, sculpture and photography, for which reason it is well worth a visit. To the west a supermodern extension is currently taking shape. Opening times: Tue–Sun 9am–5pm.

> **! Baedeker TIP**
>
> **Dong'anmen night market**
> Beijing's local government has in fact got rid of most of the open-air cookshop markets, regarding them and unhygienic and scruffy. This one is allowed to exist under strict controls. The stalls that remain open all night on Dong'anmen, a side street off Wangfujing, serve snacks which even are exotic even by Beijing standards: fried cicadas, scorpions, squid and silkworms, for example.

★ ★ Lama monastery (Yonghe Gong)

This holy place in the northeast of the Inner City, 3 km/2 mi northeast of the imperial palace, is easily the most important Buddhist temple monastery in the city. With its abundance of imagery, it is not only a treasure house of artistic history but also an extraordinar-

Many people in Beijing keep a bird as a pet. In good weather they are allowed to get some fresh air outside by the front door.

COURTYARD HOUSES AND HUTONGS

Beijing was once a sea of single-storey, grey-roofed houses, transected by a few straight main roads with a labyrinth of crooked alleyways beyond them. It was not as impressive as might be expected of the seat of a »Son of Heaven«. Nevertheless it fascinated all those who got to know the old Beijing: full of life, colourful and noisy in the suburbs, quiet and cultivated in the residential areas. Here and there, there are still traces of this – in the hutongs. The people of Beijing use this word of Mongolian origin to denote the alleys of the old quarter.

The type of house associated with the hutongs is the courtyard house. In a sense it represents the converse of the form of house or estate that is usual in the West: its occupants do not look out at the front onto the street, at the back into the garden, and over the garden fence to the neighbours' garden, and they certainly have no view of the house opposite. Instead the courtyard house is built inside out: the yards and gardens are enclosed by buildings, and a high wall encircles the ensemble. The only opening to the street is the gate of entry, which is visually closed off by the »spirit wall«.

The courtyard is the focus

Those who enter find themselves first of all in an outer court, which is separated from the actual living quarters by a wall. At the exact centre of the wall, a gate, colourfully painted and decorated with woodcarvings,

leads into the **main courtyard**, around which the principal buildings are arranged. The residents of these well-protected compounds were aware of the life of the hutong primarily through its sounds: by means of shouts or of rattling, clashing and ringing noises – the main thing was to be as loud and penetrating as possible – itinerant traders and delivery services drew attention to themselves, each trade with its own special instrument or a verse of song, performed as a kind of acoustic calling card. Few purchases required residents to leave the courtyard house. Everything was delivered – including drinking water. **Peddlers** brought toys that they had made, ready-cooked snacks on portable stoves, porcelain and vegetables. Night-soil men emptied the chamber pots, while rag-and-bone men and scrap dealers took away any leftovers that could be re-

used. This world came to an end in the mid-1950s, when it fell victim to collectivization. Public conveniences in hutongs replaced the old ecological system of sewage disposal. The population explosion of the 1960s, coupled with the inability of the communist system to provide enough housing, sealed the fate of the old courtyard house and its way of life. Soon four or more families were crowded together where previously just one family lived, the intimate courts became semi-public spaces and were crammed full with temporary structures, huts and piles of coal briquettes. The spirit walls were demolished to ease access.

The post-Mao era

Thanks to renewed freedom for small traders to do business, the 1980s saw a brief revival of itinerant suppliers and collectors, but a new age followed. It

Young and old love to play Chinese chess.

brought in its wake – and will continue to bring – the destruction of entire hutong districts through development. Admittedly, not all of them were idyllic places to live, with lots of space and character. Courtyard houses that have been restored or even rebuilt on a new site – now with a garage for the car and of course with modern sanitary facilities

A summer snooze in the shade of your own courtyard tree – that's the way to live!

especially after the buildings had been neglected for decades. Add to this the idea that old means backward. And in truth, the courtyard houses were indeed behind the times, lacking central heating, baths and sanitation. However, that was the situation in the past. Now that most inhabitants of the historic quarters have moved to tower blocks in the suburbs, **hutongs and courtyard houses are being redis-covered** – as accommodation for the rich. The advantage of this type of housing is that residents live in the middle of the city, but in absolutely quiet surroundings at ground level

– are a dream home. Few Chinese are able to make this dream come true, however. Foreigners seldom succeed in buying or renting courtyard houses in Beijing, but everyone is entitled to look around free of charge, ideally by taking a walk through the hutongs around the Three Back Lakes, where the residential culture of old Beijing has survived in many places. It appears in, for example, the beautiful stones with reliefs that act as hinges for the wooden doors of the entran-ces, in the spirit walls and the shady inner courts, where a glance inside is occasionally possible.

ily impressive **monument to politically supported religious devotion.** It was the only imperial monastery in Beijing. It goes back to a princely residence built in 1694. The prince in question later became emperor and when he died in 1735, his body lay in state here. In 1744 his son, the Qianlong Emperor, decreed that the abandoned remains of his residence be transformed into a lamaist monastery. There were political motives behind this. In 1720 the Manchu empire had gained **overall control of Tibet**. Since Tibetan Buddhism was widespread even beyond Tibet's borders, especially among the Mongolians, the capital's imperial monastery was intended to strengthen the ties to the dynasty of the peoples who had come into its empire.

Outer courtyard The courtyard outside the monastery is now misused as a car park but it includes three impressive show gates and a high »**spirit wall**« which represents the most southerly part of the complex. Another outer courtyard 160 m/175 yd long and 40 m/44 yd wide adjoins the first to the north (it is now greened over). When the emperor came to visit, the monks would form a guard of honour here.

Entrance courtyard Beyond another intervening gate is the entrance courtyard of the monastery itself with a bell tower to the right and a drum tower to the left. The northern side is occupied by a hall of the Four Heavenly Kings. Two octagonal **column pavilions**, one to the north of each tower, contain inscriptions in four languages and dating from 1744, in which the Qianlong Emperor explains the circumstances of the founding of the monastery. Temple flags are flown from two masts on feast days. A huge copper vessel by the drum tower was used to provide the monastery's occupants with rice porridge.

Hall of the Heavenly Kings In the middle of the hall a **pot-bellied Buddha** thrusts a navel out at visitors, **a symbol of life energy**, and smiles at the unimportance of earthly cares. To the right and left, the dramatic figures of the Heavenly Kings, dressed as generals, remind the incomers of the need for repentance. Demons coil beneath their feet, indicative of human passions – greed, hatred and obsession. To keep the interior of the monastery free of all evil, it is also watched over by **Weituo, the general of the faith**, whose magnificent gold statue behind the pot-bellied Buddha looks out over the next courtyard.

First courtyard Towering over the first courtyard inside the complex is a column pavilion with an inscription in four languages from 1792 (Manchurian is at the front, Mongolian right, Tibetan left and Chinese at the rear), in which the Qianlong Emperor explains Lamaism. To the south in front of the pavilion is the great ritual apparatus of the monastery, an **incense holder** 4.2 m/14 ft in height and dating from 1747. Behind the pavilion – right in front of the main hall – a bronze sculpture of Meru, the world mountain, represents levels of being up to the heavenly palace at its summit.

The first of the main halls bears the name of the whole temple complex on the plaque above its entrance: »**Palace of Harmony**«. Inside, the Buddhas of the Three Ages illustrate the highest and most authentic level that human striving can attain. The bronze statues are gilded and the middle one, representing Buddha Gautama, is flanked by his disciples, **Ananda and Kashyapa**. The appearance of the Buddhas is enhanced by their magnificent halos, in which the bird-man, the Garuda, soars over the Buddhas' heads. The ritual apparatus in front of them is just as magnificent. Along the walls at the sides, statues of the 18 holy monks (luohan) line up in rows.

First main hall

The following hall, the »**Hall of Eternal Help**« also has a trio of gilded figures enthroned inside it. In the middle is the crowned head of Amitayus, the Buddha of Long Life. Left (west) of him is the Medicine Buddha, who emphasizes the philanthropic aspect of Buddhism. On the right the **Buddha of the Lion's Roar** embodies the call of the teaching, which can be heard throughout the world. The sculptures are 2.35 m/8 ft tall and carved from sandalwood. Each of the figures sits on a stylized lotus blossom.

Second main hall

The next, square courtyard allows a clear view of the unusual, Tibetan-inspired building style of the teaching and assembly hall. Its floor plan is cruciform with the roof interrupted by dormer windows, topped with small, golden stupas and hung with Aeolian bells. The inside is dominated by a figure more than 6 m/20 ft in height representing **Tsongkhapa**, the great reformer of Tibetan Buddhism (1357–1419). On both sides there are raised thrones. The left-hand one is where the current Dalai Lama sat upon his visit to Beijing in 1954, while the other is for the Panchen Lama. Although the architecture appears to be thoroughly aligned to the statue of Tsongkhapa, it was not actually added until 1930 and only gilded in 1982. The bookcases along the walls contain exquisite volumes of the **written compendium of Tibetan Buddhism**, Tanjur and Kanjur. The walls are painted with depictions of bodhisattvas and saints. A giant wood carving to the rear of Tsongkhapa represents a mountain landscape with the 500 luohan.

Teaching hall

If the figure of Tsongkhapa was of monumental size, the next (and last) hall has contents of even greater dimensions. An 18 m/59 ft **Maitreya bodhisattva** makes any visitor feel no bigger than an earthworm. The effect is amplified by the narrowness of the 25 m/82 ft high hall. The figure can only be looked up at when the beholder has reached its feet. Crowned as Lord of the Future, a Maitreya guides observers back to the world beyond where salvation still awaits. The figure itself is a **monument to Tibetan religious diplomacy**. The 7th Dalai Lama (1708–1757) had obtained the giant Indian tree trunk, from which it is carved, in Nepal and had it transported via Tibet and down the Yangtze to the Manchu court in order to show his

Pavilion of 10,000-fold Happiness

gratitude that a Chinese army had defended his hegemony in Tibet against rebels in 1750. After the building's pedestal was constructed the 26 m/85 ft trunk was embedded 8 m/26 ft deep in the ground. The hall was then built around it.

One of the finest works of art in the temple monastery is in a side hall to the east, a gilded **Shakyamuni** in the act of preaching, which is housed inside a magnificent carved shrine cabinet. The Buddha is flanked by his disciples. In the secondary halls on the southern side of the monastery is an exhibition of gifts to the temple.

Secondary halls around the last courtyard

The buildings at the side of the front courtyard also conceal an **abundance of artworks**, most of them in typically Tibetan style. Among them are thankas and yab-yum figures in the Tantric tradition. The latter display male and female gods in **ritual ecstatic coitus**. The male god, facing the observer, usually a multiple-armed and ferocious protective god, is meant to symbolize, among other things, pity and active assistance, while the female portrays wisdom. The message is that in their sexual union all the polarized aspects of life on earth are cast aside, and the cult makes it possible to experience Nirvana. The monastery **attracts hordes of visitors**. In order to see the halls in some degree of peace, it is advisable to be there as soon as the doors open. Opening times: 9am–4.30pm daily. Underground line 2: Yonghegong.

Other secondary buildings

✱ Confucius temple (Kong Miao)

Take a short detour from the lama monastery to the dignified, quiet and seldom visited temple of Confucius. This too was built with imperial funds, as the yellow roof tiles indicate. When the Mongols conquered China, they noticed after a certain time how well they were succeeding in winning over Chinese officialdom. For that reason they gave their new capital a temple to Confucianism between 1302 and 1306, a forerunner of the one still extant. Its current appearance only dates back to 1906, when the declining Qing dynasty sought to counteract Christian influence by **boosting the cult of Confucius**. The main project was the enlargement and rebuilding of the offertory hall. It was only finished in 1916, after the dynasty had been toppled.

> ! **Baedeker TIP**
>
> ### »House of Sages' Rest«
> Liuxian Guan: That is what the Chinese name of the stylish teahouse diagonally opposite the Confucius temple means, far better than its English name, the Eatea Tea House. The interior, furnished with antiques, is gorgeous. Apart from tea it also serves light snacks. Foreigners are catered for. www.eatea.com.cn. Guozijian Jie 28, Tel. 010/840 48 59.

← *Stupas and bells adorn the roof of the teaching hall*

First courtyard

In the first courtyard there are three columned pavilions as well as the building for the killing of sacrificial animals at the extreme right. 198 stone tablets list the names and places of origin of 51,624 jinshi, successful candidates in the examination for officialdom. They date back to the 14th century.

Gate and stone drums

The »Gate of Great Perfection« (Dacheng Men) leads into the main courtyard. Inside the gatehouse ten **»stone drums«** can be seen, featuring an imitation of some inscriptions from ancient times on stones shaped like drums, which was completed in 1790.

Main courtyard and main hall

On both sides of the square main courtyards there are more columned pavilions. The dominant building is the **»Hall of Great Perfection«** with a terrace for sacrifices in front of it The 600-year-old thuja to the left of the stairway is called the »Traitor Hitter«. It is supposed to have knocked off the hat of a corrupt minister as he read the offertory rite, thus exposing him. Inside in the central shrine is the **soul tablet of Confucius**. To the left and right are the tablets of his students and other Confucius followers. In front of them, much of the props and musical instruments which were used in ceremonies on the terrace can be seen, including chime bells and Chinese zithers. For a fee Chinese musicians may play a selection from the ceremonial music. Opening times: daily 9am–5pm, last admissions 4.30pm.

The »Hall of Great Perfection« in the Confucius Temple

West of the main hall, a passage leads to a **monument to scholarliness**: The 13 canonical scriptures of Confucianism have been carved onto 189 large steles – 6.3 million characters copied onto paper by a scholar between 1726 and 1737 and chiselled into stone between 1791 and 1794. It is the only complete text of the 13 books in the handwriting of a single person. The neighbouring complex to the west is the Guozijian Imperial Academy. It central building represents the square disc of the earth surrounded by the world sea. Opening times: 9am–4.30pm daily.

Confucian canon

Guozijian Imperial Academy

Olympic Green

Everyone knows it by now: China's National Stadium, the »Bird's Nest«. Seldom can a sports venues have been given a form that makes it so instantly recognizable. What's special about it is the complicated, chaotic-looking structure of its steel. The structure, which seats 90,000, was designed by the Swiss office of Herzog & Meuron.

National Stadium

Hardly less spectacular is the **National Aquatics Centre**, the »Water Cube«, situated opposite to the west. The shimmering bluish translucent block seems to consist of irregular bubbles. The idea came from the Australian office PTW Architects.

To the north is a sports hall, the **Olympic Village**, and further sports-related locations. From a town-planning point of view it is interesting that the Olympia Park takes up Beijing's old north-south axis and extends it far to the north. To the north of the 4th ring road. Underground line 10 to Beitucheng, then line 8 (Olympic Sports Center, Olympic Green).

✱ ✱ Altar of Heaven and temple (Tian Tan)

This is the biggest, oldest and in terms of its cult most important **shrines of the imperial cult**. It is also the most architecturally perfect. The Altar of Heaven is laced with symbolism like few other buildings are. The emperor would make his offerings to heaven and its manifestations (stars and weather) on an open terrace as part of a ritual lasting several hours and accompanied by music on the longest night of the year. In spring, too, he prayed for the right weather for a good harvest at the northern temple hall (from which the place get its name the »temple of heaven«).

The extensive grounds – 2.5 km/1.5 mi southeast of Tian'anmen Square – are planted with trees. While the emperor was performing the **sacrificial rite** on the altar's torchlit terrace, he was totally withdrawn from the urban world. The Confucian empire considered itself to be the natural fulcrum of the world and the consciousness of its rulers that they were responsible for harmony in the world can be understood here even today.

Fulcrum of the world

History and tours The Altar of Heaven dates back to 1420 and essentially took on its present form in 1530. After 1949 the outer parts of the altar's grounds were largely built up with blocks of flats and other buildings. The entrances in the north, south and east are new as well. The complex is **aligned towards the south** and tours start from that point of the compass, although to take the emperor's own route means starting at the old west entrance and first visiting the fasting palace.

Fasting palace In a square complex of halls near the west gate covering 4 ha/10 acres completely enclosed by a wall and a moat, the emperor would prepare himself for the coming sacrificial rites by fasting. The »**Bell of Ultimate Harmony**« in the northern part of the outermost courtyard would ring when he was ready to start the offertory service.

Altar The altar terrace, as circular as the dome of the heavens itself, was the actual **centre of the heaven cult**. Its design is based on the heavenly yang number three and uses primarily its square, nine. The terrace has three levels ascended by three times nine steps. The stone in the centre of the terrace is encircled by nine concentric paved rings, the innermost of which is made up of nine paving stones. The second ring has twice that number, the third, three times nine and so on until the outermost ring the lowest level, which consists of three times nine times nine, or 243 stones. The number of segments in the marble balustrade also obeys the same **numeric symbology**. Spiralling cloud reliefs adorn the supporting walls and cloud dragons dance on a relief on top of the balustrade. The terrace is also enclosed by another circular wall covered by dark-blue glazed tiles. In the southeast corner of the enclosing square wall is a green walled basin, which was used as a grill for the **sacrificed calf**. Twelve large metal baskets were used for the burning of sacrificial silk. The emperor would kowtow nine times on the terrace, facing north as a subject of heaven as his subjects would usually face him. Up on the terrace the **soul tablets of heaven** and its manifestations would be set up in blue tents. Dozens of officials were involved in the ceremony, performing strictly regulated tasks in precisely stipulated placess. The nocturnal scene would be illuminated by lanterns on high masts.

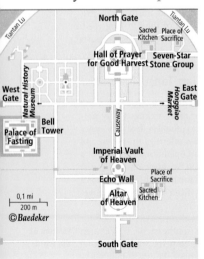

Altar of Heaven Map

- Tiantan Lu
- North Gate
- Tiantan Lu
- Sacred Kitchen
- Place of Sacrifice
- Hall of Prayer for Good Harvest
- Seven-Star Stone Group
- Natural History Museum
- West Gate
- East Gate
- Hongqiao Market
- Bell Tower
- Causeway
- Palace of Fasting
- Imperial Vault of Heaven
- Echo Wall
- Place of Sacrifice
- 0,1 mi
- 200 m
- © Baedeker
- Altar of Heaven
- Sacred Kitchen
- South Gate

Three terraces lead up to the Hall of Prayer for Good Harvests with its blue-tiled, three-part roof. The emperor prayed for a good harvest in this temple building.

The imperial vault of heaven

The blue covered circular wall north of the terrace surrounds the halls where the **soul tablet of the sacrifice's recipients** were kept. They too have been reconstructed in their former layout: the tablets of the moon on the left, then those of the rain, the clouds, the wind and the thunder, with the tablets of the sun at the right along with those of the constellation of »the Plough« (Ursa Major), the five naked-eye planets, the 28 »houses of the moon« (constellations) and the firmament itself. The most distinctive of the buildings is the Hall of the Imperial Vault of Heaven, a **round hall on a tall marble pedestal**. Inside, on a throne-like plinth, are the tablets of heaven. At the sides, on smaller plinths, are the tablets of the deceased emperors of the last dynasty. The blue conical roof is supported by curved wooden beams, which form a precise circle – a **miraculous example of the art of carpentry**. The enclosing wall is known as the Echo Wall, since any word uttered against it can clearly be heard on the opposite side. With the visitor numbers usual here, though, this phenomenon is difficult to test.

Causeway

A white marble causeway leads from the southern section with the altar through a triple-arched gate to another area in the north. Where a route from the west gate meets the causeway a terrace extends to the east. Here the emperor would enter a tent to change clothes for the **spring ceremony**.

Hall of the Harvest Prayer, Temple of Heaven The building towering over the entire altar site at the northern end of the causeway is the Hall of the Harvest Prayer, indubitably **the most perfect example of classical Chinese architecture**. It was rebuilt after a fire in 1896. A round white pedestal with three levels raises it up above the terrace and matches with the three levels of the blue roof topped by a golden capital. 28 pillars support the hall, the four large ones right in the middle being representative of the four seasons, while another inner ring of twelve signifies the months and the outer dozen stand for the twelve two-hourly periods of the day. The building thus emulates time in its constant running and repetition, echoing the annual repetition of the sacrifices to nature. The soul tablets of heaven and the earlier emperors are placed on throne-like podiums. The wooden parts are painted with dragons and phoenixes. The central baseplate exhibits a natural pattern, also held to represent dragons and phoenixes. The most glorious aspect of the building, though, is its dome, in the centre of which there is a golden dragon and phoenix relief.

> ! **Baedeker TIP**
>
> **Open-air concerts**
>
> The long, open gallery leading south from the Hall of the Harvest Prayer towards the east gate is a popular meeting place for amateur musicians. Other musicians – especially amateur singers – go in the evening to the park which stretches along the old city moat to the south of the altar, in particular about 900 m/1000 yd west of the southern entrance near the newly rebuilt city gate, Yongding Men. Often arias from Beijing operas can be heard.

Secondary halls In the two halls at the sides, left and right in front of the round hall, exhibitions have been set up to illustrate the sacrificial rite. In the hall at the northern end of the grand terrace are the **soul tablets of heaven**, which were carried into the Hall of the Harvest Prayer in the course of the cult rituals.

Long Corridor and secondary buildings Eastward of the Hall of the Harvest Prayer a long colonnade (Long Corridor) leads to the secondary buildings, which include the **holy kitchen**, where the sacrificial offerings were prepared, the holy storeroom for the ritual utensils, and the abattoir for slaughtering the sacrificial beast. Opening times for the inner parts of the altar site and the Hall of the Harvest Prayer: 8.30am–5pm daily.

Hongqiao Market In the multistorey market hall diagonally opposite the east gate to the Altar of Heavens life is colourfully exotic – from fresh fish on the ground floor to handbags and electronics at the top, there are shoes, silk and cashmere, all kinds of craft products and a huge section for pearls. Everything is very cheap – with enough resolute haggling.

Central Business District The area where the major east-west axis meets the 3rd ring road in the east is a veritable forest of high-rise offices and hotels, pulsing with commercial life. The germ of the development was the World Trade Center, with the elegant China World Hotel. 650 m/730 yd further north, on the 3rd ring road, is Beijing's most spectacular skyscraper, the 234 m/750 ft headquarters of the state television organization CCTV, a design by the Dutch architect Rem Koolhaas. Underground line 1, Guomao.

✳ White Cloud Monastery (Baiyun Guan)

Beijing's most important Daoist shrine is 4 km/2.5 mi west of Tian'anmen Square. It is the biggest and the oldest **Daoist monastery** still active today and is home to the Daoist Society. Thanks to its abundant imagery and the religious life that takes place there make it one of the most interesting holy places in the city. One particular aspect behind the atmosphere of the lovingly tended complex is the sight of the monks themselves, dressed in their traditional, unassuming **robes with wrap-round gaiters and cloth shoe**. With beards and hair knotted on top of their heads – hair is never cut – they look as though they have come straight out of some old pictures.

History

Although the monastery was established as early as 739, its history only really begins under Genghis Khan. The Mongol conqueror had it rebuilt in honour of the Daoist wise man, **Qiu Chuji**. In the 17th–19th centuries it enjoyed imperial protection. Well-to-do eunuchs chose it as their place of retirement. Under Mao, White Cloud Monastery was the only Daoist monastery in Beijing used for its intended purpose.

Marble lions flank the magnificent decorative gate. Its inscription, **»Kingdom of Heaven«** implies that people are here entering a better world, that of the white clouds, where the Daoist immortals, after years of practice, have finally transcended their mortal shape and can travel at will in time and space.

Outer courtyards

From the first courtyard the Mountain Gate leads into the second outer courtyard with its white marble bridge, underneath which hangs an enlarged **copy of an ancient Chinese copper coin**. Anyone managing to throw a real coin and hit the bell that hangs in the hole inside the imitation coin may hope for the fulfilment of their wishes. Anyone who misses at least makes a contribution to temple funds.

Halls

In the second gatehouse that follows, the sword-swinging, red-faced temple guard, Wang Shan, guards against all evil. In the next court, drum and bell towers stand to the left and right and in the north is the first of the main halls, the Hall of the Jade Emperor. In popular Daoism the **Jade Emperor** is the highest of the gods. Either side of him, star gods are portrayed. The next hall has the lowest ceiling and is used as an assembly room. Here the Six Patriarchs are worshipped. It is to their teaching that the school to which the monastery belongs is dedicated.

Inner section The next hall leads to the innermost part of the monastery. The statue of the sage, Qiu Chuji (dating from the Ming period) occupies the honoured position in the shrine. His mortal remains are buried beneath the hall, allegedly under a burl-wood bowl placed in front of the altar, which was donated to the monastery as an imperial gift. The next courtyard is the only one surrounding by an unbroken ring of buildings. On its northern side stands the two-storey **»Hall of Their Four Majesties«**. The name refers to the four gods worshipped on the ground floor, three gods of heaven and one of earth. The upper floor has images of the three highest deities of monastic Daoism, the »Three Pristine Ones«.

Western wing The halls of the western section of the temple are given over to the ordinary people. Most of the figures here are of little importance to »advanced« Daoists but all the more so for the lay public. The first hall on that side contains goddesses responsible for feminine fertility, a quick and painless birth and the eyesight of small children. In the

Baiyun Guan temple monastery

hall opposite this one to the north, **Wenchang**, patron of scholars and officials, is honoured. To his right is a statue of Confucius. Of the two halls of the court that adjoins to the west, the northern one is dedicated to the worship of **Lu Dongbin**, the most popular of the Eight Blessed Ones (or Immortals), to whom the hall facing to the south is dedicated.

Hall of the Year Gods

In the north the great Hall of the Year Gods is the last one in the western wing. It has sixty personifications of the years of the sixty-year cycle of the ancient Chinese calendar. The colourful little **clay figures** were made anew in 1990. Believers come to offer incense to the god representing the year of their birth and pray for the god's support at times of crisis.

Monastery gardens

A passage next to the Hall of the Year Gods leads to the »**Cloud Forming Garden**«. It is laid out with colonnades and artificial rock hills. A pavilion slightly raised above the ground at the rear of the last hall is the ordination and teaching terrace. The mural that decorates the wall shows the saints in a heavenly palace riding on clouds or waves and foaming water in which dragons live. At the sides the evergreen pines signify long life. In the eastern part of the garden there is another mural: **the eight saints crossing the sea**. Baiyunguan Jie. Opening times: 8.30am–4.30pm daily. ⏱

Capital Museum

A spectacular new building designed by French architect Jean-Marie Duthilleul displays the multifarious aspects of cultural, social and political history in Beijing up to 1949 by means of original items, replicas, models and audio-visual media. Visitors can learn all about customs, festivals and theatre – or about the design of courtyard entrances. Fuxingmenwai Dajie, corner of Baiyun Lu. Underground line 1: Muxidi. Opening times: Tue–Sun 9am–5pm. ⏱

✳ The Fragrant Mountain and the Temple of Biyun Si

The Fragrant Mountain (Xiang Shan) has, since ancient times, been the most popular leisure spot for citizens of the capital, in particular when the leaves turn brown in the autumn. Here, some 20 km /12 mi northwest of the centre, the 570 m/1870 ft summit provides a stupendous **panoramic view**. After the 12th century the emperors would regularly come here for hunting and to breathe the fresh air in summer.

Xiang-Shan Park

From the car park and the terminus of the bus routes (no. 331 bus from the summer palace, no. 360 bus from the Xizhimen, from where private minibuses also run) a colourful street full of shops and restaurants leads to the north gate of Xiang-Shan Park, which includes the former imperial grounds and stretches all the way up to

A pavilion on the Fragrant Mountain, a place to recover from the urban bustle

the summit. The park's landmark is located in the lower section, the **»Porcelain Pagoda«**, with its covering of glazed tiles. Right at the north entrance is the lower station of a chair-lift, which can carry visitors to the summit in 18 minutes to enjoy the best view in all of Beijing.

Biyun Si Temple From the north gate of the park a wide path leads along the perimeter wall to the loveliest of the temples on Beijing's fringes, the **»Temple of Azure Clouds«**. The present buildings mostly date from the Ming era. The 500 Luohan Hall and the Diamond Throne Pagoda were added in 1748. From 1925 till 1929 the body of the Sun Yatsen, founder of the Chinese Republic, was kept in the pagoda following his death in Beijing and before his mausoleum in Nanjing could be completed. The sequence of halls climbed in a line of terraces. The statuary is new. Only the bronze **pot-bellied Buddha** in the Hall of the Heavenly Kings survived the Cultural Revolution. One of the halls is dedicated to Sun Yatsen.

Hall of the 500 Luohan The **»Arhat Hall«** stands to the left of the main axis and is one of the most spectacular works of Buddhist art in Beijing: 500 life-size figures of monks, carved from wood and painted gold hold a silent conversation with the visitors. Near the north entrance, one small figure squats up on a beam. This is **Jigong, a sort of Chinese practical joker**. According to legend he sought a place among all the other 500 holy monks, but arrived too late and the only space left was up in the beams.

Diamond Throne Pagoda Beyond the main halls, three decorative gates form an architectural prelude to the highlight of the complex, the great Diamond Throne

Pagoda. The pedestal of the Indian-style white marble structure is decorated with bas-reliefs, and building can be climbed by a staircase inside. At the top there are two small bottle pagodas and five pyramid-shaped pagodas, of which the middle one is the tallest. The entire construction is decorated with reliefs and semi-sculpted figures: Buddhas, Heavenly Kings, guards, dragons, phoenixes, lions and clouds. From the top there is a great **view of Beijing**.

✳ Wofo Si Temple · Botanical gardens

3 km/2 mi northeast of the Fragrant Mountain there is a lovely estate with some unusually well preserved statuary. The route to the temple monastery passes through Beijing's botanical gardens, which cover an extensive area of 200 ha/500 acres, passing **the biggest greenhouse in China**, a spectacular glass palace covering 17,000 sq m/ 20,300 sq yd. Founded at the beginning of the 7th century, the Buddhist monastery is the oldest within Beijing's city boundaries. Its heyday began when the Mongol emperor Yingzong had it rebuilt from 1321, also commissioning the casting of the reclining Buddha from which the site gets its name.

An avenue of gnarled old thujas leads to a splendid decorative gate covered in green and yellow glazed tiles. It possesses an inscription written by the Qianlong Emperor with the challenge: »**delve together into the mysteries.**«

Avenue and decorative gate

Next comes an outer courtyard with a goldfish pond, the original purpose of which was for setting free fish that had been caught. It is the location of the **Hall of the Heavenly Kings**, the first main court and the main hall with the Buddhas of the Three Ages and the 18 luohan along the walls, all made of clay.

Halls and courts on the main axis

Beyond the main hall is the last building on the main axis, which contains the biggest attraction on the site, in the **Hall of the Sleeping Buddha** (on his entrance to Nirvana). As ever he lies on his right-hand side with his head propped to the left so that visitors can see his face. The bronze figure is 5.2 m/17 ft long, making it the largest statue of its kind in China. Twelve of his disciples, depicted as crowned bodhisattvas and considerably smaller than the Buddha himself, keep watch standing by his side. The plaque at the rear, in the calligraphy of the Qianlong Emperor, roughly translates as: »**In the state of absoluteness**«.

> ! *Baedeker* TIP
>
> **A walk in Cherry Gorge**
> Leave the monastery grounds heading west then turn to the north. This brings you to the picturesque Cherry Gorge, Yingtao Gou, an undramatic but delightful green valley with cliffs and hermits' caves – a nice place for a walk.

✸ ✸ Summer Palace of Yihe Yuan

The **»Gardens of Nurtured Harmony«**, usually called the Summer Palace, have a quite different history from the city's »winter palace«. It is not a fortress or a cage for concubines, but a green and spacious, highly varied and often very pleasurable estate. It was not conceived as an imperial villa but as a home for widows. Nowadays the estate, 16 km/10 mi northwest of Beijing's city centre, is primarily seen as a **miracle of landscape architecture**. It is dominated by two key features: **Lake Kunming**, which, with the associated lakes and ponds, takes up three-quarters of the gardens, and the 60 m/200 ft elevation called **»Longevity Hill«**, which rises out of the northern shore of the lake. Opening times: April–Oct. 6.30am till 6pm daily, halls 8.30pm–5pm; otherwise 7am–5pm and 9am–4pm respectively. 332 bus from Xizhimen bus station to the end of the route.

History and design of the site
Built in 1750 but almost totally destroyed by British and French troops in 1860, the estate was reconstructed from 1888 at the wishes of the **Empress Dowager Cixi** for her own use. She would spend the summer and autumn months here, from 1898 always in the company of the emperor whose power she had usurped. The themes of the site, in ever varying aspects are longevity and immortality. This is exhibited in the names of the halls and other places (»Longevity Hill«, »Hall of Benevolence and Longevity« etc.) and in the symbolism of the flora, the ornamentation and decorative items, for example pines, cranes, peaches, mushrooms, gourds. The religious references are also of note, for instance in the most prominent building on the site, the **»Pavilion of Buddhist Incense«**. The gardens too sought to demonstrate the magnificence of the Manchu empire, so that on the northern slopes of the hill there is a southern Chinese scholar's garden with a lotus pond and a Tibetan temple. Otherwise the main aim was pleasure: two theatres, a shopping street, the Long Corridor and of course the water gave plenty of leisure options.

> **!** *Baedeker* TIP
>
> **Recuperation in the style of the Empress Dowager**
>
> Yihe Yuan is a stylish place to rest. The Tingli Guan restaurant (»For the Call of the Orioles«), at the west end of the Long Corridor, serves imperial cuisine. The teahouses here are more atmospheric and intimate. There is one on Suzhou Road north of the hill and another by the lotus pond in Xiequ Yuan garden east of the hill. A hundred years ago the Empress Dowager Cixi herself would sip tea here.

Main gate (east gate) Renshou Men
Two bronze lions flank the main entrance. The fact that it **faces east** and not south already gives a hint that this is not intended to be as strict an environment as in the imperial palace. The **»Gate of Longevity and Benevolence«** reveals a view of the main courtyard with its stands of tall pines and its audience hall. A rock 3 m/10 ft high

Yihe Yuan Summer Palace Map

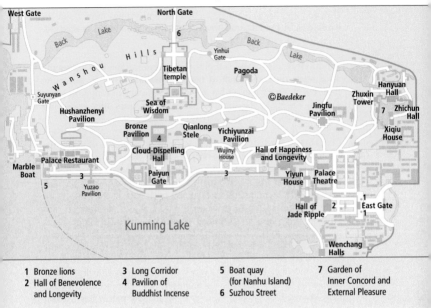

1 Bronze lions
2 Hall of Benevolence and Longevity
3 Long Corridor
4 Pavilion of Buddhist Incense
5 Boat quay (for Nanhu Island)
6 Suzhou Street
7 Garden of Inner Concord and External Pleasure

along the main axis right behind the gate resembles abstract sculpture – as do other stones in the gardens here and at other places around the palace, this one being a superb example. Behind the stone a bronze **qilin** sits on its haunches. These animals are hoofed creatures with the head and scaly skin of a dragon. It heralds an age of blessings. Bronze dragons and phoenixes are used for dispensing incense.

Renshou Dian audience hall

The audience hall (»Hall of Longevity and Benevolence«) is an emphatically plain building, which suggests humility with its simple grey-covered roof. The interior has been preserved virtually in its original form. The throne in the centre is surrounded by cranes and censers. On the wall, a canopy with dragon ornamentation behind the throne has the character »shòu«, »Longevity«, incorporated in the design 226 times. The plaque behind the throne says: »age and benevolence belong together« – thus giving the hall its name. It refers to one of the analects of Confucius.

Palace theatres

»Garden of Virtue and Harmony« (Dehe Yuan) is the name of the larger of the two palace theatres north of the audience hall. At 21 m//69 ft high and 17 m/56 ft wide, the three levels of the stage, equipped with trap doors and lift mechanisms, allowed for some startling effects. The buildings at the sides, from which the Empress Dowager and her court once viewed the proceedings, now house an **exhibition of the Empress Dowager's utensils** and gifts she received, including an 1898 Benz motor car.

Palace of Yulan Tang

Southwest of the theatre complex on the shore of the lake comes the residential court, the **»Hall of the Jade Waves«**. Here is where the Empress Dowager housed her nephew, the Guangxu Emperor, when she was staying at the summer palace in the years after 1898 until they both died under house arrest.

Palace of Leshou Tang

Cixi herself lived in the adjoining complex to the northwest, the **»Hall of Happiness and Longevity«**. All over the place, corresponding symbolism is to be found, for instance the bronze courtyard ornamentation in front of the main hall shows a pair of stags on each side along with cranes and vases, plus a relief pattern showing cranes sitting on pines. The fact that each of the objects number six also symbolizes a proverb: **»six unifies – peace on earth«**. In Chinese eyes the monumental garden stone resembles the lingzhi mushroom, eating which is said to bestow immortality. Inside, Cixi's throne and the table where she ate are easily identified. There are embroidered works showing a peacock on a wheel and »A Hundred Birds in Audience with the Phoenix« – which allegorically refers to Cixi herself, here likened to a phoenix venerated by all. The palace has its own jetty. A gate-like frame 20 m/66 ft high once had a lantern suspended from it, which acted as a lighthouse signal for nocturnal trips on the lake.

Long Corridor

The most famous architectural feature on the site adjoins the palace. Its 728 metres/796 yd of roofed colonnade with a view of the lake and the hill are only part of the attraction, though. The rest of the delight comes from the **paintings** decorating the ceilings, making it the longest painted colonnade in the world. There are supposedly more than 8000 large scenes – a picture book of popular literary fiction and the beauties of nature: landscapes, birds and flowers.

Palace of Paiyun Dian

In the middle, the Long Corridor opens onto the architectural **highlight of the whole palace complex**. The building's effect is enhanced by the imperial yellow, glazed and occasionally blue-rimmed roofs. The part of the building facing the lake is called the **»Hall of Dispelling Clouds«** (Paiyun Dian). The name calls to mind a 4th-century poem which mentions the dispelling clouds as the vehicles of the immortals, on which their free spirits travel through space and time. In the name of this hall then, the garden raises the hitherto carefully unfolding topic of longevity to an even higher level of poetic legend. The sequence of courts, halls and stairs rising ever higher towards the heavens starts from the lake shore with a decorative gate. Twelve garden stones on the outer courtyard of the palace are supposed to represent the **animals of the twelve-year Chinese calendrical cycle**. Beyond the entrance gate a white marble bridge leads over a pond. One more gate leads to the throne hall, distinguished by its double-eaved roof. The Empress Dowager sat here to receive the honours of the courtiers on her 70th birthday. The sumptuous furnishings have been preserved. The majority of the items were birthday gifts.

A covered stairway climbs up to another yellow-roofed hall. From there another stairway, this time open to the elements, proceeds to the building which dominates the whole palace, the Pavilion of Buddhist Incense, an octagonal, three-storey building, raised up upon a 20 m/66 ft terrace so that it is visually on a level with the summit. To choose a Buddhist facility as the dominant **showpiece of a palace** would have been unthinkable for a ruler in Confucian China. The Manchus had a very close bond to Buddhism, however. The building contains a thousand-armed Guanyin. There is a magnificent panoramic view of the lake from the terrace.

Pavilion of the Buddhist Incense (Foxiang Ge)

From Kunming Lake there is a wonderful view of the Summer Palace.
The octagonal Pavilion of Buddhist Incense on its square terrace catches the eye

From the Pavilion of Buddhist Incense the eye ranges eastwards to the great Qianlong stele (right) and the sutra carousels that flank it.

Bronze pavilion To the west on the slope is a small hall made entirely of bronze, the **»Precious Cloud Pavilion«** dating from 1752. This gem of a building, 7.5 m /25 ft in height, rises up from a white terrace between some other buildings amid a small courtyard. Formally speaking, it is an imitation of a wooden hall building with a tiled roof.

Tingli Guan Restaurant and Theatre Back to the Long Corridor, the last of the major groups of buildings to which it leads is the **»House for the Call of the Orioles«** with the Palace restaurant and the smaller of the palace's two theatres. The name Tingli Guan refers to the song of the black-naped oriole, *oriolus chinensis*, a reference to the music that was played here.

Marble boat The pavilion which stands on a boat-shaped pedestal is a curiosity of dubious taste, especially since the boat, which had been in existence since 1755, received dummy paddle wheels under the Empress Dowager. The buildings on top of the terrace, built in the European style as was the fashion at the time, are deceptive too. They are made of **wood painted to look like marble**. The unsinkable building is supposed to be a literary reference to a piece of advice given to the Tang Emperor Taizong (7th century): The same water that supports a ship can also cause it to capsize, meaning of course the ship of state.

A path leads north from alongside the larger of the palace theatres (Dehe Yuan). With one more turn to the left it comes out at the idyllic »**Garden of Inward Harmony and Outward Pleasure**«. It was designed as an extended imitation of a mid-Chinese scholar's garden. With its pond surrounded by weeping willows and pines, lined by pavilions, halls and colonnades at pleasing intervals, it is primarily a garden for the high summer. An encircling path, which leads over small bridges here and there links the buildings together. In one pavilion on the southern bank a teahouse has been opened.

Xiequ Yuan garden

In 1987 two rows of shops, which had been destroyed in the 19th century, were reconstructed. They are patterned on the mid-Chinese city of Suzhou on both sides of a canal at the northern base of the hill. The emperor, plus the empress and concubines, could pretend here to be like normal people. There are 60 shops where eunuchs and servants would sell them food, toys and craft art or let them **rest with a cup of tea**. The present-day vendors wear traditional costume and the shops have their old signs. It is a fun place to go shopping.

Suzhou Road

On the northern slope of »Longevity Hill« (Wanshou Shan) there is a group of 19 buildings in Tibetan style. They form a **mandala** consisting of the »four continents« of the Buddhist world metaphor, each with two sub-continents. The eleven buildings higher up are raised on a red terrace with dummy windows and are reminiscent of the Red Palace of the Potala in Lhasa.

Tibetan temple

With the causeways that delineate the western section and the bridges that cross the linking streams, the largest of the imperial garden lakes emulates the famous West Lake of Hangzhou. There are jetties for boats at various places on the north bank, near the east gate and on the island in the south. **Boats can be hired** next to the marble boat and at the eastern end of the Seventeen-Arch Bridge.

Lake Kunming

At 150 m/164 yd long and 8 m/26 ft wide, this elegant bridge, built in 1750 of natural white marble, is among the most famous old bridges in China. Stone lions guard its end and smaller ones top the pillars of the balustrade. The bridge leads to the largest of the islands in the lake, a good place to go if only to see the view of the hill **Wanshou Shan** and the palace buildings on the northern shore. In an old Dragon King Temple on the island, the lord of the water, bestower of blessings, is worshipped.

Seventeen-Arch Bridge

The Great Wall at Mutianyu is an impressive sight

The Great Wall of China

The Great Wall near Badaling ✸

The nearest section of the Great Wall of China to Beijing (60 km/37 mi northwest) and therefore the **most crowded part of the wall** was restored as long ago as the 1950s. Nowadays it can be reached by motorway. On the northern side of a pass at an elevation of 660 m/2165 ft there is a settlement with numerous restaurants, a large car park and the Great Wall Museum.

Tours

Visitors have a choice: towards the east the climb is gentler, whereas to the west it is steeper but the view is better. A **cable-car** irons out some of the bigger height differences. On clear days in autumn the view extends all the way to Beijing itself. The two sections together add up to a length of almost 4.8 km/3 mi. Bus 919 to Badaling from Deshengmen (underground line 1); if possible take the express bus, but on no account line 919Z.

Great Wall Museum

The entrance price of 45 yuan to the Wall includes admission to the museum (beyond the Wall itself above the large car park). It displays photographs and plans illustrating the **history of the Wall's construction** plus the remains of earlier Chinese border walls.

The Great Wall near Mutianyu ✸✸

The section of wall amid the best scenery is 70 km/44mi northeast of Beijing and has stunning views of forested slopes. A cable-car carries visitors up the higher western flank. From there it is possible to follow the wall down to the upper station of a chairlift **upper station of a chair lift** to get back down to the valley. The fun alternative to that is a giant slide.

This is the most precipitous section of the Wall, where it snakes over a mountain ridge with steep drops on both sides. On some stretches the wall is no more than 50 cm/20 inches thick with a gangway at ground level. The highest part of the wall is closed off. Those parts that can be visited are broader and have only been restored in so far as was possible using **original bricks from the year of construction, 1577**. A chair lift helps iron out the biggest differences in height. From the lower end of the wall, a daring rope slide – where the »passengers« are suspended in a harness – leads over a reservoir down to the exit.

✸ **Great Wall near Simatai**

✸ Ming tombs (Ming Shisan Ling)

The necropolis of the third to 16th Ming emperors (excepting the seventh) is the most popularly visited attraction outside Beijing (44 km/27 mi north) after the Great Wall. Only two of the **mausoleums** are important in a tourist sense. Most of the others are dilapidated and closed to the public. The surrounding area stands out for its scenic beauty. Columned pavilions tower up among the tree tops and over broad views of the plains.

The location for the imperial tombs was chosen in 1409. The range of mountains, on the southern slopes of which the graves are situated, rise up here towards the highest peak in the vicinity (750 m/2460 ft). The area is also protected to the west and east by two flanks of the mountain . Most of the buildings were destroyed during the **rebellion of Li Zicheng**, which brought down the Ming dynasty in 1644.

History and complex as a whole

The first building at the necropolis stands on a slight rise 1 km/1100 yd in front of the main gate, a white honour gate with five arches, 12 m/39 ft high, 29 m/32 yd wide and decorated by animal sculptures and reliefs. It was built in 1540. A perimeter wall once adjoined the »Great Red Gate«, the **main gate to the necropolis**. Its three arches were closed by heavy wooden doors.

Marble honour gate, main gate

The tourist buses, which always drive past the two gates, make their first stop at the columned pavilion. This is the beginning of the central section of the Sacred Way with its **famous animal statues**. At the beginning is the great columned pavilion of 1435, surrounded by four columns with dragons twining round them in bas-relief. The 6.5 m/21 ft stele that protects the pavilion stands upon a tortoise as tall as a man. Both the stele and the tortoise are carved from one mighty block of stone.
The **inscription** at the front proclaims »Divine Merit and Sacred Virtue of (the Lord of) the Changling mausoleum of the Great Ming«. In the text, the fourth Ming emperor praises the deeds of his father, the Yongle Emperor. The text at the rear, added in 1785, describes the whole complex and gives dates for its history.

Columned pavilion

Sacred Way **(Way of Souls)**	To the north the central section of the »Sacred Way« continues, the route along which the catafalque of the deceased sovereign would be carried. This section, almost a kilometre/1000 yd in length, is lined by **eighteen pairs of stone figures**: six animal pairs and twelve pairs of officials, 36 statues in all, which do final honours to the emperor being borne to rest. The sequence starts with lions, in the same honourable guarding function as they play in front of doors and gateways, then come xiezhi, a singled-horned creature of fable representing loyalty and supposedly keeping the holy precinct clear of all those of unseemly intent. Next along are two camels, which have no particular symbolism but are undoubtedly very virtuous creatures: obedient, patient and ready to do service. The next animal is the elephant, used in living form as the imperial draught animal, they stand for morality, virtue and precious happiness. The qilin, sometimes called a Chinese unicorn, presages, whenever it is sighted, an **era of peace and prosperity**, and thus here praises the deceased son of heaven as one who had ruled over such a happy epoch. The equine steed of the nobility (such as the Yongle Emperor) and the cavalry also has no mystic symbolism but has many obvious virtues – obedience, speed, noble calmness and readiness for service. The two types of guarding creature (lions and xiezhi) are at the beginning of the row, as befits their function, and are showing their teeth. By contrast, the qilin. camels, elephants and horses are shown as tame domesticated creatures or **creatures of fable**. After the animals come two pairs of military and civil officials and four sets of ministers.
The Changling tomb	The oldest, largest and best preserved of the thirteen mausoleums is the resting place of the Yongle Emperor, who died in 1424. The building of the tomb lasted from 1409 till 1427. Like the other mausoleums it consists of two sections, the grave temple and burial mound directly adjoining it. An **outer courtyard** is entered via an elevated gate houses with three arches. To the right there is a **columned pavilion** with a curious animal supporting its stele, mixing a scaled body and a horned dragon's head.
Main courtyard and Ling'en Dian Hall	The spacious main courtyard is entered through a hall-like gatehouse. On other side there are furnaces for the sacrificial burning of silks. They are covered with yellow and green glazed tiles and designed to look like small buildings. Even the wooden windows are imitated by a ceramic relief. The white marble terrace with three levels in the northern part of the courtyard is the oldest of its kind in Beijing. As with other imperial buildings, panels along the central one of the three stairways are decorated with **bas-reliefs of clouds and dragons**. At the bottom, reliefs featuring two seahorses rise out of a moving water surface. Atop the terrace the dominant building is the **tomb's temple hall**, dating from 1416. This is the only one of the

This guardian on the »soul path« regards visitors critically →

sacrificial halls to have survived, but with a width of 66.6 m/218 ft, it even exceeds the largest throne hall of the imperial palace in size, although it is not so deep (29 m/95 ft). All of the supporting wooden structure, including the 60 imposing columns, are made of nanmu wood, the most precious of all Chinese building timbers. Ceremonies with feasting and the burning of silks for the interred rulers took place here on the anniversaries of their births and deaths.

Third court
A tripled-arched gate leads to the third court. It has another honour gate inside it, which is normally closed. There is also a large marble altar with the five (by nature Buddhist) **»implements of worship«**, in this case made of stone and effectively unusable, there only for symbolic reasons: an incense holder with a lid covered in a dragon relief plus a candlestick and a vase on each of the sides.

Burial mound and stele
At the end of the courtyard atop a tall crenellated pedestal is the 13 m/43 ft pavilion of the burial column. It forms a transition to the circular **burial mound**, 300 m/330 yd in diameter, behind it. A stairway leads to the edge of the tumulus and the base of the columned pavilion. From there it is possible to cast an eye towards the columned pavilions of the other tombs in the necropolis. The stele bears the inscription, »Mausoleum of Chengzu, Emperor Wen of the Great Ming«. Chengzu was the temple name of the Yongle Emperor and Wen his posthumous name. Opening times: 8.30am–5.30pm daily.

The crypt of the Dingling tomb consists of a series of chambers of varying size. The sarcophagi of the emperor and empresses were in the rearmost chamber

Between 1956 and 1958 the basis was put in place for this tomb to-day to become part of the **standard programme for most tourists to Beijing**: At that time, its crypt was opened and some precious burial goods were recovered. They testify to the extravagance for which this emperor was known. The Wanli Emperor (1563–1620) lived solely for his own passions and left the rule of the empire to a few trusted eunuchs. It took six years to build his tomb, for which planning had begun when the emperor was just 19. Its cost corresponded to a full two years' tax revenues. Apart from the emperor, the empress, who died shortly before him, and the mother of the imperial heir, a for-mer concubine, are also buried here.

Tomb of Dingling

All that remains of the tomb's main buildings are the marble pedes-tals. To the sides of the third courtyard two exhibitions have been set up in which some of the **burial items**, from a total of nearly 3000 pieces, are on display. They include some wonderful head-dresses, jade pendants (adorning robes), belts, all kinds of vessels and some silk bro-cade newly woven to match the originals, which have sadly crumbled.

Courts and exhi-bition halls

As with the other tombs the last courtyard leads into the burial mound itself. The dominant building is the pedestal for the burial column's pavilion, which is integrated into the perimeter wall and protrudes into the courtyard. The temple name and posthumous name of the buried emperor are inscribed upon it.

Burial mound and stele

A newly installed ramp leads from the burial stele to the crypt, the »underground palace«. The ramp acts as an exit route for visitors. The site is entered via a stairway shaft specially built inside the burial mound. The crypt itself is completely made of natural stone and is impressive in its dimensions. It consists of a short outer chamber, another outer chamber, 20 m/22 yd in length, a central chamber of 32 m/35 yd and, beyond that at right angles to it, the rear chamber with a width of 30 m/33 yd. On a stone pedestal along the rear wall of the latter are the three **sarcophagi of the emperor and his em-presses**. Nowadays only replicas are on display. From the central chamber passages lead to two side chambers each 26 m/28 yd long, where empty plinths for additional sarcophagi are placed to symbol-ize the tombs of other concubines who are buried elsewhere. The left-hand side chamber now serves as the entrance for visitors. The vaulting is 9.5 m/31 ft high. Drainage of the burial mound was so good and the natural stones of its chambers so well matched that when the crypt was opened, it was found to be completely dry. Other than the central and rear chambers, all the others are empty. The central one has three **marble thrones**. The one decorated with drag-ons is for the emperor, while the others, adorned with phoenixes, are for the empresses. The porcelain basin in Ming-era blue-and-white contained oil and wicks to serve the purpose of eternal lamps. Open-ing times: 8.30am–5.30pm daily.

Crypt

✳ ✳ Eastern Qing tombs (Qing Dong Ling)

The imperial tombs of the final dynasty are divided into two areas, one southwest of Beijing and another 115 km/71 miles east of it. With its 15 burial mounds, the latter is the older and larger necropolis and has the more important tombs. This is where the Kangxi and the Qianlong Emperors were laid to rest, as well as Empress Dowager Cixi, the three dominant **ruling figures of the Manchu era**. In total 160 members of the dynasty are buried here. The mausoleums are newer and better preserved and, since they are further from the city, less crowded than those of the Ming emperors.

History and location

The first mausoleum, the Xiaoling tomb, was built from 1661 for the first Manchu emperor to sit on Beijing's dragon throne (Shunzhi era 1644–1661). He had surveyed the site during his lifetime and designated it as his burial place. The necropolis was used until 1935, when a last concubine was buried here. As at the Ming tombs, a geomantically **auspicious spot** was chosen, which creates a spontaneous impression thanks to the beauty of the scenery. The necropolis is protected to the north by mountains. One low hill and a conical mound in front of it, both lying along the axis of the Sacred Way in the south, act as natural »spirit walls«.

Sacred Way (Way of Souls)

Any visit should start in the south. The Sacred Way that leads from there to the oldest mausoleum, the Xiaoling tomb, is 5 km/3 mi long. Even before the main gate there is a marble **honour gate with five arches** decorated with animal reliefs. At 12.5 m/41 ft high and 31 m/34 yd wide, it is the largest building of its kind in China. The red main gate is adjoined by a partially restored perimeter wall. The Way leads directly to a large columned pavilion, upon which inscriptions in Chinese and Manchu tell of the **»Divine Merit and Holy Virtues«** of the Shunzhi Emperor. Beyond the »spirit wall hills« is the beginning of the 900 m/1000 yd central section of the Sacred Way featuring 18 pairs of stone figures – emulating the Ming tombs with ots sequence of six types of animal (lion, xiezhi, camel, elephant, qilin – an imaginary four-hoofed creature – and horse) plus military and civil officials. A double bend in the axis at the **marble bridge** which follows derives from the same concept as the spirit walls, i.e. that approaching evil, which only moves in straight lines, will encounter an obstacle.

Xiaoling

The mausoleum of the Shunzhi Emperor is the core of the necropolis. The sequence of buildings is as follows: a **column pavilion** in the outer courtyard, which has the temple name and posthumous honorary title of the deceased inscribed on it, the gatehouse to the adjoining **main courtyard**, the **offertory hall** with its lovely incense holders on the terrace, then on the other side of a triple-arched gate, the **outer courtyard of the burial mound itself**, where there is another honour gate and an altar with depictions of the five worshipping implements (incense holder, candlesticks and vases) in marble and, surrounded by a high wall, the **burial mound itself**, topped with the burial column's pavilion. This arrangement is repeated with only minor variations in all the other burial temples. In the main hall demonstrations of the sacrificial ceremonies are given four times a day, at 9.30am, 10.30am, 2pm and 3pm.

The grave of the Qianlong Emperor, who died in 1799 (along with those of two empresses and three concubines) is the biggest at the eastern Qing site and is the most interesting thanks to the **opening of its crypt**. It was built from 1743–1752. At 54 m/59 yd long and covering 372 sq m/445 sq yd it is a little smaller than the crypt of the Ming dynasty's Dingling mausoleum, but its extensive and exquisitely executed Buddhist relief work is a delight. Four stone double doors, each 3 m/10 ft high and 3m/10 ft wide, divide the chambers from one another. On the outside they each have a standing bodhisattvas pictured on them. In the first chamber reliefs of the **Four Heavenly Kings** stand guard. In the second chamber there are 24 images displaying various gestures. In the third, there is a depiction of the five sensual lusts, which every devout Buddhist should avoid: a mirror (sight), pipa or lute (hearing), perfumed powder (smell), fruit bowl (taste) and a robe (touch). Most of the inscriptions are in Tibetan, while the remainder are in Sanskrit. Tip: it helps to bring a torch to make the low reliefs easier to see.

Yuling

From the northern end of the court outside the Yuling-tomb a footpath leads west to the associated tomb of the emperor's concubines. Its buildings, in keeping with their lesser rank, are not topped with imperial yellow tiles but with green glazed versions. Amid the 35 small tumuli, each surrounded by a wall, **36 of the Qianlong Emperor's concubines** are buried.

Tombs of the concubines

The footpath leads further to the west to the nearby tomb of the Empress Dowager Cixi. This was built at the same time as its immediate neighbour, the mausoleum of Ci'an, senior wife of the Xianfeng Emperor, and is of identical design. Cixi , though, subsequently had her burial temple furnished with more sumptuous effects and had a relief stone added at the stairway to the sacrificial terrace, which displays a phoenix above a dragon – symbolizing **her position in the power structure**, even above the emperor. Inside the offertory hall, the exquisite wood carvings, reliefs and the golden dragons winding around the columns catch the eye. In one niche a wax figure of Cixi herself hovers over a lotus pond in a depiction of her as the merciful goddess Guanyin. The scene itself was created in a photographic studio. The crypt is open to the public too. Opening times: The crypts and halls close at 5pm; although the open outdoor parts of the site remain open after that.

The burial temple of Cixi (Ding Dongling)

★ Changbai Shan

Hj/Hk 24/25

Province: Jilin   **Altitude:** Up to 2744 m/9003 ft

Spectacular spot on the border with North Korea where the 2700 m/8860 ft volcanic peak of Baitou Shan rises out of the dense forests of the »White-Topped Mountains« (Changbai Shan).

From above the tree line on the sulphur-yellow rim of the Baitou Shan volcano (2744 m/9003 ft), the view takes in the mysteriously shimmering waters of **»Heaven Lake«** (Tian Chi). 9.2 sq km/3.6 sq mi in area, its waters finally plunge into the valley down a 68 m/223 ft waterfall. 17 hot springs testify to the fact that the earth beneath is still volcanically active. The last eruption was in 1792. Accommodation is provided in a settlement at the foot of Baitou Shan, which includes hotels, shops and bathhouses. The waterfall and the lake at its base can be reached from there on foot. Local minibuses ply up the winding road to the edge of the crater.

2000 sq km/800 sq mi of the Changbai Shan range are set aside as a biosphere reservation. This is the home of ginseng and the Manchurian tiger, of which several are living wild in the region. The volcano, which is an **island of cold**, is home to an endemic flora. The deciduous forests around it are settled on the Chinese side too by Koreans. The way to the volcano passes their villages with their thatched peasant houses and mostly very recent Catholic churches. It's almost possible to imagine being in some rural part of Europe. Winter visitors to Changbai Shan can also take the opportunity to ski.

! *Baedeker* TIP

Water and wine

Wine is cultivated in the province of Jilin. Investigating the shops around Changbai Shan will soon turn up a quite drinkable example, perhaps to be enjoyed at a small evening picnic on the pebbles beside the mountain stream that gushes from the waterfall through the village under Baitou Shan.

 VISITING CHANGBAI SHAN

GETTING THERE

A visit is best handled by booking a package arrangement from a travel agent at home; in China, the travel office counters in hotels can help. Access is easiest via Yanji in the eastern part of Jilin province, which has a railway station and an airport.

WHERE TO STAY

▶ **Mid-range**
Mount Changbai Cuckoo Villa
Tel. 04 33/574 6099 Fax 04 33/574 60 08. A nice place to stay in the hotel complex around Baitou Shan is Mount Changbai Cuckoo Villa (Changbai Shan Dujuan Shanzhuang).

Changsha

Province: Hunan   **Population:** 2.5 million
Altitude: 30–300 m/100–1000 ft

The capital of the province Hunan is on the Xiang Jiang, one of the largest tributaries of the Yangtze. It mainly attracts tourists from China itself as it forms the last stop on a political pilgrimage taking in nearby birthplaces of Mao Zedong and his long-time adversary Liu Shaoqi.

Western tourists rarely come here but the splendid provincial museum is a genuine attraction. In addition it is possible to book a number of worthwhile day-trips from here, including visiting the home of Mao's family.

What to see in Changsha

The provincial museum is regarded as one of the finest and best-known museums in China and is mostly dedicated to one spectacular archaeological relic: the **grave of Mawangdui**. This is the name of the excavation in the north of Changsha, over which the provincial museum was built. The painstakingly reconstructed grave of a local prince, his wife and their sons, who died between 186 and 160 BC, was opened in stages from 1970. Among those things which came to light were silk fabrics with wonderful embroidery, statues of servants, toys, bronze mirrors, more than 700 lacquer items with elegantly decorative patterns, manuscripts written on silk and the remains of 150 different foodstuffs. One of the giant sarcophagi is also on exhibit along with the **mummified body of a woman** in its air-tight chamber. The two »flying robes«, which were probably banners for the cortege, are reproductions of the originals. Their mythological paintings describe the path of the soul to the heavenly beyond. At the top are the moon and the moon toad along with the sun and its crow. Other burial finds are displayed on the first floor, including **funerary statues from the Tang period**. All the signs and labels are in English. Opening times: 9am–5pm Tue–Sun and on public holidays.

★ ★
Provincial museum (Hunan Sheng Bowu-guan)

⊕

At what was once the southeast corner of the vanished old town in Tianxin Ge Park some 250 m/275 yd of the city walls have survived. Atop the 13 m/43 ft wall (you can climb up at either end) is the tower-like **Tianxin Pavilion**. The whole section is floodlit in the evenings.

City walls and Tianxin Ge Park

The broad, forested mountain of Yuelu Shan, across the river in the west of the city, is the locals' favourite **leisure spot**. The summit is accessible by cable-car and features various restaurants and some temples. Halfway up, **Lushan Si**, founded in AD 268, is the oldest

Yuelu Shan

Changsha Map

Station

Chezhan Lu

①

Wuyi Dadao

Jiefang Donglu

Remmin Lu

②

Bayi Lu

Yingpan Donglu

Yuejin Hu

Liuyang

Nianjila Hu

Zoo

Gongnong Lu

Shaoshan Lu

Shaoshan Lu

Wenyi Lu

Jiefang Zhonglu

Martyrs' Park

Provincial Museum

Jingbin Lu

Remmin Lu

Nan Dalu

Dongfeng Lu

Bayi Lu

Wuyi Dadao

Stadium

Qingshuitang

Jiucaiyuan Lu

Airport

North Station

Qingshuitang Lu

Furong Zhonglu

Furong Beilu

Jianxiang Zhonglu

Jianxiang Nanlu

Beizhan Lu

Duzheng Jie

Tianxin-Ge Park

Cai'e Lu

Zhongshan Lu

Cai'e Lu

Xiangchun Lu

Xuegong Jie

Huangxing Lu

Jiefang Xilu

Zhiji Jie

Chengnan Lu

Laodong Square

Wuyi Dadao

Zhongshan Lu

Pozi Jie

Huangxing Lu

Yanjiang Dadao

Yanjiang Dadao

Chuziang Jie

Xiangjiang

Fujia Dao

Xiangjiang

Xiangjiang Bridge

Juzi Zhou

0,25 mi
500 m

N ←

©*Baedeker*

↓ *Yuelu Shan*

Where to stay
① Hunan Furama Hotel   ② Lotus Hotel

⏵ VISITING CHANGSHA

WHERE TO STAY

► Luxury

① *Hunan Furama Hotel*
88 Bayi Lu
Tel. 07 31/229 88 88, fax 229 19 79
www.hnfurama.com
228 rooms. Good, manageable four-star hotel a short walk from the railway station

► Mid-range

② *Lotus Huatian Hotel*
176 Wu-yi Da Dao
Tel. 07 31/440 18 88
Fax 446 51 75
269 rooms. Large four-star establishment belonging to the Huatian chain. Close to the station and cheaper than it looks.

Buddhist temple in the region. The **Yuelu Academy** at the foot of the mountain facing the city was founded in AD 976 and is famed throughout the land. It was regarded as one of the finest academies in ancient China. At the end of the 12th century it counted Zhu Xi, among its teachers, the most important philosopher of the neo-Confucian movement. The present buildings date from the Manchu period and are now part of Hunan University.

Around Changsha

About 120 km/75 mi south of Changsha **the »Holy Mountain of the South«** rises up to 1290 m/4230 ft. Of the five holy mountains this is the least spectacular. Nevertheless its importance is not to be underestimated. This is manifested in the presence of several Buddhist and Daoist temples and monasteries. It is a popular tourist attraction, especially in summer. Day-trips to Heng Shan can be arranged in Changsha. The »Grand Temple of the South Mountain«, **Nanyue Da Miao** is the main temple in which sacrifices to the mountain were made as part of the state religion. It is situated at the foot of the mountain in the village of Hengshan (also called Nanyue Qu). The combination of a southern Chinese roof (distinguished by its sharply upward-pointing corners) with yellow tiles marking the temple out as an imperial institution is rare. From the temple, it is possible to climb the mountain on foot. Allowing for a few rests along the way, the ascent to the summit **Zhurong Feng** and back can be expected to take some ten hours. As an alternative for those not wishing to travel on foot, there are motorbike taxis on offer and a cable-car which runs from halfway up almost as far as the summit.

✱ **Heng Shan**

In 1893, Shaoshan, 90 km/56 mi southwest of Changsha, saw the birth of a peasant boy, who was later to go down in world history: **Mao Zedong**. During the Cultural Revolution, at the high-point of the personality cult around the Great Chairman, his childhood home

Shaoshan and Huaminglou

became a place of pilgrimage for millions of Red Guards, and a railway line had to be built specially to carry them all there. Nowadays most tourists visiting Shaoshan book a day trip in Changsha at any of the travel agents opposite the railway station or from their hotel. Bus tours cost 150 yuan per person. These trips also stop at Huaminglou along the way, which was the birthplace of the former president, **Liu Shaoqi** (1898–1969), whom Mao toppled during the Cultural Revolution. At both places the tours visit the clay huts where they grew up and there is plenty of political memorabilia on sale. Liu's home, tellingly, is a reconstruction, as the original fell victim to the Cultural Revolution too. One attraction in Shaoshan is a trip by chairlift to the 519 m/1703 ft **»Shaoshan summit«** (Shao Feng, 3 km/2 mi southwest of Mao's birthplace) and its cluster of temples. Both Mao and Liu now have museums dedicated to them. Caution: Shaoshan station is not actually in the village of Shaoshan; having arrived there it is necessary to go another 5 km/3 mi, by minibus for example.

! **Baedeker** TIP

Breathing country air

In Shaoshan various farms offer accommodation – one good way to discover a little more about rural life in China. Although Shaoshan now thrives primarily on tourism, its fields are still carefully tilled.

✶✶ Chengde

He 25

Province: Hebei
Altitude: 200 m/650 ft

Population: 350,000

256 km/159 mi northeast of Beijing by train lies Chengde, known in ancient literature as Jehol. It has the most important imperial buildings in China outside Beijing itself. Until the end of the 17th century it was just a village, but in the 18th it became the summer and autumn residence of the Manchu emperors. With its impressive buildings – the palace, the palace gardens and the »Eight Outer Temples« – it testifies to that final heyday of Confucian China, as it once again could be regarded as a world empire for several decades. The historic legacy has been declared a UNESCO World Heritage Site.

Since the 1990s the present town has massively developed into a secondary capital for the northern part of Hebei province – although not for the best, unfortunately. To the north and east, around the monasteries, the town has retained its **village-like character**, though. The neighbouring mountains are forested and uninhabited. The monastery buildings still create their original effect in such surroundings.

▶ VISITING CHENGDE

GETTING THERE

A tourist special runs along the line from Beijing to Chengde every day at 6.30am, arriving at noon. The same train starts its return journey at 1.30pm. If you get the chance, try to spend a whole day in the town in order to see not only the palace, but its gardens and the surrounding temples. The palace is at the northern edge of the town centre. To get to the monasteries and between them, cycling is a good way to travel. If you take a taxi, have it wait while you are in the monasteries. Taxis have fixed fares for the journeys. Bicycles can be hired from alongside the Yunshan hotel. More information is available from the travel agent Beifang Lüxingshe, Tel. 03 14/205 84 98.

WHERE TO STAY

▶ Mid-range

Yunshan Hotel (Yunshan Fandian)
6 Nanyuan Donglu

Tel. 03 14/205 58 88
Fax 205 58 85
The standard hotel for foreign tourists: 440 rooms in a small high-rise building at the south of the city centre near the river. The restaurant in the hotel's garden is nice in the summer.

Baedeker recommendation

① *Qiwanglou Hotel*
Tel. 03 14/202 43 85
Fax 202 19 04. Near the main entrance to the summer palace stands the small palace of Qiwang Lou. From here the emperor would once gaze out upon his subjects as they tilled their fields. In 1984 an altered version of the building was constructed on the old site which now serves as a three-star hotel. It is quite the nicest place to stay in Chengde.

The early Manchu emperors journeyed every year in September the 350 km/220 mi north from Beijing to the hunting ranges of Mulan, accompanied by musketeers, ministers, concubines and close relatives, all in all a couple of thousand people. Along the way, they stayed in 21 »journey palaces«. One of these was situated in Chengde. The terrain, with its wooded mountains, abundant waterways and some curiously shaped rocks, was delightful. The much-travelled **Kangxi Emperor** considered that here the specialities of both north and south were beautifully combined.

Out of the past

Diplomatic and practical considerations persuaded the Kangxi Emperor to expand the journey palace into a full-scale residence. The dynasty had diplomatic obligations to the neighbouring Mongol tribes, who had helped the Manchus in the conquest of China. These were best served by open-air banquets and joint hunting expeditions. The tented villages, which were commonly set up on the steppes, were hardly suitable for the purposes of running an empire, though. In Chengde the two objectives could be combined perfectly. **Building**

From journey palace to royal residence

began in 1703. The temple buildings, apart from two older complexes, followed after 1755. They too were built for diplomatic reasons. Firstly the Mongols who the Chinese were seeking to ally to the empire were **devotees of Lamaism** (which the Manchus would make their own court religion in the 18th century). Secondly, similar considerations also applied to the Tibetans themselves, who had also come under Manchurian dominion after 1720. Here amid the imitations of their own sacred items, it was hoped the ambassadors from Mongolia and Tibet would feel at home while still acknowledging Manchu sovereignty.

! *Baedeker* TIP

A glimpse of the Great Wall
On the journey from Beijing to Chengde it is worth taking in the view through the train window. The mountainous landscape is varied and gorgeous and there are many villages to see. About half-way along at the Gubeikou Pass, it is also possible to see the Great Wall of China atop the hills on either side of the line.

After the **Jiaqing Emperor** died in Chengde in 1820, its facilities ceased to be used on a regular basis. His death was seen as a bad omen, many of the monasteries were abandoned and after 1912 parts of the palace buildings fell into ruin.

Imperial Summer Palace (Bishu Shanzhuang)

🕐
Opening hours:
In summer
7am–6pm, otherwise 7.30am–5pm

A crenellated wall surrounds the »**Mountain Resort for Escaping Summer Heat**« (Bishu Shanzhuang). Covering an area of 5.6 sq km/ 2.2 sq mi it is the largest garden palace in China, although four-fifths of the grounds are natural, forested hill terrain. The main things to see are the palace buildings in the south and the adjoining **pond garden**, fashioned in the southern Chinese style. Another area comprises a grassy plain with trees to the north of the ponds. The best route to see everything, for which you need to set aside half a day, starts at the main gate in the south, then leads through the main palace and through the pond section before taking in part of the grassland to reach the eastern gate. Alternatively, you could go back a different way through the pond garden and exit through the south gate again. If more time is available it may be possible to walk further and take in some of the attractions in the hills.

★
Main palace

The main part of the palace, consisting of five main buildings with courtyards in front of them and some ancillary buildings has survived fully intact and mainly functions nowadays as a museum for the furniture and art treasures of the imperial court. The architecture emulates the awe-inspiring monumentality of the Forbidden City in Beijing and also anticipates the later summer palace of Yihe Yuan. The esprit evoked here is at its most apparent in the **throne room**. This is known as the »Hall of Modesty and Earnestness«. All the buildings are covered with grey-black, unglazed tiles. There are no elevated marble terraces. The floor plan evinces **strict axial symmetry** but the manageable proportions of the airy and generously sized courtyards make for a pleasing impression.

The outer **main gate**, guarded by stone lions, opens in the south of the palace walls and is aligned with the compass axis of the palace itself. The first inner courtyard inside the gate is lined by reception buildings and guardhouses. Keep going straight ahead through the Noon Gate (Wu Men) into a second courtyard. A pair of bronze lions flank what is called the Inner Noon Gate.

Main entrance

The first of the main courtyards is dominated by the »**Hall of Modesty and Earnestness**« dating from 1754. The name is in keeping with the substance of the hall, not its external appearance. The throne room in Beijing is big enough to encompass four halls the

Throne room

Chengde *Map*

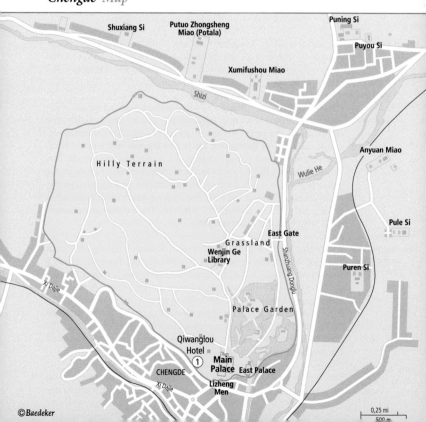

Shuxiang Si
Putuo Zhongsheng Miao (Potala)
Puning Si
Puyou Si
Xumifushou Miao
Shizi
Hilly Terrain
Anyuan Miao
Wulie He
Pule Si
East Gate
Grassland
Wenjin Ge Library
Shanzhuang Donglu
Puren Si
Xi Dajie
Palace Garden
Qiwanglou Hotel
① Main Palace   East Palace
CHENGDE
Xi Dajie
Lizheng Men

0,25 mi
500 m

©Baedeker

size of this. The pillars are unpainted and are made, like all the other wooden elements, from precious nanmu wood, which emits a fine fragrance in damp weather. The wooden wall panel behind the throne itself is ungilded, even though quite ordinary temples gild their altars with gold leaf. The **relief carvings** of the panel also include no dragons, instead showing hard-working subjects in an idealized landscape tilling the fields and weaving. This is an idealization but also represents a **reminder of political responsibility**. Other ornaments like the exquisite carvings of the windows and panels, display swastikas and stylized Shou characters, symbolizing a wish for »thousand-fold happiness« and »a life lasting ten thousand years«.

Studio of Four-fold Knowledge

The name of the small hall that follows, the »Studio of Fourfold Knowledge«, is a reference to the **art of diplomacy**. This encompasses knowledge of the requisite flexibility, the right amount of toughness, the appropriate openness and the relevant secrecy. This is where the emperor would dress for audiences in the throne room and receive ambassadors from his vassal peoples and other dignitaries for informal sessions rather than official meetings.

Hall of Longevity

The long »Hall of Longevity« to the north completes the »outer chambers«, the parts of the palace dedicated to state business. It had various functions in the past but is mainly used for a museum display of **porcelain**.

Residential chambers

Beyond a gatehouse (includes rooms for the accommodation of eunuchs) come the residential areas of the palace. The building that was home to the emperor himself occupies a place at the centre. Its name, the **»Hall of Refreshing Mists and Waves«** refers to the location of the summer palace between the mountains and ponds. The rooms include a throne room in the middle, a meeting room in the east along with a room for Buddhist meditation and a heated living-room and bedroom in the west The interior has been maintained in its original state or restored to match it. The neighbouring courtyards were home to the empresses.

»The Wonderland of the Misty Mountains«

The last of the halls in the north is a two-storey building which was used for leisure and amusement. On the ground floor there was a small theatre stage, while the upper floor provides a chance to look at the moon, into the palace garden or at the »wonderland of the misty mountains«, whence the building gets its poetic name. Instead of a wooden stairway, the upper floor is accessed via **an artificial rocky hill**. It is the only piece of architectural playfulness that the builders allowed themselves. The ground floor now displays some of the state gifts received by the emperor.

»The Rustling of Pines in All the Valleys«

Leaving the palace through its rear gate one can see the five halls on the right which are the oldest in the whole complex. The name applies to the main building, erected in 1708 for the **offices and study of the Kangxi Emperor**, who was advised here by his trusted staff while enjoying the view of the pond garden and the treetops.

A separate gate provides direct access from outside to the eastern palace complex, where the great birthday receptions took place and the palace theatre once stood. The theatre burned to the ground in 1945, so that only the stone pedestal of the building remains. The halls at the northern end have been reconstructed. **Eastern palace**

✳ ✳ Palace garden

The **landscaped ponds** of the palace gardens cover some 60 hectares/ 150 acres. The artificial landscape was laid out in the early 18th century and transports the scholars' gardens and landscaped scenes of southern China into the northern Chinese summer residence. The well-travelled Kangxi Emperor would have recognized the scenery emulated here from his own observations. All over the gardens there are **picturebook examples of Chinese exoticism**, full of spiritual variations between verdant green and shimmering, rippling waves, with pavilion roofs peeking between rustling willows, views of the distant hills and pagodas. Indeed when the wind is still, the idyll is replicated by the reflection in the surfaces of the ponds. The emperors who commissioned the work were already delighted with the result. Both the Kangxi and Qianlong Emperors made lists of their 36 favourite scenes at the summer palace. Most of them were to be found in the pond gardens. Opening times: daily till sunset (visitors may remain inside till later). ⏲

The palace garden of the Kangxi Emperor

Grassland and hills

North of the pond-garden area it is a mere step from southern China to the **fringes of Mongolia**. Kept clear of thick vegetation in order to hold the knightly tournaments which entertained host and guest alike, the grassland acts as a gardener's bow to their steppe tradition. It served as pasture for horses and a field for equestrian sports, wrestling and archery contests. Deer were introduced as well – an animal which symbolizes wealth and long life. The grassland is nevertheless not very steppe-like in appearance. Much of it is taken up by the **»Garden of Ten Thousand Trees«** (Wanshu Yuan), an open grove kept clear of undergrowth.

Yurt village To pay due reverence to the Mongolian guests, the emperors kept a yurt village in the northwest part of the grassland. The central yurt – a special construction of generous proportions – was where the emperor himself would live when sporting competitions, acrobatic performances or picnics were called for. He would also hold audiences here. In 1793 a **British delegation under Lord Macartney** was also received here. They were probably the only Europeans ever to see the mountain resort in its golden age. For their second audience, the delegation were invited to the throne room of the palace, where they kowtowed three times to the aged ruler on the occasion of his 82nd birthday. The yurt village can still be seen to this day – although, albeit not the genuine article. Nowadays it serves as a hotel and the yurts themselves are concrete imitations.

> ! **Baedeker TIP**
>
> **Panoramic photography from the Potala**
>
> From the Potala Temple, the imposing Putuo Zongsheng Miao, there is a fantastic view of the walls enclosing the residence. This does require a certain amount of time – some two hours – since the only way to get there is on foot. Walk north through the palace gardens along the hill paths to the outer wall. In a few places it is possible to climb up to the top. The top of the wall is wide and easy to walk along. Particularly in late autumn or winter, when the sun is low in the sky during the day, the light is perfect and the view of the inner-sanctum buildings with their gold roofs is magnificent.

Pagodas In the northern section of the grassland a towering pagoda can be seen for miles around. It is an octagonal structure of nine storeys rising to a height of 65 m/213 ft. It is the only remaining building work from an old **Buddhist temple**, of whose halls nothing remains but the foundations.

The Wenjin Ge library Between the grassland and the hills, somewhat apart from the other buildings, stands the imperial library of Wenjin Ge, built in 1774. The main building has two storeys and occupies the northern side of a walled garden with ponds that provided water for quenching fires It was modelled on the most famous of all the private libraries in

China, the **Tianyi Ge in Ningbo**. Among the items stored here was one of only seven examples of the massive text compendium, Siku Quan-shu, »The complete writings of all four literary genres«, including canonical scripts, philosophy, history and literature in a tome edited on the instructions of the emperor himself.

The vast remaining area of the estate is delineated by four valleys running through hills rising up to 180 m / 560 ft above the level of the grassland. The formerly numerous **pleasure palaces and hermitages** have mostly disappeared. Among the possible destinations for walks through the hills are the pavilions at the summits, which are particularly worth visiting on days with a clear view. Be careful, though. The northwest gate, which looks like it should offer a route to the Potala temple, is always closed and be aware too that it is easy to get lost in the hills. It may not be too hard to find a way back but it can still take long enough for you to miss your train. The railway timetable is not altogether reliable either. **Hills**

»Eight Outer Temples« (Wai Ba Miao)

The austerity and frugality which distinguished at least the external appearance of the palace itself did not apply to the surrounding temple monasteries. On the contrary, when it came to the religion and diplomacy of the mighty empire, glittering pomp was the order of the day. Such an abundance of religious buildings, built here as part of an **ambitious state project** can be found nowhere else in China. Of course not all of the temples are **monuments to religion and diplomacy**, some are memorials to war. Here was where the Qing dynasty celebrated their victorious campaigns in central Asia. Almost all the monasteries, regardless of the style of building, practise Tibetan style Buddhism (Lamaism). They were designed to accommodate ambassadors from various central Asian vassal peoples (primarily Mongolians) who followed the Tibetan form of Buddhism. The larger monasteries are now once again occupied by a small number of Tibetan Buddhist monks.

The term »Eight Outer Temples« was in use even at a time when they numbered as many as twelve (although four have disappeared now). The expression comes from administrative sources, i.e. from the official department which dealt with China's foreign relations. Administratively speaking it was not the number of actual buildings that counted but the institutions, which did indeed number eight. The other four temples were not necessarily under control of the foreign office but were **subsidiary monasteries**. The »Outer« part of the name refers to the Great Wall, as Chengde lies beyond the wall as seen from Beijing. **Name**

The temples are described in the following section in the order they can be reached from the town itself and in the order it is easiest to visit **Tours** them all, i.e. east of the Wulie He river from south to north and west of the river from east to west. The most interesting temples are those of Puning Si and Potala, followed by the Xumifushou Miao and Pule Si.

Puren Si   The beautiful and carefully restored »**Temple of Universal Charity**« was built in 1713 as a gift from Mongolian nobles to the Kangxi Emperor for his 60th birthday. The emperor had of course given support to the project and it was simultaneously to be seen as a return gift to the Mongolians. The complex is in purely Chinese style and some of the statuary dates back to the original opening, although some has been added during restoration. At the moment the monastery is closed to the public.

✳
Pule Si   The »**Temple of Universal Happiness**« was built by the Qianlong Emperor in 1766/67 for Dzungarian ambassadors. Its location on the slopes of Sledgehammer Peak gives it a marvellous view. The **entrance hall** features iconography following the Chinese pattern. The magnificent figures of the Four Heavenly Kings are particularly expressive. The statuary decoration of the **main hall** is also impressive. On the left is the Medicine Buddha adopting the meditation gesture, in the middle is Shakyamuni in the mudra of touching the earth, on the right is Amitabha making the wish-granting gesture, while each
Round hall ▶   of the sides has four Buddha-like bodhisattvas. The dominant building of the monastery can be seen for quite a distance around it. The round hall stands on a high square terrace and features a double-eaved imperial-yellow roof. The building makes an appropriate home for its contents, a three-dimensional, palatial **mandala**, with a yab-yum figure at its centre: a wrathful god in a position of copulation with his yogini. The group is an unusual monument to Tantrism and unparalleled anywhere in China. The **auxiliary halls** of the monastery have an exhibition of tantric religious art. Opening times: 9am–6pm daily (admissions until 5.30pm), closes 5pm in winter (admissions until 4.30pm).

✳
Sledgehammer
Peak   The path up to the monastery passes the lower station of a **cable-car**. This takes passengers up to the mountain summit, which is dubbed Sledgehammer Peak (Qingchui Feng, Bangchui Shan) by dint of the unusual rock formation that tops it. In clear weather there is a superb view. It is also possible to hire ponies to ride to the top. Opening times: May–Oct. 7.30am–5pm daily.

Anyuan Miao   Only the highly imposing 27 m/30 yd main hall remains of the original buildings of the temple monastery. Its dark interior contains an **impressive statue of the Green Tara**, the most popular protective goddess in Tibet. She sits crowned on a lotus blossom against a background made up of a vast mandorla. Her right foot is stretched out over the edge of the lotus flower so that she is always ready to come and help. Opening times: 8am–5.30pm.

Death; riding a buffalo and wearing a prayer necklace of human skulls. The threatening figure in the middle is Mahakala ; considered the protector of Mongolia and portrayed here in an elephant skin as the protector of wisdom. On the left is the goddess Devi riding a wild ass and using a venomous snake as its reins.

The mandala formed by the Tibetan buildings is not easy to spot since the terrain here is so steep. It consists of 19 elements: the imposing Mahayana-hall in the middle represents Sumeru the world mountain. It is situated at the intersection of two axes, which form a cross defined by the four buildings at its ends, one at each point of the compass. These represent the **»four great continents«**, which surround the world mountain as islands in the world sea. Each one of these buildings is flanked by two smaller halls representing the »eight small countries (or continents or islands)«. Thus the total number of buildings is twelve. Alongside them are six other buildings, four of which are topped by stupas in the form of Tibetan bottle pagodas and mark the diagonals of the mandala; while the other two lie on the east-west axis on either side of the main hall and represent the sun and moon, the heavenly light sources that illuminate the world mountain.

The Tibetan part of the monastery

37 m/121 ft tall, the **»Hall of the Great Vehicle«**, with its six roofs and its storeys which taper towards the top, is most unusual looking. The name of the hall indicates here at the centre of the mandala that the kingdom of Buddha – Buddhadom – is attainable to all those who earnestly strive for it. An image of Guanyin stands there with a thousand arms ready to help. The mighty figure – 23.5 m/77 ft high atop a 27 m/89 ft pedestal – is the **largest wooden figure in the world**. It has a volume of some 120 cu m/4240 cu ft. There are actually 40 arms so that they need to be multiplied by 25 to come to the number of one thousand. Each hand holds a symbolic object.

Mahayana hall

The figure is flanked by two pious assistants, Sudhana and the daughter of the dragon king (Nagakanya), who worship Guanyin their teacher with their palms pressed together. Both of them are said – in terms of Buddhist mythology of course – to have gained enlightenment within their lifetimes, an encouragement to all those who still strive for this.

Baedeker TIP

Navel-gazing
For a small fee it is possible to climb the stairs of the Mahayana hall to arrive at the height of the giant Guanyin's navel. Here she can be seen in greater detail and from a much better perspective. The little extra effort is well worth it.

✱ Xumifushou Miao

What a greeting! In 1779 the sixth **Panchen Lama** offered to visit the Qianlong Emperor in his summer residence to congratulate him on his 70th birthday. The emperor had this enormous temple monastery crowned with golden roofs and topped by a pagoda built for the occasion. It is modelled on the Tashilhunpo Monastery in Shigatse, i.e. the residence of the Panchen Lama himself, although like many other such imitations among the vast world of Buddhist monasteries it differs markedly from the original. The **consecration in 1780** brought the phase of temple building to an end. Some of the pictures remain in their original form while others have been brought from other monasteries, from the palace, or are recent additions.

Gate, stele pavilion

A triple stone gate leads through the wall enclosing the complex into the outer courtyard. This is dominated by a huge stele pavilion **with the founding inscription of the monastery** in four different languages. A triple-arched honour gate covered in glazed tiles then leads into the main courtyard.

Red Palace and Throne Palace

The **main building of the temple** rises from a high granite pedestal. The three storey Red Palace is adjoined to the east (right-hand side) by the Throne Palace (Yuzuo Lou), although only the outer walls of that remain. The latter is where the emperor would retire when visiting the temple. As is common in Tibetan buildings, the Red Palace has a flat roof and small windows which illuminate the interior with

A small gift for a great guest: on the occasion of the visit of the Panchen Lama, the Qianlong Emperor welcomed him by building the Xumifushou Miao monastery

a mysterious half-light. At each corner there is a pavilion with a roof in the Sino-Tibetan style and a guarding figure inside.

The entrance to the Red Palace opens on to its south wing. This features modern **paintings of the Four Heavenly Kings**. In the rooms to the left and right there are 2811 small Buddha figures as well as several lifesize Buddhas in the Tibetan style. Seven gold-painted wooden figures on the top floor depict the seven manifestations of the Medicine Buddha.

South wing

Inside the inner courtyard of the Red Palace is the square Golden Hall, so called after its gilded, double-inclined, tent-like roof with dancing dragons on the joists. This too has three storeys and represents Sumeru the world mountain. **Tsongkhapa**, the great reformer of Tibetan Buddhism, can be seen on the lower floor along with Buddha Shakyamuni at the rear surrounded by the 18 luohan. Further along on the eastern side is the throne of the Panchen Lama. On the middle floor there is another image of Shakyamuni flanked by his two truest disciples.

Golden Hall

The middle of the ground floor of the north wing beyond the Golden Hall is occupied by Buddha Shakyamuni. Beside him there are some lovely figures of the Four Heavenly Kings and 16 (rather than the usual 18) luohan. The upper floor is dominated by the figure of an **Amitayus**, Buddha of long life. Going up another floor takes you into the rear part of the monastery on the roof of the Red Palace.

North wing

Northwest of the Red Palace is another adjoining building consisting of a pedestal in Tibetan style and a hall building in the Chinese vernacular. The latter has a double-inclined, gilded roof. This complex contains the **residential and reception rooms** of the Panchen Lama. The rooms are used nowadays for exhibitions.

Hall of Happiness and Dharma Joy

The building with the name which roughly translates as **»Source of All Dharmas«** is located on the main axis of the monastery up the slope behind the Red Palace. It once served as a residential block for high-ranking Tibetan mystics. It now has an exhibition of Buddhist art on view.

Wanfazongyuan Hall

A seven-storey pagoda decked with glazed tiles towers above the highest point at the end of the monastery's axis atop an octagonal pavilion. The reliefs on the pedestal depict eight Buddhas.

Pagoda

✱ ✱ Putuo Zongsheng Miao (Potala)

The most magnificent of all the temple monasteries is a miniature version of the **Potala Palace in Lhasa**. It has more than 50 Tibetan-style buildings spread over an area of 22 hectares/54 acres and does

not obey any axial symmetry. The group stretches up the hillside where it is dominated by the main building, arranged like its exemplar into a White Palace and the – in this case especially large – central Red Palace. Little remains of the original painted decoration in its original location, yet the religious works of art collected and sometimes reconstructed here still number nearly a thousand. The Qianlong Emperor had the complex constructed from 1767 to 1771 to impress and delight the vassals of the Qing empire, who in 1770 were invited to his 60th birthday celebrations and then to the 80th birthday of his mother a year later. In the **founding inscription** the emperor states that Tibet is the second home of Buddhism (after India) and the Potala Palace is the symbol of its rule. The building long stood in ruins but has been gradually restored since 1990.

⊙ Opening hours:
8am–6pm daily
(admission until 5pm),
8.30am–3.45pm in winter

Three works of architecture start the tour, the massive outer gate with its guarding lions, the stele pavilion for the imperial founding inscription and the subsequent inner gate, which already exhibits the Tibetan style with its dummy windows. The latter is flanked by two white elephants and is topped by five small stupas of differing designs and coloured to represent the five schools of Tibetan Buddhism.

Imperial founding inscription

A decorative gate in the Chinese style, covered with glazed tiles and topped by seven roofs, separates the main courtyard into a small section at the front and a larger space at the rear. Around it there are some 30 white **stone buildings in the Tibetan style** with typical flat roofs and dummy windows, mostly two or three storeys high and irregularly spaced. Paintings are displayed in some of the restored halls. Most of the buildings were used as accommodation for a community once numbering more than 300 monks, although some were used for other purposes.

Main courtyard

The White Palace at the northern end of the main courtyard adjoins both sides of the dominating Red Palace and makes up the 18 m/59 ft pedestal upon which the latter is built. Four pavilions top the roof. The tall east wing of the White Palace provided accommodation for Emperor Qianlong when he visited the monastery. The Red Palace has a floor plan 59 m/65 yd square at the bottom. Its slightly inward tapering walls are decorated with glazed reliefs of the Buddha Amitayus, who as the **symbol of long life** fitted perfectly with the original reason for the monastery's existence. Only the three upper storeys of the Red Palace are real. Underneath – as is the case with the lower part of the White Palace and in spite of its dummy windows – it is quite solid.

White and Red Palaces

In the nature of the architectural mandala with the world mountain Sumeru in the centre, the Red Palace surrounds a Golden Hall, a

Golden Hall

← *Impressively beautiful: the »little Potala« of Putuo Zongsheng Miao*

deep pavilion seven bays wide in the Chinese building style. Its double-eaved roof with gilded copper tiles covers the Red Palace itself and as the holy of holies, it represents a goal to which all can aspire. Now that restoration has been completed, the interior of the hall once more exhibits its former splendour. The cloisonné stupas are particularly conspicuous, along with the implements of worship on the altar tables, the central **shrine with its statue of Buddha** (thought to represent Shakyamuni or Maitreya), the carved wooden »coral trees« which flank it, the amitayus figures at the sides, the **throne for the Dalai Lama**, which has never been used, the twelve Thankas that hang from the internal pillars, the coffered ceiling with two imperial dragons and its largest work of art, an embroidered wall-hanging 10 m/33 ft high and 3 m/10 ft wide, depicting, among other thing, various Buddhas, bodhisattvas, the 18 luohan and the four guardians of heaven.

Galleries   In the rooms of the Red Palace, which surround the inner courtyard, there are a large number of Tibetan Buddhist artworks on display. In the south wing among the things to see are the five **patriarchs of Tibetan Buddhism** The west wing has five green Taras, while the north wing has Buddhas of the Three Ages, nine amitayus figures and the 18 luohan. The east wing features five bodhisattvas.

Roof   The view from the roof of the Red Palace counts as one of the highlights on any stay at Chengde. From here there is a view encompassing the entire complex and the neighbouring temple monasteries. In the distance it is possible to see Anyuan Miao, Pule Si and Sledgehammer Peak. The pavilion in the northwest corner of the roof, raised above the roof level by an additional pedestal, forms the **highest point of the entire monastery complex**. Its name, written on a dragon-ringed sign in the calligraphy of the Qianlong Emperor, effectively means »**Buddha's mercy extends to all«**. In the eastern counterpart to this hall, the pavilion on the roof of the White Palace, there is a bronze figure of the wrathful protector goddess Devi riding on a wild ass and wielding a sword.

> **Baedeker TIP**

Sunday is market day
On Sundays the usually dry bed of the little river that runs between the three north-western monasteries and the palace wall is the venue for a large colourful market where you can buy spices, food, clothing and all other necessities of daily life.

Shuxiang Si   »**The Temple of the Manjushri Statue**« is named after the bodhisattva Manjushri. It was built in 1774/75 after the mother of the emperor had made a pilgrimage to the holy mountain of Wutai Shan; where there is a monastery of the same name. This monastery is not open to the public.

✴ Chengdu

Province: Sichuan
Altitude: 400 m/1300 ft

Population: 3.4 million
(11 million in the surrounding area)

The provincial capital of Sichuan is a true metropolis, self-confident, dynamic, but still a great place for idlers, strollers and gourmets. It is also the departure point and hub for the most densely populated province in China, which possesses more first-class attractions than many a whole country in Europe.

Chengdu is unjustly little known outside China. It has, though, retained an element of **Chinese exoticism** which has vanished without trace in many other places. This is due to such things as the people who serve tea in its tea gardens, its masseurs, shoe cleaners and even – no joking – professional ear-cleaners.

Despite its size it is easy to find your way in Chengdu. From the central Tianfu Square – with its museum of technology and the monumental statue of Mao in front of it – **four main roads** lead to the main points of the compass. A concentric system of roads encircles the city centre. One other aspect that aids navigation is the presence

Layout – finding your way

Titillating tickle: in Sichuan, the art of ear-cleaning is still carried out by professionals

▶ VISITING CHENGDU

GETTING THERE AND BACK, LOCAL TRANSPORT

There are direct flights to Chengdu's international airport from Amsterdam. The main railway station has services to Xi'an and Beijing and is located in the north of the city. Fast motorway coaches also run to Chongqing. Day trips can be booked from hotels. A cheaper alternative is to book at the bus stations, e.g. Xinnanmen Keyunzhan (east of the Traffic Hotel) and Ximen Qichezhan (northwest of the centre). From both these coaches run on day trips to Dujiangyan and the Qingcheng Shan. One useful bus service is the number 16 which runs from the railway station along the city's north-south axis to another smaller station in the south. An underground railway is currently under construction.

Sichuan International Travel Service

65 Renmin Nanlu 2-duan
Tel. 028/88 89 88 04
Mobile tel. 136 08 08 60 20
Fax 028/86 08 72 00
hezhongwen@hotmail.com
If Mr He Zhongwen, who owns the above mobile telephone number, is not available ask for Amei Chen. From here it is possible to book all kinds of Sichuan tours and day trips as well as journeys to Tibet.

THEATRE

Shufeng Yayun

In the culture park next to the temple monastery of Qingyang Gong
Tel. 028/87 76 45 30
www.shufengyayun.com
Variety with typical Sichuan stagecraft: operatic arias, folk music, puppet shows, mysterious and enchanting

Steaming and bubbling to satisfy customers' appetites: cookshop in Chengdu

masque theatre and other amazing performances. It is possible to order a massage for during the show. Performances daily at 8pm.

WHERE TO EAT
► Moderate
① Ba Guo Bu Yi
8/19 Guangfuqiao Beijie
Tel. 028/85 09 58 88
One of the most renowned spots in town, a magnet for gourmets. The illustrated menu is useful.

② Chen Mapo Doufu
141 Qingyang Zhengjie (opposite the provincial museum)
Tel. 028/87 31 72 16
An institution, »Pock-marked old Chen tofu« – allegedly referring to the wife of the restaurant's founder – has been served here since 1862. It is a classic dish, as tender as it is spicy but there are of course many other Sichuan dishes on the menu. Branches in other parts of town.

③ Huangcheng Laoma
20 Qintai Lu
Tel. 028/86 14 85 10
Specialist for Sichuan hotpot – fresh ingredients in a fiery stew. Handily located directly to the east of the Qingyang Gong temple monastery, it has a great ambience.

► Inexpensive
④ Longchaoshou
6 Chunxi Nanlu
Tel. 028/86 67 86 78
Dim sum Sichuan style. Dim sum is ordered from the menu and you can enjoy a sequence of delightful delicacies that you will not want to end. The tiny portions mean that you can delight in it almost as long as you like. Upstairs there are elegant dining rooms featuring live music, while downstairs it is more folksy, noisy and dirt cheap.

WHERE TO STAY
► Luxury
① Crown Plaza Hotel
31 Zongfu Jie
Tel. 028/86 78 66 66
Fax 028/86 78 97 89
www.ichotelsgroup.com
434 rooms. Large modern hotel in the centre with non-smoking rooms and swimming pool

► Mid-range
② Amara Hotel
2 Taisheng Beilu
Tel. 028/86 92 22 33
Fax 028/86 92 23 23
http://chengdu.amarahotels.com
232 rooms. Very sleek new establishment with open-air pool and city-centre location.

► Budget
③ Sam's Guesthouse
130 Shaanxi Jie
(am Rongcheng Hotel)
Tel. 028/86 11 83 22
samtour@yahoo.com
A popular place to stay for backpackers close to the central square and the park but still quiet.

④ Traffic Hotel (Jiao Tong Hotel, Jiaotong Fandian)
6 Linjiang Zhonglu
Tel. 028/85 45 10 17
Fax 028/85 44 09 77
www.traffichotel.com
134 rooms. Thanks to its cheap single beds in the three-bed rooms this has long been the place to go for backpackers. There are also inexpensive double rooms too, though.. There is a large selection of day trips and transport services on offer and the location on the river promenade is excellent.

Baedeker TIP

Too spicy?

For most »long noses« seeking to become connoisseurs of Sichuan cuisine, it is helpful to learn one Chinese phrase: Bú yào tài là, which means »not too hot please«. Anyone not making the request, though, will quickly be adopted as an honorary Sichuanese.

of the rivers that enclose the centre on three sides. The main river is the Fu He, although the Nan He nearer the centre is better known, particularly under its poetic epithet, the **»Brocade River«** (Jin Jiang). At the southern end of the city it provides quite a showcase district with promenades and tea gardens. In the evening the tea-gardens become beer-gardens, and anyone who doesn't feel like a drink can drift with the natives to the Chunxi Lu shopping paradise (to the east of the central square). To one side of this temple to consumerism, there is still a lot of the **traditional lifestyle**, including vegetable markets, cookshops and many other little shops.

Chengdu and its surroundings are steeped in history. As the traditional **centre of the Red Basin** it had already become the capital of the Shu kingdom by the 4th century BC. During those periods when the empire split, Chengdu would often become the capital of other independent kingdoms, as between 221 and 263, when the **»minor Han dynasty«** was based here. Even before then, the industry of its inhabitants, weavers of artistic silk fabrics, had given the town its nickname the »Brocade City«, a name it still bears to this day. Trading in salt and tea, the manufacture of paper and the printing of books all contributed to the wealth of the city over a span of centuries. Chengdu gained a second epithet in the 10th century when it was dubbed the »Hibiscus City«. The current city administration has recently been attempting to live up to that name again by extensive planting of the said flower.

Wuhou Ci Memorial Temple

Emperor and general

The well tended, quiet complex in the southwest of the city (Wuhou Ci Dajie; 2 km/1.5 mi from the centre) is a memorial to two important people, the general and politician: Zhuge Liang (181–234) and his master, Emperor Liu Bei (161–223) of the »minor Han (Shu-Han) dynasty«. Both are familiar to virtually of China's children as the novel, **»The Three Kingdoms«**, by Guanzhong Luo (various translations into English, e.g. »Three Kingdoms: a historical novel«by Moss Roberts) remains popular reading matter. The name of the temple refers to the more popular of the two: Zhuge Liang was ennobled as lord (hou) of Wuxiang. The relationship with Liu Bei is more concrete, as his grave is here in the temple. The history of the temple probably dates back to the year that the emperor died. The present buildings and their statuary date from 1672; although the clay figures have since been restored several times.

In honour of a general and politician: the memorial temple to Zhuge Liang

The outer gate leads into a large courtyard. On the right-hand side of it there is a stone pavilion, inside which is a pillar dating from the year 809 with an inscription celebrating Zhuge Liang. A further gate leads further inside to a second courtyard in which stands the first of the **main halls**. This is dedicated to the memory of Liu Bei, and contains a partly gilded statue depicting him. Each of the galleries down the sides of the courtyard has a row of fourteen coloured figures representing ministers (right) and generals (left).

Outer courtyard and memorial hall for Liu Bei

Beyond the inner gatehouse at the end of the complex stands the memorial hall for Zhuge Liang which also has an image of him flanked by his son (right) and grandson. Note the 1500-year-old bronze drum.

Memorial hall for Zhuge Liang

Beyond the memorial hall is a temple in honour of Liu Bei and his two oath-brothers. The hall was moved here in 1998. To the south-west, the way leads into a well-kept garden and on to Liu Bei's burial mound with six stone figures. Opening times: daily 8am–6pm, in summer to 9pm.

Burial mound

On the eastern side of the temple is one of Chengdu's new olde-worlde lanes of shops and snackeries, with craft shops, local specialities, tea-houses and a theatre.

Jinli

✱ Temple monastery of Qingyang Gong

Qingyang Gong is the most important Daoist sanctum in the city and possesses one of the proudest traditions in China. Its name, meaning **»Palace of the Black Billy-goat«** is explained by a legend. Lao Zi, the founding father of Daoism, was leading such a beast as his recognition-symbol when, on precisely this spot, he met a customs official, who, three years earlier, had persuaded him to write down the Daode Jing and thus bequeath his wisdom to the world. As they met again Lao Zi himself is said to have become a child once more, while the customs official, having read the work, had become a wise man.

Opening hours: 8am–6pm daily, in winter to 5.30pm

Chengdu Map

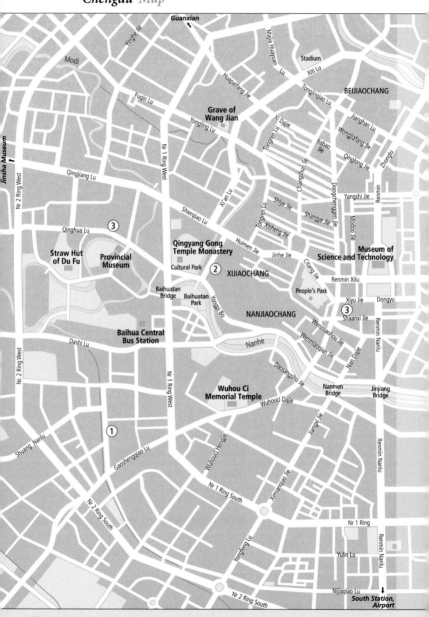

Guanxian

Yinghe Jie

Modi

Maija Huayuan Lu

Stadium

Xifu Lu

BEIJIAOCHANG

Huapaifang Jie

Fuqin Lu

Tongjingjiao Lu

Jianghan Lu

Grave of
Wang Jian

Xi Dajie

Wongjiafang Jie

Yongling Lu

Tongren Lu

Babao
Jie

Qinglong Jie

Zhongfu

Nr 1 Ring West

Xi'an Lu

Changshun Lu

Yangshi Jie

Qingjiang Lu

Shierqiao Lu

Shiye Jie

Shangye Jie

Dongchenggen Jie

Modao Jie

Renmin

Nr 2 Ring West

Jinsha Museum

Nr 2 Ring West

Qinghua Lu

③

Huimen Jie

Xisheng Jie

Museum of
Science and Technology

Straw Hut
of Du Fu

Provincial
Museum

Qingyang Gong
Temple Monastery

Jinhe Jie

Cheng Jie

Renmin Xilu

Cultural Park

②

XIJIAOCHANG

People's Park

Xiyu Jie

Dongyu

Baihuatan
Bridge

Baihuatan
Park

Yongan Bo

NANJIAOCHANG

③

Shaanxi Jie

Renmin Nanlu

Dashi Lu

Baihua Central
Bus Station

Nanhe

Wenmiaohou Jie

Wenmiaoqian Jie

Nan Dajie

Nr 2 Ring West

Nr 1 Ring West

Daosangshu Jie

Nanmen
Bridge

Jinjiang
Bridge

Wuhou Ci
Memorial Temple

Wuhouci Dajie

①

Jiangor Jie

Renmin Nanlu

Shuang Nanlu

Gaoshengqiao Lu

Wuhouci Hengjie

Nr 1 Ring South

Ximianqiao Jie

Nr 1 Ring

Renmin Nanlu

Nr 2 Ring South

Yongfeng Lu

Yulin Lu

Nr 2 Ring South

Nijiaqiao Lu

**South Station,
Airport**

Where to stay

① Crown Plaza Hotel ② Tianfu Sunshine ③ Sam's Guesthouse ④ Traffic Hotel

North Station
Changhuo Jie
Renmin Beilu
Jinhuo Jie
Jiefang Lu
Nr 1 Ring North
Zoo,
Panda Breeding Research Station
LIANGJIAXIANG
Ma'an Lu West
Ma'an Lu North
Ma'an Lu East
Caojia Xiang
0,25 mi
500 m
©Baedeker
Jianshe Lu North
Manjushri
Monastery
Fuhe
Bei Dajie
Caoshi Jie
Tongshun Jie
Zushu Jie
Wenwu Lu
Luguya Xiang
Desheng Lu
Taisheng
1-Hao
Bridge
Hongxing Lu
Jianshe Lu
Mengzhuiwan Jie
Nr 2 Ring East
Xiyulong Jie
Fangzheng Jie
Yusha Lu
Pleasure
Gardens
Zhonglie Jie
Qingyun Jie
San Huaishu Lu
Dongdachong Jie
Xinhong Lu
Xishubcheng Jie
Tidu Jie
2-Hao
Bridge
Shuanglin Lu
Renmin Donglu
Jie
Hongxing Lu
Dacisi Lu
Dongshuncheng Jie
Fuhe
Wangfing Jie
Xinhua
Park
Shuanglin Lu
Chunxi Lu
Shamao Jie
Nr 1 Ring East
Dong Dajie
YANSHIKOU
Dongfeng
Bridge
Dongfeng Lu
Shuangqiao Lu
Hongxing Lu
Dong Dajie
Jiaozi Jie
Shuinianhe Lu
Jinghua Lu North
Dongmen
Bridge
Niuwangmiao Jie
Shudu Donglu
Xinnanmen
Bridge
Xingbao Jie
Nr 1 Ring East
Yixinqiao Jie
Jinhua Lu South
Nr 2 Ring East
Xinnanmen
Busbahnhof
Xiaotianzhu Jie
Zhimin Lu
Longjiang Lu
Ximan Lu
Xinsheng Lu
Jiuyan
Bridge
Wanghua Jie
Hailanchi Lu
South
Taiping Nanjie
Wenhua Lu
Fuhe
NIUSHIKOU
Longzhou Lu
SICHUAN
UNIVERSITY
Jinxiu Lu
Kehua Lu
Wangjianglou
Park
Canguantang Jie
Jingjusi Lu
Lingshiguan Lu

The origins of the temple are lost in the mists of antiquity. The story that it was built in the Zhou era, 2300 years ago or more, is probably a pious legend. What is certain is that it was in existence in the mid-8th century when the **Tang emperor Xuanzong** took refuge from rebels here and received the poet prince Du Fu, who lived in a thatched cottage not far away. Most of the present buildings date from the 19th century. Their carved ornamentation indicates a distinct emphasis on vernacular styling, which was popular during the Manchu era. The temple monastery remains popular to this day. It is now run by Daoist monks.

! *Baedeker* TIP

Two temple festivals

At the first and second full moons of the lunar year, the temple monastery of Qingyang Gong and the neighbouring culture park attract large crowds: first to the lantern festival, with a lantern show, music, snack booths and much else, and then to the flower festival, for the 15th day of the 2nd month is regarded not only as Lao Zi's birthday, but is also the time when the local population come to the temple to buy spring flowers for their homes and gardens. Caged birds, antiquarian books and many more things are also offered for sale.

Flanked by a pair of stone lions and decorated with rooftop dragons, the **gatehouse** leads to the interior. A sword-bearing celestial general guards the gateway.

The **hall of the first courtyard** is dedicated to Lao Zi, who is depicted here wearing a golden robe as »**master of the primeval chaos**«, i.e. he is worshipped as the god of creation. At the rear of the building the Buddhist Guanyin is shown, here adopted into Daoism.

Pavilion of the Eight Trigrams

Along the axis of the complex, the next building is the octagonal two-storey »Pavilion of the Eight Trigrams«. Its name and form refer to the line symbols from the Book of Changes, which are said to represent the essence of all phenomena in the world and the changes it undergoes. Eight magnificent **columns with dragon reliefs** support the roof. Inside there is a statue of Lao Zi.

Hall of the Three Pristine Ones

Next comes the main hall, which covers an area of 1600 sq m/1900 sq yd and dates from the year 1669. Enthroned inside are the »Three Pristine Ones«, also translated as the »Three Pure Ones«, the highest gods of Daoism. To the side of them there is a row of twelve statues of heavenly figures. The biggest crowds, though, gather around the entrance. It is considered lucky to touch the two **cast bronze billygoats** there. One of them was put in place in 1723. It has just one horn that looks like a coxcomb and, according to Chinese symbolism, combines aspects of all the creatures in the Chinese calendrical cycle. The other animal has two horns as normal and has provided the first with company only since 1829.

Doulao Dian Hall

The next hall is dedicated to a star goddess. With her eight arms, she is ready to help anyone who asks for her aid. She sits between the

Queen Mother of the West, responsible for the domain of the dead, and the earth goddess, responsible for fertility. Outside the hall there are pictures of **14 constellation deities**. The hall dates back to the Ming period and is the oldest on the site.

The following courtyard is bounded on the right and left by three high terraces each with one building upon them. On the right, in the **»Pavilion of Childbirth«**, the mother of Lao Zi can be seen with the religion's founder as an infant, shown in a way that matches the meaning of the words »lao zi«, which not only mean »old master«, as they are usually understood, but can also mean »old child«. The image here plays on the latter showing the old master as a **baby with a beard**. In the pavilion opposite Lao Zi can be seen giving his teachings.

Three terrace courtyard

Two halls follow along the main axis of the complex. First all, the visitor will enter the Hall of the Jade Emperor, built only in 1995. His statue is on the upper floor. Downstairs, five so-called emperors are sitting. The three at the front are responsible for heaven, earth and water, while the two behind for regions of the northern firmament. In the last hall Li Yuan, the first emperor of the Tang dynasty, is depicted with his consort and son.

Hall of the Jade Emperor

Western Chengdu

One may be forgiven for being on tenterhooks. The old museum closed in 2002 and if the new one is as good as China's other newly built museums, it will be one of the city's top attractions. The **historical and archaeological collection**, built up since 1941, includes some 160,000 articles covering the Palaeolithic period till the revolutionary history of the 20th history. One of the periods well represented by excavated finds is the New Stone Age. Other important artefacts include bronze weapons from the Warring States Period plus grave goods and wall paintings from Han-period tombs. The generously proportioned building on Huanhua Nanlu about 700 m / 770 yd to the west of the Qingyang Gong, a 300-million-yuan project, was due to open in 2009.

Sichuan Provincial Museum

The thatched cabin where Du Fu is said to have spent four less than happy years is only a reconstruction from 1997, which you might want to see but can just as easily ignore. What is really nice, though, is the well tended park of the same name around it, where magnolias and camellias flourish. The park also has a **bonsai garden** and a good tea-house. The Du Fu study society also has its base here and it has an exhibition on the life and work of the poet set amid classical architecture. The high admission price means that the park is an attractive and very quiet oasis in the midst of the bustling city. Qinghua Lu West; 600 m/660 yd west of the provincial museum. Opening times: daily in summer, 7.30am–7pm, otherwise 8am–6.30pm.

✱ The thatched cottage of Du Fu (Du Fu Caotang)

🕐

General Wang Jian (847–918) made himself head of a short-lived empire after the end of the Tang dynasty. His realm was about the size of France. His burial chamber under a 15 m/50 ft hill in the northwest of Chengdu (Yongling Lu) is now open to the public. It is the only one in which a Chinese emperor was laid at ground level. Its main attractions are the warrior statues, the reliefs of dancers and musicians on the stone pedestal of the sarcophagus and the sculpture of the interred emperor in the rear burial chamber. In two halls further finds are on display, and the orchestra of the palace of the dead with its instruments is explained in detail, in English too. The avenue of stone figures is new. Beyond the burial mound is a tea garden. Opening times: daily 8.30am–5.30pm.

The tomb of Wang Jian (Wang Jian Mu, Yong Ling)

Jinsha, or »gold sand«, was the name of a village on the western outskirts. The site found fame in 2001 when prehistoric objects were discovered during engineering works. Soon the remains of an entire settlement were uncovered, the centre of a culture which lasted from the 13th to the 7th century BC. Today, everything has been spectacularly arranged for the visitor. Beneath an enormous roof, it is possible to climb down to the excavation site itself. Charred tree-trunks discovered in the process have been set up outside to create a black grove. The main destination, though, must be the museum building, which rises from the ground like a huge ramp. The exhibits include oracular bones, jade and bronze objects, gold masks, and, the climax of the exhibition, a gold sun-disc. Jinshalizhi Lu, opening times: daily 8am–5.30pm.

Jinsha Museum

✳ Manjushri Monastery (Wenshu Yuan)

The most popular Buddhist monastery in the north of the city attracts masses of people, and not only for prayers and incense offerings. About 100 monks live in the complex. It is the headquarters of the Buddhist societies of Chengdu itself and of the whole province of Sichuan and thus serves as a **religious centre** for millions of people. The gastronomic delights on offer here are of almost equal importance. A large tea garden adjoins the monastery to the east and a vegetarian restaurant is associated with it too.

A temple monastery has stood here for some 1600 years, but it was totally destroyed and then rebuilt in around 1700 As the **legend of the rebuilding** relates, a miracle had occurred: When the body of a Zen monk who had lived in the ruins was being cremated, the bodhisattva Manjushri appeared amid the smoke. Thus the sanctum was named after this lord of wisdom. Most of the present buildings date from around 1830. Since then the devotions in the temple have been directed whatever was popular. The statuary therefore has some de-

Legend and history

← *This nun at an altar in Wenshu Yuan is immersed in prayer*

cidedly syncretic aspects. Since the 1990s, lots more donations have been arriving so that new building work is starting to take shape.

In the gatehouse six guarding figures surround the obligatory pot-bellied Buddha. In the front are the generals Heng and Ha, followed by the **Four Heavenly Kings**. At the back there is an Amitabha. The first courtyard is shaded by ginkgos and overlooked by bell and drum towers, both with three-fold roofs. In the hall on the northern side the three great bodhisattvas are worshipped: Guanyin in the middle, Manjushri on the right and Samantabhadra on the left. All of them are feminine in appearance and sit on their familiar steeds. Two Daoist figures are given a lower ranking: the general and patron saint of soldiers Guan Yu has the shrine outside on the left and Wenchang, patron saint of scholars has the shrine opposite. The next courtyard has the actual main hall with its statue of the Buddha Shakyamuni sitting and teaching along with two of his closest disciples serving him. In the courtyard in front of the fourth hall there is a **sutra column** dating from 1873. It contains one of four Burmese jade Buddhas in the possession of the monastery. Inside, there is a piece of calligraphy by the Kangxi emperor dating from 1702, and the ordination terrace with painted images of the Buddha and bodhisattvas. Outside are the 18 luohan. The imposing **sutra hall** concludes the series of great halls. The roaring of the lion depicted within it, Manjushri's steed, embodies the call to enlightenment of Buddhist doctrine.

From the Peace Pagoda to the tea garden
East of the temple halls there are some new buildings. The most conspicuous among them is the Peace Pagoda, made entirely of bronze. Further along is the popular monastery tea-house, spread over pavilions and courtyards. This is turn leads to the excellent vegetarian restaurant. Opening times: daily 5.30am–9pm, temple halls 8am–6pm.

Wenshu Fang
Diagonally opposite the monastery a pseudo-old, car-free quarter seeks to entice the public with cookshops, tea-houses and souvenir shops.

✳ Other things to see in Chengdu

Panda breeding station (Xiongmao Jidi)
Nowhere in the world is so good a place to see pandas as here at the northeastern edge of Chengdu city (Xiongmao Dadao; 14 km/9 mi

A great panda that is still too small, in the incubator of the panda research station

from the centre). Nowhere else has had such success in breeding the animals. The park-like and very extensive grounds have **large free-ranging enclosures** for giant pandas and for the less well-known – and less endangered – red pandas or firefoxes. In summer, when it is too warm for animals attuned to mountain air, they mostly hang lazily in a fork between tree branches. They get more active when it is colder. If cubs are born, they can be viewed through glass windows in the breeding station. The site also has a museum, with information (also printed in English) about the natural habitat and distribution of the creatures as well as the history of research into them. Opening times: 8am–7pm daily, in winter till 6pm.

The three-storey »**river-view tower**« gives this popular park in the southeast of the city its name. The extensive estate is famous for having almost 150 species of bamboo growing in it, but the most attractive feature is its tea garden.

Wangjianglou Park

✳ Dujiangyan

60 km/37 mi northwest of Chengdu near the town of Dujiangyan is the core section of the what is the oldest **irrigation system** still in use today anywhere in the world. What sounds as if it might only be interesting for enthusiasts of the history of technology in fact has a lot to offer everybody. It has river and mountain scenery, an imposing temple complex and a lovely park. Dujiangyan has been declared a UNESCO World Heritage Site.

Around 250 BC, Li Bing, local prefect for the state of Qin, conceived, organized and implemented a project that, under his direction and that of his son, would be, for its time, a **gigantic and complicated**

History and conception

building work. The main factor that Li Bing had recognized was that precisely here, where the Min river enters the plain, the river waters could be utilized and distributed in such a way that a huge area of farmland could be supplied with water with no dependence on the irregular rainfall, with an extra bonus in the fact that the risk of uncontrolled flooding could also be diminished. In order to use the river water in this way, though, two problems needed to be solved. First it was necessary to cut through a hill and secondly the flow of water needed to be controlled. A third factor was that deposits of sand and silt carried by the waters needed to be disposed of on a regular basis. What the father-and-son team achieved back then thanks to their **inventiveness and engineering skill** as well as the mobilization of countless workers, can be still be seen and understood in the same place today, in spite of a number of modern rebuilding and extensions. The **earthquake of 12 May 2008** did not damage the irrigation complex, but did cause the associated temple building to partly collapse, and devastated the exterior elements. Restoration is planned to take two to three years. The following paragraphs describe first the elements on the plain and by the river, which were hardly damaged. As for the Two Kings' Temple, it is currently only possible to describe it as it was before the earthquake.

Elements of the system

At the core of the system is an island which functions like a dam. At its tip, called the »Fish Mouth«, it splits the Min river into two. In order to control the amount of water shunted out of the stream, large three-legged wooden structures would be placed into the waters – this is still done occasionally nowadays for the purposes of demonstration. In addition gravel-filled bamboo baskets several metres long and tubular in shape were attached to them to weigh them down and connect them together.

Lidui Park

A visit is best begun in the village itself with the beautifully tended and artistically planted Lidui Park. This occupies the spandrel between the Min river in the west and the main irrigation channel, known as Baopingkou (»Bottleneck Channel«). A fountain in the park sprinkles recumbent cast-iron cylinders, known as **sleepers**, which were laid on the canal bed in Ming times to mark the depth aimed for when unwanted deposits were removed each winter.

Dragon-taming Temple

In the far north of the complex, on an elevation immediately above the cutting, is the Dragon-taming Temple, the dragon in question being the mass of water. This structure was damaged in the earthquake. It contains a 2.9 m/10 ft high stone figure which was recovered from the riverbed in 1974. An inscription declares it to have been made in AD 168, and to represent Li Bing, the »father« of Dujiangyan. Visitors can leave the park westwards across a suspension bridge which today spans a now redundant side-channel. This leads to a tongue of land with a pavilion, from a view upstream is obtained. On the left there is another short channel, closed off by a modern sluice-gate, along which surplus water can flow back to the river if necessary. Further down one comes to the island where the river actually divides, namely at the »Fish Mouth Levee« at its northern end. The modern dam can be seen to the west of the »Fish Mouth«. To the east, another suspension bridge leads to the Two Kings Temple, beautifully situated on a wooded slope. On the »Fish Mouth Levee« and on the shore, there are a number of heavy wooden blocks weighted down with gravel-filled bamboo rolls. They were used to divert the water before the sluices were built.

This complex, which was badly damaged in the earthquake, is dedicated to the memory of Li Bing and his son. Once decorated with fine carvings, the buildings also include a temple stage.(opposite the main hall). Above and to the north, there is access to the Qinyan Lou (Qin Dam Tower), a belvedere decorated with pagoda-like roofs, which offers a panoramic view of the whole complex. The exit (or the rear entrance) is here.

Two Kings Temple

A victim of the 2008 earthquake: the Dragon-taming Temple

✳ Qingcheng Shan

On a day trip from Chengdu the ideal place to combine with Dujiangyan is the 1600 m/5250 ft Qingcheng Shan. Just 15 km/9 mi further westward, it is **one of the most important Daoist monastic mountains in China**. With its rocks, caves, waterfalls and thick forests it looks like it has come straight from a picture book, which is one reason it has been made a UNESCO World Heritage Site. The »Celestial Master« **Zhang Daoling** (34–156), who was a key figure in Daoism, is said to have worked here before he rose to heaven as an immortal. Nowadays rising to the heavens, albeit only a short part of the way, can be done by chair lift. It is not advisable to visit Qingcheng Shan at weekends. The monastic buildings were severely damaged in the 2008 earthquake, and some were destroyed. Sightseeing will only be possible to a limited extent, if at all.

Anterior Mountain
The climb begins near the **monastery of Jianfu Gong** at the foot of the mountain. If taking the cable-car, first take the ferry across the Yuecheng Hu lake. Climbing on foot up to the **Shangqing Gong Monastery** near the summit means ascending some 900 metres/3000 feet and four rest stops should be planned for. The most important stop comes after four km/2.5 mi at the **monastery of Tianshi Dong** (»Cave of the Celestial Master«). Beyond the aforementioned Shangqing Gong (20 minutes away from the upper station of the chair lift) it is only another 500 m/550 yd to the summit pavilion Laojun Ge (»Lao Zi Pavilion«), a pagoda-like building dating from 1992, which unfortunately is too big, although it does have a superb view.

Posterior Mountain
The region of the »Posterior Mountain« has only been added to the tourist trail since the 1980s. It is still less frequented than the »Ante-

A solemn atmosphere in Shangqing Gong monastery

rior Mountain«. Anyone with tired feet will be pleased to see there is a chair lift here too. There are fewer monasteries but much more in the way of nature. Access to the region is 15 km/9 mi from the »Anterior Mountain«. One nice round trip first heads through the **»Five Dragon Gorge«** (Wulong Gou) to Youyi Cun. From there head past the mountain station of the cable-car to a lake and then back through the Feiquan Gou Gorge (»Valley of the Flying Mountain Stream«). If visiting from Chengdu, the bigger distances involved mean it will be necessary to spend the night, ideally at the foot of the mountain not far from the the gorge in the **Buddhist monastery of Tai'an Si** or otherwise, if more comfort is desired, in Dujiangyan.

> **Baedeker TIP**
>
> **A night in the monastery**
>
> If the time is available, the chance to spend a night in a monastery – passably comfortable but definitely atmospheric, particularly in Tianshi Dong, which also has rooms with a bath. The advantage over Shangqing Gong is that it is not far to go in the morning to see the sunrise at the summit.

Until the mid-1980s ideas about early Chinese culture were mainly influenced by archaeological digs in the area of the Yellow River and its tributary the Wei He. Since then the picture has expanded enormously. This came about in spectacular fashion and a visit to the museum opened in 1997 40 km/25 mi north of Chengdu near the town of Guanghan makes it clear how. The discovery in question concerns the highly independent **Sanxingdui culture**, which has been dated to between 2800 and 800 BC. The most important finds were uncovered at the spot where the museum now stands. On display are some impressive bronze figures of birds and people with mask-like faces and large ears. The largest of these is 2.62 m/8.6 ft in height. There are also **items made of jade, ivory and pottery**. Opening times: 8.30am–5.30pm daily.

✱ Sanxingdui

⏱

Chongqing

Gj 31

Province: Self-governed city
Altitude: 200 m/650 ft

Population: 32 million
(including surrounding districts)

What would it be like if the whole of Austria were made a suburb of Vienna? The answer may be: something like Chongqing. Nominally Chongqing is a self-governing city covering an area of 82,400 sq km /31,800 sq mi with a population of 32 million people, which makes it the biggest city in the world (Austria covers 83,870 sq km/32,000 sq mi but has only 8.2 million people). Most of the area, though, consists of mountain terrain, villages and separate towns. The actual city has a population and area more like that of Berlin.

Chongqing is different from all the other big cities in China as it is not on level ground but amid hills and mountains at the confluence of the Jialing Jiang River and the Yangtze. In China it is known as the **only city with no cyclists**. Its irregular network of roads is oriented to the contours and the two great rivers which flank a peninsula 6 km/4 mi in length and up to 3 km/2 mi wide, upon which the city centre is built. The shortage of space means the streets are narrow and large squares and parks are rare. Typically it has gloomy alleys away from the main streets, especially in the older (eastern) part of the city centre, not pretty but always an interesting place to explore.

! **Baedeker** TIP

»By cable-car over the river«
It costs next to nothing to float across the Yangtze or the Jialing Jiang and back in one of the aerial gondolas. The trip is particularly worthwhile when the city is bathed in the sea of lights in the evening. Platforms on the stations provide the best viewpoints for photography.

In its location on the great river, 2400 km/1500 mi from its estuary, Chongqing has for centuries been the gateway to the Red Basin and the province of Sichuan, to which its culture still binds it to this day. Nevertheless it has seldom been of such importance as a trading city as it is today. This was even the case after 1891, when British pressure led to it to becoming a treaty port, giving it customs and trading privileges for foreign goods. It was not until 1935 that the city was provided with mains electricity. Three years later, though, it was catapulted into a new era when the national government fled here from the encroaching Japanese and made Chongqing China's **wartime capital**. Again and again it was bombed by the Japanese air force. People found protection in bunkers built into the mountains. With the arrival of the government, factories and other business flooded into Chongqing and laid the foundations for its post-war development. After 1949 it became a centre of the armaments industry. Since the reform era began, it has been developing with huge dynamism, benefiting from the rich supplies of gas and coal in the surrounding district which it administers

Temple Monastery of Luohan Si · Business centre

Rock sculptures The oldest and most important **shrine in the city** dates back to the years 1064–1067 when a Zen monk carved the first likeness of Buddha into the mountain rock. There are two rock walls 3.5 m/11.5 ft high and 21 m/23 yd and 24 m/26 yd in length respectively, which form a sort of corridor behind the entrance. The niches and caves along them now have more than 400 images of Buddhas, bodhisattvas and pious benefactors surviving in various states of repair from those early days of the monastery, which itself fell into ruin several times in the course of the centuries and in its current form only dates back to 1885, when a monk rebuilt the ruined temple with the help

⏵ VISITING CHONGQING

GETTING THERE

Chongqing has one passenger airport (Jiangbei Airport, 25 km/16 mi north of the city) and railway stations, but more important are the Yangtze docks above the gorges. These are the start and end points for ferry trips along the ►Yangtze gorges (p. 599). Fast motorway coaches run to Chengdu and Dazu (the bus station is next to the main railway station).

City transport

In the inner city area, the best way of getting around is by shanks' pony. The underground railway – currently consisting of a single line running southwest from the city centre – will not usually be needed much by visitors. The two cable-cars are an unusual aspect. They link the city centre to the opposite shores of the two big rivers.

WHERE TO EAT

► Moderate

① *Waipoqiao*
68 Zourong Lu in the Metropolitan Plaza complex next to the Harbour Plaza Hotel), 7th floor

Tel. 023/63 83 59 88
The »Granny Bridge« is one of the city's most popular hotpot hotspots, but other dishes are served too. Curious: the dishes are served on wooden plates floating to the tables along wooden gullies. Reservations advisable.

WHERE TO STAY

► Luxury

① *Harbour Plaza*
Wuyi Lu
Tel. 023/63 70 08 88
Fax 023/63 70 07 78
www.harbour-plaza.com
398 rooms. Just one block away from the liberation monument where the city is at its most lively. Features a swimming pool and gym.

► Mid-range

② *Chaotianmen Hotel*
18 Xinyi Jie
Tel. 023/63 10 18 88
Fax 023/63 71 30 35
145 rooms. Close to the quays in a prime spot for a view of both rivers. Three-star comfort.

of benefactors' donations. All the buildings burned down, though, in a 1940 air raid, but were once more rebuilt from 1945. As the **central Buddhist temple in the city** the sanctum is now visited by many believers every day. It is the headquarters of the Buddhist society of Chongqing and a small number of monks make their home here.

The name of the monastery refers to its main attraction: the Hall of the 500 Luohan. Before mid-2009, however, no sightseeing is possible, as the hall is currently being rebuilt at the expense of thousands of private benefactors. After the interior was devastated by Red Guards in 1966, the state provided replacement clay figures in 1986, but these were not appreciated. The new sculptures are made of bodiless lacquer.

Hall of the 500 Luohan

Chongqing Map

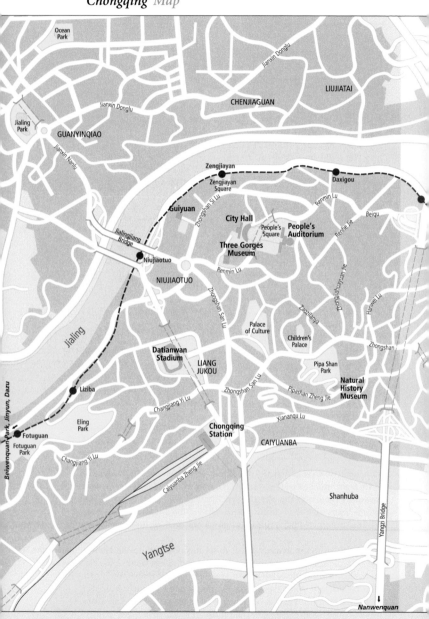

Ocean Park

Jianxin Donglu

LIUJIATAI

CHENJIAGUAN

Jianxin Donglu

Jialing Park

GUANYINQIAO

Jianxin Nanlu

Zengjiayan

Daxigou

Zengjiayan Square

Beiqu

Guiyuan

Zhongshan Si Lu

Renmin Lu

City Hall

People's Square

People's Auditorium

Jialingjiang Bridge

Three Gorges Museum

Renjie Jie

Niujiaotuo

NIUJIAOTUO

Renmin Lu

ZhongwushuTianzhuan Jie

Jialing

Zhongshan San Lu

Palace of Culture

Zaozianya

Children's Palace

Hanwei Lu

Datianwan Stadium

LIANG JUKOU

Pipa Shan Park

Zhongshan

Liziba

Pipashan Zheng Jie

Natural History Museum

Beiwenquan Park, Jinyun, Dazu

Eling Park

Changjiang Yi Lu

Zhongshan San Lu

Fotuguan

Xiananqu Lu

Fotuguan Park

Changjiang Yi Lu

Chongqing Station

CAIYUANBA

Caiyuanba Zheng Jie

Shanhuba

Yangzi Bridge

Yangtse

↓ *Nanwenquan*

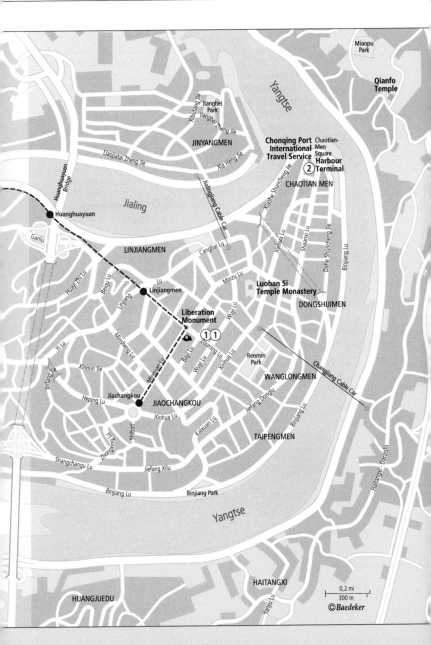

Miaopu Park

Qianfo Temple

Yangtse

Jiangbei Park

Xiuqiang Jie

Jiangbei Zheng Jie

JINYANGMEN

Liaojiatai Zheng Jie

Xia Heng Jie

Chonqing Port International Travel Service

Chaotian-Men Square

Harbour Terminal ②

CHAOTIAN MEN

Huanghuayuan Bridge

Jialing

Jialingjiang Cable Car

Ganlu

Huanghuayuan

Xiaohe Shuncheng Jie

Xinhua Lu

Shaanxi Lu

Dahe Shuncheng Jie

Binjiang Lu

LINJIANGMEN

Cangbai Lu

Minzu Lu

Luohan Si Temple Monastery

DONGSHUIMEN

Huayu Zhu Lu

Baixu Lu

Linjiang Lu

Lu

Linjiangmen

Wuyi Lu

Liberation Monument

Zourong Lu

① ①

Xinhua Lu

Renmin Park

WANGLONGMEN

Changjiang Cable Car

Yi Lu

Xinmin Jie

Minsheng Lu

Minzuan Lu

Bayi Lu

Wuyi Lu

Jiefang Donglu

Jinfang Jie

Heping Lu

Jiachangkou

Xinhua Lu

JIAOCHANGKOU

Kaixuan Lu

Jiefang Lu

Binjiang Lu

TAIPENGMEN

Shibati

Zhonglu

Min Buch

Shangchangu Lu

Jiefang Xilu

Binjiang Lu

Binjiang Park

Yangtse

Haitangqu Danzishi

HUANGJUEDU

Yanyu Lu

HAITANGXI

0,2 mi
300 m
©Baedeker

●━━●┄┄▶ Monorail

Main Hall The Main Hall too is dominated by **Shakyamuni** flanked by his two closest disciples; further disciples occupy glass cabinets along the side walls. The following four-storey sutra hall houses a jade Buddha on its ground floor. The dragon on the censer in the courtyard brings good luck to those who stroke it and then rub their hands over their head and body. The monastery is tucked away between skyscrapers in the city centre (Luohansi Jie; a side road off Minzu Lu). Opening times: 8.30am–6pm. The vegetarian monastery restaurant is popular (to the right of the Luohan hall).

Liberation Monument The 27.5 m/90 ft monument, in fact a tower which can be climbed via a spiral staircase inside it, was erected in 1945 200 m/220 yd southwest of the temple monastery to commemorate the **victory over Japan**. Nowadays it has become virtually synonymous with the business centre of the city. Almost vanishing between new skyscrapers, it stands amid a network of nicely laid out pedestrian zones with shops, department stores, banks, cinemas, bars and restaurants. This is the very pulse of urban life.

Chaotian Men Square This is at the tip of the peninsula at the confluence of the Yangtze and Jialing. Traffic on the rivers is busy. The broad **river view** from the square, 700 m/ 770 yd northeast of the temple monastery of Luohan Si, is a laid out in attractive modern style. The view downstream

is not to the east, as might be expected, but towards the northwest as the Yangtze meanders around a great loop here. Below the square and further upstream there are rows and rows of docks and quays.

People's Square

Vehicular traffic has been banished from the only large inner-city square into tunnels beneath it, and is now Chongqing's living-room, so to speak. It is a well-kept and popular rendezvous with fruit-sellers, shoe-shine boys and shady benches, but unfortunately no restaurants. Two huge buildings give the square its symmetrical shape. To the south is the **People's Auditorium**, a curious monument to Sino-socialist architecture, which imitated the imperial style. It was erected between 1951 and 1953. Its distinguishing feature is its 65 m/ 200 ft high curved conical roof, whose shape and colour are reminiscent of the Hall of Prayer for Good Harvests in the Temple of Heaven in Beijing; the smaller hall in front of it, high above the façade, imitates the tower structure of the Gate of Heavenly Peace in Beijing. The huge hall, which seats 4000 and is used for **conferences and cultural events** is open to sightseers. The strictly symmetrical side wings house the DLT Hotel, which until 2007 was called the »People's Hotel«, although it never accommodated the »mere people«, but only party functionaries on official trips.

People's Square (Renmin Guang-chan)

Slightly reminiscent of Manhattan: the skyline of Chongqing

Three Gorges Museum Opposite the People's Auditorium is Chongqing's biggest attraction, which was opened in 2005. Its name only hints at what is inside, namely the cultural history of the region and the city, in places highly elaborately staged. The immediate occasion for the construction of the building was the programme of excavations in the Yangtze Gorge prior to its flooding as part of the dam project. The lives of the bargees are recalled, one of the exhibits being a life-size replica of a boat. Then there are reconstructed streets from old Chongqing, a look back at the bitter war years from 1938 to 1945, and relics of the prehistoric and early historical periods. Splendid funerary reliefs and figures take visitors back to the Han era 2000 years ago – with hunting and harvest scenes, and the construction of a well. Half a day will have passed before you realize it. Opening times: Tue-Sun 9am–5pm.

Pipa Shan Park (Pipa Shan Gongyuan) A pavilion tops the **city centre's highest hill** (345 m/1132 ft above sea level). The best time to come here is in the evening twilight when the lights penetrate through the haze and neon signs bathe the smog that rather spoils the view during the day in bright colours.

✶ Dali

Gf 33

Province: Yunnan
Altitude: 2000 m/7000 ft

Population: 18,000

Behind the Cang Shan mountain range, which rises to a height of 4122 m/13,524 ft, with a panoramic view of the long, narrow Lake Erhai at its feet: this is the glorious location of Dali, capital of the Bai people, which has made it a favourite destination for many a backpacker.

This form of tourism has influenced the infrastructure so that there are family-run hostels, restaurants geared to foreigners and unfortunately along **»Foreigners' Street«** (Yangren Jie), where businesses clamouring for tourist money teem, there is also an irritating burden of indigenous-art vendors, tour agents, shoe-shine boys and others touting for trade. There is no doubt, however, that Dali has plenty to offer. There are boat tours and horse-drawn carriages, bicycle routes and hiking trails. The **well-groomed image** of the town is charming, mountain streams gush through the streets and there are old town walls and lovely temples to admire.

City layout Unlike nearby Lijiang, the layout of Dali is typically Chinese: like a chess board with straight streets. The area experienced its initial **heyday** before the Chinese era began, though. The capital of the kingdom of Nanzhao (629–1252) was only a few kilometres to the south. It survived as such until conquest by the Mongols. The 4.4 m/14.4 ft

»stele for the pacification of Yunnan« on Sanyue Jie testifies to that historic turning point, not only of the town but of the province as a whole. Dali's present layout was created from 1682 following wartime destruction under the Ming dynasty. Since the 1990s the city has been beautified with neatly constructed pavements and newly channelled streams. Old buildings have been restored too, including a Catholic church on the east side of Fuxing Lu, slightly to the south of the North Gate. Be aware, though, that all this refers to **Dali Old Town** (Dali gucheng) as distinct from **Dali City** (Dali-shi), as the much larger town of Xiaguan, 18 km/11 mi to the south, is called. Anyone arriving by plane or train will come in via Xiaguan but staying there would be a mistake.

! *Baedeker* TIP

Market in the third month

In the third month of the lunar year it is possible to see why the street known as Sanyue Jie (»Street of the Third Month«), which runs up the hill from the West Gate, gets its name and why it is so wide: For a week in that month (after the full moon) it fills up with stalls, and the peoples of the region, not only the Bai but the Yi as well, flock to market. Traditional wares include horses, salt, tea and medicinal herbs, but nowadays you can buy virtually anything. In addition there is dancing, singing and all kinds of sporting competitions.

Dali roofscape

What to see in Dali

City walls, gates and tower

Chinese tour groups always go to the smart **South Gate** with the two golden characters of the town's name and the green in front of it. This frontage of the town fortifications, which unfortunately no longer exist in full, is, however, a reconstruction built in 1984. The **North Gate** at the other end of the north-south axis (Fuxing Lu) is more authentic and atmospheric. In front of it some of the moat around the town has also survived. The **West Gate** facing up the mountain is also a reconstruction. One distinctive feature is the **Wuhua Lou** (»Five Flowers Tower«), which bridges the main street a little to the north of the South Gate

Baedeker TIP

Web artists

A spectacular sight for all non-arachnophobes: the huge webs spun by a local species of spider. Sometimes up to a dozen large creatures with black legs and orange bodies collaborate to build a three-dimensional web 20 m/66 ft or more in length, and several metres in height and breadth. There are some fantastic examples in the town moat at the North Gate.

On the site of a former military headquarters, from which the rebel general Du Wenxiu ruled his short-lived dominion between 1856 and 1872, there is a **local museum** exhibiting archaeological finds relating to the cultural history of the region. More than a hundred grave statues, life-like images of servants, musicians and guards, form the main attraction. One amusing exhibit is a representation of the twelve calendrical creatures. It is situated northwest of the South Gate on Fuxing Lu (opposite the marble market). Opening times: 8.30am–6pm daily.

Three Pagodas Temple Chongsheng Si

The three elegant brick pagodas 1 km/1100 yd northwest of the old town are known across the country as the **city's hallmark**. The middle one, with its 16 roofs, has a square floor plan and is 69 m/226 ft high. It dates from the 9th century. The other two are octagonal, only 42 m/138 ft high and 100 to 200 years younger. All the pagodas stand in the grounds of a temple, reconstructed in the **style of the Tang period**, in which historical information is provided and some of its almost 680 relics are displayed, having been discovered in the foundations and pinnacle of the largest pagoda during reconstruction of the towers between 1978 and 1980. Opening times: 8am–6.30pm daily.

Single Pagoda (Yi Ta)

Like the Three Pagodas the Single Pagoda originally belonged to a **Buddhist temple** which has not survived the ages. The tower is 44 m/144 ft high with a square floor plan and 16 roofs. It is situated about 500 m/550 yd uphill from the South Gate.

Marble industry

One genuine attraction to be seen in the region around the town is the working of the marble grinders and masons: Whole streets are lined by their workshops, showrooms and the magnificent villas of those who grew rich from their work. **»Dali stone«** (dali shi) is in fact the Chinese word for marble, and it is easy to see why. The Chinese take particular delight in the way that the natural grain of the marble always looks like a brush-painted landscape. They make the showrooms into veritable picture galleries.

The Cang Shan mountain range

Chair-lifts fans can get a real treat at the upper end of Sanyue Jie (uphill from the West Gate): the journey takes more than half an hour. The lower section glides over a wild cemetery. At the top it comes to the syncretic **temple monastery of Zhonghe Si**, from which the stunning panoramic view is the main thing to see: the Old Town, the surrounding villages, lakes and mountains are all visible at once. There are hiking trails into the mountains from here.

 VISITING DALI

GETTING THERE AND GETTING AROUND

Bus route 8 runs from Dali City station (with services to Kunming) to Dali Old Town. Dali City also has an airport. Cross-country buses going to Lijiang stop on the main road beneath Dali Old Town. Accommodation and tickets can be obtained from the travel agents around »Foreigners' Street«. The same applies to bookings for day-trips across the lake and for the Gantong cable-car. To get to the Cang-Shan chair lift and the Three Pagodas temple, you can take a motorcycle taxi or a horse-drawn coach. Cycle rental agents (also clustered around »Foreigners' Street«) rent out some pretty good mountain bikes.

SHOPPING

It is virtually obligatory to buy two types of souvenirs: the exquisite embroidery of the Bai women and a marble landscape – at the upper end of »Foreigners' Street« these can be obtained in the form of small, thin plates.

WHERE TO EAT

► **Inexpensive**

Numerous places line up along both sides of »Foreigners' Street« (upper end of Huguo Lu) and the adjoining southern part of the Bo'ai Lu. To escape the mayhem there, try the Ice Island Guest House, Huguo Lu 131 or the little Café de Jack, 82 Bo'ai Lu.

WHERE TO STAY

► **Mid-range**

Asia Star Hotel

Holiday District (app. 800 m / 800 yd to the south of the old town)
Tel. 08 72/267 99 99, Fax 267 16 99
www.asiastargroup.com
310 rooms in a large complex, many with a view of the lake

► **Budget**

Yinvilla Hotel

109 Huguo Lu
Tel./Fax 08 72/266 46 66
www.yinvilla.com
Friendly private hotel with a family atmosphere

✱

Gantong cable-car, Qingbi Xi Gorge

To get to the lower station of this cable-car a little further south of the town, it is best to take a mini taxi. The journey ends close to the Qingbi Xi Gorge, through which an easy trail runs. Thereafter there is a pleasant stroll on the easy and broad »Jade Belt Walk« keeping to a contour half-way up the mountains for 12 km/7 mi northward to Zhonghe Si, from where the chair-lift goes back down to Dali. Pony treks can be booked to **Qilongnü Chi** lake.

✱ Lake Er Hai and its shores

Lake Er Hai is 40 km/25 mi long, 7 to 8 km/4 to 5 mi wide and offers plenty of opportunities for enjoyment. The sporting variant is to cycle around it, while the more gentle option is to take a **tour by boat**. It is also possible to combine the two by taking the boat to the other side of the lake and cycling back. Alternatively you might want to restrict your touring to the west bank, where there are plenty of things to see at various intervals. Boats start from directly below the town at the Caicun quay, accessible by bike or mini taxi. If the boat trip is booked in the town, the fare to the quay is usually included.

Tianjing Ge Pavilion

The first stop on a boat trip is at the »**Pavilion of the Celestial Mirror**«, a pagoda-like observation tower on the eastern shore opposite Dali. It is part of a whole ensemble of buildings including pavilions, restaurants etc. A covered bridge is painted with scenes from a legend. A **princess of the Nanzhou kingdom** once fell in love with a young hunter. As she was already engaged to a general, she fled with her lover into the mountains. When winter came she froze miserably so the hunter tried to find her a warming coat, but an evil magician pushed him into the lake, where he turned into a stone mole. When the princess died of heartbreak, she turned into a white cloud which can still be seen sometimes drifting over a mountain peak, looking for her beloved. One stone spire that pokes out of the lake near the pavilion is said to mark where the stone mole lies in the water.

Jinsuo Dao Island

The second port of call is usually the island of Jinsuo Dao, the largest in the lake. There is a small hamlet on its eastern shore, where it is possible to do a little shopping. The village square right next to the harbour is nice with its market and stalls selling snacks. At the southern end of the village there is an entrance to a cave, the »**Palace of the Jade Dragon**« (Yulong Gong).

Bai villages

On a bike ride along the western shore the villages of the Bai people are delightful places to go. **Xizhou**, near the shore about 15 km/9 mi north of Dali, is known for its traditional houses. **Zhoucheng**, 23 km/14 mi from Dali is similar but a bit bigger.

The Pavilion of the Heavenly Mirror →
stands majestically above Er Hai Lake

Dali City Xiaguan, the »lower fortress«, was once a fort built to protect Dali itself. Nowadays it is a modern town. Travellers to and from Dali Old Town usually pass through it to make their connections and no more. With a little more time, though, there are certainly a couple of nice places to go. In particular the large **Erhai Park** at the southern end of the lake (north of the centre) is nice. Anyone seeking to find out more about the Bai nation and the history of the region should go to the **regional museum** (Dalizhou Bowuguan), which is built in the style of tradition Bai architecture. It mainly displays pottery and masonry work. 8 Erhe Nanlu on the embankment west of Erhai Park.

✶✶ Datong

Hb 25

| **Province:** Shanxi | **Population:** 550,000 |
| **Altitude:** 1040 m/3420 ft | |

No one arriving in Datong should expect to see a quiet little village. The city and surrounding region are covered by a layer of coal dust, ankle-deep along some roads where an unceasing stream of small lorries carry the stuff. In recent years Datong has endeavoured to improve conditions and beautify itself but the air is often of – literally – breathtakingly poor quality.

The reasons to come here are different. It has two temple monasteries in the centre of town as well as the **Buddha grottoes of Yungang**, which make the town a first-class tourist destination thanks to their wonderful paintings dating back more than 1500 years, a delight for all those who revel in the expressiveness of religious art.

Layout Datong has the regular street grid aligned to the points of the compass as is typical in northern China. The **north-south and east-west axes** intersect precisely in the geographical centre of the old town. On one of the streets south of there, a **drum tower** makes for a handy landmark. A single day should be enough to visit the sights of Datong. Taking night trains there and back from Beijing means that an overnight stay is unnecessary.

Huayan monasteries and the Nine Dragon Wall

Commonly people speak of a single Huayan monastery but in fact there are two separate complexes close together. The names of both refer to the Huayan school of Buddhism, which is based on the Huayan sutra. Both complexes were set up in the **Liao period** about 1000 years ago. During the tumult of war at the end of that era, the monasteries were largely destroyed but were rebuilt by the subsequent **Jin dynasty**. Unusually for temple monasteries in northern China, both of them are aligned to the east. The oldest buildings exhibit stylistic and constructional features, which were soon to disappear during the contemporary **Song dynasty** owing to the development of »more modern« forms. They include large single-eaved roofs with only slight curvature and a deep roof overhang supported by sturdy consoles. Both monasteries are famed for their expressive statues and vivid pictorial decoration. Xiasi Po (turn south off the »Great West Road« Da Xijie). Opening times: 8am–6pm daily, closes 5pm in winter.

The upper of the two Huayan monasteries is spectacular both inside and out. At 54 m/180 ft wide and 29 m/100 ft deep, the **temple hall** is the largest Buddhist hall in China. The building dates from 1140. In a later era, a hall of such dimensions would have been furnished with a double-eaved roof but this one just has a simple hipped roof, giving it an almost **archaic-looking monumentality**. Another contributory factor is the fact that the walls are undecorated and only broken by three double doors in the eastern frontage. The terrace, 4 m/13 ft high, upon which the hall is built underlines its importance. The ends of the roof ridges are fashioned in the shape of chi-wen creatures, holding the ridge in their enveloping maws. Both of them are 4.5 m/15 ft tall.

✳
Upper Huayan monastery

Twilight at Datong: one last truck is loaded with coal

▶ VISITING DATONG

INFORMATION

CITS Datong
21 Yingbin Donglu
Tel. 03 52/510 22 65
Fax 03 52/510 20 46
Branch at the station:
Tel. 03 52/510 13 26
www.datongcits.com
Guided tours to all the important attractions in and around the city can be booked from here, including a visit to the museum of steam locomotives.

WHERE TO STAY

▶ **Mid-range**
① *Hongqi Grand Hotel*
11 Zhanqian Jie (to the right opposite the main station)
Tel. 03 52/536 65 66 (Information)

Tel. 03 52/536 66 66
(Reservations)
Fax 03 52/536 62 22
www.hongqihotel.com/001e.htm
95 rooms in a well run three-star hotel. With discounts, the price for overnight accommodation can even drop below 200 yuan.

② *Yun Gang*
International Hotel
38 Da Xi Jie
Tel. 03 52/586 99 99
Fax 03 52/586 96 66
236 centrally located five-star rooms from which the Nine Dragon Wall and Huayan monasteries can be reached on foot

Statuary ▶ The main figures on the central altar are five gilded Buddhas sitting on high lotus pedestals in front of equally impressive mandorlas. These are the **Buddhas of Wisdom** with Vairocana, the sun-like, in the middle. He embodies absolute enlightenment. The others are arranged at the four compass points; west, north, south and east. The three in the middle are actually made of wood and were carved in 1427; but the other two are clay and are slightly more recent, along with the six statues of serving bodhisattvas. Along the sides there are rows of exquisite figures representing the twenty devas, the **protective gods of Buddhist teaching**. They are each individually designed – some in armour, others in civilian clothes – and have their hands pressed together in veneration. Their head-dress is varied and often quite amusing. The grand Buddha images effectively portrayed with much gold contrast uniquely with the esoteric and unworldly symbolism of the devas. Under foreign rule by the Kitan (Liao dynasty) and Jurchen (Jin dynasty) their Tantric Buddhism had spread throughout northern China. The ensemble here sought to popularize the new movement and make its superiority prominent.

Murals ▶ One other spectacular feature of the hall is provided by its extensive murals, which cover an area of 887 sq m/1055 sq yd. They were created by a local artist in around 1900 and include portrayals of **scenes from the life of Buddha**, Guanyin and her thousand arms, the luohan and the story of the awakening of the youth Shan Cai.

In the lower monastery, again, one building catches the attention. It is an original Liao-era building dating from 1038. It functions as a library but contains one of the loveliest groups of statues in all of China. In style it resembles the **Bhagavat Hall**, the main hall of the upper monastery, although it is much smaller. Entering the hall, the three groups of clay figures can be seen opposite the entrance. They date from the period when the building was erected and nearly all of them were probably fashioned by the same unknown artist. They are unusually well preserved. The variety of figures is confusing to begin with but the iconography in fact obeys a simple schema. The basis is formed by the **Buddhas of the Three Ages**; arranged from right to left and forming the central figures for each group. Their flaming

✷
Lower Huayan monastery

Datong Map

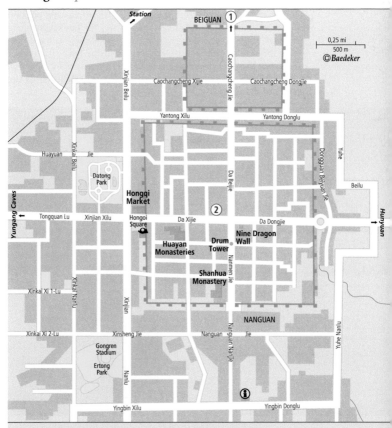

Station
BEIGUAN ①
Caochangcheng Xijie   Caochangcheng Dongjie
Caochangcheng jie
0,25 mi
500 m
© Baedeker
Xinjian Beilu
Yantong Xilu   Yantong Donglu
Dongguan Beiyuan Jie
Yuhe
Huayuan   Jie
Xinkai Beilu
Datong Park
Beilu
Yungang Caves
Da Beijie
Hongqi Market
②
Tongquan Lu   Xinjian Xilu   Hongqi Square   Da Xijie   Da Dongjie
Hunyuan
Nine Dragon Wall
Huayan Monasteries   Drum Tower
Xinkai Xi 1-Lu   Namen Jie   Shanhua Monastery
Xinkai Nanlu
Xinjian
Yuhe Nanlu
Xinkai Xi 2-Lu   Xinsheng Jie   Nanguan Jie   NANGUAN
Nanguan Nanjie
Gongren Stadium
Ertong Park
Nanlu
ⓘ
Yingbin Xilu   Yingbin Donglu

Where to stay
① Hongqi Grand Hotel   ② Yun Gang International Hotel

Baedeker TIP

Iron horses from within

The last of the world's steam locomotives was completed in the locomotive factory in Datong in 1988. Several examples are now preserved for display in the factory's museum including an original British engine from 1882. Tours can be booked via CITS (see p. 202) . These include a trip on a genuine steam engine. Caution: the museum is closed at weekends and a party must consist of at least five people.

mandorlas make up the visual backdrop. In front of each Buddha there are three pairs of figures and it is these that provide the ensemble with its effectiveness. They are virtually life-size and as they often hold their fingers in the encouraging gesture, the warning gesture or the giving gesture, they seem to be most concerned with the spiritual health of their observers. The left-hand and right-hand groups both include also two pious youths and a smaller Buddha figure, although these were probably added later by another artist. Although from the rather restricted viewing position offered to visitors they are rather hard to see, the **bookcases** along the outer walls are also quite remarkable. »Bookcases« is hardly the word: they are shaped with superb joinery in the form of a sort of two-storey hall with roofs and complicated console work. Outside, the actual halls of the outer courtyard contain an **exhibition on the history of the city**.

True treasures await visitors to the Huayan monasteries

The people of Datong are proud of the Nine Dragon Wall. At 45.5 m/50 yd long, 8 m/26 ft high and 2 m/ 7 ft thick, it puts the two similar walls in Beijing thoroughly in the shade. It is older, too, dating back to 1392, when it was built as the **spirit wall for a princely palace**. One other thing gives this glorious edifice an advantage over its Beijing equivalents, for it is only here that the dragons frolic over the element from which Chinese dragons are said to derive, water. There is problem, though: the dragons adorn the northern side of the wall, meaning they are more or less always in shadow. Dong Dajie (east of the Huayan monasteries). Tours: 8am–6.30pm daily, closing 5.30pm in winter.

Nine Dragon Wall

⏲

✳ Shanhua monastery

In the second of the city's major temple monasteries, as many as four halls have survived from the 12th century. Its greatest treasures are its **paintings**, which mainly date back to the time of construction. The monastery was founded as early as the 8th century although the present buildings came into being between 1123 and 1149, exhibiting much the same frugal, monumental style as the main hall of the upper Huayan monastery. Unlike there, though, this monastery is aligned towards the south.

Even the entrance to the complex, formed by this **gate house** is of impressive dimensions. It houses the four kings of heaven with their attributes: pagoda and pipa on the left, snake and sword on the right. The figures on the left look outwards while those on the right face inwards – a very rare arrangement. They were created during the Ming period (probably around 1528).

Hall of the Heavenly Kings

One unusual feature is the fan-shaped arrangement of the consoles in the façade of the Hall of the Three Saints – a fashion of the time. The figures inside date from the Ming period. They represent the **»Three Saints of Huayan Buddhism«**: Buddha Vairocana in the middle, flanked by the bodhisattvas, Manjushri (right) and Samantabhadra. A 2.6 m/8.5 ft pillar in the southwest corner documents the history of the monastery's destruction and rebuilding at the end of the Liao period and the start of Jin era.

Hall of the Three Saints

On the terrace in front of the Mahavira Hall, the main hall of the complex, there is a decorative door flanked by two pavilions for bell and drum, all three of which date from 1616. The fabulous imagery inside the main hall represents a highlight of 12th-century art. The iconography with the **five Buddhas of wisdom** is essentially the same as in the main hall of the upper Huayan monastery. The design of the devas at the sides, though (24 of them here), concentrates less on decorative effect. The individual realization of the characters, though, is all the more effective. Among them is the **»devil's mother«** (ac-

Mahavira Hall

companied by a devil child). She does not look evil, though, as the artist depicts her after her conversion to good. Before then she had stolen and eaten other people's children. To teach her a lesson, Buddha once hid her youngest child. When she protested, Buddha pointed out the horror of her own deeds, in response to which she and her whole family of children converted to Buddhism, since which time she has counted as a protective goddess. Other things in the hall to note include the artistic **wooden dome** over the Vairocana in the centre and the **remains of murals** dating from around 1700.

Puxian Ge, Five Dragon Wall
Among the group of buildings at the western edge of the courtyard in front of the main hall is the Puxian or **Samantabhadra Pavilion**. This two-storey building also dates from the 12th century. To the southwest of it, slightly away from the halls, a wall with five dragons can be seen. It is 20 m/22 yd long and 7 m/23 ft high and was built around 1600 as the **spirit wall** for another temple. Da Nanjie (west side, in the southern part of the old town). Opening times: 8.30am–6pm daily.

✸ ✸ Yungang caves (Yungang shiku)

The main reason for coming to Datong can be found 15 km/ 9 mi west of the city. Almost 1500 years ago around 50 **Buddhist cave temples** were hammered out of a specially prepared wall over a length of 1 km/1100 yd. 45 of them are still in existence, including some that were begun as imperial projects, with dimensions to match, as well as 207 smaller niches and shrines. Paintings, 51,000 of them, cover an area of 18,000 sq m/21,500 sq yd. Most of them express a joyously pious quality and the quantity is in some places overwhelming.

! **Baedeker TIP**

Bring binoculars

Bring binoculars to the Yungang-caves. They will be needed to see the lovingly drawn details of the pictures near the top – especially the flying Gandharvas and Apsaras. In addition most of the caves are inaccessible to the public so that they can only be viewed from outside.

The Yungang caves were the first examples in China of Buddhist cave temple building financed by the emperors themselves. Three rulers of the Toba dynasty sought to honour their ancestors and **enhance the glory of their religion** in the years between 460 and 494, not least while glorifying themselves with the important cave temples. The dynasty would later move its capital to Luoyang, where the Longmen caves then came into being. On a smaller scale, the work would continue for nearly another 30 years after they had gone. Here, on the edges of the steppes, traces can be seen of the journey that the custom took from its native India along the Silk Road, also adopting influences from Iranian and Graeco-Buddhist styles (Gandhara art). Yungang also featured a **technical**

innovation – at least in Chinese terms. This was the first time all the images had been carved directly out of the rock instead of being modelled separately as free-standing clay figures supplemented by paintings, as in the earlier Mogao grottoes in Dunhuang and the older caves at Maiji Shan. In the Yungang caves there are no paintings; every image and every detail is sculpted, mainly in low relief, but with some of the larger figures the relief is so high that they are almost free-standing. The **colours** seen in some of the caves were mostly only painted on at the end of the 19th century.

The caves are numbered 1 to 45 from east to west. The entrance to the area is in front of cave no. 6, more or less in the middle of the sequence, since nos. 1 and 2 are quite a long way distant from the rest. The most important grottoes are those numbered 5 to 20. **Guided tours** usually begin with no. 5 and end at no. 20. It is better, though, to see them the opposite way round, starting with the oldest caves and leaving the finest examples, 5 and 6, till last. These two are also currently the only caves to which the public has entry. **Tours**

Hewn from the rock 1500 years ago: the Buddhas of Yungang

Architecture The structure and concept behind the cave architecture changed within the space of a few decades. The oldest caves (nos. 16–20) were all started in 460. They have elliptical floor plans, are relatively shallow and function mainly as a **shrine for one massive Buddha**. The typical feature of the next most recent generation of grottoes is their rectangular floor plan with a central pagoda-like pillar, which supports the roof of the cavern so that visitors must circle round it. Some caves also possess a vestibule. The caves of the third generation, which did not come into existence until after 494 and were mainly financed by private money, are much smaller and less ostentatious.

Iconography In general, **five distinct types of images** can be ascertained: first Buddhas (mostly in a flaming mandorla, often with an additional gloriole), secondly bodhisattvas (sometimes with highly complex headgear and a gloriole), thirdly holy monks (mostly disciples of Buddha, also with glorioles), fourthly figures from Indian mythology, either in the form of protective deities (devas) or flying heavenly creatures reflecting the joy of the enlightened, and fifthly pictures of other people in **scenes from the Buddha legends**. Apart from representations of people, there are also images of animals: peacocks, cattle and elephants; while the most common floral motif is the lotus blossom.

Buddhas, bodhisattvas, figures from Indian mythology – monumental …

The smallest Buddhas can cover whole walls as part of the **thousand-Buddha motif**, representing the Buddhas of all aeons. The larger Buddhas, mostly sitting in their own niches unless they are monumental figures occupying whole caves, are always at the centre of an ensemble including an odd number of figures. Apart from the Buddha himself, such scenes usually have at least two standing bodhisattvas, opposite him and on a slightly smaller scale and occasionally the two closest **disciples of Buddha Gautama**, Ananda and Kashyapa. There may also be two or more praying figures, easily recognized with their hands pressed together and slightly raised hands. Some of them are kneeling as well. As can be seen from their halos, the lesser images are not portraits of their sponsors, as such things were unknown at the time, but **portrayals of higher creatures**, usually devas – a sort of spiritual police force. Usually the surroundings of the Buddha niches are decorated too, mainly with fields and friezes above them. In those places, as well as further up the walls and on the ceilings, Apsaras and Gandharvas fly. Whenever two Buddhas are seated alongside one another in a niche, they represent a **scene from the Gautama legend**. The earlier Buddha Prabhutaratna is even supposed to have returned from Nirvana to listen to Buddha Gautama's teachings.

Groups of images

... and colourful depictions

Cave 20 The starting point at the west includes the best-known Buddha on the site, and one of the most photographed in all China. Since the front part of the grotto has caved in, the monumental figure, 14 m/46 ft in height, is now in the open air, so that the **style of the earliest phase of the iconography here** is particularly easy to see: exceedingly wide shoulders, huge ears that reach down to where the shoulders are, a pointed Greek-style nose and eyes that are open, unlike in the later depictions where the eyelids are half closed. The legs, originally crossed in the lotus position, have weathered so much that they are no longer recognizable as such. The head is surrounded by a **flaming nimbus** and around the body is a **flaming mandorla**, both of which feature small Buddhas floating amidst them. Square holes in the rock indicate that there was once a wooden roof serving as protection after the collapse of the cave. There were once two Buddhas at the sides of the largest one but only one of them has survived. The survivor is holding his right hand in the gesture of granting protection.

Caves 19 to 16 In caves 19 to 16 an impression can be gained of how cave 20 must once have looked: a monumental Buddha gazes out through a large opening into the open. The central Buddha in no. 19 is nearly 17 m/56 ft high, the second biggest on the site. The loose hand-gesture of the large Buddha in no. 18 is still a long way from the strict symbolism of the later caves. His left hand is adjusting the sleeve of his monk's habit, which itself is covered in tiny Buddha depictions, while the right hand hangs at his side. Cave 17 is more richly decorated than the others, while cave 16 is heavily weathered.

The famous »musician frieze« in Yungang cave no. 12

Nos. 14 and 15 are small and date from the **last phase of construc-**
tion (c. 494–524). They do not contain much of interest. Various
smaller niches were also carved out of the rock walls around caves 11
to 13 during the late phase, too. Their figures are up to 1.5 m/5 ft in
height. The proportions of the figures changed markedly from the
earliest phase. The slim shoulders and narrow faces are particularly
conspicuous.

The fine details of this gorgeously decorated group are highlighted
by the painting executed in around 1891. Nos. 13 to 11 form what
from outside appears to be a nearly **symmetrical triad**, while 10 and
9 are also a related pair. All five date from the middle phase of construction. One unusual and pleasing detail is the small, four-armed
figure in cave 13, which supports the right arm of the 13 m/43 ft
Maitreya Buddha. The crossed legs of the latter represent, in the
iconography of the Yungang caves, the typical feature of this »Future
Buddha«. Along with the flaming mandorla behind him, he takes up
half the cavern at the rear.

The world of the enlightened is a happy place. This can be expressed
by the joy of music as in the rings of flying dancers that appear
throughout the caves. Apart from them, though, no cave delights in
musical revelry ss much as cave 12. It is mostly famed for its **frieze
of musicians** along the top of the longer wall in the front cavern.
More musicians are depicted on its domed ceiling; indeed they are
even bigger than the Buddhas, whose happiness their playing is
meant to illustrate. The **magnificent design of the front cavern**
(with its imitation palace buildings) continues in the main cavern of
the perfectly composed grotto.

The first really well-preserved example on the tour of a **grotto with**
a central pillar is cave no. 11. On each of the four sides around its
pillar there is a Shakyamuni some 5 m/16 ft in height. An inscription
on the east wall dates its construction to the year 483.

Nos. 10 and 9 are next door to one another, are of the same size and
have the same architecture, each featuring an open vestibule chamber
and a main chamber with a central pillar. The abundant **statuary** is
partially integrated into depictions of a palace. Rich floral ornamentation decorates the entrance to each of the main caverns, while
guards keep the evil spirits away. Under the consoles of the false ceiling above the entrance to no. 10, there are **garlanded flying Apsaras**.
To the left of the entrance a Maitreya sits in a niche between two columns topped by capitals, which are never seen in the timber building
style common in China. These appear to be inspired by Ionic columns: The telamones at the bottom of the left wall of the vestibule
also appear to have arrived via traditions from the Far West. The
lions, depicted no larger than domestic cats, which sit at the feet of

several Buddhas, also descend from the cultural exchanges taking place along the Silk Road.

Caves 8 and 7 Caves 8 and 7 form a pair and count as the earliest examples of the second phase of building. Both consist of two rectangular caverns of roughly similar size, neither of which have a central pillar. Each one has an imitation **coffered ceiling**, upon which Apsaras dance. At the passage through to no. 8 a manifestation can be seen of the Indian god Indra possessing five heads and six arms. He is seated on a peacock, holding a chicken in front of his chest and the sun and moon in the outstretched arms. Both are considered powerful **protective gods in Buddhism**.

Cave 6 Cave 6 is the most artistically important and iconographically interesting of the caves, featuring an **abundance of detail**. Thanks to a four-storey timber vestibule hall, which was erected in front of it in 1651, it is particularly well preserved. The two levels of the central pillar are extraordinarily elaborate and unparalleled in Chinese temple architecture. It does of course support the ceiling 16 m/52 ft above the ground but it seems to serve rather as a picture gallery. At the bottom a Buddha niche is let into each of the walls. On the upper level the walls separate into slender, pagoda-like columns at each corner, between which stands a magnificent Buddha statue with a wide sweeping cloak. The grotto is best known, though, for the intricacy with which it relates the **legends from the life of Buddha Gautama**, Prince Siddhartha. The cycle of images begins at the front left of the central column. The scenes are at eye level in the sectors above the bodhisattva and deva figures, which are each assigned to their Buddha niches. On the right-hand side of the left wall (west wall) the nativity of Buddha is depicted. Maya, his mother, is seen with her ladies-in-waiting in the Lumbini grove holding on to a branch, while the youth emerges from her side under the armpit. The story continues to the east. Nine nagas reach up from the left-hand embrasure of the Buddha niche. **These water snakes of Indian mythology** give the new-born child, who can already walk, a cleansing shower. Further left, Shuddhodana, Siddhartha's father, rides an elephant and holds his son in his arms. To the right of the north wall, the bearded soothsayer, Asita, recognizes physical attributes that point to a special future for the child, while the parents listen enthralled. Left of the niche, the now adolescent Siddhartha rides his own elephant. On the east wall, **scenes of his life in the palace** are depicted.

! **Baedeker TIP**

On familiar terms with the Guanyin
7 km/4 mi before the Yungang caves, directly to the north of the road on a small elevation, there is a small Guanyin temple dating from 1651. It does not get many visitors but its 16, slightly naive-looking but nevertheless life-like figures have a particular charisma and are well worth stopping off to see.

If no. 6 was a high point in terms of the abundance of narrative detail, then no. 5 can still trump it with the monumental impression it gives as a whole. This too was protected by a vestibule building of 1651. Those entering find themselves at the feet of a **giant Buddha figure, at 17 m/56 ft the biggest in the Yungang caves**. The face of this Shakyamuni in meditation pose was covered with gold-leaf in 1891. The shape of the nose and ears still display the characteristics of the early phases of cave construction. The same applies to his two equally monumental companions, themselves nearly 8 m/26 ft tall, which are not bodhisattvas, but standing Buddhas. Here again, their smiles underline the **joyful basis of the religious message**. Along with the main figure the three make up a group representing the Buddhas of the Three Ages. Opening times. 8.30am–5.30pm daily, 9am–5pm in winter. To save on taxi fares, it is possible to take a minibus from opposite the railway station.

Cave 5

Around Datong

The Chinese name of this monastery claims that it »hangs in space«, which is a slight exaggeration, but it is still a precarious-looking structure, supported on thin stilts attached to an overhanging cliff-face. Unfortunately a retaining wall slightly above it blocks the view

Hanging Monastery (Xuangkong Si)

Xuangkong Si, the monastery »suspended in a void«

of the dramatic gorge, in which this **little monastic retreat** once sheltered from the world. Nowadays, in addition, it has become the victim of its own fame. In the high season it is no fun to join the crowds that throng the narrow stairs and galleries which provide access to the tiny little group of halls. Some of the statuary is quite syncretic. In the rearmost and topmost of the miniature halls **Lao Zi, Buddha and Confucius** all sit next to each other. 5 km/3 mi south of the regional capital Hunyuan, 70 km/443 mi southeast of Datong. Open daily.

! *Baedeker* TIP

Light for photographing the Hanging Monastery

Since it clings to an east-facing cliff and is rather deep inside the gorge, the monastery is usually tucked away in shadow. The best light is in the early morning when the sun lights up the painted wooden sections. In winter, though, the sun only peeks very briefly over the mountain.

The **wooden pagoda of Yingxian** is one of the most famous pagodas in China. Even though it is built of such flammable material, it has survived all the wars and lightning strikes, as well as several earthquakes, since 1056. At an impressive height of 67 m/220 ft and a diameter of 30 m/100 ft at its base, **this miracle of carpentry** is the oldest wooden tower of its size in the world. Inside, the octagonal building has nine storeys, though outside it possesses just six roofs. A wall core structure reaches up to the second floor and stairs lead up as far as the fifth. The pagoda is located in the centre of the regional capital of Yingxian, 80 km/50 mi south of Datong. Opening times: 8am–5pm daily.

Dazu

Gh 31

Province: Chongqing
Altitude: 300–600 m/1000–2000 ft

Population: 60,000

In a hilly and heavily cultivated region, mainly distinguished by tall eucalyptus trees, the most southerly and most recent cave temples in China can be found tucked away in a not entirely expected cliff face. Some of the caves clearly indicate the tradition of exemplars in northern China such as the Longmen and Yungang caves, but others have a character all their own.

The cave temples are spread over several widely spaced locations. Their name comes from the district of Dazu, which was founded in 758 around the town of the same name. It is usually translated in Western literature as »Big Foot« although it actually derives from the local river, the name of which, probably referring to its waters, really means something like **»ever more plentiful«**.

▶ VISITING DAZU

WHERE TO EAT

The rear exit from the Dazu Hotel (door to the old wing) leads to a street with a number of traditional local food stalls and small restaurants providing pleasant food at a cheap price.

WHERE TO STAY

▶ **Mid-range**

Dazu-Hotel
47 Gongnong Jie
Tel. 023/43 72 18 88, Fax 43 72 28 27
The only international hotel in town has a new building with a sumptuous hall at the front and an older wing in the courtyard.

Tours

Thanks to the motorway, which gets as near as 40 km/25 mi to the local capital, it is possible to take in the caves on a day trip from Chongqing; although they are 160 km100 mi away by road. The **Baoding Shan grottoes** in particular, the showpiece site among the caves, are for that reason very crowded during the day. It is better, therefore, to spend a night in the town and leave for the Baoding Shan caves no later than 8am so that there is relative peace for an hour or so before the invasion of the day-trippers begins. The **North Mountain (Bei Shan) caves** at the northern edge of the town attract rather fewer visitors. The Daoist **South Mountain (Nan Shan) caves** are also close to the town. In addition, a little further away and in the neighbouring district to the north there are various other cave-temple sites, although seeking them out is something best left to real enthusiasts.

✹ ✹ Baoding Shan caves

Unusual features

The ensemble of caves, 15 km/9 mi from the town, has a number of unusual features. In particular, of all the large cave-temple sites in China, it is the only one to have been the brainchild of a single man, which inevitably means that the period over which it came into existence is short, too. Its »inventor«, the monk **Zhao Zhifeng**, made it his life's work between 1179 and 1252. The layout and the artistic depictions thus obey a basic concept that, in its propagandist intent, greatly differs from that of Buddhist temple-grottoes elsewhere. At a time when Buddhism had been put on the defensive by a resurgence of Confucianism, Zhao devised a bold design in which he sought to portray both the native Chinese teachings of Confucianism itself and Daoism as mere **aspects of a higher Buddhist wisdom**. The whole presentation is given over to this ideal in a way that is found here and here alone. Thus it features an extraordinary abundance of narrative scenes and images – and not only Buddhist images. One other unique feature is the location, a horseshoe-shaped depression accessed not by climbing up to it but by descending. The name Baoding Shan, **»Treasure Summit Mountain«**, is in this sense therefore somewhat misleading. Opening times: 8am–5pm daily; buses run roughly every half hour from Dazu bus station.

Two routes, one destination

Having climbed down to the site, one can get a hint of its message by making a circuit of it. In fact to take it in properly, you really need to split into two: the two sides of the horseshoe deal with different themes but both come together at the top in an artistic, spiritual and, one might say, propagandist climax in the shape of a **gigantic, sleeping Buddha**. It is best then to make the journey twice: first down to the right (where the images are on the right-hand side), then back the same way before going down to the left. There is a short-cut, for those who want to take it, leading from the end straight back to the exit. Between the car park and the entrance there is no avoiding a long street with shops and stalls, where traders do their best first to delay people from making their visit, then from going home.

Goal attained: Buddha enters Nirvana

As in Buddhist temples, people entering first get a fright and a warning. This starts at the bottom of the stairs leading to the site with a tiger. That is followed by a row of Dharma defenders, in thick armour and with their legs spread ready to battle any evil with their **terrifying grimaces** and keep it from entering any further into the sacred area beyond. If the visitor gets past these guards, another fright immediately follows: Mara the demon of death shows each of us **the truth of our ultimate fate** – the wheel of reincarnation, in which all creatures are trapped. The creatures to whom the imprisonment applies are shown in the innermost of the three rings: the heavenly creatures (at the top), the people and saints (to the right and left beneath them), with the animals and hungry spirits under them and the beasts of hell at the bottom. Yet, already, there is an intimation of hope. Buddha sits in the unmoving hub of the wheel and spreads light over all. Even over the demons hover Buddhas, those »enlightened ones« who have defeated all that is demonic. This is the oldest depiction of this kind in all of China.

Protective gods and the demon of death

An inscription of three characters beneath images of monks, Buddhas and pagodas heralds the next stage. The characters spell the name of the site, **»Treasure Summit Mountain«**. This is where the sense of the name is revealed: rather than an old name for the place it is a specially chosen label for the ensemble of caves with the meaning, **»Mountain of the worthiest apex«**. The worthiest apex refers to Buddhadom itself. Next come three large figures, which illustrate this apex with Vairocana in the middle, the sun-like, master of the eternal diamond world – i.e. the opposite to the domain of the death-demon shown earlier. He is accompanied by his two bodhisattvas, Manjushri (right) and Samantabhadra. Shortly afterwards the open-air section comes to an end. A porch protects the most spectacular image of the whole site, a **fully gilded, thousand-armed Guanyin**. The huge circle of hands, not merely ornamental as elsewhere, are all depicted in three dimensions. They cover an area of 88 sq m/105 sq yd. The number »thousand« is no exaggeration here either. To be precise, the bodhisattva reaches out in mercy to help people and rescue them from sorrow with no less than 1007 hands. This image is a magnificent testament to the early blooming of the Guanyin cult, which persists to this day. Note: photography is not permitted here.

Vairocana and golden Guanyin

The spiritual and geometric pinnacle of the complex depicts Buddha Gautama reaching the highest-possible goal of human aspiration: entering Nirvana at the moment of death and thus achieving release from the pain of death and rebirth. The size of the figure, 31 m/34 yd long, **intimates the magnitude of this goal**. At the same time, this area is the domain of the Gautama legend as it sees itself, namely as historical truth. A design trick makes the Buddha seem bigger than the space allows. The lower part of his sleeping form disappears into the ground to an extent so that it is not actually part of the figure.

Great Buddha

The mourners also look out from there, consisting of his disciples, portrayed as bodhisattvas or monks, alongside members of the family. Only their upper bodies are visible, nicely matching the »sunken« part of the Buddha. A **table for offerings** is laid with fruit, and above, a group of women hover in a cloud. They include Buddha's mother, his stepmother, his wife and other characters from his early life and from the world beyond. The images on the northern side of the valley are described next, also in the direction leading towards the Buddha, since that is the only way to put them into a sensible order.

Good and bad karma

Again the first things to be seen are frightening, a group of protective gods on the way to hell, which is depicted on the next part of the trail. They strike terror into any evildoers but are in fact **advocates of the good**, for whom they plead for justice. Those people who collected good karma during their lives are seen above them. The main figure with the golden face is the ascetic, **Liu Benzun**. He was teacher to Zhao Zhifeng, the creator of the whole site. He thus sets firmly into his own present the lesson in salvation that he wishes to convey on this side of the site.

Scenes of hell

Next comes a flood of gruesome images. In the netherworld after death, the devils make certain of overdue justice. One evildoer is put under a circular saw, another has his bones smashed, others have to tremble in a cave of ice or fry in boiling oil. In between there are some peaceful scenes to provide necessary contrast, like a young lady feeding her chickens. One source of sin is alcohol, so that too is depicted. A son in his drunken haze handles the breast of his own mother, while another drunk fails to recognize his own wife and yet another his own son. Enthroned above all this sits **Kshitigarbha, bodhisattva of the underworld**, surrounded by the judges of hell and the managers of purgatory. This incidentally has nothing to do with Buddhism, but that is not the message here. On the contrary, the Daoist folk belief on which these scenes of hell are based is hereby put into the context of the Buddhist teaching of karma and reincarnation.

Paradise of Amitayus

The contrasting Buddhist world is the »Pure Land in the West«, the **dead man's paradise of the bodhisattva Amitayu**. The happy and relaxed existence amid dancing and music which 7th and 8th-century paradise scenes present to their beholders in the Mogao caves of ► Dunhuang is nowhere to be seen here. Now that Confucianism had gained the upper hand, such things were frowned upon, so that everything had become terribly stuffy.

Gautama and the love of children

Buddhism was seen by Confucians as immoral, mainly because of the celibacy of its monks and nuns. Who would take care of parents if there were no children and grandchildren? In the next tableau, the

Some get a nasty surprise in the world to come

propaganda response unfolds in the shape of two large groups. Buddha Shakyamuni preaches the duties of children and their parents' love for them. Right at the beginning (between the stairs and the main figure), **Buddha Gautama** can be seen at the bottom helping to carry the coffin of his own father. Other scenes are purely Confucian: a man carries a yoke on his shoulders with two baskets on the ends in which his aged parents are sitting, married couples delight in their new babies, mothers breastfeed their infants, one couple mourns over the body of their son, a pregnant woman can be seen and one young couple pray to the monumental Buddha depicted above them for an heir. Among the best known scenes is one at the rear (under a row of seven great Buddhas): a mother, whose infant son has wet the bed in which they are both sleeping, moves over to the wet side so that the child can slumber in the dry.

Next comes the Vairocana cave, which serves as a »theological« link **Vairocana cave** between the sections before and what is to come. **Vairocana, the sunlike**, is the timeless lord of the highest wisdom. Here, though (unlike across the way in the middle of the corresponding second section on the other side), he is not shown directly, but his wisdom still imbues Kshitigarbha, the bodhisattva of the underworld and of children, i.e. the very bodhisattva responsible for the aspects of life and death so lovingly illustrated in the preceding scenes. All joys and sorrows are lifted and forgotten in the **sphere of the Buddhas beyond this life**. Since the teaching of Vairocana only extends to those who meditate, though, people need more easily perceived words and images. Thus the next section starts a new narrative: how Buddha came into the world.

Section 4 Passing a wall virtually devoid of imagery, visitors then find themselves in front of the peacock king, an earlier **incarnation of Buddha Gautama**. The peacock once sucked water with wonderful healing properties out of a stone. The section expresses Buddhist charity and mercy for the suffering of creatures. Next comes the tale of Buddha's birth, his mother Maya and a serving girl with the newborn child, who is already able to stand up and walk. The **nine dragon heads** above him are actually water snakes, nagas, who according to legend washed the new baby clean. Water does indeed spurt from the head of the largest dragon. To create the effect, a spring was diverted to this cave. The water fills up a ditch which leads the visitors to the same destination as in the first leg of the tour, to the giant reclining Buddha.

✳ North Mountain Caves, South Mountain Caves

The 290 Buddhist grottoes of the North Mountain Caves, 1.5 km/1 mi north of Dazu, provide delight with a large number of lovely and often quite well preserved paintings, which are also easy for visitors to see even though it is not permitted to enter the caves themselves. They were created from 892 until about 1160. As in other Chinese cave-temple complexes, each of the grottoes is a unit in its own right and the **iconographic scheme** is, unlike at Baoding Shan, mostly conventional, which is not to disparage the quality of the art. The oldest caves date from the late Tang period, although most were made in the Song era. Opening times: 8am–5pm daily.

Caves to the south As soon as Buddhism arrived in China, the Daoists found themselves challenged by this foreign teaching. Here, 2.5 km/1.5 mi southeast of the town, they imitated the **art of the Buddhist cave temple** – albeit in modest fashion. The 15 niches with their images mostly came into being in the 12th and 13th centuries, although some were added later. Opening times: 8am–5pm daily.

★★ Dunhuang

Gc 25

Province: Gansu	**Population:** 100,000
Altitude: 1400 m/4600 ft	

An oasis town with a long history of a very particular kind. Dunhuang is virtually the template for an oasis on the Chinese section of the Silk Road, a lively place in the middle of a verdant ring of artificially watered fields, beyond the unmarked boundaries of which there is nothing but barren desert, great dunes, unending gravelly plains or flatlands with sparse growths of stubby grass.

VISITING DUNHUANG

GETTING THERE

Dunhuang is easiest to get to by plane. Anyone preferring the cumbersome train route needs to alight at Liuyuan, 120 km/75 mi away. From there cross-country buses run to Dunhuang and to and from Jiayuguan, the fort at the western end of the Ming dynasty's Great Wall of China.

SHOPPING

Along the street known as Yangguan Donglu in the centre of town, there are plenty of shops offering an interesting assortment for tourists: cloths with decorative motifs from the Mogao caves and small black vessels made of the mineral called »nighttime glory« (see Baedeker tip p. 282). One definite recommendation is to buy photographic volumes with pictures of the murals in the Mogao Caves. These reproductions with English captions cover the artworks there in all their beauty and variety in a way that is more edifying than the necessarily fleeting views obtained amid the crowds on a live visit.

WHERE TO STAY

▶ Mid-range

Silk Road Dunhuang Hotel
Dunyue Lu
(the road leading to the sand dunes, about 4 km/2.5 mi south of town)
Tel. 09 37/888 20 88, Fax 888 20 86
www.the-silk.road.com
300 rooms. A colossal clay structure which is extraordinarily stylish both inside and out and where good food is served.

Then again, there are the Mogao caves, which have made Dunhuang famous the world over. They make up the most magnificent and richest of all the many Buddhist cave temples which came into being along the transcontinental trade route – the biggest **kaleidoscope of Buddhist art in the world**.

When the empire of the Han dynasty was spreading westward around 100 BC, Dunhuang became the most important garrison of the western districts and also developed into a key trading post along the Silk Road, which was then undergoing its earliest boom period. Traders coming from the east long the Gansu corridor between the Tibetan plateau in the south and the Gobi desert to the north via a **chain of oases** leading west had to decide at Dunhuang which of two or three routes to take. The Silk Road split here into a northern trail leading towards Turfan, a middle route towards Loulan, which was later abandoned leaving Loulan itself to become a ghost town, and a southerly passage heading for Qarkilik and Hotan. Coming from the west therefore, this is where several routes coalesced into one, so that when the **Silk Road** was open, Dunhuang was the biggest and richest trading post along a line stretching for 3000 km/2000 mi as the crow

Trading post on the Silk Road

flies between Xi'an in the east and Kashgar in the west. It was via Dunhuang that Buddhism arrived in China around the time of Christ, to be followed in the 4th century by the custom of cave-temple building. When the Silk Road was experiencing its most glorious heyday, at a time when the Tang dynasty had pacified the whole of central Asia, Dunhuang became richer than ever, as the biggest of the cave temples in the Mogao caverns, which date from that period, testify to this day. Thereafter, though, there was a bitter **period of decline** as conquerors attacked in search of plunder and the trade that had flourished in times of peace was annihilated. It was due to one such event, though, that Dunhuang gained its second (historically speaking possibly even more important) claim to fame: the phenomenal hoard of writings that was discovered in 1900 inside the town's walled-up library.

✷ ✷ Mogao caves

25 km/16 mi southeast of the town a **periodic desert stream** had cut into the terrain and created a cliff face some 1600 m/1 mi long and up to about 25 m/82 ft high. Between the 4th century and the 14th, believers hacked about 1000 grottoes out of the relatively soft rock. They form two to four rows stacked one above the other, which were formerly accessed mostly by means of wooden gantries in front of them, although nowadays these have mostly been replaced with concrete versions. Many of the caves no longer exist since they have either collapsed or been weathered away by erosion of the cliff. The majority of them served as accommodation or storage rooms for monks. Among the surviving caves, though, the are 492 larger grottoes which served as **places of meditation or offering**, i.e. as actual cave temples. These are thus fantastically decorated, primarily with murals. The benefactors were sometimes wealthy individuals (often widows), sometimes lay societies. The painted surfaces add up to an area of some 45,000 sq m/54,000 sq yd. In a majority of the caves there are also painted clay statues, an average of seven in each cave, mainly depicting bodhisattvas, which are grouped alongside statues of guards or monks around a central Buddha. The total number of such figures still surviving is approximately 2400, ranging in size from 10 cm/4 in up to 35 m/115 ft.

! **Baedeker TIP**

»Night-time Glory«
This is a rough translation of the name of a blackish-brown mineral, which in this region was ground to make thin-sided beakers and vases. These make a nice and typically local souvenir and can be obtained in many shops in the centre of Dunhuang.

Motifs and stylistic developments In the first phase of cave temple building along the Silk Road, Buddhism was still propagating a **lifestyle of renunciation** extending to full asceticism. One typical expression of this ideal can be found in

THE HIDDEN LIBRARY

It was in 1900 that a Daoist monk called Wang, who had gone into retreat, cleared the sand that had drifted into one of the Mogao Caves. Suddenly part of a side wall collapsed. Wang enlarged the hole, crawled inside – and in the dark, previously hidden neighbouring cave made a discovery the significance of which he, with his limited education, was not even remotely able to grasp: he had chanced upon a three-metre-high pile of old manuscript scrolls.

Obediently the monk Wang reported his discovery to the provincial governor, who presumably thought it too expensive to take away the manuscripts and allowed Wang to keep them locked up where he found them. Seven years later **Sir Aurel Stein**, a British archaeologist, got wind of the matter while staying in Dunhuang in search of remains of the Great Wall. After some time Stein succeeded in gaining the monk's trust, talked him into parting with more than a third of the scrolls, which thanks to the dry conditions were in an outstanding state of preservation, and took them to London.

Scholar or thief?

It was not long before the next researcher appeared: the French sinologist **Paul Pelliot**. He too gained Wang's confidence and was subsequently able to select the most valuable of the remaining manuscripts (as unlike Stein he understood Chinese), and arrange for them to be transported to Paris. Other researchers did the same.

By the time the Chinese authorities finally reacted, most of the scrolls, including the best of them, had left the country.

Immeasurable value

The manuscript hoard of Dunhuang, as Stein realized from the beginning, was a monastery library of immeasurable worth. The oldest manuscripts dated from the 5th century. When an army of **foreign invaders** approached, probably in 1035, the manuscripts were walled up to keep them safe, and then forgotten. Most of them are Buddhist texts, but a large amount of other literature was included. Much of it was completely unknown before the discovery. One of the most valuable is a text of the **Diamond Sutra** dating from 868: it is the world's oldest printed book.

the jatakas, legends originating from India concerning earlier incarnations of Buddha Gautama. The events are often related almost in the form of a **religious comic strip** with rows of pictures (sometimes arranged in an S-shape starting at the top right). The style of such depictions is still distinctively Indian: The people's torsos are naked above their wrap-round skirts or loin cloths, their skins are dark and their physiognomy is clearly Indian or central Asian. With the arrival of Chinese Mahayana Buddhism, which promises salvation even to lay people and adds to the somewhat abstract concept of Nirvana a more **comprehensible intermediate paradise**, and the creation of a new and major Chinese empire under the Sui, who had reconquered Dunhuang, the imagery changed dramatically after the late 6th century. A typical expression of the new teaching was its depictions of paradise. Amid palace architecture in the central perspective and surrounded by lotus ponds, Buddhas sit enthroned on lotus blossoms, orchestras play and elegant dancers swing their hips and spin with shoulder scarves flying. Most of the people seen in these depictions are clearly Chinese. The **architecture of the grottoes** themselves changes too. Early cave temples have a central pillar supporting the roof but in the 6th century pyramid-shaped ceilings made the pillars unnecessary and allowed for greater amounts of space for the paintings themselves.

Tours The caves are locked shut with steel doors so that it is necessary to join one of the **guided tours**, which are also provided in English. There is no lighting installed in any of the grottoes so it is best to bring your own torch, although it is also possible to borrow one at the turnstiles. Bags and cameras have to be left at the entrance. Times for tours: 8am–5pm daily. Caution: the tour guides break for

Monumental splendour: the great Maitreya in Mogao cave no. 130

lunch so it is advisable to arrive before 10am or after 2pm. The following section provides a description of some of the more popular grottoes:

No. 16 is a very large cavern with 1000 paintings of Buddha from the Xixia era (1028–1227). The cave itself, though, is older, probably at least as old as no. 17, which can also be accessed from here and which is where the **monastery library** was immured.

Nos. 16 and 17

Cave 61 (Xixia era) is famous for the life-size **pictures of its benefactresses** – including a princess from Hotan, who was married into a family from Dunhuang. On the left the monastery hill of ► Wutai Shan (p. 566) is depicted.

No. 61

The largest cave, no. 96, was completed in 695. Since it is taller than the cliff itself, it has a wooden roof with a pagoda-like appearance which is recognizable from outside the complex. A **statue of Maitreya** 34.5 m/113 ft in height is believed to be the biggest indoor figure of Buddha in the world. The hands were restored in 1980. In the entrance, various layers of the historical flooring have been exposed, the oldest of which dates back to the construction of the cave.

No. 96

This cave was constructed between 713 and 741 and it too has a monumental Maitreya; this one being 26 m/85 ft high. To the left and right bodhisattvas can be seen in murals. The painting and the floor mosaic outside the cave are from the **Xixia era**. The Apsaras dancing at the top of the walls are 2 m/2 yd long and are the biggest at Dunhuang. The benefactresses of the grotto were the wife of a military governor and their two daughters.

No. 130

Cave no. 148, finished in 775, has a reclining Buddha 15.6 m/17 yd in length being mourned by 72 disciples, bodhisattvas and other figures. Opposite the Buddha some **stunning depictions of paradise** can be seen. At the far left and right the bodhisattvas Manjushri and Samantabhadra both ride their steeds.

No. 148

This grotto with its 15 m/16 yd long reclining Buddha (the head is particularly fine) was built at about the same time or slightly later. Buddha is still being mourned by bodhisattvas and other supernatural creatures but there are also some decidedly earthly folk bawling their loss, too. Among them are some foreigners, **some of whom are depicted in caricature-like fashion**, who form a whole group towards Buddha's feet. Some of them are numbing their sorrow by scoring their skin with knives. Among them a »Westerner« with a pointed cap can be seen wearing a pointed cap.

No. 158

Cave no. 196 is from the late Tang period and is famous for its depiction of the fight between the demon Raudraksha and Buddha's

No. 196

disciple Shariputra; which takes up the whole of the west wall. Raudraksha had sought to aim **fiery flames at Shariputra** but, with no less magical skill, its holy opponent called up a ferocious wind which blew the flames back the way they came, causing terror and consternation among Raudraksha's armies.

No. 249 The painting in cave 249 is superb. It dates from the time of the Western Wei dynasty. **Asura the giant** stretches across the middle of the slanting ceiling opposite the entrance, surrounded by the god of wind and thunder (recognisable by his crown of drums), Garudas, Gandharvas and other supernatural creatures. To the left and right the thousand-Buddhas can be seen and the benefactors are depicted at the bottom. The original statues have not survived and those that can be seen were added a thousand years later.

No. 257 Cave no. 257 relates a popular jataka: the **legend of the wondrous nine-coloured antelope** (here shown in white): The antelope rescues a man from drowning and he has to promise the creature that he will not betray where it lives. However, when the queen of the country has a dream about the antelope and offers a reward for anyone who knows of its whereabouts, the rescued man breaks his vow and the miraculous beast is cornered. Then, though, the animal tells the story of how the man knew where to find it and instead of being rewarded, the treacherous fellow is punished.

No. 323 On the left hand side of the front wall in cave 323 (early 7th century) the early **history of the Silk Road** is depicted. Among the figures that can be seen is Emperor Wu of the Han dynasty and the explorer Zhang Qian who ventured westward at the emperor's behest, bringing back a report which triggered a campaign of conquest that would expand the Chinese empire as far as Dunhuang (and beyond).

The sand dunes near Dunhuang only sing when a strong wind blows

The sponsors of cave no. 428 were the 1200 members of a lay society. **No. 428**
It is one of the more recent grottoes with a central pillar. On the
left-hand side of the right wall another **Buddha legend** can be seen:
The deadly demon Mara has her pretty daughter dance before Gautama to awaken his earthly lusts and wrest his triumph from him.
Two jatakas are depicted, too. One has the generous Prince Sudana,
who lends a miraculous rain-making elephant to his enemies in the
neighbouring country when the land suffers a drought, and the other
is the story of Prince Sattva, who while riding with his brothers gives
a starving tigress something to eat.

A useful supplement after the tour is provided by the cave museum **Cave museum**
near the entrance. There is also a well-organized **museum shop**, but
primarily there are full-size replicas of the contents of each cave. At
last the chance to view the details in peace.

✳ Singing sand dunes and Crescent Moon Lake

At the southern edge of the oasis, 5 or 6 km/3 or 4 mi from the town,
there is a broad area with gigantic sand dunes towering up to 200 m/
650 ft high, making them the biggest in China. Climbing them is
sweaty work. Every time you take a step forward, you slip half a step
back. A **ride around them on the back of a camel** is a more comfortable option. Beyond the gates, where there is a camel and stagecoach
station, there is an easy path leading to the right to Crescent Moon
Lake, obviously named after its shape. The lake is fed by springs in the
ground. On the way, there are enterprises offering the chance of **sand
sledging**. The ascent is made easily and quickly over wooden planking.
Bolder individuals may opt for paragliding. Now what was meant by
the »singing dunes«? If the air is still, there is nothing to be heard, but if
there is a strong wind, a rumbling noise arises over the ridge of dunes.

✳ Jade Gate Fort and the Great Wall of the Han dynasty

For anyone interested in archaeology a trip 80 km/50 mi westward
to the Jade Gate is a must. This is part of the Great Wall fortifications
which **Emperor Wu** of the Han dynasty had built around 100 BC to
secure his conquests. The road there leads through a thoroughly
bare, flat gravel desert, where mirages often appear. The fortifications
consist of three parts.

The fort is a square building made of rammed earth, 10 m/33 ft high **Fort**
and an area of 640 sq m/765 sq yd. Two gates lead into its inner courtyard. The eastern side of the fort was enlarged in recent times. The location close to the desert river **Shule He** is interesting; it seeps into a
huge salty swamp here and to the west. In the Han period a garrison
was stationed here.

The Great Wall of the Han dynasty   About 5 km/3 mi further west, remains can be seen of the Han dynasty's Great Wall. It is made of rammed earth with thick reed layers to stabilize it. Also to be seen are the **ruins of a watchtower**, which is made of mud bricks. The northern side of the Wall was its outer face. A caravan route used to lead along it. The Wall's main purpose was to ensure that the caravans did not avoid the customs post set up at the fort.

River warehouse   About 6 km/4 mi east of the fort there is an impressive ruin measuring about 100 m/330 ft in length with 10 m/33 ft high mud-brick walls and several large openings and remnants of an enclosure with watchtowers, the river warehouse. The building mainly served as a **granary** for feeding the garrison: Along the river, which opens into a lake just beyond the ruin, Chinese peasants, who had been settled there specially for the purpose, once cultivated the land. The natural raw materials for that were then transported here by barge.

✴ Emei Shan

Gg 31

Province: Sichuan   **Altitude:** 3099 m

In the southern part of the province of Sichuan, about 140 km/87 mi south of the provincial capital Chengdu, Mount Emai rises to an altitude of 3099 m/10,167 ft. It is the highest of the holy mountains of Chinese Buddhism. Along with the great Buddha of Leshan (30 km/19 mi to the east) it has been a UNESCO World Heritage Site since 1996, not only thanks to its importance in cultural history but also because of its natural beauty and its major status as a unique biotope.

3000 plant species have been counted here, each of them adapted to the climate at four separate altitude levels. They range from sub-tropical and evergreen broad-leaf forest to sub-Alpine coniferous forest just below the tree line. The summit region (from about 2000 m/ 6500 ft upwards) forms a **cold island**. This is home to 100 endemic plant species.

A hermit's life   Even 1800 to 1900 years ago, Daoist hermits are said to have retreated here for the mountainous solitude, enough of them to build settlements. The earliest definite date for a Buddhist presence goes back to the **founding of the Wannian Si** monastery around 400. Even then it was obviously being postulated that there was a close relationship between the mountain and the bodhisattva of law, Samantabha-

Jianyin Dian monastery on Emei Shan in winter dress →

► VISITING EMEI SHAN

INFORMATION AND BOOKING

Rooms in the monasteries can usually be booked at the hotel you are staying at at the foot of the mountain. Here you can also get a weather forecast. It is best to book a bed in the monastery via the Sichuan International Travel Service (p. 232), particularly at weekends and during holiday periods.

GETTING THERE

The town of Emeishan is on the railway line between Chengdu and Kunming and there are services to Chengdu several times a day. The station is at the eastern edge of town. Usually it is better to travel by motorway coach, which is quicker and more frequent. In addition the long diversion via Emeishan can be avoided, as there are morning services from Chengdu which go directly to Baoguo Si bus station at the foot of the mountain. From the town of Emeishan itself (bus station) buses run frequently to Leshan.

WHERE TO EAT

It is not necessary to bring too much food onto the mountain since there are stands all the way up to keep the pilgrims provided with nourishment. In the larger monasteries there are refectories where it possible to eat rather well. If staying in a monastery, a vegetarian breakfast will be provided and sometimes an evening meal as well. The inexpensive prices for food get higher nearer the summit. One speciality is wild mushrooms.

WHERE TO STAY

► Mid-range

① *Hong Zhu Shan Hotel*
On the edge of the hotel district near Baoguo Si

Tel. 08 33/552 58 88
www.hongzhushan-hotel.com
This hotel has played host to Chiang Kaishek, Deng Xiaoping and other top politicians – not in the modern hotel wing, of course (283 rooms), but in villas in the extensive, park-like grounds.

② *Jin Ding Hotel*
On the Jin-Ding summit
Tel. 08 33/509 80 88
Heated mountain-top accommodation with 85 rooms

► Budget
Monastery accommodation
All the larger monasteries and many of the smaller ones on the mountain offer accommodation. Sometimes the rental is just for a bed but occasionally there are some proper double rooms. It makes sense to bring a linen sleeping bag and your own towel. The atmosphere usually makes up for the lack of comfort. Be careful, though, between spring and autumn the rooms fill up quickly in the afternoons and anyone arriving shortly before the doors close (i.e. sunset) risks being turned away. It is safer to book in advance at a travel agent's.

③ *Teddy Bear Hotel*
43 Baoguo Lu
(not far from the bus station)
Tel. 0833/5 59 01 35
Andy mobile 138 90 68 19 61
www.teddybear.com
Old-established meeting place for backpackers (22 rooms) with two buildings. Andy the innkeeper requests visitors to call him before arriving. He collects his guests from the station free of charge before they fall victim to touts from other establishments.

dra, a tradition which survives to this day. This is reflected in the fact that the earliest name for Wannian Si was in fact the **»Samantabhadra monastery«** (Puxian Si). In the course of the following millennium, the number of monasteries slowly but steadily increased. It was in the 16th and 17th centuries that Emei Shan became really popular, as a place of pilgrimage too. That is when most of the present-day monasteries were founded. At one point there were over 200, of which only 25 remain. Some of the monasteries were and are Daoist.

Emei Shan is very big and the route to the summit is long. From the foot of the mountain to the summit is a walk of at least 35 km/

! **Baedeker** TIP

When the azaleas bloom
On Emei Shan, particularly in the higher regions, there are more than 60 species of wild azalea and rhododendron. They flower in May, which is thus the best time for a mountain hike.

22 mi. The sights themselves are also spread over a corresponding area. There is no standard route for visiting the attractions. Depending on how much time is available and how much of the route you want to cover on foot, there are a variety of **tours and hiking routes**. It is possible to get as far as Jieyin Dian, at an altitude of 2500 m/8200 ft by bus and at that point you can change to the summit cable-car. Another cable-car covers the lower part of the mountain and links the car park for Wannian Si (890 m/2920 ft) with the actual Wannian Si temple monastery (1020 m/3346 ft). It is important to know that climbing or riding all the way to the summit is not always worthwhile, firstly because it is normally shrouded in cloud and sec-

Emei Shan *Map*

Where to stay
① Hong Zhu Shan Hotel　② Jin Ding Hotel　③ Teddy Bear Hotel

ondly because most of the things to see are on the lower slopes of the mountain (up to a height of about 1100 m/3600 ft). In any case, it is best to plan for two overnight stops, ideally one night at the foot of the mountain and one night in one of the monasteries. A **short tour** starts with a bus trip and cable-car to the summit before descending to the Wannian temple car park then up by cable-car to Wannian temple itself and by foot along **Monkey Valley** to Wuxiangang car park and from there by bus back to the foot of the mountain. This can be covered in a day (but means starting out by 8am at the latest), but even that means staying two nights at the base of the mountain. To travel the whole journey on foot takes at least two days, but requires a very good constitution. It is necessary to decide as well whether to take the northern route or the longer southern route. The routes separate at the bottom near the pavilion of Qingyin Ge and rejoin at the saddle of Jiulinggang. The opening times of the monasteries depend on the time of year, usually lasting from sunrise to sunset.

Emei Shan …

What to see at Emei Shan

The eponymous town (with the railway station; 475 m/1560 ft above sea level, pop. 70,000) lies at the northeastern foot of the mountain. There is no reason to stop there, though, as the relevant starting point for tours of the mountain is 6 km/4 mi further south in a **hotel and restaurant estate**, which has no official name (in brochures it is called Emei Shan Holiday Area or similar) near the temple monastery of Baoguo Si – with the bus station, museum and some nicely kept parkland.

Emeishan town and the foot of the mountain

The temple that covers the greatest area on the mountain of Emei Shan has a quite non-Buddhist name, which translates as something like **»Temple Monastery for Repayment of State Benefactions«**. Since its founding in the 17th century it has served as accommodation for pilgrims and a base camp for the pilgrimage up Emei Shan. Beyond its imposing gates there is a row of four halls along the tem-

Temple monastery of Baoguo Si

... *a winter wonderland*

ple's axis. The first is the Maitreya Hall, where the Future Buddha smiles at visitors. In the second hall sits Shakyamuni, flanked by the 18 arhats. Next comes the **Seven Buddha Hall** with images of bodiless gold lacquer made in the Daoguang era (1821–1850). They are the biggest statues in the province to have been made using this complicated technique, which is very seldom used for objects of this size. The last hall is the Samantabhadra Hall, which has an image of a bodhisattva.

Mount Emei Tourist Center and Emei Shan Museum ⊙

The information centre provides plenty of useful material The museum in the same building is very effective with its well presented, and multifaceted **cultural history collection** as well as geology, plus the flora and fauna of the mountain. It is situated in the park opposite Baoguo Si. Opening times: 8.10am–6pm daily, admission free.

Temple monastery of Fuhu Si

The »**Temple Monastery of the Crouching Tiger**« is the first one on the way to the summit, 1 km/1100 yd from Baoguo Si at an altitude of 630 m/2067 ft. It probably gets its name from the shape of the mountain behind it. Its main attraction is a hall featuring 500 arhats, a new building dating from the 1980s. A bronze pagoda 6.5 m/21 ft in height is historically important. The text of the Huayan sutra and 4700 small Buddha reliefs are cast into its shell. It is thought to have been made around the year 1600.

Pavilion of Qingyin Ge

Beyond the »Temple Monastery of the Growling Thunder« (Leiyin Si), the Daoist monastery of Chunyang Dian and a couple of other small shrines, it is another 10 km/6 mi to the »**Pavilion of the Clear Song of the Streams**« (Qingyin Ge, 710 m/2330 ft), one of the best known, prettiest and most popular places on the mountain. The particular charm of the spot comes from the two mountain streams that pass either side of the pavilion with two **arched bridges crossing them** and join together by the Ox-heart Pavilion at little further down the slope. This gets its odd name from the shape of the rock on which it stands. The Pavilion of the Clear Song of the Spring has continued to inspire poets visiting Emei Shan down the centuries. For a short-cut to the spot, take a bus to Wuxiangang from the bus station at Baoguo Si. From there it is just 1.5 km/1 mi on foot.

! *Baedeker* TIP

Our feathered friends

256 species of bird have been counted on Emei Shan, making the mountain an especially attractive place for ornithologists and twitchers. One tour operator that specifically caters for such interests is Aves Tours in Münster, Germany. The English section of their website www.aves tours.de is rather thin, so it is best to use it to send them an e-mail requesting detailed information.

Shower of blossom at Fuhu Si temple monastery →

»Crack of Sky« gorge, monkey reservation

Even when ascending by the shorter north route, it is a good idea to make a short detour along the southern path since just above the Qingyin Ge pavilion it runs through a narrow gorge appropriately named »Crack of Sky« (Yixiantian) At this point the route had to be carved out of the rock. The valley is now a **reservation for the familiar Emei Shan monkeys**, a variety of macaque. Be careful because the animals are not at all timid and will even steal plastic bottles. Any provisions should be kept well hidden. Suitable food for the monkeys can be obtained at the entrance to the reserve. A detour through the cutting takes about an hour.

? DID YOU KNOW ...?

■ that each of the four holy mountains of Chinese Buddhism is dedicated to a particular bodhisattva? Emei Shan to Samantabhadra, Wutai Shan to Manjushri, Jiuhua Shan to Kshitigarbha and the island of Putuo Shan to Guanyin.

Southern route

Beyond the valley of the monkeys a long climb leads up to the **Xianfeng temple monastery** (1750 m/5740 ft), from which it is worth breaking off for a stop at the »Cave of the Nine Elders« (21 km/13 mi from the Qingyin Ge Pavilion). About 10 km/6 mi further on the north and south routes come back together again.

Northern route: Wannian Si

After the pavilion of Qingyin Ge the northern route climbs for 2 km/1.5 mi past a temple monastery called the **»White Dragon Cave«** (Bailong Dong) to the »Eternity Monastery« (Wannian Si, 1020 m/ 3346 ft), where it is possible to get a pretty decent night's sleep (bring a towel). The monastery is the oldest on the mountain and has a history dating back 1600 years. It is also a popular destination for pilgrims. Early in the morning, even before sunrise, it is possible to attend the **morning liturgy**. The main architectural attraction in the extensive grounds is a Ming-era brick hall containing the most famous Samantabhadra image on Emei Shan. It is 7.4 m/24 ft high and was cast from 62 tons of bronze in the year 980 (commissioned by the emperor himself). Later it was painted. The bodhisattva is depicted enthroned on his elephant steed – a miraculous white animal with three pairs of tusks.

The northern route heads steeply upwards over the **Huayan summit** (1914 m/6280 ft), then back down to rejoin the southern route before climbing sharply again towards the **»Elephant Bathing Pool«** (Xixiang Chi, 2070 m/6791 ft, 14 tough kilometres/9 mi past Wannian Si). The name of this monastery refers to Samantabhadra's steed. In the ancillary buildings around its three halls, the shrine can accommodate several hundred pilgrims and forms the final base for an ascent to the summit.

The path to the summit

Ancient trees and azaleas line the relatively gentle climb to the monastery of **Jieyin Dian**, from where a cable-car opened in 1988 runs for 1170 m/1280 yd to provide a short cut to the top. For those who do not use it, there is another 6 km/4 km of steep climb to overcome.

Golden Summit

The objective of an Emei Shan-pilgrimage is actually a secondary peak, although at 3077 m/10,095 ft it is only a fraction below the highest point of the mountain. This is the site of the Huazang Si summit monastery, whose shining roofs match the peak's name. In front of it is a new attraction in the form of a bronze Samantabhadra with ten faces. He is riding on Siamese elephant quadruplets and is 48 m/150 ft tall.

The summit (especially the cliff edge) is famous for the frequency with which the »**glory« phenomenon** is observed here, an effect also known as a »Brocken spectre« after the mountain in the Harz mountains of Germany where it also famously occurs, and which in China is called the »Buddha nimbus«: If the sun casts a person's shadow onto a bank of fog at a lower altitude, the image appears in the form of a circular halo with rainbow colours that looks not unlike the halo of a saint around the head of the observer.

The Ten-Thou-sand Buddha Summit

It is four kilometres/2.5 mi from the »Golden Summit« to the »Ten-Thousand Buddha Summit«, the actual highest point of the mountain. The distance can be covered most easily by monorail. On the rare clear days it is possible to see as far west as the 7556 m/24790 ft peak of **Gongga Shan**, 140 km/87 mi away. Even more so, a »successful« sunset is the highlight of any visit to the summit.

✳ Guangzhou (Canton)

Province: Guangdong
Altitude: 5 m

Population: 7million (not including the Greater Gwangzhou area)

The role that Shanghai fulfils for eastern China and the mouth of the Yangtze is fulfilled at the end of the Guangzhou, the Pearl River, by another international metropole and port. Formerly known in English as Canton, Gwangzhou, though, came into existence when Shanghai was no more than a seashore lapped by waves. For tourists now, however, the city is not only overshadowed by the larger and more spectacular Shanghai, but even more so by nearby Hong Kong, even though the latter's establishment as a British trading port was inspired by its proximity to Guangzhou, which indeed also applies to Macau. The combination of modern boomtown and deep tradition that Guangzhou has to offer is to be found nowhere else.

Guangzhou is the capital of the southern Chinese province of Guangdong. It is the second biggest port on China's south coast after Hong Kong, and the **centre of the whole region around the Pearl River delta**, which itself is now fusing into a single giant metropolitan area. The city is largely flat with hills and mountains only towards the north.

City of goats

Guangzhou's nickname comes from a legend. In ancient times the people had a hard life and were mostly hungry. One day five immortals rode out of the clouds on five goats and gave the people five ears of corn. When the people planted the corn, their suffering came to an end. When the immortals soared back to their clouds, they left the goats behind and the city has prospered ever since.

A turbulent history

The area was brought into the Chinese empire under the first emperor in 214 BC. When the Qin empire fell in 206 BC, a **kingdom by the name of Nanyue** came into being here and Guangzhou was its capital until 111 BC, when it once more became part of China in the empire of the Han dynasty. Guangzhou's role only really began to flourish, though, under the empire of the Tang, when it developed into an overseas port. At that time Arab merchants established a large Muslim community here. Under the Song dynasty the city experienced a new heyday, when only Quanzhou exceeded it in importance as a trading harbour with the outside world. The Portuguese landed here in 1517, to be followed by the Spanish, Dutch, British and French.

Over the course of time the port became ever larger. Jesuit missionaries first entered China via Guangzhou. In 1684 the British East India Company moved its headquarters to Guangzhou. When in 1757 the Qianlong Emperor decreed that all sea trade with foreign lands was to handled via Guangzhou; the Chinese merchants who were privileged to operate here amassed **vast fortunes**. In the early 19th century the East India Company flooded China with opium, smuggled in via Guangzhou – thus leading to the outbreak of the Opium Wars and the founding of Hong Kong, the opening of other harbours to foreign trade and thus the loss of Guangzhou's monopoly position. Early in the 20th century the city became a hotbed of the anti-Manchurian, republican movement. **Sun Yatsen**, the »Father of the Republic«, established the Whampoa Military Academy to the south of the city in 1924 as a first step to reuniting the country, which had been split up under the control of warlords. The revolutionary tradition of the city has not always seen it on the winning side, though.

After the split between the Communists and the Kuomintang, a workers' revolt in 1927 saw more than 5000 communists slaughtered by KMT troops. The only remnant of the city's trading legacy that was retained after the establishment of the People's Republic was the Guangzhou trade fair, which took place twice a year and was the only

In Guangzhou and elsewhere: imported brands have great prestige

fair for external trade anywhere in the country. Otherwise the city, robbed of its dynamism, declined into a kind of hibernation. There is no trace of that today, though. On the contrary, anyone who has been away from the city for ten years would have trouble recognizing the place.

All the sights to see are in the region of the old town north of the Pearl River. A cross of streets separates the district into four roughly equal sections. Jiefang Lu (Liberation Road) runs north to south and Zhongshan Lu (Sun Yatsen Road) goes east to west. A visit to the city should plan for at least a day and a half, two days if a trip to Foshan is included.

Tours and getting around

Yuexiu Park and its surroundings

In the northern part of the old town, southwest of the old central station, is Guangzhou's **»green lung«**, an extensive park covering 93 ha / 230 acres and including many ponds, a flower hall, an orchid garden and a stadium. In the southwest of the park the prominent Goat Monument recalls the legend of the city's founding. A little further south the even bigger Sun Yatsen Monument towers over the park.

Yuexiu-Park (Yuexiu Gongyuan)

On Yuexiu Hill, named after the park, there is a tower-like old building called Zhenhai Lou. It dates back to 1380, although it was rebuilt in concrete in 1928, since when it has housed the city's museum with exhibits (particularly archaeological relics) illustrating the history of Guangzhou and its environs. Opening times: 9am–5pm. Underground: Yuexiu Gongyuan.

Zhenhai Lou, city museum

🕐

▶ VISITING GUANGZHOU

INFORMATION

Guangzhou Tourist Corporation
155-4 Huanshi Xilu
(by the central station)
Tel. 020/86 66 51 82
Fax 020/86 67 75 63
Plenty of useful tips are offered in
English at www.cityweekend.com.cn/
guangzhou

GETTING THERE

Guangzhou's Baiyun international
airport is 34 km / 20 mi north of town;
there are direct flights from Europe.
The old central railway station in the
centre of town is now less important
than the very much larger Guangzhou
East station; both are served by the
underground. Express trains from
Hong Kong (Kowloon station) reach
Guangzhou East in one and three-
quarter hours. Express buses go to
Zhuhai and Macau (two and a half
hours).

SHOPPING

High-class art and craft shops are
located in the White Swan Hotel.
There is an excellent range of china,
jade, lacquerware, carvings, ink-
paintings etc. – old and new – at the
Guangzhou Antique Shop, Wende
Beilu 172 (underground: Nongjiang-
suo). All kinds of attractive souvenirs
can also be picked up at Shamian on
4th Street (Sijie). The Friendship Shop
sells both high-quality international
goods and first-class Chinese products
(Youyi Shangdian, 369 Huanshi
Donglu).

BARS AND PUBS

The locals frequent the bars on
Baietan Bar Street southeast of Sha-
mian on the other side of the Pearl
River (underground: Fangcun). Those

wishing to meet Guangzhou's expa-
triate colony are recommended to go
to the Elephant and Castle near the
Friendship Shop (363 Huanshi Donglu).

WHERE TO EAT

Cantonese cuisine in its home city is a
must, especially in a teahouse. Good
food is in any case the central aspect of
Cantonese culture. Even more than in
Hong Kong there are exotic dishes
such as dog (only in winter) and snake
(also best in winter), not to mention
sea-food.

▶ Expensive

① *White Swan Hotel*
For a treat, with a view of the Pearl
River; the interior is air-conditioned,
but especially on balmy summer
evenings the hotel garden is an inviting place to sit (▶ Where to stay).

▶ Moderate

② *Dafosi Sushige*
27 Xihu Lu, 3rd floor
Tel. 020/83 30 21 26
Underground ½ Gongyuanqian
Buddhist vegetarian restaurant with
incredible imitations of fish and meat.
The dim-sum lunch is particularly
cheap.

③ *Guangzhou*
Wenchang Nanlu 2 (Ecke Xiujiu Lu)
Tel. 020/81 38 03 88
Underground Changshou Lu
Doubtless the city's most famous
Cantonese restaurant, it extends over
three floors. Noisy and uninviting – as
is ought – but the cooks know their
business.

④ *Lai Wan Market*
Garden Hotel, Huanshi, 368 Donglu

Tel. 020/83 33 89 89 ext. 3922
Not a market but a hotel restaurant that serves dim-sum and rice dishes in a lovingly designed ambience with classical Chinese furniture and flowing water.

WHERE TO STAY
► Luxury
① *White Swan Hotel*
Shamian Dajie
Tel. 020/81 88 69 68
Fax 020/81 86 11 88
www.whiteswanhotel.com
Underground Huangsha
843 rooms, unique spot right next to the sea with a lovely garden and excellent catering

► Mid-range
② *Guangdong Victory Hotel*
53-54 Shamian Beijie
Tel. 020/81 21 66 88
Fax 020/81 21 60 62
www.vhotel.com
Underground Huangsha
211 rooms spaced over two buildings.

The older and cheaper wing has a colonial atmosphere. The Chaozhouyuan restaurant is good.

③ *Shamian Hotel*
53 Shamian Namjie
Tel. 020/81 21 82 88
Fax 020/81 21 86 28
www.gdshamianhotel.com
Underground Huangsha
The White Swan Hotel is too expensive? Then try its smaller and cheaper neighbour. Very popular so book early.

► Budget
④ *Guangzhou Riverside Youth Hostel*
15 Luju Lu Changdi Jie
Tel. 020/22 39 25 00
Tel. 020/22 39 25 48
rsjiangpan@yahoo.com.cn
Highly praised hostel not far from Fangcun underground station. With travel service, internet, laundry.

The city's best museum – mainly thanks to its spectacular, 2100-year-old grave treasures, discovered here in 1983. The mausoleum is in the grounds outside the museum and possesses a seven-chamber crypt, which is open to the public. The man entombed inside was the second king of Nanyue, **Zhao Mo**, who died in 122 BC. The jade work is particularly exquisite and there is sometimes a quite magical fascination in the design. The most magnificent piece is a burial robe made of 2291 jade platelets sewn together – an incorruptible stony shroud. Other things on view include bronze vessels, bronze mirrors, two golden seals, a bronze carillon, a sounding-stone instrument and more – about 1000 exhibits in all. 867 Jiefang Beilu. Underground: Yuexiu Park. Opening times: 9am–5.30pm daily.

Museum of the mausoleum for the king of Nanyue (Xi Han Nanyue Wangmu Bowuguan)

Ⓟ

The immense building, 49 m / 1160 ft in height, dedicated to the memory of the **founder of the Chinese Republic**, was built in 1931 in neo-classical Chinese style opposite the southern end of Yuexiu Park. It now serves as a centre for conferences and exhibitions. Its central hall holds more than 4000 people. Underground Jinian Tang.

Sun Yatsen memorial hall (Zhongshan Jinian Tang)

Guangzhou Map

Where to stay

① White Swan Hotel ② Guangdong Victory Hotel ③ Shamian Hotel ④ Guangzhou Riverside Youth Hostel

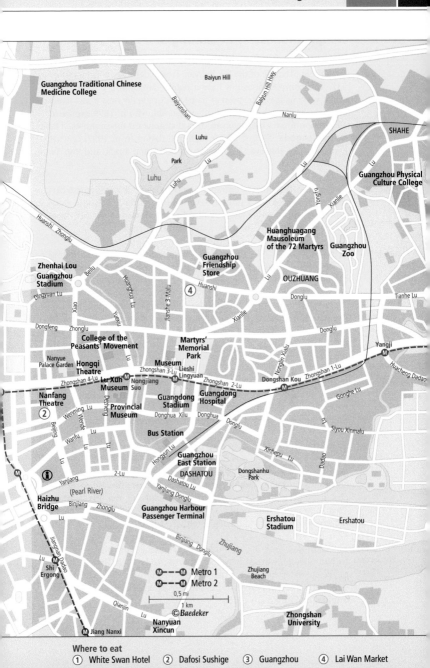

Guangzhou Traditional Chinese Medicine College

Baiyun Hill

Baiyunshan

Baiyun Hill Hwy.

Nanlu

SHAHE

Luhu

Lu

Park

Lu

Luhu

Xianlie

Yongni

Guangzhou Physical Culture College

Luhu

Luhu

Huanshi Zhonglu

Zhenhai Lou
Guangzhou
Stadium

Belu

Huanghuagang
Mausoleum
of the 72 Martyrs

Guangzhou
Zoo

Guangzhou
Friendship
Store

OUZHUANG

Dingyuan Lu

Yuexiu

Huanghua Lu

Tianhe 3-Malu

④

Huanshi

Lu

Donglu

Tianhe Lu

Dongfeng   Zhonglu

Xianlie

Donglu

College of the
Peasants' Movement

Martyrs'
Memorial
Park

Nanyue
Palace Garden   Hongqi
Theatre

Museum

Nonglin Xialu

Yangji

M

Zhongshan 1-Lu

Huacheng Dadao

Zhongshan 4-Lu   Lu Xun
Museum

Lieshi
Lingyuan

Zhongshan 3-Lu   Zhongshan 2-Lu   Dongshan Kou

Nanfang
Theatre

Nongjiang
Suo

Gonghe Lu

M

②

Wenming Lu

Dezheng

Guangdong
Stadium

Guangdong
Hospital

Beijing

Wende   Donghua Xilu   Donglu

Siyou Xinmalu

Provincial
Museum

Danao

Wanfu

Donghua

Lu

Bus Station

Hongrun Lu

Donglu

Xinhepu

Lu

M

Lu

Yanjiang

2-Lu

Guangzhou
East Station

Dashatou Lu

Dongshanhu
Park

Haizhu
Bridge

(Pearl River)

DASHATOU

Binjiang   Zhonglu

Yanjiang Donglu

Ershatou
Stadium

Ershatou

Lu

Guangzhou Harbour
Passenger Terminal

Binjiang Donglu

Zhujiang

Jiangnan Dadao

Zhujiang
Beach

M

Lu

Shi
Ergong

M——M Metro 1
M——M Metro 2

Qianjin   Lu

0,5 mi

1 km

©Baedeker

Zhongshan
University

M Jiang Nanxi

Nanyuan
Xincun

Where to eat
① White Swan Hotel   ② Dafosi Sushige   ③ Guangzhou   ④ Lai Wan Market

Temple monastery of Liurong Si

What is probably the most visited **holy place** in town, the monastery Liurong Si (Temple of the Six Banyan Trees), dates back as far as AD 537. The complex does not have a regular layout and the buildings are of varying ages. The present name was originally only a nickname and goes back to the poet and official Su Shi, who in 1099 expressed admiration for six large banyan trees that grew on the premises. The slender **pagoda**, 57 m / 200 ft high and dating from 1097, is what really catches the eye. It is made of wood and brick and can be climbed.

Main hall The main hall facing the entrance was rebuilt in 1983 as its predecessor fell victim to the Cultural Revolution. The three valuable Buddhas there now are the largest gilded **bronze statues** in the province, although they could also enter a competition for the ugliest.

Guanyin Hall Left of the main axis, the first building is the Guanyin Hall dating from 1987. The image of the bodhisattva inside, though, goes back to 1663.

Hall of the Six Patriarchs The hall on the right is in memory of the monk Huineng (638–713), the actual founder of Zen Buddhism as a specific school, the path to which had been prepared by the five patriarchs before him. The **image of the holy man** seen here was cast in the year 989 and is one of the monastery's greatest treasures.

Hall of Ancestors It is from the Hall of Ancestors that the monastery earns the most money, namely by **renting out places for ancestral tablets**. The rental period is two years. 87-89 Liurong Lu. Monastery opening times: 8am–5pm daily. Underground Gongyuanqian.

✱ Temple monastery of Guangxiao Si

One block west of Liurong Si is another generously proportioned, harmonious looking, well kept and quiet **temple**, the oldest in the city, having emerged from an earlier structure in the 4th century. Thanks to the Indian monks who taught here, it played a key role in the spread of Buddhism through southern China.

Hall of the Six Patriarchs The sixth patriarch of Zen Buddhism, Huineng, also made his contribution, as he worked here too. Appropriately, then, there is a hall to his memory here (as at the temple of Liurong Si). The present building dates from 1692 and is supposedly a **reconstruction of the original building** from 1016.

Sacrificial offerings at a hall →
of Liurong Si temple monastery

Iron pagodas Among the curiosities of the site are two iron pagodas, which are more than 1000 years old – the oldest pagodas of their kind in all China. The one to the east was cast in 967 and is 7.7 m / 24 ft high including its stone base. It is covered with more than **900 Buddha reliefs** and is located inside a hall specially built to house it. The iron pagoda to the west is even older, having been made four years earlier. It is in the same style but is no longer complete. The hall protecting it collapsed during a typhoon in the 1930s and damaged the upper storeys.

Yifa Pagoda The octagonal brick pagoda is 7.8 m / 24 ft high. It goes back to the 7th century but has been rebuilt on several occasions. It is a sort of **burial pagoda for the hair of Huineng's head**, which was shaved off when he made he monastic vows. 109 Jinghui Lu. Opening times: 6am–5pm daily. Underground: Ximenkou.

Temple of the Five Immortals (Wuxian Guan) Following the street that runs along the eastern side of the Guang-xiao temple monastery southward for about 1 km / 1100 yd, turn left at the junction with Haizhu Lu and on the northern side of the street a curious Daoist shrine can be seen, although it no longer operates as a temple. It was once used for the worship of the five immortals who many long ages ago came riding five goats and brought the local people everlasting prosperity. This **oasis of peace** features a hall, a huge bell tower where even the bell is 3 m / 10 ft high and four of the immortals with their goats, in the shape of some rather cute stone figures standing out in the open air. Huifu Xilu. Opening times: 9am–5pm daily. Underground Ximenkou.

Guangzhou: the banks of the Pearl River

Around the corner to the north is a road called Guangta Lu, »**Smooth Tower Street**«, which immediately calls to mind its main attraction, a round minaret, 36 m / 110 ft in height. It belongs to one of the oldest mosques in China, founded during the Tang era. The currently alleged year of its establishment, 627, just five years after the Hejira, is not confirmed, however. Not regularly open to the public.

Huaisheng Mosque

✳ Clan temple of Chenjia Ci

A quick journey by underground (one stop) takes you to one of the most magnificent temple sites in the city, the **Temple for the Ancestors of the Chen Clan**. The phrase »temple for ancestors« only describes part of its purpose, though. The six courtyards of the complex also housed a school for the male children of Guangzhou's Chen family. Nowadays part of the museum of folk art is housed here, which is thoroughly in keeping with the temple's theme.

In ancient China relatives often got together to give clever children a Confucian education, even if they came from poorer parts of the family. This gave them **a chance to take the exam to enter the bureaucracy**. In addition it was especially common in the south for members of a clan in a certain place to build and maintain a joint temple to honour their ancestors, which also functioned as an assembly hall and school. The temple here also had one more function: the 82 branches of the Chen clan who got together to build the complex wanted to gain prestige thereby and create an unmistakable expression of their wealth.

Background

The whole site is quite uniform: three axes, each with three halls with the ones at the side slightly narrow than the one on the centre. The roofs are conspicuous and typical of the region: not curved but featuring high, and highly ornamented, roof ridges. The decoration indeed is the **main attraction of the temple** – the finest masonry work, luxuriant wood carving, stucco and ceramics from the workshops of nearby Shiwan. They depict flowers, animals, fruits and thousands of human figures – in a colourful mixture of allegories, symbols promising happiness, scenes from the rich source of Chinese legends and history. Especially amazing are the double-sided, perforated doors with different images on either side, although each hole on one side necessarily also appears on the other. Working out the design must have involved huge amounts of work.

The complex and its style

Hardly any of the original furnishings have survived. The large **ancestor shrine on the rear wall** of the central hall at the rear has been reconstructed. Nevertheless among the exhibits assembled here, there are some fascinating things to see: artistically painted porcelain, more wood carvings, some of them gilded, furniture and other ob-

Exhibits

jects which display the preference for what is sometimes quite exaggerated decoration popular in the late Qing period. Zhongshan Qilu, on the side street Enlongji Lu. Opening times: 8.30am–5.30pm daily. Underground: Chenjiaci.

Shamian The island of Shamian on the Pearl River to the southwest at the edge of the old town was set aside by the Qing government at the end of the 18th century for foreign merchants and their consulates: There they could enjoy their freedom without disturbing the peace of the Chinese. What was once an uninhabited sandbank was then gradually expanded until only a narrow channel crossed by numerous bridges separated it from the main shore. In 1861 it was officially designated a concession for the French and British. A lot of the **colonial atmosphere** has been retained. It is nice to walk along the shady streets and occasionally to enjoy the bronze statues, which depict visitors to Shamian and its inhabitants from both then and now. The dominant building in the centre of the southern shore is a skyscraper, which is not terribly attractive from the outside, the luxury White Swan Hotel. Underground: Huangsha (west of the island).

! **Baedeker TIP**

Qingping Market
The market to the north of Shamian has is famous, but also notorious in its disregard for endangered species. It no longer exists in its original form but it is still worth shopping here, especially because of the huge amounts of dried mushrooms, dried roots and medicinal herbs on offer. Qingping Lu (northward over the bridge in the middle of the island and straight on).

✶ ✶ Foshan Zu Miao Temple

Guangzhou's neighbouring city, 20 km / 12 mi to the west (nearly 1 million inhabitants) has a name meaning »Buddha mountain«. Nowadays it hardly seems separate from Guangzhou at all. The main reason to go there is the Zu Miao Temple. This »ancestor temple« is one of the most spectacular holy places on southern China. Its name does not actually mean it is a temple for the worship of ancestors, but that it is itself the **»ancestor of all temples«** by dint of its great age. It was used for worship of the Northern Emperor, mythical lord of the fearsome north, who is resident in that part of the firmament which the sun and moon avoid. From there he determines the joy and sorrow of the people.

History The temple was founded as early as 1080. The present buildings were constructed in the Ming and Qing periods. The project was expanded on several occasions and was mostly financed by merchants, who also used the premises as a place of assembly.

The complex and its style The site is somewhat unusual in that the entrance was moved to the side in the 17th century. All the halls are laid out along a single long

Decorative detail at the Zu Miao temple

axis. The style of building is reminiscent of the Chen temple in Guangzhou – pitched roofs with no curvature, hugely ornamental high ridges – with the difference, though, that here most of the figures and rich decoration are also **painted gold**. The colourful mixture of allegories, happiness symbols and popular imagery is also reminiscent of the aforementioned temple, with the addition here, though, of the Xuanwu, the pair of animals which symbolize the Emperor of the North: a turtle with a snake coiled on its shell.

The entrance at the side leads from the park in front of the site through a decorative gate into a broad courtyard. Straight ahead there is a **spirit wall decorated with two dragons**, which dates from 1958. To both the right and left a stone dragon pillar looms up. Two more decorative gates at the far left look a little out of place as they do not seem to go anywhere. They did not originally belong to the present temple. The first of them (to the south) dates from 1521 and has an imperial inscription. A small cast-iron pagoda at the southern end of the was moved here from a Buddhist temple.

Entrance and outer courtyard

An opening leads into an inner courtyard. Its outstanding feature is a **large water basin**, in which lurk the symbolic creatures of the Emperor of the North, a turtle and snake carved from granite. On either side there is a drum tower and a bell tower.

Inner courtyard

Two stone lions flank the three-entrance gatehouse from 1450. The plaque above the centre entrance bears the official name of the temple: the **»Temple of the Miraculous Answering«**. The parallel verses on each side are in the calligraphy of an imperial minister. The most eye-catching sights on the outside are a gold painted frieze of figures, running for 31 m /70 ft beneath the eaves and an equally long and

Gatehouse

ostentatious roof ridge made of Shiwan tiles, measuring up to 1.8 m / 6 ft in height. On the front of it more than 152 figures are depicted with another 149 at the rear. It is the result of a beautification attempt dating from 1899, which is typical of its time. Inside to the right a bell dating from 1486 can be seen.

Entrance hall An intermediate roof immediately adjoins the gatehouse, underneath which there is an incense holder from 1801. In the actual entrance hall, built in 1429, there is a splendid table, 3.3 m / 11 ft long with gilded carvings, displaying among other things the **subjugation and humiliation of foreigners** – an expression of desire dating from 1899. Along both sides towards the north there are rows of figures. More than life-size and glittering with gold, they portray the Emperor of the North's generals. A perforated carved wall screen brings the scene to an end before the courtyard beyond.

Courtyard The following courtyard is dominated by a **bronze tripod** dating from 1899. At the front of the galleries on the right stand the god who manages temple and the god of the city, both members of the Emperor of the North's entourage as are the figures on the left, the »local gods« (patrons of the two regions of countryside). Behind them are some panels which would once have been carried at the front of a procession for the gods when such things were common.

Main hall In the »Purple Cloud Palace«, as a plaque above the main shrine declares the name to be, the **dramatic iconography** reaches its conclusion and climax, a grandiose table, another staggering tapestry, more of the Emperor of Heaven's officers, two sets of five implements of worship on the altars and finally the main shrine with its image of the Northern Emperor, a bald bronze figure with a black beard dating from 1452. The hall was already in existence in 1372, making it the oldest part of the temple.

Decorative gate Going back and around the pond, there is a decorated gate, which was once the main entrance to the temple. This **impressive building with its triple roof** was an imperial gift from 1449. The two characters on the inside of it (where you are standing) mean: »imperial order«, while the corresponding characters on the southern side tell those entering that this is a »holy area«.

Temple stage It was because of the construction of this splendid building in 1658 that the entrance was moved. Its luxuriant, black and gold decoration is top notch. Occasionally the stage is still used for performances. Its position on the axis opposite the main temple was carefully chosen, since it is at the end that the Emperor of the North is seated.
⊕ Zumiao Lu 21. Opening times: 8.30am–6pm daily. Buses from the provincial bus station (western side of Guangzhou Central station) to Zumiao bus station close by the temple.

✶✶ **Guilin**

Province: Guangxi   **Population:** 350,000
Altitude: 150 m/490 ft

The town of Guilin lies amid China's most famous landscape, which goes by the same name. Its karst cones rise out of rice, taro and lotus fields, the River Li lined by leaning bamboos and fairy-tale mountain scenery, fishing cormorants, southerly sunshine and the comfort of seeing and admiring everything from the deck of a boat without having to take a step. Just look around and delight in this paradisical piece of earth in the north of Guangxi province.

Limestone sedimentary layers deposited on the ocean floor were pushed up from the sea bed about 360 000 years ago. Erosion then began its work, as is typical for karst regions in the tropics and sub-tropics. This gave rise to the **tower or conical karst rock formations** that can be seen today.

 ## VISITING GUILIN AND SURROUNDINGS

INFORMATION

CITS
11 Binjiang Lu (on the Li river next to the Golden Elephant Hotel)
Tel. 07 73/2831 999
Fax 07 73/282 74 24
www.chinahighlights.com
This is the place to go to book boat trips and other day trips, among other things.

GETTING THERE

Guilin has an international airport with direct connections to all the major centres in China, and some smaller ones, as well as to some nearby airports abroad. The railway station is on the main Wuhan –Changsha – Nanning line. Long-distance buses with sleeping facilities also connect with Guangzhou, Shenzhen and other places. Low-fare minibuses and large long-distance coaches go from Guilin station to Yangshuo at regular intervals throughout the day (journey time 1 hour approx.).

WHAT TO DO

Apart from the city of Guilin itself, Yangshuo is the second important base for exploring the region. The hotels and hostels there offer plenty of opportunities to book cycle tours, rafting and canoe trips, motor-rick-shaw rides, day trips, language and qigong courses, painting lessons, climbing tours (in winter only) and much more. Evening boat trips can be booked from Guilin or Yangshuo allowing you to see the cormorant fishing.

THEATRE

Liu Sanjie
»Third Sister Liu«, is the name of this

spectacular stage show featuring the talents of more than 600 people, which takes place outside Yangshuo. A 2000-seat auditorium has been established here so that not only these stage spectacles, featuring attractive music and folk dancing by the ethnic minorities of northern Guangxi, can be viewed but also the scenery around it, which is illuminated for the purposes and made part of the show. Information: www.yxlsj.com, Tel. 07 73/881 19 82.

WHERE TO EAT

Guilin

Guilin is famed for exotic specialities like raccoon, snake, lizards or freshwater snails, but also has a rich selection of fruit and vegetables, including water chestnuts, lotus root, taro, carambola, kumquats and lychees. Adventurous souls will thus have plenty to try out and as long you do not ask for the meat rarities, there will not be too much to pay for the tasty fare. In the pedestrian zone, Zhengyang Lu, there is a dizzy selection of local food establishments, primarily low and mid priced. There are rows of simple restaurants and cafés to the north opposite the entrance to the educational college, where horse flesh is among the delicacies on offer.

Yangshuo

Whereas the numerous foreign tourists in Guilin mainly eat in their hotels, so that few independent restaurants are geared to outsiders, in Yangshuo, 90 km/56 mi south of Guilin, it is the other way round: In particular »West Street« is full of nice little establishments serving dishes from all round the globe and with menus printed in English. The prices are low to medium.

▶ Moderate

① **Guilin: Zhengyang Soup City**
60 Zhengyang Lu
Tel. 07 73/285 85 53
The speciality here is herb soup but there are also rice noodles à la Guilin, snails with chili and other dishes typical of the region. English menu.

Yangshuo: Lisa's
Xi Jie (next to the Si Hai Hotel)
Tel. 07 73/882 02 17
Long established restaurant with a wide selection of dishes, featuring western as well as Chinese and regional recipes.

WHERE TO STAY

▶ Luxury

① **Guilin: Sheraton Guilin**
9 Binjiang Nanlu
Tel. 07 73/282 55 88, fax 282 55 98
www.sheraton.com
A 430-room-hotel which stands out thanks to its central location with a view of the river.

▶ Mid-range

② **Guilin: Bravo Hotel**
14 Ronghu Nanlu
Tel. 07 73/289 88 88
Fax 07 73/289 33 33
www.glbravohotel.com
A four-star establishment (Holiday Inn) with 329 rooms on the lakeside, often offers major discounts.

Yangshuo: Paradesa Yangshuo Resort
Xijie 116
Tel. 07 73/882 21 09
Fax 07 73/882 21 06
www.paradiseyangshuo.com
The nicest place in Yangshuo, primarily because of the lovely location (next to a pond in a quiet spot away from the road), with a swimming pool and 145 rooms, although parts of the hotel are not in good condition.

► **Budget**

③ *Guilin: Flowers Youth Hostel*
6 Zhongshan Nanlu Shangzhi Xiang
Tel. 07 73/383 96 25, fax 384 52 75
www.yhaguilin.com
In a small street that turns off
opposite the railway station. Handy
for public transport but still quiet.
The rooms have air conditioning.

Yangshuo:
The numerous private guest-houses
on »West Street« and its side roads
also have weekly or monthly rates.
Since there is a lot happening on West

Street in the evenings, those who like
an early night are not best served
here. There is an atmospheric alternative 4 km/2.5 mi south of town,
which you can get to quickly by
bicycle:

Moon Resort
Gaotian, Yuelian Shan, Diqiu Cun
Tel. 07 73/877 76 88
www.moon-resort.com
Pleasant 15-roon inn with a view of
the karst landscape, 7.5 km/5 mi
south of Yangshuo at the foot of the
Moon Mountain.

The area came under the rule of the first Chinese emperor 2200 years ago. Ethnically speaking, however, this was a **settlement of the Tai peoples**. One of their tribes were the Zhuang, whose 15.6 million people now represent the largest ethnic minority in China (for which reason the province is officially called the»Autonomous region of the Zhuang«). In and around the town of Guilin, though the Zhuang have, over the course of the centuries, largely been overwhelmed by **Han Chinese** and now make up only 3% of the urban population. Guilin is situated in the northern part of the conical karst region with its centre on the west bank to the River Li. The centre of the old town is occupied by a former **princely palace**, although only the perimeter walls still survive. There is now a college on the site. Only the south gate (next to Lake Rong Hu) remains of the city's former walls. Since the late 1990s, Guilin has seen some highly beneficial de-velopments and it is particularly nice in the evenings in the vicinity of the old town centre (Zhengyang Lu pedestrian zone) and the **riv-er-bank promenades**, which exhibit a Mediterranean flair.

The city of Guilin

What to see in the town of Guilin

A little south of the old town centre on the western bank of the river there is an elephant. The giant animal may have no ears, legs or tail, but it is clearly recognisable anyway as it dips trunk into the River Li. A gap in the mountain is what creates the impression, at least when the water level is high enough. The **curious sight** can be seen from the park on the bank to the north of it.

Elephant Trunk Hill (Xiangbi Shan)

»**Fir Lake**« north of Elephant Trunk Hill and the adjoining »**Banyan Lake**« to the west have shady promenades and are ideal places for a walk, since vehicular traffic has largely been excluded from the

Lakes Shan Hu and Rong Hu

Guilin Map

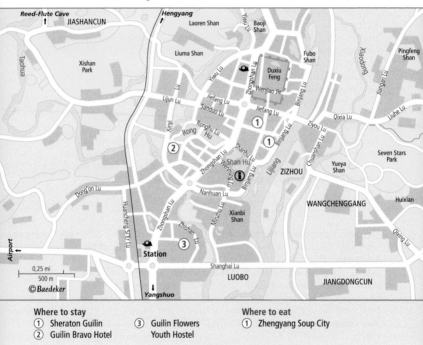

Where to stay
① Sheraton Guilin
② Guilin Bravo Hotel
③ Guilin Flowers Youth Hostel

Where to eat
① Zhengyang Soup City

banks. One block west of the main street of Zhongshan Zhonglu on the northern bank is the old south gate of the walls that once fortified the town. In the area between the gate and the main street students of the nearby language school like to try out their English on any strangers they see. This is called »**English Corner**« and provides an excellent opportunity to find out from young Chinese people anything you can't find in the book.

Fubo Shan

Following the river promenade to its northern end leads to a typical karst cone called the »**Wave Subduing Hill**«, referring to the fact that in its position right next to the river, it seems to swim on the waters. It can be viewed from the top or the bottom. »From the top« means climbing up 323 steps and enjoying a **superb panorama** from 62 m/ 203 ft up. »From below« refers to the fact that its base is hollow and it is possible to climb up and through natural catacombs to an opening and a rocky terrace right next to the river. As early as the Tang period, Buddhist sculptures were carved out of the rock here. They number some 200 in total. In addition there is an example of calligraphy hewn into the stone by **Mi Fu** (1051–1107), one of the most important artists and calligraphers of the Song dynasty. Opening times: 8.30am–4.30pm daily.

From the town centre the **»Liberation Bridge«** leads across to the east bank and following the street along leads to the Seven Star Park, named after its seven peaks, which correspond to the seven stars of the constellation known to us as the Plough, the Dipper or the Great Bear. It is a nice place to while away a good two hours. There is a **cave with stalactites and stalagmites** (Qixing Yan) as well as other caves including one at the west end which is full of old inscriptions. Often it is possible to see stone rubbings being made here. Some of them are sold in a shop next to the cave. A hill path leads further east from here, although it is also possible to circle the karst hill round its southern side. In the eastern part of the complex there is a rather miserable little zoo with a pitiable giant panda. In addition it is possible to see one of the most famous karst peaks in Guilin, the appropriately named **Camel Hill**. Opening times 8am–5pm daily.

Seven Star Park (Qixing Gongyuan)

! **Baedeker TIP**

Free buses

Something well worth noting is that the 58 bus goes to the most important tourist attractions, including the Reed Pipe Cave, Fubo Hill and Seven Star Park, for free.

Caves featuring stalagmites and stalactites are typical in karst regions. This one is the »standard cave« for tourists in Guilin, really big and close to the town. Nevertheless a word of warning should be sounded: there are other, more spectacular caves of the kind and the **imaginatively colourful lighting** does not necessarily improve the experience. It is a different experience to go on one of the tours with a good Chinese guide as what the Chinese see in the various formations is culturally quite surprising. 6 km northwest of the city. Opening times: 8am–5.30pm daily.

Reed Pipe Cave (Ludi Yan)

6 km/4 mi east of the town in a rural setting at the western foot of the mountain Yao Shan is a set of necropolises. Some of the site has only recently been restored, although much of it is still »wild«. The tombs belong to the princes who resided in the palace at Guilin during the Ming period. Between 1370 and 1645 a total of eleven princes and their wives were interred here in distinguished **funerary temple complexes**. Although not of imperial dimensions, they are nonetheless imposing. The smallest occupies an area of 0.5 ha/1.2 acres, while the biggest covers 21 ha/52 acres. The tomb of the third prince has been completely restored and looks like new. It has gates, tended parkland, a stone honour-guard and a hall for offerings, and shows how all the tombs once appeared. Nevertheless, it is the still-unrestored graves with their **atmosphere of enchantment** that appeal more to Western eyes. On the way to the tombs of the princes the

✱ Tombs of princes (Jingjiang Wangling)

route passes a conventional cemetery in the style of the region with circular, walled mini burial mounds. Opening times: 8.30am–5.30pm daily. Take the no. 24 bus from Liberation Bridge.

Yao Shan   Yao Shan is the highest peak in the region with a summit 909 m/ 2982 ft above sea level (760 m/2500 ft above the surrounding plain). From the tombs of the princes a chair-lift transports visitors to the top in less than 20 minutes. The more **adventurous** can try a giant slide 1 km/1100 yd in length that starts from the intermediate station of the chair lift and ends up back at the princes' graves.

✳ ✳ Trip on the Li Jiang

This is what really matters. The 83 km/52 m stretch of the Li Jiang river between Guilin and Yangshuo is the real reason for tourism in Guilin. To see the bizarrely shaped mountains, villages, swimmers and cormorant fishers from the middle of its clear waters (when the weather allows), is **as beautiful as any journey can be**. All the boats allow passengers to stand on the upper deck and take in the view in

The unique Li Jiang riverscape…

all directions. They all have a galley, too, serving multiple-course, hot lunches (included in the price). For a little extra expense it is possible to enjoy certain specialities like river prawns from the Li Jiang itself, which are very nicely prepared in spite of the cramped space available.

At most times of the year the first step is to take a bus the 30 km/19 mi downstream to the **jetty at Zhujiang**, since in Guilin itself the water level is too low. Boats leave there in rapid succession between 9.30 and 10am – there is often a lot of confusion so make sure to keep your group in sight. The boats dock some four hours later in **Yangshuo**, from where the return journey is by bus (the boats sail back empty). It is best to book an all-in package from your hotel. Anything else is unnecessarily complicated and will be more expensive. As it is, the trip is by no means cheap. On the contrary: a price of at least 350 yuan can be expected, even for the lowest price in the winter season (December to March). 450 to 500 yuan is more realistic, but with better service and a better boat with fewer passengers. Beware of cheap packages with food in cardboard boxes, overfilled decks and sometimes no transport back.

Book an all-in package

… with cormorant fishers

Scenery It is possible, of course, to enjoy the trip alone but it is more interesting to hear what the Chinese imagination associates with many of the mountains past which the boat glides. Brochures for river tours may help but you will miss a lot if you are not looking in the right direction at the right time. It is always better to have an English-speaking guide on the vessel. These are some of the sights (starting from the Zhujiang jetty). **»Nine Dragons Playing the Water«** (right bank): stalactites hang from a cliff face in the open, overgrown with greenery and dripping water. **»Looking Out for Husband Rock«** (right bank): a rock that resembles a woman standing with a child on her back. **»Boy Worshipping Buddha«** (left bank): a small rocky peak in front of a larger one. **»Snail Hill«** (right bank): a hill with spiralling ledges. **»Brush Holder Hill«** (right bank): a row of hills with rounded depressions between them, looking like the utensil Chinese ink-painters or calligraphers keep their brushes in when they take a rest.

✳ Yangshuo

Whereas Chinese tour groups prefer to visit the countryside using Guilin as their base and go back there after a river voyage, »Western-

»West Street« in Yangshuo: centre of tourist activities

ers« travelling on their own, in particular, prefer to use Yangshuo at the end of the journey as their base for longer visits. The town, once a former rural spot of no great importance, now lives on the back of tourism – although that gives rise to certain **unpleasant spin-offs**, mainly in the surrounding villages, though, rather than the town itself. Once one has got used to got used to having unwanted goods thrust upon one, having to haggle for virtually everything and keeping an eye out for thieves, the **many charming aspects** of Yangshou are there to be discovered. One major advantage is that it is cheaper than in Guilin. There is a lot of nice private accommodation, cafés, bars and restaurants geared to foreigners and a welcome selection of other services, among which the bicycle hirers are surely the most popular, since Yangshuo is ideal as a base for day trips, long and short, to other places along the Li River and the **idyllic countryside around it** with its markets, villages, more oddly shaped karst curiosities, caves and swimming holes, boat trips and paddling. This is one of the few places in China where you could stay for a month.

Markets

Days in Yangshuo are divided into two: about two hours between the docking of the river boats and the departure of the last bus back to Guilin, when thousands of visitors throng the streets, and the other 22 hours when it is rather cosy and leisurely. The markets that extend from the jetty to the coach parks and away from the river down the main street (Xi Jie, »West Street«), obviously do most of their business during the said two hours. Their wares make Yangshuo a **paradise for souvenir hunters**. Apart from all kinds of textiles (including inexpensive silk) there are masses of imitation antiques, jade and other rock carvings, bric-a-brac, toys and Chinese puzzles for grown-ups, which often take hours of head-scratching. In addition, of course there is fruit and veg, drinks etc. The central market for the natives (on Diecui Lu north of Xi Jie) is a different matter, dealing mostly in agricultural produce, including all sorts of fruit, mushrooms, vegetables and much more,.

Attractions

In and around the town there are a host of mostly small **places to walk or** extending out as far as anyone could wish to travel. In the town itself **Yangshuo Park** and **Mount Bilian** with its mountain and water park in the east directly overlooking the river. There are some more interesting places 7 or 8 km/4 to 5 mi south of town across the Yulong River. The **Banyan Tree** is a veteran, which demands respect. Its massive crown of foliage casts shade over more than an acre (0.5 hectares). It is estimated to be 1400 to 1500 years old. Right past the Banyan Tree is **Moon Mountain**, an eye-catching site: This is a mountain with a round hole at the top resembling a half-moon. It is well worth climbing and, for the courageous, going that little bit higher to the top of a **natural bridge**, which is rewarded with a glorious panoramic view. For safety reasons, however, such a tour is not to be undertaken alone.

✴✴ Hangzhou

Province: Zhejiang
Altitude: 5 m/16 ft

Population: 1.4 million (6 million in the greater Hangzhou area)

In China the name of Hangzhou is comparable to those of Florence or Vienna in Europe, with an air of tradition, wealth and beauty. The capital of Zhejiang province, 180 km/112 mi south of Shanghai on the Qiantang Jiang estuary, primarily fulfils the Chinese ideal of a city amid glorious scenery. The West Lake with its causeways has been imitated twice in palace gardens by the emperors in Beijing. Hangzhou has long been a place with a fine lifestyle, at least since the Song emperors chose it as their residence.

Hangzhou is associated with a rich legacy of stories and legends but the city has little in the way of historic buildings. From its 150-year heyday under the southern Song dynasty (1127–1279) not a thing has survived. Then, as now, the best description of the city in that era is that of Marco Polo, who called the city Quinsai and dubbed it **»by far the most glorious city in the world«**. Modern-day Hangzhou has been caught up in the ongoing boom experienced by greater Shanghai and, here too, skyscrapers have shot up, which from the perspective of tourism to the West Lake can only be called idiotic and annoying. To expect a romantic-looking city would therefore be a mistake. Nevertheless, to miss out on Hangzhou means missing a key, indeed an edifying, part of China. Two days is a decent time to spend there. Making the trip from Shanghai thus means that one overnight stay might be enough if need be, although obviously one would wish to have more time to enjoy the city at leisure.

✴✴ West Lake

Some 12,000 years ago a spit of land across a bay in the estuary of the Qiantang River created a freshwater lake. It would become the most famous lake in the country. Its banks are lined by weeping willows, promenades, teahouses, pagodas, boats and skiffs, islands, lotus plants and the whole scene is encircled by rolling hills. The lake is only about 1.5 m/5 ft deep and covers just 6 sq km/2.5 sq mi but it provides **countless scenic views** and any number of ways to enjoy them.

By land and water
The West Lake, or Xi Hu in Chinese, is not only to be enjoyed from the water. There are also shady promenades on the shores in the city and extending from the town along the banks. Open-topped electric carts trundle up and down them, a quiet and beneficial provision for the delight of older people, tired folks and anyone else who has bro-

Hangzhou Map

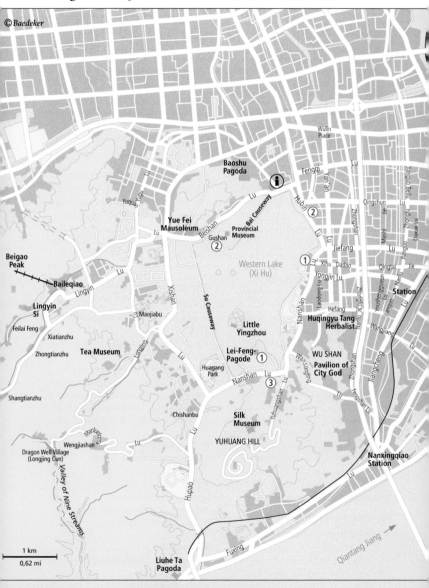

©Baedeker

Baoshu Pagoda

Wulin Place

ⓘ

Fengqi Lu

Yan'an Lu

Hubin Lu

Qingchun Lu

Bai Causeway

Yue Fei Mausoleum

Beishan Lu

Provincial Museum

Gushan

②

Zhongshan Lu

Yuquan Lu

Lu

Jiefang Lu

Masho Lu

Zhongli Lu

② Hubin Lu

Beigao Peak

Western Lake (Xi Hu)

① Xihu Dadao

Yongjin Lu

Laodong Lu

Qingtai Jie

Lingyin Si

Lingyin Lu

Xishan Lu

Maojiabu

Nanshan Lu

Hefang

Huqingyu Tang Herbalist

Station

Feilai Feng

Xiatianzhu

Su Causeway

Little Yingzhou

Wangjiang

Zhongtianzhu

Tea Museum

Loging Lu

Lei-Feng-Pagode ①

Lu

WU SHAN

Pavilion of City God

Wansongling

Jiangcheng

Shangtianzhu

Huagang Park

③

Nanshan Lu

Yuhuangshan Lu

Zhongshan Lu

Fenghan Lu

Chishanbu

Silk Museum

Nanxingqiao Station

Manjuelong

Wengjiashan

Lu

YUHUANG HILL

Dragon Well Village (Longjing Cun)

Valley of Nine Streams

Hupao Lu

Fuxing Lu

Lu

Liuhe Ta Pagoda

Qiantang Jiang

1 km
0,62 mi

Where to eat
① Xihu Tiandi
② Louwailou

Where to stay
① Xizi Binguan
② Overseas Chinese Hotel
③ West Lake Youth Hostel

▶ VISITING HANGZHOU

INFORMATION
Zhejiang CITS
1 Shihan Lu (at the northern end of
the Bai causeway)
Tel. 05 71/85 15 88 28

Complaints telephone for tourists
Tel. 05 71/87 17 12 92

GETTING THERE
Hangzhou is on the main rail line from
Shanghai to Guangzhou and trains run
several times a day from Shanghai
(journey time from Shanghai South
station between 80 mins and three
hours). It takes between two-and-a-
half and four hours to get to Suzhou.
To the east, Ningbo is 2–3 hours away.
Hangzhou has its own airport with
non-stop flights to numerous domestic
destinations (incl. Hong Kong and
Macau) and other major cities in Asia.
Long-distance buses run to various
places, one interesting one being
Huang Shan (from the-West Bus
Station, six hours' journey time).

SHOPPING
The famous green Dragon Well tea
leaves can be bought in many shops. A
small tea service made of Yixing china
would be a fine addition, all the more
so as the clay originates from this
region. Other souvenirs, including
fans, for which Hangzhou is also
famed, can be found in the old-town
lane near Wu Shan Square.

WHERE TO EAT
▶ **Expensive**
① *Xihu Tiandi*
147 Nanshan Lu (on the east shore of
the West Lake near the road Xihu
Dadao)
Butterfly: Tel. 05 71/87 02 77 11
Tea and Wine Chapter:

Tel. 05 71/87 02 69 33
A whole group of restaurants in an
ensemble of highly chic, modern glass
pavilions. The Butterfly, for example,
serves southeast Asian food in a
designer ambience. In the Tea and Wine
Chapter the food is classic Chinese.

▶ **Moderate**
② *Louwailou*
30 Gushan Lu
(southern shore of Gushan island)
Tel. 05 71/87 96 90 23
The best known restaurant in town
was established in 1848. Its most
tempting aspects are the view of the
lake and its specialities, including fish
from the West Lake itself served in
brown sauce and prawns boiled in tea.

WHERE TO STAY
▶ **Luxury**
① *Xizi Binguan (Wangzhuang)*
37 Nanshan Lu
Tel. 05 71/87 02 18 88, Fax 87 06 35 37
xizi@mail.hz.zj.cn
Former state guest house in an in-
convenient place in terms of transport
but a very pretty one at the southern
tip of the lake. The lawns of the hotel's
own park go right down to the water.

▶ **Mid-range**
② *Overseas Chinese Hotel*
15 Hubin Lu
Tel. 05 71/87 07 44 01, Fax 87 07 49 78
hq_hotel@mail.hz.zj.cn
300 rooms on the lakeside promenade,
good value for money

▶ **Budget**
③ *West Lake Youth Hostel*
62–63 Nanshan Lu
Tel. 05 71/87 02 70 27
www.westlakehostel.com
Small, quiet establishment.

ken into sweat on a summer afternoon. In addition there are also **lakeside parks with tea houses, restaurants and cafés**. One other thing is that some influential and organizationally gifted individuals very early on built two causeways into the waters themselves. These are among the lake's most memorable and distinctive features, so that similar structures also adorn its imperial imitations in Beijing and Chengde.

The side of Hangzhou that visitors come to see. It is not only the view of the West Lake that makes its so nice to walk by it. The well-tended parklands also please the eye and their trees offer shade. Benches are provided, too, and bars, ice-cream parlours and restaurants alternate all down the banks. From here too, on the eastern side of the lake, boats ply out onto the waters themselves. | **Promenades in town**

The nicest way to enjoy the West Lake is still to cross it **by gondola**, travelling in comfort and virtually in silence. Up to six passengers can be accommodated, sheltered from sun and rain by a simple canopy. The less attractive alternatives are motor boats or rowing boats. The larger tour boats in particular lack that certain flair and, furthermore, they are always so full that some unlucky folk may get no more than a glimpse of the actual lake between the heads of the other travellers. In general it is best to take a tour late in the afternoon when the waterways and islands are less full and the light is more beautiful than at midday, for example. | **Tours**

The shorter and narrower of the two causeways forms an **avenue of willows** leading from the northern end of the town promenade to the island of Gushan. The name of the causeway is linked to the poet Bai Juyi, who sang of it as early as the 9th century. Two gaps allow for the passage of small boats with the one at the eastern end being spanned by a small bridge called the »Broken Bridge«. Even in ancient China the strange name gave rise to several explanations. The simplest and probably the most accurate historically is that it just means the »Bridge over the Break«, since this is where the mainland is cut off and the causeway begins. Towards the northwest it is possible to see the slender 45 m/148 ft Baochu Pagoda. | **Bai causeway**

The only natural island on the West Lake, **Gushan**, is largely laid out as a park. A pavilion tops the summit of the hill. On the southern shore there are teahouses and

> ! **Baedeker TIP**
>
> **Tea with ambience**
>
> In the vicinity of the Bai causeway two rather special teahouses invite visitors to take a break. One of them is on the last side street before the Bai causeway when heading out of the town, on a slope beyond the embankment. It is conspicuous for its curving roofs. The second is on the courtyard of the Wenlan Ge library in the grounds of the provincial museum. It does not have a view of the lake but it is spared the noise of traffic.

restaurants with the provincial museum between them. The view from the terrace at the eastern end is famous as the »Autumn Moon over the Calm Lake«, one of the traditional Ten Scenes of Xi Hu, which need to be experienced at the right time of year, in this case in the autumn when the moon is up and the wind is still. Proceeding westward along the shore, one passes the museum before coming to the Louwailou restaurant, the most famous in town, and then the classical premises of the **Xiling Seal Engravers' Society**. On the west bank, to the right of the road shortly before the bridge which leads back from the island to the mainland, is the grave of the revolutionary and women's rights campaigner Qiu Jin (1875–1907), where there is a white statue of the brave lady. She was executed as a rebel and her mortal remains were only moved here in 1981.

✱
Provincial museum

The provincial museum of Hangzhou (Gushan Lu 25) contains a huge variety of beautifully displayed exhibits. Among the things on view are **archaeological finds** from prehistoric cultures, pottery, coins, craft work, sculptures, paintings and calligraphy as well as exhibits from the more recent history of the city. The Zhejiang West Lake Gallery also belongs to the museum but has a separate entrance. The building, which opened in 1999, mostly houses exhibitions of artworks from the 20th and 21st centuries. On the other side, to the west of the main museum buildings, is one of the four famous imperial libraries of China, built in 1782 to house an example of the text compendium, Siku Quanshu (► Chengde, Wenjin Ge Library p. 218). Opening times: Tue–Sun 8.30am–4.30pm, Mon 12 noon–4.30pm. Last admissions 4pm.

Yue Fei Mausoleum

Having crossed the bridge and, if it is summer, enjoyed the view of the lotus flowers and water lilies, turn left and walk the 300 m/330 yd to the memorial temple and tomb of Yue Fei (1103–1141) on the right. The general was fighting for his life defending the empire of the Song dynasty from invasion by the Jurchens, who succeeded in conquering northern China. Meanwhile, though, an enemy of his was plotting against him at court and Yue fell out of favour. His execution, due to the machinations of the traitor, as the official reading has it, made him China's first **national hero**. His statue in the main hall was fashioned in 1979. In one of the side halls his parents are honoured. His tomb is on the left of the main courtyard accompanied by a 400-year-old stone honour-guard (to the left of Yue Fei's burial mound). Among them is the traitor himself, with his wife and two accomplices kneeling alongside. Generations of Chinese have spat on these cast iron statues. Opening times: 7am–6pm daily.

Su causeway

The longer of the two causeways, which forks off opposite the Yue Fei temple, was named after its builder, **Su Dongpo** (1036–1101), one of the most famous poets of ancient China, who was a magistrate in Hangzhou and had the causeway constructed in the years

Idyllic nature at the centre of the city: early morning atmosphere on the West Lake of Hangzhou

after 1089. 2.8 km/1.7 mi in length, it crosses six bridges and, just before it ends, the lovely Huagang Park lies to the right.

The »Flower Harbour Park« is the landscape-gardening highlight at the southern end of the Su causeway, a fascinating **mixture of Chinese and English garden design** – with plenty of views across the water and a tea house from which one can take in one of the famous Ten Scenes. This one is called »Viewing Fish at the Flower Harbour «, referring to the numerous golden carp. Opening times: 6am–6pm daily.

✱
Huagang Park

🕐

On the southern bank of the West Lake, the pompous Lei Feng Pagoda, built in 2002, cannot be overlooked. Behind glass in its pedestal, the foundations of a previous such building on the site can be seen. The earlier building collapsed in 1924. It played a key role, though, in one of the most famous of the tales of the West Lake, the **Tale of the White Snake**. This is a love story involving a young scholar and a snake sprite, who had spent hundreds of years learning how to turn her body into that of a beautiful woman. A monk who saw this relationship as unnatural managed to use his own magical powers to imprison the snake under the Lei Feng Pagoda – »until the pagoda falls and the lake dries up« – meaning of course till the end of time. In the story, though, the miracle really does occur after many long years. So the collapse of the pagoda was even predicted by the story. The fable of the snake sprite is illustrated on the new pagoda in the form of some exquisite carvings. Opening times: 7.30am–9pm daily, in winter 8.30am–7.30pm.

Lei Feng Pagoda

🕐

✳
»Little Ying-zhou« Island

The most famous of the artificial island on the West Lake is named after a legendary island in the World Ocean, where the immortals are said to live. This is thus the chance to set foot on a kind of **paradise island**. It is indeed unusual, consisting largely of water in the form of lotus and lily ponds separated from one another and from the lake by narrow, often tree-lined, levees. Thus wherever you wander on the island, you can always see water or water plants on either side. South of the southern shore, three stone lanterns going by the name of Santan Yinyue poke out of the lake: »Three Pools Mirroring the Moon«. This is another of the Ten Scenes of Xi Hu, although it can only be seen by moonlight at the mid-autumn festival when the lamps are lit. Ferries ply to the island from the city promenade near Jiefang Lu.

Around Wu Shan Square

At the southern edge of the city centre, within walking distance of the lake, there are two more places to see. At the foot of Wu Shan Hill there is a reconstructed old-town street with the historic apothecary Huqingyu Tang. On top of the hill stands a pagoda-like observation tower called Chenghuang Ge. To find the way there look for Wu Shan Square on the northern side of the hill.

✳
The old-town street and Huqingyu Tang Pharmacy

Head east from the square through the ornamental gate to the He-fang Jie pedestrian precinct with its pretty shops and restaurants. While the street is largely **an artificial attempt to re-create an old town ambience**, the result is successful, and it is pleasant to stroll along. Most of Hangzhou's old town centre looked like this before the clearance and rebuilding of the 1980s and 90s (but not so spick and span by any means). On the right a conspicuously high wall can be seen. Behind it is the city's most beautiful historic legacy, the original Huqingyu Tang Pharmacy dating from 1874. The word »pharmacy« is admittedly somewhat of an understatement here, as this is not just a shop but virtually a palace. The building with its multiple courtyards has some 4000 sq m/4800 sq yd of sales floor. It also features some wonderful gilded carvings, verdant inner courts, in which restorative plants are grown, and its own **pharmacy museum**. Furthermore the medicines here are not just sold but also prepared (often before visitors' own eyes). Hefang Jie, Dajing Xiang 95. Internet: www.huqingyutang.com. Opening times: 8.30am–6pm daily.

🕐

City God Pavilion (Chenghuang Ge)

Go back to Wu Shan Square, then up the hill. Up a little further there is a 42 m/138 ft tower completed in 2000, decorated with curved pagoda-style roofs. Its exaggerated dimensions give it a rather ugly look to Western eyes. By contrast, though, it offers an **outstanding panoramic view of the lake and the city**. It is worth going to the top (by lift) even after dark. On the first floor there are large dioramas illustrating the city's history, including one of Hangzhou as it was 800 years ago, when it was the residence of the Song emperors. Further up there is a teahouse, very pleasant with classical Chinese music performed live. At the bottom beside the tower is another new buildings, a **temple to honour the god of the city**, who was considered responsible for Hangzhou when such beliefs were still common. The tradition is here portrayed merely as a spectacle for tourists. Opening times: 7.30am–10pm daily.

✳ Temple monastery of Lingyin Si · Mount Feilai Feng

After the West Lake, Mount Feilai Feng and the monastery of Lingyin Si count as the number two attraction. In a shady valley with a tumbling brook, one side has a rocky cliff, the other an imposing Buddhist temple, making up a remarkable **ensemble of nature and religious art**. If it were not for the thousands of visitors who flock here every day, the fact this place, just 3 km/2 mi from the West Lake, is close to a great metropolis, would seem incredible.

The name Lingyin Si, »Temple of Inspired Seclusion«, is partly self-explanatory: For those renouncing the world, the retreat into the loneliness of forest and mountain truly works wonders. Whence comes Feilai Feng, though, the»Peak Flown From Afar«? The monastery was founded in 326 by an Indian monk who thought the rocky hill opposite (170 m/558 ft high) looked so like one from his own

Names and history

Withdrawal from the world works wonders – at least according to the name of Longyin Si monastery

home that it seemed to have flown to China from there. Later on, in the 10th–14th centuries, more than 300 Buddhist sculptures and reliefs were carved out of the rock here, mostly inside natural caves. The most famous of them is a smiling **pot-bellied Buddha** dating from the Song period and located near the monastery. None of the present-day monastery buildings, however, was built more than 140 years ago. The only reminders of more ancient times are the two stone sutra pillars on the path leading up to the temple – they date from 969 – and two damaged stone pagodas from the same era situated in the first courtyard. Thanks to the streams of visitors and countless donations, the monastery has in the post-Mao era been extensively and imposingly expanded. The work is still unfinished.

Hall of the Heavenly Kings The actual entrance hall can unfortunately only be accessed from the rear. Its six statues follow the usual scheme, but the joint **shrine for the serene pot-bellied Buddha** and the Weituo figure guarding the interior of the temple behind him is unusually splendid.

Baedeker TIP

A detour worth taking
A different approach to the Lingyin monastery: about 700 m/770 yd in front of the front gate take the Beigao Feng cable-car to the »High Northern Peak«. There, 314 m/1030 ft up, not only is there a great view but offerings can be made to the god of wealth. The monastery is then a good thirty minutes' walk downhill through the woods, but it is a good way to avoid the crowds around the main entrance.

The main hall dates from 1953 and at 33 m/108 ft high it is impressive in its dimensions. Enthroned in the centre is a 9 m/30 ft Shakyamuni Buddha. This was carved out of camphor wood and gilded in 1956. Including the pedestal and the halo, it reaches a height of almost 20 m/65 ft. The figures at the sides are the 20 protective deities of Buddhism and after them come the enlightened disciples of Buddha. At the rear, a relief scene 20 m/66 ft high tells the **story of the youth Shancai**, who on his way to becoming a Buddha sought out 53 teachers, including the goddess of mercy Guanyin. Her statue is in the middle riding a giant fish, upon which she rides out over the World Ocean to rescue human souls.

Hall of the Medicine Buddha This icon of Buddhist philanthropy is surrounded by his two assistants and the twelve patron gods of the twelve two-hour periods of each day.

Rear halls Another two equally large halls dating from the post-Mao era follow next. The statuary is new. The pedestal of the penultimate statue contains the **monastic treasury**, where liturgical accessories, valuable texts and vestments are on display.

Hall of the 500 Arhats The Hall of the 500 Arhats, another recent building is to some extent **indicative of the economic boom in the region**: There seems to be no lack of finance here. The figures of the 500 holy monks are bigger than life-size and are the largest of their kind in the whole of China. The shrine that houses them is correspondingly immense. Its floor plan takes the form of the Buddhist symbol for eternity, the swastika. Opening times: 7am–5pm daily. Take the nostalgic wooden buses from the city centre (routes 1 and 2 to their terminus).

South and southwest

The West Lake only contributes one part of the »spirit« of Hangzhou. Another of the elements is represented by the hills that flank the lake, the tea plantations in their valleys and between them the caves, bamboo groves and not forgetting the **silk that expresses the Hangzhou lifestyle**. The best way to take in all of this is on a bicycle tour. Completing the whole trip with two museum visits and stops for other attractions, it can take the best part of a day. One alternative would be to take buses and taxis and cover the rest on foot. For those who prefer public transport the no. 27 bus or the no. 3 tourist bus run from the Bai causeway (northern end) to Dragon Well Village.

From the middle of »West Hill Street« (Xishan Lu) on the western bank of the West Lake a side-road leads off the road to Longjing Lu towards Dragon Well Village. Take the second right after that to get to the tea museum, which illustrates the **history and culture of tea cultivation, processing and preparation** in pleasant surroundings with captions in English. Bus stop Shuangfeng Cun. Opening times: 8.20am–4.20pm daily.

✱ Tea museum

The tea museum is right in the middle of the home of China's most famous brand of tea, Dragon Well (Longjing cha). The tea plantations, through which the next 2 km/1.5 mi to Dragon Well Village (Longjing Cun) run (at the end of which the actual Dragon's Well is located), are not the only ones that grow this sought-after brand, though, and depending on the plucking, the prices commanded cover a wide range. For that reason it is wise to be cautious when buying leaves privately as many a hawker will try to persuade you to do on the way to the final destination. Try to get informed in a shop first as to the price ranges and levels of the various quality teas. **Longjing tea leaves** are anyway more expensive here than elsewhere, but they are guaranteed to be fresh.

Dragon Well Village

Carrying on, a path leads south down Nine Brooks Road (Jiuxi Lu) through an idyllic **valley free of vehicles** but lined with sloping tea plantations and bamboo groves. It the middle there is a waterfall and a pond; with a restaurant, too. After 4 km/2.5 mi, the path meets the Qiantang-River. Bus routes K 4, K 504 and 514 run from here back to the city or to the next place on the itinerary:

✱ Nine Brooks Valley

Liuhe Ta Pagoda   3 km/2 mi south of the West Lake or1 km/1100 yd downstream from the spot where Nine Brooks Valley meets the Qiantang Jiang, there is a hill, on top of which stands the Liuhe Ta Pagoda, one of the city's landmarks. Its name **»Pagoda of the Sixfold Harmony«** refers to a unity and community of six aspects of a Buddhist monastery: teaching, guidance, worship, liturgy, morals and belief. The wooden building is nearly 60 m/200 ft high and was most recently rebuilt in 1900, although it actually dates back to the year 1163. Of the original structure only the brick core of the tower remains. From the top there is a lovely view of the river and the road-and-rail bridge built between 1934 and 1937, which is 1.4 km/ 1530 yd long. Opening times: 6am–6pm daily.

! **Baedeker** TIP

Tidal bore

The long, funnel-shaped mouth of the Qiantang Jiang gives rise to a tidal bore that thunders up the river at spring tides (new moon or full moon). Poems were written about the bore 2000 years ago. It can be watched from the Liuhe Ta Pagoda, although it is at its most spectacular 40 km/25 mi further downstream.

For the last part of the round trip it is best to take a taxi as there is no direct bus service. The **silk museum** is about 1 km/1100 yd south of the West Lake's southwest tip. It is large and very new, but not that well run – in large part it is best described as a silk salesroom. Nevertheless it is still worth a visit. English captions describe the history and techniques of silk manufacture and historic silk garments. Among the most valuable exhibits are some silks dating back 1000 years. Yuhuangshan Lu 73. Opening times: Tue–Sun 8.45am– 4.30pm, Mon 12 noon–4.30pm. Last admission 4pm.

Shaoxing

60 km/37 mi east of Hangzhou the town of Shaoxing (pop. 350,000) is a place to go on a day trip by rail or bus. It was known for its pretty appearance until well into the 1990s. It was distinguished by traditional, white, one and two-storey houses with grey roofs, and innumerable canals. The latter are still there but most of the old houses and shops have had to give way to newer buildings.

Around Shaoxing   Shaoxing is only slightly above sea level. In particular the area to the north of the city is criss-crossed by canals and ponds. The traditional agricultural district is being pushed back further and further these days by modern **industry, transport works and housing estates**. Selling their land or starting new businesses, though, has made some ex-farmers wealthy and they have had some magnificent houses built so that parts of the country have the air of rich villa estates.

Old town   The central **square**, the result of modern town planning, i.e. demolition, seems to be popular with the natives. In the west a restored piece of the old walls is on view, while to the south the 40 m/131 ft **brick pagoda of Dashansi Ta** can be seen. The monastery to which it once belonged has not been in existence for some time. The pagoda itself dates from 1228, although it has been restored many times since.

Hongqi Lu (Red Flag Street) is not named in memory of lingering socialism but is a beautifully restored old-town street leading from the southwest corner of the square southward along the canal. It has several nice restaurants and shops on it. One way to get back to the other side of the canal is via Longshan Houjie. Another alternative is to cross the canal at the first opportunity from Red Flag Street (westward) and go straight on before climbing **Fu Shan** hill, site of Fushan Park. At the top there is an observation pagoda with a great all-round view.

Lu Xun monument

Lu Xun, the most important poet of modern China (►Famous people p. 80), was born in Shaoxing and grew up here. On Luxun Zhonglu, the middle section of Lu Xun Road is his **birthplace**. The large house owned by his parents has survived largely unchanged along with some of the contents. It gives an impression of life in the latter days of the imperial era. The large garden is particularly nice. Lu Xun did not have far to go to school: diagonally across the street and over a footbridge to the other side of the canal. The school itself was tiny and the conditions were impoverished. In the neighbourhood, the **Lu Xun monument** provides information on the life and work of the poet. Opening times: 8am–5.30pm daily.

Xianheng Bar

Kong Yiji, one of Lu Xun's famous short stories, takes place in the Xianheng bar. It tells of a good-for-nothing with a Confucian education, who keeps his head above water by theft and, when he has any money, comes here to order a cup of rice wine. The bar lives nowadays more on the back of its literary fame and has turned into a proper restaurant, a large establishment with two courtyards and plenty of dining rooms. **Shaoxing wine**, the most famous wine in all China, can be obtained in bottles elsewhere but drinking it here is indubitably authentic and testifies to sophistication. It is drunk warm, by the way. Xianheng Jiudian, Luxun Zhonglu 179.

✷ Orchid pavilion (Lan Ting)

About 10 km/6 mi southwest of the city is a reconstruction of the pavilion where, in the spring of 353, 240 scholars met to drink wine and hold a poetry contest. The master calligrapher Wang Xizhi later reported the events of this assembly in his famous »**Preface from the Orchid Pavilion**« (Lanting Xu), which is how it has been handed down to subsequent generations. Nowadays it is a pleasant spot with bamboo groves, waters, pavilions, a teahouse and a large obelisk, upon which both the Kangxi and Qianlong emperors added to the fame of the place in their own calligraphy. Opening times: 8am–5pm daily.

Harbin

Hk 23

Province: Heilongjiang
Altitude: 140 m/460 ft

Population: 3.2 million

The capital of China's most northerly province, Heilongjiang, is 500 km/310 mi northwest of Vladivostok. In more than one respect it feels rather more as if it should belong to Russia: It came into being from 1896 as the Russians were building a railway to Manchuria and much of it looks rather European. Nowadays its proximity to Russia plays a key role, especially in terms of trade. Harbin's winters are Siberian and it is thanks to this that the city can offer its major attraction, the Ice Festival.

What to see in Harbin

Daoli District (Daoli Qu)   The old town with its Russian colonial ambience is a nice place to wander and shop, particular on **Zhongyang Dajie** with its restored façades. Northwards of here are the banks of the Sungari River and to the east is the popular Zhaolin Park. From there Zhaolin Jie runs south to **St Sophia cathedral**. This former Russian Orthodox parish church (built 1907) was, like all the other churches here, ravaged during the Cultural Revolution. It has been beautifully restored and now houses a museum of architecture, which features some historic photographs of the city. Opening times: 9.30am–5.30pm daily.

The Russian Orthodox Cathedral of St Sophia in the centre of Harbin

▶ VISITING HARBIN

GETTING THERE

Harbin's airport is 40 km/25 mi west of the city. Traditionally people travel by train. This is where the South Manchuria Railway has its junction with a branch of the Trans-Siberian Railway leading direct to Vladivostok. From Harbin it is possible to travel to Moscow without changing trains.

WHERE TO EAT

▶ Moderate

Cafe Russia 1914
57 Xi Toudao Jie
Tel. 04 51/84 56 32 07

A small culinary trip through Russia – hearty and inexpensive. The dining area is one big living-room.

WHERE TO STAY

▶ Mid-range

Modern Hotel (Madi'er Binguan)
89 Zhongyang Dajie
Tel. 04 51/84 61 58 46
Fax 04 51/84 61 49 97
The hotel was »modern« when it opened in 1906. 131 rooms behind the historic façade are new and unfussily furnished.

Stalin Park stretches along the right-hand bank of the Sungari River. It contains the Flood Control Monument, in memory of the dyke building and riverbank reinforcement which was carried out after a catastrophic flood in 1958. During summer days the river is always hectic. It is possible to take a boat trip to the Sun Island on the other side of the river, where Sun Island Park has all kinds of leisure activities on offer. A little bit further upstream a cable-car plies across the river. **Stalin Park and Sun Island**

In January, when it so cold that lorries and buses can drive over the Sungari River, it is peak holiday season in Harbin: Hundreds of thousands come to see the spectacular **ice sculptures** in Zhaolin Park and along the river, some of them as big as houses (and depicting temples or castles). It is particularly gorgeous after dark when lighting installed inside the ice transforms the exhibits into gigantic and colourful crystals. The festival opens on 5 January and usually lasts until mid-February. **✱ Ice Festival**

Hohhot

Ha 25

Province: Inner Mongolia
Altitude: 1050 m/3445 ft

Population: 1.4 million

The capital of Inner Mongolia is a modern Chinese city. Only 11% of the 1.4 million inhabitants are actually Mongolian.

► VISITING HOHHOT

GETTING THERE

The rail journey takes ten and a half hours from Beijing and four hours from Datong. By air, Hohhot has flights from all the major Chinese cities and from Ulan Bator. If you cannot resist the touts who circle round the people arriving at the station offering trips into the steppes, you should at least haggle the price down. Such trips can also be booked from hotels.

WHERE TO EAT

Mongolian food is not like Chinese food. It is dominated by meat (mutton and sometimes camel) or noodles and there is also some cheese, although it won't taste like it does in Europe. The best known recipe is mutton hotpot (shuan yangrou), including vegetables. Several people should be on hand to eat it.

► Inexpensive
Malaqin Fandian
Corner of Xincheng Xijie and Julong Changjie

An institution known all over the town serving Mongolian and Chinese cuisine, including an outstanding hotpot in the evenings

WHERE TO STAY

► Mid-range
Zhaojun Hotel
53 Xinhua Dajie
Tel. 04 71/696 22 11
Fax 04 71/696 88 25
258 rooms in a faceless tower block, but inside the rooms are impressive. There is a travel bureau with English-speaking staff, which is good for booking a trip out to the steppes.

► Budget
Binyue International Youth Hostel
52 Zhaowu Dalu
Tel. 04 71/660 56 66
Fax 04 71/431 08 08
The youth hostel (48 rooms) is part of a four-star hotel. There are many advantages to compensate for the disadvantageous location.

Old town

Mosque In spite of the ongoing »upgrading« there is still a whole swathe of historic buildings in the centre. The main places to mention are four religious sites. The main mosque for the city's community of more than 20,000 Muslims is near the former North Gate in what is now a Muslim suburb. It was established towards the end of the 17th century and the present buildings date back mainly to extensions carried out in 1789 and 1923. The style is predominantly Chinese with some Arab elements. Non-Muslims are permitted to visit (except inside the prayer hall).

Temple monastery of Da Zhao The »Great Monastery« of Tibetan Buddhism, about 1 km/1100 yd south of the mosque, was established in 1580 by Altan Khan at the same time as the city itself. It is Chinese in style. It gained its present appearance under the Kangxi Emperor (1662–1722). That was also when the two-storey **Great Sutra Hall** was built, which was especially privileged to be allowed an imperial yellow roof, as were the other halls. The censer in front of the main hall dates from the early 17th century. Danan Jie. Opening times: 8am–5pm daily. ⏲

Beyond the main street, opposite Da Zhao to the east, is the biggest Buddhist temple in town. Indeed it is older than the city itself, although it was initially much smaller than it is today. The dominant building is a Tibetan **bottle pagoda** with reliefs adorning its pedestal. The main hall is in the Sino-Tibetan style and is roofed with gilded copper tiles. Since the 18th century – until the present day – the monastery has been the home of a Tibetan »Living Buddha«. He is the leader of the city's Buddhist community. Opening times: 8am–5pm daily. ⏲

Temple monastery of Xilitu Zhao

800 m/880 yd to the east on Wutasi Houjie is the Five Pagoda Monastery, of which only the **Diamond-throne Pagoda** built in 1740 still stands. This stone building decorated with reliefs consists of an 8 m/26 ft pedestal with five pagodas on top of it as well as a small pavilion above the entrance door. The most unusual feature is the one and only extant Mongolian map of the fixed stars, which can be seen as a stone relief at the rear. Opening times: 9am–5pm daily. ⏲

Five Pagoda Monastery

The folklore department in the Museum of Inner Mongolia provides an overview of the Mongolians' culture, clothing, hunting equipment and much more. The highlight in the palaeontological department is a **dinosaur skeleton**. The historical department offers information on Ghengis Khan and the Great Mongolian Empire. Unfortunately not very much is captioned in English. The spectacular new building in the east of the city has been occupied since 2008. (Xinghua Dongjie, corner of Dong Erhuan Lu). Opening times: Wed–Mon 9am–5pm, in winter 10am–4pm. ⏲

Museum of Inner Mongolia

✴ Trip out to the steppes

The steppes are usually what people really want to see, with the city being just an intermediate stop. Any number of trips out to the grasslands – from 80 km/50 mi to the north – are on offer in Hohhot. They are very touristy but offer virtually everything conceivable concerning the Mongolians' lifestyle: living in yurts, horseriding and equestrian acrobatics, Mongolian wrestling and in the evenings a huge feast with masses of mutton, to be washed down with plenty of spirits. There is also some Mongolian folk singing. **Xilamuren**, the nearest place to go, is the most crowded. It can be reached on a day trip; but more distant spots are nicer, like **Gegentala** and **Huitengxile**, where you can stay the night. Tours like this are only good in the summer when it has rained and the gently rolling steppes are luxuriant green all the way to the horizon. From the end of October till June the country is not very pretty.

✶✶ Hong Kong

Province: Special administrative zone **Population:** 6.9million
Altitude: 0–958 m/0–3143 ft

There is nothing so crazy as this anywhere else in the world: a city of millions with no space. That is at the root of what makes Hong Kong so fascinating. A jungle of skyscrapers, not only in the commercial centre (like every other high-rise city), but all over town, so that low-rise buildings are rare exceptions.

Everything is squeezed between the Peak and the water, and then more mountains and more water, enthroned on the slopes, on land reclaimed from the sea, served by motorways on stilts which darken the streets beneath before disappearing into tunnels bored through mountains or beneath the straits, with abrupt changes from one metre to the next, between high-rise dwellings and sub-tropical rainforest where glitteringly coloured giant butterflies flutter, poisonous snakes lurk and monkeys perform their acrobatics. To exaggerate a little, Hong Kong has no sights to see, the city itself is the sight. Of course, there are some fascinating places to visit and apart from the view of the city itself there is one other major attraction: Hong Kong is a gastronomic capital with culinary delights to suit all pockets and encompassing the cuisine of all five continents.

Many who remember Hong Kong from the time it was a British Crown Colony ask if any of the British character has remained since 1997. In fact English remains, alongside Mandarin and Cantonese, the official language here, cars drive on the left and street names like Queen's Road, Prince Edward Road etc. remain as they ever were. Hong Kong has, though, become even more international, as can be seen from its **restaurants and bars** for example. Nevertheless, much, much more Mandarin Chinese is spoken than before. For visitors from the Chinese mainland Hong Kong has become a top holiday destination.

British, Chinese or international?

History of Hong Kong

When the British occupied the virtually deserted island of Hong Kong during the first of the Opium Wars (1839–1842), it was not their intention to establish a major city there. All they wanted was a harbour sheltered from typhoons, a **military base** and a place where British merchants could come and not be troubled by Chinese bureaucracy. In 1860, during the second Opium War, the Kowloon Peninsula was added as well. In those days it was less than half the

← *The wonderful lights of Hong Kong seen from Victoria Peak*

⏵ VISITING HONGKONG

INFORMATION
Hong Kong Tourism Board (HKTB)
The HKTB has some outstanding informative material available as well as having qualified and helpful staff. Airport counter (for incoming passengers only)

Star Ferry Terminal, Tsim Sha Tsui, Kowloon 8am–6pm daily
www.discoverhongkong.com

MTR station, Causeway Bay
Exit F, Causeway Bay Hong Kong Island, 8am–6pm daily

GETTING THERE
By air
Chek Lap Kok international airport is situated on an artificial island to the north of Lantau Island. The terminal building, designed by star British architect Norman Foster, is an attraction in its own right. An airport rail-link ferries passengers to Kowloon in just 19 minutes or to the Central District (where there is a connection to the MTR underground) in 23 minutes. Many places, though, are easier to get to – i.e. without changing – by means of one of the airport buses (Airbus), which make their way quickly into the city by motorway.

By rail
Train passengers arrive at the very central Kowloon station. Dozens of bus routes connect the station with virtually every part of town.

By sea
Cruise liners dock at the Ocean Terminal in Tsim Sha Tsui, while ferries from China have their own ferry terminal north of there. Most ferries to Macau dock at the Macau ferry terminal on the island (MTR Sheung Wan).

TRANSPORT
MTR
Hong Kong's public transport system is complicated. Various companies compete in the market.

MTR
11 underground and other rapid-transit lines connect most parts of the city and go to the New Territories, the airport and to Lantao Island. Individual tickets can be obtained from ticket machines (to be retained for the whole journey!) or else there is the convenient Octopus Card (see below).

Buses
The system of routes and fares is not easy to understand. Payment is made when entering the bus and always covers the entire remaining part of the route, whether you are travelling one stop or twenty. The routes through the harbour tunnel have three-figure numbers shown in red.

Minibuses
Take the green minibuses, which operate like the larger buses. Without knowledge of Cantonese, it is definitely not a good idea to take one of the red buses, which stop on request.

Trams
On trams payment is made when alighting. There is practically only one line (on Hong Kong Island only) with a branch line to Happy Valley.

Taxis
Few taxi drivers speak English. It is best to write down the destination in Chinese.

Octopus Card

The Hong Kong Transport Company's multi-person ticket with a store of credit saves a lot of fiddling with change. They can be purchased at the airport and cost HK$100 plus HK$50 deposit, which will be refunded along with any unused credit when the card is surrendered. Cards are used by holding them next to a special sensor when entering buses or passing through railway ticket-barriers. They can be topped up at any MTR station.

SHOPPING

The days when Hong Kong was a cheap oasis in the Far East is long gone. Thanks to the lack of any sales tax, though, many things – though not all – can still be obtained cheaper than in Europe.

Causeway Bay

MTR station Causeway Bay
Attractive shopping district. Particular highlights are the Japanese Sogo store and the Times Square shopping palace, both real giants with expensive wares. There is a computer mall in Windsor House, Great George Street (10th–12th storeys).

Granville Road

MTR station Tsim Sha Tsui
Masses of inexpensive clothing to be had.

Sai Yeung Choi Street

MTR Mong Kok
Off the beaten track for tourists, here (southward from Nelson Street) there are some reputable and cheap shops selling cameras and electronic goods.

Yue Hwa Chinese Products

301–309 Nathan Road
MTR station Jordan
Department store with both international and Chinese goods, large department for craft products and Chinese medicine.

The Night Market in Temple Street draws crowds in the evening

BARS AND PUBS

Lan Kwai Fung
MTR station Central
Virtually synonymous with night life in Hong Kong. On the pedestrianized street and the neighbouring D'Aguilar Street there are throngs of bars and restaurants. One particularly nice and popular place is Post 97, 9–11 Lan Kwai Fung.

Wan Chai
MTR station Wan Chai
This was where the film The World of Suzy Wong was filmed. In the area around Lockhart Road/Jaffe Road/Luard Road there is as much going on as back then. The area is not so seedy as its reputation, but you should be on the lookout for spivs. Plenty of the bars, discotheques and night clubs are thoroughly reputable, e.g. Mes Amis (Luard Rd, Ecke Lockhart Rd) and Joe Bananas, 23 Luard Rd.

WHERE TO EAT

▶ Expensive (more than HK$300 per meal)
① *Peak Lookout*
121 Peak Road (Victoria Peak)
Tel. 28 49 10 00
Hong Kong's finest restaurant is a tempting place to stop after a tour of the mountain peak. Its pan-Asian cuisine is rather expensive and not always good but the atmosphere is unsurpassed.

② *Indochine 1929*
California Tower, 2nd floor
Lan Kwai Fong
MTR station Central
Tel. 28 69 73 99
The Vietnamese gourmet restaurant banks on colonial nostalgia for its decor and its consistently high cuisine carries conviction. Very inexpensive lunch menu, also vegetarian.

② *Yung Kee*
32-40 Wellington Street
Tel. 25 22 16 24
MTR station Central
One of the most renowned teahouse restaurants in town. Behind its golden façade there are several storeys. Reservation advisable.

▶ Moderate (150–300 HK$)
④ *A Touch of Spice*
10 Knutsford Terrace
MTR station Tsim Sha Tsui
Tel. 23 12 11 18
Hot Thai cuisine, visually balanced by the gentle colonial ambience.

⑤ *Dong*
Hotel Miramar, 2. OG
118–130 Nathan Road
Tel. 23 15 51 66
MTR station Tsim Sha Tsui
Excellent Cantonese cuisine with inexpensive menus and small portions so that even one or two people can enjoy the delights in full. À la carte dishes are a good bit more expensive.

▶ Inexpensive (up to HK$150)
⑥ *Xiangjiang Suiyue*
182 Nathan Road
Tel. 27 35 53 32
(only for take-away orders, no table reservations)
MTR station Jordan
The menu outside is in Chinese only but there is an English one inside. Top-class Cantonese folk recipes.

WHERE TO STAY

Particularly at the expensive hotels, the room prices fluctuate wildly. Depending on the season or the state of booking, large discounts may be obtainable. Information on all of Hong Kong Hotels can be found at www.discoverhongkong.com/eng/mustknow/accommodation.

► Luxury (from HK$1800 for a double room per night)

① *Grand Stanford*
70 Mody Road
Tel. 27 21 51 61, Fax 27 32 22 33
www.hongkong.intercontinental.com
MTR station Tsim Sha Tsui East
Most of the 578 rooms have a fantastic view of the harbour and the islands.

② *Renaissance Harbour View*
1 Harbour Road
Tel. 28 02 88 88, Fax 28 02 88 33
MTR station Wan Chai
Many of the 860 rooms have a view of the harbour. The building is part of the Congress and Exhibition Centre. Plenty of exercise and swimming facilities.

► Mid-range (HK$900–1800)

③ *Garden View International House*
1 Macdonnell Road
Tel. 28 77 37 37, Fax 28 45 62 63
Minibus 1A from Star Ferry Central
Well equipped with a pool and fitness centre, 130 rooms including 25 family suites. Above Hong Kong Park with direct access to the botanical gardens and the zoo.

④ *Salisbury YMCA*
41 Salisbury Road
Tel. 22 68 70 00, Fax 27 39 93 15
MTR station Tsim Sha Tsui
365 rooms in top location, with swimming pool and crèche.

► Budget (up to HK$900)

⑤ *Booth Lodge*
11 Wing Sing Lane
Tel. 27 71 92 66, Fax 23 85 11 40
MTR station Yau Ma Tei
54 rooms in a hotel run by the Salvation Army, central but still quiet.

⑥ *Wang Fat Hostel*
Paterson Building, Block A, 3rd floor
Flat A2
47 Paterson Street
Tel. 23 92 68 68, fax 25 76 75 09
www.wangfathostel.com.hk
MTR station Causeway Bay
Popular place for backpackers with Internet and washing machines in the middle of the bustling Causeway Bay district.

Luxury doesn't come cheap: the foyer of the Hyatt Regency Hotel

size it is now and was no more economically viable than the island itself. Both were surrendered by the Chinese to the British crown »in perpetuity«. In 1898 the colony was expanded to several times its original size with the addition of the New Territories (the adjoining part of the mainland and several other islands), which were to be leased for 99 years. Around this time the colony experienced a major boost in development and under its foreign rulers it became a prosperous Chinese port.

Japanese occupation

The Second World War saw the city occupied by the Japanese and the effective collapse of economic activity. These were the darkest days for the city. In the late 1940s an era of unforeseen challenge was ushered in with the influx of **hundreds of thousands of refugees**, all needing homes, work, water and space, none of which were available. The history of Hong Kong can be described in terms of flattened mountains and filled in bays – and must include the highly ambitious and outstandingly successful programme of house building, which saw the invention, for example, of owner-occupied social housing. The slums disappeared, motorways, underground lines and cultural centres came into being. Hong Kong became wealthy. On 1 July 1997 the British lease ran out and the whole territory was handed back to China. It was then transformed into a **»special ad-**

Hong Kong *Map*

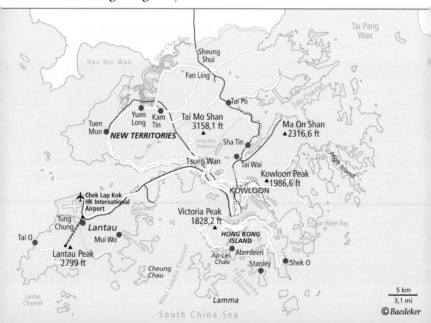

Highlights Hong Kong

Statue Square
Centre of the financial centre
► page 344

**Hollywood Road,
Man Mo Temple**
In the neighbourhood there are antiques,
a flea market and a popular shrine
► page 347

Hong Kong Park
The city's »Central Park« with its aviary,
tea museum and newlyweds
► page 350

Peak tour
The stunning panorama is the best sight
of all, especially in the evening twilight
► page 351

Stanley
Eating, drinking, swimming and cheap
shopping: all virtually in one spot
► page 352

Cultural Centre
Museum of art, concerts, theatres and a
magnificent panorama of the harbour
► page 353

History museum
A must even for those who do not like
museums.
► page 354

Temple Street
Night market with fortune-tellers and
barrel-organists
► page 355

Markets of Mong Kok
Caged birds, flowers, clothes, crabs, fish,
fruit and toads
► page 358

Lantau
Hong Kong's biggest island with Disneyland, a Buddhist monastery and a fishing
village
► page 358

ministrative region« which now has 1100 sq km/425 sq mi of land
and 6.9 million inhabitants. Even before then, a radical change in
structure had begun to take place. Nowadays, little is manufactured
in Hong Kong. Many people commute to work in the special economic zones across what is still a border. Instead tourism, financial
services, trade and science have gained in importance.

Tours

Many think that Hong Kong consists solely of skyscrapers and that a
day is enough to see everything important. This is a big mistake. The
centre, the Peak, the markets of Mong Kok, one of the islands where
no cars are allowed, one or two museums, perhaps a tour of the New
Territories or a few hours on the beach, that would be a minimum.
It is easy to keep amused for at least a week, though, and only then
does the joy of discovery really set in.

Hong Kong Island: north side (Central District)

Any tour of Hong Kong should start at Statue Square, the central
square in the **Central District**. The tough decision is where to go
next. Here is one compromise suggestion.

Statue Square

The Hong Kong and Shanghai Banking Corporation (HSBC) or »Honkers and Shankers« provided the money. The name, Statue Square, refers to the statue of Sir Thomas Jackson (1841–1915), former director of the bank, and the bank's own headquarters, the Hong Kong & Shanghai Bank building, dominates the view along the main axis of the square. It is one of the spectacular designs of **Norman Foster**. When it was completed in 1985, it was regarded for some years as the most expensive skyscraper in the world, although at 179 m/587 ft it is not especially tall. Notable features are the »light shovel« in the southern façade. The older skyscraper, characterized by its balconies, on the western side of the square is the luxury Mandarin Hotel. The ugly high-rise block opposite is home to the exclusive Hong Kong Club and the older building on the southeast corner, built from 1899–1910 as a law court, is nowadays the seat of Hong Kong's administrative assembly, the **Legislative Council** (Legco). Op-

Hong Kong Island · North Side Map

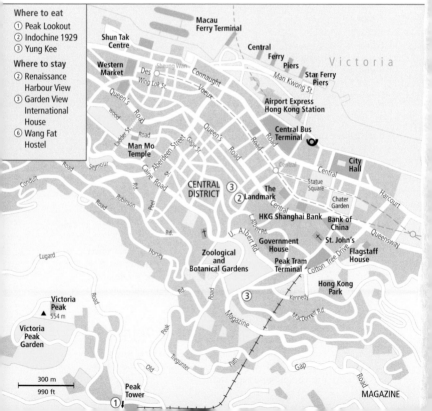

Where to eat
① Peak Lookout
② Indochine 1929
③ Yung Kee

Where to stay
② Renaissance Harbour View
③ Garden View International House
⑥ Wang Fat Hostel

Macau Ferry Terminal
Shun Tak Centre
Central Ferry Piers
Star Ferry Piers
Victoria
Western Market
Des
Sheung Wan
Connaught
Wing Lok St.
Voeux
Man Kwong St.
Airport Express Hong Kong Station
Queen's Road
Wood
Ladder St.
Road
Central Bus Terminal
Man Mo Temple
Aberdeen Street
Gage St.
Queen's
Road
Road
City Hall
Seymour
Caine Road
St.
Central
Central
Statue Square
Conduit
Road
Peel
CENTRAL DISTRICT ③
The ② Landmark
Chater Garden
Harcourt
Robinson
Rd.
Central
HKG Shanghai Bank
Bank of China
Queensway
Lugard
Horsey
Rd.
U. Albert Rd.
Government House
St. John's
Flagstaff House
Zoological and Botanical Gardens
Ladder Rd.
Peak Tram Terminal
Cotton Tree Drive
Road
Rd.
Road
③
Hong Kong Park
Victoria Peak
▲ 554 m
Kennedy
Victoria Peak Garden
Road
Peak
Magazine
MacDonnell Rd.
Old
Tregunter
Path
Gap
Road
MAGAZINE
300 m
990 ft
Peak Tower
①

posite the building to the south is another older building occupied by the Bank of China. That bank's newer building, the **Bank of China Tower**, looms behind it like an abstract sculpture, distinguished by its diagonal framework structure. Its architect was Ieoh Ming Pei, who also designed the Louvre pyramid. MTR station Central.

Tram

At the southern end of the square comes a first encounter with Hong Kong's double-decker trams. Since 1904 they have provided the link to the suburbs in the north of the island. If you can get a seat at the front on the top deck, you'll get a tour of the city with a fantastic view.

St John's Cathedral

Head along Garden Road just a few steps up the hill to Hong Kong's main Anglican church, built in 1849. Since the Japanese used it as a casino during the Second World War, the interior has been completely replaced.

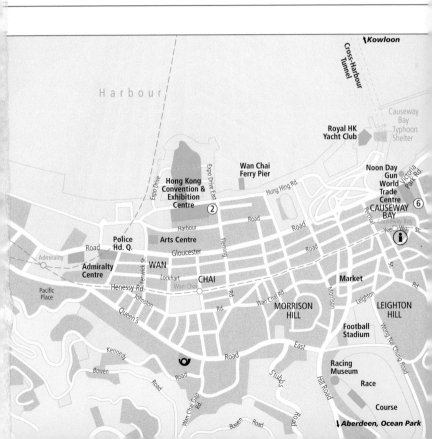

Hong Kong Island: Peak

The highest point on the island is 552 m/1811 ft above sea level, but the whole area around the summit is known as the Peak. To view the panorama of the city from here is a must – provided the summit is not obscured by cloud.

Another must is to go up the funicular railway, the **Peak Tram**, which rises some 400 m/1312 ft and has been in operation since 1888. The lower station is in Hong Kong Park. The upper station has had the **Peak Tower**, shopping and leisure centre built over it. You should ignore this, assuming you can find the hidden exit, since there are better things to experience.

When the weather is good, a tour of the peak can be the highlight of any visit to Hong Kong. It is a bit of a walk to the right of the Peak Tower up the narrow Lugard Road and 800 m/880 yd to where the steep slopes start. From here the **panorama of the city and its harbour** is stunning. At dusk it is even more overwhelming. The trail around the peak carries on without ever climbing and after a 50-minute walk it comes back to its starting point.

! Baedeker TIP

Evening in Causeway Bay

Evenings in Causeway Bay are wild. Characterized by shopping temples, fashion stores, restaurants and cinemas, this suburb is where Hong Kong's youth meets every evening. The crowds are huge but the atmosphere is great (MTR station Causeway Bay).

Peak Trail

Hong Kong Island: the south

Western films featuring Hong Kong as a location always used to include scenes from the **sampan township of Aberdeen**. Little of it remains nowadays. Nevertheless old ladies will still try to strike up a conversation on the harbour promenade calling »sampan, sampan!« and offering tours through what remains of the former floating settlement (about HK$60 per person for a 30-minute trip). To save some money, it may be easier to take the free ferry to the floating restaurant »Jumbo«, which is anchored further to the south beyond the high bridge as a gilded **monument to Chinese kitsch**.

Aberdeen Harbour

Ocean Park is a well done and spectacularly situated pleasure park on a mountainous peninsula east of Aberdeen. From »Kid's World« at the main entrance (with clowns, children's roundabouts and two genuine pandas) a cable-car rocks some 1500 m/1640 yd across the rough terrain to a three-storey coral aquarium, a shark pool, a butterfly house and the Ocean Theatre with its dolphin and sea lion shows. At the other end an escalator 272 m/297 yd long rolls down to further attractions such as the »Middle Kingdom« theme park

Ocean Park

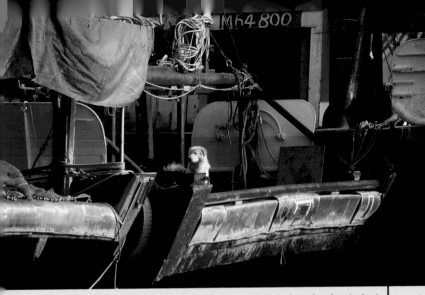

Life in Aberdeen harbour is less hectic than other places in the city

with Chinese landscapes and a teahouse, to the flamingo pool and aviaries, and to a curious bird-theatre – and there is a great deal more to see too. 10am–6pm daily (last admission 4.30pm). Direct buses go from the MTR stations Admiralty, exit B, and Star Ferry (Central). No. 48 bus from Aberdeen.

Repulse Bay
Hong Kong's most popular stretch of beach is Repulse Bay to the east of Ocean Park. On the slopes behind it there is an area of expensive housing. The »House with the Hole« is well known. Apparently its investor decide to forgo having a dozen flats in the building for reasons of Feng-Shui, so that the **dragon of the mountain** would not get angry – although more likely it was just a marketing ploy. At the southern end of the beach there is a Tin Hau temple with a collection of figures, more of a monument to kitsch than a place of worship and contemplation. Bus routes 6 and 6A from Central.

★
Stanley
The most southerly suburb of Hong Kong is popular both with tourists and with expats. It has bars and restaurants with a view of the sea, a beach for swimming and windsurfing as well as a large market with cheap textiles, some craft products plus suitcases and handbags. At the western end of the promenade is the **Murray Building** dating from 1844 – although in 1844 it was in an entirely different place. It had to be moved from its original location in 1982 to make way for the new Bank of China Tower and spent two decades in storage. It houses a small maritime museum. Bus routes 6 and 6A from Central to Stanley Market.

Kowloon: southern tip

This is the main tourist area, **Tsim Sha Tsui**, with its hotels, shops selling electronic goods and jewellery and the ever-present risk of being swindled. There is a lot more, though, and all startlingly different.

The rounded ferry boats (they do not have to turn) are themselves an institution, especially for transport to and from Central District. Somewhat less frequently they ply three other routes. To obtain a better view, it's worth paying the extra for the air-conditioned upper deck.

Star Ferry

The Clock Tower is a relic of a railway station that once stood on the site. Right behind it, the eye-catching Cultural Centre rises up. It has a large foyer, theatre, concert hall and a separate studio theatre. In particular the open area next to the water is popular for its **panoramic view of the harbour** and across to the island. The conspicuous building with the undulating roof that can be seen there from the other side of the harbour is Hong Kong's Congress and Exhibition Centre.

Clock Tower, Cultural Centre

Kowloon Map

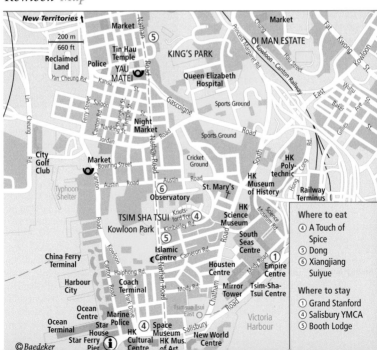

New Territories ↑

200 m
660 ft

Reclaimed Land

Market

Tin Hau Temple

Police

Nathan Road

KING'S PARK

Market

OI MAN ESTATE

Kowloon – Canton Railway

Princess Margaret Rd.

Chung

Hau Street

Fat Kwong

Kowloon St.

Wuhu St.

Baker Ave.

Gillies

East

Yan Cheung Rd.

YAU MATEI

Kansu St.

Saigon St.

Canton Rd

Shanghai St.

Temple St.

Nanking St.

Jordan

Saigon

Gascoigne

Queen Elizabeth Hospital

Sports Ground

Sports Ground

Road

Night Market

Nathan Road

Lin Cheung

City Golf Club

Canton Rd.

HK Cong

Market
Bowring Street

Austin Road

Austin Road

Cricket Ground

South

Road

HK Museum of History

HK Poly-technic

Railway Terminus

Typhoon Shelter

Observatory

St. Mary's

Museum Rd

Science Rd

Kowloon Road

Knuts-ford Tce. ④

TSIM SHA TSUI

Kowloon Park

Kimberley Rd.

⑤

HK Science Museum

South Seas Centre

Cameron Rd.

China Ferry Terminal

Haiphong Rd.

Islamic Centre

Houston Centre

Empire Centre ①

Mody Road

Chatham Road

Harbour City

Coach Terminal

Nathan Rd

Mody Rd.

Mirror Tower

Tsim-Sha-Tsui Centre

Ocean Centre

Ocean Terminal

Marine Police

Star House

HK Cultural Centre

Space Museum

HK Mus. of Art

Tsimsue Tsui East

Salisbury

New World Centre

Victoria Harbour

Star Ferry Pier ❶

© Baedeker

Where to eat

④ A Touch of Spice
⑤ Dong
⑥ Xiangjiang Suiyue

Where to stay

① Grand Stanford
④ Salisbury YMCA
⑤ Booth Lodge

Museum of Art, Planetarium
The east wing of the Cultural Centre by the water is dedicated to classical and modern Chinese art. Its treasures include lacquerwork, bronze, jade, pottery, and sculptures have mainly been donated by art-loving benefactors. The latest **Hong Kong works of art** are displayed, too. Opening times: Fri–Wed 10am–6pm. It is adjoined to the north by the planetarium, officially called the »Space Museum« and featuring an exhibition on astronomy and space travel. Opening times: Mon, Wed–Fri 1pm–9pm, Sat, Sun 10am–9pm, Wed admission free. MTR station Tsim Sha Tsui.

Peninsula Hotel
Opposite the planetarium there is an eye-catching old building, the luxury Peninsula Hotel, now overlooked by its own modern annexe with a helipad on the roof. Its classy foyer is a fine place to take high tea.

! *Baedeker* TIP

Felix

Felix is the name of the bar and restaurant at the top of the Peninsula Hotel's high-rise tower. The French architect and interior designer Philippe Starck is responsible for its spectacular appearance. Taking a drink here to see the twilight over Hong Kong is an incomparable experience. Ladies have the advantage that their toilets provide a superb view across the city's harbour. One needn't be a hotel guest: the restaurant and bar are open to all. Access via the lift in the west wing.

Nathan Road, Kowloon Park
Alongside the Peninsula opposite the planetarium, Hong Kong's best-known shopping street leads away northward. Nathan Road's epithet, the **»Golden Mile«** cannot disguise the fact that it is noisier and more suffocating than anywhere else, since Kowloon's main thoroughfare runs along this shop-lined canyon. To get over the stress of shopping, though, take a rest in the neighbouring Kowloon Park, either in its sculpture garden, on one of the hills or next to the bird pond. One entrance is next to the mosque at its southeast corner. MTR station Tsim Sha Tsui.

★ History museum
Head through the labyrinth of smaller shopping streets east of Nathan Road and cross Chatham Road to get to the rather sterile, newly built area of Tsim Sha Tsui East. Here, at the north end of Chatham Road itself, there are two important museums. One is the magnificent Museum of History, which illustrates the history of the city. In this building, money, ideas and sophisticated curation have com-

bined to create a **museum experience in a class of its own**. It features the calls of jungle animals, photographs the entire height of the walls, full-sized theatrical stages and buildings as well as original film material, e.g. from the Second World War. Opening times: Wed–Mon 10am–6pm, Sun closes 7pm. Admission free on Wednesdays. Bus routes 5C, 8 from Star Ferry.

The building next door will mainly interest young people, but not exclusively. Here too, some **brilliant ideas about museum curation** will fascinate you. To mention just a few examples from the wide range of contents, they include a model of Hong Kong, Chinese medicines, computers, fundamentals of physics, energy and the use of energy along with »Betsy«, Hong Kong' first passenger plane. Opening times: Mon–Wed and Fri 1pm to 9pm, Sat, Sun 10am–9pm. Admission free on Wednesdays. Bus routes 5C, 8 from Star Ferry.

Science Museum

Central and North Kowloon

In these greatly expanded big-city residential areas, the main items of interest are the markets.

From 6pm the stalls go up on Temple Street. On offer there are T-shirts, cheap electronic goods, suitcases and handbags, CDs and much more. At the Tin Hau temple fortunes-tellers ply their trade and barrel-organists hold forth with operatic arias. MTR station Jordan.

✱ Temple Street, night market

Fruit at one stall, fortune-telling at the next: the Night Market has it all

The dragon has a free view of the sea through the middle of the Repulse Bay Building

NO ROOM FOR SENTIMENT

Late Modernist or Post-Modernist, Bauhaus, Constructivist or Deconstructivist: many architectural influences can be discovered in the city of Hong Kong. The architects of office blocks, hotels and museums were able to give free range to their imagination – so long as they did not get in the way of the dragon.

A striking landmark: the Lippo Towers on Hong Kong Island

Almost every internationally renowned architect has made his creative mark on Hong Kong. The British architect **Lord Foster**, for example, designed the headquarters of the Hong Kong & Shanghai Bank, which was one reason why he was chosen to work on the huge new airport on the island of Chek Lap Kok. Another is the Chinese-American **Ieoh Ming Pei**, who won the approval of his patrons in Communist China by sketching the appearance of the new Bank of China with five or six casual strokes of the pencil.

A third star architect is the Italian **Remo Riva**, whose building for the new Hong Kong Museum of Science put his ideas on modern construction into practice. Chinese-born architects also played their part, of course. Dennis Lau, for example, who not only built one of the tallest buildings in Asia with his Central Plaza Tower, but also showed here that he was an adherent of Daoism and feng shui: instead of sharp corners, he gave the building a rounded façade. His rea-

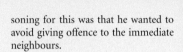
The architecture of the Peak Tower, the upper terminus of the Peak Tram, makes its own rules

soning for this was that he wanted to avoid giving offence to the immediate neighbours.

Construction in record time

The practical implementation of architects' plans happens faster in Hong Kong than elsewhere in the world. There are no time-consuming procedures for planning permission here, nor do protest movements or environmental activists raise obstacles to construction schemes. **One storey per day** is the rule rather than the exception when building in Hong Kong. Old buildings that stand in the way are demolished without any thought for their historic importance: there is no place for sentiment here.

Varied architectural forms

The forms that are employed are as varied as the contents of an architectural textbook. However, there are few buildings in a pure style. The preferred materials are steel and concrete, glass and aluminium. **Architects who work in Hong Kong** have to be not just artists but proven masters of their profession. The buildings have to withstand extremely strong wind pressures of a magnitude hardly to be encountered elsewhere. And although the risk of earthquakes is very low, much lower than in San

Francisco for example, it has to be taken in account when building a skyscraper.

Practical feng shui

In Hong Kong there is a good deal of fanciful architecture which sometimes seems to have been borrowed from a collection of curiosities. The opening in the roof of the lobby of the stock exchange does admittedly serve to let in daylight, but its primary purpose is to let good fortune have direct access to the trading floor. In the light of that, it almost goes without saying that the lucky dragon occupies a place in the middle of the room on a plinth. You just have to believe in it! **Talking of dragons**: there is a particularly conspicuous example of the influence of feng shui on architecture in the building that has replaced the venerable Repulse Bay Hotel. **Feng shui experts** pointed out to the architect that the hills behind it were the residence of a dragon, whose view of the sea should not be blocked. The architect took the point – and left a hole in the façade about 400 square metres (4,300 square feet) in size.

Text: Heiner F. Gstaltmayr

Tin Hau Temple The Tin Hau Temple is dedicated to the **patron goddess of sailors**. In the side temple on the left offerings to the deceased can be seen – houses, domestic appliances, chests, everyday objects, all made of paper and bamboo. They will later be burned. It is hard to imagine that the shady square in front, where people relax reading newspapers or playing chess, was once in the middle of the sea. MTR station Yau Ma Tei.

Jade market The jade market is below the overpass that crosses Temple Street but it is only open during the day. Anyone lacking the skill for valuing jade is well advised not to shop here. Nevertheless it is still a nice place to see. MTR station Yau Ma Tei.

Food market Nelson Street The food market on Nelson Street and the side streets that cross it is where housewives from **Mong Kok** shop for vegetables, pork, live chickens, fish, mussels, toads and crabs – whatever they need to feed their families. MTR station Mong Kok.

New Territories

The New Territories district on the mainland is made up partly of uninhabited mountain terrain and partly of satellite towns. Neither are places that a short-term visitor will need to see, but there are some **hidden attractions** that might be visited on an organized tour, including ancestor temples, walled villages and monasteries. Information is available from HKTB offices (▶p. 338).

Sai Kong The small town of Sai Kong in the east, at the base of the Sai Kung Peninsula, was once a fishing village. Now the harbour promenade features rows of seafood restaurants and it is possible to book a **tour by junk** round the labyrinth of islands in the bay offshore. 92 bus from MTR station Choi Hung, Exit B.

! *Baedeker* TIP

Been there, saw nothing?

To link the new airport the longest road-and-rail suspension bridge in the world has been built, Tsing Ma Bridge with a span of 1377 m/1506 yd. Anyone travelling via Lantau from the airport into town crosses it. People taking the train, though, get to see nothing of the construction but the inside of the black tunnel underneath the road, i.e. nothing at all – one reason for choosing to travel by bus.

Lantau Island

Hong Kong's largest island has some widely differing faces. It has two satellite towns and the new **Disneyland** park, but it also has a traditional fishing village (Tai O at the western tip), several monasteries and uninhabited mountains as well as several nice beaches. Over half of the island has been made into national parks. Ferries from Central District, Pier 6, to Mui Wo and MTR station Tung Chung.

In the mountains of Hong Kong's biggest island at an elevation of **Po Lin monastery** 460 m/1510 ft is **the area's biggest religious building**. Its landmark feature can even be seen from mainland China: what was, at the time of its completion, the largest open-air bronze Buddha in the world. It is 22 m/72 ft high, 34 m/112 ft including the stone pedestal. The monastery also has a vegetarian restaurant. Beside the monastery is the »Ngong Ping 360«, a pedestrian street with shops, bars, restaurants and a multimedia and kung-fu show. No. 2 bus from Mui Wo or cable-car from Tung Chung (MTR).

Stepping through the gate means, as might be expected, being **✸** transported **from Hong Kong to the USA**. »Main Street USA«, »Fan- **Disneyland** tasyland«, »Pirateland« and »Tomorrowland« are the four amazing experience zones. Opening times: Summer Mon–Fri 10am to 8pm, ☺ Sat, Sun 10am–9pm, otherwise daily 10am–7pm. Admission HK$295, children (3–11) HK$210, over-65s HK$170. Peak times (weekends, public holidays, holiday periods: HK$350/250/200. Note: there are a limited number of admission tickets. They can be booked in advance from www.hongkongsdisneyland.com or by telephone: +852 18 30 830. Direct rail link via the Disneyland Resort Line.

✸ Cheung Chau

Among the smaller Hong Kong islands where no vehicles are allowed, this is the most interesting, since it includes a **traditional village** in the middle with a harbour for sampans and a long sandy beach on the other side. A half-day walk to the south brings more beaches into reach. The spiritual centre of the village is the Emperor of the North temple, north of the ferry dock. The fish restaurants by the harbour are tempting places to rest. Ferries from Central District, Pier 5.

✸✸ Huang Shan

He 30

Province: Anhui   **Altitude:** 1864 m/6115 ft

The »Yellow Mountain« is not yellow at all. The meaning of the name is rather »Mountain of the Yellow One«, meaning the Yellow Emperor, mythical forefather of the Chinese, who is said to have achieved immortality here and ridden to heaven on a carriage of clouds.

You could almost believe it were true seeing the magical show that nature puts on here. When mists well up from the canyons, when the pines stretch out their branches, when rocks mysteriously vanish and then reappear, when the summits sail on seas of clouds carrying

▶ VISITING HUANG SHAN

INFORMATION

CITS
6 Xizhen Jie
Huangshan-Stadt (Tunxi)
Tel. 05 59/254 21 10
Fax 05 59/251 52 55
From here English-speaking mountain guides can be booked.

GETTING THERE
Huangshan City can be reached from Shanghai and Nanjing by train; although most visitors travel by plane (direct flights from most of the major tourist destinations). For a bus or taxi ride to the mountain, about 90 minutes should be added to the journey time.

SHOPPING
Huang Shan is a tea-growing area so that tea from the mountain makes a nice souvenir.

WHERE TO EAT
On the mountain it is best to eat at the hotels. Since porters need to carry everything up on foot, the prices are higher than usual. Western food is mostly unavailable or of very poor quality. The Xihai-Hotel has traditionally served especially good Chinese food.

WHERE TO STAY
▶ Luxury
① *Xihai Fandian*
Rear Mountain, Xihai region
Tel. 05 59/558 88 88
Fax 05 59/556 89 88
Expensive rather than luxurious, but, since it has only 139 rooms, no mass tourism. The food is very good.

▶ Mid-range
② *Beihai Binguan*
Rear Mountain, Beihai region
Tel. 05 59/558 25 55
Fax 05 59/556 19 96
The biggest hotel on the mountain, conveniently located for the Yungu cable-car.

③ *Daoyuan Binguan*
Southern foot of the mountain, hot spring region
Tel. 05 59/558 56 66, fax 253 82 88
141 rooms. Nice, comfortable at the foot of the mountain near the Yuping cable-car.

you with them, it is like being in another world. **Xu Xiake**, the most famous geographer of ancient China, summed it up memorably, having climbed the mountain in 1616 and 1618. »Whoever has seen Huang Shan will have no eyes for any other mountain.« People in China commonly misquote him, although no less aptly, »Whoever has seen the five holy mountains will have no eyes for any other mountains, but whoever sees Huang Shan will no longer even look at the holy mountains.«

Countless peaks   Huang Shan is a granite massif in the south of Anhui Province, 60 km/37 mi north of Huangshan City (Huangshan Shi, also called Tunxi). In an area covering 154 sq km/60 sq mi – an area half the size of Edinburgh – there are countless peaks, 77 of them are more than 1000 m/3300 ft high. The highest, the **Lotus Blossom Peak**, is not especially imposing at 1864 m/6115 ft, but it is not the actual height that really matters.

Huang Shan gained fame in China relatively late on. Nevertheless, for several hundred years now China's painters, gardeners, poets and scholars have recognized Huang Shan as their **ideal landscape**. Indeed their very ideals of nature are here exceeded by nature itself. Since this began, people have admired the »Four Wonders« of Huang Shan: the bizarrely shaped rocks, the odd pines, the sea of clouds and the hot springs. To begin with the latter, waters at temperatures of 42 to 44°C emerge from the southern slopes. This is indubitably a pleasant phenomenon, but in truth it is not a key feature of the landscape and is not really important in any other respect either. It is the other three factors that really deserve their fame.

The Four Wonders

The granite rock of Huang Shan is sundered with crevices. Between its peaks, the cliffs often plunge down into canyons so deep and narrow that the bottom is invisible from the wooden pathways and steps that effortlessly link the heights and from which so many of Huang-Shan's attractions can be enjoyed in such comfort that it is almost like being in an open-air theatre. The **jaggedness of the massif** can also be seen in miniature. About 150 formations are identified by name around the mountain theatre that is Huang Shan, strangely shaped little rocks, often no more than a few metres high, but their curious forms are irresistibly reminiscent of all kinds of mythical creatures, animals or objects from home or palace.

The rocks

The species of pine known as *pinus huangshanensis* or *pinus taiwanensis* is not unique to the mountain but nowhere else does it contribute so much to the flavour of the landscape. The aesthetic charm of the trees has been fascinating people for generations. The trunks are mostly bent at the base, but then they strike straight upwards. The

Huang Shan Map

©Baedeker

Where to stay
① Xihai Fandian   ② Beihai Binguan   ③ Taoyuan Binguar

branches are few but broad, growing horizontally or perhaps inclining slightly upwards. At the ends they separate into densely packed, frantically zigzagging twigs bearing clumps of needles that form a flat-topped crown, giving a **typical and distinctive shape** to the tree-tops. They grow in the most impossible places, seeming to need no soil, just a narrow cleft in a cliff face. The roots secrete a mild acid, which loosens the rock, making room for the growing tree, keeping it in place and furnishing it with nourishment. The little water that the pines need they get partly from the damp crevices from which they spread, partly from the mists that condense on the rocks. Some of the trees take their own roles in Huang Shan's natural drama. The biggest star on the mountain's stage, though, is known throughout the country; the Welcome Pine, who seems to stretch out her branches to greet climbers with a handshake.

The sea of clouds The view of clouds at lower altitudes is familiar from elsewhere but here the mountain makes an enthusiastic contribution. Rainfall drips rapidly off the steep cliffs and slopes. At the bottom the damp collects amid the thick vegetation in the shaded valleys. When the air there has been enriched with moisture, the mist wells up. This happens on 250 days in an average year, according to the statisticians, and on 50 of those days the effect is so great as to fill the air with

A backdrop that gives free rein to the imagination

clouds. In five places there is enough space to make it look like a veritable sea. They are called the **Sky Sea**, the East Sea, the West Sea, the North Sea and the South Sea. If a slight wind creates ripples on the surface of these »seas«, it looks as though the peaks are no longer still, but are drifting gently on the waves. Even more than cloud seas, though, it is the mists that make Huang Shan unforgettable in its enchantment. Often it is possible to sit and gaze into a cleft, marvelling at the way rock formations suddenly appear in different places, as if the mist were a curtain drawing back to reveal a view into the distance, then drawing closed again to conceal it once again from sight. With a little luck, it is possible to get a whole series of quite different photographs without moving a step, where a new surprise is revealed every ten seconds.

From the direction of Tunxi (Huangshan City) the road arrives at the base of Huang Shan in the south, where there is village of hotels and guest houses, named after the main attraction as the **»Hot Spring Area«** (though the spring itself is not visible having been diverted into pipes). The part of the mountain above this village is called the »anterior mountain« and most visitors ascend this via the 2.2 km/1.4 mi long Yuping cable-car. The biggest hotels on the mountain are a few kilometres from there on the northerly »posterior mountain«, accessed via the 2.8 km/1.7 mi Yungu cable-car. The two »halves« of the mountain are not separated by a valley, though, as one might think. Instead they simply represent the two faces of the mountain, north and south, with the three highest peaks as the rough dividing line. On the way up though, there is a lot of climbing and descending, rather more on the anterior than on the posterior mountain, which does not have any very steep parts.

Anterior Mountain and Posterior Mountain

It is common to take either the Yuping or Yungu cable-car up the mountain (a third cable-car ascending from the north is mainly used by local people). Most visitors make one overnight stop high on the mountain itself. Two nights, though, would not be excessive. On the contrary, it provides an opportunity to experience the same places a second time, whereby the experience may be quite different from the day before. The light may be completely different, one day in sunshine, the next in mist. Anyone who struggles with lots of walking would do best to take the **Yungu cable-car**; as its upper station is just 1 to 3 km/1 to 2 mi from the attractive spots and hotels around the »North Sea« and »West Sea«. It is much more interesting, though, to take the route that starts from the upper station of the **Yuping cable-car**. However, sedan chair or litter carriers offer their services all over the mountain, although they usually charge a three-figure sum. Altogether the distances are really quite manageable, and thanks to the carefully laid and superbly maintained stairways it is sufficient to wear normal walking shoes. From the upper station of the Yuping cable-car to the hotels on the posterior mountain, for example, the

Visits

distances are between 6 km and 8.5 km/4 to 5 miles depending on the destination and the route taken. People climbing on foot will need to make an ascent of 750 to 800 m/2450 to 2600 ft before reaching the upper stations of the cable-car routes, a distance in each case of 7.5 km/4.5 miles. Climbs begin at the valley stations, which can be reached from the hot spring area by minibus.

Finding your way on the mountain is not difficult as all the routes are well signposted. Nevertheless, in the event that you are not travelling with a tour guide, you may be well advised to engage a mountain guide via a travel agent. There are hardly any rock formations which do not possess a name, often a highly imaginative one. This applies to some of the pines too. It is only with accompanying explanation that that the magical mountain theatre of Huang Shan comes properly to life. The list of scenes that follow is only a small selection.

Mountain guides

Places and scenes on the »Front Mountain«

Where the southern ascent reaches the heights of the mountain, the most famous of all Huang Shan's pines extends a welcome to the travellers, an expansive tree called the Welcome Pine. There is also a **wonderful viewpoint** here. It and the Welcome Pine are accessed from the Yuping-cable-car by taking a short turn to the right.

Welcome Pine

> **!** *Baedeker* TIP
>
> ### Clothing and baggage
> On Huang Shan a rain cape is essential; they can be bought everywhere here. Bring no more luggage than a rucksack, and carry nothing in it that you don't definitely need for one or two nights' stay. Leave your suitcase at the last hotel at the foot of the mountain or in Huangshan town.

Not far from the Welcome Pine and the nearby Yupinglou Hotel, a route forks up to the **Lotus Blossom Peak**, the highest point on Huang Shan. From there another path leads back down before the route continues via the »Hundred-Step Scaling Ladder«. The **Tiandu Peak** is 1810 m/5938 ft high and involves the most hair-raising ascent – not for the timid or anyone with slight vertigo. To get there means first climbing down beyond the Welcome Pine unless you have come up from the bottom on foot anyway.

Above the cable-car station the main route heads left. Initially there is a climb. A descent then leads to a narrow ridge into which steps have been carved. If the area is in cloud, though, there is nothing to see to the left or right, nor forward or back beyond the next step, which is an experience in its own right.

Hundred-Step Scaling Ladder

← *Mist transforms the Huang Shan into a fairytale world*

Giant Fish Shortly after that, the path ascends again up a steep, narrow stairway, which enters from below into a cave, leading through there back into the open. Here it can often be one-way traffic, so that there is a diversionary route, which is actually much easier to climb. The cave is called **Giant Fish Cave**. The reason for this only becomes apparent after rounding the large rock, at the end of which the cave is situated. It has the shape of a fish with its mouth above the cave. Up on its back there is another smaller rock and the whole scene is called: »Giant Fish Carrying Gold Turtle«.

Places and scenes on the »Posterior Mountain«

Guangming Peak Northward of the giant fish, the dramatic scenery initially peters out. The path carries on up a long but comfortably ascending stairway to an altitude of 1840 m/6037 ft at the so-called **»Bright Light Peak«**, where there is a weather station and a TV tower. Directly to the east the terrain plummets into a small valley where monkeys can often be seen swinging.

The Peak Flown From Afar At Guangming Peak the route splits in two. To the right a short path leads to the hotels, while the more interesting left route leads along the clefted edge of the plateau. The main attraction is the »Peak Flown From Afar«, a boulder 12 m/39 ft high, which seems to stand loose on a plinth above a sheer drop as if it had just landed there.

! *Baedeker* TIP

Throw the keys away ...
Wherever an iron chain protects the edges of a viewpoint, padlocks will be hung from it. Lovers engrave their names on them (once they are locked to the chain) then throw the keys away into the depths. Is this one way to lower the divorce rate? Try it out for yourself!

»Dispelling Cloud Pavilion«, not far from the Taiping cable-car (take the fork to the left) is not a significant building but it has a great view. It is held to be one of the best and is **the ideal place to watch the sunset**. From here alone, more than a half-dozen rock formations and pines with their own names can be seen, among them one rock in the shape of an upside-down boot like the ones worn by generals in a Beijing opera. Its full name is the »Immortal's Boot Left Out to Dry«.

New round-trip To distribute the hordes of visitors more evenly, a new path was opened in 1999/2000, starting at the Paiyun Pavilion. At the bottom it forms a loop so that it does not matter whether you take the left fork or the right fork. The route leads through previously inaccessible parts of the massif, sometimes along quite precarious paths, even along overhanging cliffs. It is still used by fewer visitors than elsewhere.

Lion Peak Heading east from the Paiyun Pavilion the route first passes a hotel settlement (including the Xihai-Hotel) with another following a bit later. Left of there the path leads up long rise, partially rocky and partially wooded with pines. At the top the Lion Peak has several good viewpoints overlooking the »North Sea«. One protrudes like a narrow, rectangular tongue: the **Qingliang Terrace**; considered a classic spot to watch the sunset. The chance of getting a good look through the thronging crowds, though, is minimal.

Further east, shortly past the large Beihai Hotel on the left, a slighter lower terrace can be seen. This allows for two pieces of scenery to be seen: one the upstanding »Writing Brush Peak« (right) and the accompanying »Brush Rack Peak« (straight ahead). At the top of the rocky Brush Peak there is a small pine, which gives rise to the sight's full name: **»Dream Blooming from a Writing Brush«** or alternatively »The Dream of Being a Successful Writer«. There is nothing actually blooming there now, though. The original tree died long ago and has been replaced by a rather poor plastic imitation.

Writing Brush

The Welcome Pine is the most famous of all the trees on Huang Shan

Peak of Conviction

A left turn at the following fork leads to the Yungu cable-car while the left route goes to one of the key spots on any Huang Shan trail. The name of the »Peak of Conviction« (not really an actual peak but a group of rocks of multifarious shape) refers to an ancient Chinese sceptic who had perceived the **Wonders of Huang Shan** to be nothing but a fairy-tale, but at this point, he became convinced they were true. The rocks are very crowded during the day. In late afternoon it is much quieter and nicer. Two more scenes should be mentioned: the »Pine Dipping into the Sea« grows with a huge long upward-reaching branch from a vertical cliff and »Two Immortals Playing Chess«, where there are two roughly human-shaped rocks with a flat-topped pine looking like a table between them.

Turn off to the right

To the right of the stalls by the Peak of Conviction, a dead-end path leads down to a spot the Chinese tour groups usually miss out. At the end, though, is another tremendous viewpoint that you can sometimes have all to yourself.

Places to go around Huang Shan

✳
The old villages of Xidi and Hongcun

Southern-Anhui is known for its beautiful old villages. Several of them are passed on the way to the mountain from Huangshan City. Elsewhere two of them are, quite independently of Huang Shan, included on the list of **UNESCO World Heritage Sites** in their own right. They are 40 km/25 mi and 55 km/34 mi southwest of the mountain (or from its southern foot) and are called Xidi and Hongcun. Both are similar in size and nature and both have, in addition, been thoroughly restored in recent years, meaning they give the impression of actually being new. Both consist of several hundred houses from the15th to the 19th centuries, have one or two thousand inhabitants and are surrounded by streams and ponds. In both cases, more than a dozen houses are open to the public. The extensive **wood carvings** are particularly nice. Their richness and motifs show how wealthy and well educated southern Anhui once was. The villages are now popular locations for films and have been seen in many a kung-fu movie across the globe. Both get crowded with visitors during the day, so to get more of the mood an overnight stay is called for. Hongcun in particular has plenty to offer in this respect. Buses run direct from Huang Shan.

✳ Jiuhua Shan

Jiuhua Shan is one of the four holy mountains of Chinese Buddhism. It is dedicated to the bodhisattva Kshitigarbha, who has been worshipped here since 720, when a Korean monk arrived and set up the earliest shrine to him. There had already been some Daoist settlements here beforehand. Nowadays there are around 60 temple monasteries, which for most of the year have a contemplative atmosphere. The name Jiuhua Shan roughly means **»Nine Blossom Mountain«** and goes back to a poem by Li Bai, in which he compares the mountain peaks to nine lotus blossoms.

Half-way up the northwestern side of the mountain, the village of Jiuhuajie forms the economic hub of the site. Most of the monasteries are nearby and even for the more distant places, the village is still used as a base.

Jiuhuajie village

The monastery of Huacheng Si was founded in the 8th century and is considered the oldest on Jiuhua Shan; although most of the buildings surviving today date from the 17th–19th centuries. Only the hall of **Cangjing Lou** goes back to the Ming era, having been built between 1426 and 1434.

Monastery of Huacheng Si

The best known temple monastery on Jiuhua Shan, Roushen Baodian, was established in 794, although the present buildings date from the latter half of the 19th century. Several **valuable texts** from the Song and Yuan periods are kept here.

Roushen Baodian monastery

Zhiyuan Si is a very beautiful monastery at the lower end of the village northeast of Huacheng Si. It dates from the mid-16th century. The three gilded statues of Buddha in the main hall form the highlight.

Zhiyuan Si monastery

The »Palace of Hundred Years' Life« is on a mountain ridge west of Zhiyuan Si from where it can be reached via a path. Another alternative is to get there by a funicular railway from with a lower station to the south of Zhiyuan Si. In Baisui Gong it is possible to see the gilded **mummy of the monk Haiyu** (a.k.a. Wuxia), who is said to have died here in the early 17th century at the ripe old age of 126. The monastery was built in 1630 in his memory.

Baisui Gong monastery

The more remote rural sights can be reached on foot but it is easier and quicker to get there by minibus. One worthwhile destination is the 1325 m/4347 ft peak of **Tiantai Zhengding**, from which it is possible to see Huang Shan on a clear day. The quickest way up is by cable-car. At the moment a 99 m/300 ft monumental statue of Kshitigarbha was almost finished by 2008.

! *Baedeker* TIP

The thirtieth day of the 7th month...
... is the main day of the year for a Kshitigarbha pilgrimage. Anyone not coming to make offerings and prayers of thanks to the bodhisattva is probably better off coming at another time.

Jiuhua Shan can be reached from Huang Shan by a cross-country bus service running daily to either Tangkou, the closest small town to the south, or Taiping, which is to the northwest at the other end of the Taiping cable-car.

Transport links

★★ Huanglong · Jiuzhaigou

Gg 29

Province: Sichuan   **Altitude:** 1990–4600 m/6500–15,000 ft

Natural wonders in northern-Sichuan: In the remote valleys of the Minshan Mountains nature has created a magical landscape out of water and limestone, algae and bacteria and decorated it with moss, lichen and hundreds of plants, staggering in their quantity and beauty. All this is then topped with snow-capped mountains.

Huanglong and Jiuzhaigou are two nature reserves which have been UNESCO World Heritage Sites since 1992. They adjoin one another and tourists can visit them both together, but to get from one to the other still means a journey of 120 km/75 mi – not much effort, though, considering that **getting there from Chengdu** by land already needs a whole day and an overnight stop, although flying is quicker. While a wander through the little Huanglong valley can be enjoyed in a morning or an afternoon, the extensive valleys of Jiuzhaigou need at least one whole day, if you stick to visiting those spots that are easily accessible by bus and don't need too long a walk. To avoid the crowds, means doing a lot of walking and will require at least two days. Only then, though, does it get really beautiful.

> ! **Baedeker TIP**
>
> ## Go by road not air
> The earthquake of May 2008 has disrupted overland access. But once the damage has been repaired, the road journey through the dramatic mountain landscape really should not be missed. Taking the plane to Huanglong means missing out on a lot. It would be a pity to by-pass the ancient villages with their rustic culture and the fortified town of Songpan.

★★ Huanglong

»Yellow Dragon« is how the nature reserve around Huanglong translates into English. It is only possible to visit a fraction of the 580 sq km/230 sq mi of terrain in the park but that is the part where the back of the yellow dragon can be seen. This **travertine outcrop**, covered by a thin layer of flowing water, is in the middle of a mountain valley which rises from 3100 m/10,100 ft to 3500 m/11,400 ft, whose bottom otherwise largely consists of limestone terraces. The ponds which they create are different colours as a result of algae and bacteria. They higher one goes, the more colourful it gets. The reflections of the sky, the clouds and the foliage all make their contribution, as does the view of the 5588 m/18,161 ft Xuebao Ding (»Snow Treasure Peak«) glittering in the eternal snow directly on the line of sight up the valley.

▶ VISITING HUANGLONG AND JIUZHAIGOU

GETTING THERE

Thanks to the airport situated between Jiuzhaigou and Huanglong, both places can be reached quickly nowadays, meaning that the whole trip from Chengdu only needs two and a half days if a day in Jiuzhaigou is enough. Staying there for two days and driving there and back means planning for five days. Owing to the complex travelling conditions, particularly getting a connection from Huanglong, it is highly recommended that the whole tour be booked as an all-in package, from Chengdu if not before (►Chengdu, Sichuan International Travel Service S. 232). From Chengdu to Jiuzhaigou is 460 km/290 mi. The best place to stay overnight on the way there is at Songpan, although Chuanzhusi (near the airport) is all right too. On the way back, Maoxian is the place to stop off, although it means starting out in the morning. The road that leads through the pass to Huanglong may not be passable in winter.

THEATRE

The Jiuzhaigou Hotel (see below) also possesses a neighbouring building in which there is a dinner and theatre show every evening featuring folk dancing and songs of the Tibetans and the Qiang, another of the region's ethnic minorities. The show also stages a traditional wedding ceremony. Beverages on offer include butter tea and barley schnapps.

EXCURSIONS

Pure adventure but still well organized: horse treks lasting several days in the picturesque wilderness of Min Shan. Go to the Shun Jiang Horse Treks office by the north gate of Songpan, Tel. 08 37/723 11 61, or 723 12 01. The manager, Guo Shang, speaks English.

ACCOMMODATION

Staying in Huanglong is not recommended as the accommodation is poor. It is better to set out early from Songpan or Chuanzhusi.

▶ Mid-range

Songpan: Taiyang Dajiudian
Shunjiang Beilu
(near the North Gate)
Tel. 08 37/723 98 88
Best place in town, in fact the only place for those who want to be sure of hot running water.

Jiuzhaigou: Jiuzhaigou Hotel
On the main road to Songpan
Tel. 08 37/773 48 39
112 rooms, a rather confusingly constructed building. In the high season – like everywhere else in Jiuzhaigou – it charges luxury prices.

Even air passengers can still enjoy the mountain experience. From the small town of Chuanzhusi, where the roads to Huanglong and Jiuzhaigou separate, the route initially leads through a frosty, high-altitude pass, 4200 m/13,650 ft above sea level with an expansive view, and carries on up another 1000 m/3250 ft of hairpin bends to a small grouping of hotels with extensive car parking and the entrance to the core section of the reserve. **Getting there**

Tours The route goes up and down for a total of about 8.5 km/5.5 mi, most of it over wooden walkways to keep one's feet dry. The area is well supplied with signposts and information panels in three languages, although it is difficult to get lost anyway. It is best to take a few provisions along the way. Those who have trouble walking can take a sedan chair.

Bottom end After crossing a small wood, the tour starts in earnest with the »welcome ponds«. They are bright green in colour as a result of natural over-fertilization, which causes algae to flourish. The first group of ponds ends at the equally green **Feibuliuhui Waterfall**, 60 m/100 ft wide and 10 m/33 ft high. Above that the colour changes to yellow and soon the route passes the entirely ochre **Xishendong (»Body Wash Cave«) Waterfall**, which is 7 m/23 ft high. It is said that if a virgin spends a night in the cave that can be seen here, she will emerge pregnant in the morning. In spite of China's rigid one-child policy, the grotto has not been shut off

Bonsai ponds On the eastern side of the waterfall (the left-hand side when ascending) are the Bonsai ponds: **limestone and travertine** impede the growth of the trees and shrubs that emerge from the water so that they appear as dwarf plants.

The limestone terraces of Hanglong

»Yellow Dragon« is the name of the aforementioned travertine surface, of which the ochre waterfall is just the bottom end. It is 2.5 km/1.5 mi long and 50 to 100 m/55 to 110 yd wide. The rock has been precipitated from the water, which bubbles with carbon dioxide, and forms small steps so that the streams cascade in an **unending series of miniature cataracts**, looking like the scales on the back of a giant dragon. Since Chinese dragons are aquatic creatures, the association that gives the whole valley its name must have seemed quite obvious.

»Yellow Dragon«

The »ponds that compete in colour« at the top end of the dragon do just what their name suggests. This third group of extensive calcified terraces exceeds all the colour that has gone before.

Zhengyancaichi

There is then a long stretch without any interesting limestone formations. First of all comes the Buddhists' **»Middle temple«**, then the Temple of the Yellow Dragon, where the »Immortal of the Yellow Dragon« can be venerated. As the Tibetans who have settled in this area relate, a wise man here once had a dream that there would be a terrible flood. He warned all the inhabitants to head for safety. When a devastating flood did indeed come it seemed clear that this wise man was in truth the **»Immortal of the Yellow Dragon«** himself, and so the people built this temple to him as the human incarnation of this beneficent yet uncanny water creature.

Temple

Five colours? Chinese understatement, for here at the **Five-Colour Ponds**, right next to the »Temple of the Yellow Dragon«, nature's sorcery has conjured a scene of kaleidoscopic drama for the highlight at the end of the walk – not just five colours but a whole spectrum. There are 693 ponds according to the park administration's count, gleaming in turquoise, white, ice blue, yellow or green; each pool seems to have a shade of its own. It is amazing how colourful clear water can be. Opening times: 7am–6pm (shorter hours in winter).

> **!** *Baedeker* TIP
>
> **The early bird and the hiker**
> In Huanglong it is only possible to avoid the crowds by arriving as soon as the gates open. In Jiuzhaigou even that is no good. The only thing that helps here is to take some time and wander off the beaten track on the well-made walkways.

★ ★ Jiuzhaigou

It almost seems as though Nature had wished to display all of her facets at once in this remote karst-dominated mountain region of »Nine Village Valley«. More than 100 pools, some clear, some coloured, waterfalls and cataracts, limestone tuff levels, floating islands and allegedly **more species of plant than in all of Europe**, the surprises, large and small, seem to have no end.

Tours »Nine Village Valley«, settled by Tibetans, actually consists of three valleys, the upper pair of which form a Y-shape with the lower one. The area, covering 720 sq km/280 sq mi (almost the size of a city like Birmingham), is not so elevated as Huanglong. The entrance (where the waters flow out of the valley) is at an altitude of 1990 m/6470 ft. From there the valley rises relatively gently up to more than 3000 m/ 10,000 ft. The peaks rise to as high as 4600 m/15,000 ft. An asphalt road passes through all three valleys along a total length of 55 km/35 mi. Apart from the occasional official car, there is no traffic here other than the park's own buses. A day ticket can be obtained for travelling on them. What is nice is that the park administration has also laid very **convenient and well maintained wooden walkways** to make paths on the sides of the valleys where there is no road. There are no crowds here, because most of the Chinese visitors are on day trips and thus have little time for hiking. Crossings lead now and then back to the main road. Opening times: 7am–6pm daily. From 16 Nov till the end of March the upper part of the Rize Valley (above Swan Lake) is closed to the public.

Shuzheng Valley This is the main valley, 14 km/9 mi long from the extensive entrance zone (selling admission tickets and souvenirs, with green areas and car parking). Even at sunrise, the entrance is thronged with visitors. For the first stretch as far as **»Bonsai Beach«** it is worth taking a bus.

Precious Mirror Cliff The first attraction (on the left) is a completely smooth cliff face 400 m/1300 ft high, which seems to obscure the end of the valley like a giant spirit wall. It is called the»Precious Mirror Cliff«. According to the tales of Jiuzhaigou's Tibetans, the **»ancestor spirit of the mountains«** once used this magic mirror to cast down a demon, who now sits trapped under the rocks. The evil creature had in his time pursued a **mountain sprite of astounding beauty**. The unfortunate nymph suffered at the hands of the monster for ten thousand years before the ancestor spirit could defeat the evil beast. In the course of the fighting, though, the sprite's make-up mirror cracked into 108 pieces, which are now the 108 lakes of Jiuzhaigou.

Bonsai Beach The first in a long line of »aquatic attractions« is a limestone tuff level where the plants are dwarfed due to the lack of nourishment. At the lower end of it, near a Tibetan **water mill**, it is possible to cross to the other side of the valley and cover the rest of the distance via the wooden walkways.

Four lakes Above Bonsai Beach there follows a lake with reeds growing in it. It is 2 km/1.5 mi long and is called **Reed Lake**. The next lake up the path is the Lake of the Two Dragons: snaking limestone reefs along the bed of the lake were the inspiration for the name. According to one legend, they were evil dragons who kept ravaging Jiuzhaigou with hailstorms before a Tibetan king managed to defeat them and chain them for ever deep in the lake. Above the next cataract is Glittering Lake. If the morning sun has dispelled the mist, its light causes the waves to glitter. One more lake further on and another dragon comes to light. In the »**Lake of the Sleeping Dragon**« there is another dragon-like limestone deposit.

19 ponds

The first highlight comes up shortly afterwards: a 5 km/3 mi sequence of limestone tuff steps, each of which traps water so that cataracts are formed. The steps are not barren, though, but overgrown with woody shrubs through which the water splashes. At two spots, there are wooden walkways across the steps to the other side. By one of them some Tibetan watermills can be seen. The trail is brought to an end at the top by the 25 m/80 ft **Shuzheng Waterfall**, whose fine spray nourishes the moss cushion on the rocks.

Tiger Lake, Rhinoceros Lake

The next two lakes have somewhat surprising names. The higher of them, at an elevation of 2315 m/7520 ft, is the largest in the Shuzheng valley, covering 20 ha/50 acres. Its name goes back to a story. It is said a Tibetan lama once appeared here riding on a rhinoceros. He was apparently dying, but when he drank from the waters of the lake, he was cured.

The scenery at Jiuzhaigou is delightful.

Nuorilang Waterfall	The Nuorilang Waterfall, is where the two upper valleys meet. The falls are 30 m/100 ft high and wooded at the top. A path leads along the more westerly of the two upper valleys (Rize Valley) – to the right – for 17 km/10 mi.
From Mirror Lake to Five Blossom Lake	Above the Nuorilang falls there are another 18 limestone tuff cascades, which get their water from the Mirror Lake, now properly protected and able to live up to its name. At the top end of it, another wooden walkway begins and this is the route to be taken. The first stop is **Zhenzhutan Waterfall**, 310 m/1000 ft wide, 28 m/90 ft high and plummeting into a narrow valley. The route leads upwards from the falls. Above them, the water crosses an inclined limestone tuff level, which the Chinese call the »Pearl Beach«. Here too there is a wooden walkway leading across it. Having set foot on the walkway, the visitor will immediately know where the poetic name comes from. The water, splashing over the broad surface which is coloured green with algae and has miniature shrubs growing from it, atomizes into droplets that glitter like pearls. The fact that plants can still grow in a stream gushing fast enough to wash away all the soil is one of the mysteries of the spot and there are only a handful of other places where it can be seen. Go back to the original path and follow it upwards as far as Five Blossom Lake, also dyed in startling colours by algae. The best view is from the road that passes the lake at a higher level.

> **! Baedeker TIP**
>
> **Zaru Temple**
>
> Near the »Treasure Mirror Peak« a road leads into the neighbouring Zaru Valley. Near the beginning of the road on the right is one of the most important Buddhist temples in Jiuzhaigou.

Panda Lake and Waterfall	Unless, having got back to the road, you want to take a bus, you should carry on along the footpath on the far side of the valley. It leads Jiuzhaigou's highest waterfall. Its drop of **78 m/250 ft** is divided into three levels. Most visitors, though, do not actually see any water. There is only water here during the rainy season in summer. At other times all the water that enters Panda Lake, above the falls (2587 m/ 8410 ft), seeps out of it again down through the karst ground. It is said that even in the 1970s real pandas were sighted at Panda Lake.
Arrow Bamboo Lake	Another footpath on the opposite side of the valley to the road goes up to the Giant Bamboo Lake with its own lovely waterfall. It is possible to walk under the falls on a wooden walkway. The next stretch of 9.5 km/6 mi is not so interesting as the rest, so it is a good idea to take a bus again here.
Grass Lakes, Jungle	The top end of the of the sequence of lakes consisting of two interesting examples: **Swan Lake** and **Fragrant Grass Lake**. Both are

White water: unspoiled nature in the reserve at Juizhaigou →

thickly overgrown with waterweeds, upon which islands of grass actually float. The road ends at the edge of a jungle and it is possible to enter a little into it to see the extraordinary variety of species that live there

Zechawa Valley The area to the east of the upper valleys is characterised by its karst terrain, making it quite arid in places. The attractions are not nearly as concentrated along the 18 km here as along the other two valleys. At the bottom of the valley on the left-hand side, there is a large complex of buildings, the reserve's **visitor centre** with restaurants and shops. It is handy to take a bus from here to the top of the valley then walk some of the way back.

Chang Hai The journey up the valley passes two lakes – or two big dry depressions: there is only water here in summer or early autumn when there has been a lot of rain. After that the waters seep down into the ground. Right at the top of the valley at an elevation of 3060 m Höhe, there is a lake lined by dense evergreen forest, the **»Long Lake«** (Chang Hai), the biggest in the Jiuzhaigou reserve. It is fed by lots of streams but none leads out of it, at least not at ground level. Its level thus never rises above the height of the glacial moraine, which dams it at its lower end. Its **surface is often dazzling** and gives it a mysterious air. The Tibetans say that monsters sometimes emerge from the waters. In winter a layer of ice up to 60 cm/2 ft thick forms on the lake.

Five-Colour Lake A cleverly constructed footpath leads from here down the valley to the last natural wonder of Jiuzhaigou: a pool measuring 40 x 25 m/ 130 x 80 ft and up to 6 m/20 ft deep with a turquoise surface so intensely coloured that it would look artificial if the water were not so crystal clear. No streams lead into or out of the pond.

Jiayuguan

Ge 26

Province: Gansu	**Population:** 160,000
Altitude: 1450 m/4700 ft	

The modern industrial town is not very interesting as such but anyone travelling the Silk Road will certainly make a stop here. The fort with which the town shares its name is at the very end of the Ming era's Great Wall of China.

A section of the Wall 15 km/9.5 mi long closes off to the west the broad valley through which the Silk Road passes. To the north, it meets mountainous terrain, to the soth a gorge. There was formerly

▶ VISITING JIAYUGUAN

GETTING THERE

Jiayuguan can be reached by plane from Xi'an, Lanzhou and Beijing. When travelling the Silk Road, though, overland routes are more appropriate, e.g. by train (station at the southern edge of town). Cross-country buses offer the most convenient link to Dunhuang.

ACCOMMODATION

▶ **Mid-range**
Changcheng Binguan
Jianshe Xilu 6
Tel. 0937/622 63 06
Fax 0937/622 60 16
160-room hotel – one of the few attractive places in town though only Chinese food is served.

only one way through, which was secured by the mighty **Jiayu Guan fortress**, which also served as a garrison. To this day, the location, right on the boundary between oasis in the east and desert in the west, continues to fascinate visitors. From the west, the view of the clay walls with their battlements and three towers is hardly any different from what it was in the 16th century. Anyone coming here will immediately understand how the **Great Wall** was once not just a national border, but also a frontier between cultures.

The core of the fortress is a 160 m/520 ft square with crenellated walls almost 12 m/40 ft high (partly of rammed earth but partly clad with mud bricks). They are 6.6 m/20 ft thick at the bottom and 2 m/7 ft thick at the top. The two entrances, one in the west and one in the east, are reinforced by bastions. Inside the large central courtyard there was once a command post. The square of walls is surrounded by an outer wall, the western face of which is as tall as the inner wall. A spacious outer courtyard in the east, reached via the main gate in the east contains a **temple dedicated to »Emperor Guan«**, protective god of soldiers. A theatre stage facing the temple was used for making offerings to the deity. A two-storey building at the side is dedicated to Wenchang, protector of scholars.

Layout

The fort is older than the Great Wall itself. Its construction started in 1372; it reached its current size in the 16th century, though its present appearance dates back to restoration during the 1980s.

History

Ramps capable of taking horses lead up to the battlements atop the wall around the inner courtyard. On the inside of the barbican separating the bastion from the outer courtyard in the west, a single mud brick is placed on a ledge above the gate. The legend behind it is that when the builder who erected the gate calculated the materials required, his estimates were so accurate that only one brick was left over, this one. Opening times: 8.30am–6pm daily.

The left-over brick

A bastion on the border: the fortress of Jiayu Guan

The first watch-tower (Di-yi dun)
The wall that adjoins the fort and blocks the whole valley is anything but imposing. This is how the Great Wall looked in most places during the Ming era – quite different from what it does near Beijing. It ends in the south at watchtower no. 1, a half-ruined rammed-earth tower. The part that mostly makes a visit worthwhile is a clay canyon some 50 m/160 ft deep right behind it. Go right to the end of the safety fence at the edge to see the whole scene. It is a great place to watch the sunrise.

»Hanging Wall« (Xuanbi)
The northern end of the section of Wall climbs steeply up the slope of a mountain. Its mud walls and watchtowers were restored at the end of the 1980s, or rather rebuilt from scratch. From the top there is a great panoramic view of the desert, the oasis and the town along with the fort and – when the air is clear enough for a really good view – the 5000 m/16,000 ft peaks in the distance.

Kashgar

Fd 26

Province: Autonomous Region of Xinjiang

Population: 350,000
Altitude: 1290 m/4232 ft

This was once the most important junction on the old Silk Road and is now the most westerly of China's big cities. It seems to be a veritable incarnation of the exotic. Amid the endless sandy Taklimakan Desert in the east with high mountains shielding each of the other compass points, the Tianshan Mountains in the north, the Pamirs in the west, and the Kunlun range in the south, was one of the most difficult places in the world to get to until well into the 20th century.

Since the development of air travel and its incorporation into the Chinese rail network in 1999, getting there is no longer such an adventure. The city itself has changed, too, and large parts of it look much like any other city in the country. Nevertheless there is more of Central Asia here than China. The city is **3440 km/2138 mi from Beijing**, but it is only 91 km/57 mi to the border with Kyrgyzstan, 144 km/90 mi to Tajikistan and 266 km/165 mi as the crow flies to Afghanistan. These are not just isolated numbers: 77% of the population are of Uighur descent and speak a Turkic language. Taking a trip into the country around here one will meet many a Kyrgyz or Tajik.

Kirghiz yurts against the backdrop of the 7564 m/24,816 ft Musztag Ata in the Pamirs. The dried yak dung in the foreground is used by the two women for heating their oven.

Ethnic conflicts Kashgar is as old as the Silk Road itself and its history is every bit as complex. The people and their rulers changed every couple of centuries. Sometimes conquerors followed hot on each other's heels: Tibetans, Turkomans, Mongols, and Chinese are only the best known. In the mid-18th century the Manchu emperors absorbed Kashgar into their giant empire. From 1862 to 1875 it was the **capital for the rebel Yaqub Beg**. China (or the Qing empire) did conquer the region back in 1877, but ethno-political conflicts were not allayed by this and tensions remain to this day.

What to see in Kashgar

Old town There is no guarantee that what remains of the old town will continue to exist, but there's still a lot of it and none of it counterfeit. Its two-storey, flat-roofed mud brick houses, mosques, a plethora of small workshops and shops selling this and that from smiths and lathe cutters to milliners or drive-belt specialists – and where other cities might have a bus, here people get around by donkey.

✷
Bazaar and Sunday market To the east of the old town take the dead-straight Aizirete Lu to get to the bazaar, a giant new complex, but still on one level, as per tradition, and still with stacks of atmosphere. It is at its liveliest at the famous Sunday market, which attracts thousands to the city. Not only local wares are on sale there, but all sorts of services are on offer, knife-grinders, open-air barbers and hairdressers and, of course, food stalls with typical Uighur fare.

✷
Cattle market The Sunday cattle market was moved to the eastern edge of town a few years ago. For most visitors it surely remains the most exotic of the Sunday markets here. Primarily sheep or goats, donkeys or horses are traded, camels in late autumn, along with accessories such as harnesses and all kinds of animal finery.

Id Kah Mosque The most important mosque in the city stands on a not very big, but prestigious square on the western edge of the old town. It is said to be the biggest mosque in China. The gatehouse, which dominates the western side of the square along with its two minarets, gives little idea of the 1.6 ha/4 acres of grounds behind it. Part of that area is occupied by gardens beyond the gate, through which the main building is accessed. This is a **prayer hall** covering an area of 2600 sq m/ 3300 sq yd, along with an open vestibule. 140 wooden columns support the roof. Everything is in the Arabian-inspired, central Asian style. The mosque was founded in 1426 or 1442 (the date is uncertain), with the present buildings having been built in the mid-18th century. Women are allowed to visit the area (except during prayers) if they are suitably dressed.

Almost 80% of the population of Kashgar is Uighur →

► VISITING KASHGAR

INFORMATION

New Land International Travel Service
20 Payinapu Lu
Tel. 09 98/253 52 78, Fax 253 52 77
www.newlandtravel.net
Excursions to the Pamirs can be booked here, as can Silk Road journeys, trekking tours and mountain hikes.

GETTING THERE

Kashgar airport is north of the city. There are several flights daily to the provincial capital of Ürümqi. Kashgar station is 7 km/4 mi east of the city. The train to Ürümqi takes a whole day. Long-distance coaches run to and from the Pakistan border from the international bus station on Jiefang Beilu. Journeys to Pakistan are only permitted, though, for those holding a Pakistan visa, and it is not possible to obtain one in Kashgar. The same applies to journeys into nearby Kyrgyzstan (Irkeshtam Pass towards Osh, Torugart Pass towards Bishkek). Be careful because buses across the border into Kyrgyzstan do not run every day.

SHOPPING

Elaborately embroidered caps, carpets, brassware, ornamented daggers, gold-woven fabric – the bazaar has a seductive surfeit of goods to tempt the money from your wallet. Haggling is essential in Kashgar.

ACCOMMODATION

► Mid-range
Qinibagh Hotel (Qiniwake Binguan)
144 Seman Lu
Tel. 09 98/298 21 03
Fax 09 98/298 22 99
This 260-room building is the best hotel in town – and has the longest tradition: The premises include the former British Consulate established in 1908; which is now used as a restaurant. Inexpensive dormitory beds.

✳ Abakh Khoja Mausoleum

China's most important Islamic mausoleum testifies to the national independence of the eastern Xinjiang region before the Manchu conquest. It was built in around 1640 by the Emir of the Yarkand Khanate, **Abakh Khoja**, for his father. In total there are 58 tombs here with five generations of the Khoja clan, including Abakh himself. This large and dignified complex also includes two madrasas and a mosque.

Main building A gate covered in glazed tiles leads to the first garden. To the right there is another garden laid out symmetrically in the Persian style. It is at the northern side of this that the mausoleum itself stands. It has a strictly symmetrical floor plan with a circular minaret at each of the four corners and a dome in the middle, which has a lantern on the top. Apart from the white plastered niches, the outside is mainly covered in green and some blue glazed tiles.

The tomb of Abakh Khoja is in a central spot under the dome. More notable, though, is a small grave in the right-hand corner at the rear, that of the »Fragrant Concubine«, a granddaughter of Abakh's by the name of **Iparhan**, who was sent to the court of the Qianlong Emperor for the purpose of a political marriage. She was a real person: Giuseppe Castiglione, the Qianlong Emperor's Italian court painter, painted her portrait and photographs of it can be viewed or purchased in and around the mausoleum. The fact that she is buried here, though, is mere legend; one which is popularly related to this day in the way of propaganda to underline the assertion that Xinjiang is historically part of China. The real »Fragrant Concubine« died in 1788 aged 55 and is fact buried in the tombs of the Qing emperors east of Beijing.

The »Fragrant Concubine«

On the western side of the first garden is the tomb's mosque, a half-open building with beautifully carved, slender wooden pillars. The Abakh Khoja Mausoleum is on the northeast edge of Kashgar. Opening times: 9am–5pm daily.

Mosque

⏱

Yarkand (Shache)

This town of some 100,000 inhabitants, 125 km/78 mi from Kashgar, was already a renowned **centre on the southern part of the Silk Road** 2000 years ago. Occasionally, as in the 13th century when it was the capital of the Chagatai Khanate, Yarkand even exceeded Kashgar in size and importance. Chagataian was in use as a literary language, using Arabic script, until well into the 20th century. The shabby but lively Uighur old town still retains a traditional appearance.

The centrepiece of the old town is composed of a lovely ensemble of buildings including firstly the large mosque (not open to non-Muslims), secondly the elegant mausoleum of the song collector, poet and musician, **Aman Isa Khan** (1526–1560), with the tombs of the former kings nearby, and thirdly, on the opposite side of the street, the gate of the former citadel and royal residence, which can be climbed by the public.

✱
Old town

✱ ✱ Trip into the Pamir Mountains

This can either be done in comfort as a day trip by taxi or cheaply using the bus: A trip on the road to the Karakorums through the dramatic highland scenery of the Pamir Mountains in the direction of Pakistan as far as Lake Karakul, 190 km/118 mi away, is practically a duty. The »Black Lake« (not to be confused with an identically named but much larger briny lake in Tajikistan) is located at an altitude of over 3645 m/11,950 ft in an area traditionally settled and grazed by Kyrgyzian people, who still erect their yurts here in the six summer months. The most spectacular thing to see is the view of two mountains over 7000 m/23.000 ft in height, as they are reflected in the waters of the lake, the 7719 m/25,325 ft **Kongur Tag** (the highest mountain in the Pamir range) and the especially lovely 7546 m/ 24,757 ft **Muztagh Ata** (»Ice Mountain Father«). There is a restaurant and some spartan overnight accommodation. Camels are available for a round trip.

Bulungkol On the way there, the route passes Bulungkol, a broad flood plain at the confluence of two rivers, which is flanked by massive sandstone hills topped by snowy peaks. On the journey it is essential to take a passport to avoid being sent back from the **Gezcun** border control centre, which actually comes before Bulungkol and where photographs are strictly prohibited. If making the trip by cross-country bus (via Karakol to Sost or Tashkurgan), an overnight stop will need to be planned. Be careful: it can be difficult to get a bus back from Karakol – they bypass it on the main road and do not always stop. It is better to book a trip at a travel agency.

Kunming

Gg 33

Province: Yunnan **Population:** 3.9 million
Altitude: 1890 m/6200 ft

Anyone travelling in Yunnan will usually start here in the capital and may well quickly find out even here that the southwest corner of China is a bit different. That is noticeable even by the climate: »four seasons of spring«, as the Chinese say, which is a slight exaggeration but not by very much.

It never gets very hot in Kunming (pop. 3.9 million, 1.35 million in the city itself.) but it never gets that cold, either. The average temperature in July is 19.7°C while in January it is 7.7°C. Nevertheless, from November it is often wet and dismal. To the north the province ascends right up to the Tibetan Plateau but the lifestyle here in perceptibly more »southern«, more relaxed, cheerier and even the food reflects this, increasingly incorporating more southeast Asian flavours as you go further south. Finally there is considerable historical testament to an independent cultural tradition. Yunnan only became a permanent part of the Chinese empire under the Mongols in the 13th century. The province remains an **ethnic patchwork** to this day. No other part of China has so many different peoples living in it.

Appearance and layout Until into the 1990s western visitors would be fascinated by the large and exotic old town but now little remains of it. What emerged in its place mostly looks like any other provincial capital but thanks to the generously sized squares and plenty of park space, it also has its

► VISITING KUNMING

GETTING THERE

Kunming is the terminus for trains to and from Beijing, Shanghai, Guilin, Dali and other places. There is also an international airport nearby. Shilin, 120 km/75 mi south of Kunming, can be teached by tour buses that leave from outside the railway station (opposite the long-distance coach station) until 12 noon. For those who like more comfort, a day trip to Shilin can be booked as an organized tour from any hotel.

THEATRE

Dinner theatre

Song and dance featuring the ethnic minorities of Yunnan can be enjoyed in various places in conjunction with a meal of culinary specialities, e.g. 8pm every day in the Kunming Hotel, 52 Dongfeng Donglu, tel. 08 71/316 20 63.

WHERE TO EAT

The most famous of Kunming's specialities, and also its cheapest, are »over the bridge noodles« (guoqiao mixian). According to legend they were invented by a woman who had to cook for her husband working on a small island. In order to keep the soup warm on the way across the bridge and so that the vegetables did not lose their flavour, she kept the stew warm under a layer of fat and then served the ingredients at the man's table. This is still how the dish is served today, even without crossing any bridges, today.

► Moderate

① *1910 La Gare du Sud*
8 Hou Xin Jie (north from the East Pagoda then turn right twice)
Tel. 08 71/316 94 86

Good cuisine with a special atmosphere in the remains of a former railway station on the French-built Yunnan Railway – it is nice to sit outside, too.

Baedeker recommendation

► Inexpensive

② *Yuquan Zhai*
88 Pingzheng Jie
Near the temple of Yuantong Si is the most famous vegetarian restaurant in town. Well-known Buddhist eatery with vegetarian imitations of fish and meat dishes. Some very good »over the bridge noodles« are served here, too.

ACCOMMODATION

► Luxury

① *Bank Hotel*
399 Qingnian Lu
Tel. 08 71/315 88 88
Fax 08 71/315 89 99
www.bankhotel.com
Large new hotel, 285 rooms in a central location

► Mid-range/budget

② *Camellia Hotel*
154 Dongfeng Donglu
Tel. 08 71/316 30 00
Fax 08 71/314 70 33
www.kmcamelliahotel.com
Popular 200-room hotel, which covers two different price categories: for backpackers there are dormitory rooms but the double rooms in the renovated wing are on a more comfortable level. There is a large range of extra services on offer, including cycle rental.

Kunming Map

Qiongzhu Si

North Station

University

Yuantong Park

Zoo

Yuantong Si ②

Yuantong Jie

CHUANXINGULOU

Chuanjin

Huancheng Bei Lu

Panlong

Lingguang Jie

Huancheng Dong Lu

Beimen Jie

Cuihu Dong Lu

Wenlin Jie

Qianju Lu

Cuihu Bei Lu

Cuihu Park

Cuihu Nan Lu

WUHUASHAN

Qingnian Lu

Tocyuan Jie

SHUIJINGCUN

Beijing Lu

Kunshi Lu

Western Mountains (Xi Shan)

XIAOXIMEN

Shangyi Jie

Xinhua Jie

Huashan Nan Lu

Wucheng Lu

Changchun

Lu

Lu

Renmin Dong Lu

Baita Lu

Tanhua Si

Daguan Jie

Dongfeng Xi Lu

Hongxing Theatre

Guanghua Jie

Zhengyi Lu

Weiyuan Jie

Qingnian Lu

NANTAIQIAO

Huguo Lu

Workers' Cultural Hall

Dongfeng Dong Lu ②

Provincial Stadium

Xinwen Lu

Guofang Stadium

Provincial Museum

Jingxing Jie

Shuncheng Jie

Wuyi Lu

Nanping Lu

Zhengyi Lu

Huguo Lu

①

Baita Lu

Huancheng Xi Lu

Jinbi Xi Lu

Jinbi Square

Jinbi Lu

Tuodong Lu

Tuodong Lu

City Museum

Airport

FUXING XINCUN

MILESI

Huancheng Xi Lu

West Pagoda

Houxin Jie

East Pagoda ①

Dongsi Jie

Shilin Jie

Beijing Lu

Wujing Lu

WUJING XINCUN

Huancheng Nan Lu

Minhang Lu

TUQIAO

Tangshuang Lu

WULIDUO

XINQIAO

Huangcheng Nan Lu

Wujing Lu

0,25 mi
500 m
©Baedeker

XIYUEMIAO

Bus Station

HUANGGUAYING

Haigeng Lu

Panlong

Main Station

pleasant side. The main axis for orientation is the road running north from the railway station; **Beijing Lu**, which passes through the old town and the eastern edge of the present business area. The east-west axis, Renmin Lu (»People's Road«) runs through the middle of it. Kunming is situated on the northern shore of the great lake Dian Chi, but the waters are not a major factor in the city's appearance. The central attractions all lie relatively close together to the south, west and north of the city centre.

What to see in Kunming

The oldest building in the city is the 35.5 m/116 ft brick tower simply called the West Pagoda. Stylistically it resembles its contemporary, the large pagoda at Chongsheng Si in Dali. After an earthquake in 1499 caused the partial collapse of the tower, it was reconstructed in 1504. During renovation work in 1984, though, one brick was found which was **stamped with a date equivalent to 849**. The temple to which the pagoda once belonged no longer exists. Nowadays it is part of a green park, highly popular with the natives for its pleasant and lively atmosphere.

West Pagoda

Originally the East Pagoda was just what it appears to be again today, a twin of the West Pagoda, which was built at the same time. However, the original East Pagoda totally collapsed in an earthquake in 1833 and was rebuilt from 1882 as a complete **replica of the West Pagoda**. Both of the pagodas are to the south of the central Jinbi Square, the western one on Dongsi Jie and the eastern tower one block further east on Shulin Jie.

East Pagoda

Three imposing gates mark the newly built southern end of Zhengyi Lu, which acts as the central north-south axis for the centre of Kunming. Northward it runs direct to the provincial administration buildings. The gates to the south of the road bear the words »Blue Chicken« and »Golden Horse«, while the third, the entrance to Zhengyi Lu, claims »Loyalty and Love«. Azure blue (bi) and gold (jin) are also used for the names of the roads running east-west across Jinbi Square. The gates are patterned on an old tradition but in their current form they only date from 1999. On the southern side of the square there is a complex of new buildings in the old town style, housing restaurants, but Zhengyi Lu itself is an almost sleek and pleasantly designed **pedestrian zone** with the most elegant international shops in town.

Jinbi Square

? DID YOU KNOW ...?

■ ... that, after conquering Yunnan, the Mongols settled their Muslims in Kunming? There is still a large community of Chinese Muslims here. Around the turn of the 20th century, though, thanks mainly to the French-built Yunnan Railway which linked Kunming to Hanoi from 1910, Yunnan came under French influence. The city was only incorporated into the Chinese rail system in 1970.

Provincial museum

Head north one block up Zhengyi Lu to the large roundabout and then go west to get to the provincial museum (Dongfeng Xilu, corner with Wuyi Lu), a building built as late as 1964 but which was still clearly, from its Sino-Stalinist style, designed during the era of Chinese-Soviet comradeship. In the Buddhism section there are some **relics of the Nanzhao kingdom** on show: bricks with inscriptions, bronze mirrors, small statues and some large colour photos of buildings and large-scale Buddhist art. Most things are labelled in English. The most spectacular exhibits for the era of the Dian culture (1st century BC) are several decorated bronze drums. On the ground floor there is a museum shop, which also has embroidery by some of Yunnan's ethnic minorities on sale. Opening times: 9.30am–5pm daily.

Cuihu Park

From the museum, the street Wuyi Lu leads straight to the »Jade Green Lake« (Cui Hu). With its parkland and islands, it is a favourite place for Kunming's inhabitants to spend time. Among the attractions are boat trips, watching the old people play mah jongg, listening to amateur musicians, speaking to the students at »English corner« on a Sunday or filling up at a cookshop by the lake shore. Opening times: 6am–6pm daily.

Temple of Yuantong Si

Heading east from the lake, the most important temple within the city limits of Kunming appears at the southern edge of the zoo. Yuantong Si has delightful park-like grounds and a lovely atmosphere. Although it was established more than a thousand years ago during the Nanzhao era, its buildings and decorative imagery are not historically important. One special feature, though, is the **octagonal pavilion**, standing in the middle of a pool of water. The statuary in the main hall consists of three gaudy Buddhas. In one new building built especially for it, there is an impressive bronze Shakyamuni, a gift from the king of Thailand. North side of Yuantong Jie. Opening times: 8am–5pm daily.

★ Temple of Qiongzhu Si

The »Bamboo monastery« (Qiongzhu Si) has the most fabulous luohan figures in all China: 500 almost life-sized, coloured clay statues, made between 1883 and 1890 by **Li Guangxiu**. The accuracy of the images, sometimes featuring staggeringly realistic gestures, postures and expressions as well as some quite fantastical ones, is astounding. The wit, imagination and artistic mastery is enough to catch the breath of any visitor. 12 km/7 mi northwest of the town centre. Opening times: 8am–5pm daily.

★ Western Hills (Xi Shan) and Lake Dian Chi

The lake of Dian Chi covers an area of 300 sq km/120 sq mi, although at its northern end it is only very narrow. Its status as an

New made to look old: gate on to Jinbi Square →

attraction derives not from the waters themselves but from the Western Hills which loom steeply over the west bank 15 km/9 mi southwest of the city and rise to a height of 2350 m/7710 ft.

From Huating Monastery to Nie Er 's tomb

The first 8 km/5 mi up from the foot of the mountain can be driven. The first stop is the large Huating Temple, with buildings dating partly from 1883 and partly from 1923. Its main hall contains the images of 500 luohan. 2 km/1.5 mi further up comes the **Taihua Temple**, which has some particularly nice greenery around it and is famous for its Dali marble reliefs. The third stop is the tomb of the composer Nie Er (1912–1936), who wrote China's national anthem but died at a sadly early age. There is a statue of him with 24 steps representing the years of his life. Near the grave is the »hub« of tourism to the Xi Shan range: a large car park, which is also the terminus for buses and coaches, the lower station of a chairlift to the summit of Taihua Shan and the upper station of a cable-car which crosses to the Nationalities Park on the other side of the lake.

Sanqing Ge Temple

A level path leads further along the slope to the »Temple of the Three Pure Ones«, which has halls stacked one atop the other on nine terraces. It offers the opportunity to rest with a cup of tea.

Dragon Gate

The most eccentric of Western Hills' attractions, not only because it has the best view of the lake, came into being between 1781 and 1853 when a Daoist monk and a number of assistants hacked a **tun-**

Distant view close at hand for city-dwellers: the Western Mountains near Kunming

nel-like gallery and several grottoes out of a vertical cliff. The caves were later decorated with colourfully painted and often gilded figures. Among those to be seen are Guanyin, who brings children, star gods and dragons. The Dragon gate is the portal in front of the final grotto. The rocky path is so narrow that it is almost impossible for two people to wriggle past one another in places.

The eastern shore of the lake is not far away from the Western Hills and it is possible to take a cable car across to see two more attractions, the Yunnan Museum of Minority Nationalities and Nationalities Village. In two different ways they both give an impression of the ethnic variety of the province. The museum displays **national dress, musical instruments as well as arts and craft works**. The village has houses and groups of houses in the styles of the various peoples of the region. In addition folk dances and songs are performed every day. Opening times: Tue–Sun 9am–4.30pm. No. 51 bus from Chuncheng Lu near the station to Gaoyao at the foot of the Western Hills, or special bus from the art theatre (Yishu Juyuan, Dongfeng Xilu, corner of Guanghua Jie, near the provincial museum) direct to Nie Er's tomb, no. 24 bus from the station direct to the Village of Nationalities.

Nationalities Museum and Nationalities Village

★ ★ The »Stone Forest« of Shilin

The most famous natural wonder in Yunnan province is 120 km/75 mi southeast of Kunming and can be visited on a day trip. The stones are not actually petrified trees, as one might think, but bizarre **limestone formations** up to 30 m/100 ft high, which are taller than they are wide so that one can walk the artificial paths between them as in a gigantic maze, and possibly get lost too. It is worse than among the trees in a forest. In fact there are several such »stone forests« in the area, although the second-largest of them, covering an area of about 90 ha/220 acres, attracts the most visitors.

The limestone of Shilin, which has been eroded into such dramatic forms here, came into being about 270 million years ago as sediment on the sea bed. As it was pushed upward during the aeons of Earth's history – currently to a height of some 1750 m/5750 ft – erosion began to take effect about two million years ago, primarily due to water in this rainy area. The overall size of the stone forests is about 400 sq km/150 sq mi, but in most places the limestone is covered with soil and in others it only protrudes a little from the surrounding fields.

> **!** *Baedeker* TIP
>
> **Stone forest with and without the crowds**
>
> Some 10,000 visitors come here every day, and they nearly all arrive in the late morning. As most of them don't stay very long, things get quiet from about 3pm, the start of the ideal Shilin time for individualists.

A forest of stone – with a few exceptions

Tours In the main area, more than 5 km/3 mi of paths have been laid out. Most visitors take a standard tour lasting an hour or so. Anyone with more time to spare can explore the more distant and less busy paths, allowing some three hours and taking advantage of a guide – Sani women make themselves available for this. The Sani are a local tribe belonging to the Yi people. Beware: without a guide, or at least a compass and a good sense of direction, it is very easy to get lost.

Stone Forest of Naigu The biggest of the stone forests covers 300 ha/750 acres and lies 8 km/5 mi further to the northeast. The rocks are not so densely packed but there are also karst caves and a waterfall.

Kuqa

Province: Autonomous region of Xinjiang

Population: 100 000
Altitude: 1100 m/3600 ft

The old oasis town is among the more important on the northern part of the Silk Road. Kuqa is not especially romantic, even if it is a good example of Uighur exoticism, as seen in most of the oasis towns around the edge of the Tarim Basin. It is the surroundings, though, which draw visitors here. Kuqa is the official spelling nowadays although an older form, »Kuchar«, probably gives a better idea of the actual pronunciation.

Kuqa was an independent kingdom until its conquest by the Tang empire. Its former administrative language and that of its monasteries is called Tocharian B; which was an Iranian, i.e. Indo-European language, and was used until the 8th century, being written with Indian characters. The **influence of China**, though, made itself felt very early on, during the Han period, when the king of Kuqa made a state visit to Changan in the year 65 BC. In terms of cultural history, Kuqa was of particular importance as a centre of Buddhism. It is said that 10,000 monks were living here in 365. The most important legacies of that era are the **Cave Temples of Kizil**, some of which were financed by the king of Kuqa himself. During the heyday of the Silk Road in the 7th and 8th centuries, Kuqa too was a boom town. At that time it was home not only to the Tocharians but also Sogdians, Indians, Tibetans and Chinese. Kuqa's music was fashionable in the Chinese capital and was even played at court. Later research into Kuqa and the history of the region was given a major boost by the German Turfan expeditions of 1903–1914. Research into the Tocharians became a special area of interest for German researchers after the expeditions unearthed countless writings from the desert sands, including medical tracts, translations of sutras, magic spells and mercantile documents.

✳ Buddha caves of Kizil (Qyzil)

The biggest cave temple complex in the region lies 75 km/47 mi northwest of Kuqa across the Muzat River. There are approximately 300 caves hacked into a steep cliff, of which 236 are numbered. 135 of them are more or less intact but only 17 are open to the public. The history of archaeological research in the region means they all have German names, which are written on tablets inside the caves.

History and artistic decoration

The Buddha grottoes were built and used from the 3rd into the 10th century. The most interesting of them are the earliest caves (including some of the oldest on Chinese soil), which are dominated by art derived from India and the Gandhara kingdom, and very much display the motifs of **Hinayana Buddhism**. Chinese stylistic influences start to appear only in the middle of the 7th century. Hardly any figures and sculptures have survived but the remains of old frescoes depicting legends from the life of Buddha or his earlier incarnations can be seen.

Tours

Of the 17 caves open to the public, eight belong to the western part of the site and eight to the eastern part. A separate admission charge is paid to enter each side. Seeing the »**Music Cave**« (Cave 38) with its choir of musicians also requires an extra payment. The most impressive aspect is the site of the caves. The paintings themselves, often badly damaged and all incomplete; are often regarded as disappointing and should in all cases be viewed in the company of a guide.

Kumarajiva   One more word about the bronze sculpture behind the entrance: it depicts Kumarajiva (344–413), possibly the most important Buddhist scholar and translator of his time. He was the nephew of Kuqa's king (so Kuqa was his home) and the son of an Indian. He later travelled to China. His teaching and his translation into Chinese meant he made a major contribution to the adoption of what was then the new movement of Mahayana Buddhism.

> ! **_Baedeker_ TIP**
>
> ### The best thing about Kizil
>
> The best thing at Kizil is to explore the valley beyond the entrance. Many a »wild« grotto will be passed along the way, many a side valley with its own brook and it is even possible to visit some of the caves lower down but there are no murals to be discovered along the route. There is a reduced admission fee for those not actually making the usual cave tour.

National Road 217 traverses a dramatic, eroded and bizarre mountain landscape on the way to Kizil. The **Xaldarang Scenic Spot** features steep layers of green and red sedimentary rock layers. Since there is practically no vegetation, the whole view looks like a scene from Mars.

Kizilgaha Beacon Tower   On the way there or back it is worth taking a detour to another impressively scenic spot. On a hill between two wadis, which are usually dry, a 13.5 m/44 ft **rammed-earth watch tower** has been keeping a lookout towards the mountains of Tian Shan for a good 2000 years. No other example this far from the Chinese core territory displays the effort that was put into military security for the new conquests, even in the time of the Han emperors.

The ruined monastery of Subash   One more testament to the golden age of Buddhism along the Silk Road is this set of ruins taking up both sides of a broad wadi 20 km/ 12 mi north of Kuqa. Subash was established in the 4th century and served as the private monastery of the Kuqa monarchs. In the 12th century the settlement was abandoned so that nowadays it makes for an impressive collection of rammed-earth ruins.

 VISITING KUQA

GETTING THERE

Kuqa is on the railway line from Ürümqi to Kashgar and has direct connections to both those places. For destinations outside the town is it best to take a taxi, having agreed a fixed fare. Depending on the type of car, the price can be expected to be around 300 yuan.

ACCOMMODATION

► **Mid-range**
Kuche Hotel
Jiefang Beilu 17
Tel. 09 97/713 67 90, Fax 713 11 60
www.kcbg.com
120 rooms, near the centre and really quite comfortable by the standards of the Silk Road

Lanzhou

Gg 27

Province: Gansu   **Population:** 2.8 million.
Altitude: 1500 m/5000 ft

There are few reasons to stay in this industrial city longer than absolutely necessary. Nevertheless it is the capital of Gansu Province. The main reason to stop over here in the upper reaches of the Yellow River is to make a couple of trips.

Lanzhou is on historic terrain along the Silk Road and was already an important garrison town 2000 years ago during the war against the Xiongnu. Trade and warfare dominate its later history, too. This only changed when industrialization came after 1950.

What to see in Lanzhou

The provincial museum houses an important collection, although it has been undergoing a rebuild, so that the exhibits may be better and more lovingly displayed than hitherto. On view there are examples of Neolithic pottery (Dadiwan culture, c. 8000 BC), writing tablets and other discoveries from the Han period as well as the most important piece: the »**Flying Horse**«, a grave item unearthed 300 km/190 mi away in Wuwei. The stallion, shown in full gallop, rests on just one hoof, which itself rests on a flying swallow. Xijin Xilu. Opening times: Tue–Sun 9am–5pm.

Provincial museum

✳ Buddha caves of Bingling Si

Another cave temple site? Yes, but these are special, firstly because the grottoes are hewn into a 60 m/200 ft rock cliff which rises straight out of the water, and secondly because they have survived with so little destruction over the course of history.

The cave temple site is hard to get to under one's own steam. It is better to book an organized tour from Lanzhou. This should include travel to the **Liujiaxia Reservoir**, the boat trip and two admission charges, one to the surrounding area and one to the caves themselves. The journeys there and back take roughly three to three and a half hours (depending on whether a fast boat has been chosen). Two hours should be long enough to see the caves. Those with less interest in Buddhist art can save on the entrance to the caves, as the scenery and the view of the cave site from the water make the trip worthwhile on their own.
Be careful, from November to June it is not possible to make this tour owing to the low water level.

Tours

The site   34 caves and 149 niches stretch along the cliff on the left bank of the Yellow River, here dammed into a reservoir, for a length of 2 km/1.5 mi. The lowest section of the site and its caves and niches are protected from flooding by concrete wall 200 m/220 yd long and 20 m/66 ft high. In total there are almost **800 sculpted figures**, mostly carved direct out of the rock but occasionally modelled in clay. In addition, murals cover an area of 900 sq m/10,000 sq ft. About two thirds of the site was fashioned in the Tang era, including 20 of the 34 caves. A 27 m/90 ft sitting Buddha catches the eye. This too is from the Tan period. The best cave with the best paintings unfortunately demands a separate entrance fee: no. 169, created in around 400 inside a natural cave.

✳ Xiahe - Labrang Monastery

The small town of Xiahe is about. 230 km/143 mi southwest of Lanzhou by road. There is only one reason to make to the two-to-three day trip: the Labrang Monastery, one of the six main monasteries of the Yellow Hat school of monks founded by **Tsongkhapa** (►Famous People p. 83). At 3000 m/10,000 ft altitude, the monastery is already on the edge of the Tibetan Plateau. Visiting from Xiahe thus allows a taste of Tibet without actually having to venture into Tibet itself.

Experience Tibet without going there: Labrang monastery in Xiahe

VISITING LANZHOU AND XIAHE

GETTING THERE

Lanzhou has a station on the main line from Xi'an to Ürümqi but can also be reached by direct train from the north (Baotou). The city has an airport about 70 km/43 mi to the north with flights to most of the key destinations inside China as well as to Jiayuguan and Dunhuang. At least three buses run to Xiahe every day from the southern bus station in Lanzhou but advance booking is recommended (possibly via a travel agent).

WHERE TO EAT

Lanzhou is known for its noodles, in particular for beef noodle soup – a very cheap, filling and tasty recipe, which can be obtained in cookshops all over town. One good place is the market at Hezheng Lu (one block north of the station).

ACCOMMODATION

► Expensive
Lanzhou: Sapphire Hotel
37 Minzhu Xilu
Tel. 09 31/884 99 99
Fax 09 31/885 26 26
This centrally located 143-room hotel opened in 2007. It immediately become the city's most popular place to stay.

► Budget
Xiahe: Labrang Guest House (Labuleng Binguan)
3 km west of the village (about 1 km/1000 yd west of the monastery)
Tel. 09 41/712 18 49
Fax 09 41/712 13 28
Nice, quiet hostel in tall Tibetan style and situated amid rustic surroundings on the banks of the river, although most of the 114 rooms are very small and in need of renovation.

The region the road passes through on the way is settled by Chinese Moslems (of Hui nationality) and the characteristic **minarets** of their mosques can be seen everywhere. Their curved Chinese roofs, though, mean they could easily be taken for Buddhist pagodas. Xiahe, however, is one of the major pilgrimage destinations for Tibetans, thanks to its monastery. Having two ethnic groups living in the region has not always made for peaceful co-operation. Violent clashes took place as recently as the 1990s.

Tibetans and Muslims

The monastery itself is at the southern end of town. Its layout and building style are typically Tibetan. The buildings feature rugged walls with small windows and are spread about without any sort of axis. The roofs are flat but the most important buildings, the **Buddha halls and prayer halls** also exhibit Chinese-style curved roofs, covered with gilded copper tiles. Among the monastery buildings, which form a village in their own right, there are also six academies dedicated not only to religious teaching and liturgy but also to medicine, astronomy and mathematics. The whole complex is encircled by a

The monastery site

perimeter path consisting of galleries with prayer drums. Pilgrims go round this path in a clockwise direction turning the drums as they go.

History The monastery was only founded in 1709, making it comparatively recent. One of the reasons for picking this spot was its relative proximity to the Mongolians, who also follow Tibetan-style Buddhism. The high renown that the shrine enjoys is due to its founder, a so-called living Buddha, the sixth reincarnation of whom now manages the site, of course a living Buddha in his own right. The monastery was shut down during the Cultural Revolution but now it is once again home to some 1200 monks and novices.

Tours Religious life and, in particular, the everyday lives of **Tibetan pilgrims** can be experienced in detail and for free all around the monastery premises, which are open on all sides, on the perimeter path and at the pilgrims' markets. This is also another reason why Far Western visitors like to spend one or two days longer. To see more interior of the monastery, it is necessary to join one of the guided tours on offer twice a day, also with English-speaking monks.

Leshan

Gg 31

Province: Sichuan	**Population:** 500 000
Altitude: 350 m/1150 ft	

The reason for coming to Leshan is to see the Great Buddha, once the largest statue of Buddha in the world. Around the town, though, and just a little beyond the tourist bustle, there are also a few more enjoyable extras.

The city of Leshan is around 140 km/87 mi south of ▶Chengdu (35 km/22 mi east of ▶Emei Shan) at the confluence of the Dadu He and a Yangtze tributary called the Min Jiang. The centre of town is on the west bank of the latter. There is not much of note in the city itself. The Great Buddha and other attractions are on the hilly east bank across the water.

What to see in Leshan

Great Buddha ✺ It is not necessarily handsome, it does not sit in the right way for a Buddha and engineering considerations mean there are no symbolic hand gestures. None of that seems to hurt its fame, though. 71 m/ 233 ft high and 24 m/80 ft wide (the ears alone are 7 m/23 ft long and the toenails up to 1.6 m/5 ft), the figure was hewn from the rock between 713 and 803 during the heyday of the Tang dynasty, also the

golden age of Chinese Buddhism. The building of monumental Buddhas was, in some places at the time, a matter of prestige. The initiator of the project was a monk, who proposed that the Buddha would protect people from the occasional flooding of the Min Jiang. Obviously there were plenty willing to believe this and contribute money to it.

The Buddha statue is intended to be a Maitreya image. It is part of an ensemble which includes two more monumental **guarding statues** although these are badly weathered. They stand in separate niches in the rock and can only be seen from the river. In addition, some smaller niches were also carved out to the sides of the main statue to house further Buddha and bodhisattva figures, though some of them are of considerably later date.

The ensemble

The Great Buddha tour starts with a walk through the **Lingyun Temple** (usually entering from the rear where the car park is). From the southern side of the square before it, it is already possible to see the hair of the Buddha, which protrudes slightly over the top of the platform. Alongside the Buddha, a precipitous stone stairway leads down to his feet. From there a narrow tunnel leads to a path with carved steps so high and steep that you need to take care not to bang

Tours

Small people, big statue: Leshan

For structural reasons the hand rests on the knee …

your shins on the edges. At the top it comes out back at the starting point. Opening times: May–Sept. 7.30am–7.30pm daily, 8am–6pm daily the rest of the year.

Bijin Pavilion Instead of following the stream of tourists back to the Lingyun monastery, there is a much nicer alternative for those who have the time. Rather than following the stone steps back up again, turn off along the shady and verdant path to the right. It follows the slope southwards about half-way up offering views of the river. It soon comes to a large, two-storey building in the classical style, the Bijin Pavilion (Bijin Lou), where there is an inexpensive restaurant. After a meal to keep your strength up, you can siesta on the terrace and enjoy the **river view**. When a little mist is around, it is like being in a Chinese ink painting. A four-character inscription in the rock opposite the entrance says this is »**another world**« and one can only agree.

! **Baedeker** TIP

Boat trip
The excursion steamers which leave from both banks of the Min river (from the centre and from opposite the promenade), are totally touristified, it is true, but the trip is worthwhile, not least for the outstanding view of the great Buddha.

Mahao cliff tombs The next stop on the tour takes in the important Mahao cliff tombs, which were only discovered in 1940. They are some 1800 years old. There are eight tubular crypts carved into the foot of the cliff face level with the ground. Three of the caves belong together as do two of the others, so that there are **five graves** altogether. Reliefs and

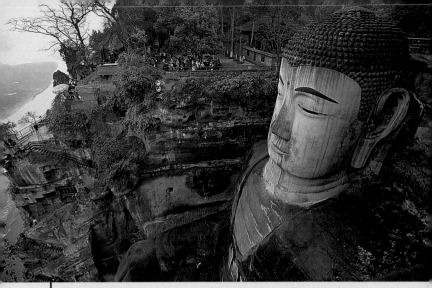

... but the posture seems a little stiff

paintings decorate the walls. The burial items which have been un-earthed are displayed in exhibition rooms at the sides. Above the lintel of the central crypt of grave no.1 (the second from right), a small relief image of a Buddha can be seen. This is one of the oldest Buddha images to be found in all of China.

A little past the cliff-tombs museum, a triple-arched bridge leads across to the hill, Wuyou Shan, where the Wuyou Temple occupies a superb position high over the Min River. In its main hall, a **gilded figure of Shakyamuni**, 3 m/10 ft high and carved from camphor wood, is flanked by the bodhisattvas, Samantabhadra and Manjushri. The main attraction is the Hall of the 500 Arhats. The multifarious figures were destroyed during the Cultural Revolution but have since been reconstructed. Opposite the monastery gate, a path leads up a stairway. Take the first fork to the left to get to a bus stop for the regular buses that run to the cruise-boat quay.

✱ **Wuyou Shan Island**

Zigong

100 km/62 mi west of Leshan is China's **city of salt** – probably the oldest still active salt manufacturing centre anywhere in the world: For more than 2000 years rock salt has been drilled out here from deep in the earth. In ancient China the state had a monopoly in the salt trade, which was then disseminated in the form of licences to private merchants, some of whom made huge fortunes from the salt trade. That is how Zigong gained the two attractions that draw modern-day tourists: the magnificent guild hall for the salt merchants of

▶ VISITING LESHAN

GETTING THERE

Cross-country buses run frequently to and from Chengdu and Emeishan City (journey time from 2 hours approx.). An airport is under construction.

ACCOMMODATION

▶ **Mid-range**

Jiazhou Hotel
Baita Jie 19

Tel. 08 33/213 98 88
Fax 08 33/215 60 06
The Jiazhou Hotel and its roughly 200 rooms are not that good but not as expensive as the ostentatious foyer makes it look at first glance. In spite of that it is the best hotel in town.

Shaanxi and a salt well which has been transformed into a museum where the ancient techniques are still largely maintained and demonstrated to visitors. In addition, outside the town there are some important **dinosaur excavations**. The museum dedicated to the topic is a third good reason to visit. It is worth stopping over in the town when travelling on from Leshan to Dazu or Chongqing, but it can also be taken in on a day trip by taxi from Leshan or ▶Emei Shan.

Xiqin Huiguan Guild Hall and Salt Museum

Temple, hotel and clubhouse: those were the three main functions of this grandiose complex, which unmistakably shows off the wealth of the Shaanxi salt merchants. It was built between 1736 and 1752. Luxuriantly **gilded wood carvings** illustrate the popular scholarly wisdom of ancient China. Nowadays the rooms are used for a museum of salt. Exhibits include original tools, illustrations, historic photographs, schematic drawings and cross-sections – all with English captions. 107 Jiefang Lu. Opening times: 8.30am–4.30pm daily.

! **Baedeker TIP**

The Arhat Oracle

What will the future bring? What is to become of me? People seeking the answer to questions like this should simply choose any of the statues in the Hall of the 500 Arhats and start from there to count all the others till they reach their own age. The Arhat where the counting stops should give an intimation of the future in the way that it looks. Apparently it works for the Chinese anyway.

Zigong was once a drilling and mining town. Salt was raised via deep wells reinforced with bamboo. The salt was dissolved in water and the brine was then winched to the surface. Over the course of history, the salt wells got deeper and deeper until they attained a depth of more than 1000 m/ 3300 ft in 1835, the first time such depths had been reached anywhere in the world. The **Shenhai Jing Salt Well Museum** here demonstrates the ancient techniques, although motor-driven winches replace the ox-hauled system of olden days. The premises also include a boiling-plant fired by natural gas, which is obtained as a by-product of the salt extraction. It has been widely used in Zigong for industry and for domestic fuel since the 16th century. The gas was piped through bamboo tubes to where it is needed. Even private ovens were fuelled by gas. 289 Da'an Jie (exiting the city towards the east).

It was in 1915 that an American palaeontologist first found dinosaur fossils to the northwest of Zigong. By now 160 separate places have revealed more than **twenty different confirmed species of dinosaur**. At one of these deposits, a sedimentary layer four metres thick dating from the Jurassic period, a veritable dinosaur graveyard was brought to light. The museum was built on top of it in the 1990s. 20 skeletons have been reconstructed but the view of the original site is even more impressive. Other things on view include a fossil tree trunk 23 m/75 ft long and some petrified ferns. Dashanpu (12 km/7 mi northeast of town). Opening times: 8.30am–5.30pm daily.

Dinosaur museum

Lingyun Si temple monastery: base for the »Big Buddha« tour

✶✶ Lijiang

Gf 32

Province: Yunnan　　　　　　　　**Population:** 30 000
Altitude: 2400 m/7875 ft

Lijiang goes to the heart – a town that has been almost completely given over to tourism since the 1990s, but which has not been corrupted and continues to enchant and delight all its guests. In addition, a centuries-old tradition of music is still maintained here.

As the chief town of its district, it lies 320 km/200 mi northwest of Kunming as the crow flies (550 km/340 mi by road) and looks up at the 5590 m/18 340 ft snow-capped peak of **Yulong Xueshan**. It is the capital of the Naxi (or Na-khi) people, who number some 300,000. Of the 30,000 living in the town itself, two thirds are Naxi with about 15,000 of them living in the old town, which was added to the list of UNESCO World Heritage Sites in 1999.

Town layout　Those entering Lijiang for the first time are greeted by a belt of faceless new buildings of the kind that uglify much of China's landscape. Beyond that, however, is a jewel, the old town of the Naxi people, covering just 1 sq km/250 acres – a thoroughly »un-Chinese« **labyrinth of narrow streets**. It is a challenge to any visitors with a poor sense of direction, but possesses a startling magic, mainly due to the waters, for between the masses of grey-roofed houses, clear mountain streams gurgle through carefully lined channels. Splitting in the north into several rivulets, some wide, some narrow, they mainly follow the stone-paved streets, kept free of vehicles and of dirt, and occasionally disappear behind the houses.

A sea of roofs is all that can be seen of Lijiang

The fronts of these houses are a sight in themselves. The artistically **Houses** carved door panels are at their best early in the morning before the shops open. Most of the buildings are **two-storey timber-framed houses** with brick walls and natural stone foundations. Many have inner courtyards planted with flowers, and some even have several encircling galleries, making it possible to get inside with dry feet even when it has been raining heavily.

Two aspects have dominated Lijiang' history, trade and earthquakes. Its location on the **tea and horse route** to Tibet, on which those two highly prized wares were traded, helped Lijiang become large and prosperous; that and the local crafts, in particular the brass

> **? DID YOU KNOW …?**
>
> ■ … that the priests of the Naxi's shamanistic religion are called Dto-mba in the Naxi tongue? They perpetuated a unique literary culture, which has led to the Naxi culture being dubbed in general the Dto-mba, or more simply the Tomba or Dongba culture. The script they use is genuinely pictogrammatic and is used practically exclusively for religious purposes (liturgy for songs and dances). It also represents the oldest form of choreographic notation known anywhere in the world.

work. Then, though, there are the earthquakes. The whole area is seismically highly active. In the 20th century alone there were five large earthquakes. The most recent on 3 Februar 1996 had particular consequences, although they were positive ones, since it brought not only national but also international attention to the town. In the reconstruction, the fabric of the old town was upgraded to modern standards, which included the building of a sewerage system, fire-protection measures and the laying of electricity and telephone cables, all without harming the historic appearance.

✶ ✶ Old town

It is not so much the places in the old town that await discovery but the whole old town itself. Simply wander around, look at the shops with their extensive assortment of craft products, rest in a pleasant restaurant, stand on a bridge and watch the glittering of the streams or admire the women in their ethnic costumes, which are still worn, in particular by the older ladies. It is nice to wake up with the sun and see how the town awakens. Even before the shops and eateries open, it is possible to stand shoulder to shoulder with the natives on the central square and breakfast from cookshops or mobile stands.

»Rectangle Street« is the name given to the central square. It was **Sifang Jie** once a marketplace for food and brassware. Six narrow streets lead off from there. Beyond the stream on the west side a path leads to a tower-like building called **Kegong Fang**, erected partly in honour of a citizen who passed the exam to become an official during the imperial era and partly for use as a fire station.

► VISITING LIJIANG

INFORMATION

There are several travel operators, particularly in the northern part of the old town, which offer trips to various destinations. One other good address to note is the youth hostel (►Accommodation).

GETTING THERE

Lijiang has no railway station. There is an airport south of the town with airport buses running there and back. Cross-county buses from Dali come in at the more southerly of the two bus stations. From the northern station coaches go to Shangri La.

THINGS TO DO

Dayan Naxi Ancient Music

No one interested in music should miss this. Thanks to the former remoteness of the town, Chinese music traditions have persisted here which have long since disappeared from the core parts of the country. Once vilified under Mao, this legacy is now experiencing a tourist-inspired renaissance. Some of the musicians are very old. Concerts are given in various halls with the most authentic taking place in the Naxi Concert Hall under the direction of Xuan Ke, who has not only made the revivification of ancient music his life's work, but is happy to talk about it in two languages (Chinese and English). Tickets should be bought on the morning of the show at the latest. Some examples of the music can be heard at www.xuanke.com. Dong Dajie, Naxi Concert Hall, 8pm daily, admission from 100 yuan.

Folk dancing

Nothing is as touching in Lijiang as the ring dances which take place in the evening and where natives and guests join together on the main square, Sifang Jie. Dancing also takes place near the stone gate, where a flautist plays the tune.

SHOPPING

Large parts of the old town have been transformed nowadays into one big arts and crafts bazaar, but with a typically local range of products. The intricate embroidery of the Naxi women is particularly lovely. Brass and silverware are manufactured in Lijiang too. Even those who do not want to spend much money can buy a T-shirt hand painted with Tomba writing.

WHERE TO EAT

A delight to all palates: everywhere in the old town it is possible to eat cheaply, well and in atmospheric surroundings. Most of the restaurants line up along the canal running from the water mills along the edge of Lion Hill to the main square. One very nice little café with fine cuisine and a view of the water is the Left Bank Cafe downstream from the big stone bridge (Xinyi Jie, 8 Baisuifang, enter over the footbridge). The Well Bistro serves Western food and is particularly popular in the evenings (Xinyi Jie, Mishi Xiang, by the fountain).

ACCOMMODATION

Important: make sure to stay in the atmospheric old town, even though the rooms are tiny. An »old-town tax« of 80 yuan per person is added to the room price.

► Luxury

Zen Garden Hotel

W-yi Jie, 36 Xingren Xiaduan

Tel. 08 88/518 97 99
Fax 08 88/518 95 66
Perrsonally managed elegant old-town accommodation with 16 rooms.

► Mid-range
Sanhe Hotel
Xinyi Jie, 4 Jishan Xiang
Tel. 08 88/51 20 891
Fax 08 88/51 20 892
Some of the 47 rooms face on to an idyllic inner courtyard with a fountain. In the old town.

► Budget
Lijiang Old Town International Youth Hostel
Xinyi Jie, 44 Mishi Xiang
Tel. 08 88/510 54 03, Fax 518 01 24
Good and popular spot for backpackers, a member of the International Youth Hostels Association

Mosuo Yiyuan Hotel
Nanmen Jie, 8 Yigu Xiang
Tel. 08 88/515 65 88
Very pleasant private guest house, with 16 rooms and typical inner courtyard on the edge of the old town.

The street beyond the gate leads up to Lion Hill (Shizi Shan), which **Lion Hill** borders the old town in the west. Up on the hill, though not at the top, there is an **observation platform** with a splendid panoramic view of the old town. On the summit itself stands the »Tower of the Aeons« (Wangu Lou). Although it is too chunky in appearance and too brightly coloured, the climb to the top is rewarded with an all-round view of the whole town as far as the distant mountains.

Take the left-hand street of the two that enter the main square at an acute angle on its eastern edge to get to the double-arched **»Great Stone Bridge«**, the biggest in the town. The other street, the one on the right, leads to a gate which looks like a barbican, although Lijiang never had walls. On the other side of the gate is the biggest attraction inside the old town: Mu Fu, the palace of the chieftains.

> **!** *Baedeker* TIP
>
> **Finding your way through the labyrinth**
> If you get lost, look at the direction of the streams. Going against the flow means you will eventually reach the northern entrance to the old town with the great waterwheels, from which the bigger streets and the streams themselves fan out towards the south. The rightmost stream (in the west) leads to the central square.

Mu Fu chieftains' palace

Everything to be seen here is new, from the ostentatious stone honour gate with its guard of lions (who could not prevent the building's destruction in the Cultural Revolution) to the final hall in the garden on Lion Hill. The complex is 370 m/400 yds long and is built entirely in the Chinese style. The original was ravaged at the end of the Qing period; earthquakes and the Cultural Revolution did the rest. The reconstruction was initiated in 1996.

Historical background

The Chinese emperors ruled over minority peoples in their empire by appointing a **chieftain**, furnished with appropriate privileges, to govern his fellow people and subjects and keep them under control. Among the Naxi the dynasty of chieftains (or kings) were granted the Chinese surname of Mu by the emperors. They resided here for 22 generations from the Yuan era till the Qing period.

Government complex

The largest part of the building, as seen today, was not set aside for dwelling but for the task of government and display. At the end of the large outer courtyard, with its drum and bell towers, there is a »council assembly hall«. Behind that is a multistorey library and only then come the family's hall, which contains an altar for the worship of ancestors along with plaques bearing the names of former souls and paintings of the various chieftains. Its rather modest residential courts are to the north at the side of the large halls. The halls at the side of the main courtyard house a collection of folklore exhibits.

Crossing a bridged walkway over one of the inner city streets brings you to the two-storey **Guangbi Lou**, where there is a model of Lijiang on display. After that comes the imposing building called **Yuyin Lou** (»House of the Sound of Jade«), where the chieftain would receive letters from the emperor. Nowadays it contains facsimiles of Buddhist murals from around the region.

! **Baedeker TIP**

Dream homes

The public toilets in Lijiang's old town deserve honourable mention. There are around twenty of them and on the outside they are built in the traditional dwelling style, but inside they are modern and clean. On Xinyuan Xiang, the street which turns off upstream between the chieftains' palace and the stone gate, our favourite lavatory is adorned with the title »The Home of Dreams«.

Garden

The palace garden extends up the slopes of Lion Hill and contains the hall known as **Sanqing Dian** (the »Three Pure Ones«), from the terrace of which there is a splendid view of the palace complex and the town.

Heilong Tan Pool

There is a much photographed ensemble by the »Pool of the Black Dragon« with a white five-arched bridge and the three-storey **Five Phoenix Pavilion**. On a good day it is possible to see the white peak of Snow Mountain beyond it. The pool and its parkland are about 1 km/1100 yd north of the old town. Further north from the pool a museum provides information on the Tomba culture. Opening times: 8.30am–5.30pm daily.

The old quarter of Lijiang →

Places to go outside of town

All around Lijiang, especially to the north and west, there are plenty of places to go on trips during a two-week stay. Bookings for many of them can be made in the hotels and travel agents of Lijiang itself – which is particularly advisable for the more distant spots.

Baisha

Two destinations in the north suggest themselves for half-day bicycle trips. The idyllic market village of Shuhe 6 km/4 mi to the north-west is a miniature version of Lijiang. Restful accommodation in private guesthouses can be found here. Baisha, a Naxi village 4 km/2 mi further north is known for its 400–600-year-old murals. They can be seen in the Liuli Dian temple and in the »Dabaoji Palace« (Dabaoji Gong) – a tall, double-eaved hall dating from 1582.

✳
Tiger Leaping Gorge (Hutiao Xia)

A three-day tour can be made to the Tiger Leaping Gorge (Hutiao Xia) on the Yangtze tributary the Jinsha Jiang, 90 km/56 mi to the north. It is **one of the deepest canyons on earth** and runs for a length of 16 km/10 mi. Between the villages of Qiaotou and Daju a hiking path and, more recently, a road run through the gorge. The path is above the road, though, and the latter usually remains out of sight. Some simple guesthouses can provide accommodation along the way. For the hike alone, at least a day and a half will be needed. Anyone preferring to rest sometimes to enjoy the scenery should plan for two whole days. The name of the gorge refers to its narrowness. It is said that a tiger once managed to cross the raging rapids beneath and reach the other side in one leap. A plan to build a dam here has been shelved, at least temporarily.

Yulong Xueshan

Looming to the north of Lijiang, **Snow Mountain** (Yulong Xueshan) was only climbed for the first time in 1963. Nowadays there is a cable-car, although it does not go all the way to the summit (5590 m/18,570 ft), of course. It stops at some mountain pastures at altitudes of about 3000 m/10,000 ft and 4500 m/1500 ft. No. 7 bus from Lijiang, Fuhui Lu, corner of Xin Dajie (on the road to Heilong Tan).

✳ Shangri La Zonghdian

The northwestern district of the province is mainly settled by Tibetans. The local capital Zonghdian at an altitude of 3200 m/10,500 ft (200 km /125 mi from Lijiang) now officially bears the name Shangri La and can be reached by a direct flight from Kunming. 4 km/2 mi north of the town is the **Ganden Sumtseling**, the most important Tibetan monastery in the province. Primarily, though, people come here for the landscape and its natural beauty. **Lake Napa** nestles amid luxuriant green meadows, while the **Pudacuo National Park** boasts of two high mountain lakes (Pita Hai 40 km/24 mi to the east, and Shudu Hu 49 km/30 mi to the north-east), coniferous forests and azaleas.

THE BUS TO SHANGRI-LA

Long-distance buses to Shangri-La? There they stand, on the bus station in Lijiang. Can this be possible? After all, Shangri-La is a literary invention, almost a Utopia. The British author James Hilton invented it in his novel *Lost Horizon*, published in 1933. In the book, Shangri-La is the name of a Tibetan monastery whose occupants live many times as long as most mortals.

The appearance of the name Shangri-La on the map at the edge of the Tibetan highlands is part of an amazing story that began in Vienna in 1884 with the birth of a son to a court servant. The boy grew up to be

Joseph Francis Rock's reports were the stimulus for the novel

his own man: ambitious, intelligent and eccentric. His name was **Joseph Franz Rock**, or Joseph Francis Rock after he emigrated to the USA. He was an adventurer, but also a man who worked thoroughly and systematically. When he came to northern Yunnan in 1922, he resolved to stay. He collected plants and Naxi manuscripts, took photographs, wrote for *National Geographic*, living comfortably enough

from the proceeds, and undertook journeys of exploration with a large caravan, including a folding bathtub. The older inhabitants of Lijiang still remember him, as he stayed until 1949 and was an unmistakable figure known in the whole area. His reports were the stimulus for James Hilton's novel.

The true Shangri-La

In 1995 an employee of the tourist association of Yunnan discovered some astonishing similarities between the Shangri-La of the novel and the Diqing area in north-western Yunnan. In 1997 the province of Yunnan adopted the theory that this was the place described by Hilton, and it was officially renamed in 2001. Since then, a literary Utopia has been accessible by overland bus.

Luoyang

Hb 28

Province: Henan
Altitude: 170 m/560 ft

Population: 1.5 million

A city of 1.5 million inhabitants is, by Chinese standards, a small town but this one has a great past. It was actually the Chinese capital on several occasions, first in the 2nd century BC and most recently in the 10th century. Apart from the Buddhist grottoes of Longmen to the south of the city, the only remnants of the era when Luoyang vied with Chang'an in size and glamour are underground, mainly graves and burial items. In addition, though, Luoyang is also the starting point for trips to the Sacred Middle Mountain, Song Shan with its key sites in the cultural history of the nation.

Luoyang lies amid the oldest man-made landscapes in China, not far from the Yellow River but far enough to be safe from flooding. Whenever kings and emperors, who were resident in or around Xi'an, could not remain there because of external enemies or internal difficulties, they would move eastwards to Luoyang. This was the case under the Zhou monarchs (Eastern Zhou dynasty, 770–49 BC), the Han emperors (Eastern Han dynasty, AD 25–220) and during the Tang era, when Luoyang was an auxiliary capital and built up into her new powerbase by **Empress Wu**. With a million inhabitants even then, the city was one of the biggest on earth and was a centre of international trade and scholarly pursuits. The foundations for this had been laid by the Toba emperors (Northern Wei dynasty),

 ## VISITING LUOYANG

GETTING THERE

Luoyang is on the main line from Zhengzhou to Xi'an and is linked by direct services to Peking and Shanghai among others. The airport to the north of the town only has a few regular flights.

ACCOMMODATION

▶ **Mid-range**
① *Cygnus International Hotel*
15 Zhongzhou Zhonglu, corner of Jiefang Lu
Tel. 03 79/63 89 66 66

Fax 03 79/63 89 66 77
www.ly-cygnus.com
New hotel in the commercial centre, not too large at 153 rooms.

▶ **Budget**
② *Mingyuan Hotel / International Youth Hostel Mingyuan*
Jiefang Lu 20
Tel. 03 79/63 19 13 77, fax 63 19 46 68
Two-star hotel with 200 inexpensive rooms, just 500 m/550 yd from the station. The 9th storey is set up as a youth hostel.

who moved their capital here from Datong in 494. From the 10th century, Luoyang sank into obscurity and was indeed no more than a small town until the 1950s.

The urban district stretches along the north bank of the River Luo (Luo He) for about 15 km/9 mi from west to east. It is rather narrower in a north-south direction. The station is situated in the north and the old town is in the east. The few places to visit in the city itself are scattered around the place and some distance apart.

Getting around

What to see in Luoyang

Luoyang's old town is a nice place to walk and shop. About 1.5 km/1 mi square, it still offers a small chance to breathe some old-time atmosphere. One nice place to see is the **Luze guild house** at the southeast corner, a magnificent complex, typically featuring a theatre stage above the entrance. The original furnishings have been lost but now a folklore museum has moved in with its whole collection (133 Jiudu Donglu). It is also possible to browse in the large Luze antique market nearby.

Old town

Luoyang Museum houses an important archaeological collection. Among the items on display are examples of Neolithic pottery, ritual bronzes, grave figure ensembles of the Toba era (5th–6th centuries), ceramic sculptures of the Tang and Song eras and a model of the imperial palace and palace close as it was in about AD 700. 298 Zhongzhou Zhonglu wonderful works in jade from the 1st and 2nd millennium BC, as well as discoveries from later eras ranging up to porcelain from the Song period. 298 Zhongzhou Zhonglu. Opening times: 8.30am–5pm daily. In 2009, the museum is due to move to spectacular new premises to the south of the Luo river, and thus at last find a home that will do justice to the historic importance of the city and its surroundings.

✱
Luoyang Museum

? DID YOU KNOW …?

■ … that even Bai Juyi (772–846), the great Tang poet, acclaimed the peonies of Luoyang? They are what gave rise to Luoyang's attractive by-name, »city of peonies«. More than 150 species can be admired here in spring.

An excellent idea: 22 tomb chambers of art-historical importance all gathered together in one spot and linked by an underground passage to make them easy to view. The tombs and their mythological murals document a period from the 1st century BC until the 12th century AD. Also on the premises is the tomb of the Toba emperor Xuanwu dating from 516. The tomb is painted with a representation of the firmament. Jichang Lu (northern edge of town, 6 km/4 mi from the station). Opening times: 9am–5pm daily.

Tomb museum (Gumu Bowuguan)

Luoyang Map

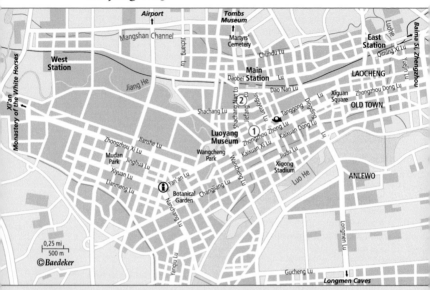

Where to stay
① Cygnus International Hotel ② Mingyuan Hotel, International Youth Hostel

Monastery of the White Horses

Founded in the year 68 AD, this is considered the oldest Buddhist monastery in China. The name »Monastery of the White Horses« refers to the **legend of its foundation**, according to which the emperor saw Buddha in a dream and shortly afterwards, two men appeared at court riding white horses, bringing with them the first copies of the sutras from a distant land, whereupon the emperor commissioned a monastery. The present buildings – 10 km/6 mi west of town – date from the Ming era.

Entrance The two white horses stand before the gate in the form of stone ponies. As usual the Hall of the Heavenly Kings functions as the inner gatehouse. The housing of the shrine is unusually splendid.

Dafo Dian Hall The »Hall of the Great Buddha« is additional to the usual scheme. Five figures are on view: The bodhisattvas Manjushri (left) and Samantabhadra (right) join Shakyamuni in the middle to make up the three saints of the Huayan school; Shakyamuni is flanked by his two most loyal disciples, Ananda and Kashyapa. On the reverse **Guanyin, the goddess of mercy** can be seen. The parrot with prayer necklace symbolizes the idea that even animals can achieve Buddha status.

In the main hall, the »Three Splendid Buddhas« are to be seen in a splendid shrine resembling a two-storey hall. . The most important art treasure of the monastery, however, is almost invisible: the 18 luohan in their glass cases, figures from the Mongol period. The hall is not normally accessible.

Main hall

Jieyin Dian Hall has the »Three Saints of the West« on view: the salvation Buddha, Amitabha, in the middle with his two assistant bodhisattvas: Mahastamaprapta on the left and Guanyin on the right.

Jieyin Dian Hall

West of the axis there are two burial mounds, which allegedly contain the mortal remains of the two Buddhist ambassadors mentioned in the founding legend. A little tucked away to the east is the elegant 24 m/80 ft Qiyun Pagoda, a brick building dating from 1175. Monastery opening times: 7am–7pm, daily Nov–March reduced hours depending on the hours of daylight.

Burial mound, Qiyun Pagoda

🕐

✹ Longmen caves (Longmen Shiku)

At the »Dragon Gate« (Long Men), a steep gorge of the Yi River measuring 1 km/1100 yds in length, the late 5th century saw construction begin on what would become the third-biggest cave temple complex in China, after those at Dunhuang and Datong. The first sponsors of the building were the same as those who built the Datong caves: the devout emperors of the **Northern Wie dynasty**. However, what is probably the most important monument for the blooming of Chinese Buddhism in the Tang period, and several emperors' ambitions of glory, is here, 12 km/7 mi south of Luoyang (81 bus from the station). Monks, nuns, lay societies and officials all contributed as benefactors, either from a desire for enlightenment, as some of the inscriptions profess, or from the hope of health or wealth or simply to underline their own revered position, either thanking Buddha or hoping to gain good karma for a later reincarnation.

🕐

Opening hours: 6am–8pm daily in summer, in winter 7.30am–5pm, April–Oct. evening opening with illumination, 7–10pm

Most of the cave temples, and the most important ones, are on the west bank of the river, i.e. they are hewn into an east-facing cliff so that it is best to see them in the morning sunlight. Some caves are carved out of the opposite cliff, though. Nearly all of them follow a simple iconographic concept, although it is occasionally modified. Opposite the entrance of the rectangular layout is a **larger-than-life Buddha**, the ideal of the teaching. To the right and left stand two assistant bodhisattvas, who face the people and are depicted in a more human way, i.e. smaller. Ananda and Kashyapa, Buddha's disciples, usually stand between these three figures to make up a group of five. The entrance is normally watched over by two grim-faced guards. People must pass the guards and their fiercely testing expressions to get to the sacred interior. One recurring motif is the lotus blossom.

The complex and its iconographic scheme

The caves of Longmen are a Unesco World Heritage Site

Buddhas and bodhisattvas often sit or stand on such blooms and they often decorate the roofs of the grottoes.

Condition　The literature disseminates some often quite fantastic numbers to illustrate the size of the whole ensemble of caves. It is better, though, to lower expectations a notch or two. The caves have unfortunately been extensively **robbed by art thieves**; as can be seen in the number of Chinese Buddhas in the world's museums and auction houses, not a few of which come from here. Most of the niches and grottoes are therefore empty, and when they are not, the heads are often missing. The large caves have survived, though, although it is not permitted to enter them. Since it is therefore only possible to see the caves through the entrance, some of the direct experience of the religious message, to which the expressions of the generously friendly, smiling bodhisattvas make a big contribution, is lost.

Qianxi Si　Qianxi Si is the first large cave of the west bank. It was built in the years between 627 and 649 and displays the »Three Saints of the West«: Buddha Amitabha with his assistant bodhisattvas, Mahasthamaprapta and Avalokiteshvara, along with Ananda and Kashyapa.

Binyang Caves　Shortly afterwards comes a group of three grottoes, the northern, middle and southern Binyang caves. The middle one is the most beautiful on the entire »Dragon Gate« site. It was built from 505 to 523 as a **project of the Wei emperor**. Here the eleven figures – the Buddhas of the three ages, six bodhisattvas and the two disciples – smile down with such friendliness that it warms the heart. The story has been handed down about how much work was required to make this grotto. It is said to have involved 802,366 man-days. To see the relief that shows the Wei emperor and his court as benefactors of the cave would mean taking a trip to the Metropolitan Museum in New York.

350 m/400 yd further upstream, a short stairway leads up to **»Ten Thousand Buddha Cave«**, dating from 680. Around 15,000 miniature relief figures cover the side walls. The group of five statues is the same as in the Qianxi Si cave but the central Amitabha, in particular, has a rather fuller, even plumper design, which accords with the aesthetic ideal of the Tang period.

Wanfo Dong

The next stairway leads to **»Lotus Blossom Cave«**, named after the particularly splendid decoration of the ceiling, featuring a lotus blossom extending out as a relief with its fruit capsule in the middle. The faces of the figures may be destroyed but otherwise their fine workmanship is clear to see. Pay heed to the flaming mandorla around the central Buddha figure and to the apsaras, who spin around the lotus blossom in a heavenly dance. This cave is one of the earliest on the site, having come into existence between 516 and 528.

Lianhua Dong

The solitary climax is now approaching. At the upper end of a wide, steep stairway there is a cave covering an area of 40 x 35 m/44 x 38 yd, which is 15–20 times bigger than any of the others on the site. Since a cave roof of such size would have collapsed, the cave was left open at the top and covered with a wooden roof, although that has long since disappeared so that the figures now stand in the open air. The central figure of the usual five is a Locana Buddha 17 m/56 ft in height. Guards stand right at the front on the left and right, each with one of the Heavenly Kings stamping on a demon behind them. In spite of the monumental size of everything, the sculpture is first rate. Note, for example, the body ornamentation of the bodhisattvas. The sponsors of the grotto, which took almost 20 years to build from 675, were the **Tang emperor Gaozong** and his ambitious chief wife Wu Zetian. It is said that the Locana Buddha sports her face. The cave is not only a stupendous testament to the golden age of Chinese Buddhism, but also as a documentation of the religious gloss over the manoeuvring for power by the empress-to-be. The name of the cave is inspired by Confucianism, »Buddha temple for the worship of ancestors«, reflecting the idea that the honour of having built the temple will additionally be conferred as positive karma for the builders' forebears too.

Fengxian Si

 Baedeker TIP

View from the East Bank

It is not so much the remains of the the cave temple which are a reason to go across to the east bank of the Yi river, as the view across them to the other side. In particular the view of the southern end with the monumental figures of Fengxian Si is worthwhile.

The following cave is much closer to the spirit of Buddhism. On both sides of the entrance to the **»Medicinal Recipe Cave«** (7th century) inscriptions list more than a hundred remedies for the healing of all kinds of illnesses – a testament to Buddhist philanthropy.

Yaofang Dong

Guyang Dong The next and final cave to be visited is the oldest of them. With its many small niches, where Maitreya Buddhas sit cross legged, the Guyang Dong cave is still strongly reminiscent of the style of the later cave temples at the Yungang Caves (►Datong).

✳ Song Shan: Shaolin monastery

The 70 km/44 mi east to the most central of the five holy mountains can be covered on a day trip from Luoyang. The mountain has a whole range of things worth seeing. The 1512 m/4961 ft summit of Song Shan is not among them but the whole mountain area is well suited for walking and it is well worth taking a hike (it is also possible to stay the night at the local administrative capital of Dengfeng). In addition, a cable-car leads up from the Shaolin monastery. The most comfortable way to experience Song Shan is to book an organized day trip from a hotel in Luoyang. Buses also run from Luoyang to Dengfeng.

Shaolin monastery (Shaolin Si) Shaolin kung fu, the art of unarmed combat (and the control of the body required for it), has gained a legendary reputation for itself and the monastery that is its home. The fact that no other Buddhist monastery in China is anywhere near so famous as this one also has another reason, though. In the early 6th century the Indian monk Bodhidharma is said to have developed **Zen Buddhism** here by sitting and meditating motionless in front of a wall for a period of nine years. Historians are unable to confirm that he was in fact the founder of the school, but this has done nothing to dampen the popularity of the legends that abound concerning him.

Nice youngsters …

What is certain is that the monastery was founded in the year 495, and that the emperor of the Northern Wei dynasty was the benefactor. There is also confirmation that there was such a person as Bodhidharma, who arrived here in 527. That he laid the spiritual foundation for the emphasis on practice by rejecting written wisdom in favour of his own direct experience, which itself led indirectly to the development of the martial art that emerged from here, is at least plausible. Just a hundred years later, Shaolin boxers are said to have lent powerful support to a subsequent emperor, Li Shimin, the second of the Tang dynasty, in his struggle for dominance. The reputation of the monastery, though, led to its becoming a centre for a national, and soon afterwards an international, kung fu movement from the 1980s. The bustle that goes on here is correspondingly frenzied. Apart from the renowned **monastic martial arts school**, there the palatial buildings of another two dozen kung-fu schools in the area with more than 10,000 students in all.

History and present

Until well into the 1980s the monastery was largely ruined. Among other things, the missing halls have been reconstructed and equipped with new images and places of worship. The bronze statue of Bodhidharma in the main hall – on the right, in front of the right-hand Buddha – was a gift from Japan. Behind the sutra hall is »Standing-in-the-Snow Pavilion«, commemorating a youth who did not wish to rouse the sage with whom he wished to study, and who had nodded off, but waited outside in spite of the snow flurries. In the **»Thousand Buddha Hall«** at the end of the axis a Ming mural shows the »five hundred luohan honouring Buddha Vairocana«. Some hollows in the floor are said to have been due to the practising of kung-fu students.

The monastery

… who can defend themselves

In a side hall on the right, another mural shows 13 monastic exercises being performed. This is the aforementioned story of the battle in support of Li Shimin.

»Pagoda forest« 500 m/550 yd west of the monastery is its cemetery, featuring a »pagoda forest« with 220 burial pagodas all of different designs, the oldest of which dates back to the Tang period. It is the biggest and most famous complex of its kind in China. Monastery opening times: 7am–6.30pm daily.

! **Baedeker TIP**

Kung fu in action

The kung-fu schools offer interesting demonstrations with fascinating moves. A half-hour tour is included in the admission price to the monastery. The theatre is to the right of the path from the car-park to the monastery. The demonstrations staged by other schools are often even better, but mostly only for pre-booked groups.

The quiet Songyang Academy is situated to the north of the local capital Dengfeng. It is not the buildings that have made it famous but its **two thuja trees**. Even 2100 years ago they are said to have impressed the Han emperor Wu so much that he conferred titles of honour upon them. The one he called »Junior General« is now a bizarre sylvan veteran with a girth of 15 m/50 ft. The »Senior General« is now no more than a shadow of his former self.

Songyuesi Ta Pagoda China's oldest pagoda is 5 km/3 mi north of the academy. The 12-sided brick building dates from the year 520 and is 40 m/130 ft high.

✱ Song Shan: the Middle Mountain temple of Zhongyue Miao

Here, 4 km/2.5 east of Dengfeng, the Sacred Middle Mountain was personified as the Emperor of the Middle Mountain and offerings were made to it as part of the cult of the state, i.e. for the benefit of the emperor. The size of the whole temple complex reflects this. It is by far the largest in the province. The courtyard has eleven age-old thujas and extends along an axis which measures 650 m/700 yd if the whole walled area is included, or double this if the drive leading from the 2000-year-old gate pillars in the south is added. The first temple for the local mountain cult was established as early as 2200 years ago. The site gained its present appearance under the last imperial dynasty. Daoist monks are employed by the state to keep the complex in order.

Iron men To the right (east) of the axis there are four statues standing 3 m/10 ft high. The originals of these iron men dated from the year 1064. With splayed legs and ready to fight, they guard the treasury around which they stand.

The **Throne Hall of the Mountain Emperor** is a building of truly imperial dimensions. It is nine bays wide with a double-eaved roof covered with imperial yellow tiles, as appropriate for an institute of the cult of the state. The figure of the Mountain Emperor dates from after the Cultural Revolution, as is his extensive entourage lined up along the neighbouring galleries.

Main hall

An emperor must have a wife! Even an imaginary mountain emperor needs to be married. After all he cannot spend all his time sitting in the throne room. Therefore a sleeping chamber is provided behind it. There the deified couple can be seen, with their beds taking the form of alcoves to the left and right. Opening times: 7.30am–6.30pm daily.

Sleeping hall

⊙

Guo Shoujing (1231–1316), possibly the most important Chinese scientist and engineer of the pre-industrial age, designed this brick building in 1276 in order to measure the length of the solar year and put the **calendar** on to a more solid basis. He was astoundingly successful with his calculations, with only 26 seconds difference from the actual figure measured using modern instruments. 10 km/6 mi south of Dengfeng near Gaocheng. Opening times: 8am–6.30pm daily.

Guanxing Tai Observatory

⊙

✶ Macau

Hb 34/35

Province: Special administrative zone   **Population:** 480,000
Altitude: 0–174 m/0–571 ft

What a curious history, from tiny Portuguese colony to the Las Vegas of China! Although the gaming aspect has gained the upper hand now (Macau now has the biggest gambling income in the world), the remains of its Christian colonial roots were declared a UNESCO World Heritage Site in 2005. Of this curious mixture of dignified age and ultra modernity, poverty and ostentatious wealth, small town and metropolis, European and Chinese-American influence, Macau has plenty more to offer.

Macau is made up of a peninsula with the actual city (9 sq km/3.5 sq mi), which can be explored in about two hours, along with the islands of Taipa and Coloane, which have gradually grown in the meantime thanks to land reclamation. Macau's non-Chinese population now makes up only 5% of the total. The people are called Macanese; although the word strictly only applies to the long-established inhabitants of Portuguese or Portuguese-Chinese descent. The Macanese language, a Portuguese creole with Malay, Sinhalese and Cantonese influences, is almost extinct.

⏵ VISITING MACAU

INFORMATION

Macau Government Tourist Office
Largo do Senado 9
(Branches at the ferry port and the airport)
Tourist Hotline: Tel. 28 333 000
The offices have some very good informational material. The »Walking Tours« leaflet is especially to be recommended.

GETTING THERE

The international airport has flights from China, Taiwan and southeast Asia. The usual way to get to Macau, though, is to take the high-speed ferries that ply every quarter of an hour from Hong Kong's Shun Tak Center (journey time 1 hour). A valid passport is needed for entry.

SHOPPING

Prices are somewhat lower than in Hong Kong. In particular, antiques are cheaper here. They can be bought on Rua de São Paulo, the road that leads from the south towards the ruins. They are even cheaper on the street that runs parallel to it in the west.

CASINOS

Macau currently has 26 casinos. Admission is free and the dress code is casual. The large casinos are open 24 hours a day. Apart from internationally known games like roulette, there are also some peculiarly Chinese betting games. The whole casino operation is totally geared towards Chinese visitors. The most spectacular

In the casinos of Macau there is much to be won – and much to be lost

casino is the Venetian, entirely based on its Las Vegas exemplar. Also worth seeing is the Pharao's Palace casino in the Hotel Landmark, 535 Avenida da Amizade.

BARS & PUBS

Popular bars and pubs huddle together in the »Docks« pub quarter on Avenida Dr. Sun Yatsen near Avenida Sir Anders Ljungstedt. One elegant and popular hotel bar is the Nova Guia in the Mandarin Oriental.

WHERE TO EAT

► Expensive (from 200 patacas)

① *Clube Militar*
795 Avenida da Praia Grande
Tel. +853/28 71 40 00
In this lovely old building one can sample high-quality Portuguese cuisine amid an artistic ambience: a very civilized experience.

► Moderate (120 to 200 patacas)

② *A Petisqueira*
Rua S. João 14
Taipa village
Tel. +853/82 53 54
Food like back in Portugal and a family atmosphere. Lots of fine hors d'oeuvres, fish and seafood.

③ *Fernando's*
On the Hac-Sa beach
Coloane
Tel. +853/28 88 22 64
Luxuriant seafood recipes in a relaxed atmosphere

④ *Platāo*
3 Travessa de São Domingos
Tel. +853/28 33 18 18
Portuguese-Macanese food. In warm weather it is possible to eat outside in thw quiet inner courtyard.

► Inexpensive (up to 120 patacas)

⑤ *Nga Tim Cafe*
8 Rua Caetano (by the church)
Coloane village
Tel. +853/22 88 20 86
The popular restaurant with an outdoor terrace serves Portuguese, Macanese and Chinese dishes.

ACCOMMODATION

For all those travelling from Hong Kong to Macau, good prices are available from the agencies in Hong Kong's Shun Tak Centre (at the ferry port). Be careful, because at the weekends there are price increases rather than discounts.

► Luxury (from 1600 patacas)

① *Mandarin Oriental*
Avenida da Amizade
Tel. +853/28 56 78 88
Fax +853/28 59 45 89
www.mandarinoriental.com/macau
Conveniently located hotel with three restaurants and generously sized pool facilities.

► Mid-range (700 to 1600 patacas)

② *Beverly Plaza*
70–106 Avenida do Dr. R. Rodrigues
Tel. +853/28 78 22 88
Fax +853/28 78 07 04
www.beverlyplaza.com
306 rooms. Conveniently located on the edge of the old town. The restaurant on the 5th floor serves both sea-food and Cantonese cuisine.

► Budget (up to 700 patacas)

③ *East Asia*
Rua da Madeira 1
Tel. +853/28 92 24 33
Fax +853/28 92 24 30
Old hotel centrally located in the old town, 98 rooms

Macau Map

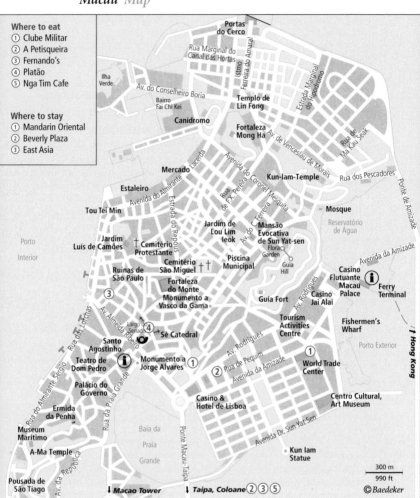

Where to eat
① Clube Militar
② A Petisqueira
③ Fernando's
④ Platão
⑤ Nga Tim Cafe

Where to stay
① Mandarin Oriental
② Beverly Plaza
③ East Asia

Portas do Cerco
Rua Marginal do Canal das Hortas
Istmo Ferreira do Amaral
Estrada Marginal do Hipódromo
Rua de Ma Kau Seak
Ilha Verde
Av. do Conselheiro Boria
Bairro Fai Chi Kei
Templo de Lin Fong
Canidromo
Fortaleza Mong Ha
Av. de Venceslau de Morais
Rua dos Pescadores
Ponte de Amizade
Mercado
Avenida do Coronel Mesquita
Kun-lam-Temple
Estaleiro
Avenida do Almirante
Estrada do Repouso
Rua de F.X. Pereira
Av. do Ferreira
Tou Tei Min
Mosque
Reservatório de Água
Jardim de Lou Lim Ieok
Mansão Evocativa de Sun Yat-sen
Flora Garden
Avenida da Amizade
Jardim Luís de Camões
Cemitério Protestante
Cemitério São Miguel
Piscina Municipal
Guia Hill
Casino Flutuante Macau Palace
Ruínas de São Paulo
Fortaleza do Monte
Monumento a Vasco da Gama
Guía Fort
Casino Jai Alai
Ferry Terminal
Av. Almeida Ribeiro
Largo do Senado
Sé Catedral
Tourism Activities Centre
Fishermen's Wharf
Porto Exterior
Rua das Lorchas
Santo Agostinho
Teatro de Dom Pedro
Monumento a Jorge Alvares
Av. Rodrigues
Rua de Pequim
Avenida da Amizade
World Trade Center
Rua do Almirante Sergio
Palácio do Governo
Ermida da Penha
Rua da Praia Grande
Casino & Hotel de Lisboa
Centro Cultural, Art Museum
Museum Maritimo
Baia da Praia Grande
Ponte Macau-Taipa
Avenida Dr. Sun Yat-sen
A-Ma Temple
Kun Iam Statue
Rua da Republica
Porto Interior
Pousada de São Tiago
300 m
990 ft
©Baedeker
↓ Macao Tower
↓ Taipa, Coloane ②③⑤
↑ Hong Kong

History Macau was established in 1557 as a Portuguese trading and mission station. It played a key role in the development of Christianity in the Far East. After the founding of Hong Kong it fell into a kind of slumber, like Sleeping Beauty, as the shallow waters around it meant that the larger, modern ships were unable to dock here. After the Second World War, the **betting industry** gave Macau a new lease of life, initially in a very modest way, but since the dynamic development of the Pearl River delta has taken hold, Macau too has been reinventing itself. Two of the key milestones were the opening of the airport in 1995 and the handover back to China 1999. Since then, Macau has, like Hong Kong, been a special administrative region in China, with its own currency. And they drive on the left.

What to see in Macau: southeast

The whole of the southeast part of the territory – all the land south of Guía Hill – has been artificially reclaimed. Here in the outer harbour (Porto Exterior) is where the ferries dock. The first thing that can be seen from the ferry is a **pleasure park** built out on the sea to the left, which has a Chinese fort in the Tang style, an artificial volcano, a ruined Roman amphitheatre and skylines from Amsterdam, New Orleans, Cape Town and Lisbon – all made of concrete and originally dating from 2005. It is also filled with restaurants, shops and fun attractions. The huge building behind it is Sands, presently Macau's largest casino.

Fisherman's Wharf, Sands

> **! Baedeker TIP**
>
> **Not at the weekend**
> Macau gets booked up on Saturdays and Sundays and nights before a holiday. This applies to the ferries, too, especially in the evenings when casino guests flood back to Hong Kong. Make sure, then, to plan a visit to Macau during the week.

Slightly obscured by Sands is the **Centro Cultural** where international orchestras play guest concerts. The **Museum of Art** next door, well worth a visit in its own right, exhibits works by both Portuguese and Chinese painters from Macau. Opening times: Tue–Sun 10am–7pm.

A monumental bronze Guanyin statue (the Kun-lam Statue) looms over the shoreline Avenida Dr. Sun Yatsen promenade. On the other side is where most of the night life takes place, where bars and pubs crowd closely together.

Kun-lam statue, »Docks« pub district

Head from the statue of Guanyin inland along the long green axis and turn right shortly before the end into Rua de Luìs Gonzaga Gomes to get to the Tourism Activities Centre with its **Grand Prix Museum**. The best thing there is the driving simulator, which makes it possible to experience what it is like racing a Formula-1 car. The **Wine Museum** in the same building offers a glimpse into the art of Portuguese vintners as well as wine-tastings. Opening times for both: Wed–Mon 10am–6pm.

Tourism Activities Centre

✴ ✴ Historic centre

The centrally located Largo do Senado is lined by a group of historic buildings. The southern side on Avenida Almeida Ribeiro is occupied by the Leal Senado, **the old town hall**. The staircase with its blue-

Largo do Senado, Leal Senado

and-white tiles, called azulejos, is gorgeous, and the council chamber and the senate library should not be missed. Opening times: Tue–Sun 9am–9pm.

Santo Agostinho and its environs

To the right of the Leal Senado, a small street leads uphill towards another group of historic buildings, the church of Santo Agostinho (left), St Joseph's Seminary (straight on), the Biblioteca Sir Robert Ho Tung (right) and the **Theatro Dom Pedro** (opposite the church). The theatre building from 1860 is seldom used these days, though.

São Domingos

From the narrow north end of Largo do Senado it is just a stone's throw to the prettiest Baroque church in town, which features a magnificent altar. The statue of Our Lady of Fatima in the left-hand side chapel is used every 13 May in a procession – one of several such events in the city. There is a **church museum** housed in the bell tower.

Ruins of São Paulo

Macau's landmark is the spectacularly decorated façade of a cathedral which burned down in 1835. Situated in splendour at the northern end of a wide open stairway, it dates back to between 1620 and 1627 and clearly exhibits missionary features. At top of the pediment flies a dove, symbol of the Holy Spirit. The central part of the pediment shows Christ as the conqueror of death and saviour of man, while the lower pediment level is dedicated to Our Lady. On the right, she is praying to defeat a dragon and on the left her prayers give protection to a trading vessel. Next to this is an image of the devil tempting mankind into sin. Some of the foundations can still be seen behind the façade. In the crypt there is a small **museum of Christian art**. Shelves there also hold the bones of Japanese and Vietnamese Christians who fled persecution in their homelands in the 17th century.

! *Baedeker* TIP

Coffee and cakes maybe?

In the Travessa de São Domingos, a lane that branches off from the narrow end of the Largo do Senado, and with the Leal Senado behind you, is the Caféchocolá, a good place to rest over coffee and cakes.

Fortaleza do Monte with the Macau Museum

The fortress offers a great view of the northern part of the city and the nearby Chinese mainland. Taking the escalator from the north end of the São Paulo ruins leads straight to the **main entrance of the museum of the city's history**, which is housed in the fort. It contains whole façades of houses and shops supplemented by dioramas and audio-visual media to give a living impression of old Macau, its history and life in former times. Opening times: Tue–Sun 10am–6pm.

Jardim Luis de Camões, Cemitério Protestante

A short walk to the northwest leads to the popular park, the Jardim Luis de Camões, named in memory of a Portuguese poet. Camões lived in Macau from 1558 and in his poem, **»Os Luisiadas«**, he re-

Colonial atmosphere on Largo do Senado

lated the story of the Portuguese conquests. A gate opens from the right hand side of the square in front of the park into the quiet Protestant cemetery. It can be seen there that mariners and traders travelling to the Far East often died at a terrifyingly young age.

What to see in the northeast

A Chinese merchant prompted the laying out of this garden in the traditional Chinese style during the 19th century. It features a miniature landscape with artificial mountains, bamboo groves and a goldfish pond. Amateur musicians sometimes meet in its pavilions. Estrada Adolfo Correiro. Opening times: 6am–9pm daily.

Jardim de Lou Lim Ieoc

🕐

Take two left turns from the entrance to the garden, then head straight on for a block before turning right after Avenida Horta e Costa. At that point is the Flora Garden, from which a **cable car** runs up Guía Hill. At the top, turn right and go to the end to reach Macau's highest point with the Guía Fort, a lighthouse and a small chapel with old wall and ceiling decorations.

Flora Garden and Guía Fort

Kun Iam Temple The »Guanyin Hall«, a little bit north of the Flora Garden on Avenida de Coronel Mesquita, is a lively and relatively large temple. It was already in existence when the first treaty between China and America was signed here in 1844. The building is topped by colourful high ridges. Its main image is at the end of the middle section, a Guanyin. The secondary halls to the east are set aside for wakes and general ancestor worship. At the easternmost point a path leads into what was once the temple's garden at the rear, where the **Lovers' Tree**, a curious tree with five intertwined trunks, is being cultivated anew after the original died in 1994.

Portuguese architecture, Chinese illumination: a familiar sight in Macau

Where to go in the south

The southern tip of the island is partially made up of a very posh residential area. In particular above the eastern shore road, the Avenida de Praia Grande, there are several **prestige buildings**, including a red building which was the former governors' residence, now home to the head of the administration. A palatial yellow building a little further south houses the Portuguese Consulate.

The Macau Tower rises up 338 m/1110 ft on some artificially reclaimed land. At the top there is a restaurant with an outstanding all-round view, a chance to plummet into the depths on the end of bungee rope or to strap in and ride the »Sky-walk« into the blue. Opening times: 10am–9pm daily. www.Macautower.com.mo

Macau Tower

One more stop on a number 21 bus brings you to Largo do Pagode da Barra near the southern tip. Here, a **temple complex** comprising several small buildings stretches up the slopes of Barra Hill. It is dedicated to the protective deity of mariners, from whom Macau itself (actually »A-Ma Cao«) also gets its name.

A-Ma Temple

Opposite the temple is a new building housing the maritime museum. It provides information in the form of photographs, models, dioramas, apparatus, aquariums and charts on aspects of fishing, seafaring and discoveries in marine biology as well as dock provision and hydrography. A mechanical puppet theatre relates the legend of A-Ma. Opening times: Wed–Mon 10am–5.30pm.

Museum Maritimo

Taipa · Coloane

Three bridges sweep over to the more northerly of the two islands of Taipa. Between the university in the north and the horse racing circuit in the southwest there is a whole forest of residential tower blocks. In the east, an airport extends out into the sea. Nevertheless, right in the centre of southern part of the island is the old **Taipa village**, particularly popular for its Portuguese restaurants and oven-fresh baked goods, obtainable on the Rua da Cunh, which is closed to traffic.

Baedeker TIP

Posada de São Tiago

The old fort at the southern tip of the Macau peninsula is now a romantic luxury hotel. Those who don't have a room here can still enjoy the unusual ambience, either in the Os Gatos restaurant, or over a drink on the shady terrace with a view over the water. Tel.: +853/28 37 81 11, www.saotiago.com.mo.

East of Taipa village, on the other side of a small hill topped by a church, is the former coast road where there are five nicely restored old villas now used as a museum (Taipa Houses Museum). This is a

🕐 chance to see how the well-to-do once lived in Macau. Avenida da Praia. Opening times: Tue–Sun 10am–6pm.

Cotai From the Taipa Houses Museum the eye is drawn across to another world: Cotai, the giant area of reclaimed land which now links Taipa to Coloane. Here is the Sands' **»Venetian«**, a gigantic hotel-casino-shopping and conference-patterned on the Las Vegas model, complete with canals, bridges and singing gondolieri, all with air-con of course. Other major projects are to follow.

★
Coloane Coloane is Macau's green island, void of casinos and equipped with hiking paths, a golf course, two beaches (the little Cheoc Van in the south and the larger Hac Sa in the east) and the idyllic Coloane village, clustered around the little church of São Francisco Xavier. A monument on the pretty square in front of it recalls a victory by the villagers over pirates who kidnapped children of the village in 1910. At the northern edge of the village there are a series of sampan wharves, some of which are still used.

Nanchang

Hc 31

Province: Jiangxi   **Population:** 1.6 million
Altitude: 20 m/66 ft

The lively provincial capital is not counted among the premier tourist destinations in the country. Travellers passing through, on the way to the mountains of Lu Shan, for example, should nevertheless plan in a day to explore its secrets..

Nestling amid hills, Nanchang is the capital of Jiangxi Province in the middle of southern China. Its centre is on the left bank of the Gan Jiang river, which forms the province's main transport artery from north to south before flowing into Lake Poyang Hu. The name of the city means »Southern Prosperity«.

What to see in Nanchang

Tours and getting around The city centre, where most of the atrractions are, is between the Gan Jiang and the north-south axis, Bayi Dadao (Avenue of the 1st August). Along this axis lies People's Park (Renmin Guangchang) with its grandiose exhibition centre. Life in the city centres on this park and the Park of the 1st August (Bayi Gongyuan, a bit further to the northwest).

Tower of Prince Teng (Tengwang Ge) The nine storeys of the tower rise up 57.5 m/189 ft above the shore of the Gan Jiang. The eye-catching building was built in the style of

► VISITING NANCHANG

INFORMATION

Nanchang International Travel Agency
161 Ba-yi Dadao
Tel. 07 91/620 23 66

GETTING THERE

Changbei Airport, 28 km/17 mi north of Nanchang, has flights to all the major cities of China. The railway station is at the southeastern end of town, about 2 km/1.5 mi from the city centre. Places to see in and around the city can be comfortably reached by bus. The long-distance coach station is at Ba-yi Dadao, somewhat to the south of the Square of 1 August (Ba-yi Guangchang). Buses run regularly from here and from the railway station to the mountains of Lu Shan.

ACCOMMODATION

► Luxury

① *Lu Shan:*
Lushan Villa Hotel
82 Zhihong Lu
Tel. 07 92/829 42 98
Strange that no one has struck upon

the idea of pepping up the dusty colonial heritage of Guling with rented villas, cafés and restaurants for the foreign trade, with the sole exception of the ten restored buildings at the Lushan Villa Hotel.

► Mid-range

Gloria Plaza Hotel
39 Yanjiang Beilu
Tel. 07 91/673 88 55
Fax 07 91/673 85 33
www.gloriahotels.com
Modern, centrally located hotel near the Tower of Prince Teng. 327 rooms, many with a view of the river, although the prices are at the top end of the category.

② *Lu Shan:*
Lushan Hotel
446 Hexi Lu
Tel. 07 92/829 52 05
Renowned hotel amid the villas of Guling. It consists of newish purpose-built hotel premises in front, with villas behind (rooms of equivalent quality).

the Song dynasty but gained its present appearance in the year 1989. Its name recalls a younger brother of the Tang Emperor, Taizong, who built the first tower on this site in 653 when he was governor of Nanchang. Since that time, the tower has been destroyed and rebuilt on no less than 28 occasions. Among the art exhibits there is one of the gems of Chinese literature, the **»Preface to the Tower of Prince Teng«** by Wang Bo (650–676). Opening times: 8am–5pm daily.   ⏲

On 1 August 1927 revolutionary troops under the leadership of **Zhou Enlai and Zhu De** managed to take control of Nanchang from Chiang Kaishek's army for a brief period during the civil war of that time. Even though the campaign ended in retreat for the revolutionaries after a few short days, it is still regarded as the **birth of the Red**

Museum of the August 1st Revolt (Bayi Nanchang Qiyi Jinian Guan)

Army, which was to be renamed the »National People's Army« in 1946. Even today, military insignia in China still bear the numerals of the date, 8-1 (chin bayi). The former Jiangxi Grand Hotel on Sun Yatsen Road (Zhongshan Lu) was the headquarters of the rebels for those few days. The exhibits and documents now on display there are mainly captioned in Chinese. Opening times: 8.30am–5.30pm daily.

People Blessing Temple (Youmin Si)

This formerly important Buddhist temple, north of Bayi Park, has origins dating back to the year 503. During the Cultural Revolution it was destroyed but the complex was rebuilt in the 1990s and now possesses such items as a standing Buddha statue 10 m/33 ft high. Opening times:8am–5.30pm daily.

Rope and Gold Pagoda (Shengjin Ta)

More than 1000 years ago when this pagoda was being built, it is said that a box was dug up in which there were four bundles of gold rope as well as other valuable items. It is from this that the pagoda gets its name. The present seven-storey building is nearly 60 m/200 ft high and dates from the 18th century. The pagoda and the surrounding **»Temple Monastery under the Pagoda«** (Taxia Si) are on the southern edge of the city centre and open only at irregular intervals.

✱
Garden of the Blue Clouds (Qingyun Pu)

The best place to recover from the bustle of the city centre is about 5 km/3 mi south of the city centre itself by the **Dingshan Bridge**. It is believed that the first building on the site was built here in 321 and the spot served as a temple premises for several centuries. Nowadays there is a museum featuring the work of painter and calligrapher Zhu Da. Zhu Da (1626–1705) was a scion of the imperial Ming dynasty. After the toppling of the dynasty by the Qing in 1644, he retreated from public view and lived as a recluse and eccentric. In 1661 he obtained accommodation at Qingyun Pu and remained there till his death. Zhu used the pseudonym **Bada Shanren**; employing the four characters of the name in his calligraphy in such a way that they could be read as ku zhi, »I weep for him«, referring to the fall of the Ming dynasty. With his expressive and evocative brushwork, Zhu remains to this day one of the most important masters of the late imperial era. Qingyun Pu Lu. No. 20 bus route. Opening times: 8.30am–5.30pm daily.

✱ Lu Shan

A summer resort: that has been the key aspect of this mountainous region with peaks as high as 1474 m/4836 ft, 120 km/75 mi north of Nanchang, for over a thousand years. The first poet to write of Lu Shan was none other than **Li Bai** (▶Famous people p. 80) and many others would later follow his lead. For a while Lu Shan was highly popular with foreigners. The villas built here as of 1895 by European and American merchants from Shanghai, Wuhan or Nanjing still testify to this. Rich Chinese were attracted here too, among them **Chiang Kaishek** (► Famous People p. 77). While abroad the fame of the mountains declined after 1949 – it is rare to see foreigners people here now – in China itself, the region's reputation grew, as now the leadership of the Party and state would come here for their own summer retreats. Lu Shan has been declared a UNESCO World Heritage Site.

Guling is the name of the holiday estate of Lu Shan, situated in the   **Guling**
northeastern part of the summit region. Some of the old **villas and hotels** have fallen into disrepair while others have been nicely restored. Both Protestant and Catholic churches have remained in existence, too. The northern part of Guling (formerly written Kuling, which was a pun on »cooling« coined by an English journalist, Edward Selby Little) is the core of the town nowadays and is densely built-up. There are shops there and some nice little restaurants.

Lu Shan Map

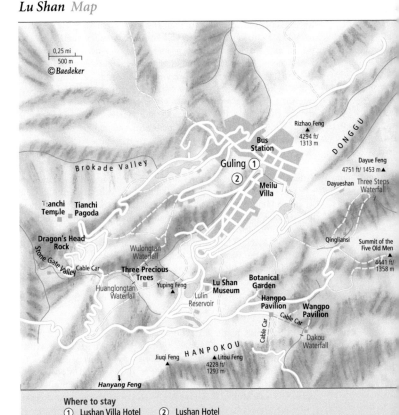

0,25 mi
500 m
©Baedeker

Rizhao Feng ▲
4294 ft/ 1313 m

DONGGU

Bus Station

Guling ①

Dayue Feng
4751 ft/ 1453 m ▲

Brokade Valley

②

Meilu Villa

Dayueshan Three Steps Waterfall

Tianchi Temple Tianchi Pagoda

Dragon's Head Rock

Wulongtan Waterfall

Qingliansi Summit of the Five Old Men

▲
4441 ft/ 1358 m

Stone Gate Valley Cable Car

Three Precious Trees

Huanglongtan Waterfall Yuping Feng ▲

Lu Shan Museum

Botanical Garden

Lulin Reservoir

Hangpo Pavilion   Wangpo Pavilion

Cable Car

Cable Car

Dakou Waterfall

HANPOKOU

Jiuqi Feng ▲ ▲ Litou Feng
4228 ft/ 1293 m

↓
Hanyang Feng

Where to stay
① Lushan Villa Hotel   ② Lushan Hotel

Meilu-Villa Said to have been built in 1903 by a British aristocrat, the impressive mansion in the northern part of the villa settlement of Guling on Hedong Lu was the **summer residence of Chiang Kaishek** and his wife after 1933. In 1959 and 1961 Mao Zedong also moved in here. Nowadays it is open to the public. The furnishings of former times have been kept intact. Opening times: 8am–5.30pm daily.

Lu Shan Museum Now housing the Lu Shan Museum, this villa, covering an area of 1 ha/2.5 acres, was built for Mao during 1960/61 (in the middle of a famine) on Huanhu Lu (the road along the eastern shore of the Lulin reservoir). However, he only made use of the house twice. His living room and bedroom are on view along with that of his third wife Jiang Qing and there are exhibitions on the history of Lu Shan, the architecture of its villas and its geology. Opening times: 8.10am–6.30pm daily, admission till 5pm.

Hiking on Lu Shan

In terms of scenic beauty, Lu Shan is not on a par with Huang Shan or Wuyi Shan, but there are still some nice walks (and cable-car rides), as it has everything a proper mountain needs: rocky clefts, peaks, caves, forests, streams and waterfalls. To see everything needs at least three and ideally four days. Even then, a few brief journeys will still need transport to cover them. It is best to negotiate a day rate for a taxi (e.g. with the help of the hotel's reception desk). This should cost about 100 yuan. Since the taxi is not needed for the whole day, agreement should be made with the taxi driver as to when to meet for a pick-up and where to go to and come back from (possibly taking the driver's own advice on this).

Route 1 This route covers the northwestern part of the area. This includes a 1450 m/1560 yd rock path above the Brocade Valley (Jinxiu Gu), the so-called **Manjushri Terrace**, Stone Gate Valley (Shimen Jian), where it is possible to descend via the Xinglong cable-car if the dramatically rugged climb down the steep steps of Dragon Head Cliff (Longtou Ya) is too much. Thereafter take a cable-car back up and continue eastwards to the waterfalls of Black Dragon Pool (Heilong Tan) and Yellow Dragon Pool (Huanglong Tan). Then go through the woods to the Yellow Dragon Temple (Huanglong Si). The tour ends at the Lulin reservoir, where those arriving early enough can also take in the Lu Shan Museum.

Route 2 This route leads to the attractions in the southeast and east: from Hanpokou, a viewpoint terrace, take the cable-car down to White Crane Valley (Baihe Jian) with its tall waterfall before going back to rejoin the taxi and visit the summits of the Five Old Men (Wulao Feng), clustered close together and requiring no mountaineering skills. On a clear day, it is possible to see from there as far as **Lake**

Poyang . Climb northwards up to Qingliansi, a small settlement. The last part of the route is difficult to accomplish in what the remains of a day, even though a cable-car is available. The objective is the 155 m/510 ft »Threefold Waterfall«. One other place to go on the route is close to Hanpokou, the botanical gardens.

✱ Nanjing

He 29

Province: Jiangsu
Altitude: 15 m/50 ft

Population: 2.7 million

The city in eastern China found fame as the »Capital of the Ten Dynasties«. Nanjing has, like other Chinese cities, visibly changed during the economic boom. The modern development, though, is still combined with a rich historical and cultural tradition. Two days to explore it is by no means too many.

Nanjing is the capital of the coastal province of Jiangsu. Amid a plain with many lakes, the city is on the shore of the Yangtze River, which is already very broad here. The damp, hot summers make it the proverbial »furnace« of China. The name (sometimes spelled Nan-

Elephants on the »soul path« of the Xiaoling imperial tomb

Nanjing Map

Ferry Quay
Duijiang Jinianbei
Zhongshan
Rehelu Square
Yangtse
Tangzhouqiao
Rehe Nanlu
Jiangjiawei
Erhangzhe
Yangongmiao
Jianning Lu
Beijing
Daqiao Nanlu
Beilu
Yancangqiao Square
Zhongfu
Jianning Lu
Heilongjiang Lu
Zhongyang Men Bus Station
Main Station
Nanjing Huochezhan
Longpan Lu

SANCHAHE
Huju Bellu
Zhongshan Beilu
Fujian Lu
Xin Mofan Malu
Luxiying
Zhongyang Lu
Xin Mofan Malu
Xuanwu
Hu
Xuanwu Hu Park

Dinghuai Men
Guping Gang
Jiangsu Lu
Shanxilu Square
Zhongshan Beilu
Hunan Lu
Xuanwu Men

CAOCHANGMEN
Huju Bei Lu
Beijing Xi Lu
Caochangmen Dajie
Shituzizhidong
Beijing Xilu
Drum Tower
Bell Pavilion
Gulou
Beijing
Dong

SHITOUCHENG
Huju Lu
Park of National Defence
Qingliang Park
Xiluo Lu
Hankou Xi Lu
Ninghai Lu
Shanghai Lu
Guangzhou Lu
University
Zhujiang Lu
Zhujiang Lu
Jimianzhe Lu
Chengxian Jie
Taiping Bei Lu
Zhujiang Lu
Tianchaogong

Jiangdongmen
Fenghuang Xijie
Wulong Park
Hanzhong Lu
Xinjiekou
Xinjiekou
Hanfu Jie Bus Station

Memorial to the Massacre of Nanjing
Hanzhong Xi Lu
HANZHONGMEN
Tangzi Jie
Mochou
Hongwu Lu
Taiping Nan Lu
Ruijin Lu
Changhai Lu

JIANGDONGMEN
Ting Dong Jie
Mochou Hu Park
Huju Nan Lu
Chaotian Gong
Jianye Lu
Zhangfu Yuan
Baixia Lu

Shuiximenwai Dajie
SHUIXIMEN
Shengzhou Lu
Sanshan jie
Jiankang Lu
Longpan Nan Lu

Changtai Lu
Laifeng Jie
Fengtai Lu
Museum of the Taiping Rebellion
Zhonghua Nanlu
Jiqing Lu
Temple of Confucius (Fuzi Miao)
Changle Lu
Bailuzhou Park

Nanjing-Wuhu Expressway
Zhonghua Men
Zhonghua Men
Yuhua Dong
Zhengxue Lu
Yuhua Xilu

0,25 mi
500 m
©Baedeker

Yuhuatai Park
Martyrs' Memorial

Airport

① ② ③ ④

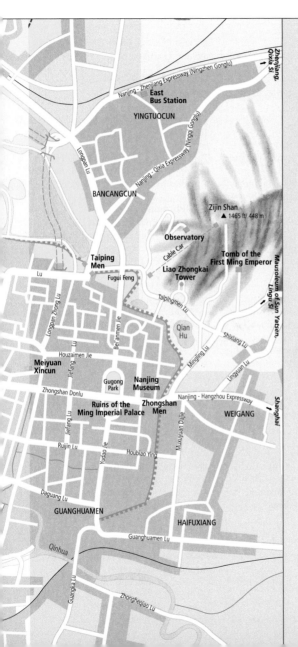

Where to stay
1. Jinling Hotel
2. Mandarin Garden Hotel
3. Jinjang Hotel
4. Fuzimiao International Youth Hostel

Where to eat
1. Sunward Fishery Restaurant
2. Wanqing Lou

Ⓜ ━ ━ Ⓜ Metro

● VISITING NANJING

INFORMATION

China International Travel Service
202 Zhongshan Beilu (diagonally opposite Nanjing Hotel)
Tel. 025/83 47 69 99, fax 83 53 86 37
www.citsnjview.com

GETTING THERE

From Lukou Airport, 42 km/26 mi south of the city, there are flights to many cities in China and a few major cities abroad, including Frankfurt. The main station is in the northeast of the city, outside the city wall. The most important coach station is 1 km/ 1100 yds further west on Zhongyang Men. South of the Yangtze bridge is the quay for shipping on the Yangtze.

WHERE TO EAT

Salted duck (Yanshuiya), fish and seafood will delight gourmets in the city. In autumn steamed mitten crabs (dazhaxie) appear on the menu. Snacks and small dishes can be found extensively around the Confucius Temple.

▶ Expensive

① *Sunward Fishery Restaurant*
189 Jiangdong Beilu
Tel. 025/86 55 11 11
Not so much a restaurant as a culinary palace, laid out over 1.2 ha/3 acres and catering for up to 2000 guests. It is a branch of a famous restaurant chain specializing in fish and seafood.

▶ Inexpensive

② *Wanjing Lou*
1 Gongyuan Yijie
(on the corner opposite the Confucius Temple, upper floor)
Tel. 025/86 62 69 50
Dimsum in traditional Nanjing style.

It's customary to order complete menus. The place closes at 8.30pm.

ACCOMMODATION

▶ Luxury

① *Jinling Hotel*
2 Hanzhong Lu (on Xinjiekou Square)
Tel. 025/84 71 18 88
Fax 025/84 71 16 66
This could not be more central. The 600-room hotel has been one of the top addresses in town for years.

▶ Mid-range

② *Mandarin Garden Hotel*
Fuzi Miao, Zhuangyuan Jing 9
Tel. 025/52 20 25 55
Fax 025/52 20 18 76
www.njzyl-hotel.com
Sterling comfort for those seeking entertainment: the shopping area near the Confucius Temple is right around the corner. 500 rooms at prices close to the top of the category.

③ *Jinjiang Hotel*
259 Zhongshan Beilu
Tel. 025/86 82 66 66, fax 83 42 43 82
Opened in 1936 and once a hotel for state dignitaries, now it is an oldie between Nanjing's steel palaces. The buildings, situated in a small park are a bit old-fashioned, but in return, the price is right. 310 rooms, in the northwest part of the old town.

▶ Budget

④ *Fuzimiao International Youth Hostel*
Fuzimiao Daba Jie 38
Tel. 025/86 62 51 33, fax 86 62 41 33
yhananjing@yahoo.com
Cheap accommodation in the lively old-town quarter with air-conditioned two-bed and four-bed rooms. Cycle hire available.

king in the past) means **»Southern Capital«** and was granted to the city in 1421, after the imperial court had moved to Beijing.

The city is known to have been in existence under various names for some 2500 years. In the 3rd century AD it was called Jianye and was **capital of the Wu empire**. It would also become the residence of several local dynasties afterwards. The period of its greatest importance began in 1368 when the first emperor of the Ming dynasty declared it his capital under the name Yingtian. Some staggering buildings were built here in the period before the capital was moved to Beijing in 1421, including the city walls, the tomb of the emperors and the no longer extant imperial palace.

History

The rebellion of the Taiping movement, which took control of half of China in the mid-19th century, reached Nanjing in 1853 and it was to be the base for their »Heavenly Kingdom of Great Peace« for the next eleven years. When the rebellion was put down in 1864, Nanjing had been largely destroyed. After the collapse of the final imperial dynasty, Nanjing was named provisional **capital of the new republic** in 1912 for a short time. It was made capital again in 1928 before being occupied by Japanese troops in 1937, and again after 1945 until the government fled to Taiwan in 1949.

Taiping Rebellion and republican era

The northwestern border of the city is formed by the Yangtze, 1.5 km/1 mi wide at this point and crossed by a huge double-decker bridge built between 1960 and 1968. In the east are the hills of Zijin Shan, on the other side of Black Toad Lake (Xuanwu Hu), an extensive area of parkland in which it is possible to cross to islands via causeways. The inner part of the centre is enclosed by extensive city walls, built mostly between 1366 and 1386 and still the biggest in the world. Originally extending for 33 km/21 mi, 20 km/12 mi remain in existence. At a height of up to 21 m/70 ft there are several spots with good views of the neighbouring parts of town.

Tours and getting around

✶ ✶ Purple Gold Mountain (Zijin Shan)

Several of the biggest attractions are in the east of the city on the eastern slopes of Zijin Shan. From west to east, they include the mausoleums of the first Ming emperor and of the founder of the republic, Sun Yatsen, as well as, less importantly, the Soul Valley Temple. Minibuses and taxis provide for ease of transport. Once there it is also possible to go from one attraction to the next in half an hour.

Zhu Yuanzhang, the first ruler of the Ming dynasty (reigned 1368–1398), is the only Chinese emperor buried in Nanjing. His tomb, one of the biggest still remaining in China, was already complete by 1383. The inner area of the tomb, north of the access road on the slopes of the hill, has frequently suffered from damage, espe-

Tomb of the first Ming Emperor (Ming Xiaoling)

cially during the Taiping upheaval. Nevertheless it is still impressive to this day for the massive dimensions of the surviving buildings. The tomb itself, located under an artificial hill almost 400 m/440 yd in diameter, has never been opened. Further south, the **»Sacred Way«** with its honour guard of 24 monumental animal sculptures and statues of eight human officials stretches for a distance of 800 m/half a mile. Opening times: 8am–6pm daily.

Mausoleum of Sun Yatsen (Zhongshan Ling)

Sun Yatsen (▶Famous People p. 83) is interred in a positively imperial fashion. The construction of the colossal building covering 80 ha/200 acres was started soon after his death. By 1929 it was possible for Sun's body to be moved here. Approaching the mausoleum the first impressive feature is the mighty open-air stairway, climbing up the slope in a flight of 392 steps. At the bottom end there is a gate of honour with the inscription »Bo Ai« (»Encompassing Love«) and 400 m/440 yd further on, the main gate, the greeting over the middle of which reads »Tianxia Wei Gong« (variously translated, but on the theme of »What is under heaven is for all«) – a recollection of the political legacy of the state's founder. Proceeding uphill, there follows the grave-stele pavilion. At the top end of the flight of steps the **memorial hall** with a luminous blue-tiled roof towers over the site. Here a marble statue of Sun gazes far across the country towards the south, as was once the rule for the traditional emperors. The actual tomb is behind it, 5 m/16 ft below another reclining statue of the president. Opening times: 6.30am to 6.30pm.

Soul Valley Temple Monastery (Linggu Si)

The story of this temple monastery goes back to the 6th century. Originally it was on the site of the emperor's tomb but was moved to its current site at the end of the 14th century. The most remarkable building is the large **»Beamless Hall«** (Wuliang Dian), a brick construction with barrel vaulting from the year 1381. It is now used for a waxwork display featuring Chinese revolutionaries. The 60 m/200 ft **Pagode Linggu Ta**, a little further uphill, recalls the fallen of the Northern Campaign (1924–1927). It was built in 1929. Opening times: 7am–6.30pm daily.

City centre

Two imperial buildings right in the city centre. The Drum Tower was rebuilt in 1889 in the wake of damage caused during the Taiping Rebellion. The Bell Pavilion (300 m/ 330 yd further northeast) contains a bell from the year 1388. Opening times: 8am–midnight daily (Drum Tower), 8.30am–5.30pm (Bell Pavilion).

Drum Tower and Bell Pavilion (Gu Lou, Dazhong Ting)

On the way to the Ming emperor's tomb, in front of the eastern gate of the city walls, Zhongshan Men, there is a museum built in classical style, which itself has a history dating back to 1933. Key exhibits of its collection include valuable bronzes and a **burial robe from the Han era** made of jade platelets. 321 Zhongshan Donglu. Opening times: 9am–4.30pm daily, www.njmuseum.com.

★
Nanjing Museum (Nanjing Bowuguan)

Less than 100 m/100 yd into the town from the museum are the ruins of the former imperial palace, a forerunner of the Forbidden City in Beijing. Nowadays just five marble bridges and a few scattered relics are all that remains of its former splendour.

Ruins of the Ming emperors' palace (Ming Gugong)

»Fuzi Miao« – »Confucius Temple« – is the name given to the bustling shopping and restaurant quarter in the centre of the city. Amid all the turmoil stands the actual Confucius Temple, first built in 1034. In earlier times young scholars would pray here for heavenly support before taking their final examinations for entry to the bureaucracy. Nowadays all around the (modern) **statue of the master** there is plenty of colour and much business being done. In the evenings the whole quarter is illuminated. Opening times: 8am–9pm daily, www.njfzm.com.

★
Confucius Temple (Fuzi Miao)

A few minutes walk to the east of the Confucius Temple is where during the imperial era great careers began and countless hopes were dashed. To prove their suitability for state service, candidates would have to write literary essays while confined for days in tiny cells. The mental pressure must have been almost unbearable and the physical stress immense. 40 cells out of what once numbered thousands have been reconstructed as a reminder of this ancient Chinese »examination hell « – complete with examples of attempted cheating. 1 Jinling Lu. Opening times: 8am–10pm daily.

Examination cells

The small Ming-era palace west of the Confucius Temple was once used by the »Heavenly King of the East«, Yang Xiuqing, as a head-

Museum of the Taiping Rebellion (Taiping Tianguo Lishi Bowuguan)

quarters. Yang had conquered Nanjing in 1853 on behalf of the Taiping rebels. He was murdered in 1856 in a leadership struggle. In addition to the historical exhibition, the neighbouring **»Garden with a View«** (Zhan Yuan), a typically southern Chinese scholar's garden, is a tempting place to rest. 128 Zhan Yuan Lu. Opening times: 8am–5pm daily.

> ! **Baedeker** TIP

Rain-flower stones

A little to the south of the Zhonghua Gate is Rain-flower Terrace Park (Yuhua Tai). A monk once preached here until petals fell from heaven. Legend has it that they turned into colourful pebbles, and these can be bought as »rain-flower stones«. They have to be placed under water, and make a popular gift for the folks back home.

Three storeys high and covering an area of 118 x 128 m/130 x 140 yd, the biggest of the surviving city gates, along the southern section of the walls, gives an impression of how powerful the defensive fortifi-

Zhonghua Gate (Zhonghua Men) cations were during the Ming dynasty. Opening times: 8.30am–9pm daily.

Memorial Hall for the Victims of the Nanjing Massacre The Memorial Hall for the Victims of the Nanjing Massacre commemorates the darkest hours of Sino-Japanese history. Japanese troops had taken control of Nanjing in December 1937. The people were then subjected to a **six-week blood bath**, while their own government could only sit by and encourage them to endure it. According to the latest research, some 70,000 people were killed and 10,000 women and girls were raped. The imposing memorial in the southwest of the city documents these horrifying events and even has some remains of murdered victims on display. 418 Shuiximen Dajie. Opening times: 8.30am–4.30pm daily.

Ningbo

Hf 31

Province: Zhejiang
Altitude: 20 m/66 ft

Population: 2 million

The old trading post, now a prosperous coastal metropolis, is not in itself a top-notch tourist destination but when making a connection here along the route from Hangzhou to Putuo Shan, it is easy to stop here for half a day and take in its main attraction: the library of Tianyi Ge, which is certainly more than just another library.

Apart from that, Ningbo is quite a pleasant city: well tended with parks, water features, modern shopping streets and nice places to go out. Those staying for longer than that half a day will not regret it either.

⊙ VISITING NINGBO

GETTING THERE
Lishe Airport is southwest of the city and offers flights to Hong Kong, Beijing and other inland destinations. Express trains link Ningbo to Hangzhou and Shanghai, with the main station being just outside the old town to the southwest. The same route can be covered quicker by express coach from the coach station opposite the railway station to the north. Shanghai can also be reached by ferry on an overnight trip. The ferry port is north of the Catholic church.

WHERE TO EAT
▶ **Inexpensive**
Gangyagou
Xianxue Jie 7
Tel. 05 74/87 29 53 39
It is rare to get so much culinary delight for so little money. This renowned restaurant turns out to be a kind of self-service establishment, but that avoids any communication problems and everything prepared is cracklingly fresh.

ACCOMMODATION
▶ **Mid-range**
Ningbo Hotel
251 Mayuan Lu
Tel. 05 74/87 09 78 88
Fax 05 74/87 09 78 68
www.ningbohotel.com
109 rooms in a good location not far from Tianyi Ge and the station. The rooms have broadband internet.

BARS & CAFES
On Zhenming Lu on the east bank of Moon Lake and north of the crossroads with Yunshi Jie, there is a whole district of pubs. There is also a large coffee house called Golden Cup Coffee (no. 330), which is a pleasant and quiet place to sit. Chinese people like to go there in the evening after supper.

✳ Tianyi Ge Museum (Tianyi Ge Bowuguan)

The library, founded in the 1560 by imperial official Fan Qin, is the most famous private library in the country. Nowadays, though, the library itself forms just the core of a much larger museum complex featuring classical Chinese buildings and garden courtyards, so that it is almost like an inner-city open-air museum.

The actual library is entered from the north. First the route passes the   **Tianyi Ge**
former home of the Fan family, a building dating from 1829. The descendants of the library's founder lived here until the 1950s. They avoided confiscation of their home by donating the library to the state. The library building itself in the courtyard neighbouring to the east has two storeys, although the books were only stored on the upper floor, designed as a single large room with ventilation at either end.
The pond in the **garden courtyard** which borders to the south had the purpose of providing water fort he extinguishing of fires. An arti-

ficial hill provided the contrast required by garden design principles. The whole group sets a standard, and even the imperial library of Wenjin Ge in the summer residence at ▶ Chengde is patterned on the design of Tianyi Ge.

Collection of bricks

The house in the courtyard adjoining to the east has one other curiosity, a collection of bricks between 1700 and about 2000 years old. Local-history enthusiasts dug them out of the rubble of Ningbo's city walls when they were demolished between 1927 and 1931.

Gardens

Head south to reach the extensive east garden. To the west of that is the south garden, which was not added till between 1996 and 1998. Both are examples of classic Chinese gardening.

Ancestor temple

At the south of the premises some other complexes are open to the public. Their halls contain exhibitions on the history of the city and of the game of mah jongg. The prime exhibit in the middle is the **ancestor temple of the Qin clan** and in particular the theatre stage belonging to it. Built from 1923 to 1925, its gilt carvings unmistakably demonstrate the wealth of the family. Tian Jie (in the west of the old town). Opening times: April–Oct. 8am–5.30pm, closes 5pm at other times of year.

Other places to see in the old town

Moon Lake Park (Yuehu Gongyuan)

Just one block east of the Tianyi Ge Museum is Moon Lake Park, a very nicely kept and partially redesigned green space with a long narrow lake.

Chenghuang Miao quarter

Further east, around the former temple to the city's god (Chenghuang Miao), is the lively city centre with its restaurants, shops and the slick new shopping centre, Tianyi Guangchang on Kaiming Jie.

Tianfeng Ta Pagoda

East of Kaiming Jie and south of the shopping centre on Dashani Jie stands this elegant, hexagonal seven-storey pagoda with another seven stories underground. The tower is decorated with artful cornices and carvings. It dates back to the **Tianfeng era** (695–696) and is sometimes called the Tang Pagoda (Tang Ta). Although it later fell into ruin, it was rebuilt in 1144 and at least its brick core dates from that period. It is worth climbing to the top for the view.

River promenade

It is just three blocks further east to the River Fenghua Jiang and a little further north there is a nicely laid-out park which extends as far as the confluence with the Yuyao Jiang.

Catholic church

From the angle of the rivers it is possible to see the Catholic church on the opposite bank. Built in 1872, nowadays it is used by a Chinese-Catholic parish and is open to the public.

✴ Putuo Shan

Province: Zhejiang   **Population:** 4600
Altitude: Up to 290 m/950 ft

Only a small island but a prime destination. The island is one of the four sacred mountains of Chinese Buddhism and since it is dedicated to the bodhisattva Guanyin, goddess of mercy, pilgrims come here from all over eastern Asia. Its magnificent monasteries, shady paths and multiple sandy beaches make it popular with non-Buddhists, too. To see it all means staying for at least two nights.

It would be nice if all of China were like this: quiet and green with small villages and no skyscrapers, all the new buildings fitting in to the character of their surroundings, lively temples, little vehicular traffic, fresh air and friendly accommodation. The island covers only 12.5 sq km/5 sq mi (permanent population 4600) and it is ideal for exploring on foot. It is not too mountainous either. **Foding Shan** (»Buddha peak mountain«) has no summit higher than 290 m/950 ft. The settlement is concentrated on the southern part of the island

 VISITING PUTUO SHAN

GETTING THERE

The island is only accessible by ferry but Zhoushan Airport is on a neighbouring island to the south. It is an airport for pilgrims so it cannot accommodate larger planes but there are direct flights from many different places including Shanghai (30 minutes in the air). From the airport a bus takes passengers to the ferry, which then makes the short trip to Putuo Shan. A standard journey starts at Ningpo, initially by bus, then by ferry, although there are certain variations on the journey. High-speed ferries also run from Shanghai.

TRANSPORT

Normal taxis do not run on the island. Minibuses ply along the main roads at irregular intervals but they are not suitable for people carrying lots of luggage.

WHERE TO EAT

On Golden Sand Beach (Jin Sha) in the south of town there many fish restaurants. For food of a better class, eat in the Citic Putuo Hotel itself.

WHERE TO STAY

► **Luxury**
① *Citic Putuo Hotel*
22 Jinsha (on »Golden Sand Beach« not far from the ferry dock)
Tel. 05 80/669 82 22
Fax 05 80/669 81 77
citic@mail.zsptt.zj.cn
108 rooms in a lovely location with English speaking staff

► **Mid-range**
② *Purple Bamboo Hotel*
Tel. 05 80/669 80 01
Fax 05 80/669 80 19
Nice 40-room hotel in the neighbourhood of the Citic Putuo Hotel

where the ferry port is. The west, north and the peninsula stretching out to the northeast are very quite areas of terrain with nothing but a few monasteries and often no people in sight. For swimming, both the Hundred Pace Beach or the Thousand Pace Beach, which despite its name is only slightly longer than the former, both on the eastern side of the island slightly south of its centre, are easy to get to. There are some more remote beaches in the north.

Putuo Shan Map

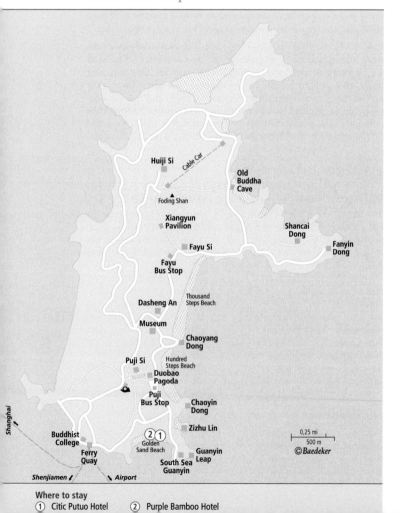

Huiji Si
Cable Car
Old Buddha Cave
▲ Foding Shan
Xiangyun Pavilion
Shancai Dong
Fanyin Dong
Fayu Si
Fayu Bus Stop
Thousand Steps Beach
Dasheng An
Museum
Chaoyang Dong
Puji Si
Hundred Steps Beach
Duobao Pagoda
Puji Bus Stop
Chaoyin Dong
Shanghai
Zizhu Lin
0,25 mi
500 m
© Baedeker
Buddhist College
② ①
Golden Sand Beach
Guanyin Leap
Ferry Quay
South Sea Guanyin
Shenjiamen
Airport

Where to stay
① Citic Putuo Hotel ② Purple Bamboo Hotel

The career of this remote piece of soil began in the year 916, when a Japanese pilgrim to China was washed onto the beach here by a storm on his way home. The devout man carried a statue of Guanyin with him onto the land and founded the first temple. Thus the seed of the local Guanyin cult was sown. During the Song era the island rose in status to become a place of pilgrimage and by the 13th century it was an important centre for the cult. The name Putuo Shan makes reference to this. It roughly means **Potala mountain**, an expression which refers back to the Indian mountain considered to be the home of Guanyin. Before 1949 there were 228 monasteries, large and small, housing more than 4000 monks and nuns. All of the statuary and images, though, fell victim to the iconoclasm of the Cultural Revolution. The traces of that barbarism have now been wiped away. Today the constant influx of offerings, large and small, to the reactivated monasteries is elevating them to unforeseen levels of wealth, which they are effectively demonstrating with new, dazzlingly golden images.

Origins

Visitors to the temple support a whole settlement here, the biggest on the island, situated in the central southern area. The temple was founded in 1080 and is the oldest of the major monasteries. The present complex mainly dates back to the 18th century. From a phase of building in which the main hall was rebuilt with funding from the emperor's court, there is also a stele with an imperial inscription from 1734. This is the best place to start a tour. It is located in the south in front of the pond placed in front of the temple for reasons of »feng shui«. Beyond the perimeter the sequence of primary buildings opens, as usual, with the **Hall of the Heavenly Kings**. The main hall, built in palatial style in 1731, contains a giant gilt Guanyin with her 32 incarnations to the side. At the front right Weituo, the general of the faith, can be seen with the (actually Daoist) protective deity Guan Di at the front left. At the back behind the main figure, Guanyin is shown in relaxed seated posture. The third hall is reserved for monks, but from outside it is still possible to spot the »Three Precious Buddhas« who are worshipped there.

Puji Si temple

The second major attraction is situated in the southeast and is already unmistakable when approaching the island by ship or plane. The South Sea Guanyin is a bronze statue 33 m/108 ft high with the goddess in standing pose. It was erected in around 2000. It towers over an impressive group possessing a sequence of large ascending terraces with some highly lifelike guarding figures carved out of stone.

South Sea Guanyin

It is said that Guanyin once paid a personal visit to the island. According to legend she leapt over the water and, in doing so, left her footprint in a rock. Guanyin's Leap, as the footprint is known, can be seen on the northern bank north of the monumental statue under

Guanyin's leap

the new **»Temple of Guanyin Who Did Not Want To Leave«**. That name refers to the Guanyin statue of the Japanese pilgrim from 916: by conjuring up the storm, she forced the monk to leave her here. The temple of the Purple Bamboo Grove, which is passed on the way there, contains a white Guanyin, accompanied by grotesque figures of the 18 luohan; while the rear hall has a reclining Buddha (upon his entry into Nirvana) on view.

Fayu Si temple North of the Thousand Pace Beach, roughly in the middle of the island, this temple is the island's largest. It was founded in 1580. The ensemble begins before the actual entrance with a decorative gate right at the front and a pond behind it crossed by an arched bridge. The first courtyard inside – beyond the wall – has a nine-dragon relief at its southern end. A wide stairway leads up to the **Hall of the Heavenly Kings**. The second hall contains a jade Buddha. The highlight is the Guanyin Hall that follows, which contains a golden statue of the goddess with the 18 luohan lined up along both sides. Reliefs on the terrace in front of the hall depict 24 scenes showing proper love for children, actually a Confucian motif. Two other central halls, the first of them with a thousand-armed Guanyin, and several side halls contain other images.

! *Baedeker* TIP

Striking out for the peak

Although the summit of Foding Shan can be reached from Huiji Si temple via what is a short and only moderately steep path, most pilgrims do not bother with the climb. This is a mistake as the panoramic view is well worth seeing. It is at its loveliest at dawn.

Summit monastery of Huiji Si Easily negotiated stairway paths lead past the Fayu Si monastery up to the summit monastery of Huiji Si. For those who want to take it a bit easier, there is a minibus route up the main road to the terminus a little further north, from which a cable-car goes the rest of the way.

Much incense is burnt in the Putuo Shan monasteries

Huiji Si is the smallest of the three main monasteries, but it still glitters with plenty of gold.

A road leads to the tip of the peninsula in the east. There a small monastery is built over a deep cleft in the cliffs by the shore. Heading north through the monastery there is a footpath to the idyllic **Shancai Caves Monastery**. The path continues t o the west back to the road. All the monasteries are open from the morning until sunset.

Eastern cape

Qingdao

Hf 27

Province: Shandong
Altitude: 80 m/260 ft

Population: 2.3 million

This modern industrial city, port and summer resort, with its forest of skyscrapers in the development zone to the east, is among the most interesting of China's coastal cities, not least because of its distinctive style. It surprisingly has the look of old Germany. At least many of its buildings exhibit that influence, as Qingdao is an offshoot of imperial Germany's colonial ambitions.

The Germans had long been on the lookout for their own base on the Chinese coast. In 1897 the murder of two German missionaries in Shandong Province finally gave them the excuse they needed to occupy the bay of Jiaozhou, which they had considered especially suitable for their aims, and to force the Chinese to lease it to them for a period of 99 years. Qingdao was thus founded in 1898 at the eastern exit of the bay and became a continually expanding model German settlement, probably the most modern city in the Far East at the time. The 99 years came to an early end, though, in 1914 when the Japanese occupied the city. The great patriotic May Fourth movement was formed in 1919 in opposition to the Treaty of Versailles, which proposed that the area should remain Japanese, rather than being returned to China. The region was indeed returned to China in 1922. Large areas of the city have preserved their Wilhelminian character to this day, however, and this style of architecture continues to be used locally even now. Note, in particular, the imitation half-timbering and the mansard roofs.

Old town

The main draw for all the visitors to the city runs outwards into the sea for 440 m//480 yd from the coastal promenade in the old town, Qingdao's pier. At the end there is a Chinese pavilion. The first pier to be built here dated back to 1891 but the modern version was only extended to its present length and size in 1931.

Pier

▶ VISITING QINGDAO

GETTING THERE

The international airport is to the north of the city and has flights to all the major centres of China as well as cities in Korea and Japan. The centrally located terminus station is the destination for trains from Jinan (or Beijing) and Yantai. There are also ferries to South Korea.

WHERE TO EAT

Qingdao counts among the best places to go for lovers of fish and seafood, and even more so because it can be accompanied by the white wine cultivated in Shandong. All that, combined with the chance to sit outside and enjoy a view of the sea, plus low prices, is on offer at the private restaurants on Qinyu Lu, which runs along the edge of Lu Xun Park from Laiyang Lu across to the island of Xiao Qingdao. An air-conditioned alternative is provided by the restaurants on Laiyang Lu itself. The amount to be paid depends, of course, on the specialities ordered and how much they cost at the particular time of year.

WHERE TO STAY

▶ Luxury
① *Equatorial Qingdao*
28 Xianggang Zhonglu
Tel. 05 32/85 72 16 88
Fax 05 32/85 71 33 83
Many rooms in the 23-storey tower of this four-star hotel have a sea view.

② *Dongfang Hotel*
4 Daxue Lu
Tel. 05 32/82 86 58 88
Fax 05 32/82 86 27 41
www.hotel-dongfang.com
Small tower block with 145 rooms (many with a sea view) close to the promenade in the old town, which caters for the lower end of the price category.

▶ Mid-range
③ *Oceanwide Elite Hotel*
29 Taiping Lu
Tel. 05 32/82 99 66 99, fax 82 89 13 88
Well-run 84-room establishment on the old-town promenade. Rooms with a sea-view are in the next price category up.

Sun Yatsen Road (Zhongshan Lu)
The street where most business is done in the old town was called Friedrichstrasse till 1914. There are still some old buildings to be found here, including one on the corner with Hubei Lu (Kronprinzenstrasse), the Seafarers' Home from 1902.

Railway station
The station can be found by taking a slight detour to the west. It was rebuilt in the1990s but at the end of the rebuilding works the façade and tower of the original German station built between 1900 and 1901 were reconstructed.

St Michael's Cathedral
Further north along Sun Yatsen Road, eyes turn to quickly to the right towards this **neo-Romanesque Catholic church** with its two towers 54 m/177 ft in height. The architect was (fairly obviously) a German and his building was erected between 1931 and 1934.

Qingdao Map

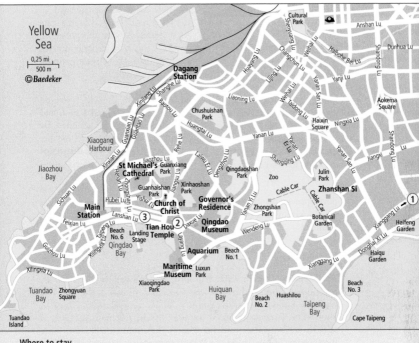

Yellow
Sea

0,25 mi
500 m
©Baedeker

Cultural Park
Anshan Lu
Dunhua Lu
Shenyang Lu
Changchun Lu
Haibohe Bei Lu
Shandong Lu
Dagang Station
Liaoning Lu
Wuhai Lu
Ijing Lu
Weihai Lu
Yanji Lu
Aokema Square
Xinjiang Lu
Baotou Lu
Shanghe Lu
Chushuishan Park
Huangtai Lu
Taidong Lu
Haixin Square
Ningxia Lu
Xiaogang Harbour
Guanxian Lu
Guantao Lu
Rehe Lu
Yanan Lu
Jiangxi Lu
Shandong Lu
Jiaozhou Bay
Jiaozhou Lu
Laiwu Lu
Dengzhou Lu
Qingdaoshan Park
Shangqing Lu
Julin Park
Xinan Lu
Sichuan Lu
Henan Lu
St Michael's Cathedral
Guanxiang Park
Xinhaoshan Park
Zoo
Cable Car
Zhanshan Si
Yanan San Lu
Haifeng Garden
Hubei Lu
Zhongshan Lu
Guanhaishan Park
Church of Christ
Governor's Residence
Zhongshan Park
Botanical Garden
Xianggang Lu
Main Station
Lanshan Lu
Yishui Lu
Tian Hou Temple
Qingdao Museum
Wendeng Lu
Haiqu Garden
Feixian Lu
Taiping Lu
Beach No. 6
Landing Stage
Daxue Lu
Aquarium
Beach No. 1
Luxun Park
Donghai Xi Lu
Xianggang Lu
Guizhou Lu
Qingdao Bay
Lajang Lu
Maritime Museum
Xiaoqingdao Park
Huiquan Bay
Huashilou
Beach No. 3
Xillingxia Lu
Tuandao Bay
Zhongyuan Square
Beach No. 2
Taipeng Bay
Tuandao Island
Cape Taipeng
①
②
③

Where to stay
① Equatorial Qingdao   ② Dongfang Hotel   ③ Oceanwide Elite Hotel

Southeast of St Michael's Cathedral is the Protestant Christ Church, built between 1908 and 1910 in the Jugendstil, the Austro-German form of Art Nouveau. On the face of the tower clock the words »Bockenem am Harz« can be read (the name of the town in Germany where the clock was made). **Christ Church**

The former Kaiser Wilhelm Promenade stretches eastwards from the pier. Many of its old buildings have survived, including an hotel and the former headquarters of the German-Asian Bank (corner of Qingdao Lu). One block further east is the restored **Tian Hou Temple**. **Coast promenade**

The most spectacular of the old German buildings in the city is on the slopes of Signal Hill. It was built from 1905 to 1907 in a rustic German style with some Jugendstil elements. The multiple levels of the building with its balconies, chimneys, gables, balconies and ornamentation mean it has interesting things to see from all perspectives. The best aspect, though, is the almost complete and well preserved **Governor's residence (Qingdao Yingbin Guan)**

»A Tsingtao, please.«

That order can be made in a variety of languages all around the globe. The former German brewery still produces what is now China's most famous beer, and it is also still spelt in the traditional fashion. Here in Qingdao they take their beer drinking very seriously, especially at the international beer festival which takes place over 16 days from the second week in August in the »beer city« (Pijiu Cheng) at the eastern edge of town, right next to the fun fair.

original interior furnishing. After the new state was established in 1949, the residence was used a state guest house. Among the people to stay here was Mao Zedong himself. 26 Longshan Lu. Opening times: 8.30am–5pm daily.

Eastwards from the old town are the beaches, numbered 1 to 3, and separated from one another by promontories. Beach no. 2 has the most flair. The leafy **villa district of Badaguan** stretches inland from there. From Beach 3 the view is of the forest of tall buildings in the development zone, which makes quite a spectacular impression when swimming after dark, as many Chinese visitors like to do in summer.

Lao Shan

The premier place for a day-trip for Qingdao's residents rises up almost directly out of the sea about 40 km/25 mi east of the city. The region is known across the country for its mineral water (Laoshan Shui). The Tsingtao brewery, founded by the Germans in 1903, is said to get its water from here, too. The mountain has for some thousand years been home to Daoist monasteries, which are another good reason to make the trip.

Taiqing Gong Temple

The »Palace of Supreme Purity« is at the southeastern foot of Lao Shan with a view of the sea. It was established during the Song era, though the present buildings date back to the **Wanli period** (1573–1620). On the walls of Three Emperors Hall (Sanhuang Dian) there are some surviving inscriptions from Kublai Khan (▶Famous People p. 78) and Genghis Khan.

Shangqing Gong temple

The »Palace of Great Purity« is known as the **Upper Temple** by dint of its elevation. It was built during the Yuan period from 1297 to 1307, although it has been expanded many times since. In front of the complex there are some gingkoes which are hundreds of years old. South of the temple a waterfall cascades down for some 20 m/66 ft.

Summit region, hiking

From the monasteries it is possible to glide up to the peak region in a cable-car. The tallest summit is 1133 m/3717 ft high and can be reached by various paths. Those not staying long usually spend their time on the southern slope from where there is a view of the sea.

Colonial architecture with a backdrop of high-rises is a typical sight in Qingdao

The good places to go hiking, though, are mainly in the north, where there are lots of caves, steep cliffs and more temple monasteries. The no. 304 bus runs from Qingdao, as do private minibuses.

★ Quanzhou

Province: Fujian
Altitude: 200 m/660 ft

Population: 300 000

In the Middle Ages Quanzhou was an important trading port until it began to stagnate. The result is that many of its historic buildings have survived.

The present town is unlike any other because of its buildings. Traditionally the building material was granite, supplemented by striped bricks. One other special aspect of the place is that religion and custom are much more active than elsewhere. With a certain amount of luck it is possible to see funeral corteges winding through the streets.

Quanzhou has an irregular street grid. In the west and south the town is bordered by the Jin Jiang River. One landmark for getting one's bearings in the city centre is the **clock tower** on the intersection of Xi Jie and Dong Jie (West and East Roads) with Sun Yatsen Road. This is traditionally the main street for business in the city and the central section (Zhongshan Zhonglu) maintains a little old town flair.

Getting around

⏵ VISITING QUANZHOU

GETTING THERE
The usual route from Xiamen or Fuzhou is by bus. There is also a motorway. Private minibuses, though, use the old main road and make frequent stops. The city can be reached by train from Wuyi Shan. 15 km/9 mi south of the city. Jinjiang Airport has flights to larger cities.

WHERE TO EAT
▶ **Moderate**
① *Red Rock*
1 Zhuangyuan Jie
(pedestrian zone)

Tel. 05 95/227 67 07
Nice café with cocktails and small dishes. Large selection of tea and coffee varieties.

WHERE TO STAY
▶ **Mid-range**
① *Quanzhou Hotel*
22 Zhuangfu Xiang
Tel. 05 95/22 28 99 58
Fax 05 95/22 18 21 28
The best downtown hotel with 377 rooms. Many attractions can easily be reached on foot from here.

Marco Polo's report Quanzhou was one of the most important trading ports on earth from about the 10th until the 14th century. There are in particular two important witnesses to this. One is Marco Polo, who started out from here on his return journey to Italy with his father and uncle in 1292. He wrote, »I assure you that for every ship that docks at Alexandria or any other harbour to load spices for Christendom, a hundred ships put into port at Zayton, because Zayton is one of the two ports in the world with the most massive turnover of goods.« Zayton was the name given to the city by the Arabs. Fifty years later, Ibn Battuta, the great Arab explorer, wrote almost the same thing. »The port of Zayton is one of the biggest in the world or, more exactly, the biggest.« The Ming dynasty, though, introduced a policy forbidding maritime commerce – foreign trade was considered per se to be espionage – and in addition the harbour was gradually silting up. Nowadays it is possible to land a paddle boat at best.

> **? DID YOU KNOW …?**
>
> ■ … very few words of Chinese have entered English or any other European language? Two of the exceptions have links to Quanzhou: tea – from the local Quanzhou dialect word »teh« – and satin – a corruption of Zayton, the Arabic name for the city, where merchants bought the fabric.

What to see in the old town

Qingjing Si Mosque The Qingjing Si Mosque is a ruin. Whereas elsewhere, ordinary timber-framed buildings are reduced to nothing but a stone pedestal, here the fact that the outer walls are made of granite means it is possible to see how the building once looked. The mosque was built in

1009 for the Arabic merchant community, although its later appearance resulted from a comprehensive restoration by an Arab architect from Jerusalem in 1309. The **Arab building style** is can be seen primarily in the high gate, which also allowed for observation of the moon. It can still be climbed today. An exhibition illustrates the history of Islam in the city, which goes all the way back to the 7th century. 113 Tumen Jie. Opening times: 8am–6pm daily.

Guandi Miao

A little further south on the same street is a small temple in which »Emperor Guan« (Guan Di) is worshipped as the patron, a lively centre of folk religion.

Yuanmiao Guan Temple

This Daoist temple is the very opposite of an antiquity. It is still being built. The project, financed by private donations – often from former residents of Quanzhou living in Hong Kong or Taiwan– is typical of the city. The **main hall of the Three Pristine Ones** is already built, a large grandiose building with carved shrines of incredible intricacy for the three primary gods, as well as featuring dragons coiling around the relief columns made of Quanzhou granite.

Maritime museum

The maritime museum (Haiwai Jiaotong Shi Bowuguan) is a modern building with a valuable collection nicely presented in three sections: 1. Shipping and the history of the city's overseas links. This in-

Quanzhou Map

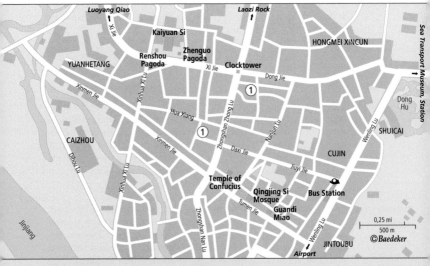

Where to stay
① Quanzhou Hotel

Where to eat
① Red Rock

cludes the **largest collection of model Chinese boats in the world**. 2. Historic porcelain made for the export market – one of the main goods handled here. Even Marco Polo sang its praises. 3. Tomb inscriptions. In the city and the surroundings inscriptions have been found in Chinese, Persian, Arabic, Syriac, Turkish and Latin – proof of the extraordinary aura Quanzhou once possessed. Donghu Jie, corner of Tian'an Beilu (outside the old town to the east). Opening times: 8am–5.30pm daily.

✱ Kaiyuan Si Temple

The best known and most interesting Buddhist temple in the whole of Fujian Province goes back to the **Kaiyuan era** (713–741). According to one legend it started as a settlement in a grove of mulberry trees. In the years until 1285 it grew into a complex of enormous dimensions.

Nowadays it measures some 7 ha/17 acres. Opposite the gate at the entrance, a spirit wall is still in place to shut off the view inside. He generals Heng and Ha act as gate guards.

Pagodas
The two lovely, octagonal stone pagodas in the first broad courtyard are Quanzhou's most photographed landmarks. The 44 m/144 ft **Renshou Ta** from 1237 to the west (left) and the 48 m/157 ft **Zhenguo Ta** from 1250 matching it to the east both imitate timber architecture and are decorated with reliefs.

Mahavira Hall
This imposing hall covering 1000 sq m/1200 sq yd was built in 1642. It contains images of five Buddhas: the Buddhas of the four compass points (with their assisting bodhisattvas) at the sides and in the middle, **Buddha Shakyamuni** (with his two apostles). At the rear a Guanyin statue can be seen, flanked by the 18 luohan. All the statues are gilded. Note the flying apsaras on the inner consoles of the hall, a very rare motif.

Hindu ornaments
Surprisingly, the supports for the rear wall are granite columns which do not quite match the style of the rest, possessing reliefs with motifs from Indian religious beliefs. They come from an earlier Hindu temple, which had been built by Indians living here during Quanzhou's heyday. Under the isolationist Ming dynasty, though, the temple had no owner and fell into decay. The columns were given a new lease of life with the rebuilding of this hall.

Ordination Hall
The Ordination Hall is the most unusual building on the site both inside and out, outside because of its triple roof, where the two lower eaves are rectangular while the upper one is octagonal. The inside is remarkable because of the **Ordination terrace**, fabulously decorated with a surfeit of statues to look like an apotheosis of Buddhism. You would have to go a long way to see anything else like it.

The venerable age of the complex is underlined by some of the trees. **Trees**
Two Bodhi trees – of the kind under which Buddha Gautama found
enlightenment – grow in front of the
Ordination Hall and west of the axis
behind a barrier, the **remains of a
1300-year-old mulberry tree** is eking
out the last years of its life. Xi Jie (in
the western part of the old town).
Opening times: 5.00am–5.30pm daily.

In 1974 the stern of a **2000-ton boat**
was hauled out of the river silt near
Quanzhou. It is about 900 years old
and can be seen in a hall at the northeast corner of the monastery grounds
(the ship is due to be moved to the
maritime museum, so if it is not here, it will probably already be on
show there). Opening times: 8am–5pm daily.

Baedeker TIP

Paper Palaces
There is probably nowhere else in China that
such elaborate bamboo and paper palaces are
made as in Kaiyuan Si. Up to 2 m/6 ft tall and
more than 3 m/10 ft broad, they are intended
for the deceased and are subsequently burnt.
Behind the ordination hall it's worth looking
to see if one is currently under construction.

What to see in the surrounding environs

Why are the monumental statues in China always Buddhas? At Laozi **Laozi cliffs**
Cliff 5 km/3mi north of town one of the great figures of Daoist can **(Laojun Yan)**
at last be seen too – Laozi, the legendary founder of the religion – in
appropriate dimensions: 5 m/16 ft high and 7 m/23 ft wide. The figure was carved out of natural rock 900 years ago.

Luoyang Qiao is a construction dating from the year 1059. It still **Luoyang Qiao**
measures 834 m/912 yd long and is 7 m/23 ft wide, crossing the **Bridge**
Luoyang river 10 km/6 mi northwest of town. The pillars still survive
from the original. In 1291 they caught **Marco Polo's** eye, too. He described them appropriately, »The pillars are made of sturdy stones,
lying one on top of the other and so fashioned that they are broad in
the middle tapering to points at the ends. One end points upstream
and the other towards the sea since when the tide rises there is a
strong current heading inland.«

✶✶ Qufu

Hd 28

Province: Shandong   **Population:** 100,000
Altitude: 60 m/200 ft

**The home town of Confucius is the most honoured town in the
country. Countless attractions are linked to the master, who was
born here and buried in 479 BC.**

Sacrificial rite in honour of Confucius

Indeed, the master demands devotion. The worship of the sage man was the task of his direct male descendants, but as the times changed it was taken on as an imperial duty, too. The leaders of Confucius' family were given fine titles and material privileges. An imperial inscription of 1468 read »Since Confucius, more than ten dynasties have passed. However wise or unwise those rulers were, ... each of their reigns was based on his wisdom.. Thus the **ceremonies in his honour** grew ever more splendid and magnificent over time.« The temple buildings and furnishings for the Kong family grew correspondingly. The head of the clan held honorary positions as well as temple land and thousands of serfs. Hundreds of »purveyors to the imperial court« had to provide everything needed for the offertories as well as everything the Kong family needed to maintain their way of life: animals for slaughter, wine, cereal, music, fireworks, funeral songs and provision of draught horses. The residence also had hundreds of hereditary servants as well as a troop of guards and other staff to help with all the management The head of the clan, who had held the hereditary title of duke since 1055, would sit in judgement over all his »subjects« and also had much else to do with the sacrificial rites. Every year Confucius alone was celebrated with fifty festivals, large and small, and there were also regular sacrifices in the ancestor temple and at the tombs of the family's more direct antecedents. Other cult services were handled, too. All in all, the whole town and its surroundings were kept busy solely with organizing the sacrificial feasts.

VISITING QUFU

GETTING THERE

When Qufu was to be given a railway station in the early 20th century, the clan head campaigned against it. The peace of Confucius would have been disrupted, he claimed. Thus the main line from Beijing to Shanghai makes a loop around Qufu and stops at the station in Yanzhou, 16 km/9 mi to the west. To get to and from Tai'an (or the sacred mountain of Tai Shan, 80 km/50 mi) take a cross-country bus.

WHERE TO EAT

Qufu holds a night market all year round (actually an evening market), where it is possible to eat plain but very inexpensive food in atmospheric surroundings. It is on Wumaci Jie, an easterly continuation of the street on which the Queli Hotel stands.

▶ Moderate

① *Post Hotel Restaurant*
8 Gulou Beijie
Inexpensive tourist menus

WHERE TO STAY

▶ Mid-range

① *Queli Hotel (Queli Binshe)*
1 Queli Jie (directly to the east of the Confucius temple)
Tel. 05 37/48 66 818, Fax 48 66 524
Stylish 160-room hotel with its own theatre auditorium which tourist groups can book to see performances of classical Chinese music and dance.

Qufu (pronounced Chufu) is not to be missed but it can all be taken in no more than one day (with one overnight stop. Most of the places to see are close together, with the more distant ones accessible via rickshaw, taxi or rented bicycle.

Tours

✶ ✶ Temple of Confucius

The dimensions of this magnificent complex – 650 m/710 yd long – and the layout with two dozen gates, high halls and gnarled old trees reflect the dignity and grandeur which the cult services, for which the temple was built, sought to express and evoke. It is both the **largest and the oldest temple to Confucius on earth** and even today it can capture the breath of those visiting it with its atmosphere, even though the temple's entire inventory was destroyed during the Cultural Revolution.

🕐
Opening hours:
8am–5pm daily.

Make sure to avoid the side entrance. It is essential to pass through all the gates starting in the south to get an idea of the temple's dimensions. Even before the temple itself, the experience begins with the south gate of the former walls of the town, which is situated directly on the temple's axis. Even though it is not very high, it is still worth climbing to the top.

South gate

»The Clang of Metal and the Quivering of Jade« is written on the first of the eight gates that need to be entered in order to reach the first hall. The four characters refer to the **sacrificial music**. »Metal« means bells and »jade« refers to sounding (percussion) stones. The educated Confucians would have associated this with a text of the philosopher Mencius. It compares the sounding-stones perfection of Confucius himself with the harmonies of the ceremonial music, which begins with the sounding of bells and ends with the sound of the stones. Similar scholarship is behind the names given to each of the gates and halls. Before visiting the temple, then, a few years studying the Confucian classics would help.

First decorative gate

The »Gate of the Star-like One« from 1754, with its stone clouds around the pillars, is the entrance to the actual temple grounds. Two decorative gates follow with the inscriptions »Cosmic Creative Power« and »Temple of the Greatest Sage«. The »The Gate of the Timeliness of the Sage« leads to a second courtyard; which is divided up by the »Jade Belt River«, a culvert. In front of that to the left there is a pavilion with two stone figures from the Han period. The »Gate of the Mighty Dao« leads into the third courtyard.

Outer courtyards 1–3

Beyond the »Gate of the Golden Mean« and the »Gate of the Unity of the Script« on the northern side of the 4th court is the **Kuiwen Ge library**: The »literature studio of the dominant Kui luminary« is a magnificent, three-storey wooden building with a ground floor alleg-

4th court and library

edly dating back to 1191. Inside there is an exhibition of stone rubbings with scenes from the life of the great master. The fasting halls to the right in front of the library are where the clan leaders and other leading figures would go to gather before the great sacrificial ceremonies.

Column pavilions

The next (fifth) court contains 13 pavilions, which protect **53 imperial inscriptions** from damage by weathering. The oldest is from 672. To the right (the east) it is possible to leave the temple via the side entrances. Further north the complex splits into three sections. The left-hand wing functioned as a temple for Confucius' parents.

Main wing and courtyard

From the middle of the 5th court the »Gate of Great Perfection« leads to the central courtyard, which is surrounded by buildings all sides. After a fire in 1724, all the buildings around were reconstructed during the period up to 1730. In the course of the rebuilding the Yongzheng Emperor elevated the temple to a rank equivalent with his own and allowed it to have imperial yellow roofs.

Juniper

A single juniper tree stands to the right of the marble steps that lead into the main courtyard. The tree is said to have been planted by Confucius himself. The great fire of 1724 destroyed the tree but it is said that the stump started putting out shoots again in 1732. Honi soit qui mal y pense!

Apricot Terrace

In the middle of the courtyard there is a pavilion. Its name refers to an old text describing Confucius sitting in an elevated position under an apricot tree while his disciples play music around him.

Main hall

The grandiose centrepiece of the court is the »**Hall of Great Perfection**«, a building 47 m/51 yd wide and 27 m/89 ft high, fit to be the hall of a palace. Such magnificent stone columns wound round with dragon reliefs are something even the emperor himself did not possess. For that reason they were probably always draped in fabric when he paid a visit. One typical feature of all Confucius temples is the large terrace in front of the hall. This is where the sacrificial ceremonies took place. For the four greatest ceremonies of the year as many people as there are days in the year would gather by torchlight at midnight: masters of ceremonies, offertory servants, dancers and musicians. The necessary apparatus, bells, sounding stones, gongs, flutes, zithers, oboes, drums and all kinds of items for show were stored in the buildings at the sides. The sacrificial animals would be slaughtered and prepared in the temple's kitchens (at the northern end of the site). The innermost hall now displays replicas of its furnishings of those days. In a spectacular shrine in the middle sits the sage himself, surrounded by a group of similar shrines housing his disciples. This is because it was not only the great master and »first teacher« himself who was honoured here, but also his grandson, two

Splendid as a palace hall: thanks to an imperial privilege, the main hall of the Confucius Temple has had a yellow-tiled roof since 1730

of his disciples, his spiritual heir Mencius (Meng Zi) and twelve more of his followers.

Sleeping hall

Since Confucianism sees the family as the original pattern for order in society, a **temple for the wife of the sage** is situated a respectful distance away at the rear of the main hall on a shared pedestal. The arrangement followed the practice, common in ancient China, that the women's quarters would lie at the rear (north) of the premises.

Hall of the Memory of the Sage

The last hall, outside the main courtyard but still on the main axis, displays scenes from the master's life carved in stone. These are the same stones from which the much more easily recognized rubbings in the Kuiwen Ge have been made.

East wing

Among other things to be seen on this side of the complex are what are said to be the wells of Confucius' own house and a free-standing red wall. This is intended to be a reminder of a house wall that was demolished some 2000 years ago and in which the Analects of Confucius were found hidden from the wicked first emperor (▶Famous People p. 82), who had assembled copies from all over the empire and burned them.

Kong residence · Yan Miao

The residence of the Kong family was both the home of its clan leader and the administrative buildings of the ceremonial city. The dimensions of the complex; 280 m/306 yd long and up to 140 m/153 yd wide, indicate their importance. The individual buildings, though, are actually of quite modest size. All of them have just one storey so that they consciously avoid even a hint of attempting to rival the temple itself. Of the complex's three wings, the main one in the centre is most worth seeing.

Qufu Map

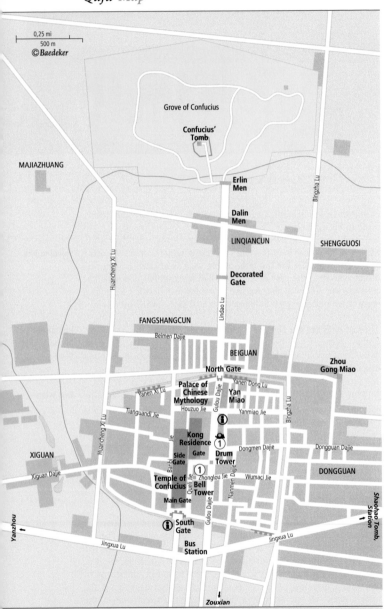

0,25 mi
500 m
©Baedeker

Grove of Confucius

Confucius' Tomb

MAJIAZHUANG

Erlin Men

Dalin Men

LINQIANCUN

SHENGGUOSI

Bingzha Lu

Decorated Gate

Huancheng Xi Lu

Lindao Lu

FANGSHANGCUN

Beimen Dajie

BEIGUAN

Zhou Gong Miao

North Gate

Palace of Chinese Mythology

Yanen Dong Lu

Gulou Dajie

Yan Miao

Yanen Xi Lu

Houzuo Jie

Yanmiao Jie

Tianguandi Jie

Bingzha Lu

Kong Residence

Dongmen Dajie

Dongguan Dajie

XIGUAN

Side Gate

Gate

Drum Tower

Zhonglou Jie

Wumaci Jie

DONGGUAN

Xiguan Dajie

Temple of Confucius

Bell Tower

Queli Jie

Namen Dajie

Gulou Dajie

Main Gate

South Gate

Jingxua Lu

Yanzhou

Bus Station

Jingxua Lu

Shaohao Tomb, Station

Zouxian

Where to stay
① Queli Hotel

Where to eat
① Post Hotel Restaurant

The outer gate leads to an outer courtyard from which both the main wing and the secondary wings can be accessed. Another gate straight ahead leads to the large main courtyard. Inside it is a closed **wooden gate**, which stands in the open. This was only opened for imperial emissaries bringing correspondence from Beijing or for a few other events of importance. The audience rooms for official receptions and for court sessions (with the appropriate apparatus) adjoin the court to the north.

Main wing, front section

Behind the third hall, a high wall with a gate that was customarily closed in earlier times brings the official parts of the residence to an end. Behind it are the women's chambers. Next to the gate is an opening in the wall through which water was poured every day into a basin behind it. This was formerly the only water that the women, and their servants and children, had for drinking and washing. In some of the rooms here, the furnishings have been preserved – the furniture of Chinese nobility in the 1920s and 30s with a few Western armchairs and grandfather clocks.

Women's chambers

Right at the rear there is a garden. The ensemble adjoins the northern part of the Confucius temple. Opening times: 8am–5pm daily.

The Yan Hui- temple (Yan Miao), a temple in honour of Confucius' favourite disciple, is a miniature version of the Confucius temple itself. Three gates are passed on the way to the innermost section. The last is called the »**Gate of Looking Up to the Sage**«, since the disciple now looks up to his teacher, Confucius. The equivalent of the Apricot Terrace here is the music pavilion (Yue Ting). Beyond the main hall there is a »sleeping hall« to honour Yan Hui's wife, too. Gulou Dajie (northeast of the Kong residence by the north gate of the old town). Opening times: 8am–5pm daily.

! *Baedeker* TIP

Alone in the temple
Would it not be good to have a temple to yourself for once (or almost)? This is possible in the temple of the Prince of Zhou, whom Confucius considered the embodiment of the perfect ruler. Practically no one comes to look at this place even though it is only a little smaller than the Yan Hui temple and just as dignified. Situated outside the northeast corner of the old town, it is easy to get to by rickshaw. Opening times: 8am–5pm daily.

✱ ✱ Confucius Grove (Kong Lin)

This huge overgrown cemetery, a virtual jungle, is bigger then the whole of the old town and is probably the oldest cemetery still in use anywhere in the world. Members of the Kong clan have been buried here since time immemorial, possibly as far back as the time of Confucius himself. Of course, the reason for coming is to see the great man's grave, but to leave the visit at that would be a big mistake. The city's administrators have had the brilliant idea of providing open-topped electric carts to transport visitors along the 3 km/2 mi perimeter path around the whole site. Their noiselessness, slow speed and lack of emissions make it possible to experience the **unique atmosphere** of the cemetery's woods, without needing to do a lot of walking. Even better, the electric carts stop at specific places, precisely where the graves of the clan leaders are, always featuring animal statues, stone honour gates, a stone altar and burial stele and nestling deep in shadow, overgrown, still as death and as mysterious. It is better still to be alone in the cemetery, when the birds call, when there is rustling in the undergrowth and the bright summer sunlight shines through the roof of foliage. Then you can stop where you like, by the new graves with their waving paper flowers, or by the moss-covered, stony witnesses of a vanished era.

The grave of Confucius There are two reasons why we can be thankful that the grave of Confucius himself is near the entrance (on the left): the must-see attraction is not far away, and the rest of the cemetery is spared all the tumult. In front of the grave stands a stone honour guard. The **burial mound of the sage** is rather inconspicuous and is indistinguishable from the two either side of it, those of his son and grandson. Two stone tablets are placed in front of the tomb with the larger hiding the smaller. Neither bears the master's name but rather his honorific, the later and longer title on the larger tablet, »Great Perfecter, Highest Saint, Culture-spreading King«. North of the old town. Opening times: 8am–5.30pm daily.

Shaohao tomb

A stone pyramid 18 m/59 ft high with a temple shrine on its truncated pinnacle. This is the unusual design of a tomb that is not a tomb at all, since this is the alleged resting place of the founding emperor, Shaohao, alleged ancestor of Confucius, whose existence is not historically supported but the **result of historical speculation**. Never mind, the tomb of the legendary ruler was started in 1012 and was modified to its present form in 1111. It is a nice place to go on a rickshaw trip. 4 km/2.5 mi east of the old town. Opening times: 8am–5pm daily.

Sanya

Gk 36

Province: Hainan
Altitude: Sea level

Population: 130,000

Tropical China: sandy beaches under coconut palms – that is what attracts ever more people especially from China and Russia to the south of the island province, Hainan, where a long holiday area extends away from China's most southerly town, Sanya.

What to see in and around Sanya

In spite of its attractive location on a sickle-shaped peninsula between the sea and the mouth of the Sanya River, the town centre has no real attractions to offer. For most visitors it is just a **way-station for getting to the beach**.

The biggest beach in town, 3 km/2 mi southeast of the centre, is the nearest place to enjoy a South Seas experience. It also features some first-class hotels and lots of restaurants along a shady car-free promenade, with a lot of music in the evening. The beach is overcrowded and the water full of plastic litter.

Dadonghai

To the east of Dadonghai this hilly peninsula stretches out into the South China Sea. On the summit at **Luhuitou Park** near the town – with its stunning panoramic view – there is a 12 m/39 ft monument recalling an old legend. Once there was a young hunter belonging to the Li people, who was driving a stag ahead of him. When the animal reached the end of the promontory, there was no way of escape for it. At that moment the young man aimed to let his arrow fly, but the stag turned its head towards him and turned into a young woman. The two ended up marrying and lived happily ever after. This is how the peninsula got the name Luhuitou, meaning »Stag Head Turns«.

Luhuitou Peninsula

The reasons for a trip to Sanya are obvious: palms, beach and the sea

▶ VISITING SANYA

GETTING THERE

The airport to the west of the town has flights from all of China's major cities, from Hong Kong and from southeast Asia.

High-speed buses to the provincial capital of Haikou take three hours by motorway. Buses also run from Sanya's bus station (Jiefang Lu) to all the major destinations on the island (including Wuzhishan Shi) and to various beaches.

INFORMATION

The many travel agents clustered around the beach of Dadonghai provide information about tours and day trips and, of course, they can also be booked from there.

SHOPPING

Pleasant souvenirs include tropical shells and necklaces of coral or glass beads; they can be bought on the beaches.

Potential buyers of cultured pearls should watch out that they are not just purchasing painted plastic. At open-air stalls haggling is the order of the day, and a rule of thumb is never to pay more than a quarter of the price originally demanded. Among the nicest souvenirs are the fabrics made by the Li people.

WHERE TO EAT

The eateries present a rich selection of fish and other seafood in water tanks. A particularly nice place to sit is on the promenade at Dadonghai, where wine can be bought by the bottle. Eateries without a sea-view are cheaper and often better. The tropical fruit and fruit-juices are delicious.

WHERE TO STAY

▶ Luxury

Sheraton Sanya Resort (Sanya Xilaidun)
Yalong Bay
Tel. 08 98/88 55 88 55
Fax 08 98/88 55 88 66
www.sheraton.com
Five-star comfort at the west end of Yalong Bay near the golf course. All 511 rooms have a free DSL connection.

▶ Mid-range

Landscape Beach Hotel (Lijing Haiwan Jiudian)
Dadonghai
Tel. 08 98/88 22 85 56
Fax 08 98/88 22 85 66
www.sanyaliking.com
A pleasant holiday hotel (200 rooms with balcony) at the west end of the beach somewhat away from all the bustle, but still with direct access to the beach and promenade.

Wuzhishan shi: Lüyou Sahanzhuang
Hebeishanzhuang Lu
Tel. 08 99/ 86 62 31 88
Fax 08 99/86 62 22 16
Three-star hotel with 110 rooms in a nice location north of the river.

▶ Budget

Sanya Eagle Backpackers Hostel (Sanya Beibaoke Lüguan)
Haitian Huiyuang Building 1206B20
Dadonghai Xincun
Yuya Dadao 96, Dadonghai
Tel. 0139/ 76 97 79 24
A youth hostel on the 12th floor of a skyscraper? But the location near the beach is no less enticing than the friendly management. Free internet, and the sixth night is free. English spoken.

Following the beach south from Luhuitou Park leads to the smaller and less crowded beach of Xiaodonghai.

Xiaodonghai beach

From Sanya a broad sandy bay extends 20 km/12 mi westwards as far as a spot called **»World's End«**. No Chinese tourist leaves Sanya without going here, although anyone who is not Chinese would do best to keep away. The tumult is immense, there are dozens of small traders harrying people all the way and the admission price is shameless. All that can be seen are a few large, rounded bits of rock poking up out of the sand. A local imperial official under the last dynasty once had two characters (tianya) carved into them, which mean the »end of the world«. Two more characters in another rock read haijiao, »edge of the World Sea«, and another four-character inscription reads: »Pillars of the Southern Sea of Heaven«.

Tianya Haijiao

It is worth taking a trip out into the mountainous homeland of the Li people, 75 km/47 mi north of Sanya. The peaceful town of Wuzhishan Shi (pop. 100,000) is at the confluence of two rivers, surrounded by fields and tropical rain forest. The bus continues to Shuimanxiang, a village of the Li and Miao at the foot of the Five Finger Mountain (Wuzhi Shan). An unmade path leads steeply up through the jungle to the 1867 m / 6070 ft summit (mountain guide needed). More about the culture of the minority ethnic groups can be found out in the museum of ethnography in Wuzhishan Shi (Minzu Bowuguan, near the bus station). Opening times: Tue–Sun 8am–5pm.

Wuzhishan Shi

✱ Yalong Bay

22 km/14 mi east of Sanya is this dream beach, 7 km/4 mi of dazzling white sands with the most luxurious holiday hotels on the island. There is glorious selection of watersports activities available: swimming, snorkelling, jet-ski riding or sailing with the banana boat. Divers will be drawn to the nearby coral reef. In the west there is an 18-hole golf course – one of more than a dozen now in existence on Hainan. The hefty green fee of 850 yuan is an indication of the price levels around the bay.

For a rather different experience from lying in the sun, swimming or water-skiing, visit the **»Seashell Museum«**, which has more than 300 shell varieties on display from all the world's seas. It is situated beneath the Yalong central square (Zhongxin Guangchang). Opening times: daily 8am–6pm.

Shell exhibition

Butterfly Valley is a shady rain-forest valley covering 1.5 ha/4 acres, where it is possible to view countless species of butterfly. In addition there is an exhibition of pinned specimens. Hainan is the Chinese province with largest number of butterfly species. In the northeast behind the Cactus Resort. Opening times: 7.30am–5.50pm.

Butterfly Valley

★★ Shanghai

Province: Shanghai
Altitude: 0 – 100 m/ 330 ft

Population: approx. 18 million

Practically everyone has some vision they associate with the name of the city on the Huangpu, the final tributary of the Yangtze before its flows into the sea. Films and novels have spread its fame far and wide, especially as it was in the 1920s and 1930s before the Japanese arrived in 1937. Shanghai was China's luxury store and its Babylon of sin, safe haven for the persecuted and the adventurous from all over the globe and for China's own revolutionaries and refugees from the land, who often discovered that it was not their fortunes that they found here but jobs sweating at workbenches or lugging great weights as coolies. Many of them even landed up in the gutters.

The city's name has even ended up as a verb in the English language. To be shanghaied meant waking up with a splitting headache as an unwilling sailor on a ship already in mid-ocean. Its image as a place of lawless greed and fabulous wealth still lives on to an extent in the minds of those who come here, even if they know that what awaits them is something quite different: a metropolis with more than 18 million inhabitants, which has only just begun to reinvent itself in recent years – with skyscrapers, inner-city motorways, elegant bars, super luxury hotels and assured worldliness – the showpiece of Chinese reform politics, on its way to becoming the **world capital of the 21st century**. Shanghai enjoys little sympathy though, its populace having a reputation in China for being snooty and money-grubbing.

A world of its own

Foreign visitors to Shanghai know that it is not exactly classical China that awaits them here. In fact the city is in a world of its own. The things that matter here are different from anywhere else in the country. Here people look to the future, not the past. Nevertheless, not only is Shanghai's identity part of what makes China Chinese, China is also a part of what makes Shanghai Shanghai. Here it is unmistakable that China matters again in the world. In addition, the city's temples, the Yu Garden and the wonderful Shanghai Museum also provide attractions for those with little taste for skyscrapers and motorways.

City of traders, pirates and workers

Shanghai is not a very old city. 2000 years ago this spot was out in the ocean – the land only coming into being later as a result of sedimentation deposited by the Yangtze at its mouth. The actual history of the city starts in the Tang period, when it was an anchorage for

← *A game of mah jongg in Shanghai*

The skyline of Pudong

coastal shipping. The **founding of a Confucian temple** in 1294 provides the first documentary evidence that an important town was emerging.

1294	Founding of a Confucian temple
1554/1555	Building of the city walls
1842	Treaty of Nanjing
1927	Bloody suppression of the workers' movement
1937	Occupation by the Japanese army
1949	Entry of the People's Liberation Army
1990s	Establishment of the special economic zone of Pudong

In the Ming era Shanghai prospered so much that it became a major target for pirate attacks. This led to the building of city walls in 1554/55. The Yu Garden, created shortly afterwards, also testifies to the prosperity of that time. When the Treaty of Nanjing opened Shanghai to overseas trade in 1842 and foreigners began to settle outside the »Chinese city«, a whole new chapter of the city's development began. Thanks to its location at the mouth of the Yangtze, the turnover in goods soon overtook that of all other Chinese ports. By 1870, 70% of all China's foreign trade was being handled via Shang-

hai. Investments by both Chinese and foreign businessmen caused the city to grow into China's biggest industrial centre from the late 19th century. This predestined it to be the **birthplace of the Chinese workers' movement**. Social and political conflict dominated the years before its bloody suppression 1927. At that time Shanghai had 2.5 million inhabitants (including the greater area) and was one of the biggest cities on earth. Its »golden age« ended in 1937 with its occupation by the Japanese army. In 1949 the People's Liberation Army entered the city and foreigners fled. From then on Beijing sucked all the wealth gained here out of the city. That was the situation until the beginning of the 1990s when the establishment of the special economic zone of Pudong heralded a whole new era.

Shanghai's street grid is not very regular. On the western bank of the Huangpu an oval of streets frames the city inside of the former city walls. North of there as far as Yan'an Donglu – previously known as Edward VII Avenue – the French concession stretched away from the river towards the west and some of the way around the old town. The flair of the former Avenue Joffre (now Huaihai Lu), in particular, led to Shanghai gaining its nickname as the **»Paris of the Orient«**. To the north the French concession was adjoined by the international lease zone, with Nanjing Lu as its main axis. Pudong was the name of the territory to the east of the Huangpu, while Puxi corresponded to old Shanghai on the west bank. The name Shanghai itself means »Up Out of the Sea«.

»Up out of the sea«

Highlights Shanghai

✳ ✳ Bund (Waitan)

The Anglo-Indian word »bund«, which means a fortified shoreline, has since the 19th century been the name given to the former French concession on the east bank of the Huangpu, which is now occupied by branches of international companies. It was extended in 1992 and made into a splendid harbour promenade. Now, more than ever, it is the **hub for any visit to Shanghai**. The two oft-photographed faces of the city look down on those walking by, the colonial face in the west, now under protection as a heritage site and the futuristic face, reaching for the sky on the opposite bank. Walking from south to north, the following buildings particularly catch the eye:

Former Shanghai Club
The 1910 clubhouse was built in British neo-Renaissance style with six Ionic columns in its façade. It was alleged to have the longest bar in the world at 33.7 m/37 yd. The club, founded in 1864, did not admit women or Chinese. 2 Zhongshan Dong-Yi Lu.

Old Observatory
To the side of the promenade stands the former observatory, a small building with a minaret-like tower, which served as a **signalling tower**, warning of a typhoon for example. Inside some historic photographs of the Bund are now on display.

Former Hong Kong and Shanghai Banking Corporation
The massive building with the dome is an eye-catcher among this row of buildings. It was built in 1921 as the local **headquarters of the HSBC**, now one of the biggest banks in the world. Between 1949

● VISITING SHANGHAI

GETTING THERE

Shanghai has two airports, the very chic Pudong International Airport by the sea right in the east and the older Hongqiao Airport in the west, which, being relatively near to the city, mainly deals with inland flights. Airport buses link both to the city centre, while Pudong Airport is also linked via a maglev railway to the underground network (line M2, Longyang Lu). Trains run from Shanghai's main railway station in the north of the city to all the provincial capitals of China and to Beijing.

INFORMATION

Shanghai Tourist Information
561 Nanjing Donglu
Tel. 021/64 39 89 47
www.meet-in-shanghai.net

Other information bureaux:
At the underground interchanges, »Railway Station« (south exit) and »People's Square«, at Hongqiao Airport and at 149 Jiujiaochang Lu next to the Yu-Garten, at 1612 Nanjing Xilu and 561 Nanjing Donglu.

CITY MAGAZINES

Cultural reporting, event information and addresses are published in the monthly city magazine »That's Shanghai« (www.thatsh.com) and the fortnightly paper »City Weekend«. Both can be obtained from restaurants, bars and hotels for free.

TRANSPORT

Buses
Without knowing the language, Shanghai's buses are difficult to use. The exception is route 911 (Hongqiao Lu–Huaihai Lu–Renmin Lu).

Underground Shanghai Metro
Lines M1 and M2, which cross People's Square, are the core services of the underground network. The Pearl Line runs above ground in an arc around the centre. Entrances can be identified by a large red M on a white background. Stations are announced in English and their names are also printed in roman script.

Taxi
All journeys are calculated via the taximeter. The all-in price for the first 3 km/2mi is 10 yuan, then every kilometre afterward costs another 2 yuan or beyond 10 km/6 mi 3 yuan. At night the fares are higher.

Tourist buses
Bus operators offer guided tours in English, but they are so expensive (USD 50 and more) that for two people it is better and cheaper to hire a taxi for half a day or a day and enjoy the advantage of total flexibility. Green buses run every day from about 6.30am from Shanghai Stadium to the day-trip destinations around the city (1200 Zhongshan Nanlu, no. 2, Underground line M1: Shanghai Indoor Stadium, Pearl Line: Caoxi Lu).

Harbour tours
Tourist boats dock on the Bund (level with Yan'an Donglu) and offer one-hour trips around the harbour in the mornings and evenings as well as three-hour trips to the Yangtze delta, as well as evening trips, for prices between 40 and 120 yuan.

GOING OUT

Bund
In the renovated colonial palaces along the Bund, glamorous bars and

restaurants have been coming into being. In »Bar Rouge« chandeliers made of red Murano glass put the haute volée into champagne mood (18 Zhongshan Dong Yilu, 7/F, www.restro18.com).

Face and Maoming Lu

Face is a bar in a colonial villa, romantically situated in Ruijin Park (118 Ruijin Erlu, Building. 4). Around the corner, on the once famed drinking boulevard of Maoming Lu, it has become a little quieter but the »House of Blues and Jazz« is still a popular meeting place for jazz enthusiasts and has jam sessions on Sunday nights (no. 158).

Hengshan Lu

A street of restaurants, pubs and discos like »Real Love« (no. 10). The over-30s can drink their beer with fine service at »Sasha's«, a 1920s villa. Its garden is famous in summer (9 Dongping Lu). To rock the night away, go across the courtyard to »Zapata's«. At Ladies' Night on Wednesdays with its »free flow of margaritas« till midnight, people happily dance on the bar (5 Hengshan Lu). It is cosier around the corner in »O`Malley's«. Beer gardens and pubs are popular places for foreigners to go to drink a Guinness, watch some sport or play darts, just as they are anywhere else in the world (42 Taojiang Lu).

Tongren Lu

Here the pub scene is beginning to flourish with new places overflowing from Maoming Lu like the »Blue Frog« (no. 86). The club »Mint« is very popular. Inside the elite villa in Bauhaus style (1937), there is a chance to let rip dancing to electronic pop and house (no. 333).

THEATRE/CONCERTS

Shanghai Concert Hall

523 Yan'an Donglu
Tel. 021/63 86 28 36
www.shanghaiconcerthall.org
M1/M2: People's Square
Neo-Renaissance building (1931) with marvellous acoustics. It reopened in 2004 after being moved about 66 metres/72 yds. The Shanghai Philharmonic play here.

Shanghai Grand Theater

300 Renmin Da Dao
Tel. 021/63 72 87 01/2
www.shgtheatre.com
Ensembles from home and abroad stage concerts, opera and ballet.

Shanghai Oriental Art Centre

425 Dingxiang Lu
Tel. 021/64 33 35 74
www.sh-symphony.com
M2: Science and Technology Museum
Astonishing architecture and superb acoustics provide a backdrop for world-class performances.

It's never boring in Shanghai

SHOPPING

Nanjing Lu is China's best known shopping street. Since 1934 it has been the address of Store no. 1 (no. 830), as ever the premier place to go for foreign luxury goods. Extravagant needs are catered for in Plaza 66 at no. 1266. Cultural desires are covered on Fuzhou Lu. That is where the shops for painting and drawing accessories are clustered, e.g. Shanghai Fine Arts Articles Shop (no. 402), and many bookshops including the Foreign Languages Bookstore (no. 390) with its selection of English-language books on China. In the cloth market cheap fabrics are available in three storeys (important: haggle and watch out for faults). On the ground floor there are ready-made articles (399 Lujiabing Lu, corner of Nankang Lu, M4 Nanpu Danjiao). At the Yu bazaar, souvenirs, jewellery, tea and home-made art are all on offer. The shops in the style of the Qing dynasty on Fangbang Lu are nice. Antiques and curiosities can be sought out in the four-storey antique market (457 Fangbang Lu). At the weekends there is an indoor flea market there. Finding something is guaranteed at the Dongtai Lu antique market on the corner of Dongtai Lu and Liuhe Lu. From there it is not far either to Xintiandi with its high-class shops which put a modern interpretation on Chinese craft products and established patterns, e.g. at Shanghai Trio (181 Taicang Lu, Unit 1, Building. 1, for colourful textiles and accessories) and Shanghai Tang (181 Taicang Lu, no. 15, for simply wonderful clothes). On Taicang Lu artists, designers and fashion creators have formed a quarter of their own. One of the first was the photographic shop of Deke Erh and the corresponding gallery (210 Space Lane, no. 2). The small, lively quarter with galleries, boutiques, cafés and pubs is a bit shabby, though.

WHERE TO EAT
► Expensive
① *Club Jin Mao*
Jin Mao Tower, 88 Shiji Dadao
Tel. 021/50 47 12 34
M2: Lujiazui
On the 86th floor of this skyscraper the panoramic view of the city is breathtaking, the art-deco ambience is overwhelming and the Shanghai delicacies are exquisite.

② *M on the Bund*
20 Guangdong Lu, 7/F
Tel. 021/63 50 99 88
M2: Henan Zhong Lu
Mediterranean-style feasting with a view of the Bund to enjoy. Nice for a coffee on the terrace.

③ *Yè Shanghai*
338 Huangpi Nanlu (Xintiandi)
Tel. 021/63 11 23 23
M2: Huangpi Nanlu
Creative Shanghai cuisine in a very pleasant, modern Asian ambience. It is pleasant to sit downstairs and see the view of the alleys of Xintiandi

► Moderate
④ *Element Fresh*
Shanghai Center Room 112
1376 Nanjing Xilu
M2: Jing'an Temple
Fresh, light cuisine for health-conscious young business people. A sunny terrace and a nice breakfast after 7am with tasty salad and »smoothies« made of fresh fruit.

⑤ *Nanxiang Steamed Bun Restaurant*
85 Yuyuan Lu, 1st floor
Tel. 021/63 55 42 06
Popular dumpling eatery next to the

Yu Garden. The only way to avoid the long queues is to book well in advance.

⑥ *People 6*
150 Yueyang Lu
Tel. 021/64 66 05 05
M1: Hengshan Lu
Even the entrance springs a surprise in this ultra-modern restaurant with good cuisine.

▶ **Inexpensive**
⑦ *Bi Feng Tang*
1333 Nanjing Xilu
M2: Jing'an Temple
A restaurant chain aiming at a folk feel, charming, cheap and good. Colourful illumination at night.

⑧ *Seagull Sightseeing Restaurant*
60 Huangpu Lu (terrace by the river behind the Seagull Hotel)
Good for a snack or a beer in the evening with a superb view of the Bund, the Pudong and the ships on the Huangpu.

⑨ *Zao Zi Shu – Jujube Tree*
77 Songshan Lu
Tel. 021/63 84 80 00
M1: Huangpi Nan Lu
Fresh and carefully prepared dishes in spartan surroundings.

WHERE TO STAY
▶ **Luxury**
① *88 Xintiandi*
380 Huangpi Lu
Tel. 021/53 83 88 33
Fax 021/53 83 88 77
www.88xintiandi.com
M1: Huangpi Nanlu
Small hotel in an orientally inspired, high-class style. 53 tastefully designed rooms, some of them with a view of the garden.

② *Anting Villa Hotel*
46 Anting Lu
Tel. 021/64 33 11 88
Fax 021/64 33 97 26
M1: Hengshan Lu
Charming hotel in the French quarter with 146 very quiet rooms, 40 of which are in a villa in a park with old cedars

③ *Heng Shan Moller Villa*
30 Shaanxi Nanlu
Tel. 021/62 47 88 81
Fax 021/62 89 10 20
www.mollervilla.com
M1: Shaanxi Nanlu
Enchanting fairy-tale castle dating from 1939 with eleven grand suites and 34 sunlit rooms inside a new building in the rear courtyard. Ask for a room facing the garden.

④ *Grand Hyatt Shanghai*
Jinmao Tower, 88 Shiji Dadao
Tel. 021/50 49 12 34
Fax 021/50 49 11 11
www.shanghai.grand.hyatt.com
The tallest hotel in the world, in the Jin Mao Tower, offers every luxury imaginable on floors 53 to 87 – and an outstanding view of Shanghai.

▶ **Mid-range/Budget**
Can anyone live cheaply in Shanghai? Not without moving in with friends. Nevertheless, there are a couple of exceptions, especially if a dormitory bed is sufficient.

⑤ *Hanting Hotel*
233 Shaanxi Nanlu
Tel. 021/54 65 66 33
Fax 021/54 65 68 33
This modern 104-room mid-range hotel opened in 2006. Its advantages are its relative cheapness by Shanghai standards, and its location in the old French quarter. It's just a short walk

Room with a view: the Grand Hyatt in Shanghai

from Maoming Lu with its restaurants and bars.

⑥ Captain Hostel
37 Fuzhou Lu
Tel. 021/63 23 50 53
Fax 021/63 21 93 31
www.captainhostel.com.cn
M2: Henan Zhong Lu
This friendly hostel is popular with travellers from all over the world. 22 sunlit rooms and a suite. 12 dormitories and berths with portholes. Bar

and roof garden with fine views of the river and Pudong.

⑦ YMCA Hotel
123 Xizang Nan Lu
(Tibet Road South)
Tel. 021/63 26 10 40, fax 63 20 19 57
www.ymcahotel.com
M1: People's Square
M2: People's Park
Built in 1929 in Chinese style, centrally located accommodation with 165 rooms and a dormitory.

and 1995 the building was used as a town hall but now it once again houses a bank. The restored telling hall is worth seeing. 12 Zhongshan Dong-Yi Lu.

The »Customs House« comes immediately afterwards, distinguishable by its clock tower. The imperial customs office had been under foreign control since the 1850s. This was its headquarters. The 1927 building is now the headquarters of the Shanghai customs administration. 13 Zhongshan Dong-Yi Lu.

Shanghai Map

Where to eat

① Club Jin Mao
② M on the Bund
③ Yè Shanghai
④ Element Fresh
⑤ Nanxiang Steamed Bun Restaurant
⑥ People 6
⑦ Bi Feng Tang
⑧ Seagull Sightseeing Restaurant
⑨ Zao Zi Shu-Jujube Tree

Where to stay

① 88 Xintiandi
② Anting Villa Hotel
③ Heng Shan Moller Villa
④ Grand Hyatt
⑤ Captain Hostel
⑥ Hanting Hotel
⑦ YMCA Hotel

Palace Hotel

On the corner of Nanjing Lu (Nanking Road) is the former Palace Hotel, built in 1906. it is now used as the south wing of the Peace Hotel opposite, so that it has retained its intended use to this day. 19 Zhongshan Dong-Yi Lu.

Sassoon House (Peace Hotel)

Another distinctive building, marked out by the pyramid on its roof, is Sassoon House. Built in 1928, it originally housed the luxurious Cathay Hotel. No other hotel in the city can boast such an **illustrious list of guests**. Some of its former glory still rubs off on the Peace Hotel, to the latter's profit. The building got its name, though, from the man who commissioned it, Ellice Victor Sassoon, whose grandfather Elias was the son of a Jewish merchant from Baghdad. Elias came to Shanghai in 1844 and made his fortune here. Ellice Victor became one of Shanghai's most important property magnates. He lived in the penthouse and enjoyed the best view in the whole city. 20 Zhongshan Dong-Yi Lu.

Bank of China

The Bank of China is a monument to the power of money. Completed in 1936, the building documents the increased self-confidence of the Chinese Republic. The main structure has an international look – not unlike its contemporary, the Empire State Building in New York. The roof, however, corresponds to the national style of China. The bank belonged to the financial empire of H. H. Kung (Kong Xiangxi), brother-in-law of Chiang Kaishek and the richest man in all China. His inflationary policies in the years following 1945 laid the foundations for the collapse of the republic.

Huangpu Park

The Bund ends in front of **Waibaidu Qiao** bridge (formerly the Garden Bridge) in a park which has unfortunately lost its river view following the building of the modern promenade. This was the location of the oft-cited sign »No dogs or Chinese«. The confluence of Suzhou He (»Soochow Creek«) with the Huangpu is the site of the **Monument to the Heroes of the People**.

Nanking Road, Nanjing Lu

Shanghai's **famous shopping street** turns off from the Bund at the Peace Hotel as a rather narrow side street. A long section (from Henan Lu to Xizang Lu) was turned into a pedestrian area when the underground railway was built. The architecture is a mixture of new and old. Underground line M2 Henan Zhong Lu and People's Park.

People's Park, People's Square

The land formerly occupied by the racecourse on Nanjing Lu is now where Shanghai puts on its best face: the People's Park in the north, People's Square to the south. The former Jockey Club at the west end of the park houses the Art Museum (daily 9am–5pm, last admissions 4pm). In the middle of the park is the glass palace of the Museum of Contemporary Art (daily 10am–6pm, Thur to 10pm). Underground 1/2/8 People's Square.

This popular meeting point is the **centre of Shanghai civic life**: in the middle of its northern side is the city hall, with the Urban Planning Exhibition Hall to the right of it and the Grand Theatre on the left, built in 1998 to a design by the French architect Jean Marie Charpentier, and also called the Opera House, though the building does not boast its own resident ensemble. A solitary building faces these three across the square, the Shanghai Museum. Underground line M1 People's Square, M2 People's Park.

People's Square

Shanghai past and future. The vast **model of the city** on the 4th floor of the Urban Planning Exhibition Hall (Chengshi Guihua Zhanlanguan) is spectacular. The museum also offers an insight into the gigantic development projects outside of the city's core. The plans for Expo 2010 are also on display. In the basement, which can be entered free from outside, the mood is nostalgic: there a replica of an old Shanghai street has been built. Opening times: Mo–Thur 9am–4pm, Fr–Sun 9am–5pm.

✴
Urban Planning Exhibition Hall

✴ ✴ Shanghai Museum

Shanghai Museum is one of the best museums in the world for classical Chinese art. The architecturally distinctive building, opened in

The Shanghai Museum is one of the best in China

1996, itself makes reference to ancient Chinese symbology. The circle represents heaven, the square is the earth. However the »handle« jars somewhat, in that in conjunction with the ornamentation of the façade it gives building the look of a bronze pot. Nevertheless what has emerged is something unmistakably Chinese. Inside the treasures are effectively presented. The well written audio guides are worth using.

Collections The main things to see on an initial visit are the departments devoted to **bronze vessels of the Shang and Zhou eras** (1st floor), pottery and porcelain (2nd floor) and jade items (4th floor). The pieces are arranged chronologically so that it is possible to get an excellent idea of the development of styles and changes in taste over the course of the centuries. Lovers of paintings will find ink paintings and calligraphy on the 3rd floor. Other things to see include sculptures (burial items and Buddhist art) on the 1st floor, seals on the 3rd floor and the art of »national minorities«, furniture and coins on the 4th floor. The 2nd floor is where special exhibitions are held. Anyone needing a rest in the meantime can retire to the tea lounge on the 1st floor.

Museum shop On the ground floor the best museum shop in all China can be found. There are some outstanding – but for that reason not very cheap – replicas of classical art and a superbly stocked department of ⊕ books on art. Opening times Shanghai-Museum: daily 9am–5pm (last admission 4pm), internet: www.shanghaimuseum.net.

✱ Xintiandi

Ultra-chic restaurant and shopping district south of the People's Park, primarily consisting of gutted old buildings with restored façades. There is a pedestrian zone so that it is possible to enjoy a cappuccino outdoors in relative quiet. Taicang Lu, Huangpi Nanlu, Underground line M1 Huangpi Nanlu.

Memorial to the Founding of the Communist Party On the same block is the spot where on 23rd July 1921 a **conspiratorial meeting** led to the founding of a new political party, the Communist Party of China. One of the 13 participants was Mao Zedong. In the present day memorial, the conference room, photographs and ⊕ documents are all on view. 76 Xingye Lu. Opening times: 9am to 5pm daily (last admission 4pm).

Shikumen Open House Shikumen Open House is a small and nicely designed museum of life in Shikumen houses, a type of building which dominated Shanghai in the 20th century until the rebuilding of the city began. The emergence of the Xintiandi is explained, too, and a tea lounge provides a ⊕ place to rest. Taicang Lu, Lane 181, no. 25. Opening times: Sun–Thu 10.30am–10.30pm, Fri & Sat 11am–11pm.

✳ Old Town · Yu Yuan Garden

This is the part of Shanghai which existed before the foreigners arrived at the end of the Opium War. But be careful, buildings from those days are the exception rather than the rule. The kind of old-town feel one might hope for is virtually non-existent these days. Visitors practically never go beyond the northern part with the Yu Yuan Garden, the Huxin Ting tea house, the temple to the city god and the new bazaar buildings, which seek to spread some **old Shanghai ambience**, although they are much too big to do that.

This was the spiritual centre of old Shanghai and the focal point of business and development. It was ravaged in the Cultural Revolution but afterwards the interior of the temple was rebuilt. There a variety of protective patrons are on view, including the 60 gods of the years in the passage hall. The red-faced **image of the city god**, who was responsible for the well being of the community, stands in the final hall, accompanied by a shrine for his wife and one for his parents. Opening times: 8.30am–4pm daily.

Temple to the city god (Chenghuang Miao)

🕐

The experience of the garden begins even before the gate. The famous zigzag bridge, running diagonally over a pond, provides entry to perhaps the best-known Chinese tea house, the »**Mid-Lake Pavilion**« **Huxin Ting**. Shanghai's own residents are hardly ever to be

Yu Yuan Garden: pond and tea house

Huxing Ting tea house

found there as the prices are too high for them. As a visitor to the city, though, the chance to rest amid atmospheric surroundings enjoying fine tea served with snacks is not to be missed..

The garden, its creation and development
Until the 19th century, the pond and the tea pavilion belonged to the »Garden of Satisfaction«, the main gate of which presently stands to the north of the tea house. It came into being from of 1559 as a place of rest for a high official. Its subsequent history is full of changes of ownership, dereliction, decay, makeovers, changes of use and forced repossession. Twice in the 19th century foreign soldiers were even stationed here. In 1875, 21 guilds purchased the land and divided it among them so that they could build their assembly halls. From 1956 to 1961 the Yu Yuan Garden was reconstructed with government funds and reopened.

Design
As can be seen from the statuary (ornamentation of the roofs, dragon walls etc.), the merchants who redesigned the gardens in the 19th century made it rustic and sometimes actually braggadocian. They were able to spend more money than an imperial official was normally able to amass so nothing was spared in terms of gardening and architectural effects. Here the full palette of design features of Chinese garden landscaping was self-confidently put on show. In this sense the Yu Yuan site is **not a scholar's garden** (not least because nobody lived here after the 19th century either), although the concepts and ideals of such places are certainly reflected in many of its aspects.

Three Ears Hall
The hall directly behind the entrance has a name that calls to mind profit and wealth, three ears of corn on one stalk. It was built in 1760 as the assembly hall of the then owners association comprising rich merchants and officials.

Rocky hill
The two-storey building at the rear with its multiple-pointed double roof was built in 1866 over a lily and goldfish pond. Across the water an artificial rocky hill catches the eye. It is the only thing that actually remains of the original 17th-century garden and is indeed the only surviving piece of work by the famous garden architect, **Zhang Nanyang**. The peculiar feature of it is that it consists of yellow stone. When the garden was being prettied up for prestige reasons in the 19th century, white stones were used on the right – a striking incongruity. The **»Pavilion with a River View«** on the top of the hill once genuinely lived up to its name.

Double colonnade
Along the pond and then to the right there is a double colonnade, an apt example of **architectural humour** If two people split up so that one goes right and the other left, they continually see each other through the windows but never meet until the colonnade comes to an end.

In the eastern part of the garden, where the colonnade comes out, there are more ponds, a bamboo grove and several halls. The space in front of the hall, roughly in the middle, is adorned with three conspicuous garden stones. They are arranged symmetrically but, since they are natural objects and inherently asymmetrical in themselves, the overall appearance is not symmetric at all, another designers' joke. The middle stone bears the name **»Jade Exquisite«** and is among the most famous garden stones in China. It is so perforated it looks like an oversized sponge.

Garden stones

> ## !   *Baedeker* TIP
>
> ### Raindrop music
>
> True garden lovers go to Yu Yuan when it is raining. Then it is not only less crowded, but those who do come can hear what the banana trees are for. They are not for enjoying the fruit but for the sonorous »plop« of raindrops falling on the big leaves.

A gate in the south wall of the eastern section leads to the **Inner Garden**, which was not originally part of the Yu Yuan garden but belonged to the temple of the city god next door. It is small and especially dense with growth. It also possesses a pretty theatre stage. Opening times: 8.30am–5pm daily.

✴ Pudong

Shanghai's new world. The finance and hotel district on the right bank of the Huangpu may not yet be a match for downtown Manhattan but its vertical dimensions already are. The rest is probably just a matter of time.

From the jetty where Yan'an Donglu meets the Bund, ferries cross to the other side of the river. A continuation of Nanjing Lu leads through the **»Sightseeing Tunnel«** to the other side – a psychedelic experience that doesn't come for nothing. Those coming from further away can take the Underground line M2 to Lujiazui.

Links

At 468 m/1404 ft the tower dominates the futuristic quarter opposite the Bund. Also eye-catching are the pagoda-like Jin Mao Tower and the 492 m/1614 ft World Financial Center, China's highest building, completed in 2008. Nevertheless the best view of the city is from the Oriental Pearl Tower, which is distinctive in every respect and easily recognized. The main structure consists of three concrete tubes 9 m/ 30 ft across, which pass through two large spheres. In addition, there are some smaller spheres on the three other supports as well as on the spire. The **main observation platform** is inside the uppermost of the three large spheres at a height of 263 m/863 ft. Above that there is a revolving restaurant. At 350 m/1148 ft; there is another observation platform in one of the smaller spheres. Opening times: 8.30am–9.30 pm daily.

✴
Oriental Pearl Tower

Shanghai History Museum

🕐

In the building at the base of the tower the city's history is being brought back to life: trade and development, work and pleasure, glory and misery, all presented in easily understood fashion. Even the sounds of the city can be heard. Opening times: 9am–9pm daily.

✳ Jin Mao Tower

What is currently the second-tallest building in the city (420 m/ 1378, 88 storeys) is also the most architecturally interesting as an attempt, regarded by most as successful, to adapt the Chinese brick pagoda style to steel and glass. The design came from the American architectural bureau Skidmore, Owing & Merrill. At the bottom there are offices, while the upper floors, above the 53rd floor, are occupied by the **Grand Hyatt Hotel**, which possesses an atrium 33 floors high. The observation floor is on the 88th storey. Shiji Dadao 88.

> ❗ *Baedeker* TIP
>
> **Panoramic drink**
> The 70 yuan you will have to shell out to visit to the observation platform of the Jin Mao Tower is better spent by taking advantage of the gastronomic facilities of the Grand Hyatt Hotel, e.g. for an evening drink in the Cloud Nine bar on the 87th floor.

Jade Buddha Temple

Of the few temples in Shanghai the Jade Buddha Temple (Yufo Si) in the northwest of town is the most interesting, although it only came into being in its present form between 1918 and 1928 and its historic roots only go back to 1880. It was then that a Chinese monk came back from Burma with two jade Buddhas. He quickly found some devout benefactors willing to provide a suitable home for the two pretty white stone figures. The temple would benefit from the wealth of the city in later times, too, as can be seen from its **luxuriant assortment of golden statues**. Thanks to a trick, the statuary even survived the Cultural Revolution: the monks glued pictures of Mao over the double doors. Anyone trying to open the doors by force would have had to rip Mao's face in two.

Spirit wall and gatehouse

That a spirit wall should stand on the opposite side of the street in front of the temple is quite a common occurrence. Here, though, the lack of space means there is no outer courtyard. The Hall of the Heavenly Kings opens directly onto the street. Its gates are always closed. To get in means paying an entrance fee at the side door so that the entrance hall has to be visited from the rear. As usual it contains a smiling **pot-bellied Buddha**, the Four Heavenly Kings and the figure of Weituo guarding the inner part of the temple.

Main hall

Images of the departure and return of the pilgrim Xuanzang on his journey to India adorn the roof of the main hall. The glittering gold

An interpretation of Chinese brick pagodas in steel and glass: →
the Jin Mao Tower

of the **main statues** in the hall covers the »Three Precious Buddhas«. Along the sides the 20 protective gods of Buddhism (devas) line up in rows. At the rear Guanyin can be seen riding across the sea on a giant fish with the 18 luohan either side of her and Gautama meditating under the Bodhi tree above her.

Great Jade Buddha

To see the main attraction, the larger of the two jade Buddhas, climb to the upper floor of the next hall. The Buddha is an image of Shakyamuni.

Sleeping Jade Buddhas

On the ground floor of the side hall to the west, the other jade statue from 1880 can be seen. It depicts **Buddha on his entry to Nirvana**. He is not shown sleeping, however, but smiles at the observers in the same sweet and pleasantly enchanting way as the larger Buddha. This makes it look different from all the other Buddhas in China. Recently another reclining Buddha has been added, actually sleeping this time. It too is Burmese but it is bigger and the workmanship is not so fine. Another figure stands undeservedly in the shadow of the jade Buddhas, a wooden **Guanyin figure** dating back some 400 years, a Chinese piece of expressive elegance.

The Jade Buddha Temple in Shanghai

In a side building of the first court, another figure can be seen, which **Bronze Buddha** is clearly older than the temple itself, a bronze Buddha some 400 years old.

The temple is maintained nowadays by donations and admission **Religious life** fees as well as by the sale of religious services. This primarily involves festivals for the dead. 170 Anyuan Lu. Opening times: 8am–5pm daily. ⏲

Longhua Temple and Martyr's Park

With its pretty complex and rather peaceful atmosphere, the Buddhist **»Dragon Blossom monastery«** is the nicest place to go in the southern part of town. It is most famous for its 40 m/131 ft pagoda, built in 977. Although the complex was ravaged in the Cultural Revolution, it is now once again home to more than 80 monks. 2853 Longhua Lu. Opening times: 7am–4.30pm daily.

Next door Martyr's Park and its **Memorial Museum** recall victims of the massacre of 12 April 1927, when Chiang Kaishek violently suppressed Shanghai's communist workers' movement. Opening times: 6am–4.30pm. Underground line M3 Longcao Lu.

! *Baedeker* TIP

Sacrifice en masse
New moon and full moon are the times for offering sacrifices: this when the faithful come to the Jade Buddha temple, bringing incense and fruit as offerings. This is not a good time for quiet sight-seeing, but for those who wish to observe lively devotion, there's no better date for a visit.

✶ Zhujiajiao town on the water

A trip out into the country, to the east bank of Lake Dianshan- (40 km/25 mi west of Shanghai), which is administratively part of Shanghai but, in spite of recent modernization and its opening up to tourism, the town of Zhujiajiao, a town on the water, still leaves an impression that seems to have come from a bygone age. With its canals, plied by cargo barges, the traditional houses, numerous alleys and twenty old **stone bridges** the spot is outstandingly picturesque. In addition it offers a colourful collection of goods for sale. Exhibitions provide information on rice cultivation and fisheries and display pottery and jade items discovered in the area, which display the artistic ideals of several thousand years ago. The **Kezhi garden**, the temple of the town's god and the five-arched Fangsheng bridge, the »Bridge of Letting Live«, which is 72 m/80 yd long. Its name is to be understood literally. Old women offer fish for sale here, which their buyers then grant a new lease of life by throwing them back in the river, thus gathering good karma for the next life. Day-trip bus no. 4 from Shanghai.

Shenyang

Province: Liaoning
Altitude: 50 m/164 ft

Population: 4.8 million

Shenyang is the capital of the southern Manchurian province of Liaoning and something of a Cinderella among China's imperial cities. In a list of the six major cities – Xi'an, Luoyang, Hangzhou, Nanjing, Beijing and Kaifeng, although the last-named is of little interest to tourists – Shenyang is not even mentioned. Nevertheless, it is the only city other than Beijing (and if summer palaces count, Chengde) where there is a real imperial palace. Furthermore, that is not the only attraction in the city.

Even though the town had a certain military importance even under the Jurchens (forerunners of the Manchus), its history only really came to the fore with the emergence of **Nurhaci** (1559–1626), the ruler who initiated the ascent of Manchuria to the status of a great power. He made what was then called Mukden his capital in 1625. Once his grandson, Fulin conquered China in 1644 and ascended to the throne in Beijing, Shenyang's heyday only continued for another couple of decades but it still held the rank of auxiliary capital. With the building of the South Manchurian Railway starting in 1898, Shenyang came first under Russian, then under Japanese influence. On 18 September 1931 Japan's Guandong army provoked what is known as the »**Mukden Incident**«, which they used as an excuse for the occupation of Manchuria. The rich mineral wealth that Japan had coveted contributed to heavy industrialization of the countryside around Shenyang after 1949.

Skyline and getting around

Shenyang is not the sort of place where people feel at home. The air is bad and there are practically no parks except at the edge of town. In the vicinity of the old town, the roads are aligned to the compass points but beyond they run at all angles. The individual tourist destinations are widely spaced and it is necessary to take taxi trips between them.

✴ Imperial palace

Two thirds of the palace was built between 1625 and 1636. Its size and architectural style document the ambitions of the strengthening Manchurian leadership to take China itself as a model and to consciously measure itself against that standard. The central and western sections, the two oldest parts of the building, reflect this most clearly, even if the dimensions cannot nearly match those of the palace in Beijing. However, they are even more richly ornamented.

Yangge dancers in Shenyang: the rustic dance is still kept up by the older inhabitants

The central section clearly shows its Beijing influence. The »Gate of the Great Qing« – as early as 1636 the chosen name of the dynasty was already being used here – leads to the main courtyard with the Chongzheng Dian, **»Hall of Exalted Government«**, occupying its northern side. The dimensions are quite modest, five bays wide with a simple roof, albeit a gabled one covered in imperial yellow. The typical Manchu style is displayed in the colourfully glazed dragon ornamentation on the gable walls, the gable itself and on the roof ridge. Daily audiences with Abahai, Nurhaci's son, would take place here. There is nothing like the ostentation seen in the great throne halls of Beijing, which were reserved for ceremonial occasions, as the needs were different at the time. The inside of the throne hall is certainly magnificent, though, especially the gilded throne cabinet, which is like another building inside the first.

Central section, gatehouse and throne hall

Beyond the throne hall comes the most conspicuous building of the whole palace, the three-storey Phoenix Tower atop its 4 m/13 ft stone terrace. At the time of its construction it was an innovative, and indeed **spectacular building**, which was then the tallest in town. This is where Abahai's quarters were and where he would hold banquets. The ground floor also acts as an easily guarded entrance to the women's chambers, which adjoin it to the north.

Phoenix Tower

The central building in the rear courtyard is the »Palace of Clarity and Tranquillity«; containing Abahai's bedchamber at its eastern end. It also served for the performance of Manchurian customs. In ceremonies led by shamans, Abahai would make sacrifices to various spirits here each day. The women lived in the side buildings. A tunnel-like passage leads northwards into the palace garden.

Qingning Gong

Shenyang Map

0,5 mi
1 km
©Baedeker

Beiling Park

Northern Imperial Tomb

Xinkai

Nujiang Jie

Huanghe Jie

Beiling Jie

Chongshan Lu

Beita Pagoda

Chongshan Xi Lu

Bainiao Park

Huanhe Jie

Changjiang Jie

Ningshan Lu

Huanghe Jie

Beita Jie

Wanghua Jie

Qishan Lu

Nujiang Jie

Qishan Lu

Lianhe Jie

Kunshan Xi Lu

Bitang Park

Heilongjiang Jie

Lianhe Jie

Huashan Lu

Kunshan Dong Lu

North Station

Lianhe Jie

Tianshan Lu

Da Reizhan Jie

Huigong Jie

Xiao Bei Jie

Bei Jie

Huanggutun Station

Xinggong Jie

Tuanjie

Huigong Square Lu

Tianhougong Lu

Da

Zhongzhan

Lu

Huigong Lu

Lingyuan Jie

Guangyi Jie

Nanjing Jie

Zhengfu Square

Beishuncheng Lu

Xiaojingqiao Lu

Bei 2. Lu

Shengli Jie

Shifu Da Lu

Heping Jie

Bayi Park

Zhong Jie

Xiao Dong Lu

Main Station

Xinggong Jie

Zhongshan Lu

Taiyuan Jie

Sun Yatsen Square

② **Mao Statue**

Zhongshan Lu

Xiaoxi Lu

Xishuncheng Lu

Imperial Palace

Minzhu Lu

Tongze Jie

①

Zhonghua Lu

Liaoning Provincial Museum

Shenyang Lu

Da Dong Lu

Xiao Nan Lu

Library

Xiaoheyan Lu

Nanjing Jie

Daxi Lu

Qing Nian Dajie

Chaoyang Jie

Binhe Jie

Shenyang Zoo

Nanwu Lu

Zhongshan Park

Shisanwei Lu

Renao Lu

Fengtutun Jie

Wanquan Lu

Shengli Jie

Tongze Jie

Shenyang Stadium

Shisiwei Lu

Waniutang Park

Nanjing Jie

Taiyuan Jie

Heping Square

Guangong Jie

Qingnian Park

Xiao Nan Jie

Da Nan Jie

Wanliutang Lu

Changjiang Jie

Xinhua Square

Heping Lu

Nanwu Lu

Lu Xun Park

Wenyi Lu

Wu'ai

Nanhu Park

Liaoning Exhibition Hall

Wenhua Lu

Where to stay
① Traders Hotel   ② Liaoning-Hotel

▶ VISITING SHENYANG

GETTING THERE

Trains stop at the modern station of Shenyang North or the older central station. Shenyang is on the main line from Beijing to Harbin and even has a direct connection to Moscow. From the airport, 26 km/16 mi south of the city, there are flights to all the major cities of China and even to Seoul in Korea.

TRANSPORT

There are many bus routes but it is worth noting the number 227, which links the Abahai Mausoleum, Shenyang North station and the imperial palace.

ACCOMMODATION

▶ Luxury

① *Traders Hotel*
(Shangmao Fandian)
68 Zhonghua Lu

Tel. 024/23412288
Fax 024/23411988
588-room hotel belonging to the Shangri La chain, conveniently situated in the centre of town between the main station and Sun Yatsen Park

▶ Mid-range

② *Liaoning-Hotel*
(Liaoning Binguan)
97 Zhongshan Lu
Tel. 024/ 23 83 91 04
Fax 024/ 23 83 91 03
This hotel opposite the statue of Mao on Sun Yatsen Square was opened as early as 1927. Its 77 rooms are modern and comfortable but the dining room is a genuine antique, atmospheric and well worth seeing. And don't forget: the food is good too.

Some smaller gates lead from the main courtyard in front of the throne hall to auxiliary wings in the north. These were extended in 1756, since space was needed to accommodate the wives, children and concubines the emperors brought on their visits.

Secondary courtyards

One even later addition is the imperial ancestor temple of Tai Miao, which was completed in 1778. It is situated in the east alongside the »Gate of the Great Qing«.

Ancestor temple

The eastern section comes across like a Manchurian military camp – except that the buildings are pavilions rather than tents – and like an architectural reflection of the military organization developed by Nurhaci. Nurhaci had recognized that the traditional tribal arrangements would not be effective for any major campaigns. He therefore assembled a professional army, the so-called **Eight Banners**, to which the soldiers' families were also assigned. Precisely this structure can be seen here. The first eight pavilions (as seen from the south) are set aside for the generals of the banners, four on each side. The last two pavilions were the administrative centres for the two highest

East wing

ranking princes and in the octagonal **»Hall of the Great Government«** in the middle, the commands for the various generals would be gathered together for the benefit of the ruler himself. The ensemble is supplemented by two music pavilions near the south gate and by the imperial coach sheds.

Western section West of the main courtyard in the central section, the first place to be seen is an intermediate courtyard of the west wing. The main buildings of the western section are north of there. This part of the palace was only added at a later date, being completed in 1782. This is where the Beijing-based emperors would relax when visiting the graves of their ancestors in Shenyang (see below) or stopping off on the way to hunting grounds in their tribal homelands. The first courtyard is the palace theatre. North of there is the **Wenshuo Ge Library**. Both buildings demonstrate the change in culture undergone by the Manchus in the space of 150 years. Operatic plays and book knowledge had played no role at all in the lives of the dynasty's founders. Nowadays the halls house an exhibition of imperial art treasures. Opening times: 8.30am–5pm daily, in winter 9am–4pm.

Mausoleum of Abahai (Bei Ling)

Both Nurhaci and his son, Abahai (1592–1643), were interred in dignified mausoleums outside Shenyang. The Zhao Ling (mausoleum) of Abahai, usually called Bei Ling, the »northern tomb«, is larger and closer to the city. The work on the whole site, which covers some 18 ha/44 acres lasted from 1643 till 1651. The Chinese influence is plain to see. The alignment towards the south, the organization of the burial mound toward the rear with the tomb's temple at the front and the **honour guard of stone animals** on the way there all match the Chinese template. The discrepancies are clear too, though. Among them are the fort-like, double wall with corner turrets and barbicans, the unique sequence of the guarding creatures – each featuring two squatting lions, squatting xiezhi, squatting qilin, standing horses, reclining camels and standing elephants (there are no statues of officials) and the luxuriant ornamentation, particularly eye-catching in the Long'en Dian offertory hall. Look at the reliefs on the marble pedestal and the colourful decoration of the console area under the roof eaves. The mausoleum is to the north of the city centre on Beiling Dajie. Mausoleum opening times: 7.30am–5.30pm daily.

! **Baedeker TIP**

Steam colossi

In Liaoning province the occasional steam locomotive is still in operation. Sooner or later they will probably end up here in Shenyang at the steam locomotive museum, where 15 are already on display in a fine new hall and on the surrounding premises, including examples made in Europe, Japan, China and the USA. The museum is in the west of town (Senlin Gongyuan, corner of Zhonggong Beijie/Jianshe Xilu).

** Suzhou

Province: Jiangsu   **Population:** 750,000
Altitude: 20 m/66 ft

This would-be hi-tech centre, 80 km/50 mi west of Shanghai, was a sort of secret capital of China for hundreds of years. It was where life was best, a source of luxury and fashion, the place where pensioned officials would retire. Its artistic garden paradises have now made it a UNESCO World Heritage Site and they are the main reasons to pay the city a visit.

Most of the officials did come from here or at least the surrounding regions, since the wealth of the place, originating from the Silk Road, allowed people from Suzhou to have the highest level of education in the country. In its time Suzhou was China's second biggest city after Beijing. After 150 years of decline, the city only now seems to be catching up.

Suzhou is popularly known as the »Venice of the East« but that conjures a false view, because the city, although criss-crossed by canals, is not built upon islands in the sea. The canals were not important for the transport of people inside the city either. Nevertheless, Suzhou has lain on the **Grand Canal** for 1400 years. The canal has now been extensively widened, and is once more becoming a key trans-

City of canals

Canals cross the old quarter of Suzhou

port artery for internal shipping. The old town covers an area of 3.3 x 4.5 km/ 2 x 2.8 mi, making it unusually large. It is indeed completely surrounded by water, a broad canal which also functions as a city moat. It is easy to get around on the regular street grid. Although in a city with such a tradition, a uniform style might be hoped for, there is no such thing in Suzhou. Nevertheless, at least around the gardens, there are tough restrictions in place and new buildings feature white plastered walls to fit in with the conventional appearance.

✴ Old Town North: Garden of Zhuozheng Yuan

Covering an area of 4 ha/10 acres, this is the largest of Suzhou's scholars' gardens and the one which attracts the most visitors. It came into being between the years 1509 and 1530. Since it was later split up, the story of its later development is somewhat complicated. A distinction is made between the eastern, middle and western sections.

Name　All kinds of bizarre translations of the Chinese name are in circulation. One English rendering, though, is »The Humble Administrator's Garden«. The Chinese original refers to an old text whose sense is more or less as follows: »The policy of the humble man is to water his garden, sell his vegetables, guard his sheep, honour his parents and live in peace with his brothers.«. Since the first gardener here was an official who had turned his back on the vagaries of state service to retreat into a private world, his choice of name sounds a little defiant. He called the spot, in full, **»Garden of the Politics of My Humble Self«**, in which I shall only concern myself with the aims of the humble man – to hell with grand politics.

East garden　The main entrance to Zhuozheng Yuan in the south initially leads into the east garden. This is the largest and least ostentatious of the three sections. A D-shaped pool allows for plenty of space. There are not many pavilions but it is verdant and shady. On the north bank of the pond there is a teahouse in which to take a rest.

Middle garden　On the other side of a long wall with ornamental windows the eye is drawn to the middle garden, largely consisting of water (a lotus pond) with several islands, hills, rockeries and many pavilions, halls and terraces. Intertwining paths lead all around it and across bridges to the islands over narrow arms of the pond. Looking west from the east end of the pond, the pagoda of the northern monastery is precisely along the axis of view, a famous example of scenery being »borrowed«, although it is actually situated outside the garden.

West garden　The smallest section of the garden resembles the middle garden in its layout. A pavilion tops the characteristic hill in the north. South from there, a side gate leads into a large **bonsai garden** with some

Suzhou *Map*

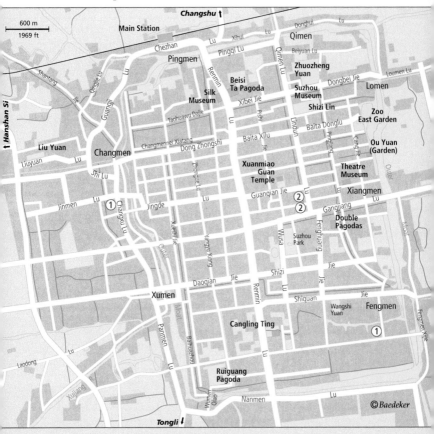

Changshu ↑

Main Station

Chezhan

Pingmen

Shantang

Guangji

Qiaofu Lu

Qingjia Lu

Xihui Lu

Pingqi Lu

Donghui Lu

Qimen

Beiyuan Lu

Qimen Lu

Zhuozheng
Yuan

Beisi
Ta Pagoda

Silk
Museum

Xibei Jie

Suzhou
Museum

Dongbei Jie

Loumen Lu

Lomen

Shizi Lin

Zoo
East Garden

↑ Hanshan Si

Liu Yuan

Liuyuan
Lu

Shi Lu

Changmen

Jinmen

Jingde

Changmen Xiatang

Taohuawu Dajie

Dong Zhongshi

Baita Xilu

Baita Donglu

Xuanmiao
Guan
Temple

Lindun

Pishi

Lindun

Guangqian Jie

Ou Yuan
(Garden)

Theatre
Museum

Xiangmen

Lu

Outer

Longjie

Pingjiang

Jingde

Zhongjie Lu

Xuejin Jie

Changxu Lu

Lu ①

Yangyu Xiang

Fenghuang

Wusa

Gangjiang

Double
Pagodas

② ②

Suzhou
Park

Xumen

Panmen

Daoqian   Jie

Shizi

Rennin Lu

Shiquan

Jie

Jie

Wangshi
Yuan

Jie

Fengmen

Moat

Xujiang

Laodong

Cangling Ting

Ruiguang
Pagoda

Nanmen

Wumen
Qiao

Bamauzhou

Lu

Baita Wuanzhou

① Songhelou

② Southern Cross

① Bamboo Grove Hotel

② Garden View Hotel

Tongli ↓

600 m
1969 ft

©Baedeker

Where to eat
① Songhelou
② Southern Cross

Where to stay
① Bamboo Grove Hotel
② Garden View Hotel

fascinating works of botanical art. It is possible to take a rest there and have some tea. 178 Dong Beijie. Opening times: 7.30am–5.30pm, 8am–5pm in winter (last admission 5pm or 4.30pm). ⏲

Directly adjoining the garden is this late work of the Sino-American architect **Ieoh Ming Pei**, whose family originates from Suzhou. The modest white building takes up ideas from classical architecture and garden design, but confidently reinterprets them. The exhibits include art treasures from Suzhou along with prehistoric finds. A part

Suzhou Museum

⏵ VISITING SUZHOU

GETTING THERE

Suzhou is on the main line from Shanghai to Beijing and can be reached in just 45 minutes from the main station in Shanghai. It is possible to go by boat to nearby Hangzhou: departure is around 5.30pm, arrival 6.30am and cabin berths are available for about 90 yuan. From 306 Renmin Lu (east of the bridge on the north bank), Suzhou shipping (Suzhou Lunchuan Yunshu Gongsi), 306 Renmin Lu, Tel. 05 12/65 20 90 76, 65 20 66 81.

INFORMATION

CITS Suzhou
18 Dajing Xiang
Tel. 0512/65159177, fax 65157805
cits@citssz.com

SHOPPING

More than anywhere else, Suzhou is traditionally a place to buy silk. It is possible to buy direct from the factory at Silk Factory no. 1, 94 Nanmen Lu (opposite the canal boat quay). Very large assortment.

MUSIC, DANCING, THEATRE

The beautifully done shows that take place every evening in the garden of Wangshi Yuan offer everything in one. The audience are scattered around various pavilions and halls, wandering from one part of the programme to the next. Classical Chinese culture is never more nicely and lovingly presented. March–Nov. 7.30pm daily, tickets at the entrance.

WHERE TO EAT
▶ Moderate
① *Songhelou*
In the Holiday Inn Jasmine Hotel
345 Changzu Lu, 3rd floor.
Tel. 0512/ 65 58 88 88

The hotel branch of an old-established restaurant with typical Suzhou cuisine. The restrained modern ambience and discreet service are equally impressive. The quality is outstanding in view of the price.

▶ Inexpensive
② *Southern Cross*
76 Luoguaqiao Xiatang
Tel. 0512/ 65 81 00 67
Centrally located café-restaurant a stone's throw south of the eastern end of the Guanqian Jie pedestrian zone. Particularly cheap lunchtime menu.

ACCOMMODATION
▶ Luxury
① *Bamboo Grove Hotel*
168 Zhuhui Lu
Tel. 05 12/65 20 56 01, fax 65 20 87 78
www.bg-hotel.com
356-room hotel with garden courtyards, good catering and hotel shops

▶ Mid-range
② *Garden View Hotel*
66 Lindun Lu Luogua Qiao
Tel. 05 12/67 77 88 88, fax 67 77 99 188
Exquisitely designed rooms in traditional court architecture. Central location on a canal. At the top end of the price category, but worth every penny, or rather yuan.

▶ Budget
Tongli: Wanshun private hotel (Wanshun Minju Kezhan)
177 Yuhang Jie
Tel. 05 12/63 33 16 08
wsmjkz@tom.com
Tongli has a few nice places to stay which are privately run. One of them is the Wanshun, which has recently been set up in a building in the old town.

of the complex is formed by the classical buildings to the east, which were occupied by a leader of the Taiping rebellion from 1860 to 1863. The east wing, formerly the headquarters of an association of »expatriates«, i.e. people from another province currently residing in the city, includes a splendid theatre auditorium. Good museum shop. 204 Dongbei Jie. Opening times: 9am–5pm, last admission 4pm. ⏲

Beisi Ta Pagoda

The imposing, 76 m/250 ft »**North Temple Pagoda**« is an outstanding viewpoint. It was built around 1150. The associated monastery, which houses a few monks, is a post-Mao re-foundation; most of the halls are also new. At the northern end of Renmin Lu, west of the Zhuozheng-Gardens. Opening times: 7.45am–6pm daily (closes ⏲ 5.30pm in winter).

Silk Museum (Suzhou Sichou Bowuguan)

The modern building opposite the pagoda to the west shows how silk is manufactured.Fabrics more than 2000 years old are on show here. There is an adjoining silk shop. 661 Renmin Lu. Opening times: daily 9am–5pm (last admission 4.30pm). ⏲

✳ Garden of Shizi Lin

Just one block south of Zhuozheng Yuan is the »**Lion Grove**«, perhaps not the prettiest but certainly the oddest, even the zaniest garden in the city, if not in all of China. What sets it apart is its artificial rocky hills and bizarre garden rockeries. The paths lead around the garden's pond, through tunnels, into grottoes and over hills. Some of the stones look like modern sculptures, others like lions at play. It might appear that the latter aspect is what gave the garden its name. In fact though, it came into existence in the 14th century as the **Garden of Lion Wood Monastery**, the name referring to the biography of the abbot, so the garden is really named after a monastery. Its present design only dates from time of the Chinese republic. It was purchased in 1918 by the Bei family, who built their ancestor temple here and redesigned the garden according to the contemporary fashion. The stone ship in the pond dates from this time, a stylistically alien element for a scholar's garden. The frequent use of concrete is also an indication of the redesign.

Tour

The entrance leads straight into the ancestor temple. A passage heading west initially leads into a separate garden courtyard, enclosed by its own wall before continuing into the garden proper. To save the highlight until last, start by turning left, keeping the garden's pond on the right. The Winter Cherry Pavilion, on a rise at the west end, and the Lotus Blossom Hall on the northern bank, function as the main viewpoints. Then comes the most exciting part, the **rocky hill** east of the pond. It is quite riddled with labyrinthine paths, sometimes leading up, sometimes down. Yuanlin Lu. Opening times: 7.30am–5.30pm ⏲ daily, 8am till 5pm in winter (last admissions 5pm or 4.30pm).

✳ Xuanmiao Guan Temple

A role that in Europe might be taken by the parish church is fulfilled in Suzhou by this impressive Daoist temple, a spiritual fulcrum in the midst of the shopping district. The large outer courtyard, which is open on all sides, also functions as the main central square of the city itself.

History The sacred place was founded as early as 276. Later on it was gradually expanded till, during the Mongol period, it ascended to become one of the eight most important Daoist monasteries in the empire. Of these it was the largest south of the Yangtze in area. The 20th century was not a good time for the temple.

Some of the building was demolished and the **Cultural Revolution** inflicted serious damage. Since the restoration and reinstitution of the temple, it is once again being administered by a community of monks.

Gatehouse The temple is along the line of sight of a road leading from the south. It leads to a new decorative gate. After that comes the large gatehouse dating from 1775, already a prestigious building in its own right, with a double-eaved roof. Inside, six generals guard the passage.

Main hall The main hall, built in 1179, is the largest and oldest Daoist temple hall south of the Yangtze. The same period of building also gave rise to the 7-m/23-ft **clay figures of the Three Pristine Ones**, who sit enthroned like Buddhas atop a 1.75 m/6 ft pedestal representing Sumeru, the world mountain. All the other figures have been recreated since the Cultural Revolution.

On both sides of the outer court, other smaller temples have been rebuilt. On the eastern side, Wenchang, protective god of literature, is worshipped in company with Confucius (right) and the philosopher Zhu Xi (1130–1200), with Guanyin and the three gods of happiness in the side halls. On the west side is a temple to the god of wealth, Guanqian Jie. Opening times: 7.30am–4.45pm daily.

Guanqian Jie The temple has its gate hall on the east-west running »Road alongside the Daoist Monastery«, the city's traditional market street. It was made one of the country's first pedestrian areas at the start of the 1980s and is a nice place to walk and shop.

Loom in the Suzhou Museum →

✳ ✳ Old Town South: Garden of Wangshi Yuan

The »Garden of the Master of Nets« is the smallest, finest and most perfect example of the »great« gardens – the epitome of a scholar's garden. Even the residential layout is easily understood. The complex attained its current form in 19th century.

Residential building

The entrance from a narrow side street first leads to what is effectively a garage, where litters or sedan chairs were kept. From there, head straight on into the reception room, a fine parlour for guests. Left of the sedan chair garage, a guest entrance leads to the southern part of the garden. If viewing the site for the first time, this is the route to take. The family used another door at the northern end of the house.

Southern section

The southern section sets the mood. The first pavilion, a large building used for company, overlooks a rockery and an **artificial rock hill** to the north of it. The main part of the garden does not start till after that, though. There is no direct access from here, either, only views to hint that there is more to see. A colonnade now meanders around another pavilion before it reaches the heart of the garden, the pond. This is the point to consider the fishing motif.

The fisherman motif

Even the first known garden on the site, dating from 1140, was called the »fisherman's retreat«. Since then its owners have always portrayed themselves as modest tradesmen, in this case recalling a sage who was happier to catch fish than to risk his neck in dignified office. The present name refers to the same idea. The fishing ideal really does permeate the site like a leitmotif. Thus, the pond has no lotus plants in it; no one casts nets over a lotus pond (the water lilies are a recent addition and rather alien to the theme). The garden house built out over the water from the southern bank is called the **»Studio for Washing Hat Ribbons«** and incorporates another fisherman's tale. The minister-poet Qu Yuan, doyen of the art of verse and the very model of an incorruptible state official, once complained vociferously about the corruption of his age. This was heard by a fisherman who sang to the official, »When the water in the Canglang is clear, I can wash the ribbons of my (official's) hat in it. When the water in the Canglang is muddy, I can wash my feet in it.« In other words: wise men should not fret at bad times but maintain their purity in private.

Other buildings

Other buildings relate to other motifs. The halls north of the pond are primarily dedicated to intellectual pursuits. Hidden behind the trees there is the »Studio of Book Reading and Picture Viewing«. Probably the loveliest place in the garden, though is the **»Pavilion of the Rising Moon and the Caressing Breeze«** at the west end of the pool. The name is only partly self-explanatory. Naturally the thoughts are of high summer, when it is possible to sit here in the moonlight and enjoy a breeze that relieves the heat. The name was inspired, though, by a song called »Song on a Clear Night« by the neo-Confucian, Shao Yong (1011–1077): »When the moon climbs high in the sky and the breeze caresses the waters, the mind becomes clear as few will grasp«. The name of the pavilion thus alludes to the position of the view over the lake, as its surface is caressed by the breeze. Side street off Daichengqiao Lu. Opening times: 8am to 4.30pm daily.

✳ Garden of Canglang Ting

The »Waters of the Canglang«, as cited by the garden of Wangshi Yuan, even provide the name of this enclosure. In a city as rich in water features as Suzhou, the fisherman motif (for the flight from politics into a simple life) is easily called to mind, and hardly any of the pensioners who built their paradise gardens here can have had an easy time in the service of the state. The **»Canglang Pavilion«**, as the garden is properly known, is not quite so perfectly designed and varied as some others – the artificial hill is too large and the garden pond too small – but it does have other strengths. In addition, it gets much less crowded. Established in the 10th century, it is also considered Suzhou's oldest garden. Nevertheless, like all the others, it has had to undergo several deaths and rebirths since it was founded and its present appearance only dates from the 19th/20th centuries.

The Zhuozheng Yuan and eight other gardens in Suzhou constitute a World Heritage Site

Entrance	Entrance to the garden is via a bridge, which crosses a public canal. Beyond the gate house, the view is initially blocked by the garden's broad hill, overgrown with bamboo plants. The logic of this arrangement is explained by the fact that the entrance is in the north, whereas the residential area is, as usual, in the south.
Residential buildings	In order to save the best for last, turn first to the right. A colonnade leads past the hill down to the low-lying garden pond and then to a group of halls, which line up in a neat rhythm and sometimes stack up opposite one another at differing depths. They themselves are renowned for the unusual variety of the window designs. One curiosity is the **Memorial Hall for the 500 Sages** which has portraits of 594 exemplary men: politicians, scholars, physicians, generals, philosophers, engineers, astronomers and dutiful sons. Following the sequence of rooms to the east brings you to a large, square inner courtyard with the »Hall of the Elucidated Dao«.
Canal view and double colonnade	The path leads from there further east around the hill to the canal and a double colonnade. Here the architecture of the garden gets amusing and perhaps even excessively bold. In incorporating the canal, at this point rather wide, into the garden landscape, the inhabitants to some extent took into account the fact that they would be seen on the outer part of the colonnade by people as they floated past. At this point though, they arranged for the garden itself to be visible only through windows. From the inner part of the colonnade, by contrast, the scenery of the canal could then be seen as if it were a series of moving, framed pictures. The path opens out at the **»Studio Facing the Water«** (Mianshui Xuan), where it is possible to take a rest after enjoying the view of the waters from both sides of the path.

! *Baedeker* TIP

Canal trips

If a little more time is available, Suzhou should also be experienced from the water. The standard trip once around the old town takes 80 minutes. In addition, there are a variety of shorter trips. They can be booked at many hotels. There is a quay for sightseeing-boats in the south-east to the north of the Xinshi Qiao bridge; another is by the Renmin Qiao Bridge in the south of the old town.

What still awaits is a little mountaineering. The objective is the Canglang pavilion itself (pavilion at the summit), which gives its name to the whole garden – an airy spot, particularly in summer.

Hall of art	Even from outside it will already have aroused surprise. Next to the garden, there is a Greek temple! The Neo-classical building from 1932 was formerly the city's art school. Nowadays it contains a gallery and an exhibition recalling the founder of the college. It is accessed from the garden. Canglangting Lu. Opening times: 8am–5pm (last admission 4.30pm).

The southwest corner of the old town is very touristy but then it is also very picturesque. Here a stone arched bridge crosses the canal which also served as the city's moat, and from high up it is possible to look out over surviving section of city wall with the Pan Men gate and a pagoda – a popular motif for photographs.

Wumen Qiao Bridge

✶ ✶ West of the Old Town: Garden of Liu Yuan

At 2 ha/5 acres, this is the second largest of Suzhou's gardens. It was built outside the city itself in the 16th century and was initially a temple garden. It is the most varied of all the city's gardens and for that alone it is worth a visit.

There is no other garden where the concept is so thoroughly explored as here. This makes the structure extraordinarily complicated. Even the main courtyard with the garden pond is surrounded by additional gardens but divided from them by walls and paths. Towards the east the design becomes very fragmented. More than a dozen garden enclosures, some large, some as small as a room, invite a tour of discovery, the details of which are impossible to describe in full.

Design

This was once the garden of a family called Liu, but »Liu« is written with a different character nowadays. Since the word means »stand still« or »spend time«, it is easy to assume that this is a garden in which it is possible to while away the time, but historically this is not the meaning that was intended. Instead, it refers to the fact that this was the only garden in the western suburb that remained intact after the rampaging of the Taiping Rebellion.

Name

The garden is entered from the south via the residential building, where the eye is initially met by the terraces and pavilions on the southern and western sides of the courtyard and by the view straight across the central pond to an artificial hill with pavilions – an effective arrangement. The best route from here is to turn left while looking backwards, then to head north to a miniature island called **»Little Penglai«**. In ancient mythology, Penglai was the name of the island in the eastern ocean where the immortals lived. The naming thus evokes the idea of the garden as a paradise. From a terrace for angling with its own pavilion, it is possible to look out from three sides over the water.

Main courtyard

Halls and courtyards of various sizes divide the eastern part of the garden in such a way that at first glance it seems like a labyrinth. Paths wind in and out with playful humour and there are constantly new things to see. Liuyuan Lu. Opening times: 7.30am–5pm daily (last admission 4.30pm).

Eastern part of the garden

ⓘ

What power the art of poetry possesses! This temple monastery is not the least bit important, yet Suzhou's tourists flock to it every day,

Temple of Hanshan Si

and not only people from all parts of China but especially visitors from Japan, too. They are here to recite the words of a **poem by Zhang Ji** (8th century), which mentions the bells of this temple as heard by the poet one winter's day while he was mooring his boat at the bridge. The complex is certainly attractive and was supplemented in 1995 by a 42 m/138 ft pagoda in the Tang style. In front of the temple there is also a lovely high-arched bridge. The temple of Hanshan Si is 2 km/1 mi west of the Liu Yuan garden (Fengqiao Zhen).

Opening times: 7.30am–5pm daily.

Tongli

Here in Tongli it is possible to see how Suzhou itself once looked: This pretty little market town, 20 km/12 mi south of Suzhou, has old houses lining neat alleys, and the main streets are canals. The chief attraction apart from the pretty skyline is a scholar's garden along Suzhou lines called **Tuisi Yuan**. Visitors do have to pay an entrance fee to enter the village but it hasn't been made into a museum or otherwise been touristified. Buses run several times a day from Suzhou.

✶✶ Tai Shan · Tai'an

Hd 27

Province: Shandong **Population:** 380,000
Altitude: 120–1545 m/400–5070 ft

Der Tai Shan, the Sacred East Mountain, is the most popular of the five holy mountains of China and that is, of course, the objective of any visit. The mountain is the sole reason for Tai'an, the settlement at its foot, a temple site and place of pilgrimage. Emperors and scholars have all made pilgrimages here and the mountain was felt worthy of the most extravagant sacrifices ever celebrated in China. Anyone standing on the summit would feel close to heaven itself and anyone visiting today follows in the footsteps of giants. Tai Shan is thus primarily a cultural experience.

Tai Shan is in the west of Shandong province. It is not such much the height of its summit at 1545 m/5069 ft which explains its special status, as the fact that the massif, largely consisting of metamorphic rock, rises almost directly out of the endless low-lying plains of northern China and has no parallel even far beyond the visible horizons: There are no higher peaks for 1000 km/600 mi around it. At its base, Tai'an rises gently from an altitude of 120 m/400 ft. A cruciform plan dominates the layout: one axis is Shengping Jie, running east-west, while the ancient north-south axis with the main line of ascent, runs right through the temple of Dai Miao. The two axes cross just before its main gate.

It is even said that **Confucius himself** stood on the summit of Tai Shan and discovered how small the world seems from there – but that is probably a myth. What is fact, though, is that the first emperor (Qin Shihuangdi, ►Famous People p.82) climbed the mountain and told the heavens of his achievements from the top. By then the pilgrimage to Tai Shan and the worshipping of the mountain must already have been a well-established custom. About a hundred years after the first emperor, the **Han Emperor Wu** (140–87 BC) raised the cult of the East Mountain to a new level. He travelled no less than five times to make the Fengshan sacrifice, the most extravagant made in China's history, which was made here and here alone. The rite has only been performed four more times since, in AD 56, 666, 725 and 1008. The costs of organizing this massive celebration were immense; the political conditions it required, though, were virtually impossible to achieve, Not only did the empire need to be at peace with its neighbours, there must have been no droughts, no locust plagues, comets or any other kind of evil omens. Nature and the skies reflected the political situation in the minds of the Chinese. In the central part of the Fengshan sacrifice, though, it was necessary for the Son of Heaven himself to ascend to the skies at the mountain summit and declare that peace and great prosperity were abundant on the earth. If the rite was indeed performed, it was a **political demonstration of the first order**. For the celebrations of 725, for example, guests were present from as far afield as India, Arabia and Japan.

The Fengshan sacrifice

 ## VISITING TAI SHAN · TAI'AN

GETTING THERE

Tai'an is on the main line between Beijing and Shanghai. The nearest airport is the one at the provincial capital, Jinan. It is also possible to take a bus down the motorway to the Confucius city of Qufu.

SHOPPING

In Tai'an it is possible to buy particularly beautiful decorative stones, mostly flat and not very heavy slabs, whose grain looks like a picture – e.g. a forest or mountain landscape.

ACCOMMODATION

► **Mid-range**

① *Taishan Hotel*
26 Hongmen Lu
Tel. 0538/822 4678, Fax 822 1432
tsbg@163169.net
Three-star hotel with 110 rooms north of the Dai Miao temple near the decorative gate of Daizong Fang on the main climbing route, which is very convenient for an ascent of Tai Shan.

② *Shenqi-Hotel*
10 Tianjie
Tel. /Fax 0538/8223866
On the slopes of Tai Shan there is now a large selection of hotels but few of them come anywhere near Western standards. The best one is the Shenqi Hotel, which even has its own sauna. Reservations should definitely be made in advance and it is as well to ask the price first, too. Accommodation at the summit is expensive!

Tai Shan Map

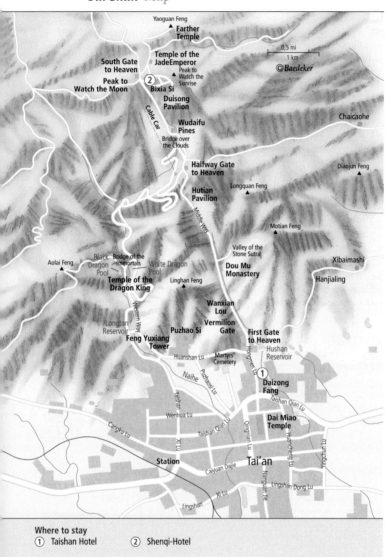

Yaoguan Feng ▲ **Farther Temple**

South Gate to Heaven

Temple of the JadeEmperor ▲ Peak to Watch the Sunrise

Peak to Watch the Moon

② **Bixia Si**

Duisong Pavilion

0,5 mi
1 km

©*Baedeker*

Chaicaohe

Wudaifu Pines

Cable Car

Bridge over the Clouds

Halfway Gate to Heaven

Diaojun Feng ▲

Hutian Pavilion

Longquan Feng ▲

Middle Way

Motian Feng ▲

Valley of the Stone Sutra

Xibaimashi

Aolai Feng ▲

Black Dragon Pool

Bridge of the Immortals

White Dragon Pool

Dou Mu Monastery

Hanjialing

Temple of the Dragon King

Linghan Feng ▲

Western Way

Wanxian Lou

Longtan Reservoir

Vermilion Gate

Puzhao Si

First Gate to Heaven

Feng Yuxiang Tower

Huanshan Lu

Hongmen Lu

Martyrs' Cemetery

Hushan Reservoir

Naihe

Puzhao Lu

① **Daizong Fang**

Taishan Qian Lu

Cangku Lu

Taishan Lu

Wenhua Lu

Taishan Qian Lu

Qingnian Lu

Dai Miao Temple

Xi Lu

Hancheng Lu

Yingchun Lu

Station

Caiyuan Dajie

Tai'an

Nanguan Jie

Xi Lu

Lingshan Dong Lu

Lingshan

Where to stay
① Taishan Hotel
② Shenqi-Hotel

The life of a pilgrim in 1628

The popularity of Tai Shan increased even more later on. A travelogue from 1628 gives an insight into the all-in package that pilgrims would be offered at that time. The guest house would »accept a fixed price including accommodation, use of litter or sedan chair (for the trip to the summit) and the mountain tax. ... Every day thousands of visitors arrive and take their place in hundreds of rooms, consuming hundreds of vegetarian meals and regular dinners.« For the feasting, the highest -priced of three different packages would include »desserts, confectionery, five kinds of fruit, ten sorts of meat, snacks and operatic entertainment«. Even now, nowhere can match that.

The worshipful status of the mountain is not only a result of its imposing size but also because of its situation in the east, where the day begins, bringing the seeds of life itself, fresh, unused living force. Tai Shan, though, was worshipped in personified form as the Mountain Emperor: It was to his heavenly authority that the official sacrificial celebrations were dedicated. Folk belief derived one other consequence, from the image of Tai Shan as the **source of life**: any power with command over existence or non-existence also has dominion over death itself. Thus the god of Tai Shan was also the prince and judge of the seventh of the ten hells, where the dead would be adjudicated on the misdeeds they had committed in life and would undergo hideous torture by way of penance. Propitiating the god of Tai Shan with offerings was therefore a good idea at any time.

The Mountain Emperor

Tai Shan gained real popularity, though, thanks to the »**Princess of the Azure Morning Clouds**«, whom people dubbed the »Mother of Heaven«. She was »invented« about 1000 years ago and was considered to be the granddaughter of the Mountain Emperor. This inspired innovation was, during the Ming era some 500 years ago, the prime motive for a pilgrimage and largely displaced the cult of the Mountain Emperor itself. To this day people still beg the princess for help, primarily in typically feminine matters. Observe the baby dolls that are offered for sale on stands along the pilgrims' way. Women bring them to the goddess as votive offerings to plead for male children or to support the recovery of an infant.

The Cloud Princess

✱ Dai Miao Temple

This imposing site, covering, 9.6 ha/24 acres at the southern foot of the mountain, came into being about 2000 years ago as part of the local Mountain Emperor cult. The temple reached its current size in the Song period, but later dynasties also added buildings. The 20th century saw deterioration in the state of the buildings and not all of the outbuildings have survived.

In front of the temple itself, outside the wall, a smaller temple appears along the north-south axis first. It is called **Yaocan Ting** and covers a space of some 3440 sq m/4115 sq yd. It would certainly be an attraction in its own right anywhere else. This is where the emperor announced his presence before entering the main temple.

Ante-temple

Since the Ming era, the Cloud Princess has had the status of a kind of receptionist here.

Wall and outer courtyard
The main temple looks from outside rather like a fort. Eight gates, five of them in the south, lead in through a crenellated wall 1.3 km/ 1420 yd in length. As may be expected for a complex of this size, the gates lead initially to an outer courtyard. This itself is split by another gate.

Eastern side court
The eastern side court in particular has many preserved inscriptions. The most ancient, only ten of whose characters can be deciphered, dates from the time of the first emperor, making it more than 2200 years old. A high terrace makes it possible to see a view of the temple grounds and look up at the mountain.

Main hall
In the main courtyard the huge »**Hall of the Heavenly Gifts**« (Tiankuang Dian) on its stone pedestal already indicates its high rank thanks to the double-eaved hipped roof, covered in imperial yellow. The terrace was where sacrificial rites took place, which even the last dynasty would still pursue long after the age of the Fengshan sacrifice had ended. For the real attraction, go inside the building. The rear and side walls are painted with a mural 62 m/68 yd in length, showing the god of Tai Shan on an inspection journey in the company of an entourage numbering several hundred. The right-hand side (east) shows them riding out and the left-hand side shows their return. The Mountain Emperor rides in a four-wheeled carriage. His statue in the middle of the hall depicts him in imperial finery. The headwear with its pearl veil is typical for his rank. In the gallery, which

A good choice of site: pavilion with a view on Tai Shan

adjoins the main hall at the side, dioramas with life-size figures seek to convey an impression of the Fengshan sacrifice.

Rear courtyard

As appropriate to his status, the Mountain Emperor also has chambers for his female consorts, where he himself retires at night. These are located in the halls around the rear courtyard. Behind them it is possible to see two architectural curiosities, a bronze pavilion on the right (east) and an iron pagoda on the left (which is sadly no longer complete). Opening times: daily May–Aug 7.50am–6.40pm, Nov–Feb 8am–5.10pm, otherwise 8am–6pm.

✴ ✴ Tai Shan mountain

Anyone in good enough condition can make a tour from the base up to the summit in a day, but all the sights on the way mean that a more comfortable tempo is preferable. Assuming the requisite fitness, the same sights also exclude the possibility of taking the easy route by road and cable-car. For those not wishing to stay up at the mountain peak but still hoping to catch the sunrise at the summit, it is therefore ideal to go part of the way with the aid of transport and walk the rest. The right way to experience the story would, of course, be to walk up the mountain, slowly getting closer to the summit. In addition, a certain amount of hard work is all part of the Tai Shan experience.

Ascent

From the north gate of the Dai Miao temple, head straight on: This has been the common route to take for centuries, if the not for the whole 2000 years and more. It also has an abundance of attractions. As on all of China's famous mountains, the way is broad, firmly paved and equipped with stone stairways so that normal walking shoes will suffice for the ascent.

Decorative gates

The bottom end of the route is adorned with several decorative stone gates. The first of them, before the edge of the town, is called **Daizong Fang** and dates from 1730. Where the steps begin is the »First Gate to Heaven« (shortly before it on the left is a large temple erected by the salt merchants of Shanxi in honour of Guan Di). The following gate bears the inscription: »This is where Confucius climbed«. Straight afterwards comes another with the words »Stairway to Heaven«.

Inscriptions

More inscriptions appear on stone tablets to the left and right. Indeed inscriptions come thick or thin all the way up the climb, mainly etched into the rock itself. Two thousand years of tourism on Tai Shan, often including some very wealthy and educated individuals who left behind graffiti of the highest order, have made for the greatest open-air display of calligraphy in the world. The tradition continues even now. Further up, even **Mao Zedong** himself is immortalized in a rock inscription.

Red Gate

The sequence of white decorative gates ends at the »Palace of the Red Gate« (Hongmen Gong), a building looking much like a city gate and acts as the main gate to the mountain itself. There are two small temples in its side wings. The left-hand one (west) is dedicated to the Cloud Princess, while the other one is for Buddha Maitreya.

House of the Immortals

The two-storey Wanxian Lou from 1620 also has a religious function. Formerly it was dedicated to the Queen Mother of the West and the immortals, but now it too is a place of offerings to the Cloud Princess.

Palace of the Great Bear Mother

After another kilometre (1100 yd) of climbing, the route reaches a former **nunnery**, a complex of buildings of unknown age. Its name refers to the constellation of the Plough or Great Bear. Note the age-old Japanese pagoda tree in front of the gate.

The route carries on climbing gently through a wooded valley, but then it gets steeper and after another 5 km/3 mi beyond Daizong Fang, it reaches the **Middle Gate to Heaven** (Zhongtian Men), where the scenery suddenly changes. At this spot a veritable village has come into being with restaurants, pubs, shops and car parking, as this is where the road that leads up the mountain further to the west comes to an end. From here a cable-car runs up to the area around the summit. To get to the valley station means taking a bit of a walk to the west.

> ! **Baedeker TIP**
>
> **Maiden Tea**
>
> On the way up to the Middle Gate to Heaven, a straw hut lies to the right, ages old, partially decked with cowhides, decorated with tree roots and open on three sides. From this building »Maiden Tea« is served, made by the owner from self-gathered leaves and given to climbers in bamboo beakers.

Bridge over the Clouds

The following part of the journey starts off with quite a shallow slope. Where it starts to get steep again there is soon a stone bridge which crosses the valley in front of a waterfall. Its name (Yunbu Qiao) should not be taken all too seriously. The inscriptions virtually chiselled into the waterfall are notable here. There is usually only a small amount of water trickling down and in winter the river can stop flowing entirely.

Wudaifu Pine

A little bit above the bridge is where the Wudaifu Pine grows. When the first emperor climbed Tai Shan in 219 BC, he is supposed to have sheltered under this tree from a shower of rain, from which it gets its name »Wudaifu«; which is a term for an official of the 9th rank.

Qianlong inscription

One major inscription in the rocks on the far side of the valley is called the »**Thousand Fathom Inscription**« (Wanzhang Bei). It documents the ascent of Tai Shan by the Qianlong-Kaiser in 1748.

The last and steepest part of the route is nothing but high steps, although it is no longer possible to count 18 bends. The expression »Staircase of the 18 Bends « goes back to earlier times. At the top is the **South Gate to Heaven**. This is where the summit region starts. Usually a fresh wind blows over the saddle of the mountain and dispels some of the tiredness people may be feeling by now. That is good because there is still further to go.

»Staircase of the 18 Bends«

The route goes on upwards to the right along a whole street of hotels and restaurants. The main path runs above the southern slopes straight through the **Temple of Bixia Ci**, where the Princess of the Azure Blue Clouds is worshipped. This has been restored and is in good condition – including its theatre stage (to the right across the path). Daoist monks live here and manage the sacred site.

Temple of the Cloud Princess

The path continues to the east around an ugly radio station towards the northern side of the summit area. On the way there are a number of curious rock formations to marvel at, including the **»Bridge of the Immortals«**, a natural bridge made of blocks of stone.

Rocks

At the point where there is no going any higher stands the Temple of the Jade Emperor, honouring the chief god of popular Daoism. The building was erected around the summit itself.

Temple of the Jade Emperor

Sunrise on the holy mountain Tai Shan

Tang inscription Below the summit to the south, a path leads to the most famous inscription on Tai Shan. It is perhaps the most splendid in all of China. Here the Tang emperor Xuanzong set down the reasons for his Fengshan Sacrifice of the year 725. The text itself is more than 13 m/43 ft high and 5.7 m/19 ft wide. All of its 1009 characters are gilded.

★
Lingyan Si Temple One of the loveliest monasteries in China lies in a deep valley on the western side of the mountain and can only be reached by taxi. The trip is well worth it, though. There are three reasons: firstly the location of the temple amid the mountain scenery with its view of tall, rocky cliffs. In addition this is the end of the valley and so there is a most pleasant feeling of stillness. The second aspect is the **monks' cemetery featuring 167 burial pagodas**, the oldest of which dates from the 8th century. The third attraction is the extraordinary clay statuary on display in the main hall. It features 40 coloured, life-size statues of monks, originally dating from the Song era, who sit like living men on a bench that runs right round the hall. The encore is the sight of a slender 54 m/177 ft brick pagoda from the 11th century. 40 km/25 mi northwest of Tai'an. Opening times: 8am–5pm daily.

Taiyuan

Hb 27

Province: Shanxi
Altitude: 800 m/2625 ft

Population: 2.4 million

Situated in the middle of Shanxi Province on the upper reaches of the Fen He River, the provincial capital is plagued with terrible air, and apart from tickling the throat, it also has few sights to tickle the fancy. Outside it, though, there are two extraordinary attractions, the women's temple of Jin Ci and the old banking city of Pingyao. It is also a base for trips to Wutai Shan.

What to see in Taiyuan

Provincial museum Shanxi Sheng Bowuguan The museum is in two separate locations. The smaller is the Daoist monastery Chongyang Gong, exhibiting mainly ceramics, bronzes, religious statuary and coins, for the most part archaeological finds. Some of the furnishings of the shrine have also been preserved; it was dedicated to the »immortal« **Lu Dongbin**, a Daoist from the 8th century (who adopted the monastic name Chunyang), who is said to have ascended to heaven instead of dying. Qifeng Jie (near the western side of 1st May Square). Opening times: May–Oct. 8am–12 noon, 2.30pm–6pm daily, otherwise 9am–12 noon, 2.30–5pm.

Confucius Temple, Wen Miao Only a few minutes walk away, the main part of the museum is housed in the former temple of Confucius, a fine, dignified complex

▶ VISITING TAIYUAN

GETTING THERE	ACCOMMODATION

GETTING THERE

As a provincial capital, Taiyuan has flights to all the major cities in China. It is a railway junction with direct trains to Beijing, Datong and Xi'an. The main station is in the southeast corner of the old town.
Long distance coaches
Beijing and Datong can also be reached from Taiyuan by long-distance coach. They run at more frequent intervals than the trains and, thanks to the motorways, the journey times are shorter, too. From the bus station west of the railway station, buses also run to Pingyao and ►Wutai Shan (S. 566).

ACCOMMODATION

▶ **Luxury**
Taiyuan: World Trade Hotel
69 Fuxi Jie
Tel. 0351/868 88 88
Fax 0351/868 98 88
Taiyuan's most reputable hotel, 398 rooms, in the centre of town.

▶ **Mid-range/Budget**
Pingyao: Yide Hotel
16 Saxiang Jie
Tel. 0351/568 59 88
Fax 0351/568 44 49
www.yide-hotel.com
Live like a well-heeled Pingyaoer. A small but attractive private hotel situated in a stately home dating from 1726, in a central but quiet old-town location.

from 1882 with bamboo trees growing in the grounds. The collection relates the history of the province. The Confucius Temple is on Wenmiao Xiang, east of 1st May Square. Opening times: May–Oct. Tue–Sun 9am–12 noon and 2.30pm–6.30pm, in winter closes 5pm.

Immediately to the north of the Confucius Temple is a Buddhist monastery with the richest tradition in the city, founded in the Tang era. In 1864 a major fire left only the **»Hall of Great Compassion«** (Dabei Dian) standing, a fine example of early Ming architecture. It contains monumental figures of the three bodhisattvas, Guanyin, Manjushri and Samantabhadra. The Guanyin is portrayed with 1000 hands and eyes. The monastery is famous for its collection of old sutra manuscripts, of which some are on display. Shangguan Xiang. Opening times: 8am–5pm daily.

Temple of Chongshan Si

✳ Temple of Jin Ci

The »Jin memorial temple«, 25 km/16 mi southwest of the city, is unique among China's religious shrines, in particular because of its theme. It is concerned with the life-giving power of water and of women. In addition there are some of the loveliest ancient depictions of women to be seen anywhere in China.

The beginnings of the temple are lost in the mists of time. All that is known is that by the 5th century AD at the latest there was a dedication to Prince Shuyu, who had lived in the 11th century BC and received this area as a fief, becoming Duke of Jin. The name Jin itself, now the abbreviation for the whole province, allegedly goes back to a stream which has its source here on the temple grounds. This source gives rise to the dominant theme of the temple, of water as the embodiment of fertility and femininity, symbol of the inexhaustible, the constant renewal of life. This idea also exists in Europe in the form of the »Fountain of Youth«. Here the variations on the theme are astounding and beautiful.

Thematics and history

The memorial temple is situated in a park. From the car park it is initially necessary to struggle through all the bustle of traders in front of the park gate and then cross the park to get to the entrance. It is located on the eastern side of the temple grounds and the temple itself is aligned in this direction, too.

Entrance

From the gate, first head westward to **»Water Mirror Terrace«**, the temple's stage, where the consoles are decorated by fine, coloured wood carvings and painted scenes from plays. As appropriate, the main figure in the main hall also faces this stage since the theatre is intended for his entertainment – only in symbolic terms of course so that it matters little that his view is severely obscured.

Main axis

The »Bridge of Meeting with the Immortals« crosses an arm of the Jin stream heading westward. The name refers to the »fountain of youth« aspect of the spring water.

Bridge

On the far bank four larger-than-life, cast-iron warriors guard the sacred area. Three of the statues date from the end of the 11th century; although two of them later had to have their heads replaced.

Iron men

The axis continues past drum and bell towers to the offertory hall, which dates back to the year 1168. This is where sacrifices were made to the main statue.

Offertory hall

The last man-made construction before the main hall is a square basin, which once again evokes the dominant theme. The water is crossed via a cross-shaped bridge. The ensemble bears the name »yu zhao fei liang«: **»Fish Pond and Flying Girders«**.

Pond and bridge

The **»Hall of the Holy Mother«** with its double-eaved roof and columns wrapped with dragons has remained virtually unaltered since the year 1102 and is a masterpiece of Song-era building skills. The

Main Hall

← *Pavilion in the part of the Jin Ci women's temple. The capitals of the pillars in the foreground are shaped like babies* name refers to the motif of the giving of life as well as to the main statue. The latter sits on a raised pedestal, quite like a Buddha, in the midst of 42 standing figures representing eunuchs and maids. The group is the major artistic and historic treasure in the monastery. All the figures are sculpted in very fine detail and are dressed in the fashions of the Song period, since they date back to the time that the hall was built. The colouring has been renewed in later times, however. In keeping with the theme of the temple, the rear wall is decorated with wavy lines.

Side halls

To the right of the main hall stands the **»Temple of Progeny«** with more beautiful statuary. It is painted with scenes featuring children. The small annexe to the left (south) evokes the topic of »water« in a new variation. In this hall the legendary hero Taitai is worshipped. He was the immortal who diverted the waters and dried out the swamps so that fields could be created.

Spring

A stone's throw further to the south is the lucrative spring which inspired the entire complex. Its name; Nanlao Quan, **»Spring of Never Aging«**, comes close to promising the miracles of the Fountain of Youth. The water emerges at a constant temperature of 17°C.

Tower of the Water Mother

The two-storey building to the west also belongs to the spring. It recalls a young farmer's wife who was always able to fill her water bucket at will. Her mother-in-law envied her ability to do such magic and abused it until she caused a flood. How the young woman then sat, hair still uncombed, on the bucket to dam the flow is depicted on the ground floor. At the top she can be seen as the Water Mother in a circle of four maids. The legend ends by saying that the Water Mother was unable to stem the flow entirely so that the bucket became the spring that can be seen outside.

Thuja

Where everything is predicated on fertility and life, veteran trees are just the right kind of flora. To the north of the main hall there is such a tree, which leans quite dangerously to one side. According to legend it is 3000 years old.

Grotto

A stairway leads up from here to a cave on the hillside. This too is naturally seen as a symbol of femininity. It is said that the sage Fu Shan (1607–1684), lived here for a while and left a treatise on gynaecology.

Side temple and pagoda

North of the main axis there is a row of several ancillary temples. The most westerly (nearest the hillside) is dedicated to the aforementioned Prince Shuyu, first **Duke of Jin**. In an inscription next to the gate dated 16 February 646, the second Tang emperor thanks him for his aid and protection in the fight against the Sui dynasty. East of there is a temple for the protective deity Guan Di, a temple for the East Mountain, where the lord of Tai Shan is worshipped and a temple to

Wenchang, protective patron of literature. Right in the south there is a brick pagoda, which can be climbed. Opening times: 8am–6.30pm daily in summer, but shorter hours at other times of year. ☉

✹ ✹ Pingyao

Travelling to Pingyao (pop. 40,000, 100 km/60 mi south of Taiyuan) is like taking a trip back in time to ancient China. Almost the entire town consists of old-fashioned streets and alleys but it does not have the feel of a museum at all. On the contrary it is very lively. In addition it is possible to find out here about credit arrangements of the 19th century, as Pingyao experienced a brief heyday back then as the headquarters of some important exchange banks.

A day trip from Taiyuan is just about sufficient if you start out early enough. However it is much more rewarding and more atmospheric to spend the night here. In a taxi it is possible to combine Pingyao with a tour of Jin Ci. **Tours**

It is best seen by those approaching from the north. The town's walls are 6.4 km/4 mi long, 10 m/33 ft high, and topped with crenellations. They were **originally built in 1370** when they were intended for defence against the Mongols, who had just been driven out of **Walls**

Pingyao Map

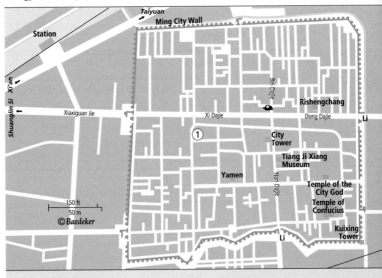

Where to stay
① Yide Hotel

The course of the Great Wall always follows mountain ridges. It is 5m/16ft wide at the level of the walkway.

THE GREAT WALLS OF CHINA

The construction of long boundary walls in the territory of steppe and desert nomads to the north of Chinese agricultural lands goes back to the period around 300 BC. At that time China began to expand northwards and secure the conquered regions with walls. More than a dozen later dynasties are known to have built walls, but almost every dynasty chose a new course for its border defences, depending on the political situation. It is therefore in fact incorrect to speak of »the« Great Wall of China.

Almost all of the walls were made of rammed earth and erected within the space of a few weeks by the forced labour of peasants. It was easy to climb over them, but the decisive point was that they represented an obstacle to horses. In this way they kept raiders out, like a solid border fence, and additionally made it pos-

A walk on the wall can be fairly hard work, as it involves a great deal of up and down

sible to control **border traffic**. The earth walls decayed as centuries passed and were abandoned when the borders shifted. Many dynasties were able to manage without walls altogether by handling the situation on the northern border through political and military measures. The last wall, the **Great Ming Wall** of the 16th and 17th centuries, is by far the most expensive and imposing, but is at bottom a monument to failure. On the one hand, it shows that the China of the rulers who built it, in its Confucian sense of superiority, would not condescend to enter into the relationship of trade and tribute that the Mongols desired. Having gained their enmity in this way, construction of a wall seemed to be the last resort in keeping them out. On the other hand, the **enormous burden** placed on the country by building the wall contributed to the fall of the dynasty, which had concentrated too much on exter-

nal enemies. Lastly, the wall proved to be by no means insuperable, despite the colossal cost. Openings for rivers and the sleepiness of the guards were notorious weaknesses. Decoy attacks drew border troops to one section of the wall, depriving other sectors of protection. In the end the Manchus, who had been called in to defend the Ming dynasty, actually marched into the empire through an open fortress gate.

Legends of the Wall

The fame of the Great Wall is matched by the amount of nonsense that has been uttered about it. It is often claimed to be the work of the First Emperor, which would make it more than 2200 years old. It is true that a general of this emperor, the first unifier of China, built a wall in the north after driving the steppe peoples out of their pastures. However, as some remaining parts show, extensive stretches of this wall, which was constructed with great haste, partly of rammed earth and partly out of courses of rubble, were little more than a border demarcation. The remains of other walls, too, must have decayed into piles of rubble as long ago as Marco Polo's time, the late 13th century, which is why Polo's account makes no mention of a border wall. The assertion that the Great Wall of China was visible from the moon or even Mars appeared decades before the start of space exploration. Later it was claimed that the wall and the dykes of the Netherlands were the only works of humankind that were visible with the naked eye from space. None of this is true: even from a high-flying plane, only the restored parts of the wall can be made out. Moreover, most of the wall consists of **ruins overgrown with grass**. In 2003, following the first space flight by a Chinese astronaut, who could see no more of

A border wall that failed to keep out the enemy

the wall than everyone else before him, i.e. nothing at all, China too has abandoned this cherished myth. So was the building of the wall ever effective in securing the border? On the whole yes, as far as the earth walls of earlier dynasties are concerned. No, when it comes to the Great Wall of the Ming, which is paying off only now – as a tourist attraction.

China. A moat around the town has mostly been preserved too, other parts having been restored in recent times. Just as it was 600 years ago, the town is entered through one of its six gates, two in the east and in the west and one each in the north and south. Coming from Taiyuan it is entered either by the north or by the northwest gate.

! **Baedeker TIP**

View from the walls
Near the northwest gate there is an ugly suburb with factories and warehouses. The view of the old town from the southeast gate, Taihe Men, is much nicer. The northeast and south gates also offer pleasing panoramas.

Pingyao consists as ever primarily of its old town; its suburbs being quite small. The walls form a rough square and most of the streets run more or less parallel with the fortifications. One street only carries on for 1.6 km/1 mi straight through the town, the axis running from the northwest gate, Fengyi Men, to the northeast gate of Qinhan Men along Xi Dajie and Dong Dajie.

Appearance There are 3800 historic dwellings, including 400 which are of particular historical importance. Some date back as far as the Mongol period. In addition there are more than a dozen other buildings, including a temple for the folk religion, of a kind that elsewhere would have been closed down and demolished after 1949. Pingyao is already in the area where there are **cave dwellings**. Since wood for building is expensive, the preferred building materials are clay or mud and stone, imitating a mud cave by means of barrel vaulting. Strict planning regulations are enforced in the town. New buildings have to be built using old techniques and shops cannot advertise with neon signs but have to use flags. The town has been dolled up a bit for the tourists now, but that has not made a museum out of it, or made all of it a feast for the eyes.

Banking houses Pingyao was one of the bases for the Shanxi banks, the smallest of three. Here there were about 20 exchange banks, which were set up exclusively for use by merchant banks and the state. Their decentralized organization meant, the importance of the local bank headquarters here was not that great for day-to-day business. Some of the former banking centres are open to the public, fine old buildings – some complete with their old furnishings – solid, beautifully decorated, yet anything but grandiose. Among the more conveniently located are the **Baichuantong Bank**, which operated from 1860 to 1918 (109 Nan Dajie, south of the town's tower), and the older **Rishengchang** (40 Xi Dajie), where the clearing process was said to have been invented in 1823. Opening times: both 8am–6pm daily, longer in summer, shorter in winter.

Nan Dajie and the town tower Die »**Great South Street**« is the main road in the town. It runs from the south gate as far as a T-junction with the east-west axis. The

Lanterns adorn the taverns of Pingyao too

northern section of it passes under the town's tower, a pagoda-like building 19 m/62 ft in height, which served as a watchtower for spotting fires.

From the Yamen to the Confucius temple

From the big crossroads on the southern section of Nan Dajie, head west to get to a large complex of old government buildings covering an area of 2.5 ha/6 acres, which was called the Yamen of the district. Nowhere else in China has such an ensemble been so perfectly preserved as here. In order to avoid going back by the same route, head south opposite the Yamen and then go east after one block. Shortly before the eastern end of this road is the Confucius temple, a dignified estate covering 1 ha/2.5 acres. The main hall dates back to 1163 and is the oldest of its kind still extant at a Confucius temple anywhere on the country. Just a little further to the east is the southeast gate. A pagoda-like tower in the southeast corner of the old town was used for observing the stars. Heading north around the Confucius temple you will come to the temple of the town's god, a complex with a number of ancillary temples.

Temple of Shuanglin Si

Outside Pingyao itself there are more temple monasteries which managed to survive the Cultural Revolution complete with their glorious old decoration. The nearest of them is 7 km/4 mi southwest of town. It covers an area of 120 x 123 m/131 x 135 yd and the statues are not just limited to individual figures standing on pedestals featuring Sumeru, the world mountain. Instead, all around the walls there are extremely elaborate wooden reliefs, bigger than life-size, depicting in miniature mountain caves and clouds, streets or buildings, inside (or in front of) which a total of **1600 figures, including complete statues,** of varying sizes are sitting, standing or performing some task. Practically everything seems to be in motion. Figures bow, their robes flutter in the breeze, their faces grimace. It is a truly spectacular sight, a kind of Ming-era Baroque, so to speak. Travel from Pingyao by rented bicycle or motorized rickshaw. Opening times: 9am–5pm daily. ⏰

Tianjin

He 26

Province: Directly controlled municipality   **Population:** 10 million
Altitude: 4 m/13 ft

The northern Chinese port of Tianjin (formerly spelt Tientsin), 130 km/81 mi southeast of Beijing, is hardly more than a small town along the chain of Chinese tourist destinations but it is no drab little out-of-the-way spot. Its particular features are its surviving colonial-era streets and its tradition for arts and crafts.

What to see in Tianjin

Temple of Dabei Yuan

The **»Temple of Great Mercy«**, northeast of the old town, is the liveliest of the Buddhist temples in the city. It dates from the 17th century but the statuary only dates from 1980, the originals having been destroyed in the Cultural Revolution. The layout corresponds to the usual scheme. The prime figure in the main hall is Buddha Shakyamuni. In the following hall a 24-armed Guanyin is worshipped. ⏲ Tianwei Lu 26. Opening times: Tue–Sun 9am–4.30pm.

Culture Street (Gu Wenhua Jie)

This pedestrian street of craft shops, between the old town and the river, consists of new buildings in the old style. On the square at the northern end is the **»Palace of Empress of Heaven«** (Tianhou Gong), a temple founded in 1326 and rebuilt after the Cultural Revolution. ⏲ It is dedicated to the protective goddess of mariners. Opening times: 9am–4.45pm daily.

Old town

Confucius temple

Covering more than 1 ha/2.5 acres, the Confucius temple, which dates from the 15th century, has a pleasantly quiet atmosphere. The main hall has some Chinese zithers on display, as formerly used in ⏲ sacrificial rites. Opening times: Tue–Sun 9am–4pm.

Old town museum

A traditional complex, built in the republican era by a wealthy citizen of Tianjin, now functions as the old town's museum. As such it is its own outstanding exhibit.
Inside the rooms there are a many different items from kitchen appliances to wedding dresses and toys offering an insight into life in ⏲ the city in earlier decades. 202 Dongmennei Dajie. Opening times: 9am–5pm daily.

★

Theatre museum

When the guild of Cantonese merchants in Tianjin built their **prestigious assembly and lodging house** in the traditional building style in 1907, they also included a theatre auditorium. Plays are still performed on the stage from time to time even now. In the adjoining

▶ VISITING TIANJIN

INFORMATION

CITS
22 Youyi Lu
Tel. 022/28350821, 28358349
Fax 022/28352619

Tianjin Tourism Bureau
18 Youyi Lu
Tel. 022/28 35 88 12, fax 28 35 23 24

GETTING THERE

Tianjin is at the junction of the lines from Shenyang to Shanghai and Beijing to Shanghai. The express trains from Beijing's South station take just 30 minutes and travel at ten-minute intervals throughout the day. From Tianjin's airport, southeast of the city centre, there are flights to all the major Chinese airports.

SHOPPING

Tianjin is known for the Yangliuqing New Year pictures, made in traditional fashion using a multi-coloured block printing method. One place they can be bought is opposite the temple of Tianhou Gong on Culture Street. Other specialities include the caricature-like clay figures of people in everyday situations: Zhang Caisu Clay Figure Workshop, 202 Machang Dao.

WHERE TO EAT

Food Street (Shipin Jie)
Qinghe Dajie
A kind of shopping arcade with 50 restaurants in all price categories – from standard noodle soup to the most expensive specialities

▶ Moderate/Inexpensive

① **Café Kiessling (Qishilin)**
33 Zhejiang Lu
Tel. 022/23 30 03 30

What originally started as a German bakery has somehow survived the changing times and still occupies the same address. Nowadays it is a combination of a café, Western-style restaurant and ice-cream parlour. Menu in English.

② **Goubuli Baozi Pu**
322 Heping Lu
Tel. 022/23 03 11 18
This is the best of a number of branches. Old and renowned specialists for baozi dumplings, »that no dog would care about«, as its odd name testifies. Downstairs it is very cheap but there is better fare upstairs on the 3rd floor.

③ **Cosy Cafe and Bar**
68 Changde Dao
(corner of Kunming Lu)
Tel. 022/23126616
Smart bar and restaurant with Western cuisine, live music and a dance floor.

ACCOMMODATION

▶ Luxury

① **Nikko Tanjin**
189 Nanjing Lu
Tel. 022/83 19 88 88, fax 83 19 22 66
www.nikkotianjin.com
The 373-room hotel, established in 2007, is the pinnacle of the local hospitality sector. The colonial quarter is only a stone's throw away.

▶ Mid-range

② **Tianjin First Hotel
(Tianjin Di-yi Fandian)**
158 Jiefang Beilu
Tel. 022/23309988, fax 33 12 30 00
100 very spacious rooms in an old building dating from 1922; although the hotel itself only opened in 1996.

Tianjin Map

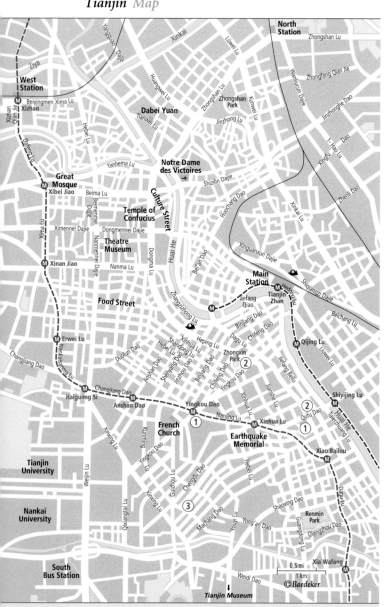

0,5 mi
1 km

©Baedeker

Tianjin Museum

Where to stay	Where to eat		Metro Line 1
① Hotel Nikko Tianjin	① Café Kiessling	③ Cosy Cafe	Ⓜ—Ⓜ Metro Line 1
② Tianjin First Hotel	② Goubuli Baozi	and Bar	Ⓜ—Ⓜ Binhai Mass Transit

rooms, photographs, programmes and other exhibits cover the history of the theatre. 31 Nanmennei Dajie. Opening times: Tue–Sun 9am–4pm.

Heping district (Heping Qu)

The Heping district has most of the legacies of the colonial era. It stretches from the southeast edge of the old town as far as Machang Dao in the south and from the Huai He River in the east to Nanmenwai Dajie and Weijin Lu in the west. From north to south it encompasses the former Japanese concessionary zone (as far as Jinzhou Dao and Nanjing Lu), the French zone (to Yingkou Dao) and the British zone. Heping Lu, once called Asahi Road in the north and Rue de Chaylard in the south, is now Tianjin's main shopping street.

There is a more densely packed atmosphere among the 100-year old bank buildings on Jiefang Beilu, formerly Rue de France in the north and Victoria Road in the south. Steeped in tradition, this is where the grande dame among Tianjin's hotels is located, the Astor Lishunde.

Jiefang Beilu

Westwards of Jiefang Beilu at the end of Binjiang Dao are the twin towers of the French church (Lao Xikai Tianzhu Jiaotang), built between 1913 and 1916 in the neo-Romanesque style and then painted. It is the largest church in town.

French church

The »five great streets« of the British concession, a little south of the French church, are neither particularly broad nor lined with impressive buildings, but here the **colonial atmosphere** can be experienced in virtually unaltered form. A protected area spans six streets: Chengdu Dao (London Road), Chongqing Dao (Edinburgh Road), Changde Dao (Colombo Road), Dali Dao (Singapore Road), Munan Dao (Hong Kong Road) and Machang Dao (Race Course Road) between Kunming Lu in the west and Hebei Lu in the east. Here it is possible to see 230 villas once owned by Britons, Frenchmen and Germans. To find out more about the history of the concessionary zones, visit the **Tianjin Museum of Modern History**, 314 Hebei Lu. Opening times: Mon–Fri 9am–5pm.

Wuda Dao

For its 600-year centennial in 2004 the city treated itself to this truly spectacular new museum building. Its shape is reminiscent of a swan in flight. Inside the inventories of the former museum of art and the local history museum have been combined. Art is exhibited on the first floor and includes ancient bronze vessels, porcelain, calligraphy, ink painting and rubbing stones. One flight up, photos, large-scale dioramas and other exhibits illustrate the city's history. Youyi Lu, corner of Pinjiang Dao. Opening times: 9am–4.30pm daily (last admission 4pm).

★
Tianjin Museum (Tianjin Bowuguan)

Tibet

Province: Autonomous region of Tibet
(Xizang)

Population: 2.65 million
Altitude: Up to 8844 m/29,017 ft.

What is Tibet? The question cannot be answered so quickly as one might think. In this case, what is meant is the autonomous region of Tibet with its capital at Lhasa. In terms of cultural geography, Tibet is larger than that and covers the entire Tibet-Qinghai Plateau, although the area does not have clear borders all the way around. In addition Tibetans have also settled in western Sichuan, southern Gansu and northern Yunnan.

When Tibetan Buddhism (Lamaism) is the theme, then the borders melt away altogether, since the Mongolians, too, would have to be counted as part of this religion. On the other hand, Tibetan culture is not so uniform as it appears from the outside. The lives of those Tibetans who farm land have little in common with those of the cattle-rearing nomads of the country other than religion, and even that is not the same as the Buddhism taught in the monasteries.

There are many reasons to experience Tibet. Tibet is not China, at least not in cultural terms. Hints of this can be seen in Chengde. Insights into the lives of pilgrims may also be gained in Xiahe (►Lanzhou) or the Mongolian lamaist monasteries, where the style of building and the iconography are the same as those in Tibet. Nevertheless the experience of the illustrious elevated plateau and high mountains under a blue sky, villages with their flying pennants and, of course, the monastic fortress of the Potala all demand a trip into the Tibetan heartland. Precisely because of the scenery and the chance to experience village life, visitors should not confine themselves to Lhasa.

Why come to Tibet?

Religion and society

In spite of a few recent tendencies towards secularism, a deep religious devotion still dominates the lives of most Tibetans. Their form of Buddhism is neither equivalent to the Theravada or Hinayana manifestations of southeast Asia nor to the Chinese-Japanese-Korean Mahayana-Buddhism, the schools of the »Greater« or »Lesser Vehicles«. Instead it is sometimes called the »Diamond Vehicle« (vajrayana) school, popular because of the great importance of its religious leaders, or simply **Lamaism**. The unique character of Tibetan-Buddhist teaching first emerged when it incorporated parts of the native, shamanistic Bön religion, which had existed before Buddhism

← *Gateway to a world of marvels: the entrance to a Tibetan monastery*

Tibet is not China. Tibet is Tibet: a fascinating natural world, ...

arrived. Its particular features include the great importance of rites, which are attributed with a magical effect, the practical application of the reincarnation theory for determining spiritual successors to deceased lamas, and a much larger pantheon as compared to Chinese Buddhism, including countless frightening and sometimes wicked deities. This makes Tibetan iconography highly complex.

Dalai Lama and Panchen Lama One special aspect in Tibet is that, since the 16th/17th centuries, worldly and spiritual authority have largely been invested in the same individuals. This applies (or did apply) to the status of abbots but also – at least in theory – to the institution of the Dalai Lama, which emerged at that time. Nevertheless, the Panchen Lama, a **manifestation of Buddha Amitabha** has an even greater spiritual authority. The monasteries have had a dominant role, too, as centres of learning, not least in such worldly disciplines as mathematics, astronomy and medicine. There were, and still are, convents for nuns but the monks composed a much larger proportion of the celibate population. In the past as many as one in four adult men lived their lives in a monastery.

History and present

Tibet was, for the greater part of its history, an independent country, although it was not always unified as a state. The first to unite it into an empire was the 7th-century king **Songtsen Gampo**, who came to the throne in 629. This is considered the earliest assured date in the history of the country. Songtsen Gampo did not rule over all of what is now considered to be Tibet, essentially controlling only the Yarlong Valley around Shigatse and Lhasa, i.e. the core territory of Tibet. The king did undertake some campaigns of conquest but his lasting

… a fascinating culture and fascinating people

fame was cemented by his marriage politics. The Nepalese princess Bhrikuti and the Chinese princess Wencheng, whom he wedded to create blood bonds with the neighbouring empires, are still revered today as the Green Tara and White Tara, protective saints of Tibet. Both of them are assigned key roles in the spread of Buddhism in Tibet. Tibet became stronger and in the 8th century it even occupied large sections of China's Tang empire, including the oasis of Dunhuang, which Tibet controlled for 67 years. After an era in which the state collapsed, which was preceded in the 9th century by a persecution of Buddhists, the religion found its feet again in the 11th century. Tibetan Buddhism gained its dominant features only in the 14th/15th centuries thanks to the reformer **Tsongkhapa** (▶ Famous People p.83) and the Virtuous or Yellow Hat (Gelugpa) school which he founded and from which the institution of the Dalai Lama would emerge in the 16th/17th centuries.

From 1722 Tibet was part of the Manchu empire. The empire was represented in Lhasa by two officials known as ambans, who also exercised political influence; so that the supremacy of the empire was not merely pro forma. In 1913 the 13th Dalai Lama declared **Tibetan independence** – the country was at that time part of the British sphere of influence – but the Chinese Republic refused to recognize this. Although the legal situation was uncertain, the facts were clear. The Republic of China no longer exerted any authority over Tibet. However, Tibet itself was non-existent in terms of external politics (except for a certain limited exchange with Britain). The lack of any diplomatic relations caught up with the country in 1950, when China re-established its claim to Tibet by force. Tibet then protested to the United Nations, but its lack of allies meant it received no support.

The problem of autonomy

The fact that there is still a question mark about the situation in Tibet emerges not only from the simple fact of Chinese sovereignty, but from the way that China has exercised its power. **Mao Zedong and the Communist Party**, who exercised control over China overall in quite arbitrary fashion, behaved no differently in Tibet, except that there the situation was different. China's government was considered there not an indigenous administration, but as a foreign power against which the populace were resistant. The conflict culminated in 1959 with the violent suppression of a revolt, the result of which was that the Dalai Lama, accompanied by many more monks, fled the country. Since then a Tibetan government-in-exile has been based in the Indian city of Dharamsala. The problem then took on international dimensions. For Tibetans, things got worse during the **Cultural Revolution**, when its monasteries were dissolved and Mao's Red Guards destroyed the most sacred of images. This barbarism was the same in Tibet as it was elsewhere in China but here, because of the great social importance of religion, and not least its existential significance for individual Tibetans, it was drastic to a quite different degree.

Suppression

While these excesses were later blamed on the »Gang of Four« and as such officially condemned, the basic problem has not altered: The »autonomy« of the region, which in word has been promised to Tibet, is de facto of little worth. China wishes the occupation of Tibet in 1950 to be seen as a liberation from centuries of oppression (which involved slavery and serfdom) and therefore to legitimize it in moral terms. This view is not really in keeping with the facts, though, as this **forced liberation** has merely replaced the old constraints with new types of oppression, now additionally pernicious in that they have been imposed from outside and, being quite arbitrary, they must be considered illegitimate. It is clear that there can be no way back and any idealization of the situation as it was before 1950 is the last thing that is needed. Old Tibet was an unhappy place where war, murder and robbery were no less common than anywhere else in the world. Restoration of a religious state in Tibet would be difficult to square with human-rights considerations and even under other circumstances, in the age of the aeroplane, the internet and **economic and tourist globalization**, Tibet would not remain an island of the blessed. This does not justify

Human rights and the modern day

> ## ❓ DID YOU KNOW …?
>
> ▪ that on every house in central Tibet there are flags of five colours? Blue stands for the sky, white for the clouds, red for the sun, green for the water and yellow for the earth. On many doors is painted a sickle with a circle with a fiery tail hovering within it: they represent the sun and moon. The drawing of a scorpion on the wall of a house is supposed to protect the occupants from disaster.

← *The history of Tibet is a story of violence and repression. The prospects for young people are not rosy.*

▶ VISITING TIBET

INFORMATION

China Tibettour
http://en.tibettour.com.cn has highly varied information in English, including detailed maps.

Shigatse Travels
Lhasa, 100 Beijing Donglu
(in the Yak Hotel)
Tel. 0891/6330489
Fax 0891/6330482
www.shigatsetravels.com
Shigatse Travels and its business partners organize jeep tours to all parts of Tibet, e.g. to the holy mountain of Kailash. English spoken.

GETTING THERE

To travel into the Autonomous Region of Tibet a »Tibet Travel Permit« is required. Bookings for Tibet made via a travel agent will automatically include one. Once there it is no longer needed. Inside certain regions, including Lhasa and its surrounding district as well as Shigatse, there is freedom of movement but for other areas additional permits are required. These can be obtained in Lhasa or from the travel agent booking the tour.

By plane or train
Normally people get to Tibet by air. The most frequent flights are from Chengdu, where many travel agents arrange for trips to Tibet, e.g. Sichuan International Travel Service (see Chengdu). Bookings are also possible from Kunming or Beijing. There are also direct flights from Xi'an, Xining and Hong Kong. Lhasa's airport (Gonggar Airport) is in the Tsangpo valley about 100 km/60 mi from the city. One other popular way to get there is by coach or by four-wheel drive vehicle from Kathmandu and the travel agents there are set up for this, although there may be problems with the issue of a Chinese visa. Taking the trip in the opposite direction, out of China towards Kathmandu, is more certain to work. The railway from Golmud to Lhasa is another comfortable alternative, although the long distances mean that it takes a long time. The scenic experience is more vivid, though. Travelling overland from Sichuan or Yunnan is spectacular in terms of scenery but tough, expensive and bookable through Chinese travel agencies.

SHOPPING

Even if a saddle may not necessarily be what the house back home needs, visitors to the great pilgrims' market around the Jokhang Temple in Lhasa will surely find something else of interest: jewellery, prayer banners, old coins, furs and many more exotic items.

WHERE TO EAT

The traditional Tibetan stomach filler is tsampa, a batter made of roasted flour, served mixed with yak butter. It is not the kind of recipe to be found in restaurants, though. Momos are popular too, filled dumplings which can be found in restaurants in the old town. In Lhasa there are also good places for eating Nepalese or Indian food, and Chinese as well as of course.

▶ Moderate to inexpensive
① Lhasa: Dunya Restaurant
100 Beijing Donglu
(Yak Hotel), Tel. 0891/6333374
Good restaurant with English-speaking staff. Tibetan and international dishes are served.

Religious souvenirs: Tibetan prayer wheels

► Inexpensive
② *Lhasa: Kailash*
Banak Shol Hotel
43 Beijing Donglu
Tel. 0891/6323829
The upper floor has a bar and a roof garden. International fare.

ACCOMMODATION

Comfort comes at a price in Tibet. Anyone hoping to live cheaply will have to lower their expectations.

► Luxury
① *Lhasa: Brahmaputra Grand Hotel (Yaluzangbu Da Jiudia)*
Gongbutang Lu Yancheng
Guangchan B
Tel. 0891/630 99 99
Fax 0891/630 98 88
Well-run 185-room hotel on the eastern edge of town near the river (2 km from Jokhang). The hotel doctor can help in case of altitude sickness.

► Mid-range to budget
② *Lhasa: Yak Hotel*
100 Beijing Donglu
Tel. 0891/6323496
Fax 0891/6336845
www.shigatsetravels.com/yak.htm
Popular place with a mixture of foreign and Tibetan management, conveniently located on the edge of the old town. Very inexpensive rooms with no bath or more comfortable rooms with bathroom facilities. The Dunya restaurant is popular.

Shigatse: Manasarovar Hotel
20 Qingdao Donglu
Tel. 0892/8839999
Fax 0892/8828111
www.shigatsetravels.com/mana
sarovar.htm
Hotel built in 2001 with Tibetan style elements. The best choice of accommodation in Shigatse even if it is slightly off the beaten track.

Lhasa Map

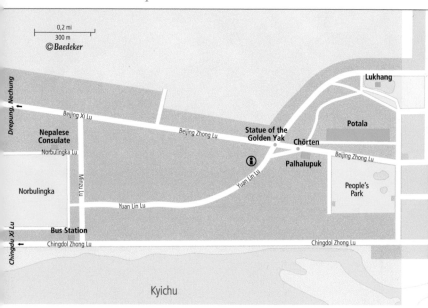

the actions of the Chinese government but it does put in perspective the changes that are occurring within Tibet. Anyone travelling to Tibet will see there, as elsewhere, aspects of the modern world and will recognize that Tibetans too are seeking their ideals not merely in the past.

Climate and health Even in Lhasa, which at 3700 m/12,140 ft above sea level is low-lying by Tibetan standards, altitude sickness in the form of serious headaches is to be expected. After flying in by plane, a slow process of acclimatization with plenty of rest, at least on the first day, should definitely be planned in – regardless of age or physical condition. Afterwards, too, physical difficulties may be foreseen. This is even more the case at higher altitudes. Other factors relevant to health include the strong sunlight and the large differences in temperature between day and night. North of the Trans-Himalayan belt the winters are of Siberian severity.

Lhasa: Old Town and Jokhang

Beware of false expectations! Tibet's political and spiritual centre (pop. 150,000 not including the surrounding region) nowadays largely resembles any other Chinese provincial town with faceless new buildings, broad, straight roads and satellite dishes.

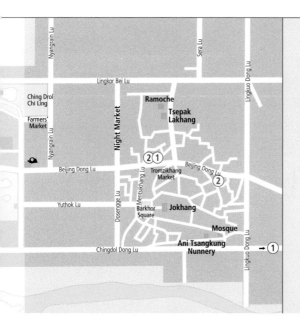

Where to stay
① Brahmaputra Grand Hotel
② Yak Hotel

Where to eat
① Dunya Restaurant
② Kailash

Jokhang Temple

This temple in the centre of the old town is really called **Tsuglag-khang**, after the name of the holiest deity, but is commonly known as Jokhang. It is the oldest and most revered Buddhist shrine in Tibet and as such is visited by a constant stream of pilgrims. Although Princess Bhrikuti is supposed to have founded it in 640, it is more commonly associated by the populace with the name of the Chinese princess Wencheng, who came to Lhasa shortly afterwards and supposedly brought the statue of a twelve-year-old **Buddha Shakyamuni**, which is the temple's greatest treasure and which receives the utmost reverence. It shows Gautama, not as a Buddha, but wearing a diadem and body decoration at a time when he was a prince and had not yet retreated from the world. Thus he becomes approachable for humans in the way a bodhisattva is. That is one of the reasons for the popularity of the image, the current incarnation of which probably dates from the 12th century. It stands in a central shrine on the east wall of the main hall opposite its entrance, which because of the irregular outer design of the temple

? DID YOU KNOW …?

■ … that the first Europeans to cross Tibet and see Lhasa were Linz-born Johannes Grueber and his fellow-Jesuit, Albert d'Orville? They crossed Tibet on foot in 1661 while walking from Beijing to India. Grueber not only worked out the geographic latitude of the city very precisely but also gave Europe its first picture of the Potala Palace – along with a report of their travels.

back to the time when Lhasa was founded, to the early days of the Potala and of Tibetan Buddhism. Depicted in sculpture is the king between the 38-armed Avalokiteshvara and the 5th Dalai Lama, along with the wives of the king Padmasabhava and other individuals. Further important rooms with splendid portraits follow in the upper storey of this part of the palace.

Via a mezzanine floor with murals, depicting amon other things the building of the Potala, the visitor walks down a staircase to the Great West Hall. It was the hall of enthronement and constitutes the architectural centre of the Red Palace. Its walls are covered in paintings, showing episodes involving the Dalai Lamas, the Tibetan kings and various manifestations of the bodhisattva Avalokiteshvara. The four rooms that surround the Great West Hall the religious message can be read as a history of Tibetan Buddhism. It begins at the Padmasambhava Hall, which is dedicated to the eponymous Indian saint who came to Tibet in the 8th century to cast out the demons of the native religion and give them the task of guarding Buddhism thereafter. The next stop is the **hall of the reformer Tsongkhapa**, whose successors posthumously declared him to be the first Dalai Lama. The third room is also dedicated to him and his next four incarna-

Great West Hall

A monk and novices in a Tibetan monastery

tions. The fourth contains the burial stupas and the bodies of the 5th, 10th and 12th Dalai Lamas. The tallest of these relic pagodas is 14 m/46 ft high and all of them are decorated with a surfeit of gilt and with precious stones. The one in the centre, the stupa of the 5th Dalai Lama, is the most magnificent jewel in the whole palace. Similar shrines in the Red Palace house the mortal remains of eight of the Tibetan priest-kings. The gilded roofs of the Red Palace make it clear where they are located even from outside.

Norbulingka

The extensive »Jewel Park« in the west of Lhasa is where the summer palaces of the 7th, 8th, 13th and 14th Dalai Lamas can be found. The spot was chosen by the 7th Dalai Lama thanks to a spring in the vicinity, which he used for its healing qualities. The main object of a visit is the palace of the present Dalai Lama, which was completed in 1956. It is not very big, relatively bright indoors and, despite its magnificent furnishings, not remotely comparable with the Potala Palace. Among the events depicted on a mural is the visit of the Dalai Lama to Mao Zedong in Beijing. Opening times: 9am–1pm, 2.30pm–6pm daily.

✴ Drepung

Drepung, formerly the largest monastery in Tibet, was founded in 1416 by a pupil of Tsongkhapa. Until 1959 it was the most politically influential **centre of the Gelugpa school**, the »Yellow Hats« and, since its abbots often set the agenda for politics at Potala, it found itself with many enemies through the ages and has been set aflame and partially destroyed several times during its history. Four academies belong to the monastery, the buildings for which are arranged irregularly around the great assembly hall.

In the west is the building that houses the former private chambers of the 5th Dalai Lama. Above it stands the »Joyful Palace« with the enthronement hall of 5th Dalai Lama. In both buildings the most impressive features are the mural paintings, as in the **Great Assembly Hall** with its 184 columns. The dominant figure there is a Maitreya, which towers up into the upper floor. To the west, diagonally opposite the assembly hall, is the building housing the Tantric Academy. This is famous for its unusually impressive murals of the Dharmapalas. To the east below the assembly hall there are three more academy

? DID YOU KNOW ...?

■ Wood, metal, stone, clay – those are the most common materials for a statue of Buddha but there are still three others: bodiless lacquerware, plaster (or stucco) and – particularly in Tibetan monasteries – butter! Yak butter statues never get very old, though. They mostly exist only in winter. Once they melt, the butter can be used to fuel butter lamps, so the noble people who donate them gain a double helping of good karma.

buildings, each of which also has an overwhelming abundance of images. 10 km/6 mi west of Lhasa. Opening times: 9am–5pm daily. ☉

✳ Sera

A different pupil of Tsongkhapa from the one who founded Drepung established the Sera Monastery in 1419. It is not quite so prominent as its arch-rival and is a little smaller. It also suffered fewer setbacks during its history.

The nearest section to the car park is the »Lower Academy«. Its great hall houses a Shakyamuni statue but it is another smaller **Shakyamuni figure** that attracts the greater veneration. Beyond a debating court, there are two academies with some important imagery, on the left the Tantric Academy and on the right what is called the Refugee's Academy. The latter was founded by a monk who had left the Drepung monastery as the result of a dispute. The central sanctuary on the rear wall of the building's great hall shows the reformer Tsongkhapa, flanked by Shakyamuni to the left and Amitabha to the right, along with the eight Tibetan bodhisattvas and some guardian deities.

Lower Academy

On the other side of another debating court, in which it is often possible to view the question-and-answer procedure of the monks in the afternoons, the main assembly hall stands across the path at the end. It possesses a monumental Maitreya taking up two storeys in its holy of holies. 5 km/3 mi north of Lhasa. Opening times. 9am–4pm daily ☉ (some buildings stay open till 6pm).

Main assembly hall

Around Lhasa

Any trips out of Lhasa should in general be organized through a travel agent. Most such trips require an off-road vehicle, meaning the prices for such journeys are high and so only become affordable if four people come along. Nevertheless they are certainly worth the trip, primarily because of the scenery, the chance to encounter villages, castles and lonely monasteries.

Ganden, the most important spiritual centre for the Yellow Hat school, was, like Drepung, founded in 1416, but since the 1960s it has been mostly synonymous with one thing, the brutality of Mao's anti-religious policies. No other holy place in China was obliterated in such heinous fashion, so that even its big, solid buildings were reduced to **rubble and ruins**. Meanwhile, several of the main buildings have been rebuilt and magnificently furnished to match the originals. A visit to the monastery is worth making, if only for the overland journey and the impressive location of the monastery amid the mountain scenery. 50 km/31 mi east of Lhasa. Open during the hours of daylight.

Ganden

Lake Nam Co   Lake Nam Co is at an altitude of 4590 m/15,059 ft, 195 km/121 mi by road from Lhasa and is a popular place for a trip. The peaks rise up to a maximum of 7114 m/23,340 ft. One overnight stay will be needed, ideally at the monastery by the lake. Comfort is not to be expected, though.

✳
From Lhasa to Shigatse
There are two routes for taking a trip to Shigatse. The faster and shorter way (240 km/149 mi) runs through the valley of the Tsangpo River (Yarlung Zangbo, Brahmaputra) – past villages and, further east, a sandy desert. The older route, 100 km/60 mi longer and more difficult, goes through the mountainous territory to the south of there and needs a whole day including stop-off visits. After crossing the Tsangpo, it first climbs up to a pass, from which a vast panorama can be seen ahead, including, among other sights, **Lake Yamdrok** and behind it the snow-capped peaks of the Himalayas.

The route then travels along the lake for a stretch before traversing a pass at an altitude of 5010 m/16,437 ft to get to **Gyangzê** (Gyantse, 4040 m/13,255 ft), two thirds of the way along the route. The little settlement is an old market town and from here sheep and yak wool is traded via the pass leading south to Sikkim. An imposing mountain towers above the northern edge of the town. The all-round view from the top makes it worth climbing. A bit further north is the **Pelkhor Chode Monastery** with its magnificent Kumbum, a chorten (stupa) built in 1440, the »Stupa of the 100,000 Images«. This is the only accessible relic stupa in Tibet and is designed as an architectural mandala. Its steps correspond to the ranks of higher entities, ranging from simple gods at the bottom to the transcendent Buddhas at the top.

Shigatse (Xigazê) · Tashilhünpo monastery

Shigatse is Tibet's second biggest town (pop. 60,000., 3900 m/12,795 ft above sea level) and the secondary centre of power in the country, although it is much more recent than Lhasa. In the 15th century it was a fortress town with its own governor in residence, but in the 16th it became the residence of the Panchen Rinpoche (Panchen Lama).

✳
Tashilhünpo
This monastery was founded in 1447 by a nephew and pupil of Tsongkhapa and counts among the half dozen most important monasteries for the Yellow Hat school. It is the base for the Panchen Rinpoche (Panchen Lama), the highest spiritual authority in Tibet. The title was created by the 5th Dalai Lama originally for his own teacher, who was abbot of this monastery, although as in the case of the Dalai Lamas themselves, the title was extended backwards so that the first Panchen Lama to be so named is now numbered the fourth of the line. Tashilhünpo now has the largest number of monks of any monastery in Tibet.

Ganden monastery, destroyed under Mao, is once again resplendent

Great Maitreya

The highlight is, as usual, presented right at the beginning of the clockwise circuit of the site, **a gilded copper statue of a seated Maitreya**, at 26 m/85 ft in height the largest of its kind in the world. It was made in 1914 out of 11 tons of bronze and 229 kg/500 lbs of gold. The Buddha exhibits the teaching mudra and holds a jar of nectar in his left hand as an indication that he will guide humanity back to the path of salvation.

Burial stupa of the 10th Panchen Lama

The burial stupa of the 10th Panchen Lama from 1993 is not much less impressive. The last Panchen Lama (before the current one) died in 1989. As he did not flee in 1959 (or was unable to do so), he was used as a figleaf for Beijing's Tibetan policies. The state is supposed to have put up half the cost of building the stupa, while the rest was raised through donations.

Other burial stupas

In addition, it is possible to visit the burial stupas of the 4th Panchen Lama (a very dark spot west of the assembly hall) and those of the 5th to 9th Panchen Lamas (east of the assembly hall). These were destroyed in the Cultural Revolution but their restoration was completed in 1992.

Assembly hall

The large assembly hall has allegedly been preserved since the 15th century. Among the things to be seen are some splendid murals and three sanctuaries on the northern side of the hall, the leftmost chapel being home to another monumental Maitreya (10 m/33 ft tall), accompanied by **Avalokiteshvara and Manjushri**. The main figure in the central chapel is a young Shakyamuni, wearing a crown and surrounded by disciples as well as eight bodhisattvas. The right-hand chapel has statues of Tara.

Monastery courtyard In the courtyard monks can mostly be seen carrying out their daily duties, chopping wood, kneading yak butter or tending the lamps. The court is on two levels and surrounded by several halls with a larger number of other statues.

✴ Trip to Nepal and Mount Everest

From Shigatse the road runs further west along the valley between the Himalayas and Trans-Himalayas as far as Lhazê, where it forks. Further west, it goes to the holy mountain of Kailash, while the southwestern fork leads through the border town of Zham (Zhangmu) and on to Nepal and Kathmandu. Before then, the route passes the **base camp for Mount Everest**.

Mt. Everest Mount Everest, the highest mountain on earth at 8844 m/29,017 ft, is on the Nepalese border with China, 220 km/137 mi south of Shigatse. It has long entranced mountaineers from all over the world. Its Tibetan name, Qomolangma, means **»Mother of the Universe«**. This is older than the Western name, which commemorates the British Surveyor-General of India, although he personally had nothing to do with the mountain itself. It was a Bengali, Radhanath Sikdar, who first calculated the height of the summit in 1852 and came to the conclusion that it was the highest on earth. The first successful ascent was on 29 May 1953 when the New Zealander Edmund Hillary and Sherpa Tenzing Norgay reached the top.

Turfan

Fj 24

Province: Autonomous Region of Xinjiang
Altitude: 154 m/505 ft

Population: 240 000

The oasis town of Turfan, on the northern route of the Silk Road, is a really pleasant place apart from the extreme heat in the summer. There is not much to see, though. The main attractions are outside of town. The population of the town is 80% Uighur and it is worth taking a walk though the streets around the central square.

What to see in and around Turfan

Emin Mosque and minaret (Sugong Ta) On the eastern edge of town, 3 km/2 mi from the centre, is the Emin Mosque. It was built in 1777/78 and is named after its benefactor, **Emin Hoja**, a Turfan ruler. The mosque is no longer used as such today. Its main attraction is the 37 m/121 ft circular minaret built of clay bricks, whereby the bricks are laid in a variety of ornamental

▶ VISITING TURFAN

GETTING THERE

Turfan is close to the railway line from Xi'an to Ürümqi but the station is in Daheyan, a good 60km/37 mi northwest of the town. The train from Ürümqi to Kashgar also stops there. Anyone wishing to go to Ürümqi, though, is better off taking one of the cross-country coaches that run all day long at frequent intervals.

GOING OUT

In summer, Uighur songs and dances are performed in the courtyard of the Grand Turpan Hotel. A walk round the town centre can be recommended at any time of year.

SHOPPING

A supply of raisins for years to come can be had very cheaply, although it probably isn't the ideal souvenir. Better to eat them there and enjoy a bottle of Turfan wine at the same time – fermentation of grapes has enormously developed in the last few years and some rather decent wines have resulted.

WHERE TO EAT
► Inexpensive

On the central square and at the bazaar on Laocheng Lu, a block further west, it is possible to eat cheaply and tastily, perhaps with hand drawn noodles or with lamb kebab.

ACCOMMODATION
► Mid-range
Grand Turpan Hotel
(Tulufan Da Fandian)
20 Gaochang Lu
Tel. 0995/855 36 68
Fax 0995/855 39 08
tlfdfd@china.com
Good 150-room hotel near the centre; the beds in the wing at the rear are nice and quiet.

► Budget
Gaochang Binguan
22 Gaochang Lu
Tel. 0995/8523229
Fax 0995/8527481
53 rooms, quiet, clear and air-conditioned in spite of the cheap price.

bands. This type of architecture can be found nowhere else in China. It is possible to climb up to the roof of the mosque. The village-like surroundings are nice, too, so that it is worth coming from the town on foot or by bicycle. Open daily during hours of daylight.

Turfan has been famous for its raisins for 2000 years. Grapes are cultivated throughout the oasis, although they are traditionally not pressed (wine presses only started being used in the 1990s). Instead the grapes are hung out to dry in houses with perforated clay walls so that the air itself does the work. Grape Valley to the northeast of the town is correspondingly organized for tourists. Here there are rows of vines, a stream flows by and gourds flourish. People are allowed to view the drying house and, of course, all kinds of raisins are on sale.

Grape Valley (Putao Gou)

**Karez Park
(Ka'erjing
Leyuan, Karez
Well)**

Karez refers to the underground tunnels by which the inhabitants of Turfan (and other places in the Tarim Basin) have been gathering water from the ground for the last 2000 years to feed their oases. The invention comes from Persia where the system is called **qanat**. It eliminates the effort of pumping spring water up to the surface as long as the oasis is close to some mountains, so that the mountain streams can replenish the higher levels of ground water. A well is drilled above the oasis, i.e. on the land that rises towards the hills, as far as the layer leading to the underground water, and further shafts are dug along the projected path leading to the oasis itself, the lower ends being connected together so that the tunnels have a slight gradient which is shallower than that of the ground itself. Where the underground tunnels emerge, the water is channelled along overground culverts to the fields or may also be tapped for household use. The shafts are used for removing the debris during building and are then used for maintenance later on. The yields from the system are virtually independent of the varying rainfall in each season and, unlike surface water channels, the water in the underground tunnels does not get polluted and can thus be drunk. Karez systems are usually 3 to 5 km (2 to 3 mi) in length, although in a few rare cases they can extend to over 10 km/6 mi. To give a people a good idea of how the system works, the Karez Park has been set up, where there is also a small **Karez Museum**. It is also possible to visit some of the tunnels. 8 km/5 mi northwest of the town in Ya'er Xiang. Opening times: 10am–7pm daily.

✳ Ruined town of Jiaohe (Yarkhoto)

10 km/6mi west of Turfan, two rivers border a rocky plateau 30 m/ 100 ft in height, 1.7 km/1 mi long and up to 300 m/330 yds wide. This makes for an easily defended natural fortress. As such, Jiaohe has been settled since the 2nd century BC. It was taken on repeated occasions, though, for example in 640 by China's Tang-empire, but the new rulers also made use of the special location and rebuilt the city. The final occupants were the Uighurs who came in the mid-9th century. They were at that time Buddhists. Then, in 1209, the Mongols under **Genghis Khan** destroyed the town and did not rebuild it, so that during the course of the 13th century it was completely abandoned. What remain are some occasionally very impressive clay ruins.

Tours

The town is entered through the south gate close to the southern tip of the plateau. At the point where the main route splits, head towards the left. There on the left-hand side is a mud platform with hollows in it, which was either a watchtower or a stupa. It adjoins a straight, north-south roadway, which marks the next route to be taken. A large complex on the right is assumed to be an administrative centre of some kind. The main road leads to a large stupa, behind which, on the other side of a large square that has been restored, are the vast ruins of a former Buddhist temple. A little to the east and then again to the north there is a smaller temple, beyond which there is a cemetery, recognizable by the remains of a forest of pagodas. Heading south again leads back to the main road in the east, from which an excavated route leads down to the old east gate. The same east road can be taken to get back to the south gate. Opening times: ☉ 8.30am–9pm daily, last admission 8pm.

Ruined town of Gaochang (Khocho, Karakhoja)

Jiaohe's big sister, 41 km/25 mi east of Turfan, is more recent: When China first conquered the Silk Road under the Han emperor Wu, Gaochang Wu was set up as a garrison town, since the narrow rocky plateau of Yarkhoto did not offer sufficient space. After the Uighurs had conquered eastern Xinjiang in 865, they established the capital of their khanate here. Although it too was devastated by the Mongols in the 13th century, Gaochang continued for longer than Jiaohe and was only abandoned at the end of the 14th century, when the political and economic centre of the Turfan basin shifted to Turfan itself.

Tour

As can be seen in places even now, the town was fortified by a double ring of roughly square walls with a circumference of some 5 km/ 3 mi. The rulers' palace in the middle of the inner circle of walls is protected by another set of walls. Less of the actual buildings have survived here than in Jiaohe and it is difficult to imagine how the town may originally have looked. Nevertheless some idea of its sizable dimensions can be gained from the showy main roads that the

The wind eats at the ruins of Gaochang

town possessed. It is a good idea to go from the present-day **entrance gate** in the east into the centre using the donkeys that ply back and forth throughout the day. The ruined palace in the centre, now partially restored with clay bricks, is the only major attraction inside the town. Parts of the inner walls have also survived, along with the majority of the outer walls, highly impressive at 11 m/36 ft in height, and a ruined monastery near the southwest corner. What is noticeable about the other buildings is the vaulting of the cellars, which are dug in natural layers of clay and – at least nowadays – are often open on the side facing the street. Open daily during daylight hours.

Astana graves (Asitana Gumu Qun)

5 km/3 mi north of Gaochang there is an old graveyard which was used from 273 until 778. The graves are visible from outside in the form of **small tumuli**, each of which has a crypt inside, which was accessible via a ramp. The graves are very valuable for archaeologists since the aridity there has meant that all the burial items have been preserved, even those made of perishable materials like wood or silk. Several written sources have also been recovered. Some of the burial items are now on display at the provincial museum in Ürümqi. Three crypts are open to the public. There it is possible to see the original murals dating from the Tang period. Open daily.

Flaming Mountains

A mountain range 100 km/60 mi long, up to 851 m/2792 ft in height and almost entirely barren, apart from in a few of the valleys that cross it. It gained its name, the Flaming Mountains, from the red colouring, which glows bright in the evening sunlight. The eroded shapes of the southern slopes are also reminiscent of red flames. After the pilgrim **Xuanzang**, who spent some time in Gaochang on his way to India, came this way, the Flaming Mountains also appear in the novel »Journey to the West«. In the story the monkey king grabs hold of a magic fan and uses it to extinguish the sea of flames so that the pilgrims can continue their journey. At the Bezeklik Caves there is a sort of Xuanzang-Disneyland which recalls the perilous trip. National Highway 312 leads along the base of the mountains.

Bezeklik Caves

The little cave-temple complex of Bezeklik is hidden away in one of the valleys that cross the mountains, 11 km/7 mi north of Gaochang. Inside it is not particularly spectacular but the V-shaped and sometimes canyon-like valley with a yellow clay cliff forming its western side (east-facing slope) is impressive. It is into this cliff that the caves have been carved. On both sides there are natural, high and thoroughly barren scree slopes but down in the valley it is green and flowers bloom. From the 5th till the 14th century **83 little cave temples** were built here, 40 of which are decorated. Seven of the caves are officially open to the public and guided tours take in six of them. Most of them consist of just a single chamber with a barrel-vaulted roof. There are no statues and the murals are in poor condition. What is unusual is that parts of the cave system are not dug out of the cliff but are fashioned as »imitation caves« using clay bricks and located in front of the slope. One other unique feature can be seen clearly in the multiple chambers of cave no. 20. After the Uighur ruling dynasty of Khocho converted to Buddhism in the 8th century, the kings ordered the restoration of the Bezeklik Caves and their extension. No. 20 was considered the cave temple of the ruling house and its murals depict devout princes and princesses. Open daily.

Ürümqi

Fj 24

Province: Autonomous Region of Xinjiang

Population: 1.2 million
Altitude: 800 m/2625 ft

»Fair pasture« is the Mongolian name for the provincial capital of Xinjiang. The Chinese pronounce the symbols they use for transliterating the city's name as »u-lu-mu-chi«. Ürümqi is north of Tian Shan on the southern Dzungaria, a traditional area of pasture for the Kazakhs. Of all the world's large cities, this is the one farthest from the sea.

Ürümqi is the boom town of western China. The majority of the inhabitants are Chinese and, apart from a few Uighur shops and street signs, the impression is that of being two 2000 km/1200 mi further east. This changes rapidly, though, on a trip into the city's surroundings. In 2009 there were conflicts between the Chinese and the Uighur ethnic minority.

What to see in Ürümqi

The only real attraction in the city. The museum has treasures on view which were excavated from the Astana tombs (▶Turfan p.550) as well as archaeological finds from the desert town of Loulan, the ruined town of Jiaohe (▶Turfan p.550) and other places along the Silk Road. Most of them are characterized by their outstanding state of preservation. The same applies to several corpses **naturally mummified** by the aridity of the desert. The most famous and oldest of them is that of a woman from Loulan who died 3800 years ago. 132 Xibei Lu. Opening times: 15 Apr–15 Oct 9.30am–7pm, public holidays 10am–6pm; otherwise daily 10am–6pm, closed on public holidays (last admission one hour before closing).

Museum of the Autonomous Region of Xinjiang

The main place to go for a day trip from Ürümqi is Heaven Lake, Tian Chi, 5 sq km/2 sq mi in size and surrounded by coniferous forests. It is 100 km/60 mi east of the city at an elevation of 1980 m/ 6500 ft on Mount Bogda, a mountain in the **Tian Shan range**. The mountain landscape is slightly reminiscent of Switzerland, although

Heaven Lake, Tian Chi

▶ VISITING ÜRÜMQI

GETTING THERE

From the international airport, 16 km/10 mi north of the city, flights are available not only to Beijing and other provincial cities but also to Tashkent, the Emirates and Istanbul. Ürümqi is also the terminus for direct train services from Beijing, Shanghai, Kashgar, Xi'an and Chengdu. In the other direction trains go further down the central Asian line to Kazakhstan.

ACCOMMODATION

▶ Luxury

Hoi Tak Hotel (Haide Jiudian)
1 Dongfeng Lu

Tel. 0991/2322828
Fax 0991/2321818
www.hoitakhotel.com
350-room tower with five-star comfort on the central People's Square. The management is from Hong Kong.

▶ Mid-range

Bogda
10 Guangming Lu
Tel. 0991/2815238
Fax 0991/2815769
Three-star hotel with 258 rooms, and some dormitories are available too. Good travel bureau.

In the streets of Ürümqi

that hardly applies to the yurts which the Kazakhs erect here for the summer months and rent out to the trippers. Tian Chi is very touristy but in summer the low temperatures are highly refreshing and anyone willing to wander further afield can leave the hustle quickly behind. From Ürümqi buses run at around 9am from the north gate of People's Park and return in the evenings.

⭑ Wudang Shan

Ha 29

Province: Hunan   **Altitude:** 1612 m/5289 ft

Wudang Shan, a mountain 1612 m/5289 ft in the north of Hunan province, is the most prominent centre of Daoism but it is barely known in the West. Unlike the »Five Holy Mountains«, which have been holy places for China's state cult for more than 2000 years, this mountain found imperial favour relatively late on. The monasteries tucked away on the mountain stand out for the way they are so neatly embedded into the landscape.

On Wudang Shan the god of the North Pole and the circumpolar stars is worshipped: Xuanwu, the **»Dark Defender«**, also called the »Northern Emperor« (Bei Di). In one legend he was the son of a mythical empress who took retreat here in order to meditate and gain immortality. He did not move for years, he neither ate nor drank and did not notice the bamboo that grew through his feet or the birds that nested in his hair. Finally he achieved his end and journeyed off to heaven in a carriage drawn by five dragons.

The first hermits seeking to divest themselves of the world are **History** known to have been here by the 1st and 2nd centuries. During the Tang era, the cult of the Northern Emperor gained in popularity and since then it has been held that this was the place where he attained his sought-after immortality. When the first temples were built, what had been wilderness was gradually linked to the world by paths and bridges, which along with the guest houses and monastery kitchens allowed it to become a destination for pilgrims. In the 13th century the Mongol emperors encouraged the **cult of the Northern Emperor** to support their own rule – after all they too came from the north. The actual heyday of Wudang Shan, though, followed during the Ming dynasty: In 1412, under the guidance of a specially authorized imperial official, 14 years of intensive building began. The larger monasteries, called palaces, and the imperial edifices added later are what make the cultural history of Wudang Shan what it is. 129 sites remain (though some are ruins), including »palaces«, eight more large monasteries, 20 cliff temples and 23 stone bridges.

Tours The mountain is well catered for with paths so that ordinary walking shoes will suffice. Most of the attractions require staying for a day and a half and spending two nights. Luckily a cable-car provides assistance getting around. Its upper station is near the **summit monastery of Taihe Gong**. Anybody who is physically up to it, though, should make the ascent on foot as it is more authentic and it is the only way to experience the true drama of the mountain. The path itself is one of the contributors to this drama. It doesn't simply go up but sometimes makes steep descents so that to get to the top actually means climbing a lot more than the 700 m/2300 ft difference in altitude from the little hotel settlement called Wuyaling near Nanyan Gong. From **Wudangshan** village at the foot of the mountain (with its railway station and hotels) it is possible to get to Wuyaling by minibus (25 km/16 mi, journey time almost an hour). From Wuyaling up to the summit the paths are well signposted. At the top it gets very crowded. There are other, little-travelled paths, though, which also lead to monasteries, caves, villages and beautiful scenery. The average temperature at the summit is only 8.5°C, almost 8°C less than at the station. It can also rain for days here. It is not advisable to visit in winter (November till March).

> **? DID YOU KNOW ...?**
>
> ■ ... that Wudang Shan has been a centre for Chinese martial arts (Wudang Kung Fu) for more than 800 years, only exceeded in age and fame by the Shaolin monastery? As there, the tradition continues in very lively fashion. It is not necessary to become a monk to visit the martial arts school (www.wudanggongfu.com).

What to see on Wudang Shan

Palace of the Jade Void (Yuxu Gong) Yuxu Gong at least appears to be the largest estate here. Situated in a broad valley near the station at an elevation of 189 m/620 ft, it once covered a space of more than 15 hectares/37 acres with all its minor temples and functional buildings included. The central section, where the courtyard alone is 3000 sq m/3600 sq yd in size and the perimeter wall is more than a kilometre/1100 yds in length, survived as a ruin along with the stone pedestals of the earlier halls and four vast pavilions for the protection of imperial inscriptions measuring 9 m/30 ft in height.

Chunyang Palace Chunyang Palace is a temple built at an elevation of 490 m/1600 ft around the year 1700. Its folk name is »**Ground-to-a-Needle Well**« (Mozhenjing): The Northern Emperor is supposed to have been ready to give up his efforts to become immortal when a farmer's wife gave him a lesson in patience. She rubbed a heavy iron pestle against a well stone with the intention of grinding it down to a needle, as she did not have one in the house. In illustration of this, two iron pestles stick out of the ground in front of the main hall. The accompanying well is on the left. Inside the hall there is a statue of the farmer's wife.

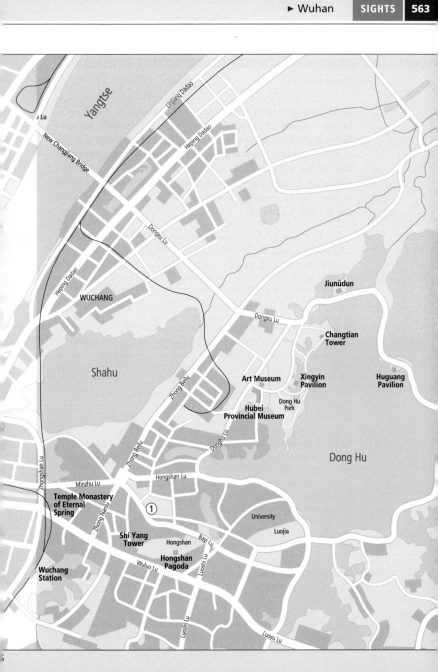

Yangtse

Linjiang Dadao

Heping Dadao

New Changjiang Bridge

Dongxu Lu

Heping Dadao

WUCHANG

Jiunüdun

Dongxu Lu

Changtian Tower

Shahu

Zhong Beilu

Art Museum

Xingyin Pavilion

Huguang Pavilion

Dong Hu Park

Hubei Provincial Museum

Dong Hu

Zhongshan Lu

Zhong Beilu

Donghu Lu

Minzhu Lu

Hongshan Lu

Temple Monastery of Eternal Spring

Zhong Nanlu

① 1

University

Luojia

Shi Yang Tower

Hongshan

Bayi Lu

Hongshan Pagoda

Wuchang Station

Wuluo Lu

Luoshi Lu

Luoshi Lu

Luoyu Lu

✶✶ Wulingyuan

Ha 31

Province: Hunan   **Altitude:** 320–1262 m/1050–4140 ft

Wulingyuan possesses a landscape that is unique in the world, a fairy-tale world of quartz-sandstone spikes. 3100 of them have been counted, spread over two large areas and clustered in another smaller region. The whole site covers just 264 sq km/102 sq mi. Most of the spikes are over 100 m/330 ft tall, many are more than 200 m/660 ft and others are nearly 400 m/1300 ft high. Nearly all of them rise up steeply and look as though they have been hewn upright with a giant axe.

Until 1984 the area did not even have a proper name. Although it is called Wulingyuan in UNESCO's list of World Heritage Sites, the Chinese mostly call it after a place towards the south of it, **Zhangjiajie**. Nowadays almost all the rock formations even remotely reminiscent of anything else are given flowery names. A couple of stones are even said to look like Mao and Stalin.

Nature About 380 million years ago, sandy sediment started to deposit in an ancient sea. When it had attained a thickness of more than 500 m/1600 ft, the land rose and the water retreated. Erosion then set to the work of sculpting the landscape. The lowest point is only 320 m/1050 ft above sea level and the highest peak only tops 1262 m/4140 ft. The climate is correspondingly mild, as important a factor for the charm of Wulingyuan as its high precipitation. This is the reason for the luxuriant vegetation, including more than 3000 higher plant species. In the valley it remains mild enough, even in winter, for a **subtropical, evergreen flora** to grow, while the plants that grow on the slopes are typical of temperate zones. Among the 116 vertebrate species counted here, there are several rarities, including the Chinese giant salamander and the Asian black bear. One reason that they have retreated to this habitat is that farmers find too little space among the rocky pillars to plant fields. This has meant that people mostly stayed away from this wonderland, although they did come to gather herbs or chop wood for their own needs. Even now 97% of the land is wooded.

Tours The terrain is not easy to fathom, not only when actually hiking through it but even on a map. It mainly consists of three regions, separated from one another by some distance. The three nature reserves are called Zhangjiajie, Suoxiyu and Tianzi Shan. Close to the main entry points, especially in and around the original village of Zhangjiajie, there are lots of crowds and the bad side of tourism is clear to see. A little further away, though, there are plenty of quieter paths. One other fun activity is rubber rafting, which makes for some gentle enjoyment here and is a wonderful way to enjoy the landscape. All in all, three days and four nights should be enough for a visit.

What to see in Wulingyuan

The standard tour that everybody takes leads to Huangshi Zhai, a high plateau with an elevation of 1048 m/3438 ft and a fantastic view. It is easy to get to by cable-car. An alternative that involves no climbing, making it just as popular, runs along the »Gold Scourge Spring« (Jinbian Xi). Heading left from there into the Shadao Gou valley the route passes through some of the more remote parts of the park before reaching »Black Dragon Village« (Heilong Zhai), the most distant spot within a day's walk. People taking this route also pass a spot that sets a world record. The **»First Bridge under the Sky«** spans 40 m/44 yd between two steep cliffs above a 357 m/1171 ft drop and is thus the highest natural bridge in the world. If you prefer to continue down the pretty Jinbian Xi valley, you will arrive at Shuiraosimen, »Stream Winding around Four Gates«, where four valleys come together. From there a different route can be taken to get back.

Zhangjiajie Nature Reserve

The area of the Suoxi Gorge in the northeast of Wulingyuan is a popular place for rubber rafting. There are hardly any rocky needles here but it does have the 11 km/7 mi long system called **»Yellow Dragon Caves«** with many stalactites and stalagmites. It is also possible to take an underground boat trip on an artificially dammed lake. Although a large number of the mighty caverns are virtually empty and dull, two places then come across as even more spectacular. One

Suoxiyu Nature Reserve

 VISITING WULINGYUAN

GETTING THERE

The city of Zhangjiajie (formerly called Dayong) in the south of the Wulingyuan district has a railway station with direct trains from Beijing, for example. Nowadays, though, most visitors come by plane. Zhangjiajie Airport is only just outside the town and has flights to all of China's major cities.

ACCOMMODATION

► **Mid-range**
Wulingyuan Hotel
Suoxiyu, 192 Wuling Dadao

Tel. 0744/5615888
Nicely situated building in traditional style with 209 rooms in the northeast of Wulingyuan, 35 km/22 mi from Zhangjiajie city.

Cui's Hotel
Zhangjiajie
near the National Park
Tel. 0744/571 21 85
Fax 0744/571 88 18
Very highly regarded 52-room establishment in a good location, at the bottom end of the price category.

of them is called the »Waterfall of the Heavenly Saints«: The waters only come down in a thin drizzle, made visible by a strong spotlight, but the water comes straight out of the broad span of a dome 50 m/ 164 ft in height. At the bottom it drops onto the tip of a giant limestone deposit looking like an upturned bowl as big as a hill. An even better sight is the 1.2 hectares/3 acres of the **»Dragon's Palace«**, which is filled with a spectacular forest of stalagmites. They have been compared to a **»gaggle of ministers«** and at one end of the cavern they are presided over by the Dragon King, that is to say, the dragon himself is not there but his throne awaits in readiness, a rounded stalagmitic heap not only as high as a house but every bit as sturdy.

Tianzi Shan Nature Reserve The north and northwest of Wulingyuan are reached via one main valley, appropriately called **»Ten-Mile Gallery«**, since the bizarre, picturesque scenery presents one spectacle after the other as if it were a giant art exhibition. This also continues down the side valleys, e.g. with the group of stone needles called the »48 Generals«. Eastwards of there is a 26 m/28 yd natural bridge hovering 100 m/330 ft above the valley floor, the »Bridge of the Immortals«.

✶ Wutai Shan

Hb 26

Province: Shanxi   **Altitude:** Up to 3058 m/10,033 ft

This sacred mountain is dedicated to the bodhisattva Manjushri. It is not only one of the four biggest monastic mountains of Chinese Buddhism, but also one of the religion's oldest holy places. No other is remotely so important in terms of art history. The central settlement of monasteries, Taihuai, is at 1700 m/5577 ft between five summits, the highest of which is 3058 m/10,033 ft high. It is these that give the mountains the name: the »Five Terrace Mountains«. The terrain is not steep but is quite barren. The slopes, which were densely covered in forest 1000 years ago are now grassy, although in recent times some parts have been reforested.

As long as 1900 years ago, monks came here to retreat alone into the remote mountains. It was in the Tang period that Wutai Shan experienced its heyday, in common with Buddhism in general. There were more than 200 monasteries, and pilgrims brought devout offerings from as far afield as Japan, Nepal and Indonesia. Later the **veneration of Manjushri** made it a place of pilgrimage for the Tibetan-Mongolian branch of the religion, too. In the 17th and 18th centuries even the Kangxi Emperor came here, to be followed by the Qianlong Emperor and his mother. The latter emperor even had an imitation of the mountain's »Temple of the Manjushri Statue« built in

Chengde. The monasteries along with their rich statuary and ornamentation survived the Cultural Revolution undamaged.

The most important monasteries are in and around Taihuai and are **Tours**
relatively close together. Many others within a radius of 5 to 15 km
(3 to 9 miles) make nice destinations for a hike. From Taihuai round
tours in minibuses are also on. Nowadays **pilgrims and tourists** are
mixed together and from the end of April until mid-October it gets
rather crowded, although the tumult tends to be concentrated on
one or two places, so that in the less visited monasteries and on the
mountain paths it is still possible to find some of the peace to match
the world-renouncing spirit of the spot. It is better than to come
here out of season, say late October/early November in the dry autumn weather. The temperatures do drop below zero after dark at
that time of year, though.

Monasteries in Taihuai

The following destinations are very close together along a north-
south axis. All of them are open during the hours of daylight depending on the numbers of people and the time of season.

The »Bodhisattva Summit«: 108 steps lead up to Pusa Ding – or
down if you have been chauffeured up via the road leading from the **Pusa Ding**
north. This is where Manjushri is said to have lived when he personally was teaching on Wutai Shan. The present name refers, though,
to the monastery at the top. Its founding was in the late 4th or early
5th century, while the present buildings are from the Qing period.

Wutai Shan Map

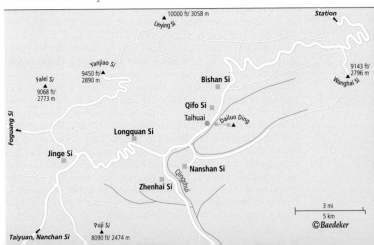

⏵ VISITING WUTAI SHAN

GETTING THERE

Accessible via bus or taxi from Datong (5 hours approx.) or Taiyuan (4 hours). From Datong long distance coaches only run in the mornings and not in winter. The links to Taiyuan are better. Anyone wishing to go off the beaten track to see the monasteries of Foguang Si and Nanchan Si will have to make a booking with a travel agent or organize a taxi since the buses do not stop there.

ACCOMMODATION

▶ **Mid-range**
Qixiange Binguan
Taihuai, on the road to the south
Tel. 0350/6542400, Fax 6542183
Best choice in the vicinity: 100 well equipped rooms in a quiet location a half hour's walk from the village.

▶ **Budget**
In Taihuai there is lots of private accommodation near the big monastery.

Since the 15th century this has been the main centre for Lamaism on Wutai Shan. Among its famous guests were the **Kangxi and Qianlong Emperors**. Both their visits are recalled by giant inscribed stelae and it is to the pair of them that the group of halls owe their imperial yellow roofs. The nicest spot is at the top of the stairs where there is a magnificent decorative gate and a view of the whole monastery settlement.

Xiantong Si The oldest monastery on Wutai Shan, Xiantong Si, is said to have been established as early as the 1st century AD and may therefore rival the White Horse Temple near ▶Luoyang as the oldest Buddhist shrine in China. Extended and rebuilt under the Qing dynasty, it became the biggest monastery in Taihuai. Among its cultural and historic treasures are the great two-storey »Beamless« (stone) Hall, two richly decorated bronze pagodas from 1606 and another two-storey hall fashioned entirely from bronze in the year 1609, which houses a Manjushri statue. The walls have a relief depicting the **10,000-Buddha motif**. The other halls also contain further statues. In the Guanyin Hall, the first one beyond the entrance, the »Three Great Bodhisattvas« can be seen, in the Manjushri Hall behind it, there are seven manifestations of Manjushri. In the almost excessively ornamented main hall from 1899 the »Three Precious Buddhas« take the throne with the »Three Great Bodhisattvas« behind them riding their steeds, while the sides are taken up with gilded figures of the 18 luohan. The Beamless Hall has a bronze Locana Buddha on a thousand-leaved lotus. It is in the hall that follows that the most famous figure in the monastery is on view: a five-headed, thousand-armed Manjushri. In the two smaller brick halls next to the bronze hall some of the monastery's other artistic treasures are on display.

The bottle pagoda, the sign of the monastic close, looms out of the early-morning mist over Taihuai

Facing the monastery to the east is the temple of Luohou Si, which like Pusa Ding was in receipt of imperial favour during the 17th and 18th centuries and also has the **magnificent statuary** to match. One real curiosity is the giant wooden lotus bud with leaves that can fold out. Then inside, four Buddha statues are on view. A pair of stone lions has survived from the Tang period.

Luohou Si

Here in the »Pagoda Court Temple« (Tayuan Si), is the premier landmark of Wutai Shan: the great **bottle pagoda**. Claims vary but it is said to be either 54 m/177 ft or 75 m/246 ft tall. It was built around the turn of the 15th century and is encircled by a gallery of prayer mills. Its existence documents the close links between Wutai Shan and Tibetan Buddhism. North of the pagoda there is a large library, which contains a rotating sutra carousel big enough to occupy two storeys. A small memorial in the side courtyard recalls that Mao Zedong stayed the night here in 1948 during the civil war.

✳
Tayuan Si

The very name of the »Ten Thousand Buddha Hall« indicates what is to be expected there. The relatively small temple of Wanfo Ge is named after one of its two halls; which contains the **»Three Great Bodhisattvas«** and countless little gilded Buddha figures in small niches covering all the walls. The second large hall is more Daoist, though. It is for the worship of the Dragon King. To the sides of its small, gilded and magnificently crowned statue are some shrines for the Dragon Queen (his wife) and for his mother. In front of the hall can be seen some ceremonial apparatus formerly used in processions. Facing that is the temple's stage.

Wanfo Ge

Monasteries in the vicinity of Taihuai

The important monastery of Bishan Si is 2.5 km north of the great bottle pagoda. Its main hall is rich in statuary and dedicated to Vairocana. The main attraction, though, is the following ordination hall, which has the only ordination terrace on Wutai Shan and a Burmese Jade Buddha as its centrepiece.

Bishan Si

Zhenhai Si
On the mountain slopes 5 km/3 mi south of Taihuai is the dignified monastery of Zhenhai Si, nestling on an east-facing slope in the shade of some thuja trees (west of the road). It is nice primarily because of its atmosphere.

Longquan Si
At the start of the 20th century the masons were able to demonstrate their skills in full here at the monastery of Longquan Si – and what skills! There was clearly no thought of honourable restraint on the decorative gate in front of the entrance or the bottle pagoda in the courtyard. As overloaded with ornamentation as the buildings are, in keeping with the fashion of their time, the abundance of fine details is admirable. The **»Dragon Spring Temple«** is 5 km/3 mi southwest of Taihuai above the road heading towards Wutai and Taiyuan.

Monasteries on the way to Taiyuan

The following pair of monasteries count among the greatest architectural treasures in China, and among the oldest wooden buildings in the world.

✱
Foguang Si
The main hall of the »Temple of Buddha's Light« (Foguang Si) is an original building dating from 857, meaning it came into existence shortly after a period of Buddhist persecution in that century. With its massive consoles, broad overhang, the shallow roof inclination and the inward-leaning columns, it is a **prime example of the architecture of the Tang era**. Around 30 life-like and colourfully painted figures have also survived from the 9th century. The 500 Luohan along the side walls were added in the Ming period. The Manjushri Hall on the northern side of the main courtyard is also gorgeous. It came into being along with its exquisite statuary and murals during the Jin period in the year 1137. 48 km/30 mi southwest of Taihuai.
⊙ Opening times: 8am–6pm daily, in winter there is a midday break from 12 noon–2pm.

✱
Nanchan Si
Only the name and the main hall remain of the »Southern Zen Monastery« (Nanchan Si). It is hardly more than a village temple, not even 12 m/40 ft wide, but it has what it takes. Built in 782, it is the **oldest surviving timber-framed building in China**, even if, as is unavoidable with wooden buildings, many or even all of the wooden parts have been replaced over the centuries. The architectural features are similar to those seen on the main hall at Foguang Si, although the inclination and curvature of the roof are even smaller. Here too the original statuary has survived, 17 painted figures (a Shakyamuni in the centre, bodhisattvas, disciples and guards) gaze out at the visitors from three sides of a U-shaped plinth just 0.7 m/2 ft high – a rare and impressive encounter with religious art. The temple is 94 km/58 mi southwest of Taihuai in a typical village setting with loess terracing and cave
⊙ dwellings. Opening times: open daily during the hours of daylight.

✶✶ Wuyi Shan

Province: Fujian   **Altitude:** 420–718 m/1,378–2,356 ft

The whole mountain range on the border between Fujian and Jiangxi provinces is called Wuyi Shan, but only a relatively small area of 60 sq km/23 sq mi has been declared a UNESCO World Heritage Site for its extraordinary scenic charm and biodiversity.

In spite of the unusual steep cliffs, some of which look like verdant sculptures, there is not much climbing to do. The hotel estate is at 420 m/1380 ft above sea level while the highest peak , Sanyang Feng , is 718 m/2356 ft. Most of the area is covered with sub-tropical rain forest, but tea is grown here, too.

A programme lasting two days involves climbing two or three peaks (with steps and paths as is usual in China) and taking a bamboo raft   **Tours**

 VISITING WUYI SHAN

GETTING THERE
North of area around Wuyishan city there is an airport with direct flights to places including Hong Kong. Wuyishan station has direct trains to Quanzhou, Fuzhou, Xiamen and Nanchang.

SHOPPING
This is the most renowned tea-growing region in Fujian Province, famed throughout the land for its semi-fermented Tie Guanyin« (»Iron Guanyin«), Wulong (Oolong) tea», but there are many other kinds, too. There is no escaping the opportunities to taste tea, so do not miss them. The best varieties are expensive but prices can be haggled down.

WHERE TO EAT
▶ **Inexpensive**
In the holiday resort a side road leads of the main street where there are nothing but cookshops and small restaurants. It is possible to sit outside there and savour the freshly prepared delights for not very much money.

ACCOMMODATION
▶ **Mid-range**
Wuyi Mountain Villa
(Wuyi Shanzhuang)
Wuyi Shan Wuyi Gong
Tel. 0599/5251888
Fax 0599/5252567
The best hotel in town has already won several architectural prizes. It is situated to the north of the »Wuyi Shan Palace« in park-like grounds with several buildings. There are 200 rooms, many in the luxury category.

Dragon Resort
(Jiulongwan Dujia Jiudian)
Tel. 0599/513 66 66
Fax 0599/525 96 66
52 rooms spread over several villa-like buildings, also an elegant tea-room and an attractive garden with swimming-pool.

down **»Nine Bend Creek«** – possibly the prettiest and most exciting river journey to be had in all of China. The standard destinations are rather crowded but there are also miles of hiking paths where other people are seldom seen. For this reason Wuyi Shan only starts to become really nice if the stay takes at least three days. All the paths are signposted in Chinese and English. On the plain east of the river **Chongyang Xi**, which borders the core region in the east, the Wuyi Shan holiday resort has come into being, a little town with plenty of hotels. Some more hotels can be found to the west of the Chongyang Xi right on the edge of the core region. From either place a taxi or minibus journey is necessary to get to the starting points for the hiking routes.

★ ★
Raft journey

The enjoyable highlight of any visit to Wuyi Shan must be the 100-minute journey on a narrow bamboo raft down the nine bends that gave their name to the clear splashing waters and many gravel beds of the **Jiuqu Xi**. There are two places to start. The raft pilots will decide which to use depending on the water level in the creek. Taxi drivers always know which is the right one. The pilots are mainly young men who will explain about the grandiose scenery on the way down, enhancing their talk with jokes and tall tales – unfortunately in Chinese only. The last rafts embark at about 4pm and it is wise to get there at least half an hour earlier. The same applies at midday when there is a break for lunch from 12 noon till 2pm. The bends in the river are numbered backwards so that the journey ends shortly after bend no. 1.

Places to go south of the river

Jade Girl Peak

Jade Girl Peak is probably the most photographed peak in the Wuyi Shan range. Slender and rounded, the distinctive formation towers above the second bend.

★
Huxiao Yan Rock

Huxiao Yan translates as »Roaring Tiger Rock«. Steps carved into the stone lead up its curving flank. At the top there is a chance to rest at a tea house (although it is expensive). A quick detour leads out to what the signpost translates as **»Fortune-Determined Bridge«**, a natural bridge spanning a cleft in the rocks. **Binxi Dong** is a cave with statues of Buddha. The best comes at the end. There is an ascent up concrete steps which protrude out from an overhanging cliff, not for those who suffer from vertigo. Down in the **»Valley of the Crescent Moon«**, which half disappears beneath the cliff, it is possible to get to the »Natural Zen Temple«, a monumental Guanyin statue, which was sponsored in 1994 by a wealthy woman from Xiamen.

★
Strip of Heaven, Yixiantian

Yixiantian, the Strip of Heaven, is probably the most attractive sight other then the nine bends. Looking as though it has been cut out by the knife of a giant, a dead straight cleft 178 m/584 ft long and up to

49 m/ 161 ft high but barely a metre/3 ft wide splits a mountain down the middle. It can be entered from the side via »**Wind Cave**«. The void acts as its own air-conditioning. The air in the cleft also emerges here in the summer as a cool wind blowing at a constant temperature of 18°C. Steps have been carved into the floor of the cleft so that it is possible to climb through it from left to right. The warning not to take any bags or spectacles when doing this is not for nothing. It gets very narrow and is not for the claustrophobic or corpulent.

Places to go north of the river

Where Nine Bends Creek has its confluence with the Chongyang-River, there is a park at the north end of a bridge with the misleading name of »Wuyi Shan Palace«, a memorial hall for the philosopher, Zhu Xi, and a row of shops in the Song style (allegedly). It is possible to take a rest in a tea house and buy souvenirs. It is also an entry point for the network of hiking paths leading to places like the majestic »**Great King Peak**« (Dawang Feng), which marks the southeast corner of the region and is a landmark of Wuyi Shan second only to Jade Girl Peak.

Wuyi Shan Palace

Looking down on the 6th bend of the creek and up to some smooth cliffs, some of them overhanging, which look as though a giant had hewn them out with a monster axe, this is the apex of a »Heavenly Tour« up the northern slope of the mountain of that name. The dense lines of other climbers sprinkled like colourful ants on the barren upper stairs of the ascent make an enjoyable way to enjoy the tourist crowds. At the top the view takes in other peaks. Youngsters apply digital portraits onto souvenir postcards with the aid of computers to prove that people have been there and a tea house provides typical local refreshment. Beyond the two-storey »**Heavenly Tour Pavilion**« (Tianyou Ge) the route leads back down again. The quickest way up to the Heavenly Tour peak is via a bridge from the road, which leads to the attractions south of Nine Bends Creek and the starting points for raft trips.

Heavenly Tour Peak Tianyou Feng

In China there are several caves with the name »**Water Curtain Cave**«, which makes a literary reference to the novel »Journey to the West«. This shell-shaped recess in a mountain can be found a few kilometres north of the river. It is only a few metres deep but is high and wide so that it hardly seems like a cave at all. Particularly after the summer rains, though, a spring emerges from it in a stream.

> ! **Baedeker TIP**
>
> **Tourist Center**
>
> Do not be put off by the name. This tea house on Heavenly Tour Peak at the bottom end of the descending path is the nicest one for miles around. With a full cup of tea and a view of the river and its rafts, of rocky peaks, bamboos and little tea plantations, it rolls all the delights of Wuyi Shan into one.

There is a tea house in the cave where it is possible to have some tea made with the fresh spring water. None of this is very spectacular but coming in the late afternoon when the hordes of visitors are on their way home, it can be quite idyllic.

✶ Xiamen

Province: Fujian
Altitude: Sea level

Population: 1.5 million including surrounding territory

The port of Xiamen is the hub of southern Fujian and one of the most pleasant places on any part of the Chinese coast. The core city, with its population of 650,000, is situated on an island linked to the mainland by a causeway. The dominant colonial atmosphere, which the city retains in spite of the skyscraper modernity it possesses as a coastal metropolis of the aspirational new China, still lends it a certain charm.

Xiamen is not mentioned in history until 1387, when a coastal fortress was established here. In the 18th century a roaring trade with southeast Asia began and to maintain better control of it, the administration of Quanzhou was moved here in 1727. The Treaty of Nanjing opened up the city to the European trading powers in 1842, it became well-known under the name of Amoy, from the way it is pronounced in the south Fujian dialect. Soon Xiamen developed into the main port for emigration from the country, mainly involving people heading for America to work as coolies. In the 20th century the city grew slowly until it became caught up in the economic dynamism of the Deng Xiaoping era. In 1980 it was made one of the first special economic zones, so that Xiamen was one of the places that paved the way for the reconstruction of China and its modernization.

What to see in Xiamen

Promenade Lujiang Dao runs along the shore at the west end of the island and is the showpiece of the city. It is not long but has been planted with some greenery to make it into a nice little promenade. The view across to the island of Gulang Yu is especially nice. Ferries dock where the main shopping street, Zhongshan Lu, meets the promenade.

Zhongshan Lu On Zhongshan Lu the mistakes that have been made elsewhere have not been repeated. The old houses have been kept, or else replaced with new buildings that match with the old in size and style and their colonial colonnades allow for shopping to be done in the dry and in the shade.

Xiamen Map

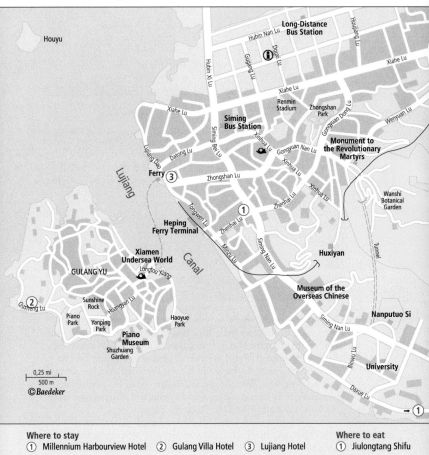

Houyu

Long-Distance Bus Station

Hubin Nan Lu

Houjiang Lu

Hubin Xi Lu

Gugang Lu

Douyi Lu

Xiahe Lu

Xiahe Lu

Siming Bei Lu

Xiahe Lu

Renmin Stadium

Zhongshan Park

Gongyuan Dong Lu

Wenyuan Lu

Lujiang Dao

Xiahe Lu

Siming Bus Station

Xinhua Lu

Datong Lu

Gongyuan Nan Lu

Monument to the Revolutionary Martyrs

Ferry ③

Zhongshan Lu

Xinhua Lu

Xinhua Lu

Wanshi Botanical Garden

Lujiang

Tongwen Lu

Zhenhai Lu

①

Zhenhai Lu

Heping Ferry Terminal

Zhenhai Lu

Minzu Lu

Siming Nan Lu

Xiamen Undersea World

Canal

Huxiyan

Tunnel

GULANG YU

Longtou Xiang

Museum of the Overseas Chinese

Nanputuo Si

② Gusheng Lu

Sunshine Rock

Huangyan Lu

Haoyue Park

Siming Nan Lu

Piano Park

Yanping Park

Piano Museum

Shuzhuang Garden

Daxue Lu

University

Daxue Lu

0,25 mi
500 m
©*Baedeker*

→ ①

Nanputuo Si Temple

On Siming Nanlu, 2 km/1.5 mi south of the western end of Zhong-shan Lu, is the liveliest and most important temple in the city, Nanpu-tuo Si. The extensive grounds of the complex are in a lovely location at the foot of **Wulao Feng** hill and stretching up its wooded slopes. It is said to have been established during the Tang period. The present form dates back to around 1700, although a majority of the buildings were reconstructed in the 20th century. The name the »Southern Pota-la Temple« refers to the mountain in India where Guanyin, goddess of mercy, lives and thus indicates the temple's main object of devotion.

Gulang Yu feels almost like a small town in Europe

Gates and ponds The entrance in the south is unusual: In front of the temple there are two ponds one after the other. This is in keeping with **feng shui rules**, which are observed very religiously in Fujian. However the smaller of the ponds is also used for liberating fish which have been caught. This benefits the karma of the releaser. Instead of one temple gate, there are two. They are situated either side of the ponds. Along the axis there is then a raised terrace upon which stands an inner gatehouse, the Hall of the Four Heavenly Kings.

Main Hall In the main hall there are images of the »Three Precious Buddhas« and behind them the »Three Holy Ones of the West«, the salvation Buddha Amitabha and his assistant bodhisattvas.

Hall of Great Mercy The spiritual centre of the temple is formed by the »Hall of Great Mercy«. The name of this octagonal pavilion-type structure with its triple roof refers, of course, to the Guanyin figure inside.

Other parts of the complex The **monastery library** is the last building along the axis. Beside it a path leads up the slope to some pavilions, burial pagodas and smaller halls. Much incense is burned in front of a tall stone block inscribed with a single character several metres high and gilded. The character is »fo«, »Buddha«. Buses 18 or 45 from Zhongshan to the terminus.

🕐 Opening times: 8am–5pm daily.

▶ VISITING XIAMEN

INFORMATION

C&D Travel

Sealight Building, 7th storey
33 Shuixian Lu (at the beginning of
Zhongshan Lu)
Tel. 0592/226 39 43, ax 226 39 37
www.sino-trip.com/index_en.asp
Ask for Jeffrey Chou or Stephen
Chen. A trip out to the tulou
(rammed earth) fortresses of the
Hakka can be booked here.

GETTING THERE

Xiamen has an airport close by with
flights to all the major Chinese cities
and Hong Kong. Direct trains run
from the station in the city to a
variety of places including Nanchang,
Shanghai, Kunming and Xi'an and
Wuyi Shan. Buses run to Quanzhou
from the forecourt in front of the
station.

SHOPPING

The main shopping street, Zhongshan
Lu, has several good tea shops, which
sell china cups and teapots as well as
the typically Fujian semi-fermented
Wulong (Oolong) tea.

WHERE TO EAT

▶ Inexpensive

① Jiulongtan Shifu

49 Huandao Lu
Tel. 0592/251 53 35
A nearby excursion destination (4
km/2.5 mi): a bastion with cannon,
and beneath it, on the beach, this
wonderful restaurant for lovers of fish
and seafood. Choose not from a
menu but by pointing.

ACCOMMODATION

▶ Luxury

① Millennium Harbourview Hotel

12-8 Zhenhai Lu
Tel. 0592/202 33 33
Fax 0592/203 66 66
www.millenniumhotels.com
The central location and a well-drilled
English-speaking team are two of the
good points of this 352-room estab-
lishment; the cuisine is another.

▶ Mid-range

② Gulang Villa Hotel

Gulang Yu, 14 Gusheng Lu
Tel. 0592/2063280, fax 2060165
Hotel built in 1989 with a view of the
sea and very close to the city – with its
own boat jetty

③ Lujiang Hotel (Lujiang Binguan)

54 Lujiang Dao
Tel. 0592/202 29 22, fax 202 46 44
This 153-room hotel is not particularly luxurious, but the location is
superb: at the mouth of the Zhongshan Lu with a view of the promenade; ferries to Gulang Yu dock
immediately opposite. In addition, the
establishment is famed for the restaurant on the top floor – with a roof
terrace.

✴ Gulang Yu

A place to feel good, a manageably sized island with sandy beaches
and rocky ledges, a place with narrow roads and no cars, lovely
houses, museums, parks, cafés, restaurants – and piano music. The
routes are well kept and the listed status is rigidly enforced.

History The first British consul in Xiamen also found it beautiful here. He was the first to have a villa built for himself on the island in 1844. At that time Gulang Yu was still used for agriculture. In the following 60 to 80 years a settlement gradually appeared, largely dominated by **European building styles**. This is what can still be seen today and it was not only villas, but schools, churches and shops. Japanese also settled here – and well-to-do Chinese, because Gulang Yu was no ghetto for foreigners. Unlike in Tianjin there was no separation into zones for the foreign powers.

Tours To see the most important sights and drink in a bit of the atmosphere takes a good half a day. There the electric carts that make a 6 km/4 mi circuit of the island are of help. Most of the islands needs to explored on foot, though. Gulang Yu is certainly a place one would like to stay for longer. A week-long holiday from the stresses of travelling in China? A quieter spot than here would be hard to find.

The temple on the Sunshine Rock on the island of Gulang Yu

On a circuit on the open-topped electric bus it is best to make at least one stop. Get out when the bus passes the first sandy beach as it travels from the north (or at the second if you miss the stop), then go up to the nearby »Piano Garden«, a fine and well-tended park plus an art gallery, an audio-visual hall and a large walk-through aviary.

»Piano Garden«
Qin Yuan

From the Piano Garden a cable-car leads across to »Sunshine Rock«, which is the highest point on the island at 93 m/305 ft. It is worth going right to the top to enjoy the panoramic view. On the eastern side of the summit is the **Sunshine Rock Temple**, a new, but stylistically appropriate building with an open-air statue of Guanyin.

✷
Sunshine Rock,
Riguang Yan

Leaving the park around Sunshine Rock by the south gate instead of near the temple (the north gate) allows access to a sandy beach (the second one on the bus circuit) and heading east from there takes you to the **Piano Museum**, which has 70 instruments hailing from every

Museums

imaginable country and spread over two buildings inside the pretty Shuzhuang-Garden. Further along the slightly ascending main street is the next destination, the former British Consulate, a white single-storey building dating from 1870 in a superb location which has been brilliantly restored. It now houses a **Coin Museum**. Opening times: Both open 9am–12 noon, 1.30pm–5pm daily.

Haoyue Park A rather curious combination: a sandy beach on one side with some sweet little »bathing villas«. The latter can be rented for a seaside holiday. On the other side there is a bombastically nationalist bronze relief in honour of the Ming general **Zheng Chenggong**, who drove the Dutch out of Taiwan in 1661. He is thus considered a patriot, although this cheerfully ignores the fact that he was a loyalist to the Ming cause and fought against the rule of Beijing – the Manchu dynasty – setting up an independent, albeit short-lived kingdom in Taiwan. Zheng represents Chinese ambitions to bring Taiwan »back home«, which is why he is not only depicted here in the bronze but also in a monumental sculpture on a rock in the southeast corner of the park, from which he stares out with a decisive gaze across the sea towards Taiwan.

> **?** DID YOU KNOW ...?
>
> ■ ... that it is said Gulang Yu has the largest »density of pianos« in all China? It may be so, since there are thought to be 600 on the island, one for every thirty islanders. In its villas, possession of a piano was considered to be good form and not only among the Europeans. The music school in the town now makes a contribution too, not forgetting the Piano Museum. In »Piano Garden«, though, the only piano to be found is in the name.

»Dragon Head Street« (Longtou Xiang) leads away from the ferry dock towards Sunshine Rock. This is Gulang Yu's shopping street; which also has restaurants. For a short rest there are also terrace cafés on the promenade near the ferry dock. That leaves the body suitably refreshed for a trip to **»Xiamen Undersea World«**, a modern aquarium a little north of the quay.

What to see in the surrounding area

Hakka fort dwellings Fujian has some of the most unusual houses in the world, multi-storey clay fortresses each providing space for several hundred people. The Hakka, speakers of a Chinese dialect, developed this type of home (called tu lou) more than 1000 years ago. They were ideal in politically uncertain times. Since they have four or five storeys at the bottom with no windows at all, it was only necessary to block the door to keep out any bands of robbers. Nowadays these fort dwellings are tourist attractions. Many of them are located not far from **Longyan** (150 km/93 mi inland from Xiamen). Since the fort dwellings are difficult to reach via public transport, it is recommended that a trip be organized via a travel agent.

★★ Xi'an

Province: Shaanxi **Population:** 4 million
Altitude: 400 m/1300 ft

In some places the modern name, well-known as it might be, is virtually overshadowed by a historical past. This is one such case: when it was known as Chang-an it was one of the world's great cities. Now though, as Xi'an, although it remains the capital of Shaanxi province, that status is little more than a memory for archaeologists, historians and visitors.

The Chinese world centred on Xi'an and its surroundings from the 11th century BC till the 9th century AD (with a few interruptions). Xianyang, near Xi'an's airport on the opposite bank of the Wei River, was the residence of the first emperor in the 3rd century BC, making it **the first capital of the Chinese empire**. The founder of the Han-dynasty then moved his residence across to the south bank and traces of it can still be seen northwest of the present old town. The great golden age of what was then Chang'an (»Long Peace«) began with a new unification of the empire under the Sui dynasty and reached its climax during the Tang era in the 7th and 8th centuries. At that time Chang'an rivalled Baghdad as the biggest city in the world and its aura was of matching splendour. Upon its streets it was possible to see Persian merchants, Turkish musicians, Indian monks, Japanese envoys and slaves from Africa, as well as Arabs, Koreans, Ceylonese and many others. The walls encompassed an area of 8.7 x 9.7 km/5.4 x 6.0 mi – almost as large as Jersey. In the confusion at the end of the Tang period Chang'an's glory days came to an end.

Highlights *Xi'an*

Dance and song from the Tang era
Resurrected every evening in the Shaanxi Opera House.
▶ page 584

Grand mosque and Moslem quarter
China's loveliest mosque, built in Chinese style, plus the old-town ambience around it.
▶ page 585

History Museum
The most important archaeological museum in China
▶ page 587

Big Wild Goose Pagoda
The most famous pagoda in the country
▶ page 587

Terracotta army of the first emperor
The world famous army guarding the emperor's tomb is one of the foremost attractions in the country.
▶ page 590

The present city was primarily **created by the Ming dynasty**, under whom it was developed as a princely residence. The present city walls were built at that time. The land they enclose is only a sixth the size of Chang'an under the Tangs. Even after it was linked to the rail network in 1930, Xi'an initially changed only slowly. Large areas of the present-day city are no more than 20 years old.

Old town

»Old town« is little more than a name nowadays. It refers to the area enclosed by the Ming dynasty's city walls but an old town atmosphere is virtually only detectable in the streets around the Great Mosque.

Beilin ✳ The »Forest of Steles« is China's largest **collection of stone inscriptions** – a stone library. 3200 tablets (of which 1700 are on view) bear some of the important texts from ancient China and thus protect them from destruction by fire, water and insects. The oldest tablets are more than 2000 years old. The biggest project was completed in the year 837: the inscription of the entire written canon of Confucius, which needed 114 tablets. Another famous exhibit is the great Nestorian stele of 781. It testifies to the existence of a Nestorian Christian community in Chang'an during the Tang period. At the top of the stele a cross can be seen. The Forest of Steles has more than that to offer, though. It is sited in the former **Confucius temple** and apart from its inscribed tablets there are also some statues and images to be seen in the side halls near the front, monumental burial animals and sarcophagus reliefs from the Han era plus Buddhist sculptures from the 4th century until the Tang period. Opening times: 8am–6pm daily.

Ancient Culture Street The street running past Beilin is wholly dedicated to ancient Chinese culture. There are galleries for ink paintings, stationery shops with brushes, rubbing stones, ink blocks, paper, tea services and folk art. In the west the street ends at the square in front of the south gate where an old stone pagoda stands to the right.

City walls Xi'an's largest building work is its square of walls, which stretch for 12 km/7 mi. It was built towards the end of the 14th century. For a while it was threatened with demolition but then tourists started streaming into Xi'an to see the first emperor's terracotta army so, in-

● VISITING XI'AN

INFORMATION

Tourist Information Service Centre
183 Jiefang Lu (opposite the station to the east), Tel. 029/87455043
Trips to destinations outside of town can be booked from here.

GETTING THERE

Xi'an's airport is one of the biggest in China with lots of national flights and some international links, too. It is 30 km/19 mi from the city centre on the other side of the Wie River beyond Xianyang. Xi'an railway station is conveniently located on the northern edge of the old town. Direct trains runs to places including Beijing, Shanghai, Chengdu and along the Silk Road route westwards as far as Ürümqi.

SHOPPING

Around the major attractions, especially near the terracotta army, colourfully embroidered bags, jackets for children, waistcoats and other textiles in the local folk style are all offered for sale. Antiques, or items made to look like antiques, can be found clustered on stands and shops in streets leading to the »Great Mosque«. The main shopping area for Xi'an's inhabitants is the »Great East Road«, Dong Dajie, from the bell tower eastward and southward as far as the south gate. One other place to go near the south gate is Ancient Culture Street.

THEATER

Several theatres are reviving the song, dance, costume and hairstyles of the Tang period as a modern stage show.

The market alleys on the way to the Great Mosque are an emporium for antiques, crafts and fakes

This is, of course, entirely for the benefit of tourists and a little kitschy but it is undoubtedly worth seeing. One good place for it is the

Shaanxi Opera House
165 Wenyi Lu
Tel. 029/87853295
Performances daily: 8pm, shows last 70 min.

WHERE TO EAT

Xi'an is famed for its variety of dumplings. Nowhere else has been so creative in terms of shape, colour and filling. A dumpling banquet, where a whole spectrum is on offer, should be part of any stay in the old town. It can be accompanied by freshly made rice wine, milky white and served warm, another local speciality

► Moderate
① *Defachang*
3 Xi Dajie (north side of the square near the bell tower)
Tel. 029/87214060
Old-established and renowned restaurant. On the ground floor it is folksy and cheap but the main reason to come is for the dumpling banquet

served on the upper floor, usually in conjunction with celebrations, but it is not actually necessary to throw a wedding; there are also menus for two people.

► Inexpensive
The cookshops and small restaurants in the Moslem quarter are also popular. Among other things it is possible to get a delicious and really cheap noodle soup.

ACCOMMODATION
► Mid-range
① *Citadines Xi'an Central*
36 Zhubashi
Tel. 029/ 85 76 11 88, Fax 85 76 11 89
www.citadines.com/en/china/xian/central.html
Apartment hotel with 162 apartments, quiet and central. Also suitable for single nights.

► Budget
② *Xiangzimen Youth Hostel*
16 Xiangzimiao Jie
Tel. 029/ 62 86 72 88, fax 62 86 79 99
Old town hostel with atmosphere, well run, pleasant staff. Double rooms are a price category above.

stead of being torn down, the walls have been restored, primarily by cladding the **rammed earth core** with bricks again. In addition, alongside the four city gates, simple openings have been made for modern road traffic – a successful compromise between the needs of conservation and practical demands. The final gap has been closed with a bridge at the station forecourt. It is possible to climb the walls at the east, south and west gates and at Beilin. Opening times: 8am–10pm daily.

Bell tower, drum tower

From the south gate the eye is drawn towards the north and the 36-m/118-ft bell tower, constructed in pavilion-form on a fortress-like stone pedestal. It is situated at the central intersection of the four main roads. The square to the west of it and the buildings there, in the classic Chinese style but a bit too big, are new. At the west end of the square stands a drum tower with an unusually long floor plan which spans a street in the form of a gate. It is not necessarily worth climbing the towers but several times a day small concerts of classical Chinese music are held there. In the drum tower there is an exhibition in view and occasionally the drums themselves are sounded. Opening times: open daily during daylight hours, depending on the season. ⏲

The Moslem quarter stretches to the north of the drum tower. A lot of old buildings still exist here. In its narrow streets and alleys there are rows of cookshops, barbers and other shops. In the streets leading to the mosque there are lots of particularly interesting stands selling both genuine and fake antiques. For those good at haggling, a nice souvenir can be had here for not much money.

Moslem quarter

China's prettiest mosque is built in Chinese style and its quiet, green courtyards are delightful, as are the harmony of the site as a whole and its fine plant reliefs. It covers an area of 1.3 ha/3 acres and is aligned along an east-west axis. It is entered from the north. On the left-hand side a high spirit wall borders the site. The 300-year-old **decorative gate** on the outer courtyard is a masterpiece of carpentry. The second court is entered via a gatehouse with some lovely reliefs. It too has a decorative gate, this time made of stone. The two imperial inscriptions to the left and right date from 1606 and 1768. They are concerned with building and renovation measures required by the imperial court. The **»Pagoda of Testing Conscience«** in the

★
Great Mosque

Architecture evolves: a glass pyramid and a bell tower

Xi'an *Map*

Where to stay
① Citadines Xi'an Central
② Xiangzimen Youth Hostel

Where to eat
① Defachang

following courtyard acts as a minaret. A stone gate, decorated with some plant reliefs showing beautiful artistry, then leads to the Phoenix Hall, a dainty pavilion-like building. Along the central axis the path leads up to a high terrace with the prayer hall, which only believers may enter. Some of the side halls off the courtyards already mentioned are worth visiting too. They have exhibitions featuring furniture and ancient items possessed by the mosque. Opening times: winter months 8am–5.30pm daily, otherwise 8am–7pm.

In the south and east of the city

A kilometer/1110 yd south of the south gate is the smaller Wild Goose Pagoda. In spite of being 43 m/141 ft high, it is hard to find among the tall new buildings in the vicinity. It was **originally built in the Tang period** in the years 707 to 709 at the commission of Empress Wu to house some Buddhist inscriptions brought from India. Its spire was lost in two earthquakes in 1555 and 1563. The pagoda was once part of a temple and currently stands in a quiet park. Few people come to visit it. It is possible to climb to the top. Youyi Xilu. Opening times: 8.30am–5pm daily.

Small Wild Goose Pagoda (Xiao Yanta)

🕐

This is the most important archaeological museum in China. In a colossal building from 1991, which blends with the Tang style, some of the spectacular finds to have been dug from the earth of the province in recent decades are displayed. The province has been a hidden treasure house of cultural history. The chronological merry-go-round of finds begins on the mezzanine floor with a **model of a village from the prehistoric Yangshao culture** and some of the vessels located there. Some artistically carved jade from the 3rd millennium BC can also be seen. Some of the ritual bronzes from the 1st and 2nd millennia BC are famous, too. The bronze fittings for wooden beams from the Qin empire (3rd century BC) are spectacular. A relief tile from the palace of the first emperor depicts a hunting scene. The fascination continues up on the next floor with **items from the Han era**. Burial items made of clay give an insight into everyday life. A 2000-year-old iron cog and the oldest known paper in the world testify to the enormous technological strides that China was taking at the time. In the section dedicated to the Three Kingdoms era, the caricature-like small sculptures of warriors are worthy of a look. A repeating crossbow mechanism and crows' feet for bringing down pursuing cavalry are important in military history. Another room is devoted to Chang'an, the capital city. It is instructive to see where they have overlaid the present-day street plan of the city over the old maps. Among the treasures are early **porcelain and pottery** from the imperial court. The figures for the topics of »Fashion« and »Pleasure« are amusing. Exhibits from the Song dynasty up till the Qing's round off the show. From the entrance hall, steps lead up to other rooms, which are mainly used for rolling exhibitions. The original murals from the imperial tombs of the Tang dynasty, which are also kept there, can only be viewed at certain times and by prior arrangement (Tel. 029/85217140). 90 Xiaozhai Donglu. Opening times: Tue–Sun 8.30am–5.30pm (last admissions 4pm).

★ ★
History museum (Shaanxi Sheng Lishi Bowuguan)

🕐

A chunky stone tower 60 m/197 ft in height, effectively located to the southeast of the history museum at the southern end of Yanta Lu, is not only a barely altered original from the7th/8th centuries, it is also the most important monument for the great translation project

★
Big Wild Goose Pavilion (Da Yanta)

The Great Mosque of Xi'an

which took place under imperial commission after Xuanzang (602–664) had returned from India weighed down with holy Buddhist texts. The treasures were to be stored here safe from fire. The odd name of the pagoda comes from a legend. In India a wild goose once tumbled out of the sky into a Buddhist monastery. The monks thought it was a bodhisattva, buried it and built a burial pagoda. The square tower, now China's most famous pagoda, is part of the temple called **Ci'en Si**. Its halls were built at about the same time as a comprehensive restoration of the pagoda, which took place in 1580. In the new buildings north of the pagoda information on Xuanzang's journey of pilgrimage is provided. It is also a nice place to rest. It is possible to climb the pagoda but the view out of its narrow windows is limited. Opening times: 8.30am–7pm, shorter hours in winter.

Banpo Museum (Banpo Yizhi Bowuguan) In 1953 at the eastern edge of Xi'an in what was then the village of Banpo a neolithic settlement was discovered belonging to the proto-Chinese **Yangshao culture**. The traces can be seen of a large community building at the centre of the village surrounded by 46 dwellings. Beyond a protective ditch, 5–6 m/16–20 ft wide, there are some potteries and a cemetery. Two types of building are present: a house half submerged in the ground to make a cellar and a free-standing building at ground level. The buildings themselves are, of course, no longer in existence. All that can be seen is the holes for their supporting pillars and other depressions in the ground. An area covering 2000 sq m/2400 sq yd has been roofed over so that the settlement can be viewed easily even when the weather is bad. There is an exhibition of appliances made of stone, bone and clay. 5 km/3 mi east of the city centre. Opening times: 9am–5pm daily.

Around Xi'an

★
Huaqing Chi

In the satellite town of Lintong, 26 km/16 mi east of Xi'an, a thermal spring bubbles out of the Li mountain at a temperature of 43°C. Even 2800 years ago, the Zhou kings came here to bathe in the waters. In the Tang era an authentic **imperial bathhouse** was built with various pools. It was rediscovered in 1982 and the exposed excavations were covered with halls in the style of the original bathhouse buildings. Tang emperor Xuanzong's favourite, Yang, also relaxed here. A white statue amid the park's lake recalls this most famous of the beauties of ancient China.

Memorial for the Xi'an Incident

A relaxing park extends from the flat up the slopes of the mountain. Among the guests who spent time here was General Chiang Kaishek, who came in December 1936 to plan an anti-Communist campaign with General Zhang Xueliang, who was in control of Xi'an at that time. Zhang was against the move. He maintained that it was necessary to form a united front with the Communists against the Japanese, who were forcing their way towards Beijing from Manchuria. When Chiang opposed this idea, Zhang arbitrarily placed him under arrest that morning and thus forced him to agree to the united anti-Japanese front. The incident, which is recalled by a memorial in the southeast of the park, captured the attention of the whole world. Opening times: 8am–7pm daily.

Mausoleum of the first emperor

Opening hours: 8am–5pm daily

No one on a first visit to China should leave without visiting the most important archaeological site in the country, the mausoleum of the first emperor Qin Shihuangdi (28 km/17 mi east of Xi'an). What the first emperor had created in his fear of death was a burial palace intended to make clear to the spirits of the world beyond that here was a ruler of worldwide importance. Historian **Sima Qian** provided a description of the burial chamber in around 100 BC. It was filled with images of palaces and official buildings with tools and precious items. Mercury was used to imitate the rivers of the country, the ceiling of the crypt was designed to emulate the firmament. All things combined to give a picture of the empire, indeed the very cosmos. Booby traps protected the crypt from intruders. What Sima Qian did not mention was the guarding army. That was only discovered by chance in 1974 when some farmers were digging a well.

Gigantic complex

The tomb was originally immense, 2250 m/2460 yd from east to west, 2150 m/2350 yd from north to south. Several hundred thousand labourers were allegedly forced into working on the building of it. Work began in the year 247 BC when the king ascended the throne at the age of 13. It was never finished, as can be assumed by the fact that one pit was found empty of terracotta soldiers: When the emperor's dynasty was toppled by rebels in 207 BC, just three years after his death, it must have been a delight for them to plunder and despoil the grave of the tyrant. It was then, too, that the underground wooden chambers in which the guarding army was kept were plundered, the figures violently smashed and the whole place set on fire.

Mausoleum The actual mausoleum, a pyramidal earthen mound 400 m/440 yd along each side and nowadays 60 m/200 ft high (originally it was more than 100 m/330 ft tall), is usually passed by without a second look. Archaeologists have detected a double wall around it, which originally enclosed the tumulus and the accompanying temple. The guarding army was outside. Excavations of the mound itself brought to light the two **bronze teams of horses** now on view at the Terracotta Army Museum, among other things. In addition, a number of other graves have been found. There and in various depositories for burial items missed by the rebel arsonists, archaeologists have found more valuable burial items, including a group of musical entertainers made of clay.

✷ ✷ Terracotta Army

Opening hours:
8am–5pm daily.

1.5 km/1 mi east of the tomb itself, **more than 7000 clay soldiers**, all more than life-size and some with horses, were set to guard the imperial mausoleum and protect it from the east, since it was from there that the threat of vengeance would come from all the kings sent to the world beyond by the first emperor as he conquered their dominions. The army, a copy of a genuine force of the time, is spread throughout three pits. It contains soldiers of all ranks and functions as well as horses. Templates were used to make them (apart from the individually modelled faces) but the variety of shapes is still large. There are soldiers without armour in knee-length garments and various forms of scaled armour. Most of them wear light caps tied around a knot of hair. Others wear a folded or two-pointed hat. Archers appear both kneeling and standing. The horses are mostly draught animals in teams of four. The wooden chariots they were pulling have been burned, though, and can only be identified by the burnt traces left in the mud. In addition there are also cavalry horses. There are even different sorts of boots. Each of them is connected to a plate that keeps it standing firmly erect. All of the figures were painted. Their original bronze weapons were stolen by the arsonists, although some have survived. The pits themselves have paved floors. The walls between them are made of rammed clay and once supported a wooden roof upon which the earth was stacked up.

The Qian Ling tomb is where the third Tang emperor, Gaozong, is buried. He reigned from 656 to 684. His concubines and the later empress Wu Zetian (reigned 683–705) are buried here too. The crypt is not open. The choice of location is conspicuous. In the south two smaller hills make for a natural gateway and a straight ceremonial axis leads from there up to the main summit in the north at an altitude of more than 1000 m/3300 ft. Some pillars and **stone statues of animals and people** have been preserved along the ceremonial road. Among the people depicted there is also a group of foreign dignitaries, although they have all lost their heads in the intervening time.

Qian Ling tomb

3 km/2 mi south of Qian Ling the second son of Emperor Gaozong and a granddaughter who died aged 17 are buried in two burial chambers quite close together. Both of them are worth seeing, primarily for the fine paintwork, which depict polo games, hunts, scenes from court, and officials bearing tribute. Both tombs were robbed early on but only items of cash value were taken, so that many of the burial items have survived there.

✶
Tombs of Princess Yongtai and Prince Zhanghuai

During clearing and restoration after the partial collapse of a brick pagoda at the temple of Famen Si in 1987 an underground chamber was discovered, which contained the monastery's treasury. Apart from valuable relic chests, porcelain, gold and silverware – more than 100 individual items – there was also a **knuckle bone said to have belonged to Buddha Gautama** himself. Sources from the Tang period were known to refer to this relic. This is what made Famen Si a place of pilgrimage for Buddhists from all over Asia. The monastery treasures can be viewed in a museum although all of the buildings in the complex date from recent times. Opening times: 8am–6pm daily. ⊕

✶
Famen Si

Han tomb Yang Ling

North of Xi'an, in the region around Xianyang, a whole row or earthen pyramids can be seen. These are the mausoleums of the Han emperors and empresses. Inside one of them, the tomb belonging to Emperor Jing of the Han dynasty (reigned 157–141 BC), some chambers with valuable burial items were uncovered during road building work in 1990. Underneath was a white terracotta army, although one markedly different from that of the first emperor. The figures are like dolls, only about 60 cm/2 ft tall, and naked, i.e. they were once clothed in rich textiles and wooden armour. The arms are missing as they were made of wood and could be turned at the shoulder like a doll with movable arms. The pits in which they were found also contained bronze weapons, large supplies of grain and miniature models of stoves, grain measures and many appliances both civil and military. A museum has now been established at the site to display some of the finds. Opening times: 8.30am to 5.30pm daily. ⊕

✴ Xishuangbanna

Gf 34/35

Province: Yunnan **Population:** 840,000
Altitude: 485–2197 m/1591–7208 ft

In the southwest of China, bordering Myanmar and Laos, at the most southerly tip of Yunnan province is Xishuangbanna, the »Autonomous Prefecture of the Dai People«. This group of people are of the Buddhist faith and represent a good third of the 840,000 population of Xishuangbanna, making them the most numerous of the ethnic minority peoples living here. They often live in remote mountain villages and retain their traditional customs and dress.

The sub-tropical climate results in hot summers with heavy monsoon rains and very mild winters. Typical aspects of the region include the rain forests, in which several endangered species, such as elephants, tigers and leopards have their habitats. The Mekong River, known locally as the Lancang Jiang, meanders from the north through the mountainous landscape, which attracts many young travellers to undertake extensive trekking tours.

Name and history
Xishuangbanna is a Chinese transliteration of a phrase in the Thai language meaning »twelve areas of rice cultivation«. There was an independent Dai state here as long as 2000 years ago and in 69 AD, for example, it sent ambassadors to the Chinese court. In subsequent centuries the region came under control of various southern Chinese empires interspersed with various brief spells of independence before it was conquered by the Mongols in the 13th century and incorporated into the Chinese empire.

Jinghong

The small provincial capital on the banks of the Mekong (pop. 40,000, not including environs, 500 m/1640 ft elevation) is the usual starting point for any travels in Xishuangbanna, since the region's airport is nearby. The other places described here can all be reached by taxi or minibus within a maximum of three hours.

Tropical flower gardens
In the western part of the town centre there is an area covering 80 ha/200 acres with more than a thousand species of tropical flowers and other rare plants. Coffee bushes, mango trees and a strip of rain forest count among the attractions of the tropical scenery. On the opposite side of the road there is an interesting garden for medicinal herbs. 28 Jinghong Xilu. Opening times: 7.30am–6.30pm daily, herb garden: 8am–5pm daily.

⏵ VISITING XISHUANGBANNA

INFORMATION
China International Travel Service
Nakunkang Residential Area
Jinghong
Tel. 0691/2122152, fax 2125777
A good summary of the attractions
and contact addresses is available at
the web site www.xsbnly.com/english.

GETTING THERE
Jinghong Airport is about 10 km/6 mi
southwest of the region's capital and
can be reached from there by taxi or
bus. There are several flights a day to
Kunming (1 hour) and one per day to
Lijiang, Shanghai and Guangzhou.
There are also flights to Thailand,
Laos and Burma. In the centre of
Jinghong there are bus stations for
cross-country coach services: on
Minzu Lu and a bit further north on
Jinghong Beilu. There is no railway.
From Jinghong the listed attractions
in other places can be reached by taxi
or minibus in a maximum of three
hours.

FESTE
Xishuangbanna is famous for the
traditional new year celebrations of
the Dai people, the Water Splashing
Festival (Poshuijie, every year 13–15
April), which is held in all of the
villages and towns in the district. They
involve dragon boat racing, dances
and the felicitations are accompanied
by gleeful water fights, where no one
escapes a soaking. Flights to Jinghong,
as well as hotel rooms, are often
booked up at that time.

WHERE TO EAT
Dai cuisine is more southeast Asian
than Chinese. Some of the ingredients
include lemon grass, bananas and
pineapples. One speciality features

fillings cooked in bamboo tubes.
Tropical fruits are sold at the side of
the streets.

▶ Inexpensive
Jinghong: Mekong Café
111 Manting Lu
Tel. 0691/2162395
Dai, Hani and Western cuisine, a
popular meeting place with a friendly
atmosphere, from which tours into
the country can also be arranged.

Jinghong: Mei Mei Café
Manting Lu
Banana pancakes and other delicacies.
A good place to rent bicycles and
obtain travel information.

ACCOMMODATION
▶ Mid-range
Jinghong: Crown Hotel
Jinghong Nanlu, corner of
Nongling Lu
Tel. 0691/2128888, fax 2127270
Nice premises near the southern bus
station and not far from the centre.
108 rooms spread over 6 buildings in
the Dai style located in a garden with
a pool.

Jinghong: Golden Banna Hotel
55 Mengle Dadao
Tel. 0691/213 66 66, fax 212 20 19
150 rooms on six floors, in the Thai
style, in the middle of a tropical
garden. The hotel is on the edge of
town, some 500 m/500 yd from the
centre. Good Sichuan and Yunnan
cuisine is served.

▶ Budget
Inexpensive accommodation for
backpackers can be find in abundance
in Jinghong and all the other places
with attractions around it.

National Minori-
ties Park (Minzu
Fengqing Yuan)

⊙

This open-air museum is situated in the southwest part of Jinghong on the Liusha River. It centres on some traditional buildings set amid tropical vegetation and highlights the customs of the Dai, the Hani and other ethnic groups. Entertainment is provided by songs and dancing. Opening times: 8.30am–6pm daily.

Chunhuan Park
(Chunhuan
Gongyuan)

⊙

A park with history. As early as 1300 years ago, there is said to have been an imperial garden here. The present-day park in the south of the town was reconfigured in the 1980s and is sometimes still known by its old name of **Manting Park**. Temples, pagodas and pavilions in traditional style can all be seen. It is possible to feed the peacocks, to observe groups demonstrating the local folklore or simply to wander in comfort as far as a small tributary of the Lancang River. Opening times: 8.30am–7.30pm daily.

Wat Manting

At the north end of Chunhuan Park is the largest Buddhist monastery in Xishuangbanna, a recent building in the Thai style made entirely of wood. The Buddhism practised here is of the Hinayana or »Lesser Vehicle« school, which is widespread in southeast Asia and which believes that salvation can only be achieved after long periods of personal improvement – in contrast with the Mahayana belief common elsewhere in China. Take off your shoes before entering.

Places to go in the surrounding area

Valley of the
Wild Elephants
(Yexiang Gu)

The **Sanchahe Nature Reserve** is an extensive reservation about 50 km/31 mi north of Jinghong. Its biggest attraction is the chance to view several dozen wild elephants from tree houses near the river. A cable-car leads through the tree tops from the entrance in the south to the centre of the park.

Jingzhen

80 km/50 mi west of Jinghong, in the village of Jingzhen, there is a good example of **classic Dai architecture** with wood carvings and Buddhist murals. The octagonal pavilion (Bajiaoting), 21 m/69 ft high and made of wood and brick, was built in 1701 and has recently been comprehensively restored. It is used nowadays for Buddhist ceremonies.

Menglun

Menglun is about 70 km/44 mi east of Jinghong. A suspension bridge leads to the tropical botanic gardens (Redai Zhiwu Yuan), which possess more than 3000 species of plants, including flora from the rain forests, groves of bamboo and the palm-like dragon's blood trees, which were only rediscovered in Xishuangbanna in 1972.

Damenglong

The »**White Bamboo Shoot Pagoda**« (Manfeilong Bai Ta), an elegant building near Damenglong, 70 km/44 mi south of Jinghong, not far from the Burmese border, dates back to the year 1204. The main pagoda is 17 m/56 ft high and is surrounded by eight smaller pagodas

A footprint of Buddha is revered at the pagoda of Damenglong

looking like little bamboo shoots. The object of veneration here is an outsized footprint which Buddha is said to have left in a niche in the pedestal. North of the town (about 25 minutes on foot). Opening ⏱ times: 8.30am–6pm daily.

★★ Yangtze Gorges

Provinces: Chongqing/Hubei/Hunan

The three great gorges of the Yangtze River are the best known scenic attractions in the country after the karst mountains of Guilin – or should it be said they were? Nowadays thoughts equally turn to the gigantic dam project in the third gorge and the reservoir which, now that the level has reached full height, has submerged countless former attractions along 600 kilometres/375 mi of river – stretching back beyond Chongqing – as well as along countless tributaries and side valleys. So are the gorges still worth visiting?

The original drop between the top end of the reservoir and the dam was about 110 m. This is the maximum height of the dam itself. Further upstream the rise in water level will be lower depending on the original elevation. In the region of the first gorge, **Qutang Gorge**, it

Gorges and reservoir

The locks on the Three Gorges Dam bridge a height difference of a good 180m/600 ft

is about 40 m/130 ft, although it will actually be less before the summer rains begin, since then the water level will be 30 m/100 ft lower. This is because one purpose of the dam is to prevent flooding of the river downstream, which entails a large reserve in terms of water level. Now the cliff faces of the gorges are several hundred metres high at the most scenic spot, so even with the reservoir, the area will still have the character of a gorge and at the top and middle of the lake there will only be a small effect. Even the width in such places is little more than before. For the lower **Xiling Gorge** things are rather different, although the scenery there is less dramatic anyway. However its lower end is in turn beneath the dam anyway. So the look of two and a half of the gorges may have changed only a little, but the voyage is still less spectacular because the whirlpools and rapids have disappeared. However even those who knew the gorges from before will still be deeply impressed by the experience of the landscape. This also applies, possibly even more, to the diversions up one or two tributaries, which every cruise programme includes. There are however no longer any tow-boats. While much ancient cultivated land between gorges and further upstream has been flooded, much has remained above water level. And there is an additional spectacular attraction: the dam itself, and its enormous locks.

▶ VISITING YANGTZE GORGES

BOAT TRIPS

For a trip from Chongqing to Yichang lasts at most three days and four nights and costs more than 400 USD on a five-star steamer, and more than 1000 USD on genuine luxury boats. On a four-star vessel – which may not necessarily be any worse but will provide less in the way of other diversions – a passage can cost less than 320 USD. In both categories, an English-speaking guide is standard. Simpler cruise vessels, let alone ferries, are much cheaper, night voyages and the absence of landing opportunities mean that much of the experience is lost. In addition, only Chinese is spoken. The additional pro-grammes, especially the three smaller gorges, should on no account be missed.

In Chongqing
18 Men Xinyi Jie 18
(at the ferry port)
Tel. 023/63 10 05 53
Fax 023/63 10 08 13
www.cqpits.com.cn

In Yichang
Yichang Three Gorges CITS
Yiling Dadao 72
Tel. 07 17/625 13 90
Fax 07 17/625 13 85
www.china-tourism.org/index.php

More than 1.3 million people were moved: new settlement on the Xiling gorge

Online bookings
Here are few possible internet addresses:
www.chinahighlights.com
www.dreams-travel.com,
www.travel chinaguide.com/cruise/
index.htm
www.yangtzeriver.org
www.victoriacruises.com

GETTING THERE

Yichang has a railway station and an airport with direct connections to the larger Chinese cities. Yueyang is on the main line from Wuhan to Guilin and also has a an airport.

SHOPPING

Silver Needle tea is the speciality of Lake Dongting-. The plantations are on the Jinshan Dao Peninsula between the Yangtze and the lake. Ideally it should be poured into glass cups so that the »silver needles« can be seen:

the tips of the leaves, which lift up when they take on water.

ACCOMMODATION

▶ Mid-range

Yichang: Yichang International Hotel
127 Yanjiang Dadao
Tel. 07 17/622 28 88
Fax 07 17/622 81 86
www.ycinthotel.com. 428 rooms in a brand new, 32-storey tower, the tallest building in town.

Yueyang:
Yunmeng Binguan
25 Chengdong Lu
Tel. 07 30/822 11 15,
Fax 07 30/822 11 15-21 49
100 two and three-bed rooms in a central location, handy for public transport. Good food.

✱ Fengdu

This small town, 171 km/106 mi downstream of ▶ Chongqing by boat, is famous for its unique »Ghost City« on the 288 m/945 ft **temple mountain of Ming Shan**, which projects as a peninsula from the north bank of the reservoir. The old village has been submerged and relocated on the south bank.

Pictures of hell A more appropriate name for this group of Daoist temples and its statues, some of which are in the open air, would be **»City of Devils«** It displays a vivid picture of what happens in China's ten hells where the Chinese at least face the judgement of hell and must undergo a suitable penance of gruesome **torture** before reincarnating, perhaps, if the last life was evil enough, as a mere dog, or even a worm. The figures are all reconstructions as the originals were destroyed during the Cultural Revolution. Some of them are truly grisly, especially those on the sides of the complex, the main temple of Tianzi Dian, which is dedicated to the King of Hell. It is easy to overlook the room behind his statue: in the most beautiful of all the Fengdu shrines sits the consort of the King of Hell, accompanied by two maids. The hall dates from 1664.

The legendary origin of the Ghost City goes back to the Han era of more than 2000 years ago, when two officials named Yin and Wang sought retreat from their official duties to lead a life here as **Daoist hermits**. Their two names, combined as »Yin-Wang«, sound similar to »Yan Wang«, the »King of Hell«, so that for this reason Ming Shan became his holy residence, so to speak. The two legendary founders Yin and Wang are still recalled to this day in the »House of the Two Immortals« at the King of Hell's temple. Opening times: 9am–5pm daily.

The legend of the temple's founding

Shibaozhai

70 km/43 mi further downstream the river passes the town of Zhongxian, which has been totally rebuilt at a higher elevation. The **»Precious Stone Fortress«** (Shibaozhai), on the left bank 35 km/22 mi further on has partially been spared the immersion: it is a small table mountain with a 56 m/184 ft stairway up to the top on its left side, so that it looks like a **cross between a pyramid and a pagoda**. The climb is less intimidating than it sounds, since it takes time to look at the works of art on each of the twelve stories. When the reservoir is full, a dam ensures that the early 19th century wooden building stays dry. The water still makes an island of the 230 m/755 ft plateau with an area of 1200 sq m/1435 sq yd at the summit. On top there is a Daoist temple from the 18th century which has the popular **protective god Guan Yu** in its first hall and images of the Jade Emperor and a goddess responsible for quick and painless childbirth in its second.

> **? DID YOU KNOW ...?**
>
> ■ ... that the 6380 km/4000 mi long Yangtze was the third longest river on earth after the Nile and the Amazon, but above all has the most populous catchment area? More than 400 million Chinese live here on 19 % of the country's total area. The Chinese name of the Yangtze is Chang Jiang, »long river«.

From Wanxian to Fengjie

Continuing onward the river passes two other large towns: Wanxian (50 km/31 mi beyond Shibaozhai), then Yunyang after another 35 km/22 mi.

This is the new »Great« Yunyang (left bank), since the smaller older town is yet another 25 km/16 mi further on. There, on the right bank, stands a noted holy place, **a temple in honour of Zhang Fei**, a famous general from the time of the Three Kingdoms. He was murdered here by revolutionary officers in AD 220.

Another 70 km/43 mi further takes the boat very close to the first gorge. 4 km/2.5 mi before the top end of it, the town of Fengjie lies at the bottom of the lake, at least the old part of it. Attractions now start coming thick and fast.

Fengjie

Baidicheng

The »City of the White Emperor« is situated at an altitude of 230 m/ 755 ft, on the left bank of the reservoir high above the water level. It is perhaps the **last outpost before the gorge wilderness begins**. It is no longer a city in anything but name, though. The name itself dates back to the year AD 25 when a rebel chieftain made his base here. He called himself »The White Emperor« after a white dragon said to have lived in a well near here, appearing from time to time as white clouds of mist.

Memorial temple   Nowadays the only thing on the hill is a memorial temple. It is said that **Liu Bei**, ruler of the Minor Han dynasty, died here of rage after losing a battle in the year AD 223. The temple recalls how the young sons of the dying emperor beseeched the minister Zhuge Liang to take over the helm. In a room at the rear »hanging coffins« are displayed, such as will be seen in the smaller gorges later on.

Gigantic bridges span the reservoir: here near the city of Wushan

The »Bellows Gorge« is 8 km/5 mi long and the shortest of the three Yangtze gorges. Confined by cliffs, the river waters once gushed through here at 7 m/sec/16 mph. The rock walls are still 350 m/1150 ft high, so this gorge remains as striking as ever. The famous Z-shaped towpath known as the **Mengliang Steps** can still be seen here, but these days only with a diving costume.

Qutang Gorge

✳ Daning He · Three Little Gorges

The newly rebuilt town of Wushan nestles on the left bank before the next of the Yangtze gorges begins. This is where most of the cruise boats dock, and it is here that passengers change on to smaller vessels for a four-hour cruise down the »Three Little Gorges« of the former tributary, the Daning He. The tributary's lower reaches have now been absorbed into the reservoir. Even so, the landscape here is grandiose, and for many it is the climax of the cruise. The cliff walls, overhanging in places, are characterized by stalactites, and are closer together than in the large gorges. Behind each bend is a new landscape. Gentler slopes and side valleys are covered in jungle, and monkeys can occasionally be seen at their acrobatics on the banks. In the middle gorge (»Misty Gorge«) a wooden coffin can be seen in a low inaccessible cave in the cliff wall on the left-hand side. It is a relic of a funerary practice that goes back to the proto-Chinese Ba culture still extant in Ming times in these once remote valleys.

It was only during the course of the dam project that the three mini-gorges of the **Madu He** became accessible to tourism. They can be experienced from small wooden boats, into which one embarks at the end of the Daning He gorges. Here the cliffs get even closer once more. A local accompanies each boat, sitting in the bow, and contributes a folk-song to the programme. On this trip, there is a good view of a second wooden coffin.

Madu He Gorges

✳ ✳ Wu Gorge

The middle gorge is often called the **»Witch Gorge«**. The name, though, comes from the Wu Shan mountain range, which it bisects, whereby the name »Wu« in this case means »shaman«. The canyon is 44 km/27 mi long and is overlooked by 12 summits ranging from 800 to 1200 m (2600 to 3950 ft) in height. The most famous of them is the **»Goddess Peak«** (Shennu Feng) at 921 m/3022 ft. It can be seen about 10 km/6 mi before a leftward turn on the northern side of the lake. Most of the other eleven peaks can also be seen from there. According to legend, all twelve are the petrified remains of twelve heavenly maidens who once came down to earth to help the hero Yu dig the rivers to water the soil and make the land habitable. After their work was completed, they did not want to return to heaven, so they were immortalized as these twelve peaks.

Shennong Xi · Zigui

Another diversion away from the Yangtze itself. On this tributary to the left, which enters the main river at Badong, tourists were once towed upstream in so-called pea-pod boats (that is what they looked like). Now the reservoir stretches well into the valley, although the landscape with its cliffs and jungle is still attractive.

Zigui The gentler banks between the actual gorges are used mainly for the cultivation of oranges. Graves can also be seen time and again. Before the third gorge, is Zigui, the birthplace of the great poet and statesman **Qu Yuan** (332–295 BC). Old Zigui is submerged beneath the waters, as is the front of Qu Yuan's memorial temple on the northern bank. A replacement, more splendid than ever, has been built in another place, not visible from the boat.

Xiling Gorge · Three Gorges Dam

The longest of the gorges, running for some 76 km/47 mi, was once notorious, primarily for its dangerous whirlpools. Now there are no more maelstroms and a majority of the rock formations, which inspired sections of the river to bear such evocative names as the **»Ox Liver and Horse Lung Gorge«**, have been immersed. Below the dam, though, one whole meander of the river has been preserved almost in its original form until the reservoir at the Gezhou Dam, built already in 1986.

★ ★
Three Gorges
Dam
Although the last of the originally planned generators only went into action at the end of 2008, the giant dam itself and its stairway of locks have been in existence for some years and have already become the **main attraction of a Yangtze cruise**. The dam is 1853 m/2026 yd across, 181 m/594 ft high and took 15 years to build, 1994 to 2009. 1.3 million people have had to make way for the waters and be resettled elsewhere. The objective of the project is threefold. First the generation of electricity – the power station installation, in operation from 2009, is to provide 6.8 gigawatts of power. The second objective is to control the water level of the reservoir, lowering it before the summer rains to prevent disastrous flooding of the river's lower reaches. The third aim is to make it easier for shipping to navigate the river.

Criticism of the
project
The project has faced criticism, though, often heavy criticism. Some of it was applied not to the actual construction work itself but to the accompanying aspects and upheavals resulting from the plans. These included the embezzlement of monies intended for resettlement, insufficient compensation payments and corruption in the issuing of contracts. In the long term, however, the effects causing concern to people will be the extent to which safety fears have been dealt with.

Flying the red flag up the Daning He, a tributary of the Yangtze

For example, is the dam sufficiently secure against **earthquake hazards**? It is also unclear to what extent sedimentation will occur at the dam, possibly causing it to lose efficiency. The planning phase also did not take into account the problem of stagnating liquid waste. Over the 1000 sq km/400 sq mi area of the reservoir, hitherto largely unknown amounts of waste, produced by more than 100 million people, are collecting in the lake's waters, including vast quantities of non-degradable plastic refuse which will have to be kept away from the sluices and turbines. The immaterial cost of the loss of the pristine riverscape is impossible to put a price on.

Gezhou Dam

At the end of the Xiling Gorge, 40 km/25 mi below the Three Gorges Dam, the river reaches its predecessor, the Gezhou Dam. It was completed in 1986 and is by no means small, being 70 m/230 ft high and 2561 m/2800 yd long. Its main objective is to facilitate navigation in theXiling Gorge.

Yichang

Here, in the western part of Hubei Province, is where the Yangtze cruises end, although the ferries sometimes continue on as far as Wuhan or even all the way to Shanghai. After Yichang the character of the Yangtze changes completely: It becomes **broad and slow**. The huge distance to the sea involves a drop in height of no more than 40 m/130 ft from here. The city itself (population 4.1 million in the greater area) has little for which a tourist would wish to stay.

Yueyang and Lake Dongting

If staying with the Yangtze beyond Yichang, there is one more place to go 300 km/190 mi further downstream, Lake Dongting and the city of Yueyang. Before getting there the river passes the docks at **Jingzhou**, a historic, walled town from which there is a rapid motorway link to Wuhan.

Yueyang
The **long history of** Yueyang (pop. 540,000 not including environs), in the north if Hunan Province on the north bank of Lake Dongting, goes back to a settlement made here more than 2000 years ago. Under the Sui, in the 6th century, it was made the capital of one of the largest districts of China.

Yueyang Lou ▶
Yueyang Lou is a name known across the country as one of the most famous examples of the »lou« type of building. It is not actually a tower (although the lack of terms for such an edifice in the West means it is often called one), but a **multi-storey hall building**, which is built in a favourable position above the lake shore with an expansive view to the west. The first of its predecessors on the site was already in existence at the time of the Tang dynasty (built 716) when it was immortalized in lyric verse by the poet princes, Li Bai, Du Fu and Bai Juyi. The current wooden building is from 1880, a three-storey edifice with a total height of 20 m/66 ft. It has four main pillars as well as 24 external and 12 internal columns and is topped by a roof with corners that curl upward to the heavens.

Lake Dongting
Lake Dongting is the second biggest freshwater lake in China. The area it covers – officially 2740 sq km/1058 sq mi – fluctuates with the seasons, as when it is high water on the Yangtze the lake fills up and expands. It is also fed by the Yangtze's major tributary, the **Xiang Jiang** as well as other rivers which then feed the Yangtze as it continues to the sea. The average depth of the lake is 6.7 m/22 ft and is only 33.5 m/110 ft above sea level. It has played a major role in Chinese legend. Lake spirits are mentioned time and time again, although nowadays things are more civilized with boats taking passengers on trips out to the **Junshan Dao** Peninsula, well known for its special tea.

✳ **Yangzhou**

He 29

Province: Jiangsu
Altitude: Sea level

Population: 1.2 million

A place to go for those who seek discovery! Yangzhou is a city full of tradition, which left many legacies in China's history – political, economic and cultural. Hardly any foreigners come here but it still exhibits China at its best and there are enough things to see to spend several days there.

Yangzhou is the canal metropolis. Even during the Han era it was important, long before the building of the Grand Canal. During the

Tang period it became the economic and cultural centre of eastern China since here, where the Grand Canal flows into the Yangtze is where internal and seagoing shipping met. At that time Yangzhou was China's biggest trading port. In the late 17th and 18th centuries the city experienced another golden age, particularly because of the lucrative salt trade. Yangzhou made an important cultural contribution too, especially its Buddhist temple and its Qing-era artists. The »eight eccentrics of Yangzhou« (Yangzhou ba guai), who rejected convention for the sake of their own creativity in the 18th century are well known in artistic circles.

Yangzhou is great place for walking and shopping. The city does not stand out for having very many individual attractions of outstanding quality but for its enjoyable abundance of smaller ones, all within walking distance.

Tours

✱ Eastern part of the old town, He Yuan garden

Since Yangzhou is practically at sea level, there is plenty of water in and around it. The canals, which also served as a moat for the city, indicate even now the historic plan of the city, covering 3.1 x 2.4 km (1.9 x 1.5 mi). The largest canal forms a border to the old town in the south and east, the former **Emperor Canal**. This section is hardly used nowadays since the waters were given a new and shorter route further to the east. It is a super place for a walk, though. Turn your back on the water now and then and go through the surviving parts of the old town with its narrow streets and single-storey dwellings. In the west the old buildings extend as far as the section of road formed by Guoqing Lu and Dujiang Lu.

The garden of He Yuan, an estate that once belonged to an important official by the name of He Zhidao, was put together in 1883. The residential building has remained extant along with the furnishings. The artistically laid-out courtyards lie to the north and east. The unusual feature is the two-storey buildings around it: dwelling houses or outer walls. The buildings sometimes project or are set back at odd angles, so that the courtyards reflect their rhythm. This effect is particularly marked in the north-west courtyard, which is practically taken up by a garden pond and a rocky outcrop. A pavilion in the pond was used for music and dances. The (privately invited) audience sat on the shore. A high wall divides this courtyard from the living quarters, ornamental window openings providing clever views.

He Yuan Garden

The colonnade is unique in Chinese architecture as it stands. One and a half parallel walls form a roofed gallery, which makes it possible to reach the residence from the north gate in the dry. **Two-level**

Double colonnade

► VISITING YANGZHOU

GETTING THERE

Yangzhou station is northwest of the city and a relatively long way away. Trains run to Nanjing, Guangzhou, Shanghai and Huang Shan, among other destinations.

By bus

The usual and actually quicker way to get here from Nanjing and Shanghai is by bus via the new motorways and the Yangtze bridges.

WHERE TO EAT

Yangzhou fried rice, served in Chinese restaurants all over the world, is actually a recipe for left-overs and does not really reflect the quality of the Huaiyang cuisine, which is native to this city. Do not fail to try out the Yangzhou version of what the Cantonese call dimsum, i.e. all sorts of small snacks, especially various forms of dumplings, popular eaten with tea. One typical local dish is laoma huoguo, which can be rather loosely translated as »grandma's hotpot«.

► Moderate

① *Yechun Huayuan Chashe*
18 Fengle Xiajie
Tel. 0514/7342932
Renowned but expensive restaurant by the Waicheng He canal between Ge Yuan and the Slender West Lake. Typical Huaiyang cuisine. Already open at breakfast time.

② *Fuchun Chashe*
35 Desheng Qiao
(side street off Guoqing Lu)
Tel. 0514/7233326
Huaiyang specialities have been served at the »Tea Society of the Lush Spring« since 1885, both high cuisine and simple morsels.

③ *Riyueming Tea House*
Wenchang Guangchang
(central square)
Tel. 0514/7111777
This place primarily has variety shows so it is not a place for those who speak no Chinese. But in the Riyueming Tea House (Riyueming Chashe) it is possible to eat in the evenings; Huaiyang specialities are served from a buffet, which avoids any language problems. The variety atmosphere then comes along for free.

ACCOMMODATION

► Mid-range

① *Yangzhou State Guesthouse (Yangzhou Yinghin Guan)*
48 Youyi Lu
Tel. 0514/ 87 80 98 88
Fax 0514/ 87 33 16 74
The »State Guesthouse« is actually open to all. A well-run establishment, its three buildings with a total of 206 rooms are surrounded by an extensive garden bordering the West Lake.

② *Yangzhou Hotel (Yangzhou Binguan)*
3 Fengle Shangjie
Tel. 0514/ 87 80 58 88
Fax 0514/87 34 95 99
The 150-room hotel is showing its age, but the prices are low and in particular the location on the city moat alongside the city museum is pleasant. The city centre. West Lake, and Ge Yuan garden are only a short walk away.

Yangzhou Map

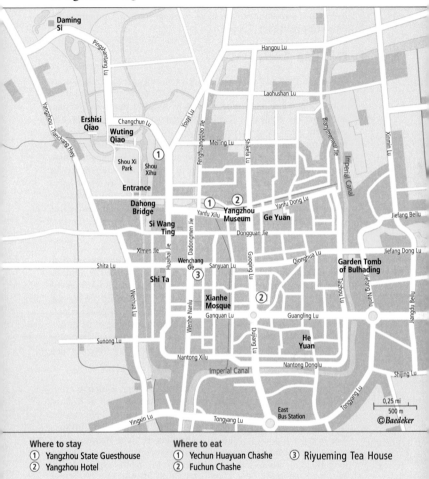

Where to stay
1. Yangzhou State Guesthouse
2. Yangzhou Hotel

Where to eat
1. Yechun Huayuan Chashe
2. Fuchun Chashe
3. Riyueming Tea House

colonnades provide access to the buildings in the garden courtyards on each side, which are separated by the gallery but, thanks to its window openings, still visually linked – a multi-functional piece of cabinet-work, so to speak.

Finally, there is a small, fine garden courtyard in the southeast. Here stands an original pavilion from the Ming era by a pond, beyond which there is another artificial hill. In the pond, though, the moon

Moon in water

can be seen, even during the day and ideally when the weather is overcast. If you don't believe it, go to Yangzhou. 77 Xuningmen Jie. Opening times: 8am–5.30pm daily.

✳ Ge Yuan Garden

In the Ge Yuan garden it can be seen that salt merchants had more money than government officials. Yangzhou's most important garden is not only bigger and more intricately designed than the He Yuan and other old gardens, it also has an interesting design concept. The estate in the northern part of the old town was laid out by a salt merchant in the 1820s. The »ge« in the name of the garden relates to the shape of the character. it resembles three hanging bamboo shoots. Written twice in succession, it results in the character for bamboo. The That the name represents only half a bamboo, so to speak, alludes to a proverb according to which man cannot live without bamboo. Access is from the north, and leads, at first eastwards past the actual garden, through a bamboo grove, where the character »ge« is omnipresent in the foliage.

Rockeries of the Four Seasons: Spring

The four sections of the garden make up four scenes representing the four seasons, not only by means of the plants within them but by four different rockeries. The round tour begins in the south at the northern side of the residential building. The rounded tips of the rocky peaks, which rise up out of the ground here, look like shoots of bamboo after the spring rains. A moon gate with the name of garden upon it then leads to the main part of the garden, which can be observed in comfort from the central pavilion, the free-standing **»Studio of the Due Rains«**, even when it is raining.

Summer

The summer section has the most intricate scenery, a bizarre artificial hill with caves in it, from which the waters in front of it, lined with further rockeries, seem to flow. The caves and trees offer shade, the latter including a splendid magnolia tree, which blooms in June. The hexagonal pond pavilion, the **»Pavilion of Clear Waves«** is also part of the theme of summer. The path through the rocks leads to a long building where the top floor bears the name »Spring Youth Paradise« and offers a panoramic view of the garden.

Autumn

In the east the route climbs over the »Autumn Hill«, the rocks of which are less bizarre than those of the »Summer Hill«. The scenery can be viewed from the **»Autumn Pavilion«** at the eastern wall. Since the evening corresponds to that part of the day which the autumn represents in the year, the pavilion opens towards the west and, when the trees were still small, the beholder could rest there to watch the sunset.

Winter

On the southern side of a small hall with the rather odd name of »The Moon Shines In and The Wind Comes Through the Cracks«

the tour of the garden comes to an end at an artificial hill made of white rocks, reminiscent of snow. The paving with its irregular, greenish stones also resembles broken ice. A high wall divides Winter from the neighbouring Spring but a moon window allows for a glance at the better days to come. The magnificence of the Ge Yuan garden is on view at 10 Yanfu Donglu. Opening times: 7.15am–5.30pm daily.

✹ ✹ The Slender West Lake (Shou Xihu)

The name of Yangzhou's most famous sight evokes comparison with Hangzhou's famous West Lake and makes it sound as though Yangzhou has had to put up with an economy version. That is not at all the case. The wonderful, beautifully tended park is an attraction in its own right. A detailed virtual tour can be found (with English text) at www.shouxihu.com.

It could not at first really be called a lake, as originally this was just a piece of the city's moat and its feeding canal. However, over the course of centuries more was made of it. Nowadays the waters are truly pleasing, flowing around little islands with **promenades, pavilions and pleasure places** lining the verdant banks. Little boats with imperial yellow, curved roofs play the canals. A large park covering 100 ha/250 acres includes more than two dozen individual attractions.

> ! *Baedeker* TIP
>
> **The Bonsai Garden**
> Where the Waicheng He canal crosses the southern end of the Slender West Lake from the east, there is a bonsai garden display. Beautifully situated and quiet, it is a lovely place to admire some jewels of the art of cultivating dwarf trees amid miniature landscapes.

Tours

The usual »entrance« is in the northwest of the old town near Da Hongqiao Lu. From there head northwards to the »Knee«, then west as far as the next bend – that will have meant a walk of nearly 2 km/ 1.5 mi and all the major sights lie along that route. If you carry on along the waters as far as the Daming Si monastery, then the whole route covers 3 km/2 mi.

Xu garden (Xu Yuan)

The garden known as Xu Yuan was originally a private estate which was later incorporated into the park and now constitutes a »garden within a garden«. The present buildings date from 1915 and constituted an ancestor temple for the Yu clan. It is situated in the inside (west bank) of the first bend.

Little Jin Shan

The »Little Gold Mountain« refers in name to the real »Gold Mountain«, an island in the nearby Yangtze. Here, where the lake bends to the left, is the spot with the best view out over the waters. The hill was created in the 18th century with the debris excavated for a newly dug canal. The present, beautifully arranged buildings come from the turn of the 20th century. The ensemble also includes »**Angel Pavilion**«. Surrounded on three sides by water, its three moon gates providing the frames for three different scenes.

Five Pavilion Bridge
Five Pavilion Bridge is the city's landmark. The broad, stone arched bridge linking the north and south banks in the middle of the lake has five pavilions on top of it. It was built in 1757. On hot summer days it is the most popular rest spot on the lake, as a mild breeze usually blows over the water.

Bottle pagoda
On the southern side along the axis of the bridge there surprisingly stands a white **Tibetan dagoba**. It came into being in conjunction with a visit to the city by the Qianlong Emperor. It was built for him as a replica of the dagoba in Beijing's Beihai Park. According to legend, it was built in a single night, but that first building was a dummy, quickly assembled after the emperor had commented that he was reminded of the park in Beijing, but the bottle pagoda was missing. Yangzhou's salt merchants then financed the building of the structure seen today. Opening times: 6.30am–5.30pm, and in the evenings at the height of summer.

Temple of Daming Si

Proceeding on foot, or better still in a gondola, along the Slender West Lake as far north as possible, one eventually reaches the generously proportioned temple of Daming Si, which is set in its own park-like garden with ponds and pavilions. The buildings and statues date with a few exceptions from the Qing period or the period subsequent to the Cultural Revolution. The most conspicuous building was built in the 1990s, the 70 m/230 ft **Xiling Pagoda**. This is a reconstruction of a predecessor on the site, which was burned down during a phase of Buddhist persecution in 843. Nowadays, though concrete and steel have been used to build it.

Memorial hall for Jianzhen
The temple is not only a popular place to go for the Chinese, but also for the Japanese. It represents the long period of cultural links between the countries. This is where Jianzhen (688–763), a highly regarded and learned monk, lived and worked. Having been invited by monks from Japan who had come to China to study, he chose to accompany them back to their country. However, this turned into a dramatic and for some a deadly odyssey. Firstly, leaving the country was forbidden to all citizens. On one occasion their plan was exposed, then when they did get to sea, their ship got into difficulties. At the fifth attempt, a tropical storm drove them onto the tropical island of Hainan. When Jianzhen finally did get to Japan after years of trying, he was already blind. The whole story is very well known among Japanese Buddhists and can also be read in a novel by Yasushi

Inoue called **»The Roof Tiles of Tempyo«**. In 1973, in what was still the Mao era, a memorial hall for Jianzhen was built – in the style of the monk's own time. The building has a replica of a lacquerware image of the monk which was made shortly after his death and is displayed in Nara, Japan, for only one day each year. Pingshantang Lu. Opening times: 8am–5.30pm daily, information on the internet under www.damingsi.com.

CHINESE NAMES FOR ASKING DIRECTIONS

Restaurants in hotels or shopping malls are listed under the name of the hotel or shopping mall. Anything else is listed under the street name. (Ht = Hotel, Tpl = Temple, Mausl = Mausoleum, Mus = Museum)

CHINESE PHRASEBOOK AND PRONUNCIATION

The most important things about the standard *pinyin* romanization and the pronunciation is given here:
Note: double or triple vowels are not pronounced separately, but together. So for example »shuang« or »liau« are both single-syllable words. The four »tones« are indicated below, but they are not always essential for understanding in Mandarin.

ao	like ow. Here: ao	*q*	like the first sound in »tune« (ty). Here: ty
c	like ts. Here: ts	*r*	at the beginning of a syllable, like the s in
ei	like ay. Here: ay		»treasure«, otherwise like r. Here: r
ch	as in »church«. Here: ch	*s*	like s. Here: s
i	after c, ch, r, s, sh, z, zh represents only a	*sh*	like sh. Here: sh
	lengthening of the consonant. Here: i	*x*	between h and sh, a bit like the start of
j	like the first sound in »due«. Here: dy		»huge«. Here: hsh
h	like h, but often rougher, as in »Bach«.	*z*	like z with a d in front. Here: dz
	Here: h	*zh*	like j. Here: j

Hello!	nǐ hǎo	你好！
Good bye	dsài dyiǎn	再见！
That's right	duèh.	对。
Of course	hǎu.	好。
No, that's wrong	bú duèh.	不对。
No, I won't	bù hǎo.	不好。
Thanks	hshiǎhshiǎ.	谢谢。
You're welcome	bú hshiǎ!	不谢！
Please!	tyǐng!	请！
Excuse me	duèh bu tyǐ!	对不起！
Pardon?	nǐ shuō shémmo?	你说什么？
I don't understand	uǒ bù dǔng.	我不懂
I would like	uǒ yào ...	我要
Please, no...	bú jàu!	不要！
Where is the toilet?	tsè sǔuǒ dzài nǎli?	厕所在那里？

Travelling

left/right	dzuǒ/yò	左 / 右
straight ahead	uǎng tyiǎn	往前
to the east/west	uǎng dōng/hshī	往东 / 往西
to the north/south	uǎng běh/nán	往北 / 往南
I should like to hire a bike	uǒ jào dzū dzì	我要租自行
/ bikes.	chíng chē.	车。
To...	dào ...	到 …
I'm getting out here	jè lǐ hshià chē.	这里下车。
Please wait	tchǐng nǐ děng uǒ	请你等我。

Shopping

I like that	uǒ hěn hshǐ huān.	我很喜欢。
I don't like that	uǒ bù hshǐ huān.	我不喜欢。
How much is it	duō shǎu tyiǎn?	多少钱？

Do you have...	yǒ méh yǒ ...?	有没有 …?
We have/don't have	yǒ / méh yǒ	有 / 没有。
Too expensive	tài guèhle.	太贵了。
I'll take it	uǒ mǎile	我买了。
I won't take it	uǒ bù mǎi	我不买。

Food and drink

Beer	pí dyiǒu	啤酒
Cola	kělè	可乐
Mineral water	kuàng tyüǎn shuěh	矿泉水
Green tea	lǜ chá	绿茶
Black tea	húng chá	红茶
Coffee	kāfēh	咖啡
Boiled rice	mǐ fàn	米饭
Fried rice	chǎo fàn	炒饭
Noodles	miǎn tiáo	面条
I don't eat meat	uǒ bù chī ròu	我不吃肉。
That's enough, thanks	gòule, hshiǎhshiä	够了，谢谢。
Cheers	gān bēh	干杯！
The bill, please	uǒ jào fù tyiǎn	我要付钱。

Post

To England	dyì uǎng yīngguó	英国，
To America	dyì uǎng měiguó	美国，
To Australia	dyì uǎng àodàliyà	澳大利亚
To Canada	dyì uǎng dyiānádà	加拿大
To New Zealand	dyì uǎng hshīnhshīlán	新西兰
To Ireland	dyì uǎng àiěryán	愛尔兰，
Stamps	yóu piào	邮票
By airmail	háng kūng	航空

Numbers

1	ī	一
2	èr	二
two items	liǎngge	两个
3	sān	三
4	sì	四
5	ǔh	五
6	liù	六
7	tyī	七
8	bā	八
9	dyiǒu	九
10	shí	十
11	shí-ī	十一
12	shí-èr	十二
20	èr-shí	二十
22	èr-shí-èr	二十二

GLOSSARY OF GEOGRAPHICAL, RELIGIOUS AND CULTURAL TERMS

Amitabha (Sanskr.) The popular redeemer Buddha of the »infinite light«. According to the »school of the pure land« – as the Buddhist school teaching the Amitabha cult is known – he takes all those into his western paradise who only call fervently upon his name.

Amitayus (Sanskr.) Buddha of long life (▶Buddha), a form of ▶Amitabha

Apsaras (Sanskr.) Female air spirits, who live on incense. As heavenly dancing girls, they express, together with the ▶Gandharvas, the joy of the Enlightened One who has left the earthly vale of tears behind.

Arhat (Sanskr., Chin.: Luohan) Holy monks who by ▶Buddha's teaching have achieved Enlightenment, as a goup of 18 Arhats known by name and also as the group of 500 Arhats.

Avalokiteshvara (Sanskr., stress on »tesh«) Bodhisattva embodying compassion and therefore the most often prayed to, helper of the Buddha ▶Amitabha; for China ▶Guanyin

Bei North

Bodhisattva (Sanskr.) »Enlightened Being«: Buddha who renounces entry to ▶Nirwana , in order to help human beings to escape the cycle of birth and rebirth; called on to help with everyday problems.

Bodiless lacquer If lacquer is applied not to wood but to a clay core wrapped in gauze, it is possible, after applying several coats of lacquer, to scrape out the core. The resulting objects are particularly light.

Bottle pagoda Tibetan form of ▶stupa: the body, standing on a ▶sumeru base, resembles an inverted brandy glass (▶p. 52 Pagodas).

Buddha (Sanskr.) »Enlightened One«, who by his own strength has recognized the nullity of the world. His chief iconographic feature: always clothed in a simple monk's habit; further features are the ascetic hairstyle, the rounded knob on the head (ushnisha) as a sign of wisdom, the long ear-lobes (pointing to the aristocratic descent of Buddha Gautama) and the bulge on the forehead, the urna, which is interpreted as a lock of hair or »third eye«; it is the sign of enlightenment. There are infinitely many Buddhas.

Buddhas of the Three Eras (past, present, future) Frequent group in the main halls of temples: to the left Dipamkara, in the middle ▶Shakyamuni, to the right ▶Maitreya.

Chörten (Tibet.) ▶Stupa in its Tibetan form as ▶bottle pagoda, mostly in a small format as a tombstone

Ci Ancestral or memorial temple

Cloisonné Enamel technique originating in the Near East: filigree wires are soldered to a metal body, and the resulting fields filled with molten glass of various colours.

Dagoba ▶bottle pagoda

Dajie »Great Street«, boulevard

Dao Street, path, road; as a philosophical concept, the »way« of all being, the law of existence

Deva (Sanskr.) Protective god of Buddhism. Most are derived from Indian mythology, but in China and Tibet others were added. Many Devas were once enemies of Buddhism but were converted; in order to expiate their misdeeds, they are eager protectors of the Buddha.

Devi Only female ▶Dharmapala, rides on a wild ass.

Dharma (Sanskr.) Law of existence and the doctrine of the ▶Buddha regarding it, often represented as the »wheel of teaching«, which is always reproduced.

Dharmapalas (Sanskr.) Eight protectors of the doctrine of Tibetan tantric tradition, in terrifying guise

Dian Hall building of traditional design

Dong TEast

Four Kings of Heaven Powerful patron gods of Buddhism, one for each corner of heaven. In armour and with threatening grimaces, they stand guard in the inner gate hall of temple monasteries. Each carries his attribute: he of the south, a sword; of the east, a ▶pipa, of the west, a snake and/or a stupa, he of the north, a rolled umbrella.

Gandharvas (Sanskr.) The male form of ▶Apsaras; they operate chiefly as celestial musicians.

Ge Pavilion, studio

Gong Palace, high-ranking temple or temple hall

Green Tara ▶Tara

Guan Daoist temple monastery

Guan Di »Emperor Guan«, also Guan Gong: the most popular patron god. Symbol of loyalty and steadfastness, hence particularly the patron god of soldiers, the deified form of General Guan Yu (d. AD 219).

Guanyin, Guanshiyin (Chin. for ▶Avalokiteshvara). In China, represented mostly as a female »goddess of mercy« for more than 1000 years

Hutong (Mongol. Chines.) alley; alley in Beijing old town

Jade Emperor Supreme deity in popular Daoism

Jie Street

Kshitigarbha (Sanskr., Chin.: Dizang Pusa) ▶Bodhisattva of the underworld, also the protector of travellers and children.

Locana Semi-material form of the transcendent Buddha; ▶Vairocana

Lu Street

Luohan Chinese for ▶Arhat

Maitreya (Sanskr.) Buddha of the future era, also represented as a ▶Bodhisattva. The »fat-bellied Buddha « in the entrance hall of the temple monasteries is likewise interpreted as Maitreya.

Mandala Point-symmetrical and often axially symmetrical representation of the (Tibetan) Buddhist world of salvation, serves as an aid to meditation and is found in both two and three-dimensional forms.

Manjushri (Sanskr., Chin.: Wenshu) ▶Bodhisattva of wisdom. Rides on a lion.

Mazu (also Matsu, Tian Hou, Tin Hau, A ma) Patron of seafarers

Miao Temple

Nan South

Nirwana (Sanskr.) »blow out«: the ineffably absolute, into which the existence of the Enlightened One flees when it has escaped the cycle of rebirth.

Padmasambhava (Sanskr.: the Lotus-born): this guru, allegedly brought up in a royal court in what is now Pakistan in the 8th century is regarded as the Nestor of Tibetan Buddhism, in particular as the teacher of ►Tantrismus.

Pipa A slim, musical instrument similar to a lute

Qiao Bridge

Qilin Four-hoofed fabulous beast with a scaled body; heralds a happy era, popularly believed to bring sons.

Samantabhadra (Sanskr., Chin.: Puxian) ►Bodhisattva of the law. Rides a white elephant.

Shakyamuni (Sanskr.) The historical Buddha Gautama, at the same time the symbol of the present age. His likeness can often be recognized by the two disciples Ananda and Kashyapa, who stand by his side. One certain distinguishing feature is the gesture of touching the earth.

Shan Mountain, hill, range of mountains

Shiku Grotto, cave temple

Si Buddhist temple monastery; also applies to mosques

Soul tablet Wooden tablet on an altar with the name of the person thus venerated, be it an ancestor, or (esp. in a Confucius temple) a philosopher

Spirit wall Also »spirit screen«, a wall built behind the gateway of houses or temples to prevent straight-line access or a direct view of what lies beyond

Stupa (Sanskr.) Indian building used a a reliquary. Original form of pagoda, resembles a bowl turned over on a base and with a point on top.

Sumeru (Sanskr.) Central world mountain of Buddhism, home of the gods; the marble bases on which the Buddha figures stand in temples, raise them symbolically as »sumeru bases« high over the earthly world.

Sumeru base ►Sumeru

Ta Pagoda, tower, minaret

Taichi ►Taiji Quan

Taiji Quan »Fist fight of the highest absolute«, hence also known as »shadow-boxing«: a form of mental and physical exercise derived ultimately from a martial art, with a fixed sequence of slow movements

Tantrismus Esoteric school of Buddhism, widespread above all in Tibet. It teaches the use of ritual actions, including the recitation of mantras, and sexual ecstasy to overcome the contradictions of the cosmos and thus to experience nirvana.

Tara Female ►Bodhisattva of Tibetan Buddhism. The Green Tara is regarded as the incarnation of a Nepalese princess, the White Tara of a Chinese one. The Green Tara is the most popular female patron god in Tibet.

Thanka (Tibetan) A picture painted on a scroll, Tibeto-Buddhist in content

Three Costly Buddhas Group of three sometimes replacing the ►Buddhas of the Three Eras in the main hall: ►Shakyamuni (centre), ►Amitabha (left) and the Buddha of medicine

Three Great Bodhisattvas The ►Bodhisattvas Guanyin, Manjushri and Samantabhadra

Three Pure Ones San Qing: the »utmost Pure One«, the »Jade Pure One« and the »High Pure One« are the three main gods of Daoism. They are regarded as incarnations of Lao Zi..

Three Saints of the West The Redeemer Buddha ►Amitabha with his assistant bodhisattvas ►Guanyin (right) and Mahasthamaprapta

Tin Hau Cantonese for ►Tian Hou

Tian Hou »Empress of Heaven«, honorary title of ►Mazu

Ting Pavilion

Vairocana (Sanskr.) The »sun-like«: transcendental, i.e. eternal ►Buddha, Lord of the centre of worlds

Vajra (Sanskr.) Derived from the »lightning sceptre« of the Indian god Indra, in Tibetan Buddhism this »thunderbolt sceptre« symbolizes the indestructible absolute and is thus also known as the »diamond sceptre«. It takes the form of a figure-of-eight shaped sceptre, to be held in the middle, with a number of points at each end, each curved back on itself.

Way of souls In a necropolis, part of the access path leading to the main mausoleum; lined along its central section by stone figures

Xi West

Year gods 60 personifications of the years of the Chinese 60-year cycle; the current cycle began in 1984. Sacrifices are made to the god of one's birth year.

Yin and Yang Philosophical concepts, denoting a bipolarity metamorphosing into itself, in accordance with the basic meanings »shady side« and »sunny side«: both move with the sun. Yin is the female, humid, submerged, dark, earthly, cool, fruit-bearing, Yang the male, dry, looming, bright, heavenly, hot, begetting.

Yuàn Courtyard

Yuán Garden

INDEX

LIST OF MAPS AND ILLUSTRATIONS

PHOTO CREDITS

PUBLISHER'S INFORMATION

Illustrations etc: 258 illustrations, 54 maps and diagrams, one large map
Text: Dr. Hans-Wilm Schütte
Editing: Baedeker editorial team (Michael Scuffil)
Translation: Simon Clay
Cartography: Christoph Gallus, Hohberg; Franz Huber, Munich; MAIRDUMONT/Falk Verlag, Ostfildern (map)
3D illustrations: jangled nerves, Stuttgart
Design: independent Medien-Design, Munich; Kathrin Schemel

Editor-in-chief: Rainer Eisenschmid, Baedeker Ostfildern

1st edition 2009
Based on Baedeker Allianz Reiseführer »China«, 8. Auflage 2009

Copyright: Karl Baedeker Verlag, Ostfildern
Publication rights: MAIRDUMONT GmbH & Co; Ostfildern

Printed in Germany

BAEDEKER GUIDE BOOKS AT A GLANCE
Guiding the World since 1827

- Andalusia
- Austria
- Bali
- Barcelona
- Berlin
- Brazil
- Budapest
- Cape Town • Garden Route
- China
- Cologne
- Dresden
- Dubai
- Egypt
- Florence
- Florida
- France
- Gran Canaria
- Greece
- Iceland
- India
- Ireland
- Italy
- Japan
- London
- Mexico
- Morocco
- New York
- Norway
- Paris
- Portugal
- Prague
- Rome
- South Africa
- Spain
- Thailand
- Tuscany
- Venice
- Vienna
- Vietnam

DEAR READER,

We would like to thank you for choosing this Baedeker travel guide. It will be a reliable companion on your travels and will not disappoint you.
This book describes the major sights, of course, but it also recommends the most interesting events, as well as hotels in the luxury and budget categories, and includes tips about where to eat or go shopping and much more, helping to make your trip an enjoyable experience. Our author Dr. Hans-Wilm Schütte ensures the quality of this information by making regular journeys to China and putting all his know-how into this book.

Nevertheless, experience shows us that it is impossible to rule out errors and changes made after the book goes to press, for which Baedeker accepts no liability. Please send us your criticisms, corrections and suggestions for improvement: we appreciate your contribution. Contact us by post or e-mail, or phone us:

▶ **Verlag Karl Baedeker GmbH**
Editorial department
Postfach 3162
73751 Ostfildern
Germany
Tel. 49-711-4502-262, fax -343
www.baedeker.com
www.baedeker.co.uk
E-Mail: baedeker@mairdumont.com